HOUSING FOR ALL

Design, Construction and Management

HOUSING FOR ALL

Design, Construction and Management

A.K. JAIN

Foreword By:

Dr./Prof. PSN Rao

Director, School of Planning and Architecture, New Delhi
Chair, Delhi Urban Art Commission, New Delhi

KHANNA BOOK PUBLISHING CO. (P) LTD.

Publisher of Engineering and Computer Books

4C/4344, Ansari Road, Darya Ganj, New Delhi-110002
Phone : 011-23244447-48 **Mobile:** +91-9910909320
E-mail : contact@khannabooks.com
Website : www.khannabooks.com

Dear Readers,

To prevent the piracy, this book is secured with HIGH SECURITY HOLOGRAM on the front title cover. In case you don't find the hologram on the front cover title, please write us to at contact@khannabooks.com or whatsapp us at +91-99109 09320 and avail special gift voucher for yourself.

Specimen of Hologram on front Cover title:

Moreover, there is a SPECIAL DISCOUNT COUPON for you with EVERY HOLOGRAM.

How to avail this SPECIAL DISCOUNT:

Step 1: Scratch the hologram
Step 2: Under the scratch area, your "coupon code" is available
Step 3: Logon to www.khannabooks.com
Step 4: Use your "coupon code" in the shopping cart and get your copy at a special discount
Step 5: Enjoy your reading!

Price: ₹ 650.00

ISBN: 978-93-86173-56-0

Housing for ALL *by* A.K. Jain

First Edition: 2019
Reprint: 2023, **2024**

To view complete list of books, Please scan the QR Code:

Published by:
Khanna Book Publishing Co. (P) Ltd.
CIN: U22110DL1998PTC095547

Visit us at: **www.khannabooks.com**
Write us at: **contact@khannabooks.com**

Printed in India.

PREFACE

With 18.78 million housing shortage in urban areas and 43.67 million in rural areas, India ranks number one in the world in housing shortage. It is a sad paradox that in spite of all resources, skills, policies and programs taken up since independence of the country, the housing shortage continues to accelerate. Concentration of poor and their isolation have condemned generations of low income areas to entrenched poverty, fragmented environments and asymmetrical societies. Shelter is a direct manifestation of poverty and also major cause of their deprivation. In the year 2011, India's urban population was 377 million of which about 65 million face housing shortage. Out of 833 million rural population, 216 million are below poverty line who face housing shortage. This is more acute in large cities like Mumbai, where half a million people sleep on the streets, and ten times as many live in crowded, dangerous slums and shanty towns. It is a national reproach that even after 70 years of Independence we have not been able to provide housing to all.

The Government of India has launched the Pradhan Mantri Awas Yojana (PMAY) for building 11.20 million houses in urban areas and 10 million houses in rural areas by the year 2022. Under the scheme a dwelling unit of 30 sqm is to the built for the EWS category (income up to Rs 3 lakh pa) and 60 sqm for LIG unit (income above Rs. 3 lakh to Rs. 6 lakh pa), whereas in rural areas 25 sqm units are to be built. It also involves the rehabilitation of 65 million slum dwellers.

Most of the supply driven housing projects serve the middle and high income groups and the investors/speculators for whom housing is a commodity. As a result, a large number of dwelling units remain unoccupied. The Census 2011 pointed out that as many as 11.09 million houses are lying vacant on the face of the total urban housing shortage of 18.78 million dwelling units. Clearly the need of the social housing has been marginalized, and there is a need to identify the barriers and evolve the reforms for social housing. The barriers include—lack of understanding of the housing problem and issues, skewed definition of shelter, stereotype designs, primitive systems of construction, lack of building resources, lack of community participation, lack of finances and distortions of investments. There is also lack of serviced land for low cost shelter, lack of linkages and livelihood, and social and physical infrastructure. It is necessary to focus on renewal and retrofitting of existing housing stock, with suitable reforms in tenure system, and zoning regulations.

This calls for developing a new paradigm which is pro-poor, community led, participatory, and is based on the principle of equitable allocation of resources, services, space and land, including housing to everyone with the house with linkages, livelihoods, water, electricity, toilets and security. This make us to rethink about the model of public-private binary and evolve a third option where community is the core factor in the shelter process.

Collective community approach in housing and financing can be a viable alternative. A small group of families come together and form a joint housing group (or cooperative) for housing development and sanction of loans. They build together and pay together. This will reduce the hassles in loan procurement, paperwork and dealing with land, construction, architects, engineers, suppliers and contractors. The credit-cum-subsidy model will reduce the government burden, ensure community participation and housing delivery.

As many as 15 million dwelling units in urban India are dilapidated and congested, which need retrofitting and upgradation. As such renewal and redevelopment of existing housing stock has to be a major area of focus by providing better infrastructure services, linkages, livelihood, and social and cultural facilities.

Land requirement for housing in urban areas has been worked out as 84,724 hectares. In view of the stringent provisions of LARR Act, 2013 for acquisition and development of land, other options such as partnership with land owners, land pooling, transferable development right, etc. need to be invoked. Compulsory reservation of land for EWS/LIG housing, infill development, redensification of existing housing areas, slums and unauthorized colonies and diversion of unused lands under special economic zones and industrial areas can be the other options. The land cost has to be excluded from the dwelling cost of EWS and LIG housing. The residents are to be connected to livelihood and provided with social and physical infrastructure (parks, education, health, water supply, electricity, sanitation, etc). While optimising the FAR and density, proportionate enhancement of the services, pubic green spaces, and community facilities is necessary for development of a wholesome environment. To mitigate large carbon footprints and negative impacts on environment, it is necessary to adopt ecological, economical and efficient construction technologies. According to a study conducted in 2007, the usage of eco-friendly building technology could lead to reduction of 16.80 metric tons of CO_2 per year and 20% cost reduction.

A combination of approaches can be worked out to minimise the cost of the house, which include subsidies, loans, mandatory reservation of land, land banking, higher FAR/FSI and densities, in-situ slum rehabilitation, upgrading of existing housing, site and services, evolutionary, core and infill housing, low cost construction, building material banking and saving on time and resources. It is essential to optimize the capacity of housing boards, bank, developers, and cooperatives towards facilitating low cost housing. An important strategy to reduce the cost of housing is by optimising the planning parameters. It is necessary to resort to rigorous planning, technological innovations, improved procurement, labour management and process efficiency. This requires removing delays in approval of plans and new rapid construction methods, along with reforms in Development Control Regulations, and Building Bye Laws. However, the most important is to change the strategy from mass housing to housing by the masses. Smart IT-based processes, skills and capacity development, revamping housing boards and establishment of housing factories and building material banks should be taken up.

There are serious distortions in investment of public finances for housing, whereas 95 percent of the houses are required for the EWS and LIG, only 5 percent of bank loans are given to these income groups, while 95% of finances go for the MIG and HIG houses. It should be mandatory that out of the total loans given by the banks and financing institutions, at least 75 percent of funds are compulsorily reserved for affordable housing.

A large number of low income families cannot access housing loan and are unable to pay its upfront cost and mortgage payment. Many poor families survive on day to day earnings. Even in illegal colonies, slums, the squatters pay weekly or monthly rental to slum-lord. The quantum of rental housing is diminishing due to various reasons such as taxation, Rent Control Act, paper work and transactions involved. Due to legal disputes, even the available housing is kept vacant. Rental housing needs to be pushed especially for the poor, informal sector, students, causal workers, young professionals, women and aged. It may be compulsory that about one-half to one-third of housing units are rental, for which incentives such as Bonus FSI, Rental Housing Vouchers, Low Income Housing Tax Credit (LIHTC) and rebate in income tax can be given.

The book *Housing For All : Design, Construction and Management* provides a road map towards the goal of housing for all which is accessible and affordable. It emphasizes that the housing be linked with the livelihood, social empowerment and economic security. More than 240 graphics help to explain the concepts clearly.

This work has drawn on support of innumerable people and institutions, including the Ministry of Housing and Urban Affairs, Government of India, Delhi Development Authority, UN Habitat, IHS (Rotterdam), and other organisations. The Association for Settlements and Housing Activities (ASHA) deserves special acknowledgement for collating data base. The Foreword written by Dr./Prof. P.S.N. Rao. Director, School of Planning and Architecture, New Delhi, and Chairman DUAC, is concise and clear. He states that the book is a significant and valuable contribution to the literature on housing and urban development. He strongly recommends this book to the students, research scholars, architects and practicing town planners. Special thanks must go to Khanna Publishing, especially Mukul Seth for accomplishing the challenge of bringing out the book with the professionalism.

A.K. Jain

योजना तथा वास्तुकला विद्यालय, नई दिल्ली
संसद के अधिनियम के तहत "राष्ट्रीय महत्व का संस्थान"
(मानव संसाधन विकास मंत्रालय, भारत सरकार)
School of Planning and Architecture, New Delhi
An "Institution of National Importance" under an Act of Parliament
(Ministry of Human Resource Development, Government of India)

प्रो. डॉ. पी.एस.एन राव
निदेशक
Prof. Dr. P.S.N. RAO
Director

Foreword

This book titled "**Housing for All: Design, Construction and Management**" by A.K. Jain is a comprehensive assessment of the housing situation in India which not only traces the path taken by governments so far, but also outlines a road map for the future.

The book begins with an overview of the housing scenario in India. It discusses various housing programmes and draws a distinction between affordable housing and adequate housing. The book also draws particular attention to housing issues of special groups such as the elderly, disabled, homeless, migrant and transit workers, students and single women.

There is also a discussion on the issue of social and physical infrastructure. The book notes that housing units alone do not constitute housing but infrastructure plays a critical role in the occupancy of housing.

The question of reducing the cost of housing has been vexatious for long. Jain deals with this issue in detail and suggests various low-cost technologies and house building systems for making housing more affordable. Another issue is that of rental housing. Jain suggests that giving a boost to rental housing through a slew of measures can go a long way in making housing more accessible and bring vacant housing into the market.

He also discusses in detail the question of land, the basic resource for housing. Land today has become a major issue on account of the change in the legislative process for its procurement through the stringent provisions of LARR 2013. He suggests alternatives for bringing land into housing development.

Finally, Jain also refers to the current PMAY and discusses various regulatory reforms for housing development in the country.

A.K. Jain is a well-known housing specialist with over four decades of experience of "hands on" working in the Delhi Development Authority as Commissioner (Planning). He has spent a lifetime grappling with housing and urban development problems. He has been a prolific writer and has authored several books and papers. This book is yet one more addition, a very significant one, to his credit and a valuable contribution to Indian literature on housing and urban development. I would strongly recommend this book to students, research scholars and practicing town planners.

(Prof. Dr.P.S.N.Rao)
Head (Housing),
Director,
SPA New Delhi

CONTENTS

1

AN OVERVIEW OF INDIA'S HOUSING SCENARIO

India's 2011 census records a population of 1,210.98 million of which, 377.10 million (31.16%) live in urban areas. During 2001-2011, the urban population of India grew at a CAGR of 2.8%, resulting in the increase of urbanization from 27.8% to 31.16%. This has led to land shortage, housing shortfall, urban congestion, stressed services and amenities.

Table 1.1: Census 2011

Total Population	1210.98 million
Growth rate	17.64% (2001-11)
Literacy	74.04%
No. of Districts	640 (excl. J & K)
No. of Sub-districts	5924
No. of Cities and Towns	7936
No. of Municipal/Census Towns	3893
No. of Villages	6,41,000
Urban population	377 million (31.16 %)
Metropolitan cities (+million population)	53

Source: *Census of India and other sources*

Urban settlements in India comprise Statutory Towns, which are "all places with a municipality, corporation, cantonment board, or notified town area committee, etc. so declared by State Law." Census Towns are those which have:

(*i*) a minimum population of 5,000

(*ii*) at least 75 percent of the male working population engaged in non-agricultural pursuits

(*iii*) a density of population of at least 400 persons per sq. km.

'Cities' are urban areas with 1 lakh (0.1 million) and above population. Other smaller settlements are termed as 'towns'. 'Metropolitan cities' are cities with 10 lakh (1 million) and above population. There are 53 such cities in India, holding more than 40 percent of urban population.

'Urban Agglomerations (UAs)' are defined as continuous urban spread constituting a town and its adjoining outgrowths (OGs), or two or more contiguous towns together and any adjoining urban outgrowth of such towns. An Urban Agglomeration must consist of at least a statutory town and its total population (*i.e.* all the constituents put together) should not be less than 20,000. An 'outgrowth (OG)' is a viable unit such as a village or a hamlet or an enumeration block made up of such village or hamlet and clearly identifiable in terms of its boundaries and location. An OG may be railway colony, university campus, port area, military camps etc. Thus, OG has arisen outside the limits of statutory town, but within the revenue limits of a village or villages contiguous to the town. An OG possesses urban infrastructure and amenities such as pucca roads, electricity, taps, drainage, sewerage, etc. educational institutions, post offices, medical facilities, banks, etc. and physically contiguous with the core town of the UA. There are other informal categories of urban settlements such as mini-metros, Tier I, II & III towns and peri-urban towns.

Urbanisation has increased the number of people living in slums and squatter settlements, with deteriorated housing conditions for the economically weaker sections of the society. This is because of the skyrocketing prices of land in urban areas. As a result, the poor are forced to occupy the marginal lands typified by poor housing stock, congestion and obsolescence. In urban areas, the gap between the demand and supply of housing (both in terms of quantity and quality) is getting wider.

The links between urbanization and per capita income have grown stronger in the Indian economy indicating that cities hold the key to economic growth. Urbanization is gradually aligning itself with the economic growth processes in India, although the interlinkage effects are still quite low by international standards.

Table 1.2: Co-relation between Urbanisation and Per Capita Income

State/UTs	Urbanisation level 2011 (%)	Urbanisation Rank 2011	PCGSDP 2009-10 (Rs.)	Rank PCGSDP
Delhi	97.50	1	116886	2
Chandigarh	97.25	2	118136	1
Puducherry	68.31	3	88158	3
Mizoram	51.51	4	45982	17
Tamil Nadu	48.45	5	63547	9
Kerala	47.72	6	59179	12
Maharashtra	45.23	7	74027	6
Gujarat	42.58	8	63961	8
Karnataka	38.57	9	52097	13
Punjab	37.49	10	60746	10

A & N Islands	35.67	11	74340	5
Haryana	34.79	12	50365	16
Andhra Pradesh	33.49	13	51025	15
West Bengal	31.89	14	41219	20
Uttarakhand	30.55	15	59584	11
Manipur	30.21	16	27332	26
Nagaland	28.97	17	45353	18
Madhya Pradesh	27.63	18	27250	27
Jammu & Kashmir	27.21	19	30582	25
Tripura	26.18	20	35799	22
Sikkim	24.97	21	68731	7
Rajasthan	24.89	22	34042	23
Jharkhand	24.05	23	27132	29
Chhattisgrah	23.24	24	38059	21
Arunachal Pradesh	22.67	25	51405	14
Uttar Pradesh	22.28	26	23395	30
Meghalaya	20.08	27	43555	19
Odisha	16.68	28	33226	14

Source: *NIUA & HUDCO/(HSMI) 2013, Metropolitan Cities in India, Phase I Report, 2012-13, New Delhi*

The data reveals strong and probable co-relation between urbanisation and incomes. The data reveals that :

- Coefficient of Co-relation between levels of Urbanisation & PCI among States = 0.8
- Over 60% of GDP comes from urban areas
- Declining Rural holdings: 1971=>3 ha; 2010=>1 ha
- Small cities are growing the fastest
- Almost 40% of towns are unplanned "quasi towns", which face haphazard growth, without infrastructure services.

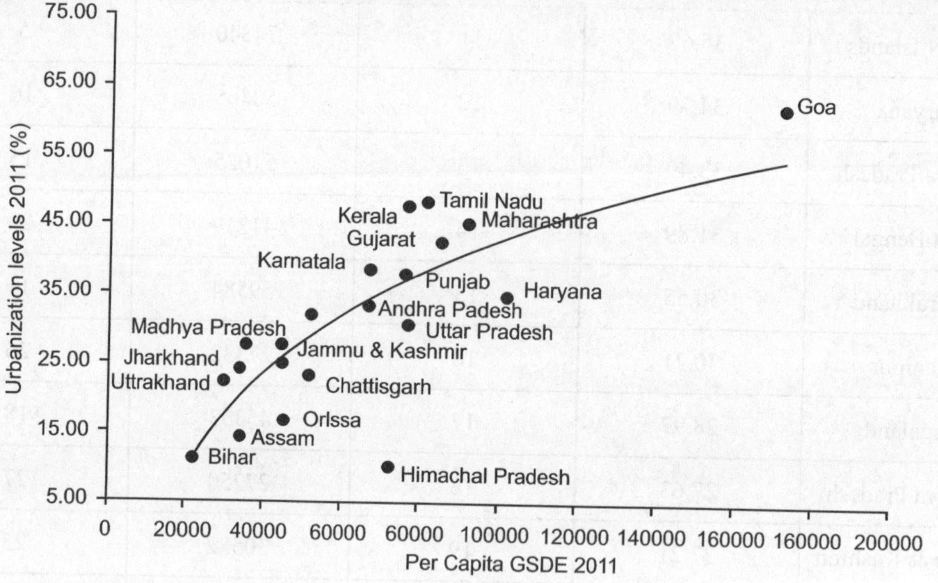

Fig. 1.1. Interrelated effects of per capita income and urbanization levels across the States

Source: *Calculations based on Census data of India and Central Statistical Organisation data, 2001 and 2011/ NIUA & HUDCO/HSMI, (2013) Metropolitan Cities in India, Phase I Report, 2012-13.*

Fig. 1.2. Slums express the failure of the government and private sector in inclusive development

Fig. 1.3. Slums lack basic services, amenities and facilities

Fig. 1.4. Slums often violate human rights

Housing Scenario

According to the 2011 Census, the housing stock in urban India stood at 78.48 million for 78.86 million urban households. Although the gap between household and housing stock is narrowing, actual shortage is high because of much of the current stock is dilapidated and people living in congested areas.

The total urban housing shortage in 2012 was estimated to be 18.78 million, (revised to 11.5 million to 2017) out of which 5 percent are non-serviceable, temporary houses, 12 percent are obsolete houses, 80 percent are in congested, dilapidated conditions and 3 percent were homeless. The urban housing shortage in 2007 was estimated at 24.71 million, and there was a reduction of 6 million in shortage of housing units between 2007 and 2011.

This classification of various economic category households such as economically weaker section (EWS), low income group (LIG), middle and high income group was based on household income criteria prevalent in 2012. EWS households were those with income up to Rs 5000 per month and LIG households are those with income between Rs 5000 and 10000 per month. The TG-12 using the consumption expenditure data from NSS 66th Round for 2009-10 found that EWS category households comprise one-third of the households in urban area and 80 percent of the households have expenditure equal to or below the LIG category. According to TG-12 the households from EWS, LIG middle and high income group category accounted for 56.18 percent, 39.44 percent and 4.38 percent respectively of the total estimated urban housing shortage.

Table 1.3: Housing Shortage in Urban India

Total Households	**81.35**
Households living in Non-Serviceable Kutcha/Temporary Houses	0.99
Households living in Obsolescent house (excluding non-serviceable kutcha/temporary houses)	2.27
Households living in congested houses requiring new houses	14.99
Homeless Households	0.53
Total Housing Shortage	18.78

Source: *Technical Group on Urban Housing Shortage (TG-12) (2012-17), Ministry of Housing and Urban Poverty Alleviation, Government of India.*

Table 1.4: Housing Shortage According to Income Groups

Category	2007 (million units)	%	2012 (million units)	%
EWS	21.78	88.13	10.55	56.18
LIG	2.89	11.69	7.41	39.44
MIG/HIG	0.04	0.18	0.82	4.38
Total Shortage	24.71		18.78	

Source: *Ministry of HUPA, 2012, Census of India, House Listing and Housing Census, 2011*

Before the launch of PMAY in June 2015, the Government of India had initiated various schemes, such as Rajiv Awas Yojana, and Affordable Housing Programme. The construction of 1,41,848 dwelling units had been approved under these schemes. These are besides other schemes of the Central Government (such as BUSP) and State Governments.

Urban Slums in India

The National Sample Survey Office (NSSO), Ministry of Statistics and Programme Implementation, provided has released the key indicators of urban slums in India, generated from the data collected in its 69th round survey (2012).

Definition and Types of Slums

All notified areas in a town or city notified as 'Slum' by the authorities (State, Union Territories Administration or Local Government) under any Act, including the 'Slum Act', are considered as Notified slums.

All areas recognised as 'Slum' by State, Union Territories or Local Government, Housing and Slum Boards, which may have not been formally notified as slum under any Act, may be considered as Recognized Slum.

A compact area of at least 300 people or about 60-70 households of poorly built congested tenements, in unhygienic environment, usually with inadequate infrastructure and lacking in proper sanitary and drinking water facilities. Such areas should be identified personally by the Charge Officer and also inspected by an officer nominated by the Directorate of Census Operations. This fact must be duly recorded in the charge register. Such areas may be considered as identified slum.

Number of Slum Households

- A total of 33,510 slums were estimated to exist in the urban areas of India. About 41% of these are notified and 59% non-notified.
- Maharashtra, with an estimated 7723 slums, accounted for about 23% of all slums in urban India, followed by Andhra Pradesh, accounting for 13.5%, and West Bengal, which had a share of about 12%.
- Of the 19,749 non-notified slums estimated to exist in urban India, Maharashtra accounted for about 29%, West Bengal for about 14%, and Gujarat for about 10%.
- Out of an estimated 13,761 notified slums in urban India, Andhra Pradesh had about 23%, Maharashtra about 14%, and Madhya Pradesh, West Bengal and Tamil Nadu about 9% each.
- An estimated 8.8 million households lived in urban slums, about 5.6 million in notified and 3.2 million in non-notified slums.
- The notified slums formed 41% of all slums but housed 63% of all slum-dwelling households in India.
- As many as 38% of slum households of urban India were estimated to be living in Maharashtra and 18% in Andhra Pradesh.
- Of slum households in non-notified slums, 40% were estimated to be present in Maharashtra and 9% each in Gujarat and West Bengal.

Average Slum Size

- At the all-India level the average slum size was estimated at 263 households. The average notified slum had 404 households and the average non-notified slum had only 165.
- For notified and non-notified slums taken together, average slum size was highest in Maharashtra (433), followed by Karnataka (392) and Andhra Pradesh (352).
- State-level average slum sizes of notified slums varied widely. For Maharashtra the average was over 1000 households whereas for Chhattisgarh, it was only 84.
- About 56% of slums in the million-plus cities and 58% of those in other urban areas had less than 150 households.
- About three-quarters of non-notified slums (77% in the million-plus cities and 74% in other urban areas) had less than 150 households. About 40% of the notified slums, both in million-plus cities and also in other urban areas, had 150-450 households.

Characteristics of Slums

- At the all-India level 44% of slums – 48% of notified slums and 41% of non-notified slums – were located on private land.
- About 60% of all slums contained mostly pucca structures. The proportion of such slums was 85% among notified slums but only 42% of non-notified slums.
- At the all-India level 71% of all slums had tap as major source of drinking water, the figure being 82% for notified slums but only 64% for non-notified slums.
- Electricity was absent mainly in non-notified slums. At the all-India level only 6.5% of all slums had no electricity.
- In about 66% of all slums the main thoroughfare was a pucca road. The proportion was 83% for notified slums and 55% for non-notified slums.
- At the all-India level 31% of slums had no latrine, the figure being 42% for non-notified and 16% for notified slums.
- About 31% of all slums had no drainage – the figure being considerably higher for non-notified slums (45%) than for notified slums (11%).
- At the all-India level, 27% of all slums had no rubbish disposal arrangement – the figures being about 38% for non-notified slums and about 11% for notified slums.
- In an estimated 32% of all slums the approach road usually remained waterlogged after rainfall. The figure was 35% for notified slums and 29% for non-notified slums.
- At the all-India level 24% of slums benefited from welfare schemes, such as the Jawaharlal Nehru National Urban Renewal Mission (JNNURM), Rajiv Awas Yojana (RAY), Pradhan Mantri Awas Yojana (PMAY), etc. The proportion benefiting from such schemes was 32% among notified and 18% among non-notified slums.

Fig. 1.5. In Mumbai, as many as half a million people sleep on the streets because they have no other place to live. Ten times as many live in crowded, dangerous slums and shanty towns in the city

Table 1.5: Indicators of housing and services in slums

Indicators of housing and services	1993	2002	2008-09
House structure - pucca	31	48	57
House structure semi - pucca	34	35	29
House structure kutcha	35	18	14
% of households with access to tap water	65	78	78
% of households with no access to a toilet	54	34	15
% of households without access to drainage	32	30	17
% of households with rubbish-collection by local government	52	61	65

Source: *NSSO (1997), NSSO (2010)*

Rural Housing Shortage

The Ministry of Rural Development (MoRD) has estimated the total rural housing shortage for the 12th Five Year Plan (2012-17) to be 44 million dwelling units. The same study identified access to finance as the fundamental pre-requisite for habitat development.

Table 1.6: Estimate of Shortage in Rural Housing

Factors taken into account	Calculation	Shortage (in million)
Households not having houses 2012	No. of households less no. of housing stock in 2012	4.15
Temporary houses in 2012	No. of housing stock less no. of permanent houses	20.21

Shortage due to congestion in 2012	Congestion factor of 6.5% based on 2001 census	11.30
Shortage due to obsolescence	Obsolescence factor of 4.3% based on 58th round of NSS	7.47
Additional housing shortage arising between 2012-17	No. of households projected for 2017 over 2012 less number of excess housing stock projected for the same period	0.55
Total Rural Housing Shortage (2012-17)		43.67

Source: *Working Group on Rural Housing for 12th Five Year Plan, Ministry of Rural Development*

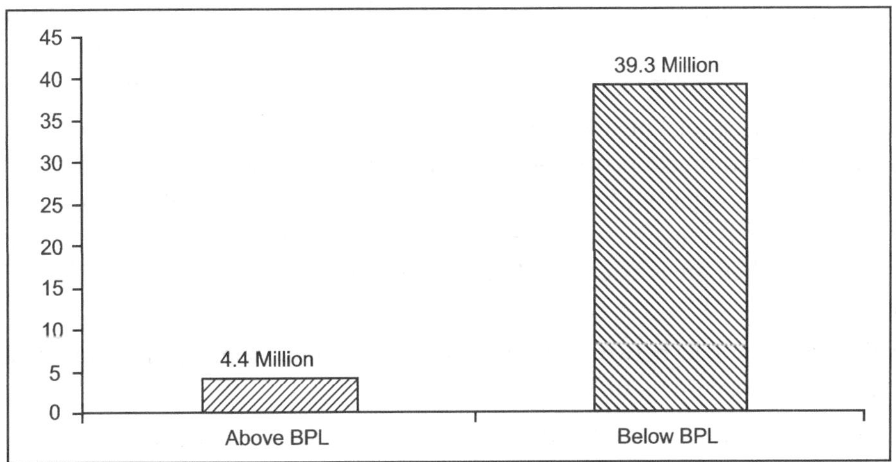

Fig. 1.6. Shortage of Rural Housing is concentrated in Below Poverty Line (BPL) families

Source: *MoRD*

The Government has taken various initiatives to tackle the housing shortage, of which the Indira Awaas Yojana (IAY) and Pradhan Mantri Awas Yojana (Rural) are the flagship schemes of the Ministry of Rural Development. IAY and PMAY (R) focus on providing houses to below poverty line (BPL) families, and since their inception 32.05 million houses have been constructed incurring an expenditure of Rs. 1,055 billion.

Table 1.7: Indira Awas Yojana

	2011-2012	**2012-2013**	**2013-14**
Houses Target (in mn)	2.72	3.00	2.48
Houses Constructed (in mn)	2.33	2.65	1.59
% Achieved	86%	88%	65%

Source: *Ministry of Rural Development*

The Housing Question

By and large, the poor live in traditional city, basti, hutments, slums, on the pavement, in dilapidated buildings, irregular colonies, etc. These are important sources of housing delivery although unplanned, deficient and unserviced.

The poor and slum dwellers lack minimum shelter, sanitation and drinking water. They are also at various risks, like the problems of unemployment, child labour, insecurity in old age, limited access to healthcare. They are on the margins of the urban community. They are caught in a cycle of perpetual poverty due to non-access to shelter, land, finance, employment and service. In 2011, India's urban housing shortage was estimated as 18.78 million, 95 percent of which is for the Economically Weaker Sections (EWS) and Lower Income Group (LIG). Nearly 65.5 million people (13.9 million household) reside in slums.

According to the government statistics, 14.99 million dwelling units comprise dilapidated, congested and cramped houses. As such, about 80 percent of the total housing shortage urban renewal, upgradation, regularization, redevelopment and in-situ retrofitting.

The current emphasis of housing development is generally on green-field development and is supply driven. Indiscriminate private sector partnership may endanger the access of housing to the poor and may be bought out by the investors/speculators. As a result of speculation, a large number of dwelling units remain unoccupied. The paradox is that as many as 11.09 million houses are lying vacant in urban areas (Census 2011) while that total housing shortage is 18.78 million dwelling units.

In order to establish links between housing and poverty reduction, it is necessary to address the livelihood and shelter issues together:

- In-situ slum rehabilitation, land reservation for social housing rental housing, night shelters, dormitories, hostel, orphanages, etc.
- Provision of basis services like toilets, water points, dustbin, street lights, etc. in the slums and informal settlements.

Land is the most expensive component of housing cost. If land cost is excluded, social housing becomes affordable and viable. This implies mandatory reservation of land for EWS/LIG in all housing projects, the cost which is excluded from the cost of the house. Compulsory reservation of land for social housing and strategies of access to land such as land pooling. Transferable Development Right (TDR), land banking, partial market sale for subsidising social housing, mixed land use and joint development can be adopted.

In order to streamline the housing transactions, as well as to discourage encroachments on public lands, it is necessary to make property registration, mutation and transfer simple, transparent and quick. The city-wide Spatial Data Infrastructure should be mandatory for all urban areas. Vertical ownership of independent floors/flats and the concept of air-rights, along with computerization of land and property records will help in creating a transparent property market. The introduction of Torrens System of property title certification would avoid litigations.

Another important reform for the success of housing for all pertains to the regulatory regime of building bye-laws. Even if all the resources-land, finances, technology, building materials, manpower and machinery are available, the delivery of houses would be delayed unless the development control and building regulations are reformed. Model Building Bye-laws, formulated by the Ministry of Housing and Urban Affairs, mandate online Building Plan approvals on a single platform.

Housing requires a comprehensive approach, of which some key action areas are the following:

- Building Database on Slums, Poverty and Livelihoods, GIS mapping of the slums, city and housing areas.
- Integrating Slums with Infrastructure services and livelihoods.
- Inclusive Zonning; Reservations for the Poor and Informal Sector.
- Transfer of Development Rights, Accommodation Reservation and Incentive Zoning.
- Transfer and allocation of Government/Municipal Lands for slum rehabilitation and social housing.
- Shelter Fund and Municipal Funds for the Poor (P-Budget).
- Participatory Planning, Peoples' Estimates & Social Audit.
- Linking Skill Development, Shelter and Micro-finance.
- Strengthening Institutional Capacity.

The Development Controls, including incentive FAR and densities, should be worked out on the basis of a Housing for All Plan of Action (HFAPoA) of the city. The increase in FAR and density should synchronize with enhanced greens/open, social/community facilities, infrastructure services, parking, etc. The concept of " accommodation reservation", *i.e.* allowing incentive FAR to land owner against the provision of community facilities in private plots, can be invoked for built-up area and regularised unauthorised colonies. In this way the community facility would be made available free of cost and without putting burden on the urban local body. Mixed use, additional FAR and commercial activity in part of the plot can be allowed against appropriation of land for public purpose.

A critical concern in redevelopment, redensification and slum rehabilitation projects relates to infrastructure service such as is water supply, sewerage, power and other services, which are under severe stress. These require strategic interventions, such as given below:

(*i*) Preparation of Service Plans of redevelopment, slum rehabilitation, social housing and regularisation projects.

(*ii*) Mandatory adoption of waste water recycling and renewable energy, water conservation, and energy efficiency as per ECBC and Green Building Code, which can save 10 to 15% of water and energy.

(*iii*) Checking of leakages, thefts and transmission losses which can save about 15 to 20% of water and power.

(*iv*) Enhancing organisational efficiency.

It is necessary to promote 'area-wise' decentralised services for water sewerage and solid waste management. Such systems can be installed and managed by the local communities themselves. An industrial approach can convert housing construction into housing production, saving both cost and time. Proven technologies and regulatory support can enable large-scale, low-cost housing production. Industrial approaches (using components manufactured off-site), standardization, and improved purchasing and other process can reduce the construction time by one-third.

Mobilising Investments for Housing

According to McKinsey Global Institute, the following three main factors can help in making the investments in affordable housing financially viable:

(*i*) Reduce Loan Original Costs:
- Improve assessment methods to quality borrowers.
- Introduced standardized property valuation methods
- Initiate mortgage-guarantee schemes

(*ii*) Reduce cost of funding mortgages:
- Establish liquidity facilities
- Expand capital market funding (with mortgage bonds/securities)
- Increase use of micro deposits

(*iii*) Leverage collective saving to reduce rates:
- Launch housing provident fund
- Offer contractual savings schemes

It is necessary to be careful about land use controls in order to check housing cost. In London, Los Angeles and San Diego, housing costs rose by about three times than their costs before restrictive land use regulations. This is equally discernible in Indian cities.

Affordability

The Demographia International Housing Affordability Survey is based on the "median multiple" price-to-income ratio. The median multiple is calculated by dividing the median house price by medium household income. Housing affordability ratings as indicated in Table 1.8.

Table 1.8: Housing Affordability Rating

Rating	Medium Multiple
Severely Unaffordable	5.1 & Over
Seriously Unaffordable	4.1 to 5.0
Moderately Unaffordable	3.1 to 4.0
Affordable	3.0 & Under

Source: *Demographia Housing Affordability Survey*

In India, the affordability of dwelling unit has been defined as the one with maximum of 30 to 40% of income as Equated Monthly Instalment (EMI) or the ratio of house price to annual income less than 5:1. The income levels of Economically Weaker Sections. Low Income Groups and Middle Income Groups are defined as below Rs. 3.00 lakh p.a. above Rs. 3 lakh to 6 lakh p.a. and above Rs. 6 lakh to 18 lakh p.a. respectively. Various efforts under the affordable housing policy include subsidies to the EWS, LIG and MIG, reducing the cost of finance, lower taxes and interest rates, incentive FAR/SFI, smaller built up area and land for housing compulsory reservation.

Definitions and Short Notes

- **Accommodation Reservation:** The Accommodation Reservation is a form of in-situ TDR which allows the land owner to develop a site reserved for road widening or an amenity in the development plan using full permissible FSI/FAR on the plot. This way the reservations for social housing, parks, utilities, retail markets, dispensaries, etc. are implemented on private lands without the need to acquire the land by payment of compensation.
- **Affordable Housing:** Individual dwelling units with a carpet area of not more than 60 sqm and preferably within the price range of 5 times the annual income of the household as notified, either as a single unit or part of a building complex with multiple dwelling units.
- **Affordable Housing Projects:** Housing projects where at least 60 percent of the FAR/ FSI is used for dwelling units of Carpet Area of not more than 60 sqm. The project shall also reserve 15 percent of the total FAR/ FSI or 35 percent of the total number of dwelling units for EWS category.
- **Architecture and Planning:** The art and science of organisation of space and design of buildings bridging between technology and the humanity. It is connective tissue between individual structures and the community as a whole.
- **Built up area and Plinth Area:** Plinth area means the built up covered area measured at the floor level of any storey, as defined in the IS code - IS 3861 : 2002, Indian Standard Method of Measurement of Plinth, Carpet and Rentable Areas (Second Revision).
- **Below Poverty Line (BPL)** means a person holding a BPL card issued by the State Government from time to time.
- **Betterment Levy:** For the sake of equity and fair distribution of public resources, the concept of betterment levy obliges the land owners to return a part of land value addition or profit that results from public investments. Betternment levies help to finance urban development and pubic services by the ULB and service agencies.
- **Building Code:** Local regulations that set forth the standards and requirements for the construction, maintenance and occupancy of building. The codes are designed to provide for the safety, health and welfare of the pubic.
- **Carpet Area for Affordable Housing Dwelling Unit:** The carpet area is the area under usable and habitable rooms excluding the area of the wall. The method of measurement of carpet area IS code 3861:2002, which includes carpet area of the living room, bedroom, kitchen, lavatory, bathroom, and balcony/verandah. The definition of the Dwelling Unit/ Tenement as provided in the National Building Code, 2016 is an independent housing unit with facilities for living, cooking and sanitary requirements.
- **Bungalow:** The majority of the British population in India lived in residences known as 'banglas' or 'bungalows', in areas where there was least concentration of population.

Kothis in the earlier period were referred to residential-cum-business establishments where goods were stored, with shops, factories or trade companies. In the early nineteenth century, kothis were large imposing residences of the English "Sahibs" and "sophisticated people". These manifested the spatial arrangement of upper strata lifestyle. Bungalows had an indigenous origin, which was derived from "bangla", a simple hut of the Bengal peasant.

"A bangla has a sloping roof on two sides and two gable ends and was made on the local seerky grass, which was remarkably light and doubled or trebled layer made the roof water proof and remarkably easy to construct." (A.D. King, Bungalow: Production of Global Culture, London, 1984).

The bungalow in the early eighteenth century had become a suburban model of a dwelling. The Anglo-Indian bungalow was a free-standing, single storey structure, raised on a plinth and situated within a large compound. It had a living room, bedrooms, dressing room, bathrooms, hall, kitchen and large verandas with projecting eaves.

- **Chawl:** A chawl is a residential building typically found in western India, especially Mumbai. These are usually 4-6 floors high with about 10-20 tenements each floor, constructed to house the migrant worker population. A typical tenement in the chawl consists of a multipurpose room, kitchen and shared/common utilities.
- **Climate:** It is the collective state of the atmosphere at a given place over a long period of time, comprising average as well as extreme weather events. Generally, 30 years of average values are considered in order to know the climate pattern of a given place.

  Micro-climate refers to the climate in specific geographically defined sites. The mirco-climate of a place is affected by local factors such as variation in topography, the presence and density of vegetation, the presence of large water bodies and nature of built development. Temperature and climate regimes determine the prevalence of particular vegetation type, which vary according to altitudes and latitudes.
- **Cluster Development:** Housing cluster arranged around community open space.
- **Common Area:** Those portions of a building, land, or improvements and amenities, parks and shopping, that are used by all of the residents, who share the common expenses of their operation and maintenance. Common areas also include recreational facilities, common corridors, parking areas, means of ingress and egress, etc.
- **Conservation** is the process of looking after a place so as to retain its historical architectural aesthetic and cultural significance. It includes maintenance, preservation, restoration, reconstruction or a combination of more than one of these.
- **Developer:** A private, public or joint sector enterprise engaged in the production and sale or rental of housing.
- **Economically Weaker Section (EWS)** means household having an annual income up to Rs. 3,00,000.
- **Environment:** The combined features of natural resources, that provide the basis for development, environmental management and conservation. It includes the atmospheric, hydrological, geophysical, biotic, human and landscape factors and components.

- **Environmental Impact:** Changes in environmental quality due to external disturbances, which include primary and secondary, short, medium and long-term ecological factors described in terms of magnitude or effect direction of change and probability of occurrence. The "development" (act of altering and modifying the resources of the natural environment to obtain potential economic and social benefits) involves the application of human, financial and biophysical resources, leading to some modifications of the biosphere. The extent of development-induced modifications depend on the locations, scale, intensity and duration of activities, as well as adequancy of mitigation and compensatory measures, which define the environmental costs and benefits. For a development to be "sustainable", it should be economically feasible and socially acceptable, without causing significant environmental impacts or land, air and water.
- **Environment Sensitivity:** The preservation of natural areas such as water bodies, air, woodlands and open areas.
- **Formal rental housing** means rental housing based on an agreement entered into between the owner and the tenant, which is registered with the competent authority under the law for the time being in force.
- **FSI (Floor Space Index) or FAR (Floor Area Ratio):** The quotient obtained by dividing the total covered area (plinth area) on all the floors by the area of the plot: *i.e.* FAR = Total covered area of all the floors/ (divided by) Plot Area × 100
- **Group Housing:** A premises of size not less than 3000 sq. mt. (in NCT Delhi) comprising of residential flats with basic amenities like parking, park, convenience shops, public utility, etc.
- **Haveli:** Haveli is the term used to denote private mansions in North and West India. The word haveli is of Persian origin, meaning an enclosed space. The havelis are usually closed from all sides with a single main entry and exit gate. They typically consist of a courtyard with rooms around. They are energy efficient and climatically comfortable structures, especially suited for the dry and hot climates. The havelis of Rajasthan are famous for their beautiful frescoes that adorn their walls, ceilings, richly carved stone jalis, and jharokhas.
- **Heritage Building** means and includes any building or any part of structure or artefact, which requires conservation for historical, architectural, aesthetic, cultural, environment or ecological purpose.
- **Heritage Precinct** means a complex historic structures which require conservation for historical and/or architectural, aesthetic and cultural values.
- **Hydrogeology:** The study of the occurrence, distribution and movement of ground water.
- **Hydrology** is the branch of earth science that studies the occurrence, circulation and distribution of water in the Earth and its atmosphere primarily on or near the land surface. The science is concerned with the water in streams and lakes, rainfall and water in the soil and rocks.

  The hydrological cycle describes the continuos movement of atmosphere on to the Earth's surface in solid, liquid and vapour state.

- **Increased Density:** More units on a plot that allows that preservation of open space, reduce infrastructure and maintenance costs, and a more diverse mix of housing.
- **Incentives** mean a payment or concession to stimulate greater output or investment in rental housing, which may be fiscal and/or non-fiscal incentives (such as grants, low-interest loans, tax abatements, etc.) that make housing accessible to those who cannot afford market rents.
- **Infrastructure:** Any project, public amenity or pubic utility or service, which is required for smooth, productive and efficient functions of an area, such as infrastructure, access roads, power, common effluent treatment plant (CETP), sewage treatment plant (STP), solid waste disposal system, communication network, shopping, institutional building, community hall, open air theatre, playground, civic-cultural facilities, pubic parking, etc.
- **Integrity:** Anything true to itself, including the honest use of materials, architectural designs and landscapes that complement their setting.
- **Katra:** A katra is a cluster of traditional courtyard houses, found in the inner cities of northern India, especially Delhi. These are entered through a single gateway and consist of two-three storey houses along narrow streets, lined with shops.
- **Land Pooling:** Land Pooling is procurement of land by voluntary consolidation and surrender of land for returnable developed plots with least displacement.
- **Live-Work Concept:** "Live Work concept" started in the 1970s and 1980s, when many urban factories and warehouses in central city were converted into residential and business premises and mixed land use became a major economic force.
- **Informal rental housing** means rental housing which is not based on an agreement entered into between the owner and the tenant, and is not registered with the competent authority under the law for the time being in force.
- **Low Income Group (LIG)** means household having an annual income above Rs. 3,00,000 (Rupees Three Lakhs) and up to Rs.6,00,000 (Rupees Six Lakhs), with a carpet area of dwelling unit between 30 to 60 sqm. States/UTs have the flexibility to redefine the annual income criteria as per local conditions.
- **Market Driven/Private Rental Housing** means rental housing provided by individual owners or institutions/entities or private rental housing operators (such as hostel owners), wherein owners finance the construction and management of rental housing, independent of government assistance.
- **Middle Income Group (MIG):** As per the guidelines of the Affordable Housing in Partnership Scheme, published by the Ministry of Housing and Urban Affairs, MIG I Dwelling with an income of Rs. 6 lakh to Rs. 12 lakh covers a carpet area of upto 160 sqm, and MIG II unit with an income of Rs. 12 lakh to 18 lakh covers a carpet area of upto 200 sqm.
- **Need Based Rental Housing** means rental housing based on need/requirement of different groups (such as students, teachers, working women/men, nurses, construction workers, migrants) who have a source of income, but find it difficult to afford the rent for housing.

- **Owner** means a person who for the time being is receiving, or is entitled to receive, the rent of any residential rental premises, whether on his own account or as a trustee, guardian or receiver of any person/institution.
- **Project approval:** All procedures involved in obtaining clearances for housing project including, but not limited to building permits, land related approvals, environmental clearances and other related approvals.
- **Property Manager** means a person or company who is employed by the owner to manage the residential rental premises and represents the owner in his dealings with the tenant.
- **Public Private Partnership:** A business venture for production and sale or rental of housing involving both private and public sector agencies. Involvement of public agencies may be in the form of active facilitation through supportive policy/ regulations or as equity holders.
- **Public Rental Housing** means social rental housing that is owned by the government, local authority or its entities.
- **Rentable Area** means the usable carpet area at any floor level, which includes the following:

  (*a*) The carpet area of kitchen, pantry, store, lavatory, bath room; and

  (*b*) Fifty percent of carpet area of unglazed and 100 percent of glazed verandah.

  It shall, however, exclude area of unglazed and glazed verandah:

  (*a*) Covered portion of the building such as storage space on landing of staircase.

  (*b*) Fifty percent of the carpet area of balcony.
- **Rental Housing** means a property occupied by someone other than the owner, for which the tenant pays a periodic mutually agreed rent to the owner.
- **Residential Rental Premises** means any building or part of a building which is or is intended to be let separately for the purpose of residence of the tenant and includes:

  (*i*) any fixtures and fittings in such premises for the beneficial enjoyment of the tenant;

  (*ii*) the garden, grounds, parking, garage, out-houses, etc. let out along with the premises to the tenant; and

  (*iii*) the definition of 'residential rental premises' does not include hotels, lodging houses, dharamshala, inn, etc.
- **Shelter** means a covered structure that provides protection from the weather or danger, for lodging of persons on a temporary basis with basic minimum facilities, such as water, sanitation, electricity, etc.
- **Social Rental Housing (SRH)** means rental housing in which the rent is set at a level below the market rates to make it affordable for poor people (Economically Weaker Section & Low Income Group). It may be owned or managed by the government, local authorities, public sector undertakings, non-profit organizations, private or charitable institutions.
- **Tenant** means a person who has entered into a rental housing agreement with the owner in lieu of rent payable towards the same.

- **Mixed Use:** Co-existence of various functions, including work, home, shopping, school, restaurant, entertainment, park, and civic building within a close proximity.
- **New Urbanism or Traditional Neighbourhood Development (TND)** refers to the pedestrian friendly, integrated and mixed land-use pattern characterized by streets, alleys and traditional houses.
- **Site planning:** The process of establishing a coherent design and plan to organize buildings, open spaces and infrastructure on a site.
- **Slum:** According to UN-Habitat, a slum household is defined as a group of individuals living under the same roof, lacking one or more of the following conditions: access to improved water; access to sanitation facilities; sufficient living area (not more than three people sharing the same room); structural quality and durability of dwelling and security of tenure.

  According to the Government of India, an area can be designated as slum under the Slum Clearance and Improvement Act when the competent authority is convinced that the area is source of danger to health, safety and convenience, or when buildings are found to be unfit for human habitation due to dilapidation, overcrowding or lack of ventilation, light or sanitation facilities. According to the 2011 Census, the slum population of India in cities and towns was 8.80 million households, of which 5.6 million are living in notified slums and 3.2 million in non-notified slums. As urban development is a state subject, state governments have the responsibility of notifying an area as a slum, which are eligible for upgrading and improvement under the programmes sponsored by the government.
- **Smart City:** A smart city is defined as one which adopts and promotes smart, innvotative technology, processes and business models for a more efficient and increased citizen engagement to improve its sustainability.
- **Smart Growth and Mixed Land Use:** Smart Growth and Sustainable Urban Form support the integration of mixed land use (MLU) and the communities in close proximity to one another. MLU also provides a more diverse and sizable population and commercial base for supporting public transportaion. It can enhance the vitality and perceived security of an area by increasing the number of the people on the street. It helps streets and public spaces to become places where people meet and revitalise the community life.
- **Sustainable Community:** Sustainability is not a matter of single issue but is an interaction of various systems, which include the variety of land use, circulation, infrastructure, energy, transport, greenery, building system and patterns of human behaviour.
- **Transit a Oriented Development (TOD):** It is a master planned development that focuses on a rapid public transit system that caters to housing, employment, shopping, and entertainment. Ideally, rapid transit station should be no greater than a 10 minute walk, or one-quarter of a mile from housing units.

  This implies a shift from vehicular dependency to walkability, cycling, and non- motorised transportation.
- **Transferable Development Right:** Transferable Development Right enables the land acquisition for public purpose without monetary compensation, but by way of grant

of additional FAR/FSI. This helps in obtaining land for road widening, new roads, development of parks, playground, civic amenities, etc.

- **73rd Constitutional Amendment Act:** The 73rd Constitutional Amendment Act (also referred to as 73rd CAA, 73rd Amendment or the Panchayati Raj Act), passed in 1992 is meant to provide constitutional sanction to establish democracy at the grass roots level. This initiative was undertaken in recognition of the need to reform the existing structure of government, which include:
  - The Gram Sabha or village assembly, as a deliberative body to decentralized governance, is the foundation of the Panchayati Raj System.
  - A uniform three-tier structure of Panchayats at village (Gram Panchyat – GP), intermediate (Panchayat Samiti – PS) and district (Zila Parishad – ZP) levels.
  - To promote bottom-up planning by the District Planning Committee DPC in every district.
- **74th Constitutional Amendment Act:** The 74th Constitutional Amendment Act (also referred to as 74th CAA, 74th Amendment or the Nagarpalika Act) came into force in 1993. One of the requirements under the 74th Amendment is the formation of Ward Committees in municipal bodies with a population of more than three lakh and making them responsible for the planning and implementation of local services.

  Key tasks to be accomplished by urban local bodies (ULBs) under the 74th CAA are:
  - Urban Planning
  - Regulations of land use and construction of building
  - Planning for economic and social development
  - Roads and bridges
  - Water supply for domestic, industrial and commercial purpose
  - Public health, sanitation conservancy and solid waste management
  - Slum improvement and upgrading
  - Urban poverty alleviation
  - Promotion of cultural, educational and aesthetic aspects.
- **District Planning Committee (DPC)** is a committee created for planning at the district level. The Committee in each District consolidates the plans prepared by the Panchayats and the Municipalities in the district and prepares a draft development plan. The Plan includes issues like spatial planning, sharing of water and other physical and natural resources, integrated development of infrastructure services, environmental conservation and the extent and type of available resources, both financial or otherwise.
- **Metropolitan Planning Committee (MPC)** for a Metropolitan Area aims to prepare a draft development plan for the Metropolitan Area as a whole. The legislature of a State can work out the composition of the Metropolitan Planning Committee and the manner in which people would be elected to it.

- **Parastatal Organisations** are state-run establishments or legal entities created by the government to undertake planning, development and service-provision activities on behalf of the government, such as, Delhi Development Authority, Mumbai Metropolitan Region Development Authority (MMRDA); Delhi Jal Board, etc.
- **Urban Local Bodies (ULBs):** ULBs are the constitutionally mandated administrative units that provide basic infrastructure and services in municipal cities and towns. According to Census of India, ULB's are classified into three main categories:
    - *Nagar Nigam*, or Municipal Corporation which governs large urban areas. The area under a Corporation is further divided up into wards. Individual wards or collection of wards within a Corporation sometimes have their own administrative body known as ward committee, as also described under the 74th CAA.
    - *Nagar Palika* or Municipal Council, governs smaller urban areas. Municipalities are divided into wards, which may be together into ward councils.
    - *Nagar Panchayats*: For very small towns, or peri-urban rural areas.
- **Urban Renewal:** The concept of urban renewal gained currency in India in the 1960s, as a process of conservation, rehabilitation and redvelopment of urban areas. It is a policy based approach that aims to regenerate the inner city with a focus on retaining the existing communities and their livelihoods. Although urban renewal has been on the agenda of master plans, it has achieved limited success.
- **Urban Revitalisation:** Revitalisation is a process of architectural and urban rehabilitation of historic centres, aimed at renewing its economic and social life.
- **Utility:** Utilities include roads, bridges, bypasses, street light, water supply system, sewerage system and treatment, storm water drainage, electrical network, and communication network, collection, treatment, discharge and disposal of solid and liquid wastes, gas pipeline, common effluent treatment plant (CETP), space for informal sector, etc.

Sources: *MoHUA, Draft National Rental Housing Policy (2015),*
Housing For All (PMAY) Guidelines (2015),
Task Force on Urban Housing (2012), and other sources.

Debriefing Questions

1. What is current situation with respect to housing shortage in Urban India?
2. Who are the major players in housing delivery?
3. What are the barriers in housing supply?
4. What are the linkages of social housing with livelihoods?
5. Define/explain the following:
   (*a*) Affordable housing
   (*b*) Basic Services
   (*c*) Community Planning

(*d*) Public Private Partnership

(*e*) Zoning and Development Controls to incentivise social housing

(*f*) Co-relation between urbanisation and economic growth

(*g*) Slums

2

HOUSING PROGRAMMES

India's 7936 cities and towns, comprising 4041 statutory and 3895 census cities/towns, have a population of 377 million. These provide 60 per cent of the GDP and 70 per cent of the jobs. It is projected that with a growth rate of 2.76 per cent per year, India would add 200 million urban population in 20 years. This poses a huge challenge of housing and infrastructure development, especially in the context of poverty and climate change. Provision of the basic infrastructure at present is estimated to cost Rs. 16.50 lakh crores and over Rs. 60,000 crores for urban sanitation.

A number of initiatives have been taken by the Government of India to address the requirements of housing and basic services. These include direct interventions for housing and basic services, interest subsidy, housing and slum upgradation and improving the livelihoods.

Table 2.1: Major Schemes with Focus on Housing

Sl. No.	Major Scheme	Year Since
1.	Subsidised Industrial Housing Scheme (Revised in 1966)	1952
2.	Low Income Group Housing Scheme	1954
3.	Subsidised Housing Scheme for Plantation Workers (Revised in 1967)	1956
4.	Slum Clearance and Improvement	1956
5.	Village Housing Project Scheme	1957
6.	Middle Income Group Scheme	1959
7.	Land Acquisition and Development Scheme	1959
8.	Rental Housing Scheme for State Government Employees	1959
9.	Jhuggi Jhopri Removal Scheme (in Delhi)	1960
10.	Rural House Sites-cum-Hut Construction Scheme for Landless Workers	1971
11.	Environmental Improvement of Urban Slums (EIUS)	1972
12.	Workshed-cum-Housing Scheme for Artisans and Handloom Weavers	1974
13.	Integrated Low Cost Sanitation (ILCS) Scheme	1980
14.	Fishermen Housing Scheme	1985

15.	Night Shelter Scheme for Foothpath Dwellers in Urban Areas	1988
16.	Shashu (NRY) (discontinued in 1997)	1989
17.	Indira Awas Yojana (exclusively for rural areas)	1990
18.	EWS Awas Scheme for Beedi Workers & Hamals	1991
19.	Shelter upgradation under PMIUPEP (discontinued in 1997)	1996
20.	National Slum Development Programme (NSDP)	1996
21.	Two-Million Housing Programme for EWS/LIG	1998
22.	Prime Minister's Gramin Awas Yojana	2000
23.	Valmki Ambedkar Awas Yojana (Vambay)	2001
24.	Jawaharlal Nehru National Urban Renewal Mission	2005
25.	Interest Subsidy Housing for Urban Poor (ISHUP)	2009
26.	Affordable Housing in Partnership	2009
27.	Rajiv Awas Yojana (RAY)-Slum Free India Mission	2012
28.	Pradhan Mantri Awas Yojana (PMAY)-Housing for All (Urban and Rural)	2015
29.	Real Estate (Regulation and Development) Act	2016
30.	Model Tenancy Act	2019

Source: *Sen A.K., Housing at the Centre, Shelter, Oct. 2016*

Pradhan Mantri Awas Yojana: Housing for All (Urban)

To meet the 'Housing for All', the following schemes have been formulated by the MOHUA:

- Slum rehabilitation of slums with participation of private developers, using land as a resource
- Promotion of Affordable Housing for weaker sections through credit linked subsidy
- Affordable Housing in Partnership with Public and Private sectors
- Subsidy for beneficiary-led individual house construction

The central government aims to facilitate the construction of 11.20 million affordable houses in urban areas for slum dwellers, Economically Weaker Sections (EWS), Low Income Groups (LIG) and Middle Income Group. The programme provides interest subsidy of 6.5% on housing loans with tenure of up to 15 years for EWS and LIG in urban areas, which equates to nearly Rs. 1 lakh to Rs. 2.30 lakh per unit. The intention is to make cities free from slums and to ensure that houses can be in the name of the women or be jointly owned by husband and wife.

The Housing for All mission gives central assistance to implementing agencies through States and UTs for providing houses to all eligible families/beneficiaries. The Mission is a Centrally Sponsored Scheme (CSS) and covers all 4041 statutory towns as per Census 2011 with focus on 500 Class I cities in three phases. Till October 2019, about 9 million dwelling units were sanctioned by the MOHUA.

The Mission defines an 'Affordable Housing Project' as one where 35% of the houses are constructed for EWS category. Economically Weaker Section (EWS) households are defined as households having an annual income up to Rs. 3,00,000. An EWS house is a dwelling with a carpet area upto 30 sqm with adequate basic civic services and infrastructure services (toilet, water, electricity, etc). Low Income Group (LIG) means households having an annual income between Rs. 3,00,000 up to Rs. 6,0,000. LIG house is a dwelling unit having carpet area up to 60 sqm. Slum is defined as a compact area of at least 300 people or about 60-70 households of poorly built congested tenements, in an unhygienic environment usually with inadequate infrastructure and lacking proper sanitary and drinking water facilities.

Table 2.2: Definition of Affordable Housing

	Income Level	Size of Dwelling Unit	Affordability
EWS	Rs. 3.0 lakh per annum	Up to 30 sm	EMI not exceeding 30 to 40% of monthly income. House price to annual income ratio less than 5:1
LIG	Above Rs. 3.0 lakh to Rs. 6.0 lakh per annum	30-60 sm	
MIG I	> Rs. 6 lakh to Rs. 12 lakh/per annum	60-120 sm	
MIG II	> Rs 12 lakh to Rs 18 lakh per annum	120-150 sm	

Note: As per amendment in 2017-18, the MIG I unit may cover plinth area of 60 to 160 sm and MIG II covers above 160 to 200 sqm.

Source: *MoHUA, 2015 and 2018.*

The Mission comprises four verticals as given below:

"In situ" Slum Redevelopment	Affordable Housing through Credit Subsidy	Affordable Housing in Partnership	Subsidy for beneficiary led individual house construction
– Using land as a resource – With private participation – Extra FSI/TDR/FAR if required to make projects financially viable	– Interest subvention subsidy for EWS and LIG for new house or incremental housing – EWS Annual Household Income up to Rs 3.0 lakh and house size upto 30 sm – LIG: Annual Household Income between Rs. 3-6 Lakhs and house size upto 60 sqm	– With private sector or public including parastatal agencies – Central Assistance for affordable housing projects where 35% of constructed houses are for EWS category	– For individuals of EWS category requiring individual house – State to prepare separate projects for such beneficiaries – No isolated/ splintered beneficiary to be covered

Fig. 2.1. Four Verticals of PMAY (Housing for All)

The MoHUA in 2017-18 included MIG I and MIG II in the definition of Affordable Housing with a plinth area upto 160 m and 200 sm respectivelly and incomes between Rs 6 to 12 lakh and Rs. 12 to 18 lakh respectively.

Slum Redevelopment

According to MOHUA, 2015, in-situ slum rehabilitation uses land as a resource with private participation. This approach aims to leverage the locked potential of land under slums to provide houses to the eligible slum dwellers bringing them into the formal urban settlement. Slums, whether on Central Government land/State Government land/ULB land or private land, have to be taken up for in-situ redevelopment. A private partner for Slum Redevelopment would be selected through open bidding process. State Governments and cities would, if required, provide additional Floor Area Ratio (FAR)/Floor Space Index (FSI)/Transferable Development Rights (TDR) for making slum redevelopment projects financially viable. A slum rehabilitation grant of Rs. 1 lakh per house, on average, would be available for all houses built for eligible slum dwellers in all such projects. States/UTs will have the flexibility to deploy this central grant for other slums being redeveloped for housing eligible slum dwellers through private participation, except slums on private land. The Ministry of Housing and Urban Affairs will decide the limit per house of central assistance, if any, for such slum redevelopment projects. State Governments/UTs or ULBs by giving additional FSI/FAR or TDR to land owners can provide an incentive for redevelopment of slums in-situ on privately owned lands.

States/UTs can decide beneficiary contribution in any slum redevelopment project and eligibility of the slum dwellers. States/UTs may also decide whether the houses constructed will be allotted with ownership rights or with renewable, mortgageable and inheritable leasehold rights. States/UTs may impose suitable restrictions on transfer of these houses. The approach for slum rehabilitation with private partnership is outlined as follows:

- Firstly, all slums as identified in the Housing for All Plan of Action (HFAPOA) of the city should be analysed with respect to their location, number of eligible slum dwellers in that slum, area of the slum land and market potential of the land, FAR/FSI available and density norms applicable to that piece of land, etc.
- On the basis of the analysis, the implementing authorities should decide whether a particular slum can be redeveloped with private participation or not. For making projects financially viable, in some cases, states and cities might have to provide additional FAR/ FSI or TDR and relax density and other planning norms. States/UTs may also allow commercial usage for part of the land/FAR.
- The State/ULB can also consider uniting nearby slum clusters for in-situ redevelopment to make them financially and technically viable. A cluster of slums can be considered as a single project.
- A viable slum rehabilitation project would have two components *i.e.* "slum rehabilitation component" which provides housing along with basic civic infrastructure to eligible slum dwellers and a "free sale component" which will be available to developers for selling in the market so as to cross-subsidize the project.
- While formulating the project, the project planning and implementing authorities should also decide the area of slum land which should be given to the private developers. In some cases, the area of slum may be more than what is required for rehabilitating all eligible

slum dwellers plus free sale component for cross-subsidizing the project. In such cases, project planning authorities should give only the required slum land to private developers. The remaining slum land should be used for rehabilitating residents of other slums or for housing other urban poor.

- Slum dwellers should be consulted through their association or other suitable means during the formulation of redevelopment projects especially for the purpose of designing the slum rehabilitation component.
- The private developers for a slum redevelopment project should be selected through an open transparent bidding process. The eligibility criteria for prospective developers can be decided by States/UTs and ULBs. The prospective developers should conceive and execute the project as required by the implementing agency using their own financial and technical resources. The project developers would also be responsible for providing transit accommodation to the eligible slum dwellers during the construction period.
- All financial and non-financial incentives and concessions, if any, should be integrated in the project and declared 'a priori' in the bid document. These incentives and concessions also include contribution from beneficiaries/slum dwellers.
- Sale of "free sale component" of project should be linked to the completion and transfer of slum rehabilitation component to the implementing agency/state.
- Slum rehabilitation dwelling units should be handed over to implementing agency to allocate such houses to eligible slum dwellers. While making the allotment, families with physically handicapped persons and senior citizens should be given priority for allotment on ground floor or lower floors.
- Open bidding for the slum redevelopment project may result either into a positive premium or negative premium. In case of positive premium, the developer who offers the highest positive premium while satisfying all other conditions should be selected. In case of negative premium, the implementing authority may select the bidder proposing lowest negative premium. Funds required to make the project viable can be made available either from slum rehabilitation grant of Central Government or own fund of States and ULBs as well as positive premium received from other projects. Any private participation, that demands substantial grants from Government, may not be encouraged.
- State Project planning and implementing authorities, ULBs should have a single project account for slum redevelopment project where premium, slum rehabilitation grant from Central Government, as funds from State Government or any other source is to be credited and used for financing all slum redevelopment projects.
- Slum rehabilitation projects would require various approvals from different agencies as per prevailing rules and procedures in the State/UT. To facilitate such changes and for faster formulation and approval of projects, it is suggested that a single authority should be constituted with the responsibility to change planning and other norms and also for according approval to projects.

Affordable Housing: Credit Linked Subsidy Scheme

According to MOHUA (2015), the Mission in order to expand institutional credit flow to the housing needs of urban poor will implement credit linked subsidy component as a demand side intervention. Credit linked subsidy will be provided on home loans taken by eligible urban poor (EWS/LIG) for acquisition/ construction of house.

Beneficiaries of Economically Weaker Section (EWS) and Low Income Group (LIG) seeking housing loans from Banks, Housing Finance Companies and other such institutions would be eligible for an interest subsidy at the rate of 6.5% for a tenure of 15 years or during tenure of loan whichever is lower. The Net Present Value (NPV) of the interest subsidy will be calculated at a discount rate of 9%.

The credit linked subsidy will be available only for loan amounts up to Rs 6 lakhs and additional loans beyond Rs. 6 lakhs, if any, will be at non-subsidized rate. Interest subsidy will be credited upfront to the loan account of beneficiaries through lending institutions resulting in reduced effective housing loan and Equated Monthly Installment (EMI).

Credit linked subsidy would be available for housing loans availed for new construction and addition of rooms, kitchen, toilet, etc. to existing dwellings as *incremental housing. The carpet area* of houses being constructed under this component of the mission should be up to 30 square meters and 60 square meters for EWS and LIG respectively. The beneficiary, at his/her discretion, can build a house of larger area but interest subvention would be limited to first Rs. 6 lakh only.

Housing and Urban Development Corporation (HUDCO) and National Housing Bank (NHB) have been identified as Central Nodal Agencies (CNAs) to channelize this subsidy to the lending institutions and for monitoring the progress of this component.

CNAs will be responsible for ensuring proper implementation and monitoring of the scheme and will put in place appropriate mechanisms for the purpose. CNAs will provide periodic monitoring inputs to the Ministry of Housing and Urban Poverty Alleviation through regular monthly and quarterly reports.

State/UTs/ULBs/PLIs shall link beneficiary identification to Aadhaar, Voter card, any other unique identification or a certificate of house ownership from the Revenue Authority. Preference under the Scheme, subject to beneficiaries being from EWS/LIG segments, should be given to Manual Scavengers, Women (with overriding preference to widows), persons belonging to Scheduled Castes/Scheduled Tribes/Other Backward Classes, Minorities, persons with disabilities and transgender.

State Level Nodal Agency (SLNA) identified by State/UT for implementing the mission will facilitate the identified eligible beneficiaries in getting approvals and documents, etc. to avail credit linked subsidy.

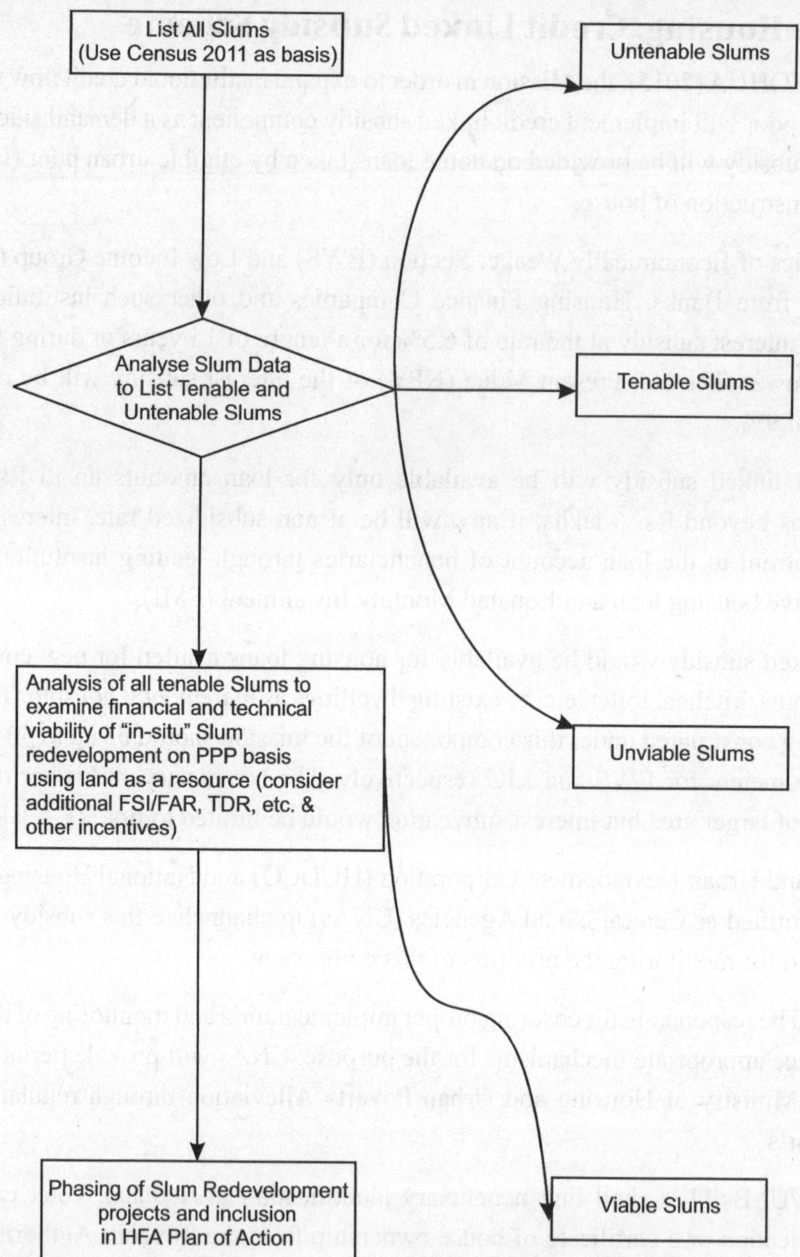

Fig. 2.2. Strategy for Slum Redevelopment Using Land as a Resource

Source: *MOHUA, 2015, Guidelines for PMAY*

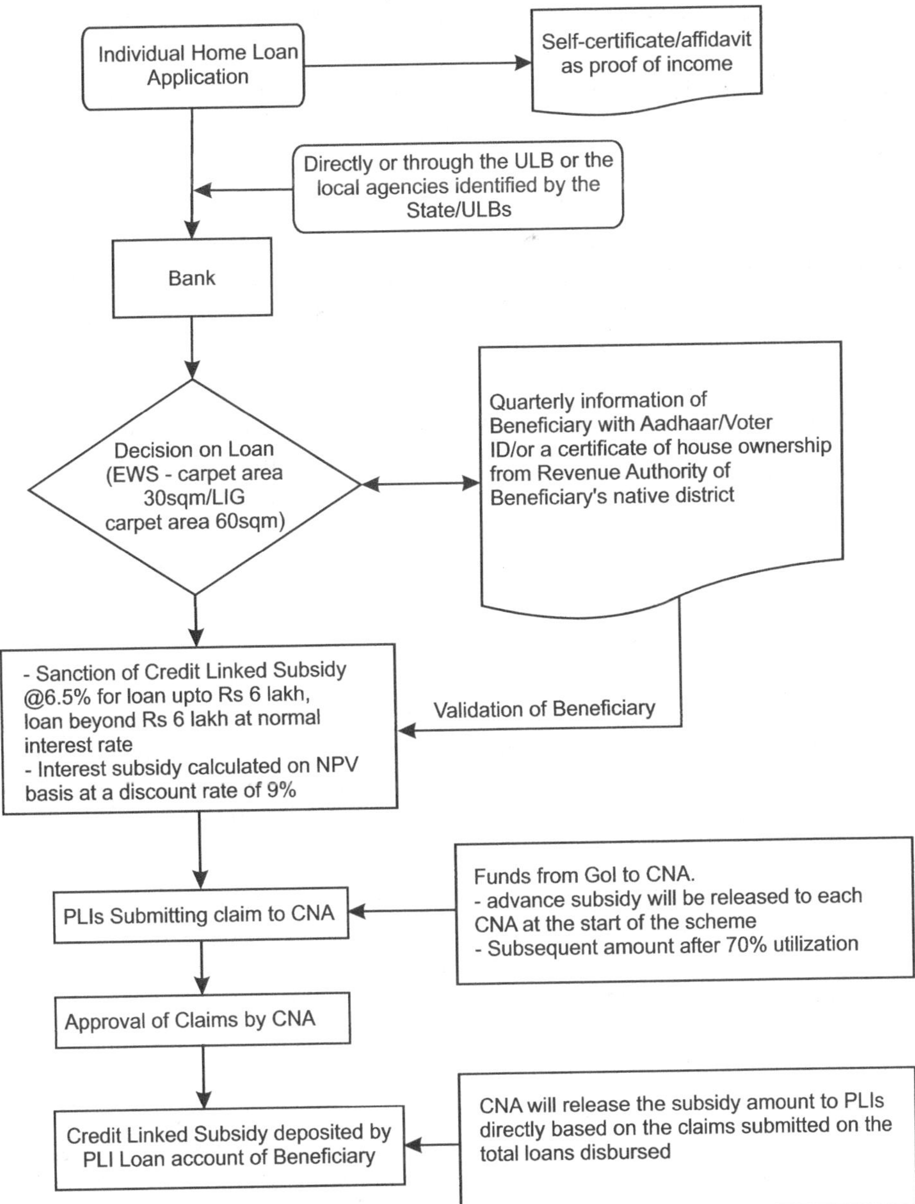

Fig. 2.3. Steps in Credit Linked Subsidy Scheme

Source: *MOHUA, 2015*

Affordable Housing in Partnership (AHP)

The third component of the Housing for All mission is affordable housing in partnership which is a supply side intervention. The Mission provides financial assistance to EWS houses in partnerships with the States/UTs/Cities.

To increase availability of houses for EWS category at an affordable rate, States/UTs, either through its agencies or in partnership with private sector including industries, can plan affordable housing projects. Central Assistance at the rate of Rs. 1.50 lakh per EWS house would be available for such projects.

The States/UTs would decide on an upper ceiling on the sale price of EWS houses in such projects with an objective to make them affordable and accessible to the intended beneficiaries. For that purpose, State and cities may extend other concessions such as their State subsidy, land at affordable cost, stamp duty exemption, etc.

An affordable housing project can be a mix of houses for different categories but it will be eligible for central assistance, if at least 35% of the houses in the project are for EWS category and a single project has at least 250 houses. CSMC, however, can reduce the requirement of minimum number of houses in one project on the request of State Government.

Allotment of houses to identified eligible beneficiaries in AHP projects should be made following a transparent procedure as approved by SLSMC and beneficiaries selected should be part of HFAPoA. Preference in allotment may be given to physically handicapped persons, senior citizens, Scheduled Castes, Scheduled Tribes, Other Backward Classes, minority, single women, transgender and other weaker and vulnerable sections of the society. While making the allotment, the families with differently-abled persons and senior citizens may be allotted house preferably on the ground floor or lower floors.

Individual House Construction

According to MOHUA, the fourth component of the mission is assistance to individual eligible families belonging to EWS categories to either construct new houses or enhance existing houses on their own to cover the beneficiaries who are not able to take advantage of other components of the mission. Such families may avail of central assistance of Rs. 1.50 lakh for construction of new houses under the mission. Such beneficiaries should be part of HFAPoA.

A beneficiary desirous of availing this assistance shall approach the ULBs with adequate documentation regarding availability of land owned by them. Such beneficiaries may be residing either in slums or outside the slums. Beneficiaries in slums which are not being redeveloped can be covered under this component if beneficiaries have a Kutcha house.

The Urban Local Bodies shall validate the information given by the beneficiary and building plan for the house submitted by beneficiary so that ownership of land and other details of beneficiary like economic status and eligibility can be ascertained. In addition, the condition of the houses, *e.g.* kutcha, semi-kutcha, etc. of the prospective beneficiary should be checked with SECC data to ensure beneficiary's consequent eligibility for construction of new housing. SECC data regarding number of rooms, details of family members, etc. should also be checked to ensure beneficiary's eligibility for enhancement.

On the basis of these applications, ULBs will prepare an integrated housing project for such individual beneficiaries in accordance with the City Development Plan (CDP) or other such plans of the city to ensure construction of proposed houses are as per planning norms and scheme is implemented in an integrated manner. Individual applicants for assistance shall not be considered.

Such Projects would be approved by States in SLSMC. While approving project for individual house construction, Urban Local Bodies and State/UT should ensure that required finance for constructing the planned house is available to the beneficiary from different sources including his own contribution, GoI assistance, State Government assistance, etc.

Implementation Process

The Housing for All Mission guidelines stipulate that as a first step States/UTs will sign a Memorandum of Agreement (MoA) to participate in the mission by agreeing to mandatory conditions and other modalities. States/UTs will send proposals to the Ministry for inclusion of cities in the mission along with broad assessment of housing and resources requirement. Ministry will approve inclusion of these cities considering availability of resources. The credit linked subsidy component of the mission will, however, be implemented in all statutory cities/towns across the country right from the launch of the mission.

State/cities will undertake a demand survey through suitable means for assessing the actual demand of housing. While validating demand survey, States/Cities should consider possible temporary migration from rural areas to the city just to take advantage of housing scheme and exclude such migrants from list of beneficiaries. On the basis of demand survey and other available data, cities will prepare Housing for All Plan of Action (HFAPoA). HFAPoA should contain the demand of housing by eligible beneficiaries in the city along with the interventions selected out of four verticals mentioned in the guidelines. The information regarding beneficiaries should be collected by States/UTs in suitable formats. While preparing HFAPoA, State/UT and implementing agencies should also consider the affordable housing stock already available in the city as Census data suggests that large number of houses are vacant.

Jan Dhan Yojana/other bank account number and Aadhaar number/Voter ID card/any other unique identification details of intended beneficiaries or a certificate of house ownership from Revenue Authority of beneficiary's native district will be integrated in the data base of HFAPoA for avoiding duplication of benefit to one individual family. Beneficiaries will be validated by States/UTs and ULBs thereby ensuring their eligibility at the time of preparation of the projects and approval of projects.

On the basis of HFAPoA, States/Cities will subsequently prepare the Annual Implementation Plans (AIPs) dividing the task upto 2022 in view of the availability of resources and priority. For larger cities, HFAPoA and AIPs can be prepared at sub-city (ward/zone) level with the approval of concerned State/UT Government.

HFAPoA should be reviewed on a yearly basis to make changes in view of implementation of Annual Implementation Plan (AIP) in the preceding years. Based on HFAPoA and availability of resources, each city will prepare Detailed Project Report (DPRs) under each component of the Mission. All DPRs should be approved by State Level Sanctioning and Monitoring Committee.

The provisions of the City Development Plan, City Sanitation Plan, etc. are to be considered with preparing HFAPoA for achieving synergy with other ongoing programmes.

Technology Sub-Mission

According to Housing for All Mission Guidelines (2015) a Technology Sub-mission has been set up to facilitate adoption of modern, innovative and green technologies and building material for faster and quality construction of houses. Technology Sub-Mission facilitates preparation and adoption of layout designs and building plans suitable for various geo-climatic zones. It also assists States/ Cities in deploying disaster resistant and environment friendly technologies.

The Sub-mission coordinates with various regulatory and administrative bodies for mainstreaming and upscaling the deployment of modern construction technologies and material in place of conventional construction. Technology sub-mission also coordinates with other agencies working in green and energy efficient technologies, climate change, etc.

The Sub-mission covers the following aspects: (*i*) Design & Planning (*ii*) Innovative technologies & materials (*iii*) Green buildings using natural resources and (*iv*) Earthquake and other disaster resistant technologies and designs. Simple designs ensuring adequate sunlight and air should be adopted. Centre and State would also partner with the IITs, NITs and Planning & Architecture institutes for developing technical solutions, capacity building and handholding. State or region specific needs of technologies and designs are also supported under the Sub-Mission.

Real Estate (Regulation and Development) Act, 2016

The Real Estate (Regulation and Development) Act 2016 aims to create a Real Estate Regulatory Authority and an Appellate Tribunal that will act as a watchdog for the housing sector. For protecting consumer interests while creating an alternative redressal mechanism for any disputes that may arise. The Act demands greater disclosure from the developer community and a higher level of project accountability to remove the information asymmetries from the housing market. The Act mandates the compulsory registration of real estate agents, which is likely to provide protection to buyers, while also preventing money laundering by the non-organised broker community. A major provision of the Act is the standardization of area measurement, with carpet area to be the measure. Developer would need to provide the status of all approvals as well as sanctioned plans to buyers and will not be able to sell their project without obtaining the required approval. The Act has also sought to ensure that the buyer's payment is utilized for the development of the particular project by necessitating the creation of an escrow account, where 70% of the customer advance will be used only for that project. The Act also seeks to make the developer responsible for adhering to the timelines and conditions committed for the project.

National Urban Housing and Habitat Policy (NUHHP, 2007) had identified 'Affordable Housing for All' as a key focus area for sustainable urban development. The major objectives of the policy were as listed below:

- Facilitating accessibility to serviced land and housing with focus on economically weaker sections and low income group categories
- Land assembly, development and disposal to be encouraged by both private and public sectors
- Forging strong partnerships between public, private and cooperative sectors for accelerated growth of housing and sustainable habitat.
- Accelerating the pace of development of housing and related infrastructure.
- Using technology for modernizing the housing sector for enhancing energy and cost efficiency, productivity and quality.

Jawaharlal Nehru National Urban Renewal Mission (JNNURM): The Jawaharlal Nehru National Urban Renewable Mission (JNNURM) was initiated on 3rd December 2005 as the largest scheme to encourage and expedite urban reforms. The mission comprised Basic Services for the Urban Poor (BSUP) managed by the Ministry of Urban Development. It provided seven entitlements or services - security of tenure, affordable housing, water, sanitation, health, education and social security to low-income segments in the 65 mission cities.

Integrated Housing and Slum Development Programme (IHSDP) was taken up in the cities/towns not covered under BSUP, with the following, features:

- Central Assistance in the form of ACA as full grant.
- 80% of the project cost to be borne by the Central Government.
- A minimum of 12% beneficiary contribution for houses; for SC/ST/BC/OBC/PH and other weaker sections, with only 10% beneficiary contribution.

The Rajiv Awas Yojana (RAY) provided Central Government support for slum redevelopment and construction of affordable housing, with the aim of making Indian cities slum free. The scheme comprised preparatory activities such as slum surveys, GIS mapping of slums and development of slum free city plans with active involvement of experts having expertise in the areas of GIS, MIS, planning, etc.

Implementation of Housing Policies and Programmes

With the Central Government's substantial contribution and matching contribution of the state governments, local bodies and beneficiaries, the social housing and slum rehabilitation schemes have become viable and affordable. Simultaneously, to make loans available to the poor a Credit Risk Guarantee Fund (CRGF) has been created.

The JNNURM-BUSP project in Thane is a typical example, where only 16 per cent of the house cost is borne by the allottees. The funding pattern of the project is four layered-Government of India contributed 50 per cent, Government of Maharashtra 25 per cent, TMC 9 per cent and remaining 16 per cent by the slum families. TMC has also used Transfer of Development Rights (TDR) and Floor Space Index (FSI) for funding the viability gap. Smart cards were issued to slum families so that benefits reach to the genuine people.

Housing loans to urban poor are given with 5 per cent interest subsidy which is available for loans up to Rs. 5 lakh where an LIG beneficiary can borrow up to Rs. 8 lakh. This enables the ULBs/State Housing Agency to access 50 per cent of the investments from the Central Government. Remaining 25 per cent can be contributed by the State government and 25 per cent by the ULB/Housing Agency/Board and beneficiaries' contribution. However, the cost of land has to be met by cross-subsidy, compulsory reservation, land pooling and reconstitution, TDR and similar instruments. By mandatory reservation of land for EWS/LIG housing, the cost of land excluded from the cost of the house—the scheme can be viable.

Housing Policies of the State Governments

Various State Governments have framed policies of Affordable Housing Development, with incentives like interest rate subsidy, enhanced Floor Area Ratio (FAR), Single Window Clearance, exemptions from stamp duty and development charges, change of Land Use Charges, etc. Invariably most of state governments have adopted the policy of one per cent interest subsidy on loans up to Rs. one million for purchase of houses costing less than Rs. two million. Haryana & Tamil Nadu Government have announced increase in FSI for housing projects targeting lower and middle income groups. Tamil Nadu has announced 50 per cent extra FSI for projects targeting EWS in Chennai Metropolitan Area (CMA), and 30 per cent extra FSI for projects targeting MIG housing projects.

State Governments' Housing Policies usually encourage the following:

Effective use of available Government land

- Unused Land parcels currently in possession of the government (*e.g.* SEZs, Industrial zones, Railways, NHAI, etc.) can be used for housing development, thereby reducing the cost of land
- Government can enter into joint ventures with developers with land as equity
- Redevelopment of slums on encroached lands by using land as a resource

Land Banking

- Purchase of large tracts of land by State Governments/Housing Agencies
- Distribution of land to private developers through a transparent process
- Land inventory, identifying potential areas of infill development and densification

FSI/FAR

- Relaxation of FSI norms to reduce land and dwelling unit cost
- FSI can be an effective tool to provide a cashless subsidy to builders and land owners against use of land for social housing, public facilities/amenities, greens, etc.

Cross-Subsidization

- Joint development of MIG, LIG and EWS flats with cross subsidization
- LIG and EWS units can be subsidized by market sale of HIG/MIG flats and commercial/ mixed land use component

Single window approval of housing projects

- To reduce delays and contain costs

Reduction in taxes on Building Materials and Construction Costs

- Reduction / exemption / deferment of taxes and duties on construction materials
- Subsidy to developers for R& D in new low cost materials and technologies
- Subsidy to developer in view of employment generated
- Lower cost of borrowing for affordable housing projects/Government participation

Sales Tax and Stamp Duty

- Reduced GST sales tax and reduction/exemption from stamp duty

Development of urban infrastructure

- PPP projects for accelerated urban infrastructure, metro rail, highways, monorail, BRT, Ring Road, etc.
- Increased budget for urban infrastructure

Integrated Townships

- Joint development

- Development of infrastructure and residential space
- Planned expansion of city limits

Access to lower cost of capital

- Relaxation of ECB norms for housing companies
- Increase in income tax ceiling on housing loans.
- Increase central, support to State Governments for affordable housing projects

Profitability of developers and housing finance companies

- 80 IB benefits for all affordable housing project developers and housing finance companies

Special focus on EWS and LIG segment

- The government and subsidiaries prioritise the EWS/LIG and affordable housing, and provide incentives to the developers.

Various State Governments provide certain incentives to promote affordable housing, as given in the following table:

Table 2.3: State Policies on Housing and Recommended Incentives

National/State	Affordable Housing Policy	Year	Key Incentives to the developer
National	• National Urban Housing and Habitat Policy • Pradhan Mantri Awas Yojana	2007 2015	• Relaxation of FAR 20–25% additional FAR for EWS/LIG. • Interest subvention in subsidy • Central assistance/subsidy to State Housing Agency/Individuals. • Land Banking.
Rajasthan	Affordable Housing Policy (with focus on EWS/LIG housing.)	2009 (Revised 2015)	• Double of the normal FAR, TDR facility for selected projects. • Waiver of EDC, Fast track building plan approval, free from conversion charges, • 10% of the land allowed for commercial use.
Madhya Pradesh	Housing & Habitat Policy	2007	• Additional FSI given for providing EWS/LIG housing. • One time transfer of additional FAR to another location is permitted under TDR Scheme.
Maharashtra	Maharashtra State Housing Policy	2007	• Developer is given TDR equivalent to FSI the area of land provided for rehabilitation project. • TDR is available against the free sale component.

Uttar Pradesh	Urban Housing Policy	1995	• Min Area 5 acres, max. 100 acres Residential unit size: 75 sqm (max) Cost: Rs. 15 to Rs. 30 lakh, Extra FAR, exemption from EDC, conversion changers, stamp duty, etc.
Karnataka	Karnataka Affordable Housing Policy	2013	• Developer is paid TDR equivalent to FSI of the land provided for rehabilitation project. • TDR is available against the free sale component.
Gujarat	Gujarat Housing Policy	2014	• Incentive of additional FSI of 50% for LIG/EWS and slum redevelopment projects. • Reservations for Affordable Housing.
West Bengal	Affordable Housing and Habitat Policy of West Bengal	2015	• Land is provided by State government. • State Government helps in building plan clearances, loans, etc. • Cross-subsidy to EWS & LIG by commercial development and market sale of HIG units.

***Source:** Adapted and updated from Task Force Report (2012) MoHUPA, New Delhi*

Rajasthan Affordable Housing Policy

Rajasthan Government formulated its Affordable Housing Policy in 2009, and updated in 2015. It has been framed with the following objectives:

- To reduce the housing shortage in the State, especially in EWS/LIG categories.
- To take up large scale construction of Affordable Housing (with focus on EWS & LIG housing with super built up area of 325 and 300 sq. ft. respectively).
- To bring down the cost of EWS & LIG houses to affordable limits.
- To promote investments in housing on PPP model.
- To involve private developers in the construction of EWS/LIG houses by offering various incentives.
- To create rental housing and transit accommodation for migrants.

The policy aims to help fill a housing shortage of an estimated one million units, which offers density bonus with transferable development rights to private developers. In return for devoting at least 40 per cent of units to housing for low-income segments (which are sold to the government at a pre-determined price), the government allows the developer to double the floor-area ratio on the site where the bonus is earned or on another site. The policy stipulates mandatory provision to construct at least 25% plots/houses/flats of EWS/LIG category and 20% of the plots/houses/flats for

MIG-A category. Private developers shall reserve 15% of the dwelling units for EWS/LIG in their township housing schemes.

The built up EWS/LIG flats shall be handed over to the nodal agency (Awas Vikas Limited) at pre-determined prices, to be allotted to the eligible beneficiaries by the nodal agency.

The developer would be free to construct MIG/HIG flats on remaining land and is eligible for the incentives like double of the normal FAR. TDR facility, waiver of EDC, Building plan approval free and conversion charges. 10% for the total landers allowed for commercial use. Private develop are also facilitated to build affordable housing on acquired lands of the ULB/government against payment of compensation (Land Acquisition cost + 10% Administration charges). Government lands are also offered the developers through open bidding, whereby the developer offers the maximum number of EWS/LIG and slum rehabilitation flats free of cost to the ULB in using a part of land for market sale (residential) and 10% for commercial use.

The policy facilitated construction of about 2.35 lakh houses in 77 cities across Rajasthan.

Gujarat

Gujarat has taken four initiatives to deal with affordable housing. The first is under the Regulations for Rehabilitation and Redevelopment of the Slums, 2010. It aims at rehabilitation of slums through regulations and incentives such as additional FSI. This enables providing housing at no cost to the existing slum dwellers. For the scheme a society of individual slum households must be formed and 75 per cent of them must agree to the scheme. The scheme applies to existing slums.

The second scheme is under the Regulations for Residential Townships Act, 2009. It relates to private developers who must purchase at least 40 hectares of land (in cases where Urban Development Authorities exist) or 20 hectares of land (in other relevant authority areas).10 per cent of the area must be reserved for housing for the economically weaker section.

The third scheme is operated under the Town Planning Scheme, where every owner within specific boundaries must provide a certain per centage (30 to 40 per cent) of the land to the Government. Government pays market rate for the land, provides the entire infrastructure, and the value of the owner's land tends to go up by about 10 to 15 per cent in a year per cent of the land is reserved for Affordable Housing.

The fourth scheme covers the lands obtained under the erstwhile Urban Land Ceiling and Regulation Act. The Gujarat government has repealed the Urban Land Ceiling and Regulation Act and transferred surplus land to urban local bodies at nominal rates for projects focused on EWS/LIG housing. The government has also come out with special provisions for the development of low cost housing, where the owner/authorised developer is expected to provide a minimum built up area of 20 sqm subject to a minimum carpet area of 14 sqm to slum dwellers along with water supply, drainage, and electricity.

Gujarat Affordable Housing Policy - 2014

Gujarat Affordable Housing Policy (Public Private Partnership), launched in 2014, envisages construction of 1 million DUs through the following measures:

- Providing affordable housing on public & private land through PPP
- Incentives of higher FSI and rationalized planning norms

- Cross-subsidization by allowing development for free sale housing covering a maximum of 40% permissible FSI, and 10% commercial development.
- Stagewise fixed payment by beneficiary.

The Gujarat Policy also covers the following:

(*a*) Technology neutral tendering process

(*b*) Incentives to private developer linked with cost and reasonable profit margin

(*c*) Lump sum turnkey based tendering to provide desired operational & design flexibility

(*d*) Government and ULB land is made available through a simplified process by giving advance possession at Re 1/-

(*e*) Simultaneous process of computerized draw, issuance of allotment letter and bank stalls for loan tie up

(*f*) Reservation for Affordable Housing Zone in Development Plan and Socially and Economically Weaker Section (SEWS) housing in Town Planning Scheme

(*g*) Inclusive land use planning with Development Control Regulations for Slum rehabilitation & Affordable Housing.

Andhra Pradesh State Affordable Housing Policy, 2015

To track the affordable housing shortage for EWS/LIG the state of Andhra Pradesh adopted a two pronged strategy to achieve the following objectives of the policy:

- Critical interventions in demand and supply areas such as subsidies, ensuring land bank availability, promoting Ease of Doing Business, financial incentives and assistance etc.
- To adopt a balanced approach between State's responsibilities and free market system for the housing sector, the latter cross-subsidising the former.

The policy has proposed four models for affordable housing encouraging private sector participation with some mandatory conditions for housing for urban poor:

(*a*) Private developer on private land

(*b*) Private developer on Government land

(*c*) Government led development

(*d*) Rental housing projects, and benefits such as exemption in service tax, trade license fees and stamp duty for affordable and rental housing units (upto 60 sq. m).

Approval process simplification includes automated land use conversion from agriculture land to non-agriculture status for land parcels falling under the development plan and empanelment of third party consultants for survey, financial and project approval, certification, etc.

Incentives also include 100% exemption of stamp duty for affordable housing component, grievance redressal system, quality infrastructure facilities, simplified and transparent application, verification and allotment procedure, etc.

Sikkim-Urban Affordable Housing and Habitat Policy

Key institutions for housing delivery in Sikkim have been identified, with their roles and responsibilities.

Initiatives under the Sikkim Policy include the following:

(*a*) Build an internal community of skilled labour by initiating Building Construction Related Skill Development Modules

(*b*) Focus on special needs of single working women, disabled and senior citizens

(*c*) The selection criteria for private developers

(*d*) Incentives for beneficiaries such as 100% exemption of stamp duty for affordable housing quality infrastructure, speedy allotment procedure etc.

(*e*) Various non-monetary and monetary benefits are given to Developers/ Non-Governmental Organisations (NGOs) engaged in providing Affordable Housing.

Karnatka Affordable Housing Policy, 2013

Launched in 2013, Karnataka Affordable Housing Policy encourages affordable housing developer through incentives and concessions through the following models:

(*a*) Private developers to construct EWS/LIG housing on 40% of their own land and will be free to sell the remaining portion.

(*b*) Karnataka Housing Board (KHB) with the help private developers to construct 50% for EWS/LIG in each of housing scheme on government land.

(*c*) Development Authorities (DAs) and ULBs to allot at least 30% of plot/flats for EWS/LIG in their residential/housing schemes.

(*d*) At least 15% of Dwelling Units and plots (or 5% of total residential area in the scheme) to be earmarked for EWS/LIG in each private township and group housing schemes.

(*e*) Housing schemes for Industrial Workers and Labour.

Some initiatives under the Karnataka Housing Policy:

(*a*) Reservation of 25% of the land acquired in an industrial estate for residential layout to accommodate workers

(*b*) Penalty imposed on developers in case of delay

(*c*) Ensuring completion of external development works within 12-18 months

(*d*) Standard type designs

(*e*) Maintenance by developers for 3 year after completion of the project, and its subsequent transfer to Residents Welfare Association (RWA).

Maharashtra

The Maharashtra State Housing Policy, 2007 promotes LIG and EWS housing along with rental housing as a key objective. The State has constituted a Slum Rehabilitation Authority (SRA) to focus on rehabilitation and redevelopment of slums, and Integrated Housing and Slum Development Program (HSDP).

Mumbai Urban Development Project

MHADA has embarked Mumbai Urban Development Project with the help of the World Bank. The project implemented through MHADA, CIDCO & MMC, comprises the following 2 main components:

- Land Infrastructure Servicing Programme (LISP)
- Slum Upgradation Programme (SUP)

Under the LISP the sites are developed to provide serviced plots of 25, 30, 40, 60 and 100 sqm and apartments. The plots of 25 and 30 sqm, are meant for the EWS category and 40 sqm plots are meant for LIG category. The planning is done in such a manner that at least 60% plots become available to EWS and LIG category. The ratio of 60 sqm to 100 sqm plots is maintained at 15% and Society plots at 25%. The schemes provide social and physical infrastructure and integrated development, including home extension loan and financing facilities.

As given below, the development follows development control regulations of Mumbai Municipal Corporation. However, for change of land use the government is the competent authority, which processes such cases on the recommendations of the SRD Authority.

- **FSI:** An FSI up to 2.5 having a differential approach is allowed and the concept of Transfer of Development Rights (TDR) has been made applicable in order to avoid congestion and over-concentration in heavily built-up areas.
- **Density:** The minimum density prescribed for such development is 500 tenements per hectare.
- **Ground coverage:** In Slum Rehabilitation/Redevelopment projects, the rule for ground coverage is confined to peripheral setbacks as per DCR without insisting upon overall ratio of ground coverage/plot size.
- **Mixed land use:** for Slum Rehabilitation in Mumbai, mixed land use policy has been adopted. Existing shop owners are eligible for built up shops up to 225 sq.ft. The usual practice is to allow 10% of the land FSI for commercial use in cooperative Societies.
- **Open Space:** The general practice is to reserve 15 per cent of the plot as open space.
- **Community facilities:** The provision of community facilities is generally seen as a government responsibility and there provision in SRD schemes is made with the help NGOs, except essential utilities like electric sub-station, pump house, etc.

Odisha: Housing for All in Urban Areas, 2015

Launched in August 2015, it aims at construction of 1 lakh dwelling units in Odisha over the next 5 years for EWS and LIG households. It offers seven models for development in convergence with Pradhan Mantri Awas Yojana (PMAY) - Housing for All (Urban) :

(*a*) Mandatory development of EWS and LIG housing
(*b*) Incentives for market based development
(*c*) Development of Affordable Housing Projects
(*d*) Beneficiary led individual Housing Construction and Enhancement Schemes
(*e*) Relocation Rehabilitation and In-situ Slum Redevelopment
(*f*) Rental Housing

The Policy envisages:

(*a*) Single window clearances.
(*b*) Online registration of applicants/beneficiaries along with biometric details, followed by Social Audit.

(*c*) Facilitation Centres set up by Odisha Housing Mission to aid applicants who do not have access to computer and internet.

(*d*) The Slum dwellers to be the members of Slum Area level Registered Society.

Haryana Government

Affordable Housing Policy, 2013 aims to make housing 'affordable' in the urban centers of Haryana. The housing projects are developed in plots ranging from five acres to ten acres. Regulations have been framed for the provision of a minimum of 20% of gross area of plotted development for LIG and EWS housing. In case of group housing developments, 15% of the flats are reserved for the urban poor.

Uttar Pradesh

The UP government has initiated the Samajwadi Awas Yojana, which provides the following mandates and incentives for affordable housing:

- Mandatory area of the scheme: minimum 5 acres and maximum 100 acres
- Residential unit area: Maximum 75 sqm (carpet area)
- Residential unit value: Rs. 15 lakhs to Rs. 30 lakhs
- Free from development charges
- Free from land-use change charges
- Free from stamp duty charges
- Increased residential density
- Free extra floor area ratio (F.A.R.)
- Single window system for the approval of the scheme

Madhya Pradesh-Night Shelter and Ram Roti Yojana: Bhopal Municipal Corporation started the Ram Roti Yojana scheme in 2010 to provide low-cost food and shelter to the poor. Operational in Bhopal, Indore, Gwalior and Jabalpur in Madhya Pradesh, a night halt at the rein basera (night shelter) is for only Rs. 2 per night, which includes provision of a bed sheet, blanket, pillow and durrie (cotton carpet), and toilet and bathroom facilities. Food is also served at bus stands and railway stations, at the rate of Rs. 5 per head, which contains six rotis, cooked vegetables, pickles, etc. The night shelters have also been built at Hoshangabad, Itarsi, Betul, Vidisha, Sehore, Satna, Rewa, Dewas, Ujjain, Khandwa, and Burhanpur.

The Way Forward

The approach of public housing schemes has been largely supply driven with private sector partnership. However, a large number of new dwelling units built by private developers remain unoccupied. The Census 2011 pointed out that as many as 11.09 million houses are lying vacant.

This poses a need to re-examine the supply driven approach towards housing, which is often without the participation of the dwellers. The public-private model is largely focused on greenfield development and marginalises the poor. There are few exceptions where PPP model in social housing has succeeded. One such project is Sukhobrishti at Rajarhat, Kolkata.

Inclusive housing paradigm has to be gender sensitive, community led, participatory and local and based on the principle of equitable allocation of resource, space and land. Every house should be provided with linkages, livelihoods, water, electricity, toilets and security. This make us to rethink about the model of public-private binary and develop a third option.

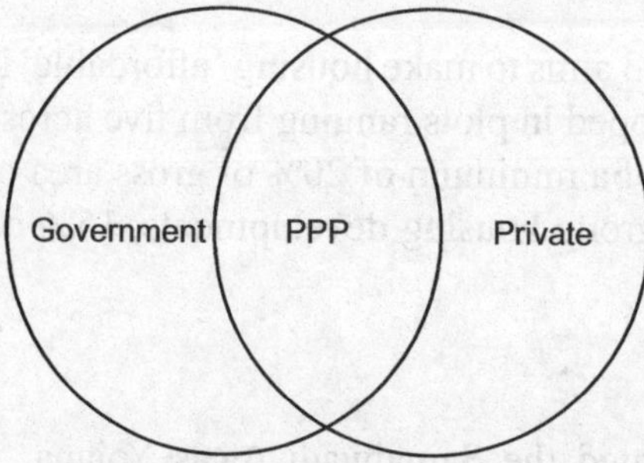

Fig. 2.4. Public-Private Binary

The Third Option

The following are the basic ingredients of the third option:

- Community as the core actor in the shelter process
- Demand–driven approach rather than supply-driven
- Local communities control the money and resources
- Promote a broader concept of upgrading and improvement of existing shelters
- Promote variations rather than standard solutions
- Synchronize shelter and poverty reduction
- Optimum utilization of urban land with focus on brownfields
- Capacity development, community empowerment and new partnerships.

The third option does not exclude the private sector, but it participates in the collective model and energises the community.

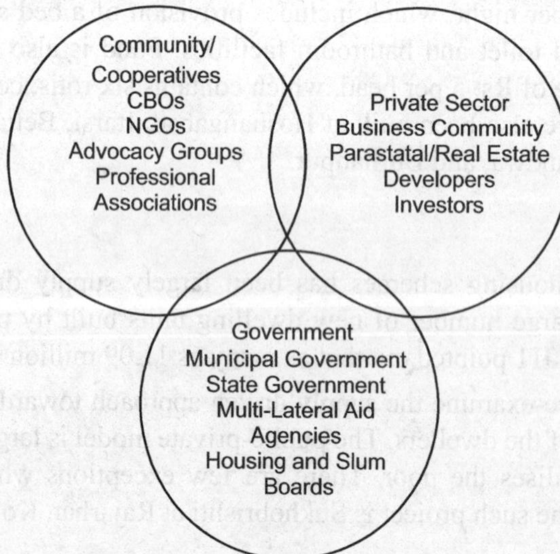

Fig. 2.5. Community Sector as Third Option to Public-Private Binary

As many as 15 million dwelling units out of total housing shortage of 18.78 million are dilapidated and congested, which need retrofitting and upgradation. As such renewal and redevelopment of existing housing stock has to be major focus area. Such areas need to be provided with better infrastructure services, linkages, livelihoods, and social and cultural facilities.

For the consumer it is the ultimate cost of the house that matters. To this end, several approaches are adopted, which include subsidies, financial loans and mandatory reservation of land, higher FAR/FSI and densities, in-situ slum rehabilitation, upgradation of existing housing, site and services, evolutionary, core, and infill housing, low cost construction and saving on time and resources

A large number of low income families cannot access housing loan and are unable to pay its upfront cost and mortgage payment. Many poor families survive on day-to-day earnings and can only afford rental housing. Even in illegal slums and invasion on public lands, they pay weekly or monthly rental to slum-lord. However, the quantum of rental housing is diminishing due to various reasons such as taxation, Rent Control Act, paperwork and transactions involved. The rental housing as per NSSO/Census (2011) is only 10 per cent by a formal rental arrangement and 17 per cent households, mostly poor live in informal rental housing. Keeping in view the difficulties in obtaining rental payment, the concessions, loans and legal disputes, even the available housing is kept vacant or sold away. Most of the house owners fear that once the house is given on rent, it will never be available to the owner.

Keeping in view the barriers in rental housing, the Government of India has formulated Draft National Urban Rental Housing Policy (NURHP, 2015) and Model Tenancy Act, 2019, which suggest various administrative and legal measures and financial incentives to promote rental housing,

Debriefing Questions

1. What is the assessment of urban housing shortage in India and its broad break-up as per the income groups?
2. What are the Government programmes to address the urban housing shortage? What are the salient features of PMAY?
3. What is the slum population in India and its characteristics, *e.g.* extent, average slum size, status of structure services, toilets, livelihoods, etc.?
4. What is the extent of rural housing shortage and progress under IAY and PMAY (rural)?
5. How the EWS, LIG and MIG have been defined under the PMAY?
6. Explain the concept of Affordable Housing and various policies and programmes of the Central/State Governments.
7. What is the role of Technology Sub-mission of Housing for All Mission?

3

AFFORDABLE AND ADEQUATE HOUSING

Since Independence in 1947, the Government of India, State governments and the private sector have made various attempts to provide housing to all. These efforts have failed to reach the poor in spite of subsidies, discounted land costs, low cost construction and low interest rates. The definitions of Low Income Group (LIG) and Economically Weaker Section (EWS) have left out the poorest of the poor, who even may not know what their income is or how to account for it. These people include the vegetable / fruit vendors, feriwala, tailor, salesman, rickshaw puller, cycle/auto-rickshaw drivers, bus cleaners/ driver, cobbler, domestic servant, rag pickers, sweepers, home guards, watchman, barbers, porters, binders, casual labourer, plumbers, painters, machine operator, blacksmith, etc.

India's total work force has 92% in the unorganized sector. Of this vast mass, the enterprises and micro-businesses comprise 98%, who have no social security cover. Many of these people are migrants and are women, children, aged and disabled. They have no bank account, no assets, no shelter and not even an identity or ration card. The world's largest democracy does not provide shelter for its majority population.

The poor are malnourished, lack minimum shelter, sanitation and drinking water; they are illiterate; and cannot afford to send their children to the school. They face the risks of unemployment, child labour, insecurity in old age, unhealthy living conditions, dangerous working conditions etc. These are the people who live in slums – the backbone of the actual, day-to-day working economy. A study conducted by Participatory Research in Asia (PRIA) and Indicus Analytics on the Economic Contribution of the urban poor found that the slum population contributes 7.5 per cent of the country's urban gross domestic product (2013).

Most of the poor live in the unplanned areas (slums, old city, villages, etc.) which remain under-serviced. These settlements continue to face the threat of demolition and pressures from the officials. Yet the residents in these settlements provide essential services without asking much. They have the right to security of residence and urban services.

What Jane Jacobs said in 1961 about the USA is relevant for India today: *'There is a wishful myth that if only we had enough money to spend–the figure is usually put at a hundred billion dollars we could wipe out all our slums in ten years, reverse decay in the great, dull, gray belts that were yesterday's and day-before-yesterday's suburbs, anchor the wandering middle class and its wandering tax money, and perhaps even solve the traffic problem. But look what we have built with the first several billions... This is not the rebuilding of cities. This is the sacking of cities'.*

Where the Poor Live

In general, the poor live in six types of housing:

- Slums and jhuggi-jhopri clusters/bastis
- Old City /villages
- Public Housing–built–up units
- Unauthorised colonies
- Public Housing–site and services,
- Private Housing

About one-sixth of the city population lives in the slums, bastis and Jhuggi-Jhopri clusters, which are mainly the settlements of the poor. The pavement dwellers/homeless comprise about 1 per cent of the total population. Traditional areas, villages and old city have about one-third of the population and unauthorised colonies have about one-sixth of the population. Public sector housing and site and services provide housing to about 32% of Delhi's population. The contribution of the private sector in EWS/LIG housing is almost negligible.

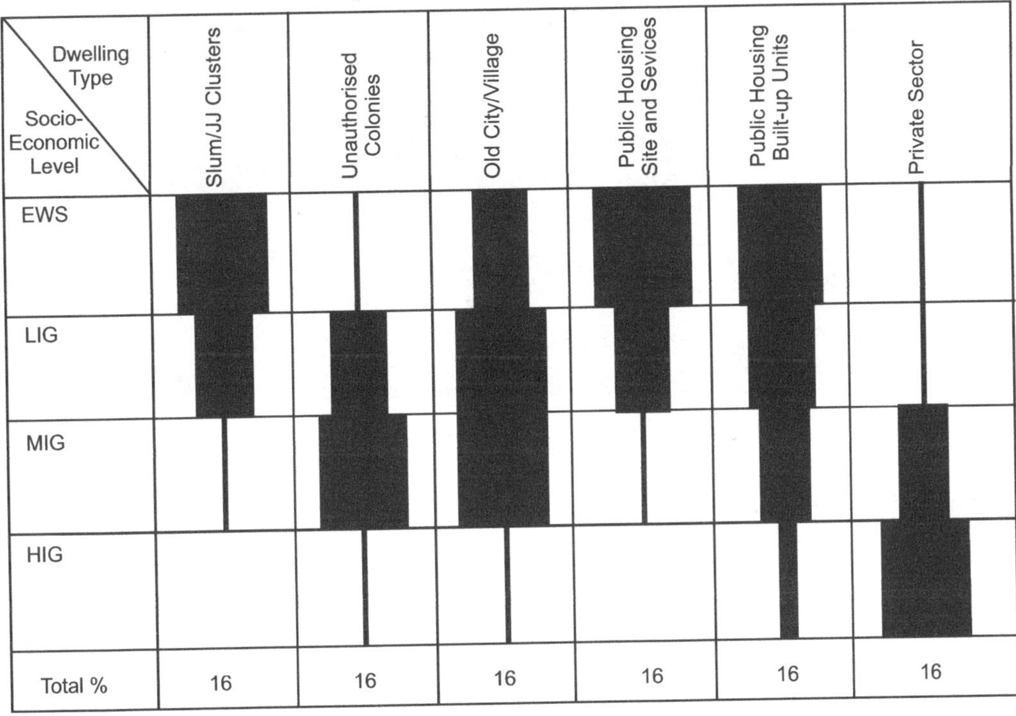

Fig. 3.1. Where the Poor Live

Notes:

- Figures are for Delhi, which have been rounded up.
- Government staff housing (3%), Homeless/pavement dwellers (1%) have not been shown.
- As per MoHUPA (2015) EWS covers a family having income up to Rs 3 lakh per annum and Rs 3 lakh up to Rs. 6 lakh per annum for LIG, MIG I covers Rs. 6 to 12 lakh per annum and MIG II covers Rs. 12 to 18 lakh per annum.

Sources: *Census of India 2011, Delhi Development Authority, A.K. Jain (2016), Building 20 million Homes and other sources.*

Lack of public housing schemes for the homeless, squatters and slum dwellers have led to improvised and informal shelter by the people themselves. The growth of slums is the failure in the housing and planning system. There is a total housing shortage of 18.78 million dwelling units (MoHUA, 2015) including around 15 million dwelling (about 80 per cent) which are old, dilapidated, and congested. These houses can be upgraded and rebuilt in-situ.

Fig. 3.2. The Homeless Mother India

Transforming Slums

According to Christopher Benninger, '*Transforming slums and poverty is visualizing the city from the "other way around!". Put the last person first, the hutment dwellers, the informal sector hawker, the small scale repairman, the physically challenged, domestic servants, street vendors, rickshaw wallah and casual workers. Put yourself in the position of elders, women, children and a diverse array of city dwellers whose lives are affected intimately and almost moment by moment by distant professional decisions that shape the city. Seek paths and channels to facilitate and empower them into becoming stakeholders, harnessing their huge energies and amplifying their contributions*'.

Benninger's words echo Gandhi's Talisman.

We need to look again at what we mean by shelter, land policy, infrastructure development, concept of planning, land use, tenure and building regulations. Innovative approaches have to be worked out to provide shelter by community resources, appropriate to the specific issues and local context. Universal solutions may not work.

Many migrants, labourers, casual workers, beggars, etc. in the city live on pavements near their jobs. For them a regular dwelling unit on the ownership basis is unthinkable. Thus, the definition of shelter should include rental units, dormitories, hostels, dharmshalas, lodge, transit camps and night shelters. As a human right, the city should provide a network of such shelters, which should be located near the Railway Stations, Bus Terminals, markets and work centres.

Shelter Integrated with Livelihood

For the poor, shelter and livelihoods overlap. Their shelter is intertwined with earning and micro-jobs; the rickshaw puller often sleeps in his rickshaw. Why should he have no other possibility? The concept of land use zoning has to include housing along with small shops, social space, facilities, utilities and work places. Every housing and slum rehabilitation project has to be based on the specific local issues and provide choices of in-situ upgrading, relocation, land sharing or re-blocking. All the slum settlements in a city need to be networked planned together and improved.

Social housing must be affordable. As a rule about half of the social housing units should be available on a rental basis, convertible to ownership after 10 years. This will give the occupier an incentive to improve his or her life. The funding pattern can be four layered. The Government of India can contribute 50 per cent. The State government and local bodies can contribute one-third. The slum families can contribute the remaining one-sixth. Transfer of Development Rights (TDR) and incentive Floor Space Index (FSI) can be useful tools. Smart cards should be issued to slum families so that benefits reach those who have genuine need.

Land

The cost of the land for social housing and slum housing can be met by cross subsidy, compulsory reservation, land pooling and by other similar instruments. To acquire greenfield sites has become very costly and difficult. It is necessary to use brownfield sites, through recycling existing urban areas, including the slum and squatter settlements and encroached land. Land cost should be excluded from social housing projects to make them affordable and viable. This implies mandatory reservation of land for social housing in all public and private housing projects. It is also necessary to optimise land use by higher density and FAR, and to reduce the cost and time in land development, construction and infrastructure provision.

Establishment of an electronic land register to show accurately who owns what. This is an essential element of the process of achieving housing for all. It is necessary to identify many parcels of under-used or idle land, including government owned land that could support affordable housing development. Unused and under used sites can be dedicated to housing development through reforms in the planning regulations, land pooling and by mixed land use.

To deal with the problem of land titles, it is necessary to introduce the Torrens System of property title registration. This will curb litigation on the question of ownership and rights to land. It is also necessary to expedite procedures for project approval and property transactions.

Shelter and Community Development

Housing for the poor supports their livelihoods. It thus helps to empower them, and with them the whole nation. It requires a holistic approach in planning and design. Housing acts as a vehicle for poverty reduction, social empowerment, community interaction, and access to health, educational and recreational facilities. Thus, housing the poor enriches society, equity and social values and provides a better quality of environment. The five elements, viz. the people, community, local activities, place and resources can be interfaced by housing development. Besides defining a minimum house (say 30 sqm minimum dwelling unit or 10 sqm per capita), a housing cluster should provide a minimum space of about 5 sqm per capita each of green area/open space/play area, social infrastructure and transport and utilities. These can integrate housing with health, livelihood, natural resources, climate and culture. Participatory planning is necessary to achieve the housing goals, establish the requirement of the resources and to accomplish the plans. No plan, however good, can be implemented unless it is supported by the people and stakeholders at all levels of decision making and implementation of spatial, financial and institutional structures.

The overall responsibility to devise ways of providing land and trunk services lies with the government. There should be collaboration with the community and private agencies, down to the level of the panchayat and the activist group. Activist groups arise when problems appear to be neglected. The communities should be linked in surveys of their housing problems, and with the housing boards, municipal bodies and service agencies should jointly develop the programs which the communities can take up. HUDCO and some NGOs have already demonstrated how this can be achieved.

The organization of urban space into the 'communities' is a key to a cross-sectoral spatial coalition of social, economic and environmental systems. Social housing projects need to focus on the following:

- Infrastructure improvement: Roads, drains, water, sanitation, street lighting and community halls;
- Health: Maternal and child health clinics, health awareness and facilities;
- Education: pre-schools, non-formal education and literacy;
- Facilitating community based participatory planning;
- Community development: institution building, gender awareness, vocational training and economic support;
- Encouraging small home-based occupations;
- Promoting micro-credit facilities; and
- Networking among communities.

Housing development can drive economic growth and improve the quality of life of people by better services, governance and urban mobility. If this causes the transformation of existing housing areas, including slums, into communities which the inhabitants value, there is a general enhancement of social and political gain. This would be possible by the preparation of Service Level Improvement Plan (SLIP), Action Plans and DRRs which focus upon water supply, sewerage, septage, storm water drains, urban transport, development of green areas and parks and other social amenities.

Development Controls for Housing

Some have argued that to solve the housing shortage, it is necessary to liberalise the Floor Area Ratio (FAR) and have higher densities. There is no doubt that it is essential to optimise land use by rationalizing the FAR and residential density. It does not, however, guarantee that higher FAR can help to create more social housing. Sometimes an increased FAR has led to creation of vacant, speculative, housing which has ignored the social needs and poverty. The Floor Area Ratio has to be seen in combination with plot coverage, density, housing form and the local urban context which could accomplish a dynamic urban environment. FAR, land use and densities involve a trade-off between open and built-up spaces, and land and infrastructure development. It is necessary to reserve a proportionate amount of land for transport corridors, social facilities, social housing and public green spaces against the grant of FAR/FSI and land use conversion.

Housing density and Floor Area Ratio (FAR) need to be considered on the basis of certain principles in a given context, which include the following:

- Whether higher density and FAR are relevant to the needs and resources of the poor?
- Whether these facilitate self-build housing?
- Whether these promote livelihoods and income generation?
- Whether the social housing is a commodity?
- Whether these are equitable and enable access to housing for all?
- Whether these make housing more expensive, unsafe and involve higher levels of maintenance?
- Whether these facilitate incremental housing?
- Whether these make legal land development difficult for the poor?
- Whether these allow rental tenure or constrain access to shelter?
- What are the gender implications and whether women and children have safe and useful common/open space?
- How economical is the provision of basic services-toilets, sanitation, waste disposal and recycling, water, electricity, drainage and sewerage?
- What are the densities and FAR that can meet the target of housing for all in a city?
- Is the regulatory framework too complex and opaque for a common developer and community based development?
- Does the planning and regulatory frameworks provide the choices and options according to local culture, climate, geography, land values, housing demand and level of technology?

Various types of existing housing forms available to the EWS and LIG categories can be evaluated against these criteria. These include slum clusters, chawls, traditional/inner city, urban villages, unauthorized colonies, site and services, public sector built-up apartments, private sector housing, cooperative housing, etc. Although unplanned housing developments appear to meet most of the needs of the poor, the planned developments ignore most of the criteria. This means incorporating the positive aspects of unplanned developments in planning framework such as chawls in Mumbai which provide cluster/courtyard walk-ups, compact, high density and affordable rental housing. Perhaps the sensible way forward is to tolerate these adaptations, rather than spend effort on outlawing them.

Densities of 600 dwelling units per hectare can be achieved in walk-ups (15 m height). For those at the base of the pyramid, LIG, there can be walk-ups, low rise–high density development. Those at mid-height – middle-income group people–can have mid-rise (up to 12 storeys). Those who are rich, at the peak, can have high rise development. The main principle is affordability, which includes cost of land, construction and services. These costs increase with the height. High rise building also restricts growth and expansion of individual units and mixed land use, which is one of the essential needs of the poor. The notion that high-rise housing leads to larger densities may not be true as it needs proportionately a higher amount of open space, community facilities and more distance between the buildings for light and ventilation.

While deciding the FAR a balance has to be struck between the cost of land per unit and construction cost. While higher density and FAR may reduce the cost of land, the cost of construction increases steeply beyond walkups (15 m height). As a rule of thumb, cost increases by 20 per cent beyond walk up height owing to lifts, foundation, fire sprinkler system, services, generator, etc. and thereafter 5 per cent per floor. There are also implications with respect to safety of women, elderly and children, home based occupations, community interaction and communications. High rise living also is technology-intensive, and has negative environmental consequences: heat island effect, air pollution, increased carbon footprint, and danger from fire and earthquake. Much higher energy is spent on lifts, pumps and air-conditioning as well.

Yet, in view of wide differences in climate, geography, culture, housing demand and land costs, it is risky to prescribe general guidelines for housing form, densities and FARs. In the areas with paucity of land, horizontal development may not be feasible, but one may have to go vertical to meet the aim of housing for all. In such cases, it is necessary to incorporate flexibility of space by creating living platforms and terraces, where the residents get common open spaces and can furnish and finish their dwellings according to their needs and resources. A simple prefab system can provide economical and fast development. Ground floor, some portion of upper floors and terraces can be reserved as community space and for common facilities.

This requires meticulous planning and design which optimizes open space, greenery and play spaces, community spaces and puts limits to congestion, vandalism, crimes and other dangers. Accordingly, FAR and density standards should not depend on commercial pressures.

The dwelling units can be built on a self-build model or evolutionary design with 'built up floor, roof and service core' on various floors. This approach recognizes the right of each family to develop its own dwelling according to its own priorities, needs and resources and allows for gradual development and changes. Evolutionary design defines the house-core relationship, *i.e.* the design of a built core, its location and the development alternatives for various stages of growth, both horizontal and vertical, around the core, *i.e.* the cell. Growth options indicate the direction as well as the feasible transformations offered by the initial core.

Affordable Housing

According to the Ministry of Housing and Urban Affairs, Affordable Housing is defined as individual dwelling units with a carpet area of not more than 60 sqm and preferably within the price range of 5 times the annual income of the household, either as a single unit or part of a building complex with multiple dwelling units.

An Affordable Housing project has been defined as the one where at least 60% of the Housing projects where at least 60 per cent of the FAR/ FSI is used for dwelling units of carpet area of not more than 60 sqm. The project shall also reserve 15 per cent of the total FAR/ FSI or 35 per cent of the total number of dwelling units for EWS category.

Inclusive and Adequate Housing

Each housing and slum re-development plan should address specific local issues and provide flexible choices of in-situ upgrading, relocation, land sharing or re-blocking. The local area plan should network all the settlements, where the local stakeholders plan together. Uniform standards that are set too high can price poor households out of formal housing. It may be better to provide basic shelter in appropriate locations, even with limited space as dormitories, hostels, etc., if it can house lowest-income households until their incomes rise. The existing housing stock and new units are complementary parts of the solution. Existing housing, even in poor condition, may serve residents better by placing them where they have social connections and access to employment. Cities need to provide housing where residents can flourish, whether by building new units or upgrading and retrofitting of existing stock.

The critical concerns in redevelopment of slums and infill development are water supply and power, which are under severe stress. These require strategic interventions as follows:

- Preparation of services plan of redevelopment, slum rehabilitation, social housing and regularisation projects

- Mandatory adoption of wastewater recycling and renewable energy, water conservation and energy efficiency as per ECBC and Green Building Code, which can save 10 to 15 % of water and energy.
- Checking leakages, thefts and transmission losses which can save about 15 to 20 % of water and power.
- Enhancing organisational efficiency.

Housing Development and Construction

Housing development includes time-bound action planning and effective monitoring to overcome delays and cost overruns. To meet the huge urban housing targets it is necessary to optimize the resources of both public and private sectors. The government and the private sector must make this change, develop new partnerships and a healthy competition in housing.

Housing development and construction must be optimized to achieve quality, productivity and flexibility, together with reducing time and costs. There is a need to innovate in construction, efficiency, quality of service and sustained maintenance. This applies to standards and specifications, infrastructure, construction, maintenance, together with energy and environment concerns. According to McKinsey Global Institute, the critical housing cost reduction strategies at design and construction stage include the following:

- Pre-manufacturing: build components off-site using industrial processes, deliver parts as needed.
- Planning Optimization: apply critical path management techniques to optimize overall plan; translate into realistic scheduling.
- In-site lean execution: use lean techniques to standardize procedures that eliminate waste in individual activities and improve construction flow balancing.
- Process Step Productivity: eliminate low value added activities and wasted time to optimize process efficiency.
- De-specification of structural design: Avoid over-specification of non-value-added components.
- Standardization of micro-design: Identify substitutes and use design-to-cost to set specifications.
- Determine sourcing strategy for each category of construction activity, detail sub-contractor management.
- Housing optimization through bundling, labour saving production, low-cost sourcing, and capacity optimisation of housing agencies, including the public, private and community sectors.
- Technical optimization: Standardize and identify substitutes with advanced costing tools.

Automated procedures can give precision to building construction and components and enable accuracy. Computer-Aided Manufacturing (CAM) and Computer Integrated Manufacturing (CIM) for pre-fabricated components, viz. ceilings, walls, roofs, etc. are integral to the process of industrialized construction. The simulation of construction process enables better control of time, machine, expenditure and the manpower, which could be reduced at least by half to one-third in comparison to the conventional construction. It is necessary to adopt industrialized building systems for efficient and economical housing delivery.

For an appropriate delivery of affordable housing project, the selection of developers and operational model is critical. It involves the following:

- Developer qualification: Qualify the set of developers through structural criteria and build a competitive market.
- Land scoring: Score land parcels for potential development and qualification for appropriate incentives.
- Public-private partnership framework: develop operating model, tendering process and legal and contractual structure for public private partnerships.
- Reverse tendering: for government lands with all approvals in place transferred to developers who return maximum number of EWS/ LIG dwelling units.

In order to streamline the land market and regulate the transactions, as well as to discourage encroachments on public lands, it is necessary to make property registration, mutation and transfer simple, transparent and quick. To bring in accountability in the real estate sector, rating of developers and projects and licensing of real estate agents/brokers/realtors need to be implemented, as provided in the Real Estate Regulation Act, 2016.

Capacity Building

It is essential to optimize the capacity of housing boards, banks and housing financial institutions, developers and housing cooperatives. In addition, the capacities of communities and cooperatives should be strengthened to make the required effort national.

Rental Housing

As many poor families cannot afford even to pay the subsidised down payment, it is necessary to review the rental legislation as follows:

- To licence shelter units initially on a rental basis, convertible into a title after 10 years, or so. Alternatively, the title can be given jointly to husband and wife/parents, or to the co-operatives/residents associations;
- Reduce the costs and enhance accountability and affordability;
- Provide common areas in a manner which would dissuade the beneficiaries to go for quick sale;
- Evolutionary pattern of housing, which can be self expanded with the needs and resources.

DEBRIEFING QUESTIONS

1. How affordable housing is defined?
2. How much is India's housing shortage in terms of various income groups?
3. How shelter can be integrated with livelihoods and community development?
4. How optimization of Floor Area Ratio and densities can help in social housing development ?
5. What critical changes are necessary in:
   (*a*) Land management and development (*b*) Housing construction
6. What are the necessary steps for capacity building of a housing organization?
7. Write short notes on the following:
   (*a*) Concept of adequate housing (*b*) Inclusive housing
   (*c*) Slum Free City

4

HOUSING DESIGN

Housing is the physical and social expression of the community and human civilisation. The housing design process involves understanding the issues, society's economic structure, the power relationships amongst social groups, and political legal and administrative structure of the State.

As such, an empirical analysis of various housing typologies becomes critical for a deeper understanding of the housing process. Various housing typologies, both in the formal and informal sectors, can be crystallised in relation to the following aspects:

1. Physical Characteristics: Magnitude, location, planning framework, morphology, building resources, density, services and physical environment.
2. Socio-economic characteristics:
   (*a*) Sequence and chronology of evolution,
   (*b*) Demography, community organisation, cultural, gender and social characteristics,
   (*c*) Employment,
   (*d*) Tenure,
   (*e*) Land values, and
   (*f*) Legal status.
3. The role of various actors and agents in the housing process:
   (*i*) Land, land use planning and development controls
   (*ii*) Services
   (*iii*) Finances
   (*iv*) Construction, building resources and housing production
   (*v*) Maintenance
   (*vi*) Regulatory framework
   (*vii*) Exchange, transactions.

The spheres of influence and issues of dominant concern can be identified from the viewpoint of the State/local body and the consumer/families, which appear to be in clash many a times. The various typologies of housing, both in formal and informal sectors, can be comparatively evaluated in terms of various factors; such as characteristics of space and location, finance, services and linkages, production process, dwellers' participation, environmental factors and management.

This enables the identification of the positive aspects in various production systems as well as the specific deprivation in particular typologies. A dynamic approach derived from the analytical framework can be evolved, based on the fundamental parameters identified in the housing evaluation:

(*a*) A clear understanding of self-help housing as a process of self-determination and self-management against the popular notion of self-help as contribution of non-remunerative labour by the poor in construction of their housing,

(*b*) Cultural, institutional, attitudinal, bureaucratic, planning, legal and socio-economic obstacles to community action,

(*c*) Factors producing disintegration of existing popular organisations,

(*d*) Resistance of communities to changes introduced from outside,

(*e*) The use of space among the poor is quite different from higher/ middle income groups. A proper understanding of this aspect should be the basis of shelter design.

Shelter and Space Use Among the Poor and Others

The utilisation of land space and built-space between the organised/formal sector and the low income group is quite different as given in the table below.

Table: 4.1: Requirement of Low Income Group vis-a-vis MIG and HIG.

Low Income Group	Higher Income Group (HIG, MIG)
Utilisation of space around shelter more important than actual design of household spaces.	Design of individual household spaces within the plot or layout as important or more so than surrounding neighbourhood spaces.
Shelter provided on self-help basis and evolves over a period of time.	Designed housing provided through contractors or as readymade units.
Generally single storeyed with provision for second floor, with floor height at less than prescribed heights.	Partially single or double storeyed for higher income groups but largely multi- storeyed from 4 storeyed walk-ups to 6 storeyed blocks.
Site and Service Layout and Shelter upgrading to cater to low rise high density pattern with lower service standards. The ares to involve relation minimum standards.	Layouts cater to prescribed development controls and service standards.
Upgrading or redevelopment of shelter with nonpermanent materials to community shared services, Which are not based on planing standards.	Upgrading or redevelopment to follow prescribed development control standards and procedures.
Informal sources of finances make it difficult to avail government support. These compromise on regular payments and user charges.	Formal sources of finance make it possible to have clear titles to land and built space and recovery of user charges. Correspondingly, expectations in delivery of services is high.

Planning and design can act as the tools for communication to allocate roles and responsibilities among the government agencies, community groups and the families. As such, a housing plan serves as an appropriate medium for intervening parties, to interact in making decisions for self-administration of the endogenous and exogenous resources incorporating time as a substantive element. The draft housing plan acts as an agenda for the local community to participate in the housing process. It covers the study of following components:

1. Participatory survey of physical and socio-economic indicators.
2. Analysis and identification of the problems, issues, needs and priorities.
3. Policies, objectives and conceptual framework.
4. Alternative models, options and strategies.
5. Norms, parameters, criteria and proposals.
6. Project implementation, process, financing, roles and likely impact of project.

Design as a Vehicle of Public Policy and Participation

The housing design can be an effective tool for evolutionary process and the involvement of the dwellers in the housing production. As a medium to facilitate interactions, appropriate concepts of design can be evolved to enhance the capacities of the organized sector and the dwellers in mutual endeavour. The role of the people and communities in attempting solutions is recognised, yet facilitative action to allow the people's creativity and motivation is conspicuous by its absence in the corporate housing design. Systems based housing concept is a positive linkage between the state intervention and the family and an effective tool for the mobilization of the resources. Existing squatter and informal settlements illustrate the resourcefulness of the people and indicate the potential that could be released in housing production.

There is a need to evolve the design concepts, which are consistent with the objectives of housing production, taking into account the potential and limitation of the available resources, materials and locally available skills. The concept should meticulously reflect the morphological peculiarities and particularities against the stereotype and sterile uniformity of the public housing. housing is not just an end product, but incorporates time as a substantive element in the act of designing.

The aggregation of housing clusters should enable the families to choose from a variety of sizes and locations. It should offer growth of space during a family cycle or economic ladder. As land is always at a premium in high density, high population situations, its optimum utilization should be envisaged for economy. This would also lead to economy of the services, transportation and community facilities creation of cohesive communities. In this context, self-employment opportunities become extremely relevant elements of the design for which mixed land use could be adopted as a valid approach. The improvement and recognition of the potentials of poor, would itself effect, huge savings in the large investments for housing construction, which could be diverted for the provision of better services, amenities, loans and other priorities of low-investment settlements. To harness the people's investments, the supports have to be given by gradual building process, recycling materials and adoption of evolutionary standards. This implies spread of activities in a time frame including building of the houses and the physical infrastructure, which is a major determinant in the mode of aggregation of clusters and their evolutionary potential.

Any housing production process based on the potentials of poor should essentially be in tune with the local technology levels, with minimum need for high-tech systems and market dependence.

The local materials also include recycled materials.

An important consideration in the conceptual evolution of housing design is the environmental sustainability, which also addresses the issues of climate change, heat islands, climatic comfort, low dependence on energy, and utilizing natural sources of energy.

Ecological Design

Housing has a uterine relationship with ecology of the city and local community. The urban vision and housing concept are tied up by an umbilical cord. The basis of a sustainable urban vision includes the concepts of walk to work, integrated transit corridor, pedestrian and cycle lanes at grade, high density, compact and mixed land use developments and integrated grids of physical and social services. Trigeneration energy systems, dual piping for recycled water and waste management combine to create "green infrastructure". Water saving toilets with recycled wastewater cisterns, save water. Satellite control micro-irrigation system cuts water and power consumption. Vertical farms provide food grown locally and reduce fertilizer and freshwater use, shorten transport and recycle grey water.

Three bin recycling is adopted with separate bins for trash, recyclable and compost which is transported and processed by an underground pneumatic system. Bio-technology, enzyme based STP, bio-remedial treatment, sludge gas/energy recovery, vermi-culture, fossilization and composting options are explored for waste treatment, green, vegetated swales, porous paving, bio-drainage and zero run off drainage and flood control. Vegetation increases the infiltration of water and reduces evaporation loss and over time will ensure replenishment of the shallow aquifer and reduction in soil salinity. Rooftop photo-voltaics provide energy for cooking, hot water, and electricity. Rooftops painted white reflect heat, lowering a building's heat gain. Rooftop vegetation, insulates buildings which helps obviating the ecological footprints, formation of heat islands and outdoor and indoor pollution.

A wide range of human needs overlap the sustainability issues. These relate to jobs, education and health, cleanliness, inclusion, affordability, equity, gender sensitivity and civic sense (particularly towards the women), conservation and protection of heritage, greens, public spaces, water bodies, rivers, etc. A sustainable city offers diversity of choices. It integrates communities and encourages a vital public life by design of a wide range of diverse public spaces, such as chowks and square, parks, boulevards, avenues, religious, social, cultural and other public facilities. It discourages the isolation of mono-activities, luxury housing, gated communities, segregated housing for poor and slum dwellers, reserved parks, etc, which create anti-social spaces.

The concepts of Circular Metabolism and Net Zero Energy aim to give as much to the environment as it takes out. An ecological city and the buildings respect the nature so as to minimize the use of energy and carbon emissions. Cities and buildings can protect the environment by using the minimum of mechanical systems and by optimising the natural resources. The buildings are designed to incorporate both old and new ecological strategies, learning from traditional forms, as well as modern technology. For example, courtyard house and aerodynamic gliders which uses the minimum amount of material to maximum affect, both work in harmony with nature. Passive design and engineering need to maintain a harmonious balance.

Green buildings can give energy saving up to 30 %, reduce carbon emissions and provide higher efficiency and comfort. The city and buildings have not only to be comfortable, green and efficient but also intelligent and integrated. Sustainable development is giving birth to a new aesthetic, where the nature (sun, wind, water and earth) integrates with technology (nano-technology, renewables, biotechnology, etc.) to create an efficient and ecological environment.

Interfacing Green and Smart

Integration of major systems on common network helps optimize use assignment and space configurations, eliminating unused or under performing space. Innovation and technology are main drivers of collective community and local capacity. The critical factors are those which affect resource use and carbon emissions, such as energy use, transportation, waste prevention and recycling, air quality, water quality, affordable housing, green space and buildings. This implies the need to rethink and reshape the urban environment comprising transportation infrastructure, zoning, building codes, waste management, open space and greens, etc. which make the city more equitous, efficient, sustainable, and participatory.

Every building exists in an ecological sphere comprising its external environment, internal ambience and building itself. Its external components comprise air, soil, water, urban matrix, energy, services, etc. which articulate a building is ecology. The internal components include internal air, micro-climatic comfort, temperature, ventilation, lighting, furnishings, furniture, fittings, etc. The building components include building design, envelope, openings, façade, roof, construction materials, etc.

Site planning and infrastructure development, including water supply, transport, sanitation and drainage, organisation of land use, circulation pattern and decisions regarding density, Floor Area Ratio, building construction and land development impact the urban ecology. A compact development can significantly help in saving fossil fuel consumption, climate change and environment.

The spatial sustainability is contingent upon an integrated approach towards urban structure, conservation of natural resources (land, water, forest, etc.), site planning, micro-climatic design, natural ventilation and lighting, greenery and infrastructure services including transport, fuels, pollution control and waste management. A low carbon urban form protects the blue and green networks by merging them together. The urban form can promote walkability and transport conservation.

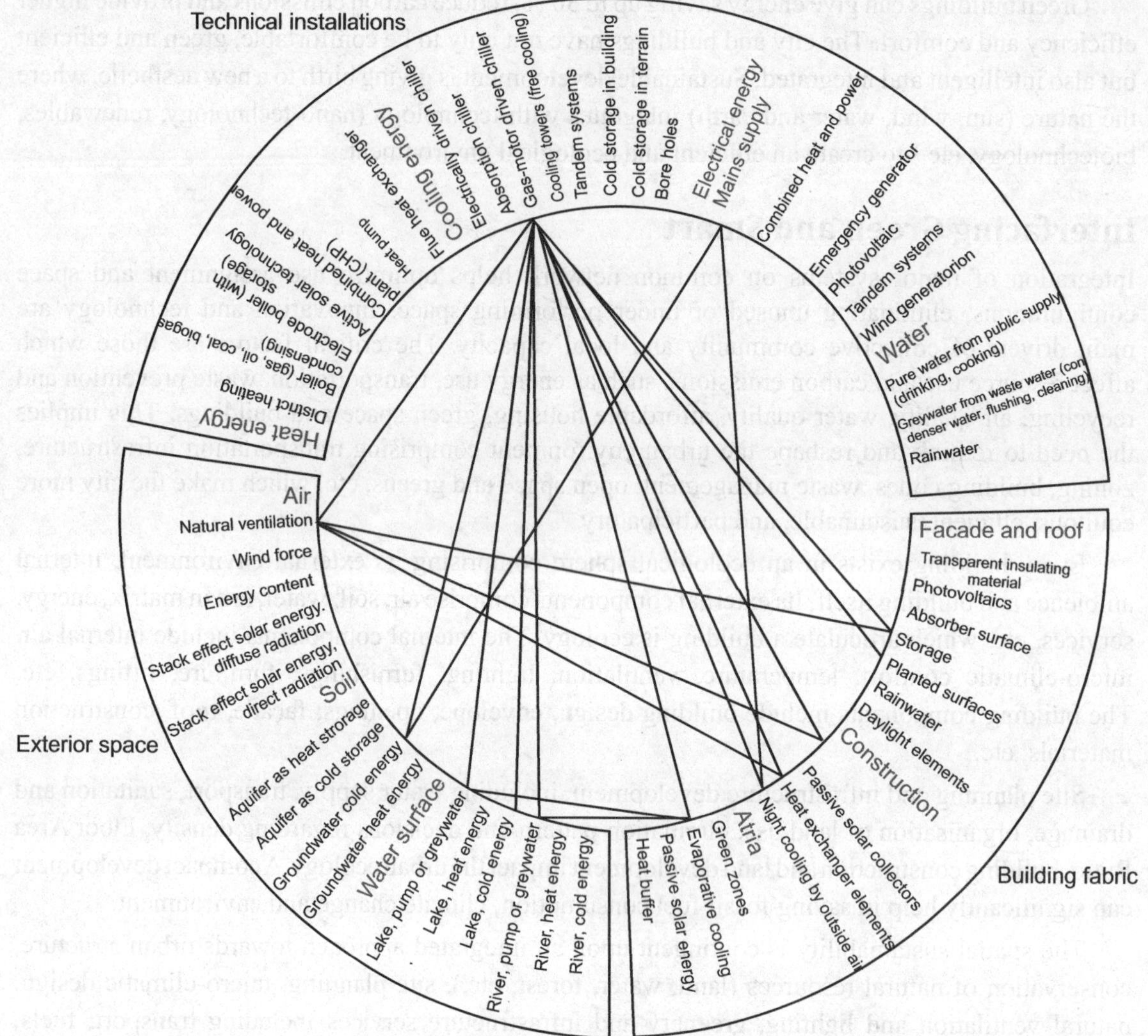

Fig. 4.1. Ecological Circle of Buildings

Source: *Daniel, Klaus, 1994, Technology of Ecological Buildings, Birkhauser, Verlag, Basel*

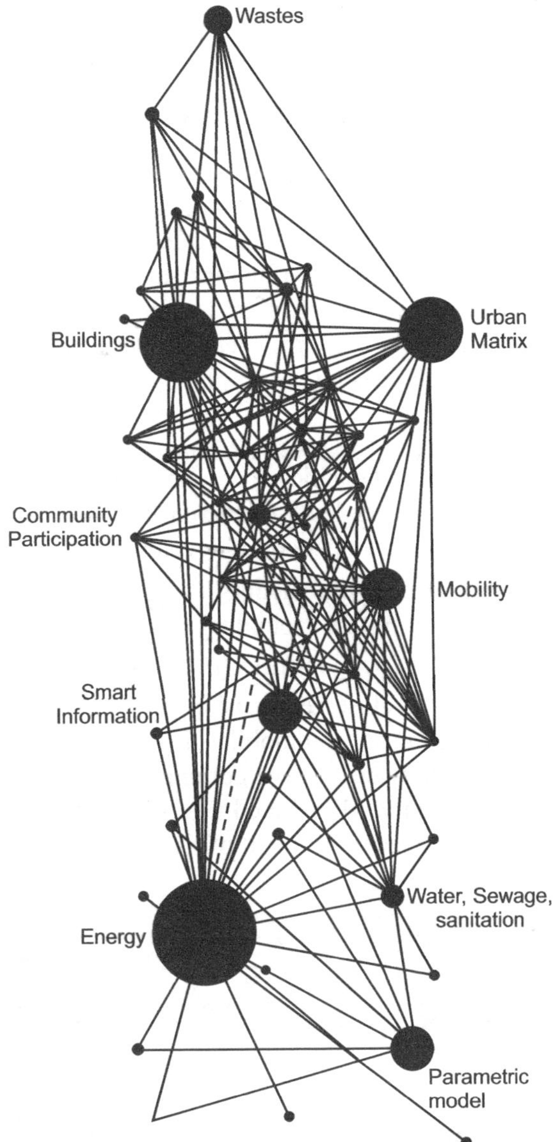

Fig. 4.2. Housing is a part of a wider urban matrix and ecology that encompasses infrastructure services, energy, greenery water and waste management, mobility and community engagement

Source: *Adrian smith and Gordon Gill (2011) Towards Zero Carbon, Image Pub., Australia*

Resource Efficiency: Natural resource saving is the starting point for environmentally responsive design. As a rule of thumb, if a certain level of resource use defined as a baseline, reduction of use by a factor x (say half) implies a reduction of the load on ecosystems by the same factor. At the same time enhancing the efficiency factor for technology and operations (say twice) gives 'factor-4' efficiency. A specific efficiency factor may be an abstract target, but successfully increasing efficiency requires knowledge of local ecology on which to base the technologies and processes used. Planning along the lines of factor-4 produces tangible results and improves the limited carrying capacity of urban land and conservation of natural resources. It is essential that the services and utilities are planned with flexibility to keep with fast changing technology. These should incorporate intelligent controls and 'state of art' maintenance systems.

Habitat Design and Community Planning

The human life, community, local activities, places and natural resources are inextricably interlinked, the urban form articulates the environment and vice-versa. It is necessary to plan the habitat taking a dynamic and holistic approach, where human element, physical environment and built-form synthesise into a workable equation of human satisfaction, environmental conservation and minimal consumption. The habitat design aims to integrate these into a composite whole by systematic analysis of local culture, economy, demography, climate and site conditions. The following aspects are critical in habitat design.

1. Spatial Geographical Context:

Urban structure, commensurate with the dynamics of growth, decentralization of activities, economy of scale and better quality of life. Higher level of mixed land use based on environmental and performance criteria, high density, compact pattern of development helps to achieve the following:

- **Urban Form:** (*i*) High dense settlements (*ii*) Less dependence on automobile (high density) (*iii*) Clear boundary from surrounding areas;
- **Spatial Characteristics:** (*i*) Social fairness (*ii*) Self-sufficiency of daily life, and
- **Social Functions:** There is close relationship between compact urban form and the sustainability by reduction of automobile dependence, efficient supply of social infrastructure and public services, active community relationship by dense habitation, and revitalization of inner city. Mixed land use practices aim to create more accessible land use patterns, which reduce the amount of travel needed to reach goods and services.

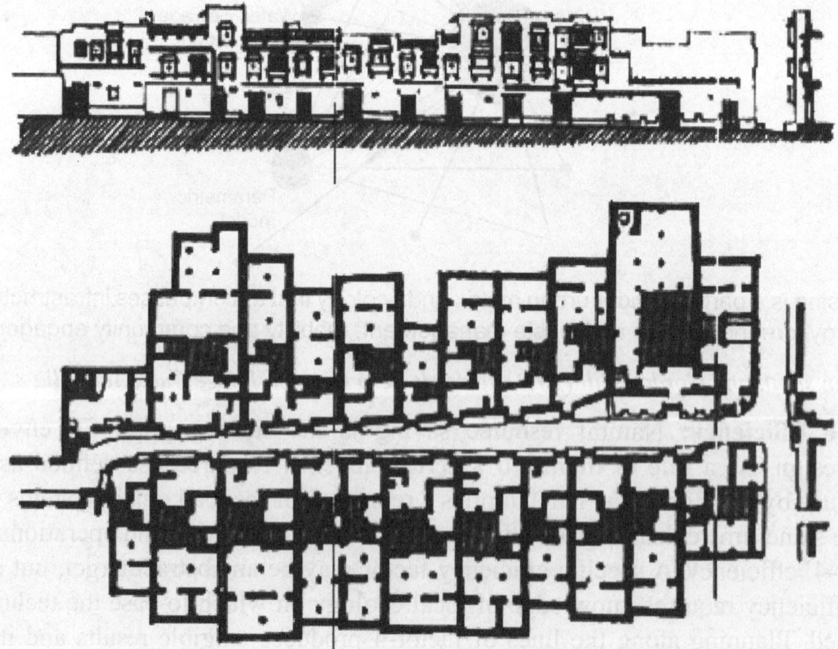

Fig. 4.3. Jaisalmer: Typical Residential Street (after Kulbhushan Jain)

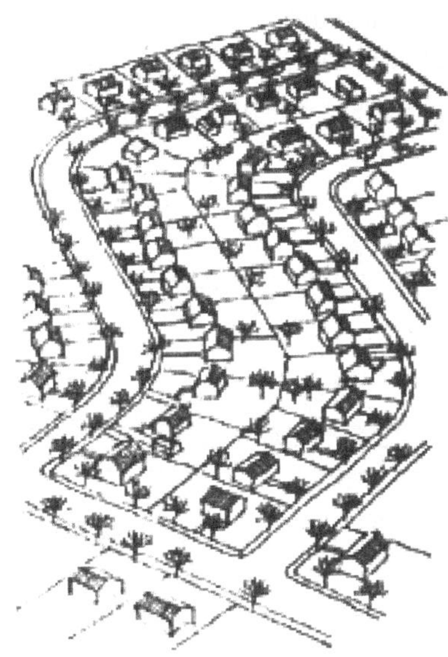

Fig. 4.4. American Suburb: car–centric, high energy, low-density urban form

A coherent urban hierarchy on modular basis ensures the provision of education, recreation, work and shopping facilities. The form, density and population of the housing cluster is derived on the basis of walkable distance (5 to 8 minutes or 400 to 600 m) which is surrounded by vehicular roads and has interlinked greens.

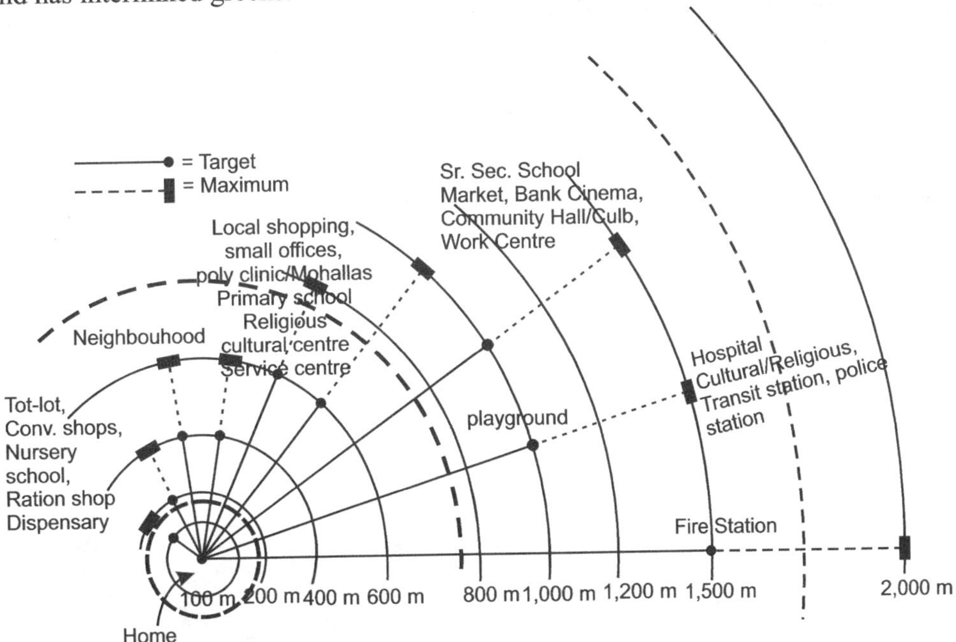

Fig. 4.5. The urban hierarchy is worked out on a modular basis and easy access to various functions so that community, especially children, women and aged, can walk to their places of education, recreation, shopping or work. As the distance increases, cycle (say upto 2 km) and public transport should provide access to the place of destination

Source: *Adapted from Barton H. et al (2003) Shaping Neighbourhoods, Spon Press, London*

Wider variety, intermixing of socio-cultural activities, relationship of commercial and public activities with public transportation and morphology of housing should address to the needs of the historical, socio-cultural context and local community.

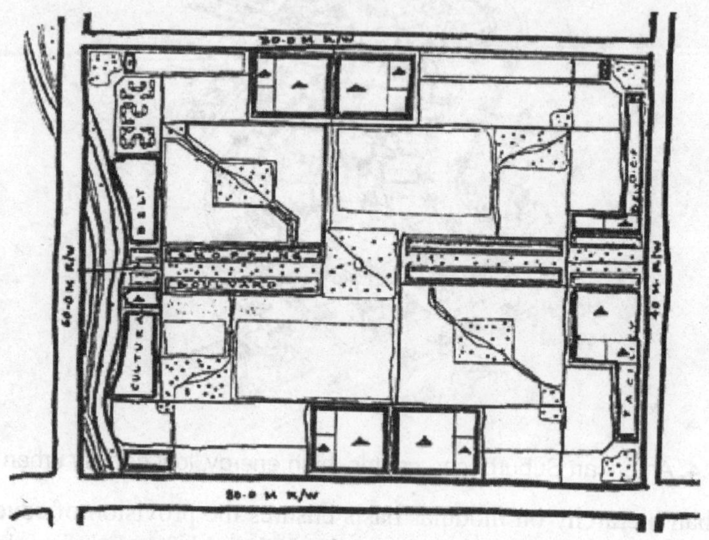

Fig. 4.6. Community Structure (A.K. Jain)

2. The Climate

Water, shade, channelling of cooling breeze as prime elements for a comfortable micro-climate, minimum exterior surface to maximum internal volume, correct orientation; atriums and internal courtyard to reducers are dissipate heat, compact group ingand clustering of buildings to minimization of wall surface, use of open spaces, platforms, chowks, porch and squares for social intensity and traditional symbolic attributes of urban design.

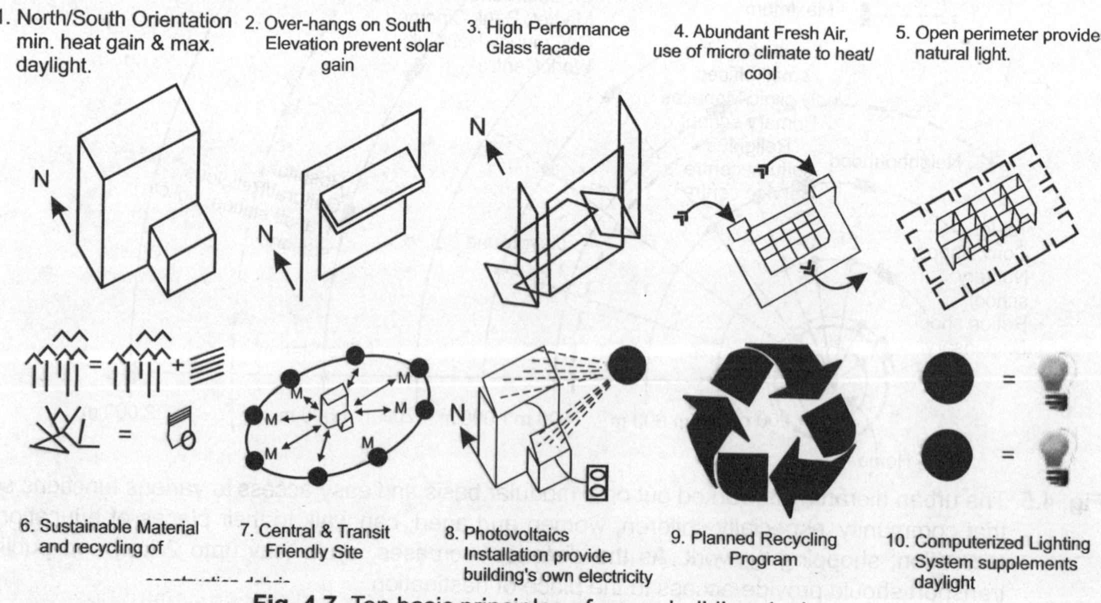

Fig. 4.7. Ten basic principles of green building design

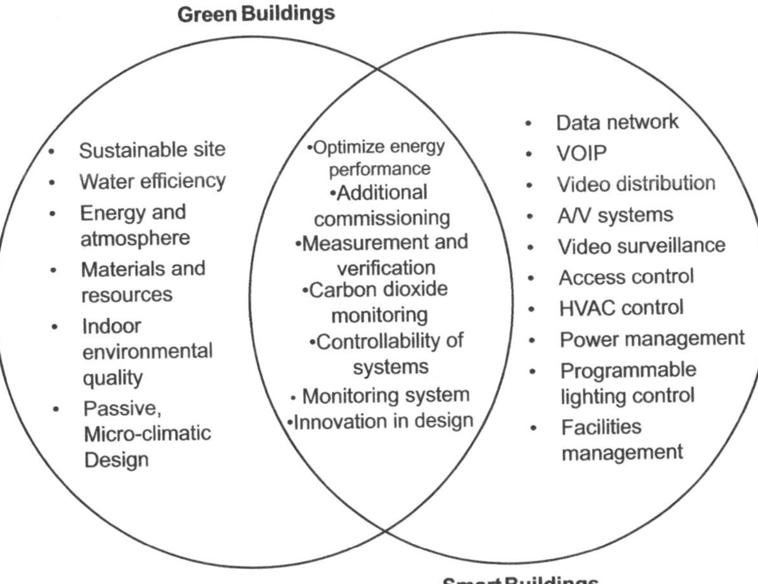

Fig. 4.8. Interfacing green and smart building

Climatically comfortable built environment and design depend upon ten factors, viz. the orientation, shade and ventilation, sustainable building materials, envelope, building perimeter, sustainable site, energy efficiency/photovoltaic, recycling system and lighting efficiency. The components of green building can be integrated with smart systems for obtaining best of the two worlds. The exterior surface should be minimum, while providing maximum internal volume. Natural ventilation, atriums and internal courtyards reduce glare and dissipate heat. Compact grouping and clustering of buildings minimise expose of wall surface and heat gain.

Due to incident solar radiation in a courtyard, air gets warmer and rises. Cool air from the ground level flows through the louvered openings of rooms surrounding a courtyard, thus producing air flow. If the roof surfaces are sloped towards the internal courtyard, the cooled air sinks into the court and enters the living space through low-level openings, and when it gets warmed up leaves through higher-level openings.

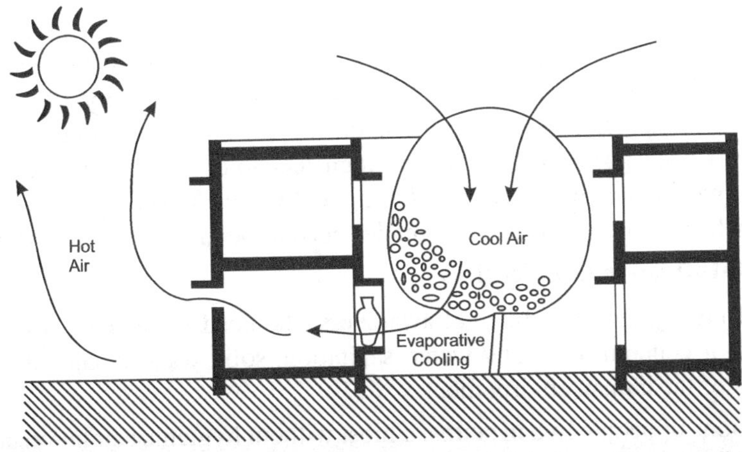

Fig. 4.9. A Courtyard in a Traditional House—shaded, cool and ventilated

The passive measures are integrated at the design stage, which are preventive, economical and long range. The active measures are usually add-ons and mechanical. A balanced mix of two approaches is necessary for a green building.

Table 4.2: Some Passive and Active Measures of Green Buildings

	Passive Measures		Active Measures
1.	TIM facade	2.	Passive solar utilization/evaporative cooling and garden (plants)
3.	Natural ventilation	4.	Natural lighting (daylight design)
5.	Cooling load reduction through storage masses (supported by ventilation)	6.	Air well
7.	Planted or white painted roof surface	8.	Rain water utilization (grey water)
9.	Photovoltaic units	10.	Solar collectors
11.	Absorber surface	12.	Wind generators
13.	Low temperature heating	14.	Cooling towers
15.	Chilled ceiling	16.	Chiller as heat pump (HP)
17.	Absorption installation refrigeration energy as heating energy	18.	Combined heat and power station (CHP)
19.	Filter installation for surface or groundwater heating (HP)	20.	Ice water storage
21.	Heat accumulator (storage)	22.	Aquifer storage (HP operated)

3. Air Pollution and Transport

Transport in large cities like Delhi, Kolkata and Mumbai, may contribute nearly two-thirds of the total air pollution in the form of suspended particulate matter and carbon emissions. This is causing a serious threat to the environment and health of the people. The objective should be to provide access to people and places by 'green' modes of urban transport. These include walking, bicycling, intermediate public transport modes, exclusive bus ways, dedicated bike tracks, CNG power and vehicles, trains, etc. Inherent with this is the aim to curtail the need for commuting and to shorten the distances by various strategies, such as decentralisation of work centres, urban form, and by telecommunications, electronic mail, mixed land-use zoning, etc. The alternative modes of transport need not be high cost and high technology solutions, but there are several low-cost options, which can be explored. Polluting and life endangering transport modes have to be discouraged, while environment friendly modes need to be given the centre-stage.

4. Decentralized Infrastructure Services

In the context of emerging environmental awareness, the need to save air, water and land from pollution is a major concern. Drinking water, sanitation, solid waste treatment and drainage are important aspects of the human environment.

In India, millions of people live in slums, almost without hygienic sanitation and water facility. The public and individual toilet facility, particularly for women and children, is a critical area of attention. About 50 to 60 per cent of area in Indian cities, especially the slums, unauthorized colonies, old cities and villages, which are inhabited largely by the poor, do not have clean drinking water supply, drainage, effluent treatment, wastewater recycling, sanitation, sewerage, public toilets and solid waste management facilities. Widespread method of land filling for solid waste disposal is an environmental disaster. In order to safeguard public health the urban society has to adopt recycling (*e.g.* water, solid waste, land), regeneration (dilapidated, old areas), recovery (wastelands, encroached areas), restructuring (networks, land use, transport), and rejuvenation (river, water bodies, traditional areas, parks, etc.). Instead of conventional drainage, the concepts of micro-runoff, bio-swales and bio-drainage need to be adopted. Ponds/reservoirs and sediment traps can be planned in the catchment zones on low-lying grounds. The concepts of watershed development, rainwater harvesting and conservation and recharging of groundwater need to be institutionalized and legalised. Various options can be explored for augmentation of physical infrastructure, such as technology upgradation, dual piping system, rain water harvesting, energy audit and exploring alternative sources of energy. Several technologies, such as decentralized and compact water treatment units, solar/aerobic/oxidation and root zone systems can be employed to purify potable water from the natural sources. Various alternative technologies, like Extended Aeration Technique, Biogas production, Bubble Diffusion process, Floatation, Anaerobic Reactors, etc. are already available, which can be explored for urban sanitation. Decentralized systems based on recycling, energy generation and organic decomposing can be explored for solid waste treatment. Bio-reactor composting and vessel system (Tunnel Reactor) are new generation technologies which can be employed for treatment of urban solid waste. All the public buildings, slums, roadsides and parks, etc. should be provided with public toilets, garbage bins and water points/public taps. Urban drains and waterfront can be landscaped in the form of interconnected parkways. Regular de-silting of drains and control of dumping of solid waste into the drains should be taken up. Public awareness programs need to be taken up in association with local community to make the society aware about the consequences of dumping the solid waste in the drains and rivers.

The performance of present sanitation system needs to be assessed with reference to environment, hygiene and their accessibility. Various alternative technologies, based on de-centralized services, like Extended Aeration Technique, Bio-gas production, Bubble Diffusion Process, Flotation, Anaerobic Reactor, etc. should be explored for urban sanitation.

5. Conservation of Surface Water Sources

The rivers and water bodies in urban areas usually have a high level of pollution, which is mainly from the untreated sewer and urban/industrial wastes. Besides, the enforcement of Water Pollution Act, an environment based strategy of land use is essential for their improvement, which links the natural/water body/river with the population by landscape development. It is necessary to control of pollution of water from industry, drainage, sewerage, flyash, garbage and waste dumping. Drainage and flood control strategy needs to be closely linked with water supply.

6. Watershed Planning and Wastewater Recycling

The revival of the age-old concept of watershed development, bio-swale, harvesting and conservation of rain water and recharging of underground water can substantively resolve the urban water crisis. Several technologies, such as decentralized and compact water treatment units, solar/aerobic/oxidation and root zone cleaning systems can be employed to purify potable water from natural sources.

Black and grey water should be collected and reused after treatment. By Decentralised Wastewater Treatment System (DWTS), treated water is recycled for irrigation, flushing, etc. Dual plumbing systems transport recycled water to buildings. An Ozonated effluent tank is installed for irrigation to landscaping and separate tertiary treated effluent tank for flushing. High efficiency fixtures, such as wash basins, sinks, urinals and WC help in saving water.

7. Vegetation and Greenery

For an urban area about one-fourth of the total area should be available for Recreational land use, which includes district/regional parks, urban forests, etc. Besides this, about 10 percent to 15 percent of the area should be planned for neighbourhood parks and playgrounds within the residential areas. In a city about 10 sq.m of recreational area per capita should be reserved as open space. A system of and scaped linkages connecting various parts of the city, neighbourhoods and important monuments should be planned. The garden, both at community and dwelling level, should provide a sense of oasis and shelter from oppressive climate. Peripheral green belts should be utilised as wind breakers, filters of dust-storms and as transition zones.

The development of greenways along natural drainage corridors and harvesting of rainwater in balancing lakes and ponds has been a new frontier in water management. Instead of resorting to conventional drainage, the concept of "zero run-off" may be adopted by using a series of retention ponds. Such ponds, reservoirs and sediment traps can be located in the catchment zones on low-lying ground, which is earmarked for greenery. This system offers distinct advantages over conventional drainage system, such as replenishment and enrichment underground water table, improving the micro-climate and ensuring an environmentally sustainable development.

This way the city would have flowing greens and interconnected parkways. These linear, connected green trails bring the landscape in the midst of concrete jungle. There is no need for elaborate gardening of the green ways, but their wild, simple and natural stretch by itself would be ecologically important. Such trails could be one of the cheapest form of drainage and recreation. These natural corridors filter water run off before it enters the river, protect biotic diversity and preserve woodland habitat. These act as air-filters for widespread vehicular pollution. They interrupt the monotony of built form and tie the neighbourhoods together. A connected spinal system of greenways can act as a recreational and health reservoir.

8. Sonic

Noise is emerging as a major pollutant and irritant in the Indian cities. Its high intensity is constant source of pain and disturbance and cause of health hazard. Against a permissible level of 50 to 60dB (a), the sound level invariably exceeds 80dB (A). Faulty and leaking silencers, over-use of motor horns, screeching tyres, rattling bodies of vehicles plying on rough road accentuate noise level from the traffic. Besides this, the noise from commercial and industrial activities, unabated use of sound amplifiers, generator sets and fire crackers often disturb the peace in urban areas.

The urban form, land use planning, landscape and green buffers help in reducing levels of noise. It is not desirable to locate residential areas along major arteries and non-residential activities inside the residential localities that would invite outside traffic. By proper land use planning, mixed land use, location of public/semi-public and commercial activities along major transport arteries, a buffer can be created for residential zone. The green buffer with thin leave trees, land formations, mounds, embankments, etc. provide effective barriers noise.

Housing Design and Bill of Rights for Housing

A salient purpose of the design is to convert a house into a home. This is possible by a gender sensitive design, keeping the women and children at focus. This leads to a realisation to configure inclusive housing and slum development from a gender sensitive perspective. Housing and redevelopment of slums are more of a habitat issues and have a vital significance vis-à-vis social and economy empowerment and quality of life aspects such as health and education, particularly of the women and girls in the slums. Thus housing is not just buildings, but about building lives of dignity.

"You employ stone, wood and concrete, and with these materials you build houses and palaces; that is construction. Ingenuity is at work. But suddenly you touch my heart, you do me good. I am happy and I say - "This is beautiful." That is Architecture. Art enters in. My house is practical. I thank you, as I might thank railway engineers or the telephone service. You have not touched my heart. But suppose that walls rise towards heaven in such a way that I am moved. I perceive your intentions. Your mood has been gentle, brutal, charming or noble. The stones you have erected tell me so. You fix me to the place and my eyes regard it. They behold something which expresses a thought. A thought which reveals itself without word or sound, but solely by means of shapes which stand in a certain relationship to one another. These shapes are such that they are clearly revealed in light. The relationships between them have not necessarily any reference to what is practical or descriptive. They are a mathematical creation of your mind. They are the language of Architecture. By the use of inert materials and starting from conditions more or less utilitarian, you have established certain relationships which have aroused my emotions. This is Architecture."

—Le Corbusier

According to Charles Correa, the Bill of Rights for Housing in the Third World should comprise the following:

- Incrementality
- Participation
- Equity
- Disaggregation
- Pluralism
- Income generation
- Open to sky space

The housing is an instrument of community organisation and communication. The aggregation of families can generate spatial patterns for the social environment. These factors, requirements and various ideas of low cost housing development are manifested in its design. These converge at access of house which is affordable to the poorest—a cobbler, rickshaw puller, casual labour and cleaner. Housing design is the conclusion of the policies, programmes, research and ideas, which aim to address to specific social and economic situations. It undergoes the rigour of financial and legal implications and may recommend certain changes in the roles and structures of the state, institutions, planning and legal systems.

The design translates the dreams and policies into the reality. This has become more important with the changing priorities, where the role of the government/civic authorities is changing to that of a facilitator, dominated by the private sectors. This needs a role reversal for socially responsive, environmentally sustainable and humane housing which incorporates the following elements:

- **Vitality:** To create a neighbourhood which can support a wide variety of functions.
- **Equity:** To achieve an equitable ambience and encourage community formation to foster a sustainable environment.

- **Efficiency:** Through optimising the resources– physical, natural, fiscal and human to the advantage of the neighbourhood and the city.
- **Flexibility:** Synthesizing local systems with global innovations and standards that can be readjusted.

This needs a design strategy that enables community participation in a decentralised programme which allows various options (including design and layout) to the households at community level and necessary technical and administrative supports. All these converge to create the homes which are affordable, functional, comfortable and sustainable. The principles of such a design include the following parameters:

(*i*) Functionally adequate space should be provided to accommodate the family and its activities;

(*ii*) Sociologically, clustered dwellings promote and sustain social interaction and fulfill man's instinct for gregarious living;

(*iii*) Climatic and passive design by orientation, courtyards, shading, wind shafts, openings, roof/wall surfaces and fenestrations to be done for micro-climatic comfort;

(*iv*) Ecologically, low rise dwelling units are better because they cater for man's primordial urge for a contact with nature and are energy efficient;

(*v*) Psychologically, different types of dwelling units must have recognisable diversity;

(*vi*) For image ability, each housing cluster should have variety of landscape materials and trees;

(*vii*) Pedestrian/cycle tracks, paved walkways and courtyards should be integral part of housing design; and

(*viii*) The housing should be accessible for all and provide special security to children, women and the elderly.

Land is a key resource for housing and should be used in an innovative manner so as to optimise its usage for greater efficiency and provision of infrastructure services. Cluster planning approach to housing design achieves high densities, while helping in promoting social and cultural lifestyle of the inhabitants. A design checklist can be evolved for various climatic regions and also taking into the consideration social, economic and cultural aspects.

Planning and Development Control Regulations

Jane Jacobs, in her seminal book 'The Death and Life of Great American Cities' puts in perspective the concept of housing density, which were often viewed as the measure of slum or luxury housing:

"What are the proper densities for city dwellings? The answer to this is something like the answer Lincoln gave to the question, 'How long should a man's legs be?' 'Long enough to reach the ground' Lincoln said. Just so, proper city dwelling densities are a matter of performance. They cannot be based on abstractions about the quantities of land that ideally should be allotted for so-and-so many people (living in some docile, imaginary society). Densities are too low, or too high, when they frustrate city diversity instead of abetting it. We ought to look at densities in much the same way as we look at calories and vitamins. Right amounts are right amounts because of how they perform. And what is right differs in specific instances."

In view of diminishing urban land and also to take up large scale housing and rehabilitation, the site and services usually may not be appropriate for large Indian cities. The four to five storeyed walk-ups have to address the problems for the elderly and disabled, while multi-storied buildings raise the issues of cost, lifts, affordability and maintenance. The FAR and densities also influence the social contacts, safety and security, sustainability and environment, travel distances, and transmission losses of power and water. They also reduce the pressure on land, public transport and services. The Twelfth Five Year Plan (2013) cites a World Bank study explaining how FSI and ground coverage can be combined to increase densities. However, due care should be taken to provide flexibility in use of space, creating streets on upper floors, social space, especially for women and children, and integrated facilities, utilities, and work places. The decision on number of floors should be based on the feasibility of fire safety, cost of construction vis-à-vis land cost and meeting the demand for affordable housing, while making full use of the Floor Area Ratio/Floor Space Index and densities.

The combination of Floor Area Ratio or Floor Space Index with different plot coverages offers opportunities for interesting architectural forms at the building level and accomplish a dynamic urban environment. At the settlement level, it will be possible to accomplish higher densities with a balanced trade-off between open and built-up spaces, land and infrastructure utilization.

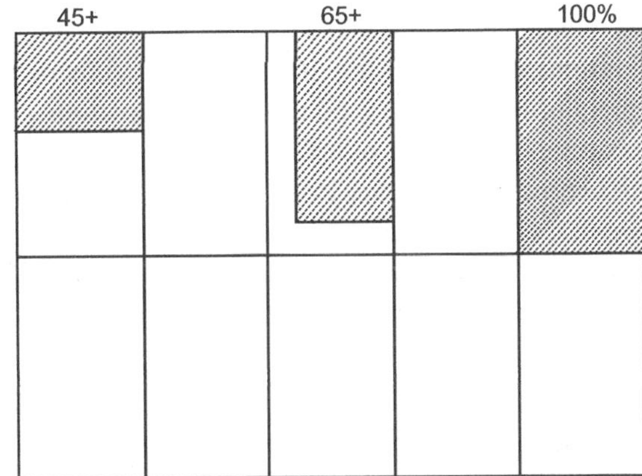

Fig. 4.10. Different Ground Coverages—Horizontal Densification.

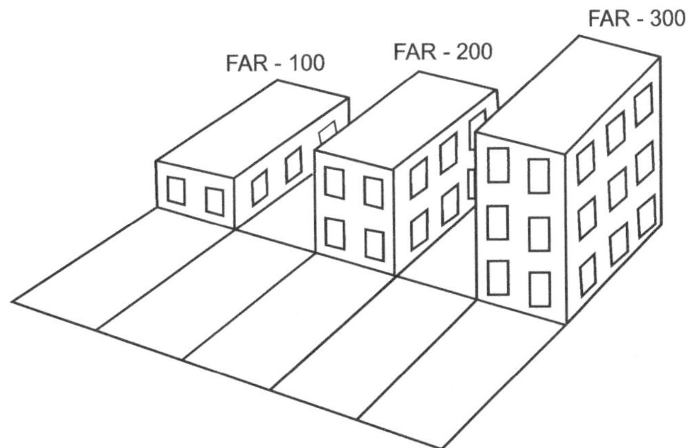

Fig. 4.11. Different Floor Area Ratios - Vertical Densification

Source: *Acioly, Claudio & Forbes Davidson, Density in Urban Development, Building Issues, Vol. 8, 1996, Lund Centre for Habitat Studies, Sweden.*

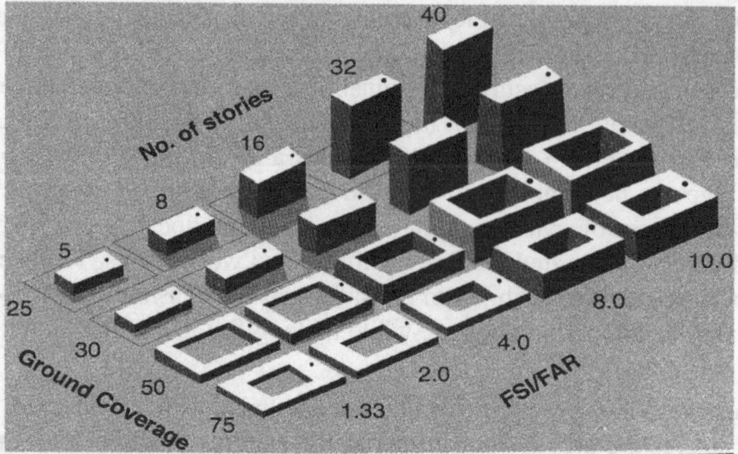

Fig. 4.12. Relationship among Ground Coverage, FAR and number of stories

The housing design may cover the green-field housing areas, upgradation, redensification and redevelopment of existing housing areas, unauthorized colonies, villages or the inner city. The requirement of shelter is dominated by small dwelling units. In view of the limited availability of land and increased requirement of housing, plotted residential development should be discouraged. There is also a need to re-examine the options of apartments in multi-storied housing, as being done in large cities like, Mumbai, Delhi, Kolkata, and Pune and how the land can be optimised by a new design approach, where even in multi-storeyed apartments, the residents have an advantage of open space, greenery and common areas, especially for women and children. The standard solutions and designs should be avoided which can be done by community participation and limited role of the housing/development authorities in design.

It is necessary to adopt a multi-pronged strategy for variety of housing designs by way of competition and cooperation among private sector, public agencies and the community/ cooperative societies. The overall responsibility for facilitation of adequate housing lies with the government which should devise ways of collaboration with the private agencies. Planning norms, land use zoning, density, Floor Area Ratio (FAR), and building controls need to be reviewed so that new areas can be opened-up for low income housing as well as the redevelopment of existing areas can be triggered. It is essential to optimise utilization of land with flexibility in development control norms. A fixed density and height restriction can lead to under-utilisation of FAR or imposition of artificial limits to optimal use of land.

Higher densities can give a range of financial benefits by optimum use of limited land, thus reducing the house cost. They can also reduce the pressure on land, public transport and services. FAR/FSI, ground coverage and density can be optimally combined keeping in view the infrastructure services, spaces for park, facilities, utilities and work places. The decision on number of floors should be based on the feasibility of fire safety, management of lifts, cost of construction and land cost and meeting the social housing demand.

Cost of the House—the Ultimate Test

While at professional level, complex issues are involved in low cost housing, for the consumer it is the ultimate cost of the house that matters. To this end several approaches are adopted:

1. Subsidized housing approach
2. Upgradation and retrofitting of existing housing
3. Site and services
4. Evolutionary, Core, Support and Infill System
5. Low Cost Design and Construction
6. Community and Cooperative Sector
7. Access to finance, loans, mortgage and subsidy
8. Rental Housing

These approaches cannot be seen in isolation, but depending upon the context and feasibility, these can be aggregated and synthesised together.

1. Subsidised Housing: In this housing system, ready-built housing units are developed by the State or private developers, usually on a subsidised basis. The private developer, either gets the subsidy or land from the government or sells those units at market rates which allow a profit. This system looks at shelter as a commodity where the prevailing business systems of finance and development offer incentives to develop these kinds of projects. But despite publicity to the contrary, the market led housing sector has been unable to reach the poorest barring some exceptions. In public housing programs, the efforts have been to develop prototypes and standardize various kinds of housing, such as site and services, resettlement and rehabilitation schemes which have generated the barracks of uniformity.

Land in Indian cities is the most expensive component of housing. If land cost is excluded, social housing becomes affordable and viable. The land can be reserved by mandatory earmarking of about 10 to 15 per cent of land for EWS/LIG in all housing projects/layouts. Accordingly, the cost of land can be excluded from the cost of the house (which could be as much as 80 to 90 per cent of total house cost).

The concept of bundling of land-FAR-housing can subsidise slum rehabilitation and social housing. In every housing project 35% of dwelling units have to be mandatory for social housing below 40 sqm against additional FAR. In case of any exemptions, the developer shall contribute proportionate cost for such housing. Partial use of FAR for market sale and commercial use can subsidise the cost for low income housing.

For the financing of social housing or slum redevelopment the priority should be to ensure that such schemes are self-financing. This can be brought in by provision of incentives like allotment of government land for social housing, additional FAR, development rights, commercial component, etc. To make social housing schemes bankable, it is necessary to take advantage of mandatory reservations, optimise utilisation of land by higher density and FAR, besides reducing the cost and time in land development, construction and infrastructure provision.

While there are many examples of low cost, subsidized housing by public sector, *i.e.* housing boards, HUDCO, Slum and JJ Wing (DUS1B), it is rare to find authentic, outstanding project by the private sector. One such project is the Shukhobrishti housing developed in an area covering 60 ha at Rajarahat, approximately 25 kilometre from Central Kolkata. The housing project consists of 20,000 flats for 100,000 population with 12,000 lower income group flats in G+4 walk-up structures and 8,000 MIG flats in G+14 multi-storey structure. The project was awarded to the developer Sapoorji Pallonji by Kolkata Metropolitan Development Authority (KMDA). The initial selling price for LIG (30 sqm, 1 BHK) was Rs. 4 lakh and Rs. 8 lakh for 44.5 sqm (2 BHK) MIG apartment. The developer was awarded 20 ha land by the government to develop commercial projects in return to the residential development. A density of 300 dwelling units per ha has been achieved. There had been no restriction on height. It is a flagship PPP project of mass housing for the urban poor. Homes are sold nearly half of the market price on a freehold basis without any restrictive covenants on the titles. As a result, homes are now available in secondary market at approximately double the original price.

Fig. 4.13. Shukhobrishti at Rajarahat New Town, Kolkata, developed by Shapoorji Pallonji in association with the KMDA and West Bengal Housing Infrastructure Development Corporation (WBHIDCO). The project covers 150 acres of land in Rajarhat and has 20,000 dwelling units: 10,444 (LIG) apartment with carpet area of 320 sq.ft., 3840 MIG apartments of 480 sq.ft. and balance 5716 apartments having an area of 690 sq.ft. each.

2. **Upgradation and Retrofitting of Existing Housing:** Upgrading is a way of improving the dwelling, its physical environment and basic services in existing communities, while preserving their location, character and social structures. Besides improving the physical conditions and quality of life in these poor communities, the physical improvements made under an upgrading process can act as a springboard for income generation, welfare, etc. Usually existing housing are rebuilt on the same land, or on adjacent land. The security of land tenure provides the community with a strong incentive to invest in their housing, through rebuilding or new construction. Although the reconstruction option involves making considerable investment the strategy allows people to continue living in the same area and to remain close to their places of work, with improved infrastructure and services.

3. **Site and Services:** In the site-and-service projects the creative and resource potential of families can be exploited. Every house can be an expression of the lifestyle of its dwellers, shaping the house according to personal preference, but within an organised framework.

The greatest advantage of the site and services strategy is that it is rapid, low cost and provides housing security and ownership. Relocation sites are often far from existing communities, job opportunities, support structures and schools. Community members who want to keep their old jobs or attend the same schools must bear the burden of additional travelling time and expense and must adapt themselves to a new environment. In case of relocation, the allottees finance the cost of constructing their houses at the new site and in some cases the land cost. The development agency should have their own land bank to undertake such schemes. This approach usually saves cost of land and laying of services.

Architect Christopher Benninger's Site and Services Scheme at Arumbakkam Chennai was planned in 1973 for five thousand families. This was followed by another 10,000 households at Villivakkam, and other sites, where people built their own houses. Efficiency in plot layout was achieved by narrow and deeper plot configuration, reducing the length of the infrastructure networks. On these smaller plots, people built their own shelters, which became a model for the World Bank. At Yousufguda near Hyderabad, incremental Site and Service provided 100 5m plots, with a water tap, toilet, a bathing platform and one room. Each owner could add more rooms. Low cost housing in Jamnagar and the SOS Children's Village at Bawana, Delhi are other landmarks.

Fig. 4.14. Site and Services Project in Arumbakkam, Chennai Metropolitan Development Authority

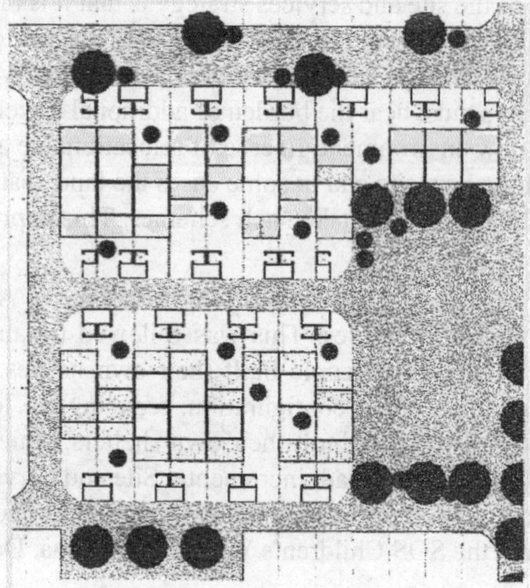

Fig. 4.15. Typical Unit Plan for Site and Services by Christopher Benninger

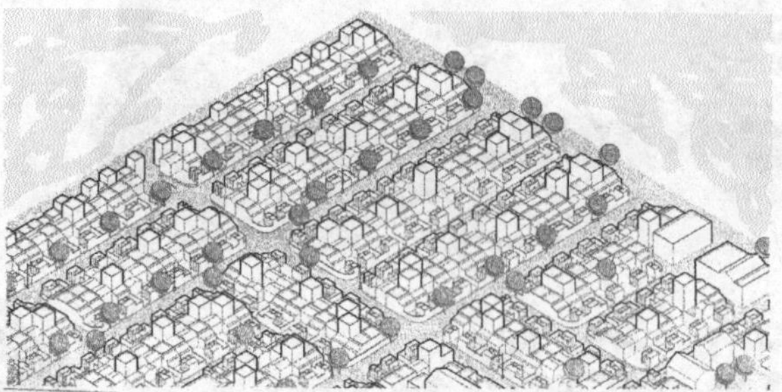

Fig. 4.16. Isometric of Site and Services scheme by Christopher Benninger

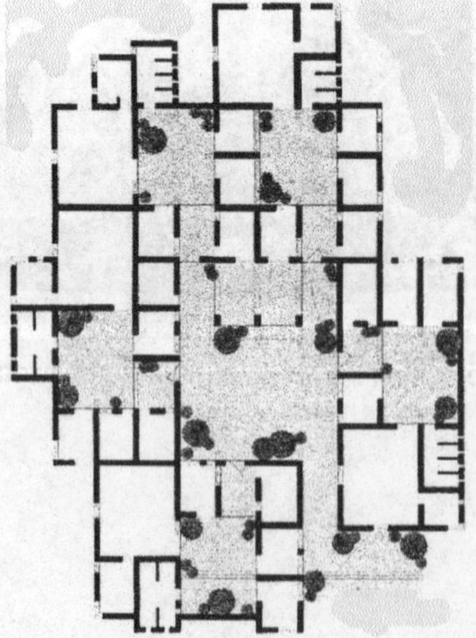

Fig. 4.17. Typical cluster plan of SOS Children's Village, Bawana, Delhi

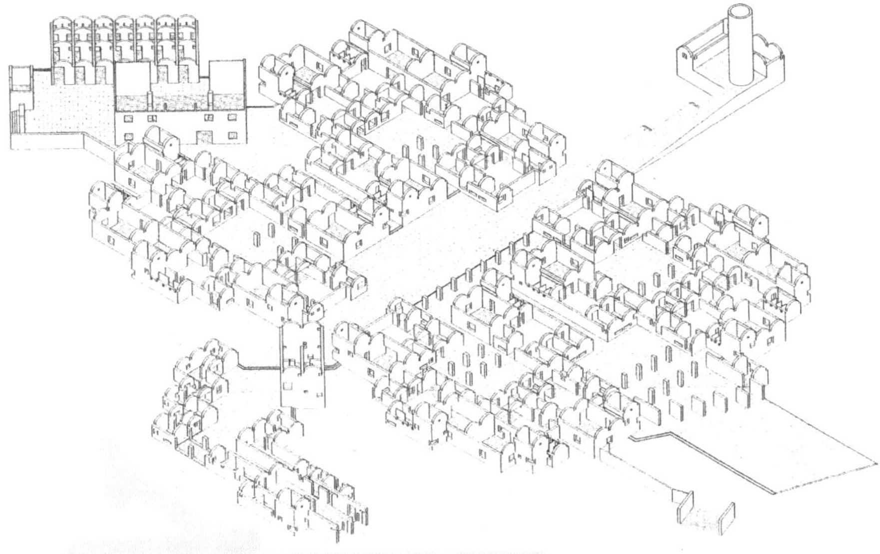

Fig. 4.18. SOS Children's Village, Bawana, Delhi, Christopher Benninger

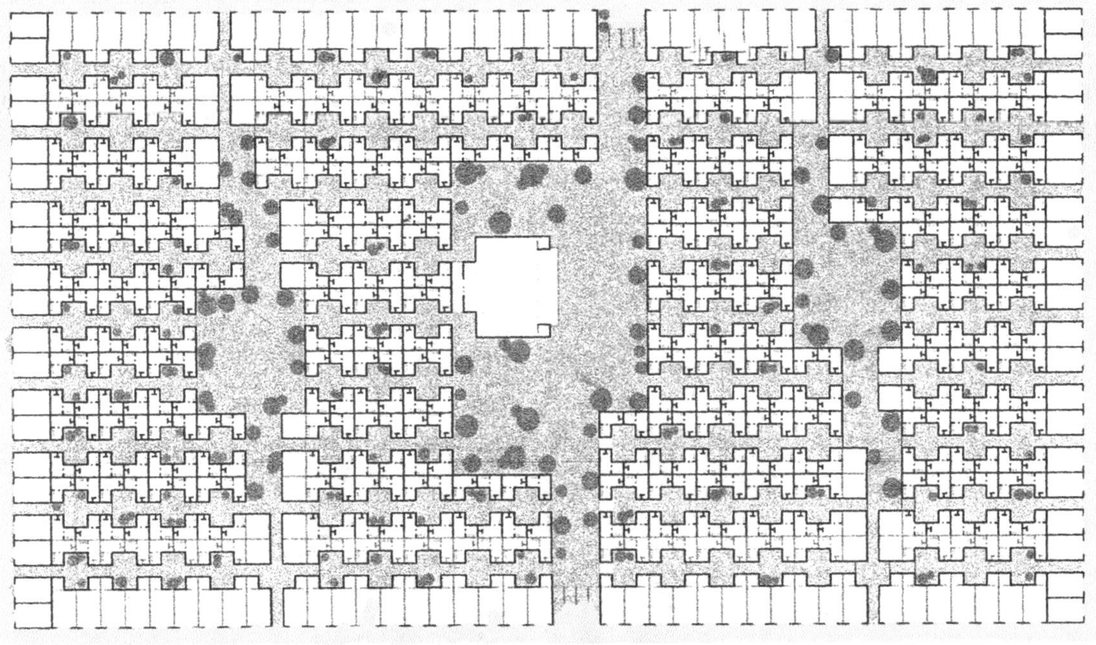

Fig. 4.19. Plan of economically weaker section shelter scheme at Jamnagar, Gujarat, by Christopher Benninger (1972)

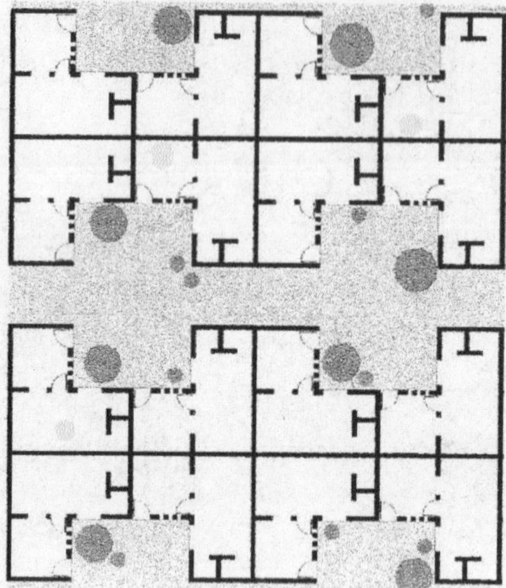

Fig. 4.20. Cluster Plan, EWS Scheme, *Jamnagar* (1972) Christopher Benninger

Renowned architect Charles Correa, in his Belapur Housing Scheme at Navi Mumbai, devised a system of social organisation. The organisation of the community revolves around a system of open space, which gradually builds up from a small courtyard of 8 × 8 m size for seven dwellings, to 12 × 12 m for 21 families, 20 × 20 m for 63 families, and onwards. The simple houses can be built by the local artisans and by self-help, which allow alterations and flexibility.

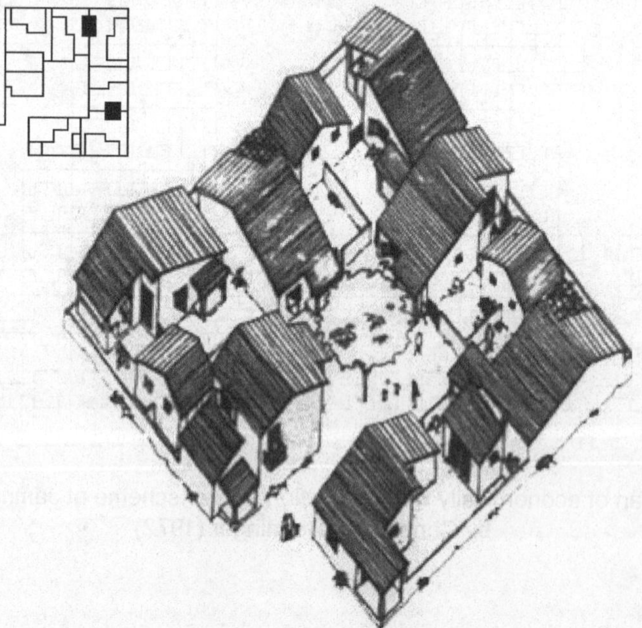

Fig. 4.21. Belapur (Architect Charles Correa)

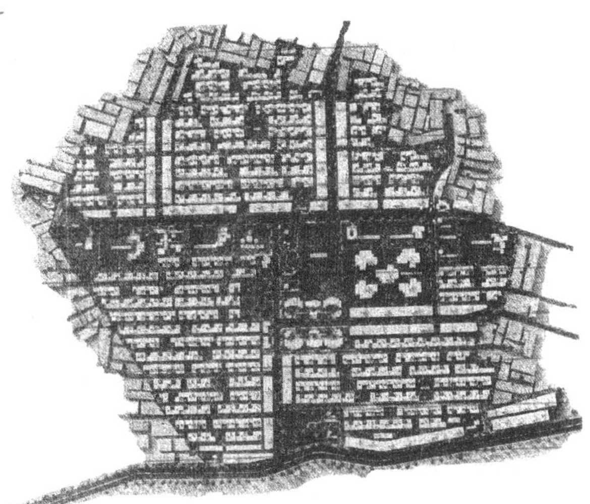

Fig. 4.22. In the Vrindavan Housing Scheme, New Delhi, housing has been integrated with self-employment opportunities among the poorer sections and informal sectors. The layout recreates traditional values of community living. The concept of mixed land use intends to create linear markets and an attractive street picture. The scheme, covering an area of 36 ha, was planned for a population of about 25000 persons on a high density (715 persons per Ha.) and a low-rise development pattern. Gradual augmentation of services and innovative systems of sewerage, solid waste disposal and drainage were contemplated. Being surrounded by the built-up areas and without any peripheral/trunk services, the decentralized service units were planned for water supply, sanitation and sewerage. (Architect: A.K. Jain)

In Vrindavan housing scheme, New Delhi, around 4600 units, ranging from 26 sqm for EWS to 150 sqm for mixed land use, and some area for group housing were planned. The scheme was based on the 'Site and Services' approach. A fully serviced plot is allocated to the EWS household, with a basic core. The container can be built by the occupant at his own pace. Clusters of 8 to 12 dwelling units are planed around open sockets reserved for the services. The service lines from the core to service slots are short and economical. To encourage, refine and develop local and modern methods of construction and to inspire traditional skills, a building center was proposed within the housing scheme.

The celebrated architect B. V. Doshi, in his Aranya Township at Indore, refined the concept of site-and-services. The concept is based upon maximization of scarce resources and stimulating the self-help element among the low income families. To correspond with the economic growth of the families, the housing design adopts the principle of an incremental prototype. The most innovative aspect of the project is an alternative system of the services. The service core and slots have been predesigned, which connect with the main lines running on alternate streets. The space for the service core is so planned that it allows alterations and modifications in the house, if required, at a later date. A versatile system for sewerage has been evolved which is based on local services, without dependence upon the city systems. For maximizing the common walls and minimising the foundations, the service core is grouped into fours over suspended platforms. Simple on-site precast elements and components encourage the self-build spirit.

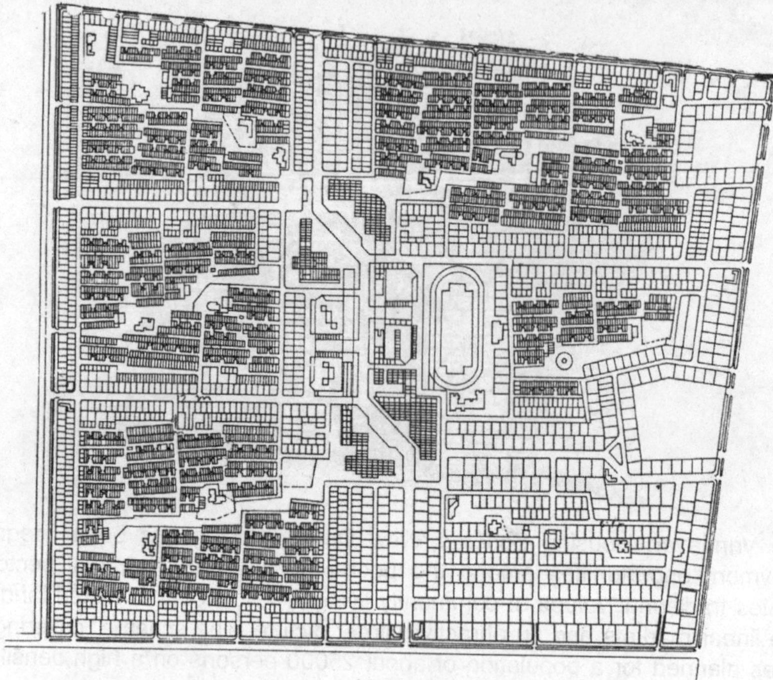

Fig. 4.23. Aranya Township, Indore, (Architect B.V. Doshi)

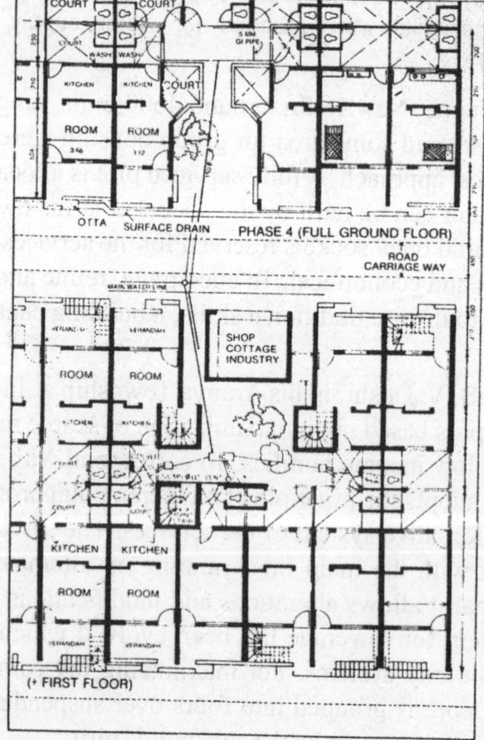

Fig. 4.24. Self-help housing at Aranya Township, Indore, which is built according to household's resources, needs and priorities

4. Evolutionary Support-Infill Housing: In this housing delivery system, individual families construct their house around a service core or room built by the public agency, instead of buying a ready-made house from the developer. This way the cost of construction is substantially reduced and deferred for future.

A pioneering effort is the work of the SAR, Netherlands, who developed a conceptual framework of 'supports' based housing for low income settlements. The concept, initially developed by Hebraken, is based upon a detailed analysis and identification of the actors, domains, morphological and spatial relationships and components of housing development. The hypothesis builds up into a complex but clear system of the dwelling unit in terms of establishing space modules. The design allows several permutations and combinations on the basis of concept of domain and right of transformation and the concept of differentiated responsibilities.

The 'Support-Infill' building process is based on a 3 dimensional skeletal grid, evolved on a modular basis and utilising simple precast components, it permits large variations, adjustments, negotiations and extensions of the dwellings. The skeletal system does not require sophisticated machinery, plant and skills for its production and assembly. For exploring a large number of combinations possible, the use of computers is helpful. The skeletal structure can either be erected by the people themselves or by a centralised organisation.

The core and support comprising a modular skeleton structure, supporting walls, floor, roof and rudimentary services should follow certain ground rules. The occupants endow their living arrangements with touches of individuality and taste, that are often found in the low-income families. They may reuse the old building materials from their old dwelling units.

5. Low Cost Design and Construction: The concept of low cost housing design and construction is based upon the use of self-help, local materials, appropriate technology and building systems. Various individuals, like Laurie Baker, Anil Laul, voluntary agencies and organisations like the HUDCO have done commendable work in this field. With their sustained efforts, traditional methods and materials, have been interrelated with sustainable, less expensive and innovative building systems. Such efforts have also resurrected the vaults, domes, arches and many such traditional elements of building, which are becoming extinct.

Laurie Baker's houses are simple to build, honest with building materials, comfortable for the climate and economical for low income group. His houses are not the final and finished products, but facilitate growth and improvements along with the family's needs and resources. His approach and simple principles to low cost housing can be easily adapted.

In Auroville, the Township Development Group through the design concepts, have experimented with the reintroduction of village craft of building construction. These include earth platforms, mud walls, brick lintels, arches for openings and country tiles and thatch for roofing. Reinhold Pingle has also adapted such techniques in his 50-house cluster at Mahaveerpuram. In Wardha, from where most of the Gandhian thoughts and philosophy radiated, the Centre for Science for Villages and Group of Research and Exchange on Technology has developed simple, low cost and pure concepts of housing. The housing incorporates mud walls, vaults built by thin burnt clay bricks and mud mortar, Nubian arches, bamboo lintels and arches for openings, pozzolona plaster over woven bamboo mats for partition walls, simple reinforced concrete and prefabricated joists. The Nubian arch is based on the catenary curve in which only compression stress occurs. This does not require any centering and is insulated by a mud phuska layer.

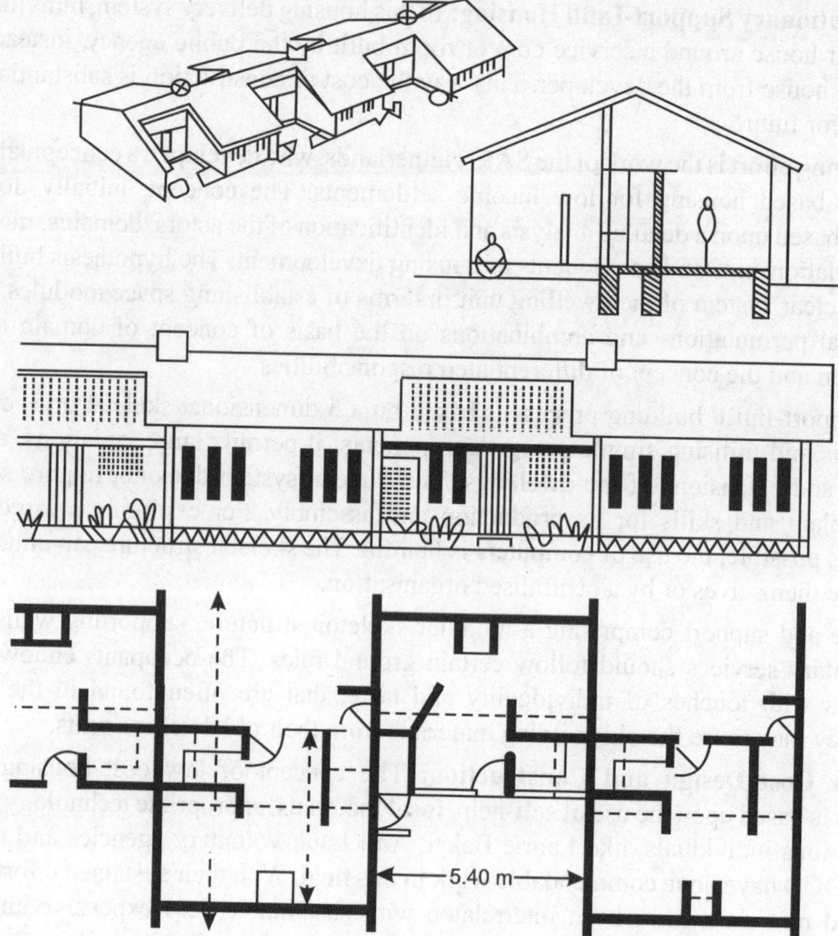

Fig. 4.25. Laurie Baker followed the principles of 'less is more' and 'small is beautiful' in the organization of space

Source: *Gautam Bhatia, 1991, Laurie Baker Life, Work and Writings, Viking, HUDCO, New Delhi*

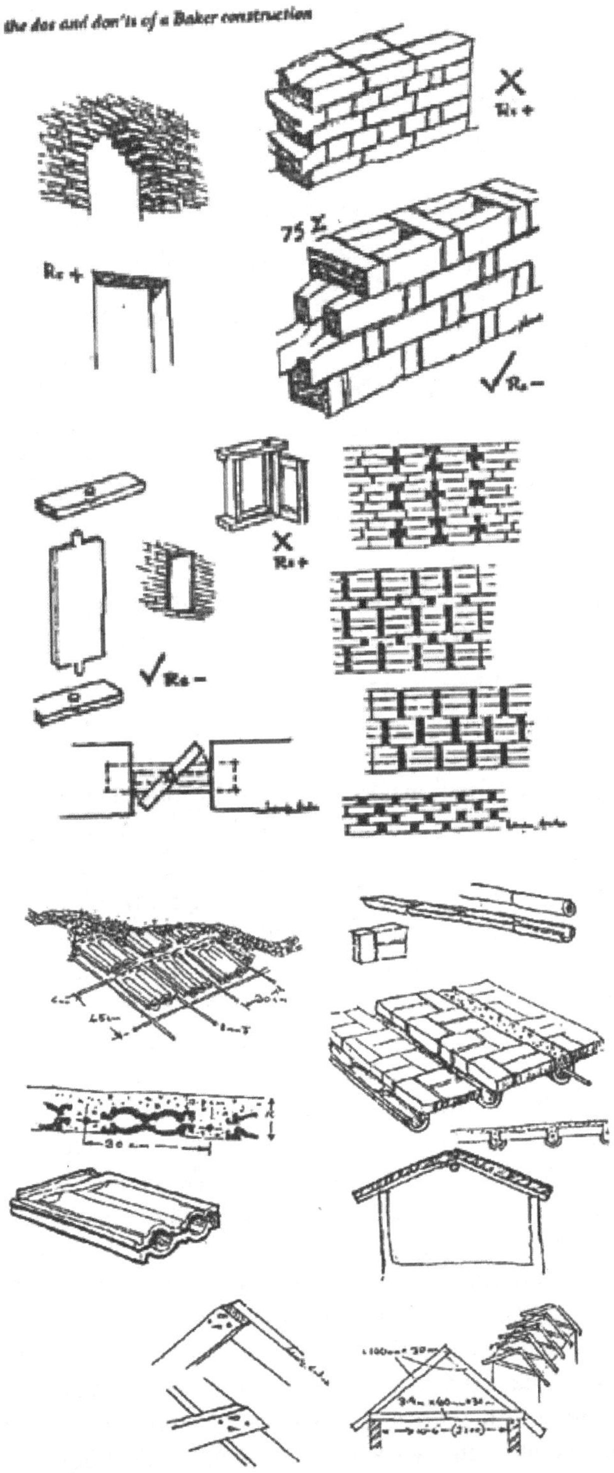

Fig. 4.26. Sketches by Laurie Baker in the Publication 'How to Reduce Cost', COSTFORD, Government of Kerala, 1986

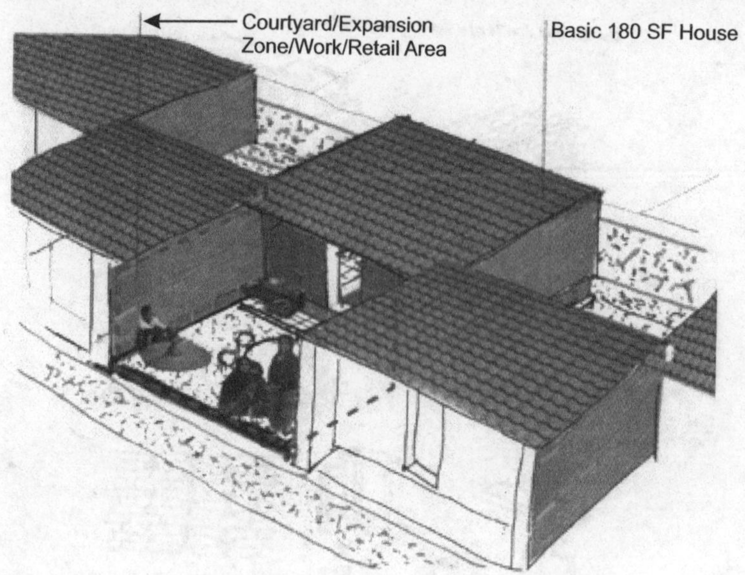

Fig. 4.27. Project Ground Up by Eric Ho Architecture Commons, envisages homes constructed of compressed earth blocks that can be manufactured by micro enterprises

The recognition and facilitation of the potentials of the local communities by self-help housing can effect huge savings in the investments, that could be diverted for the provision of better services, amenities, loans and other priorities.

Charles Correa, in an international low cost housing design competition, developed the concept of in-situ precast concrete profile suitable for short-span housing construction by self-help. The system does not require sophisticated machinery and skills, and can be manually produced.

The simple pre-cast components, like concrete supports, roof joists as panels can be locally produced and assembled. Reinforced and mixed with waste materials, like rice straw, rice husk, palm fiber, sisal fiber, reed fiber, sugarcane fiber, sawdust, sand, crushed soft stone and flyash. The problem of hydrophobisation of gypsum, which makes it structurally unsafe and unable to withstand high humidity, has been resolved by a patent method. This requires mixing of a small quantity of hydrophobic material in the gypsum precast and modular gypsum components facilitate simple, adaptable, flexible and low rise design of housing. The components need no plastering. The components can be easily cut on the site. The components can be manufactured by mobile and variable production technology. The manufacture of the elements in the vicinity of the building site simplifies storage, transportation and handling of the basic elements. A close link between production of the elements and construction of the building matches the demands of the building industry in the developing countries. Execution of the building is simple and does not require special skills. Even in the case of the large element system, production and assembly can be done manually. During the execution, only limited ancillary materials are needed, such as cement, concrete and reinforcing bars. The assembly of a house of 80 square metres, without foundations, including the positioning of the gypsum walls, floor and partition elements, construction of R.C. structure, placing doors and windows and completing the assembly takes only 140 to 160 hours. There are no essential differences between the large and small element systems from technical and economic points of view.

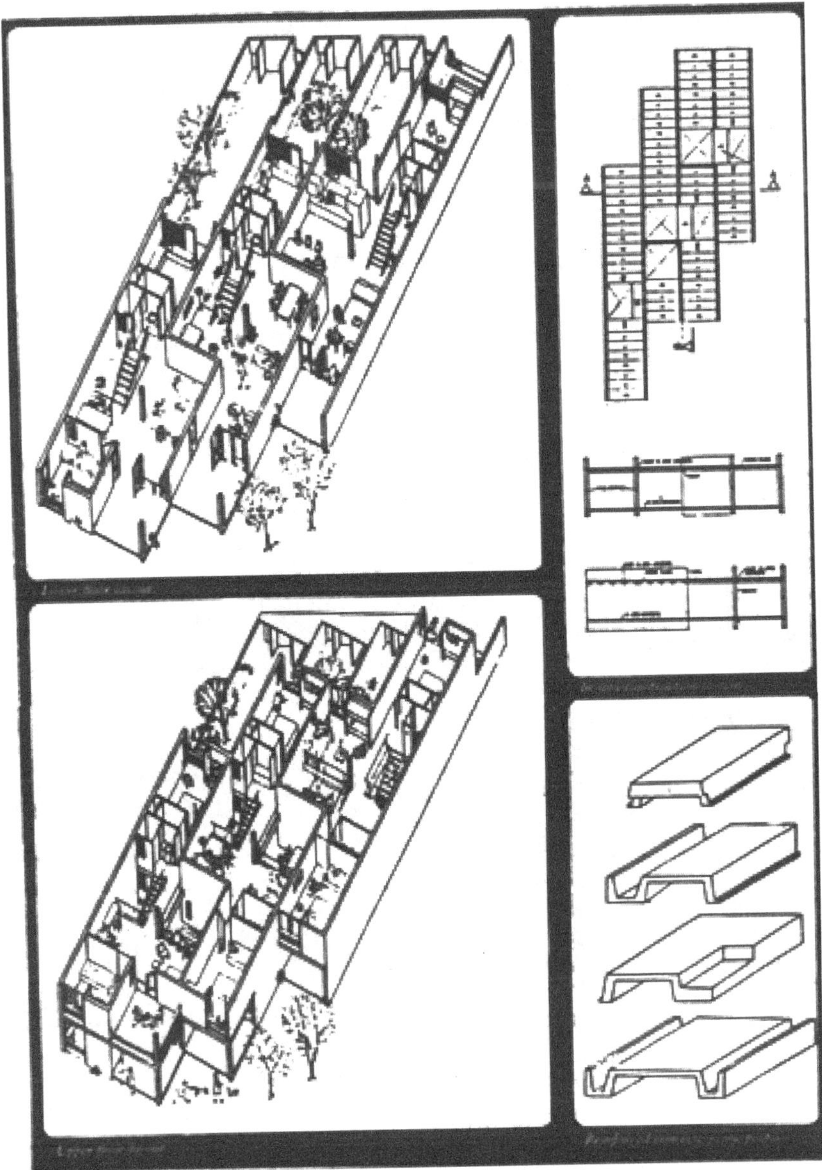

Fig. 4.28. Low Cost Housing Competition Entry (Architect Charles Correa)

Conventional foundations can be provided for the gypsum house according to the situation and local requirements. The gypsum elements are lightweight, fire resistant and low energy materials. Their hollow cores can be utilised for formation of beams, load bearing columns or can be filled with the insulating materials. The load bearing lintels are cast in situ hollow channels. For reinforcement of gypsum panels, besides steel, various alternative and local materials, such as bamboo or its reeds, wire mesh, or jute fiber can also be used. The integration of bamboo and such other local materials with gypsum can significantly improve the quality of the houses in the rural and semi-urban areas.

The vaults and domes using mud blocks, have also been experimented successfully by Rajendra and Rupal Desai. Inspired by Nader Khalili, Ray Meeker has developed the concept of fired earth house. The concept is based upon the potter's ability to convert simple earth into enclosed space.

Meeker suggests adoption of this principle for individual house construction by on-site production of mud bricks for construction of walls, openings and vaults for roof.

The Development Alternatives in New Delhi have done remarkable work in promoting the concepts of construction using mud, mud blocks, vaults, Nubian domes, arches and intermediate technology, like slender RCC beams, brick panels, filler slab, etc. Nubian vaults have been built using adobe blocks and tapered hollow cylinders, finished with china mosaic, broken pottery and tiles.

The Building Centre, HUDCO and architect Anil Laul have developed new methods and building systems like hollow blocks, light metal frame roofing, geodesic domes, fiberglass reinforced panels, funicular shells, thermocol-filled thrift panels and beams. These compliment and merge with the local materials and building crafts, like mud blocks and arched openings.

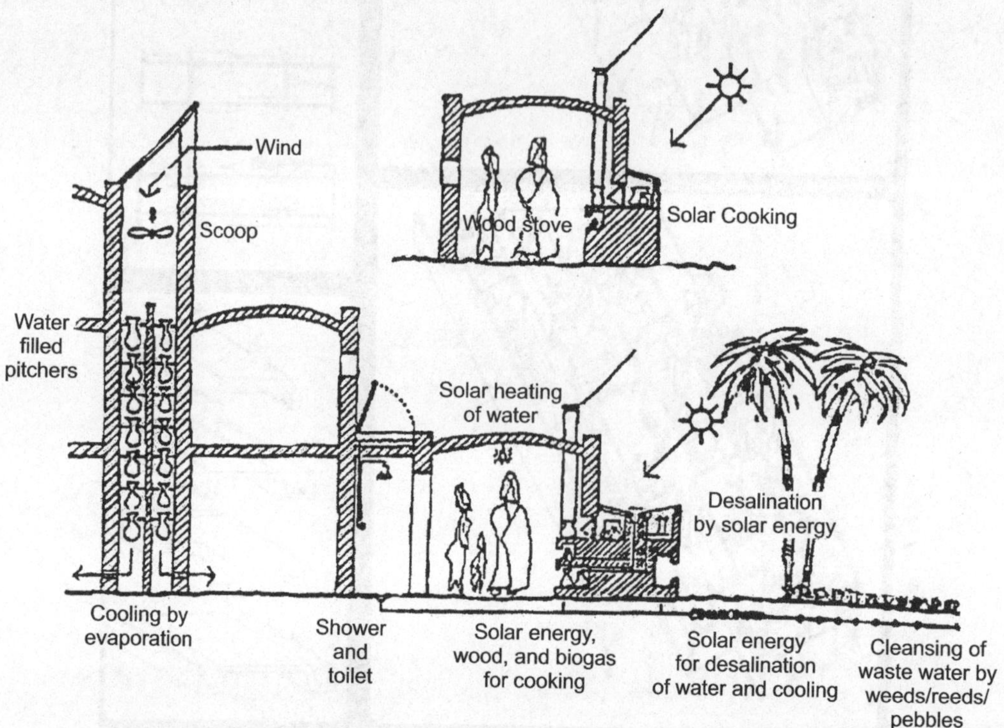

Fig. 4.29. Norwegian architect Harald N. Rostvik's low cost housing for homeless uses vernacular cooling shaft, solar energy and bio-gas for cooking, desalination of water and recycling of waste water, along with local, low-tech recycle building materials. The design won an award in a competition organised during the Year of Homeless (1987)

6. Self-help and Cooperative Sector: Shelter planned, financed and self-built by groups of people such as the cooperative housing society, reduces the investments of both the government and house owners. However, this housing delivery system may need financial engagement to finance, legal instruments to give legal status to the groups which develop them, and community organization to support the process. The professionals, specially the architects, may act as the catalysts, who help in access to land, services, finance and other resources.

Fig. 4.30. A Cooperative Housing Project in Chandigarh

7. **Access to Finance:** Housing finance can be secured through a variety of agencies/ institutions:
   - Housing finance institutions
   - Commercial banks
   - Individual savings and loans
   - Pension and insurance fund agencies
   - Cooperative societies
   - Micro-credit financing institutions credit to the poor
   - Credit guarantee scheme
   - Employers' loan/grants
   - Bonds, share market, municipal borrowings
   - Real estate investment trusts (REIT)
   - Foreign direct investments.
   - Housing and urban development funds (Central/State/ Public Sector Undertakings)

For financing and subsidising social housing, slum rehab and redevelopment, the following principles can be adopted:

(*i*) One-third from the Central Government under its programs such as Housing for All.

(*ii*) One-third from the State Government.

(*iii*) One-third by the project agency /ULB, of which half can be beneficiary contribution and remaining half may be generated by property development, additional FAR, mixed land use and cross subsidy.

The housing finance companies (HFC) and commercial banks have made available easier home loans. Interest rate subsidies have been a popular way of enhancing housing finance affordability. Micro finance for shelter addresses a gap that larger scale mortgage lenders are unwilling to provide for. Wholesale bulk "Project Finance" is usually accessed at the level of the developer/

housing agency for land assembly, infrastructure development and housing construction, which are normally short term loans.

The financing of the social housing can be supplemented by mortgage guarantee fund, Social Housing Fund, Mutual Fund, Provident, Insurance and Pension Funds and General Obligation Bonds. Rationalization of Stamp Duty and its exemption for LIG and EWS housing is necessary. Value Added Tax (VAT) would avoid repeated taxation. Social housing should also be available on rental basis as many poor families cannot afford huge down payments and EMIs. This requires design interventions which align with Government policies and programs for optimum use of resources.

8. Rental housing: A large number of low income groups cannot access housing loan and even if they are able to access, they are unable to meet the mortgage payment. Rental housing is a way to reduce huge down payments. However, in view the difficulties in obtaining rental payment, the concessions, loans and legal disputes, the availability housing. Most of the house owners fear that once the house is given on rent, it will never be available to the owner.

Keeping in view the various barriers in rental housing the Government of India has formulated Draft National Urban Rental Housing Policy (NURHP, 2019) which suggests various policies, administrative and legal measures, together with financial incentives to promote rental housing, especially among the poor informal sector, workers, women and the aged.

In terms of housing design, it is necessary to adopt a multi-pronged approach whereby the housing includes a preparation of rental housing besides the transit camps, hostels, dormitories, old-age homes, night shelter, etc.

DEBRIEFING QUESTIONS

1. What are the critical issues which need to be addressed by housing design?
2. Who are the major actors in housing supply vis-à-vis their roles in land, services, financing construction, regulations and transactions?
3. By a matrix chart compare the housing requirements of the Poor and Higher Income Groups.
4. How design can be a vehicle of public policy and participation in social housing?
5. Explain the (*a*) Concept of Ecological Circle of Buildings, and (*b*) Passive and Active Measures for Green Housing Design.
6. Explain how the urban hierarchy is worked out for neighbourhood/community planning?
7. Explain the characteristics of social housing, refer to Charles Correa's Bill of Rights for Housing in the Third World.
8. What are the various approaches towards reducing the housing costs?
9. Write short notes on the following:
   (*a*) Site and Services
   (*b*) In-situ Slum Rehabilitation
   (*c*) Affordable Housing
   (*d*) Cluster Housing

5

Rural Housing

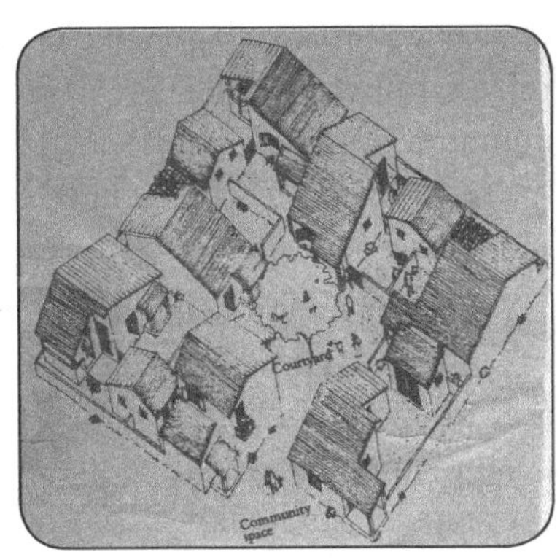

According to the Census 2011, the rural population in India stands at 833 million, that is about 68% of the total population. The Ministry of Rural Development (MORD) has estimated the total rural housing shortage for the 12th Five Year Plan (2012-17) to be 43.67 million dwelling units. The same study identified access to finance as a pre-requisite for rural habitat.

The Union Cabinet, approved the implementation of the rural housing component of Pradhan Mantri Awas Yojana. Under the scheme, financial assistance is provided for construction of pucca house to all houseless and households living in dilapidated houses.

The expenditure involved in implementing the project in a span of 3 years from 2016-17 to 2018-19 is Rs.81,975 crore. It is proposed that onc crore households would be provided assistance for construction of pucca house under the project. The scheme being implemented in rural areas throughout India envisages sharing of the costs between Centre and the States.

The Pradhan Mantri Awaas Yojana-Gramin provides assistance of Rs. 1,20,000 per dwelling unit in plain areas and to Rs. 1,30,000 in hilly states/difficult areas/IAP districts. It is estimated that the additional financial requirement of Rs 21,975 crore would be met by borrowing through National Bank for Agriculture and Rural Development (NABARD). The cost of unit assistance is to be shared between Central and State Governments in the ratio 60:40 in plain areas and 90:10 for North Eastern and hilly states. The beneficiary would be facilitated to avail loan of up to Rs.70,000/- for construction of the house which is optional. The unit size has been enhanced from the existing 20 sq.m to 25 sq.m.

To meet the additional requirement of building materials, manufacture of bricks using cement stabilised earth or fly ash will be taken up. A National Technical Support Agency provides technical support to the Centre and States to facilitate construction of the houses and to ensure their quality.

Village Profile

The spatial structure of a typical village in India corresponds to occupational division. The unclean occupations cluster on the periphery—low lying areas or in the west. The cleaner or dominant groups occupy the prime locations, usually high lands, central areas or north side. The patches of occupational clusters are separated by open ground and community facilities, *e.g.* chowk, chopal, temple and bazaar, allowing all levels to inter-act. Some time the boundaries are simply common walls of houses or courtyards, or streets between groups of houses. The village structure represents a closely knit orthogonal fabric with an introvert character of built environment. The patches and cluster within a village are clearly defined in terms of social structure. An inhabitant traditionally relates to his mohalla, *i.e.* a geographical area that defines the neighbourhood patterns of urban communities. Increasing social mobility now makes it difficult to relate the occupation of a man to his mohalla, but groups related by practice or customs and geographic origin continue to cluster in mohallas.

The power structure within the community reflects a hierarchial order, which is often made up of sub-caste, numerical strength, wealth, education, age and political power. Often few households are grouped together around a common courtyard with separate areas for men and women. The custom of purdah required that women be shielded from the gaze of passers by, so that a street view presented high blank walls. Women's courtyards are located in the rear, behind the men's quarters.

Community Space

The focal point of mohalla in a village is the chopal. This is often a semi-public open space at the junction of streets, or at the termination of gali, which acts as a connector between different mohallas and communities. Though chopals apparently appear as left over spaces in a confined environment, the fact that there is no encroachment is an indication of the great value that the community attaches to them. It is worth nothing that squatters do never encroach over a chopal. The chopal has a sacrosanct and symbiotic imagery in a village, where panchayat often meets to take the decisions and to pronounce judgments. Its sanctity is accentuated by a temple, invariably located adjacent to the chopal. Around a chopal there is generally a commercial, communal or service activity serving to daily needs. The chopal tends to serve the immediate community and becomes a focal point where the inhabitants of mohallas meet. There is general community agreement and unwritten principles of its use and sequence of events: washing of clothes, playing, smoking hookah, meetings of occasional festival, marriage or other rituals. The temple is an important landmark in a village. It does not only enshrine a deity, but serves as an institution of learning and centre of community activities for the villagers.

The privacy is protected by a series of spatial envelops according to the spatial continuum. First degree of privacy is provided by the interior courtyard which is the exclusive domain of women. Second degree of privacy is defined by the land outside the door, which is accessible to the members of family and their relations. Third degree of privacy is the boundary of the mohalla, which is the domain of the local residents. These zones of privacy are reflected in a sequence of public, semi-public and private domains of spaces, including streets, chowks and chopals.

The compact maze of buildings produce a pattern of houses having a close relationship. The contacts established by women are on a more personal level. Through the use of parapet walls, or even scaling low walls. Women have a second layer of circulation open to them which is forbidden to the men-fork. The proximity of structures acts as a deterrent to unauthorized entry of the outsiders. The meandering and narrow streets help in maintaining the privacy.

Spatial Pattern and Structure

An outside observer sees the streets as a pattern of dark voids between buildings and is apt to arrive at an erroneous conclusion. Behind then narrow dark lanes, bounded by blank walls, are sunny courtyards where most of the activities take place. The courts act as the node of horizontal and vertical circulation. The transitional elements, *e.g.* verandah, entrance and gate are highly pronounced in the built environment. The services are invariably located on the periphery of the houses.

The traditional spatial structure has a sieve like porous form. Closely knit fabric of structures help to keep out the harsh sun and provides shaded courtyards and streets. During the night, the open courtyards radiate out the heat and create a cooling effect. Thus the form, based upon the principle of thermal comfort through passive means, presents a framework of energy conscious design. The indigenous settlement is a working model of closely knit and self-contained community.

Its spatial structure is a logical outgrowth of viable sets of social and economic norms governing community and individual behaviour. Their complex organism presents pluralistic and multiple patterns of morphology reflecting socio-cultural and historical layers. Traditional rural settlements are not just agglomeration of buildings, streets, land use and deities. They are the spatial embodiment of certain social systems with their ceremonies, rurals, festivals, social network, institutions and family life. It is the inter-relationship of cultural adaptation to physical form which manifests in the continuity of communities providing security, stability and diversity of human experience. Uncontrolled invasion of non-compatible activities has led to disintegration of the homogenous community structure of village.

The spatial structure of a village provides valuable clues to the resolution of planning, housing, and community development issues. Low-income groups and migrants find in the indigenous villages an environment where opportunities exist for economic betterment. The life in villages, which is regulated by institutions and social interaction, is often more compatible than the barren imagery of new areas resulting from outdated planning concepts and manipulation of the spatial environment.

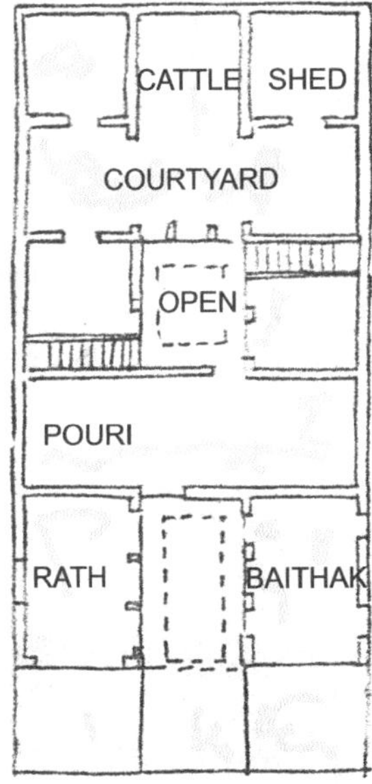

Front baithak and rath (chariot) room added to a Central court house

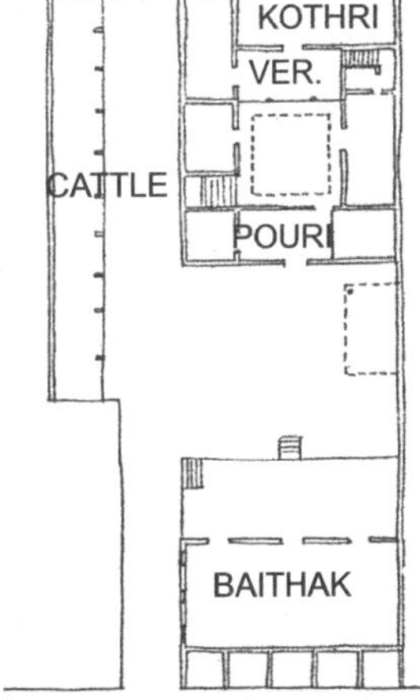

A self-contained house having baithak in the front, ladies room and cattle shed in the rear

Fig. 5.1. Rural houses are characterised by clustering on the basis of caste and occupation, privacy of women, joint family, lack of proper plumbing and toilets, use of cheaper, local building materials and space for cattle

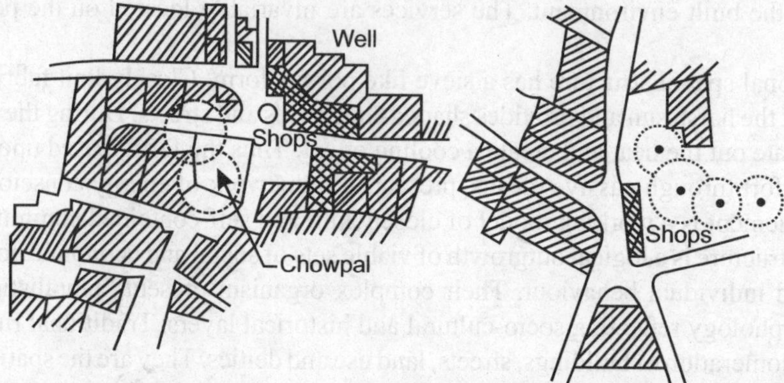

Fig. 5.2. Chopal, the focus of community, is embellished by trees, a well and place of worship. People get together, gossip and exchange news of the day. Enclosures are irregular, linear or square

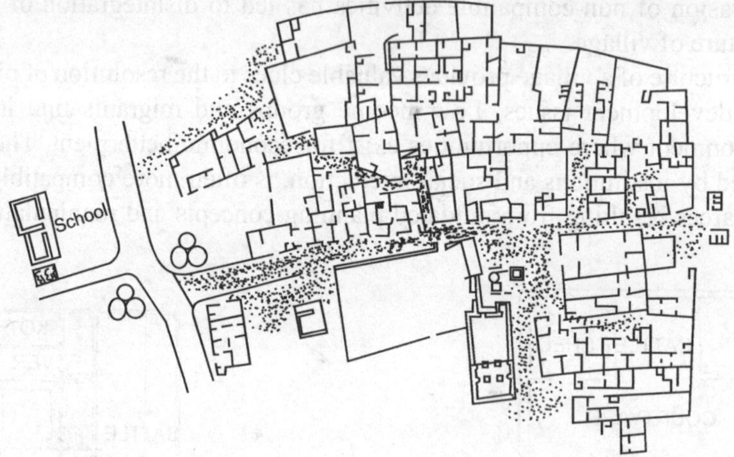

Fig. 5.3. The rural morphology, though irregular and organic, manifests the social organization of the community in the form of courtyards, chopal, temple, village pond, narrow shaded streets, joint family, occupations and frequent religious, cultural festivals and celebrations where the whole village participates

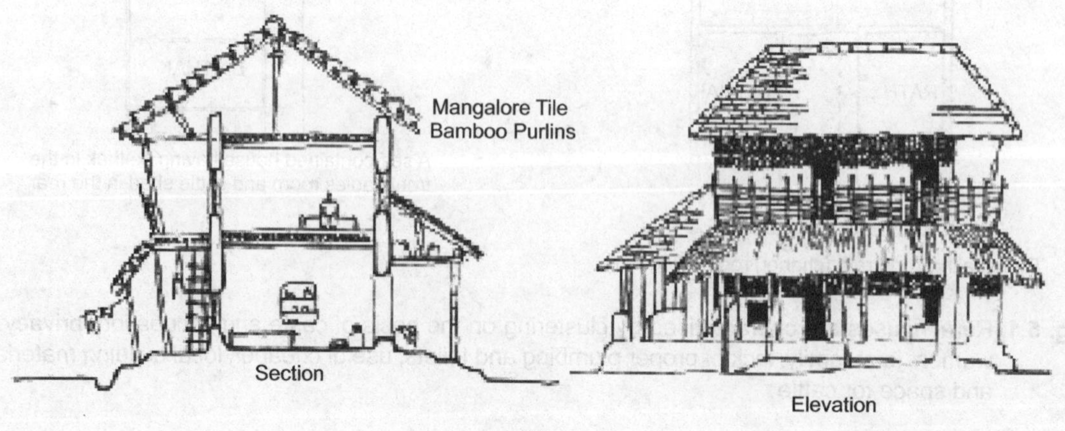

(A)

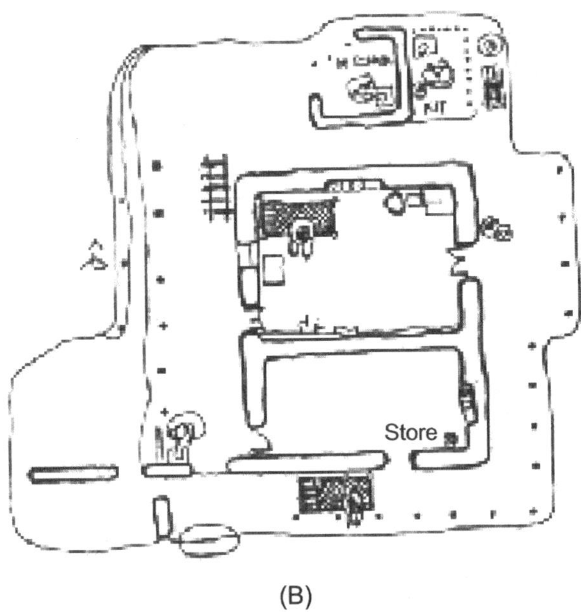

(B)

Figs. 5.4 (A) and (B). A Typical House, Radhaballabhpur. Midnapore. In villages, many of the house functions take place in open and semi-open space and the house is enveloped by a wide veranda

Analysis of the morphology demonstrates that the indigenous settlements have a variety of typologies and characteristics. No single approach can offer optional basis for understanding their morphology itself within a village settlement, it is difficult to have a uniform typology and approach. Variations in physical, cultural and socio-economic conditions are discernible among the villages and also within every settlement. The core area of a village inhabits mostly local population, in a high density closely knit pattern of clusters with permanent structures. It has a low-rise, compact and organic urban pattern, that evolved through the history. This areas has predominantly high income, high caste, land owning population and the physical form reflects their status in the village. The houses are in the form of katras, with courtyards as their hub. This area constitutes the urban core of the settlement. The marginal areas of the settlement are distinguished by their poor inhabitants and kutcha dwellings.

The essential services like water supply (individual taps) and privies are generally non-available. This area, from official point of view, is usually illegal and non-conforming. The land tenure is usually disputed or it under unauthorized possession of a non-resident landlord, who extracts rent from the residents. Low-income of the residents and status of tenure do not permit immediate improvement of the buildings or reconstruction. Since such fringe developments are illegal from official point of view, there is a whole range of formal and informal agents patronizing them. Due to their illegality, political pressures coupled with underhand dealings have been instrumental in achieving the levels of services corresponds to the strength of the patrons and their proximity to the power structure. By and large, such developments, although of recent origin, enjoy a better level of services, as compared to the marginal areas of villages.

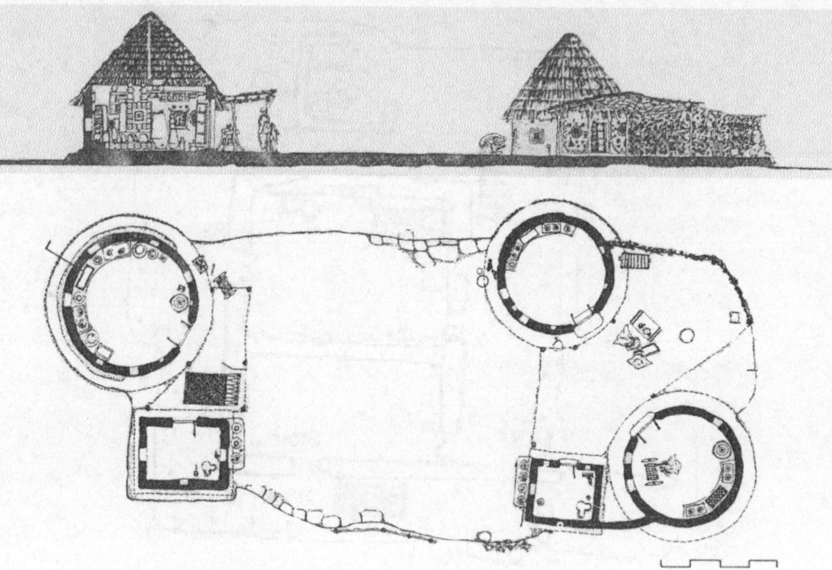

Fig. 5.5. Headman House in Ludia, Gujarat

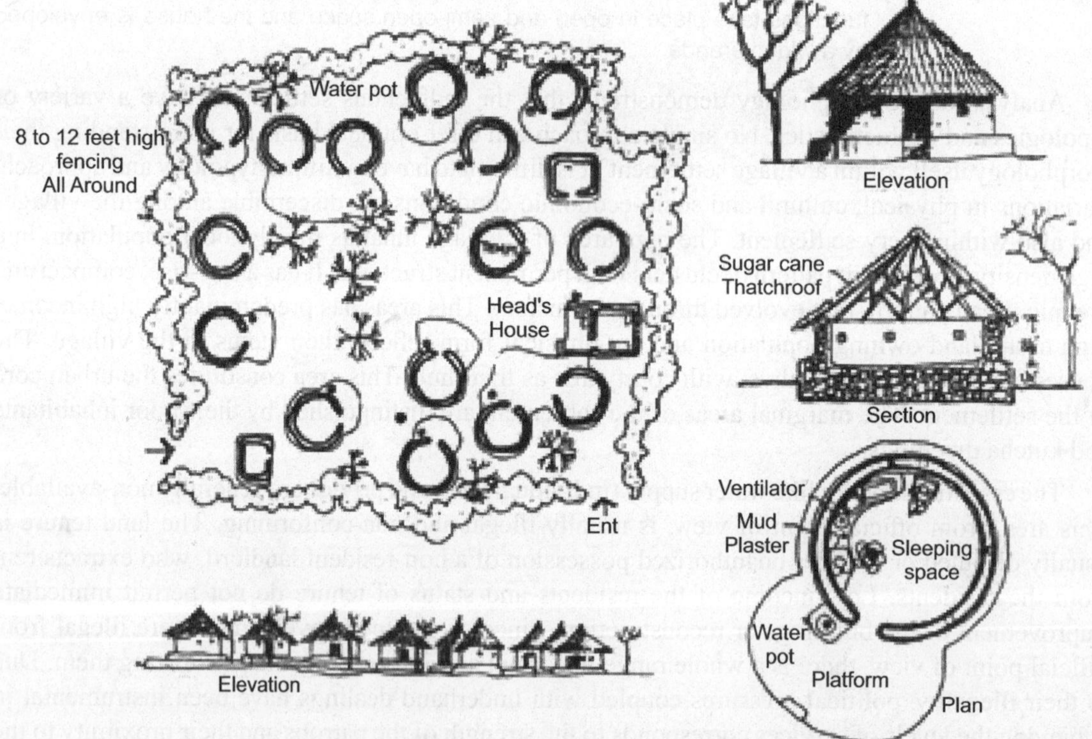

Fig. 5.6. Cluster houses in the Plasma Desert (Junagarh) of Gujarat facilitate joint family living with everyone's own space and privacy. The circular walls secure the family from hot winds and provide stability to the structure from onslaught of storms and earthquake

Source: *Jain Kulbhushan and Minakshi Jain (2000), Architecture of Indian Desert, AADI Centre, Ahmedabad*

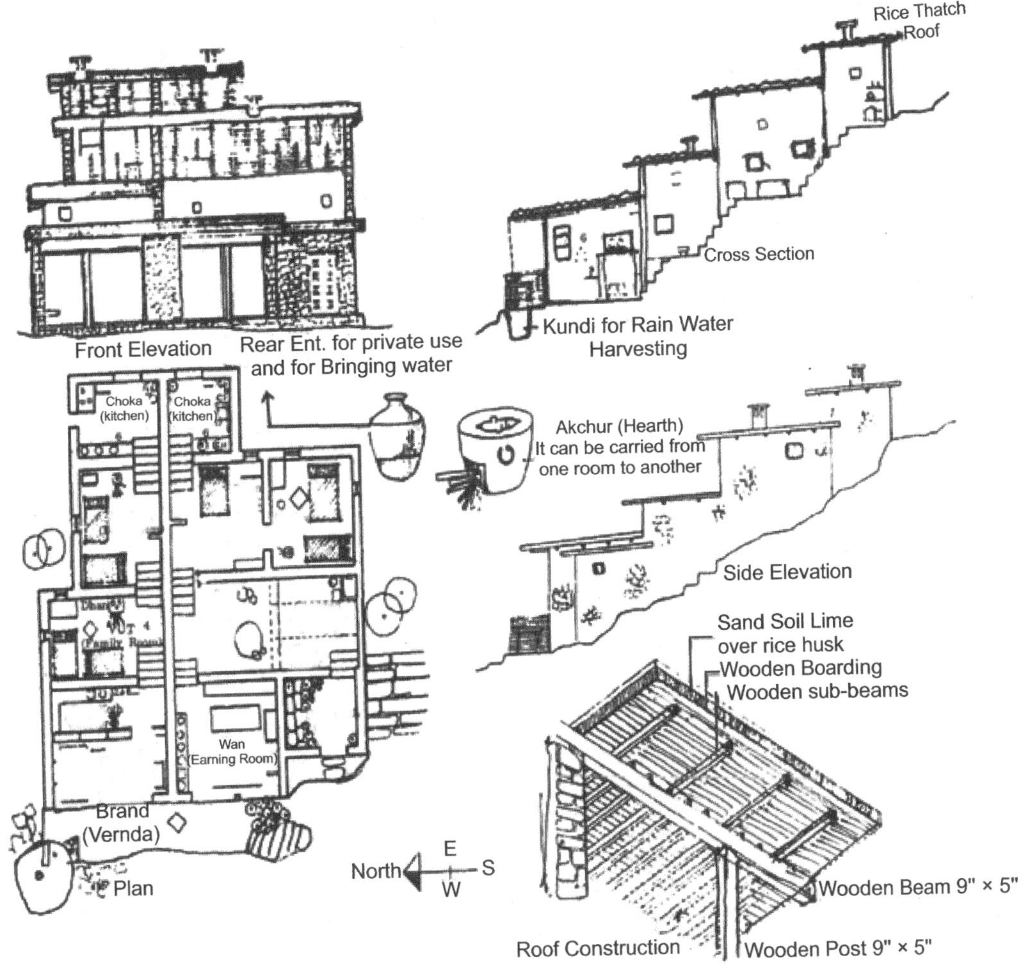

Fig 5.7. A Twin House in Ramban, Kashmir

Issues of Concern

The main issues of common concern for the villages are as given below:

- Protection of traditional habitations, which are often viewed as slums and unauthorized,
- Tenancy/land titles, and;
- Extension of rudimentary infrastructure (water supply, sewage, electricity, public roads/ transport and social amenities.

The fundamental premise of sustainable village development is based on a process of self-help, public participation and spiritual, ritual and religious connotations. This facilitated a harmonious relationship of man and environment. Today unless environment is a concern of everyone, government and centralized efforts, finance and legislation can not be successful. To make a breakthrough, it is essential to rediscover simple and pragmatic measures, which establish a holistic integration with the five elements of nature. Man is indeed an embodiment of the elements and forces of nature—the environment. He is the one with the capacity for consciousness, self-reflection and transcendence.

With this premise, there is a need to rediscover the organic culture which provides an innate and all embracing survival. Existing settlements clearly illustrate the potential for improvement that could be released by an overall change in the present attitude of planners. To evolve alternative concepts and strategies for growth and planning of traditional villages, it is necessary to understand the processes which have generated these settlements as the spatial embodiment of the communities.

The village plan should be a part of a District Plan framework which addresses the pertinent issues of public transport (highways, railways, major roads, etc.) and the level of services.

Table 5.1. Hierarchy of Facilities based on Easy Accessibility and Settlement Type

8-12 km radial	Facilities	University, Vocational / Professional Higher Edn., Shopping and Work Centre.	Peri-Urban Area
4-6 km	Urban Facilities	Cinemas Hall, Theatre/Multiplex, Sports Centre, Work Centre Library, Weekly market, marriage hall, Police and Fire Stations, etc.	Central Village
1-3 km	Rural Node/Hub	Senior School, Health Centre, Hospital, Police Station, Fire Station Community Centre, Bank, Post Office, Schools, Parks and Playground.	Rural Hub/Node
Within 1 km	Local hub	Primary School, Ration/Fuel shops, Services and Energy Centre, Park/Sports Complex, etc.	Village

The layout and services planning will vary according to the situation. The site should be laid out taking full account of local circumstances and socio-cultural factors. The physical form of the settlement can have a significant impact on security, cultural activities and social cohesion. Although, layout plan arranged in a grid pattern may appear to ease some aspects of services management and the provision of access roads, such a pattern is not normally conducive to social cohesion. In planning a village cluster, start with a modular based on social unit, which may be the family and build up using a basic unit of several dwellings to form communities, village clusters and block.

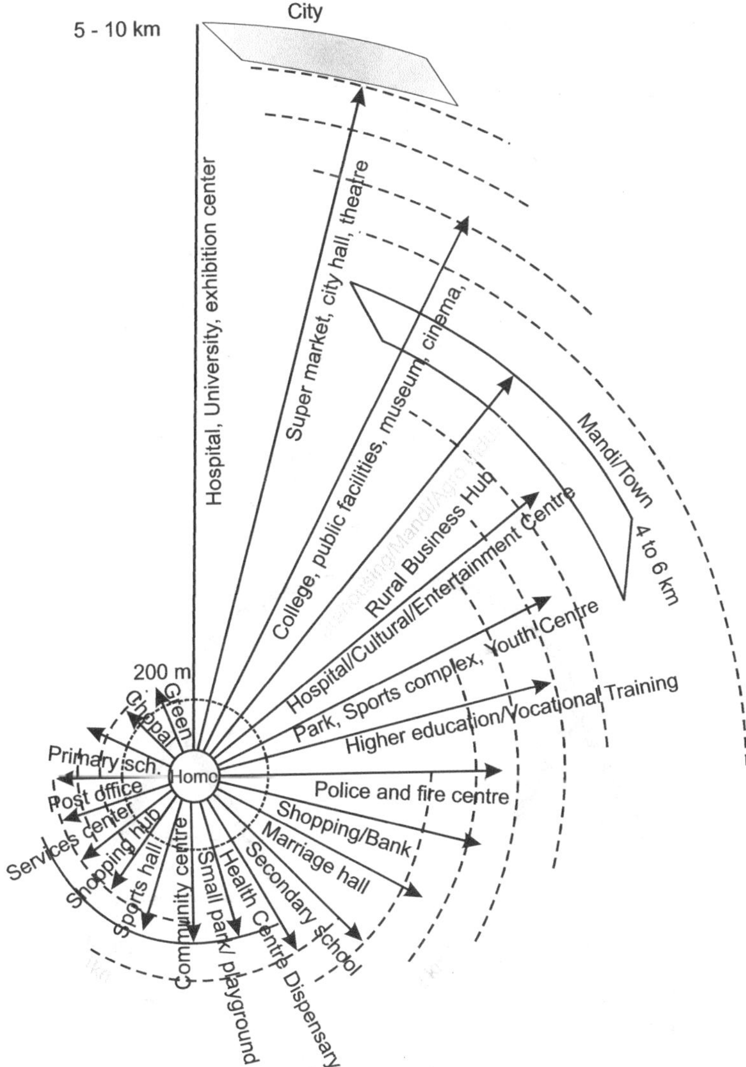

Fig. 5.8. Local Facilities for Rural Development

Table 5.2: An Example of Planning Module

Unit	Module	Population
1 family	–	4 to 6
16 families	1 community	80
32 communities	1 village	2500
4 villages	1 cluster	10,000
4 clusters	1 block	40,000

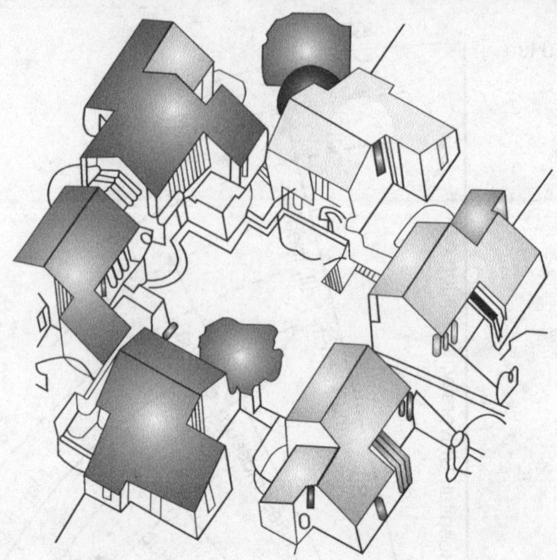

Fig. 5.9. Common green around houses acts as a community courtyard

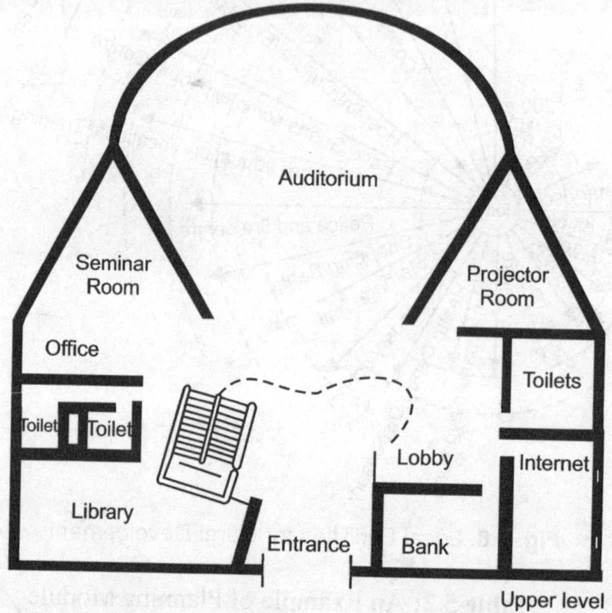

Fig. 5.10. Every village cluster should provide a community centre with multi-purpose hall for cultural performances, cinema, youth programs, etc. It should also provide recreational, banking, library, health and computer facilities for the local population

The social structure and gender roles of the population should be reflected in the planning of the village settlement and should take into account needs for markets, meeting places, recreational areas and so on. These facilities are essential in supporting the re-establishment of the displaced communities. Existing forms of social representation should be supported, given the importance of consultation with displaced people particularly women and their involvement in humanitarian interventions. The accessibility standards of various amenities should facilitate walkable distance to children and woman for day-to-day activities, while higher level of facilities can be accessed by cycle or bus.

It is necessary to provide rural housing integrated with employment opportunities. The layout of housing creates traditional values of community living. It is necessary to understand the local pattern of housing which responds to the ways of living local climate and culture. The common denominators of village planning and housing should incorporate the following:

- Integrated development together with a composite community centre.
- Ample green areas, parks, tot-lots, play and sports field.
- Chowks and squares to recreate traditional community living.
- An attractive and cohesive street picture.
- Housing integrated with self-employment opportunities by artisan workshops and community sockets for every cluster.
- Modular system of housing evolution and development.
- Gradual augmentation of services and innovative systems of low cost sewerage, solid waste disposal and drainage.
- Building Centre to promote the development of traditional skills and indigenous construction technology.

Solar House

Solar energy provides a potential of rural houses to meet thin energy needs, for desalination of water, cooling, water heating and cooking. Photovoltaics, wind driven fans and earthen pitchers can be installed in a wind tower to provide cool air in hot-dry climate zones. The Norwegian architect designed a village house incorporating such simple and practical features (Fig. 5.11.)

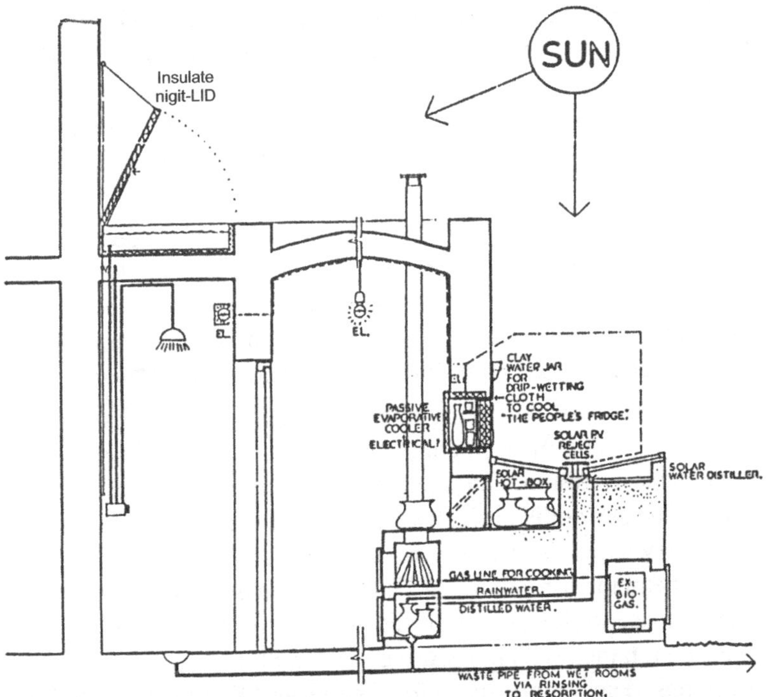

Fig. 5.11. The rural houses should facilitate living with sanitary, cooking and toilet facilities, together with basic services like drinking water and electricity

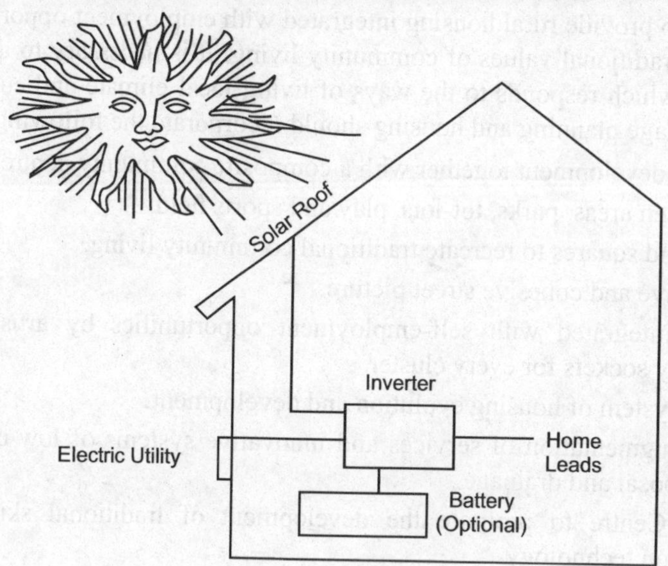

Fig. 5.12. Integrated Solar Photovoltaic not only generates electricity, but also serves as roof, wall, window, sky light and building façade

Environmental Services and Sanitation

A major problem of the rural areas is insanitation, lack of individual toilets, cattle scattered all over and lack of solid waste disposal system, resulting into contamination of water and germination of mosquitoes. The noble laureate V.S. Naipaul stated. *"Indians defecate everywhere. They defecate, mostly,beside the railway track. But they also defecate on the beaches; they defecate on the hills; they defecate on the river banks; they defecate on the streets; they never look for cover. Muslims, with their tradition of purdah, can at times be secretive. But this is a religious act of self-denial, for it is sad that the peasant, Muslim or Hindu, suffers from claustrophobia if he has to use an enclosed latrine."*

Today, we have a unique opportunity to use a whole new range of environment friendly technologies in our settlements. The adoption of eco-technology for infrastructure services is essential for improving the living condition as well as for environmental sustainability. The development of simple, small eco-technologies integrated with bio-architecture can facilitate community management and provide environmentally sustainable alternatives.

In most of the Indian villages, where municipal sewage does not exist, local on-site sanitation systems have been adopted. The most popular 'on-site' system is the septic tank and its various versions. The septic tank comprises an underground concrete or brick bank separated by a suspended baffle wall. The system is basically a horizontal continuous flow sedimentation tank in which sewage moves very slowly so as to be retained for a period sufficient to permit most of the suspended matter to settle in the form of sludge at the bottom of the bank. Some of the lighter solids including grease and fat rise to the surface of the sewage to form a floating scum. The scum and the sludge so formed are retained with the sewage in the tank for a period of several months during which they are decomposed anaerobically to form gases and liquids through the process of sludge digestion. This also reduces the volume of the sludge. The septic tank effluent is generally disposal of in a soak/seepage pit normally filled with brick or stone aggregate. Methane gas produced in the tank is removed through a vent pipe which releases the gas high enough so as to avoid nuisance from smell. The septic tank suffers from a number of problems. Periodically the tanks have to be desludged.

Although the cost of construction is generally low but because of spatial and financial constraints the soakage pit is usually not constructed and the highly septic effluent flows into stormwater drains or open land.

A serious flaw is that if any crack occurs in the floor or wall of the tank, the hydraulic pressure inside leaks the liquid contents to the surrounding soil creating a no-flow situation in the tank which stops its functioning. Another factor is that when septic tanks are cleaned manually, they expose grave risks. The disposal of the tank contents in insanitary manner contaminates subsoil water.

When the septic tank pit is filled, it is either excavated or a new pit is dug. In cases where the pit is to be reused, pit contents are disposed of in nearby low-lying areas. Otherwise the old pit is simply covered over with soil. The liquids leach into the soil by way of the unlined pit while the solids are retained. When the pit is filled the top slab is moved to a newly dug pit and the old one is covered over with soil. The main problem with all single pit latrines is that when full, there is dislocation of latrine use for some time which may extend to a number days. The single pit contents endanger the health of the scavenger and final disposal of sludge is an environmental hazard.

The two-pit pour flush (TPPF) latrine provides an alternative intermediate on-site sanitation system. It is comparatively easy to construct, operate and maintain and is economical in quantity of water required. The system consists of a squatting pan connected to a junction box outside the latrine, further leading to two underground leaching pits. The pan has a steep bottom slope of 30 degree to the horizontal, a narrow neck of 70 mm and a 20 mm waterfall trap set into the floor of the latrine. This makes it amenable to complete flushing with only two litres of water. The junction box has a Y-junction so that flow can be directed to one pit at a time by blocking one branch of the Y-junction. It has a removable cover to facilitate easy inspection. The junction box is connected through a pipe or drain to two brick-lined leaching pits with the bricks laid in a honeycomb pattern.

The pit bottom is left unlined. The pits can be square or circular and are fitted with reinforced concrete top slabs. When the latrine is flushed, the excreta passes to the pit. The liquids percolate out into the surrounding soil through the honeycomb openings and down through the open pit bottom while any gases produced are also absorbed into the soil. Only the solids accumulate in the pit. Each pit is designed to last for about three years before it gets filled. When this happens the connection in the junction box is switched so that excreta can pass to the second pit while the first one is taken out of use. The filled pit is left untouched for 14-18 months during which time all the pathogens die out and the contents turn into a rich organic humus which is safe to handle.

The pit is then opened during any dry period and the dry contents can be easily removed. With its established high fertilizer value, it can be used as manure. The empty pit is then ready to be put back into use when required.

Bio-Gas

The bio-gas plants work on animal/human excreta which is fermented in semi-liquid form. It is fed at one end and the fermented spent slurry is extracted at the other end periodically without disturbing the whole system. The combustible gas can be used for cooking, lighting, etc., while the digested sludge is available as organic manure.

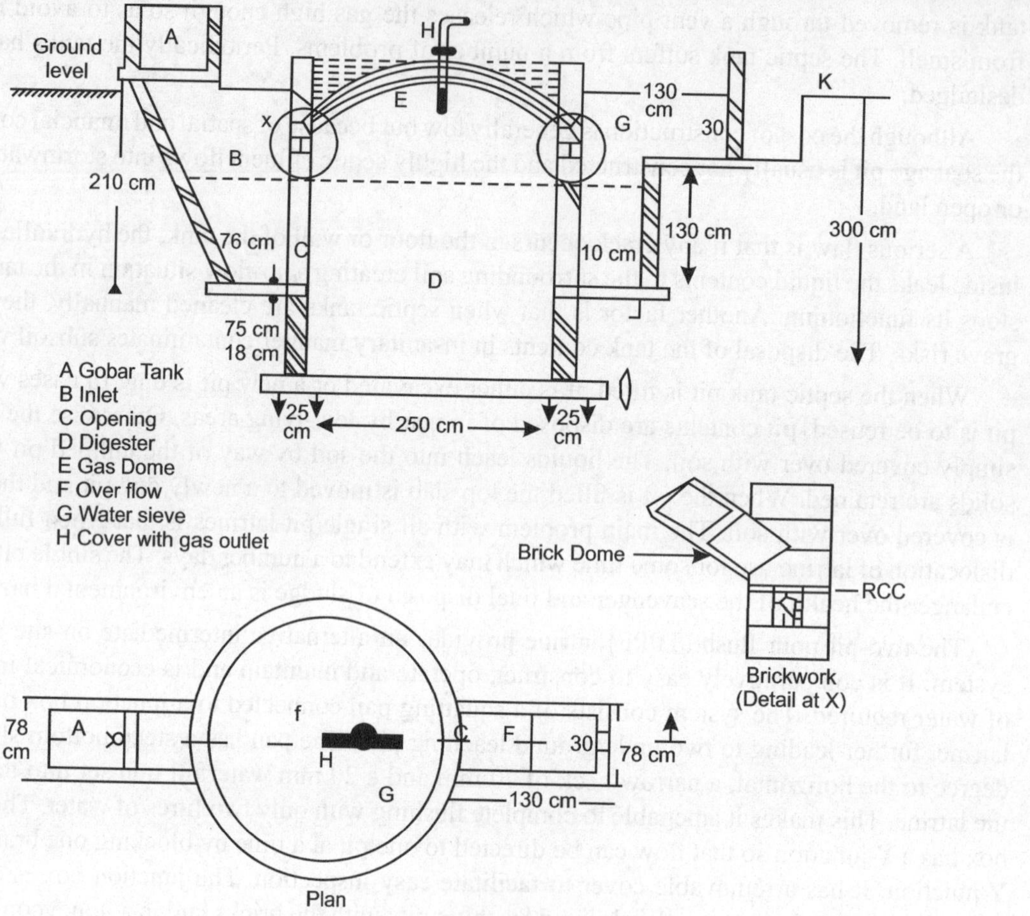

Ground level
A
H
E
130 cm
K
X
G
30
B
210 cm
130 cm
300 cm
76 cm
C
10 cm
D
75 cm
18 cm
A Gobar Tank
B Inlet
C Opening
D Digester
E Gas Dome
F Over flow
G Water sieve
H Cover with gas outlet
25 cm
250 cm
25 cm
Brick Dome
RCC
Brickwork (Detail at X)
78 cm
A
f
H
C
F
30
78 cm
G
130 cm
Plan

Fig. 5.13. A Bio-Gas Plant produces green energy for local use

Gas
Latrine
Human Waste
Animal Waste
Sludge
Drying Pad
Fertiliser
Liquid
Algae farm
Algae Feed
Poultry and Cattle Feed

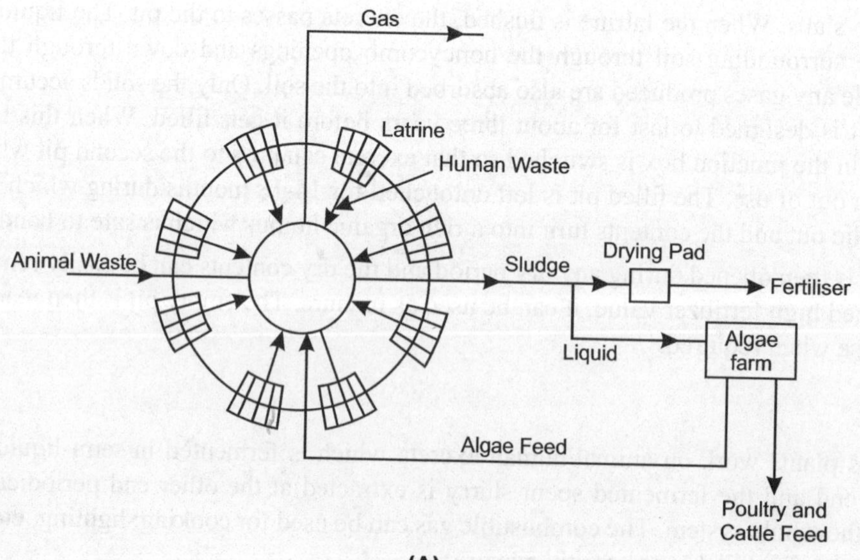

(A)

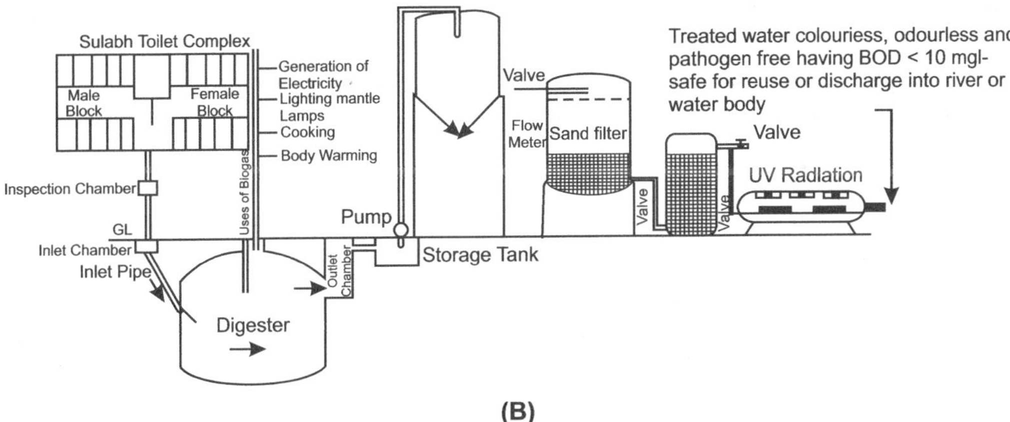

(B)

Figs. 5.14 (A) and (B). Bio-Gas plant with SET technology: Costs on collection of sewage and operation and maintenance of the system are minimal, and no manual handling of human excreta is required, Biogas is used for different purposes, treated effluent is safe for reuse in agriculture, gardening or discharge into a water body

Source: *Sulabh International*

Bio-gas plant is a composite unit of a digester and a gas holder. The gas holder floats on the top of digester, wherein gas is collected and delivered at a constant pressure to the gas appliance through the pipe-line. The underground digester made of brick, is covered by a reinforced masonry dome. While the bio-gas plants working only on the night soil are not very successful, mixing of night soil with the cow dung producing bio-gas gives encouraging results. Such plants can be integrated with community latrines where WCs are without flush tanks and connected directly to the digester. Small quantity of cow dung and other organic wastes are mixed for increasing the production of biogas, which can meet the fuel requirement of a kitchen.

Root Zone System

Developed in the sixties in Germany, the Root Zone Process has been emerging as an economical and efficient method to treat industrial and domestic effluents. Bio-diversity is the key to the Root Zone process. More than 2000 types of bacteria and tens of thousands of fungi exist in the reed bed. These microbial organisms oxidize impurities in the waste water. Since the process occurs underground, aerobic and anaerobic zones exist side by side, inducing different types of chemical reactions and balancing bacterial growth, thus decomposing the contaminants to their basic form.

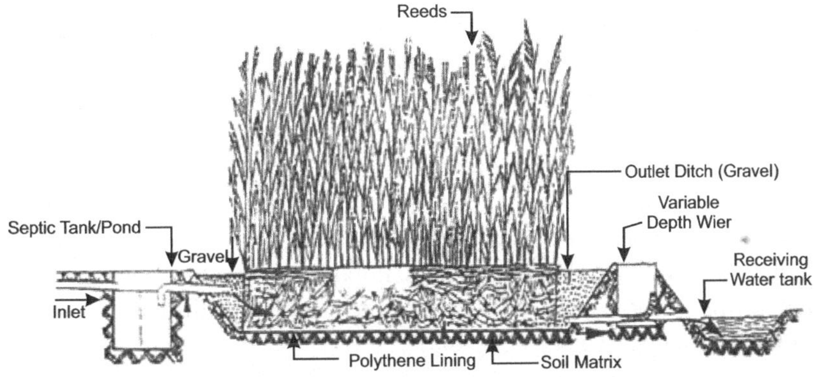

Fig. 5.15. Root Zone System

Three integrated components are essential to the system—the reeds, the reed bed and the microbial organisms. The system involves running contaminated water through the root zones of especially designed reed beds. The reeds and the reed bed together provide efficient effluent treatment, and the released water is environmentally acceptable. Phosphates, sulphur compounds, nitrogenous materials reduce their elemental forms, while BOD and COD are drastically brought down. Heavy metals precipitate from solution and are bound into the soil matrix. What comes out of this constructed marsh is treated waste water which is not only environmentally acceptable, but much cleaner than possible with any other technique.

The capital cost of the Root Zone system is roughly half that of conventional systems while operation and maintenance costs are around one fifth. The technology has the potential to reduce treatment costs considerably and therefore may gain wide application.

Biological Composting System

The micro-organism process using oxygen in the air sludge and organic wastes into carbon-dioxide, water, and energy. The energy thus produced enables the microbial cells to divide, to move and utilize yet more sludge and waste. This is a natural process by which fallen leaves get converted into humus and revitalize the nutrition of the soil. Based on this principle, continuous bio-reactor composting system is a second-generation technology for treatment of the sludge and organic waste. It has been in use in Europe since 1972. The digesters use the anaerobic bacteria to stabilize the sludge, whereas bio-reactors use aerobic bacteria for the same process. The aerobic bacteria is faster, thus the process is more efficient and also the capital cost is reduced. The heat is generated in a vessel or a tunned by bacterial action, raising the temperature to 70 degree C, which kills all the pathogens. Thus, the bio-reactors convert the sludge into hygienically pollution and germs free material, which is not possible in the digestion process.

A common problem is ever-increasing shortage of the land. Conventional sludge beds use large areas and create foul smell. An alternative of the open beds is flocculation and dehydration of sludge by mechanical means. By filteration, shearing and de-watering of the sludge, its volume is greatly reduced. After that sludge can be compost and converted into humus-like product. The system uses very little space as compared to the conventional sludge drying beds.

The reaction chamber, which can be constructed in masonry and concrete, is comprised of two main components. The first is the compaction chamber with delivery hopper to feed the material, a pusher plate pushes the water/sludge into the compression chamber. The reactor is closed on all the sides having smooth surface on the inner walls. Ventilation ducts or channels in the floor supply air to dry the sludge. The compressed material is then delivered to the maturation chamber, where micro-organisms process the sludge. Heat produced by composting process, or if necessary, by artificial heating to 60° to 70° C ensures a pathogen free end-product. The final product can be used for local parks, agriculture or for treatment of wastelands. The reactors can be designed and installed in standard modules or batteries. This system eliminates pathogen contained leachate. As such, there is no danger to pollution and contamination of sub-soil water.

For treatment of sanitation surface wastes and sludge, methanisation and aerobic biological treatment are appropriate methods which can reduce the sludge formation by one-third, as compared to conventional methods. Bubble diffusion process, flotation, anaerobic reactors, root zone cleaning system and other forms of biological, tertiary and physicochemical methods can be adopted for treatment of sanitary effluents.

Farmers' Dwellings at Mostefa Ben-Brahim, Algeria

In 1970, the government of Algeria lunched a program the construction of 1,000 farming population, to provide 200 units of social housing. The national construction company of the Ministry of Agriculture, "Chantiers Populaires de la Revolution Agraire" (People's Agrarian Revolution Building Works), the programme. The first pilot village was built in 1973 and was located at Mostefa Ben-Brahim, 30 km from Sidi Bel Abbes, in western Algeria (project leaders: P. Pedroti, D. Helmans, H. Houben). The village was handed over to the farming population in July 1976 and consisted of 192 houses of 85 m^2 each built of hollow cement blocks and 30 houses of 120 m^2 each built of stabilized remmed earth. The houses have no openings to the north. This provided protection from harsh weather and enabled the gardens to be sheltered from the gaze of passers-by, thus respecting the Islamic tradition of privacy. All the houses face the South-east. The housing took account of traditional values, such as every house had two entrances, one for the family and one for visitors.

Fig. 5.16. Farmer's Dwelling at Mostefa Ben-Brahim, Algeria

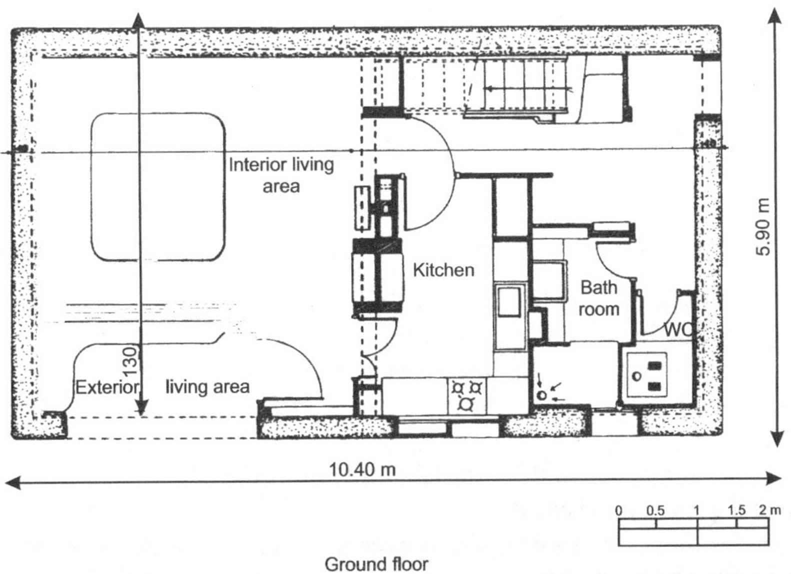

Ground floor

(A)

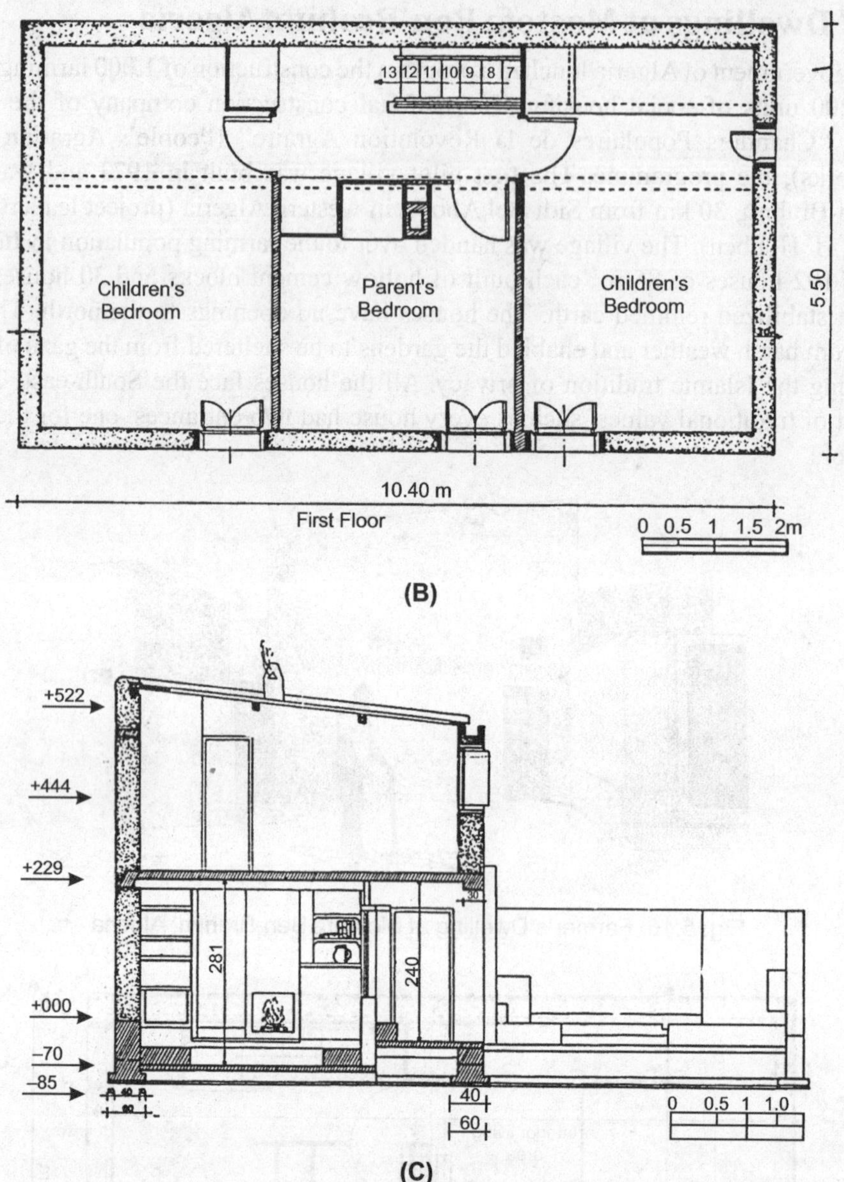

Figs. 5.17 (A to C). Plan and Section of Farmer's Dwelling at Mostefa Ben-Brahim, Algeria

Foundation: wide strip, reinforced concrete (R.C.)
Footing: light weight hydrophobic concrete
External ground floor walls: 40 cm thick in stabilised rammed earth
Ring beam: 10 cm RC
Floor: 12 cm RC
External 1st floor walls: 40 cm thick in stabilised rammed earth
Ring beam and guttering: 10 cm RC
Roofing: wooden timber, galvanised sheets over concrete 6 cm thick. Water proofing by Paxalu (aluminium and bitumen roofing finish)

Source: *CRATerre d'apres LeProject (CPR)*

Rickshaw Pullers' Village Vellore

The village was planned to rehabilitate 130 rickshaw pullers in Vellore. It provided 28 sqm houses to Rickshaw Pullers at subsidized rates.

Fig. 5.18. Each house covers an area of 28 sq m

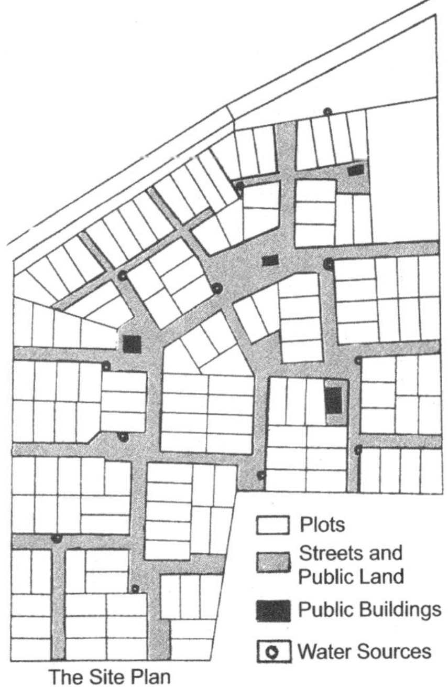

Fig. 5.19. The main street leads into the settlement, passing through a main square, temple and a meeting hall. There are small squares where the streets join. The houses include small shops

Streets were laid out orthogonally in the village. Any given segment of street or main thoroughfare had a maximum of 15-20 house fronts. Neighbourhoods are made up of pucca (permanent) structures. The main bazaar stretched along the road and the basic organization is linear. Cows and buffaloes are housed in sheds located behind houses in compounds. Shade is provided by trees.

Designed by: CEDMA, Chennai, Centre for Housing Innovation of the University of Oregon, US and Pacific Architecture, Sydney.

DEBRIEFING QUESTIONS

1. What is the extent of rural housing shortage in India and what are the programmes to meet it?
2. How villages reflect and manifest the social structure of communities?
3. Explain the morphology of a housing cluster in a village.
4. What are the major issues which need to be addressed in rural housing?
5. Write short notes on the following:
   (*a*) Social, community, religious, educational and health facilities.
   (*b*) Sanitation, sewerage and toilets
   (*c*) Bio-gas
   (*d*) Root Zone System for Waste Water Recycling
   (*e*) Renewable Energy for rural dwellings.

6

Slum Rehabilitation and Community Development

Today one in four persons in urban India is below poverty line and one in every five persons lives in a slum. It is not a coincidence that the proportion of slum dwellers and poor in urban areas is quite similar. According to the Oxfam Report (2015), India has 172 million people below the poverty line and preliminary data of socio-economic and caste census (2015) indicated that at least 35 lakh households in urban areas have no source of income, and 10 per cent of houses in urban areas don't have access to drinking water and electricity.

Many of the urban poor and slum dwellers comprise the women, children, aged and disabled. They have no bank account, no assets, no shelter and not even identity or ration card. Both, the poor and slum dwellers are malnourished, lack minimum shelter, sanitation and drinking water; they are illiterate, and cannot afford to send their children to the school. They are also at various risks, like the problems of unemployment, child labour, insecurity in old age, limited access to healthcare, non-healthy living conditions and are on the margins of the urban community. They are at the bottom of the pyramid, who are caught in a cycle of perpetual poverty due to non-access to shelter, land, finance, employment and services.

Money and income are the easiest measures of growth, but poverty is far more complex issue. The World Bank in its ground-breaking Report 'Voices of the Poor' highlights the multi-dimensional nature of poverty. *'Poverty is hunger, poverty is lack of shelter. Poverty is being sick and not being able to see a doctor. Poverty is not having access to school and not knowing how to read. Poverty is not having a job, is fear for the future, living one day at a time. Poverty is loosing a child to illness, brought about by unclean water. Poverty is powerlessness, lack of representation and freedom.'*

Shelter for Poor

The poor live in Jhuggi-Jhopri clusters, basti, hutments, slums, on the pavements, in dilapidated buildings, irregular colonies, etc. Slum and squatters are an important source of housing delivery although deficient, unserviced and unplanned. Their growth is twice as fast as formal sector housing. These settlements represent a solution rather than a problem. They contribute significantly to the city economy, both through labour market and by informal production and servicing the city.

Majority of the poor suffer from a growing sense of frustration, as their lives, families and their hopes for future disintegrate. Millions of people lack secure and adequate shelter and basic sustenance, which keeps growing with the population growth, urbanization, and mounting pressures of economy and competition.

Fig. 6.1. Slum Clusters (Mumbai)

Participatory learning with the target groups provides useful clues towards adopting a 'needs based approach.' According to ASHA, the needs of the poor population can be categorized in the following priorities:

(*i*) Survival and livelihood: Freedom from hunger and malnutrition, food security, employment, credit facility

(*ii*) Supportive: Shelter, drinking water supply, power, transport and sanitation.

(*iii*) Transformational: Education, literacy, skill development, environmental upgradation and access to information.

(*iv*) Empowerment: Equal access to resources, including land, finance, services and justice, participation in decision making, etc.

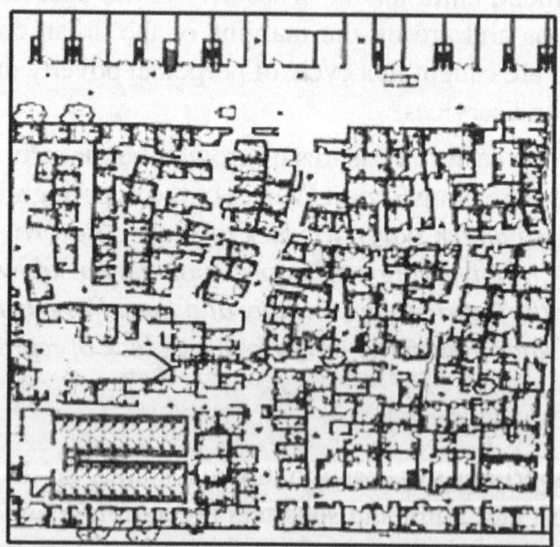

Fig. 6.2. Squatter clusters in New Delhi cater to the poorest, having average plot/dwelling size of 10 to 20 sqm, without any municipal services

Source: *Patwari S, Bo Tang and Maurice Mitchell (eds.) (2010), Learning from Delhi-Dispersed initiatives in urban landscape, Ashgate, Surrey*

The Association for Settlements and Housing Activities (ASHA) observed that with a little external support the poor are often capable of meeting their survival needs. The organized sector has a vital role in helping the poor in meeting these needs. The experience indicates that the supportive needs, like shelter really help the poor in climbing up the economic ladder. The provision of basic services and facilities is a major concern. The amenities and services can be disaggregated as per survival, supportive, transformational and empowerment needs of the poor and the priorities of planning, development and investments can be worked out. There is a need to develop a new perspective and a strategy of collaboration with the residents that would trigger a grass root level process of pro-poor and participatory community development.

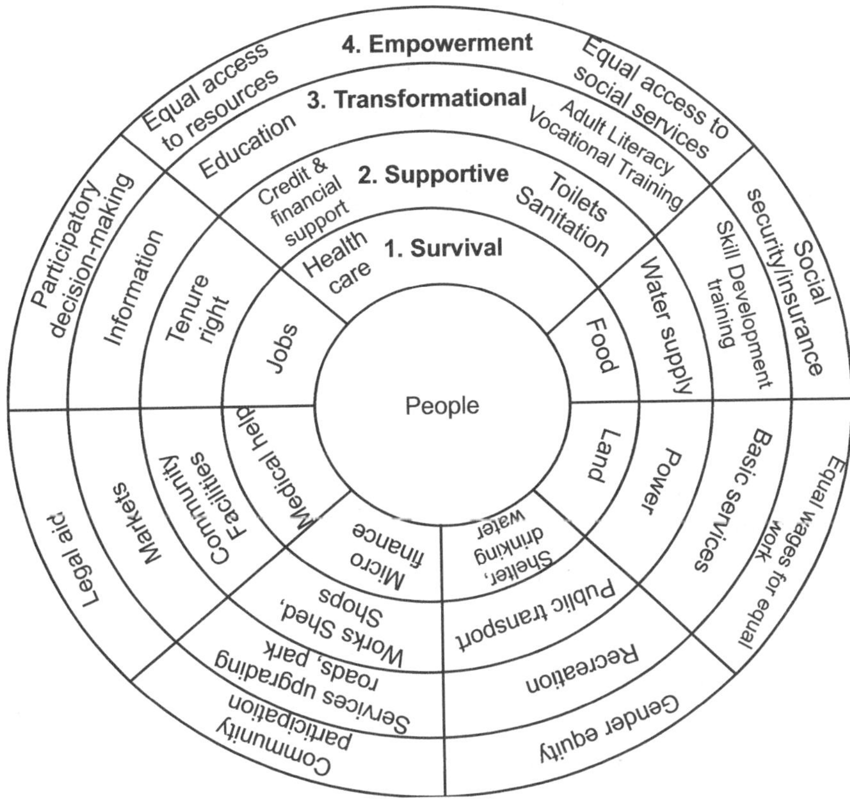

Fig. 6.3. Diagrammatic Representation of the Needs of the Poor

To address the needs of the urban poor, it is necessary to adopt an approach that combines the following three components:

- Rights (shelter, participation, information, jobs, etc.)
- Reforms (governance, land, legal, procedures, finance, etc.)
- Road map (spatial integration, shelter, infrastructure, etc.)

The walls of exclusion need to be dismantled by an enablement strategy (land, shelter, environment, technology, information, employment, services, etc.) and by spatial integration-between plans and implementation, between social and economic growth and between space and time.

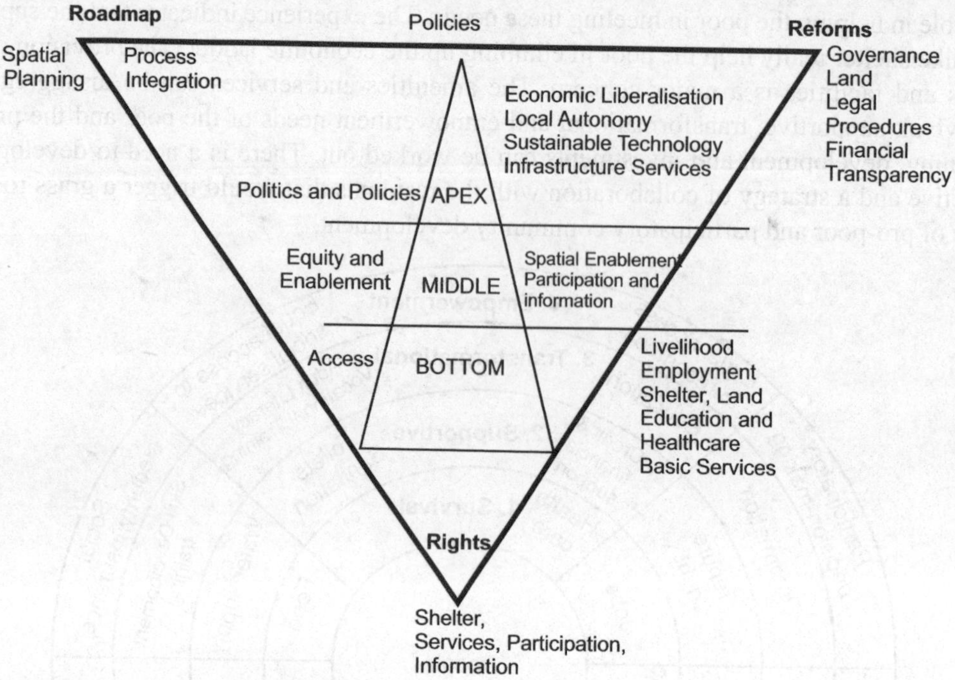

Fig. 6.4. Inverted Pyramid-Reversal of the Paradigm

Linking Shelter to Poverty Reduction

In order to establish links between housing and poverty reduction, it is necessary to start with the following measures to address the livelihood and shelter issues of the informal, unorganised sector and their livelihoods.

- In-situ slum rehabilitation, land reservation for slum rehabilitation, low-cost, affordable and rental housing, night shelters, dormitories, hostels, orphanages, etc.
- Provision of basic services like toilets, water points, dustbin, street lights, etc.
- Earmarking of space for street vendors, informal shops, hawking zones, weekly markets, workshops, repair shops, waste recycling facilities, etc.
- Provision for Adhar/identity cards, bank accounts, credit and micro-saving, insurance facilities.
- Involvement of CBOs/NGOs for collective slum/shelter development and to act as the link between the community and local agency/ authorities.
- Skill development, education, literacy, healthcare and other community facilities.

These involve some basic changes in the attitudes, planning, governance and infrastructure services for their equitable access. The professionals in the field of habitat have the responsibility to redirect the resources and power at their command to take the steps to a new era. It must involve transformation and innovation in the relationship among people, government, financial institutions, etc. towards community development.

Beggars Can Turn to Business

"In Bangladesh, 80 per cent of the poor families have been reached with micro-credit. We are hoping that by 2010, 100 per cent of the poor families will be reached. Three years ago we started an exclusive programme focusing on the beggars. None of Grameen Bank's rules apply to them. Loans are interest free; they can pay whatever amount they wish, whenever they wish. We gave them the idea to carry small merchandise such as stacks toys or household items, when they went from house to house for begging. The idea worked. There are now 85,000 beggars in the program. About 5,000 of them have already stopped begging completely. Typical loan to a beggar is $12. We encourage and support every conceivable intervention to help the poor fight out of poverty. We always advocate micro credit in addition to all other interventions, arguing that micro credit makes those interventions work better."

Mohammed Yunus

A Collective Approach

The key to success of slum rehabilitation is the adoption of local, participatory rapid assessment, which allows the communities within a constituency to link together, survey their housing and livelihood problems, and then enter into a collaborative process with the municipal government and other concerned organisations/service agencies to jointly develop options and programmes which resolve their problems.

A GIS based inventory and total station survey of all potential lands for slum redevelopment and resettlement should be prepared. After identification of potential sites, it is necessary to assign suitable land use for such sites, and provide proper services and linkages. The plans of housing development and resettlement should be based on the assessment of ground realities, existing land use, land ownership, land values, socio-economic characteristics and physical conditions of the settlement. Based on the inventory, the community can access the land and funds for the infrastructure development and the construction of dwelling units. The criteria for selection of specific strategy of relocation or in-situ upgradation have to be based on certain indicators, which is differentiated according to type of slum, habitation and its population. The following table indicates various types of urban shelter and possible approaches.

Table 6.1. Urban Shelter Types and Possible Approaches

S. No.	Type	Approach
1.	Rundown walk ups in core areas.	Cooperatising: Reconstructing at site with municipal support with transit accommodation provided during construction with ownership of constructed units through soft loans subsidised rentals.
2.	Pavement/doorstep dwellers, squatters in core areas (generally new entrants to the city as individuals)	Sanitation, night shelters, pay and use toilets, health facilities, Site and Services Schemes.
3.	Spontaneous colonies in peri-urban areas (generally new migrants), single storeyed improvised shelter.	Sanitation and granting tenure right over a period of time.

5.	Site and service schemes, plots with wet core roof.	Reduced and evolutionary standards.
6.	Built units in 4 to 5 storeyed walk-ups in periurban areas or 8-16 storeyed block in central areas on subsidized rentals.	Regular pubic housing.

Source: *E.F.N. Ribeiro / AMDA (2000).*

In a people-centered process, the adequacy of housing, utilisation of resources, productivity and economic efficiency can be redefined according to the satisfaction of people's needs and resources, and not according to an imposed idealistic standard. The reference in the support-based approach is the flexible and evolutionary indicators for the satisfaction of human needs and not the amount of consumption.

UN-Habitat's Slum Indicators

UN-Habitat has developed a household level definition of a slum household in order to be able to use existing household level surveys and censuses to identify slum dwellers among the urban population. A slum household is a household that lacks any one of the following five elements:

- Access to improved water: access to sufficient amount of water for family use, at an affordable price, available to household members without being subject to extreme effort;
- Access to improved sanitation: access to an excreta disposal system, either in the form of a private toilet or a public toilet shared with a reasonable number of people;
- Security of tenure: evidence of documentation to prove secure tenure status or defacto or perceived protection from evictions;
- Durability of housing: permanent and safe structure in non-hazardous location; and
- Sufficient living area: not more than two people sharing the same room

Community Development: In order to promote a broader, more holistic and integrated process of community development beyond physical improvements, it is necessary to integrate social, environmental and economic well-being of the local communities. By a creative, participatory process each slum redevelopment or upgradation scheme can be unique having its own identity. It is possible to upgrade old communities or to design new ones in ways which follow the spatial patterns which can often bring charm and delight to informal settlements, winding lanes, houses built in clusters around a quiet cul-de-sac, shady places to gather and sit, places for markets, temples, playgrounds, etc.

Each individual community development plan should address to specific local issues and provide flexible choices of in-situ upgrading, relocation, land sharing or re-blocking. The local community development plan should network all the settlements, where the stakeholders plan together. According to famous American thinker, Jane Jacobs, *"Planning for vitality must aim at unslumming the slums and clarifying the visual order of cities, and it must do so by both promoting and illuminating functional order, rather than by obstructing or denying it."*

Inclusive community development implies access for all to jobs, shelter, services and social infrastructure. A modular system can be developed for the provision of social facilities like health, education, recreation, socio-cultural, religious, sports and communications.The partnership in slum redevelopment would not only consist of construction of dwelling units, but should be a continuous relationship that takes care of functional order and partnerships among the communities, government and service agencies. It should enable:

- Upgrading unserviced housing; slum clusters and unauthorised colonies,
- Reduce high concentrations of social housing, and build a better social mix,
- Mobilise investments, Central, State, Local, banking and corporate funds,
- Provide/upgrade basic services, facilities and open spaces, and,
- Implement best practices in housing and urban design.

The participatory local planning process includes its integration with city development plan, social development, community organisation development, savings, income generation and social welfare. The informal sector activity is also linked with higher level of productivity and income. This will require promotion of linkages between industrial production and informal sector which will result in sustaining income and employment. Microfinancing and small loans can immensely help even the beggars, as has been done in Bangladesh.

Improved services and employment/economic development empower and enable the poor to integrate themselves with the network of transactions in the urban system as a whole. This underscores the need of upgradation and improvement as starting point of urban process. The strategy should comprise of physical, social and economic upgradation with clear linkages between the programmes of infrastructure improvement and poverty reduction. A working committee networks local communities with the representatives of the local authority, service agencies and the NGOs. The architects, planners and engineers act as the catalysts in facilitating planning and development which is a collaborative process.

The corner stones of implementation process are the following:

- Collective land management;
- Collective financial management;
- Collective social and community management.

To link slum redevelopment with the community development, it is necessary to prepare the following plans:

- **Infrastructure development plans:** paved lanes and roads, water supply and electricity, storm and sewage drains, solid waste disposal at household and community levels.
- **Environmental development plans** may include tree planting and greenery, community gardening, waste-water and trash recycling, alternative energy systems, playgrounds, recreational areas, etc.
- **Social development plans** may include vocational training, employment and welfare centre, youth and day-care centre, clinics, hostels for poor or elderly members, community centers, cooperatives, multi-facility centers, communication system, fire-fighting facilities, etc.
- **Economic development plans** may include developing markets or community stores, establishing conservation or tourism areas, enhancing people's earning through community enterprises, loans for small businesses, support for household workshops and vocational training.

A decentralised community based management system involves transformation and innovation in the relationship among people, governments, financial institutions, etc. The success of this collective enterprise depends upon the involvement of people.

Table 6.2. From Supply Based to Supports Based Approaches

Characteristics	Supply based approach	Supports based approach
Aim	– Reduce housing shortage – Provide sufficient formal housing – Aim is measured by productivity	– Improve living conditions – Increase affordable and appropriate housing options – Aim is measured by resourcefulness
Basic Concept	– Housing is a product; its value is for what it is – Housing is a commodity political instrument; a product – Experts and politicians know better about housing. They have to control provision to ensure efficiency – When people build houses for themselves, they are substandard – Housing operations can be centrally managed	– Housing is a people centred process based on participation, enablement and partnership – People know better their housing needs and fulfill them if supported. They have to control provision to ensure fit – When government builds houses for users, they may not fit their needs – Housing process has to be locality and community based
Strategies	– Provide houses on behalf of people – Centralized resources and housing construction by government, large scale control cost and efficiency – Mass housing and slum removal	– Support people in their housing process – Decentralize resources and decision making – Build people's capacity to manage the housing which is localized, small-scale, diversified and incremental – Sites-and-services and upgrading
Actors and Roles	– The government is provider and implementer – People are unknown during provision and recipients of housing	– The government is enabler to local actors – People and communities are participants and controllers – Small-scale contractors are builders, NGOs and CBOs are mediators

Source: *Based on UN Habitat and other sources*

Many migrants, labourers, workers and beggars in the city do not have shelter and live on pavements near their jobs. As a human right, they deserve to be accommodated in the night shelters, which should be located near the railway stations, bus terminals, major markets and work centers. Existing facility buildings can also be used for night shelter. Besides night shelter, there is a need to provide a network of old age homes, orphanage, women's hostel, anganwadi, transit-camps and dormitories.

In order to prevent growth of slums, mandatory reservation of social housing in all group housing schemes to the extent of minimum 15% of permissible FAR or 35 % of dwelling units on the plot is necessary. The city should ensure housing for urban poor to the extent of 50-55% of the total.

This requires provision of infrastructure development, services and facilities on differential norms and procedures. By infill development and composite redevelopment of isolated plots the provision of housing can be enhanced, without need for fresh land and new infrastructure development.

Slum Rehabilitation Scheme (SRS) in Mumbai

The approach of the Government of Maharashtra's Slum Rehabilitation Authority is based on "Public Private Partnership" (PPP), which aims to address the primary issue of right of slum dwellers to decent housing and also tenural rights and means of livelihood.

Fig. 6.5. Rehabilitation of squatters near Santa Cruz Airport

On-site rehabilitation gives the slum dwellers access to basic civic amenities, besides promoting neighbourhood improvement. The slum dwellers are also required to provide maintenance charges, which is collected upfront at Rs. 20,000 per slum dweller from the builder/developer of the Slum Rehabilitation Scheme. This fund is collectively managed by the SRA together with the residents' association. The slum dwellers are extended with other benefits, such as reduced Stamp Duty, Property Tax and Water User Charges. The Slum Rehabilitation Scheme of the Government of Maharashtra provides leasehold rights at a highly subsidised rate.

The development control regulations of Mumbai Municipal Corporation are followed, as given below:

- **FSI:** An FSI up to 2.5 having a differential approach is allowed and the concept of Transfer of Development Rights (TDR) has been made applicable in order to avoid congestion and over-concentration in heavily built-up areas.
- **Density:** The minimum density prescribed for such development is 500 tenements per hectare.
- **Ground coverage:** In Slum Rehabilitation/Redevelopment projects, the rule for ground coverage is confined to peripheral setbacks as per DCR without insisting upon overall ratio of ground coverage/plot size.

- **Mixed land use:** For Slum Rehabilitation in Mumbai, mixed land use policy has been adopted. Existing shop owners are eligible for built up shops upto 225 sq.ft. area. The usual practice is to allow 10% of the FSI for commercial use in Cooperative Societies.
- **Open Space:** The practice is to reserve 15 per cent of the plot as open space.
- **Community facilities:** The provision of community facilities is generally seen as a government responsibility and the provision of community facilities in SRD schemes is not insisted upon, except essential utilities like electric sub-station, pump house, etc.

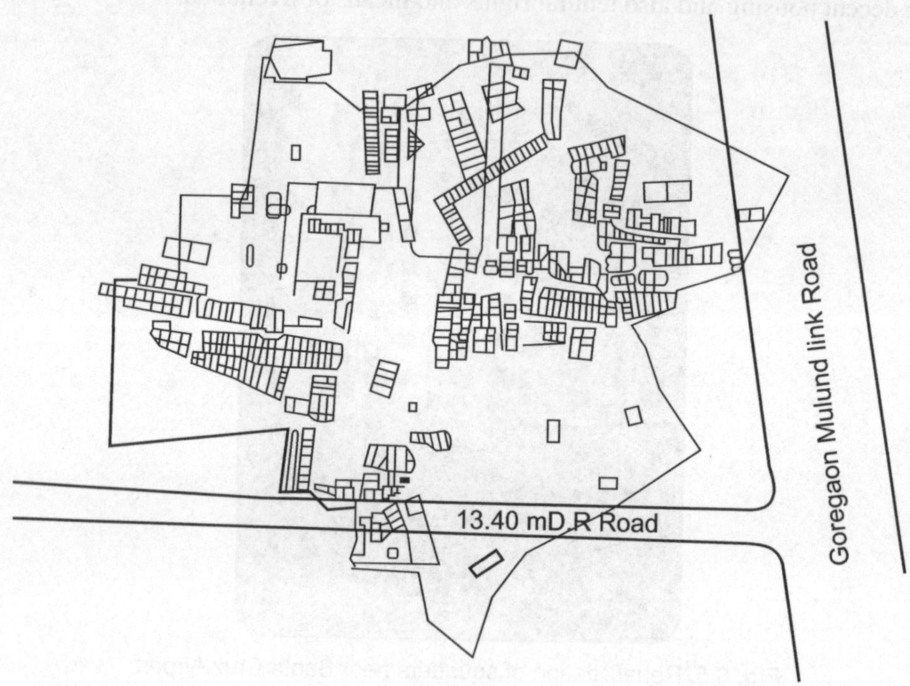

Fig. 6.6. Existing Plan of Hutement Colony on Goregaon Mulund Link Road

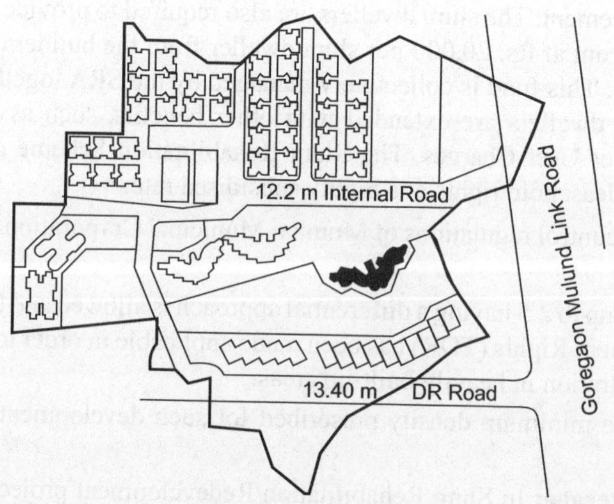

Fig. 6.7. Layout plan of proposed redevelopment (Kanyacha Pada) Goregaon- Mulund Link road, Malad (East), Mumbai

Procedure for Processing and Approval of Slum Rehabilitation Schemes (SRS)

1. All slums and pavements whose inhabitants' names and structures appear in the electoral roll prepared with reference to 1st January, 1995 or a date prior thereto and who are actual occupants of the hutments are eligible for the slum rehabilitation scheme.
2. 70% or more of the eligible hutment-dwellers in a slum or pavements in a viable stretch at one place have to show their willingness to join slum rehabilitation scheme and come together to form a cooperative housing society of all eligible hutment-dwellers through a resolution to that effect.

Resettlement of Slums under Mumbai Urban Transport Project

Mumbai is home to some 20 million people, of which 7 million live in 3,000 slums, mostly built on public lands, roads, airport, railways, land, markets, etc. In 2002, the MHADA embarked the Mumbai Urban Transport Project (MUTP) with the help of the World Bank which aims to improve the transport services in the city. The project required large scale resettlement of slums, commercial establishments, public facilities, as well as cultural and religious structures. These included about 100,000 people or 17,500 households, some 1800 shops, more than 100 religious and cultural properties, which existed on railway lands, and some occupying public and private lands and roads. There was a variety of such occupiers-legal land owners in multi storey buildings, 'pagdi' holders, tenants and lessees, as well as squatters without title. Almost ninety-five percent of these do not have legal title. The project required relocation of utilities, including underground water and electricity pipelines, telephone cables, drains, and few large transmission towers. Resettling of 100,000 people required finding several resettlement sites in Mumbai and mobilising huge financial resources to provide free housing of 225sq.ft. each. Affected shopkeepers and land owners were also allowed to buy additional floor area up to 525 sq.ft. in proportion to their loss.

Fig. 6.8. Slum resettlement under Mumbai Urban Transport Project

Fig. 6.9. A Slum Resettlement Complex with 225 sq.ft. units built under public-private partnership
Source: *World Bank*

Under the scheme, land has been used as a resource. *Private developers were given additional* transfer of development rights (TDR) or Floor Space Index (FSI) against building dwelling units for slum dwellers at their own cost. Land owners in affected areas were also offered TDR or additional FSI in lieu of cash compensation for the land they have lost. R & R activities hit several roadblocks:

(*a*) Resettlement of households and commercial establishments affected by the road widening of the two major east-west road corridors, the Santa Cruz Link Road (SCLR) and the Jogeshwar-Vikhroli Link Road (JVLR).

(*b*) Land owners, lease holders, large commercial units and religious structures, who resisted relocation and being equated with slum dwellers.

(*c*) Moving from horizontal to vertical tenements.

The MMRDA held consultations to discuss resettlement options with residents and shopkeeper associations and the managing committees of the religious structures, and explored alternative resettlement solutions, often going beyond the scope of R & R policy. This removed the bottlenecks, and the policy and procedures were modified.

The project implemented through MHADA, CIDCO & MMC comprises 2 main components:

- Land Infrastructure Servicing Programme (LISP)
- Slum Upgradation Programme (SUP)

The NGOs provided support to newly relocated people in the provision of child-care and health facilities and other facilities, such as open spaces, lighting, lifts, internal roads, sanitation and drainage. Society management offices, daycare centres and women centres were provided in all resettlement projects, besides community halls and health centres. A Livelihood Cell was set up to promote income generating activities for women at all the resettlement sites. A women industrial cooperative called Sankalp was formed to undertake a range of economic activities including supplying office stationery, selling vegetables and providing catering and housekeeping services.

Under the LISP the sites provide serviced plots of 25, 30, 40, 60 and 100 sqm and apartments. The serviced plots of 25 and 30 sqm are meant for the EWS category and 40 sqm plots are meant for LIG category. The planning is done in such a manner that at least 60% plots become available to EWS and LIG category. The schemes provide social and physical infrastructure and integrated development, including home extension loan and financing facilities.

Slum Rehabilitation and Networking

With the Central Government's contribution and matching contributions from State Governments and beneficiaries, the social housing and slum rehabilitation schemes have become viable and affordable, under which more than 16 lakh houses have been sanctioned. Simultaneously to make loans available to the poor an Rs. 1000 crore Credit Risk Guarantee Fund (CRGF) has been created, which provides collateral security to those who seek loans from the banks for EWS or LIG houses.

The JNNURM-BUSP project in Thane is a typical example, where only 10 to 16 per cent of the house cost is borne by the allottees. The funding pattern of the project is four layered-Government of India contributed 50 per cent, Government of Maharashtra 25 per cent, Thane Municipal Corporation (TMC) 9 per cent and remaining 16 per cent by the slum families. TMC has also used Transfer of Development Rights (TDR) and Floor Space Index (FSI) for funding the viability gap. Smart cards were issued to slum families so that benefits reach to the genuine people.

Slum Rehabilitation Scheme of Chandigarh Housing Board is another example of subsidising social housing by combining JNNURM and State Government financing. In Chandigarh 25,728 slum dwellers were identified in 18 slum clusters for their rehabilitation in walk-up apartments.

Fig. 6.10. Slum Rehabilitation (Thane) Financial Contribution: 50% by Central Government under JNNURM, 25% by State Government, 9% by Local Body & Dev. Rights and remaining 16% by Slum Dwellers

Ahmedabad Municipal Corporation has facilitated Slum Networking by bringing together slum communities on a common platform, in order to listen to their problems and help them with basic services, economic, social health and education supports. This has empowered the slum communities and imbibed an attitude of mutual co-operation among the slum dwellers and city authorities.

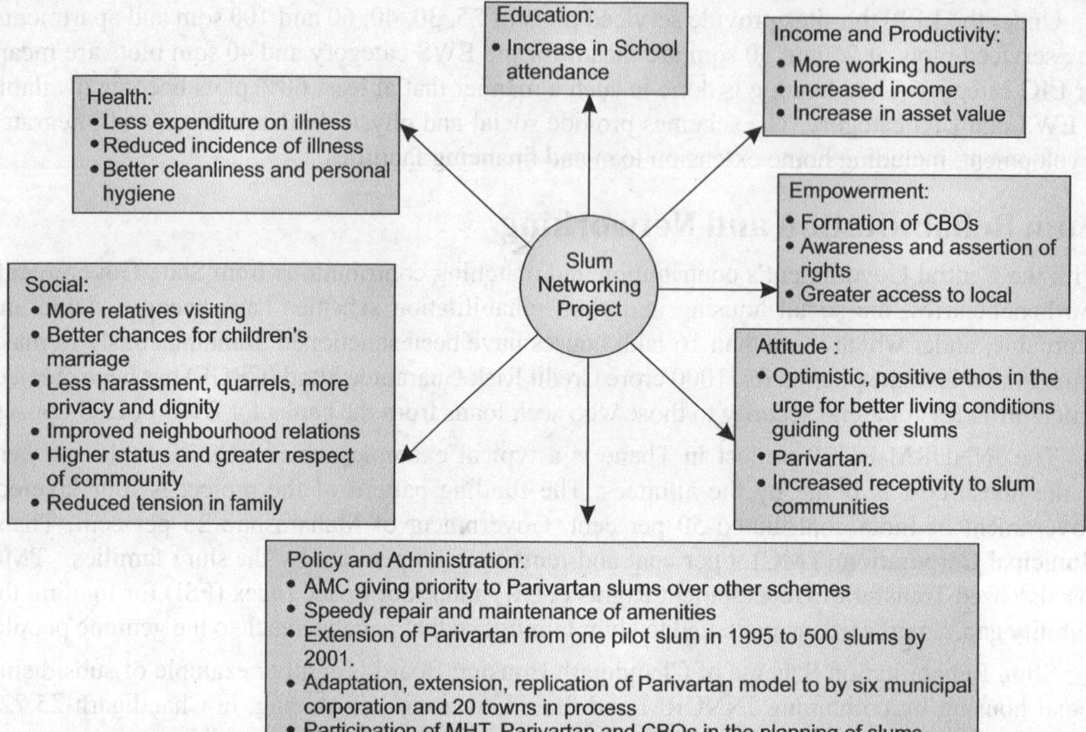

Fig. 6.11. Slum Networking Project, Ahmedabad

The lessons learnt through implementation of the SNP in Ahmedabad have been incorporated in the Gujarat State Urban Slum Policy and regulations for slum development. The design of a Special Purpose Vehicle (SPV) for implementation of SNP was prepared with the support of the Cities Alliance and Water and Sanitation Programme.

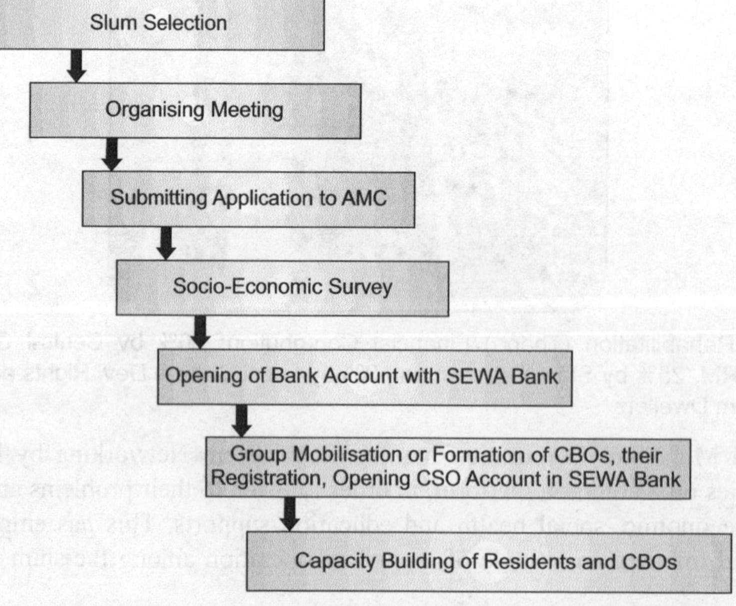

Fig. 6.12. Slum Networking and Upgradation Process, Ahmedabad

Slum Rehabilitation and Resettlement in Delhi

The Slum Areas (Improvement and Clearance) Act, 1956 is applicable to slum areas in Delhi. The Slum Areas Act refers to the inadequacy of shelter in terms of its structural quality, hygienic condition and availability of services. Chapter-II Section-3 of Slum Areas Act, 1956 defines slum areas by notification in the official gazette. The slum areas are declared which require (*a*) repair, (*b*) stability, (*c*) natural light and air, (*d*) system of dump, (*e*) water supply, (*f*) drainage and sanitary conveniences, (*g*) facilities for storage, preparation of cooking of food and disposal of wastewater. The building is deemed to be unfit if it is defective in one or more of the said matter and not found suitable for occupation in that condition.

According to the 138th Report on "Legislative Protection for Slum and Pavement Dwellers" and earlier Supreme Court order, the slum and pavement dwellers should be protected through the legislative measure, and if any eviction is undertaken by the local authorities, the alternative site and accommodation should be provided.

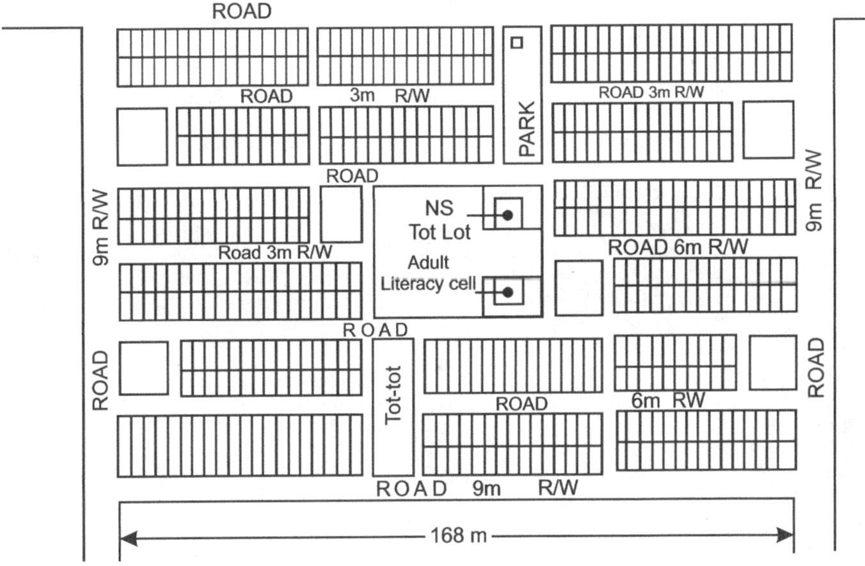

Fig. 6.13. Layout Plan of a Site and Services Scheme, whereby about 3.5 lakh slum/squatter households were resettled in Delhi during 1960-1996

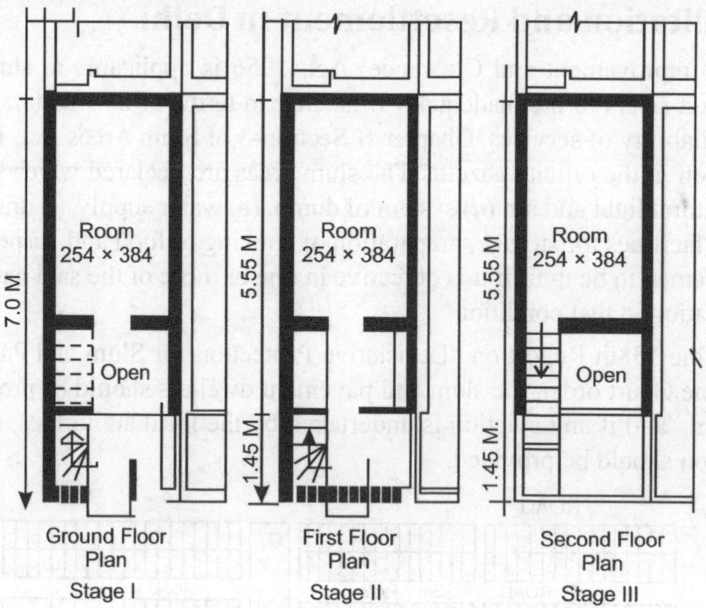

Fig. 6.14. Standard Design for 21 sqm plots

Fig. 6.15. Ambedkar Nagar Site and Services Resettlement Scheme (1977). The initial horizontal approach has gradually transformed into high density walk-ups

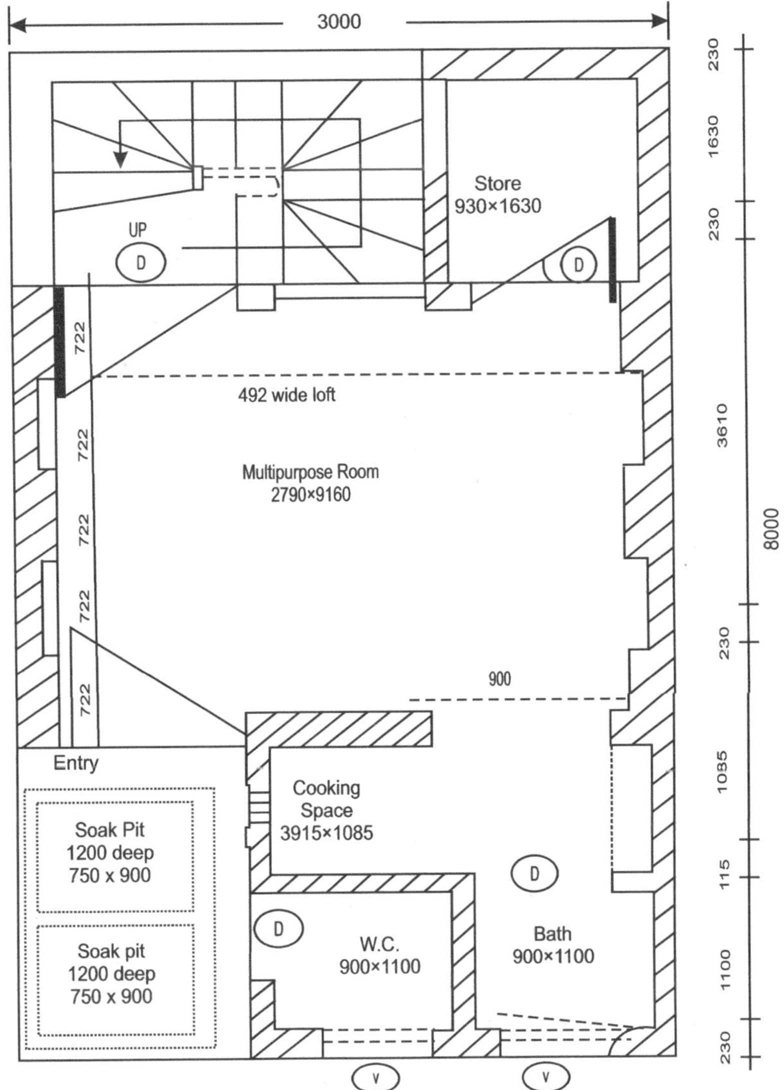

Fig. 6.16. A typical Site and Services (24 sqm) dwelling in Delhi during 1980s, which provides individual water supply, electricity and latrines

Slum Rehabilitation based on Cluster Concept

The cluster concept incorporates dwelling units around a common courtyard of 28 sqm (@ 4 to 5 sqm per dwelling unit). This promotes community living and avoids encroachments and horizontal extensions. Such units have been built by the Slum Wing now DUSIB based on the design of Nizamuddin Building Center (Architect Anil Laul). These are low cost and can be built by the residents themselves using single methods and building systems like hollow blocks, light metal frame roofing, geodesic domes, fiberglass reinforced panels, funicular shells, thermocol filled thrift panels and beams. These complement merge with the local materials and building crafts, like mud blocks, arched openings and carved doors. This concept has been adopted by the Slum and JJ wing in various schemes. Subsequently, the concept of walk-up housing has been adopted in order to achieve higher densities for optimum use of resources.

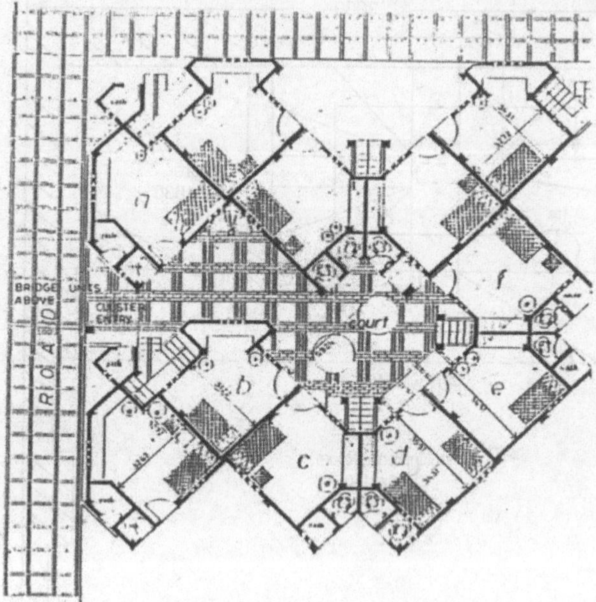

Fig. 6.17. A typical slum tenement cluster at Delhi developed by the Building Centre and Slum Wing, (now DUSIB), Architect: Anil Laul

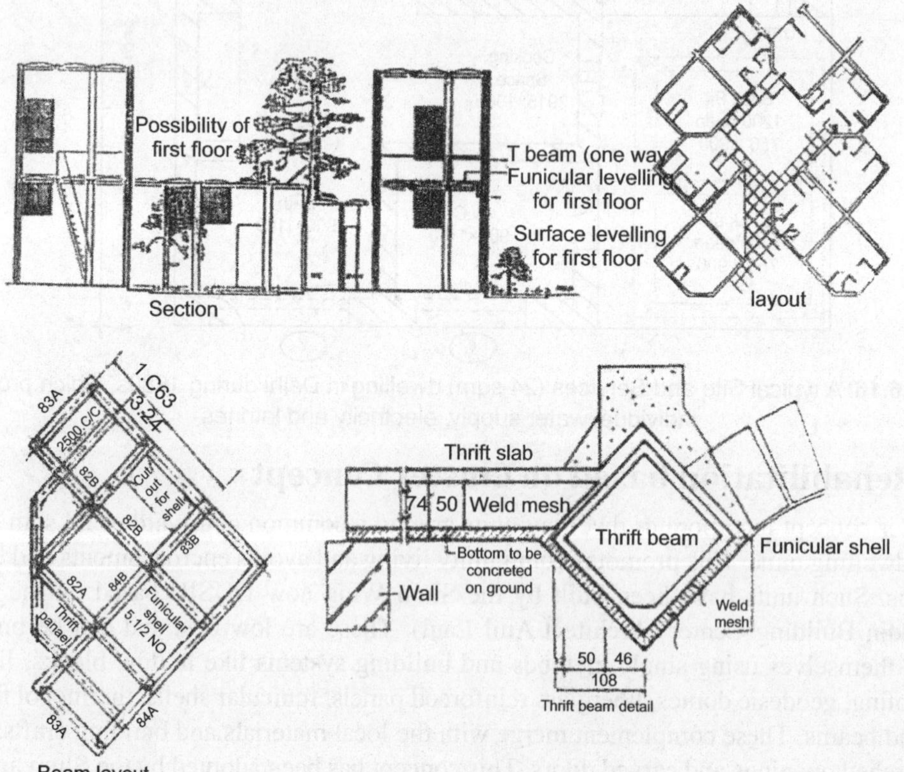

Fig. 6.18. Cluster built with funicular shell and thrift beams at Prayog Vihar, New Delhi (Architect: Anil Laul)

Collective Community Rehabilitation: To make Delhi a city without slums, an eight point programme has been proposed in the Master Plan for Delhi 2021, as given below:

(*i*) Resettlement, whether in the form of in situ upgradation or relocation, should be based mainly on built up accommodation of around 25 sqm with common areas and facilities, rather than on the model of horizontal plotted development.

(*ii*) The concept of land as a resource should be adopted to develop such accommodation with private sector participation and investment, to the extent possible.

(*iii*) Incentives by way of higher FAR, part commercial use of the land and, if necessary and feasible. Transfer of Development Rights should be provided.

(*iv*) A cooperative resettlement model with adequate safeguards should be adopted with tenure rights being provided through the institution of cooperative societies.

(*v*) The provision of accommodation should be based on cost, with suitable arrangements for funding/financing keeping in view the aspect of affordability and capacity to pay.

(*vi*) In case of relocation, the sites should be identified with a view to develop relatively small clusters in a manner that they can be integrated with the overall planned development of the area, particularly keeping in view the availability of employment avenues in the vicinity. Very large resettlement sites could lead to a phenomenon of planned slums.

(*vii*) Suitable arrangement for temporary transit accommodation for families to be rehabilitated should be made. This may preferably be near or at the same site and the utilization of these may be synchronised with the phases of implementation of the scheme of in situ upgradation.

(*viii*) Community Based Organizations (CBOs) and Non-Government Organizations (NGOs) should be closely involved in the resettlement process.

According to Master Plan for Delhi (MPD-2021), the schemes for collective community rehabilitation/relocation should be explored with the possibility of involving slum cooperatives. In existing resettlement colonies, redevelopment, regular servicing and maintenance, which are overdue, are to be based on the guidelines and incentives as applicable for the Squatter Rehabilitation Scheme. To make the scheme self-financing an FAR upto 400 in permissible with minimum 60% for slum rehabilitation and 40% for market sale housing (including 10% of FAR for commercial use).

Slum Rehabilitation Norms

The following norms, with site-specific relaxations, have been adopted for the preparation of slum rehabilitation schemes in Delhi :

(*i*) Minimum plot size 2000 sqm (facing a min. road of 9 m).

(*ii*) Density – 600 to 900 units per hectare.

(*iii*) The scheme should be designed in a composite manner with an overall maximum FAR of 400.

(*iv*) Mixed land use/commercial component upto 10% of permissible FAR.

(*v*) Specific situations may require clubbing of scattered squatters with JJ sites in the neighbourhood to work out an overall comprehensive scheme.

(*vi*) The minimum component of the land area for rehabilitation of squatters has to be 60% and maximum area for remunerative use has to be 40%.

(vii) Area of dwelling unit for rehabilitation shall be around 25 to 30 sq.m.

(viii) Common parking is to be provided which can be relaxed wherever required, except for the parking for remunerative purposes.

(ix) No restriction on ground coverage (except set-backs)

(x) There is no restriction on the height, subject to clearance of the Fire Department, Civil Aviation Department and Structural Safety. The development control norms facilitate both the options-walk up (5 storeys) or multi-storeyed apartments in order to achieve the full permissible density and floor area ratio.

(xi) Schemes/designs should be compatible for disabled.

To make Slum & JJ Rehabilitation self-starting, the concept of land as a resource with private sector participation and investment has been adopted, which provides incentives of higher FAR and density, part commercial use of the land and Transfer of Development Rights.

Fig. 6.19. Low cost housing built by DSIIDC at Bawana, Delhi has 3164 houses. The cost of construction worked out to Rs. 350 per sq.ft. (2008). The materials used in the construction of the houses are flyash bricks in rat trap bond, RCC planks and joists, ferrocement shelves, sunshades and steps, Pramod Adlakha and Associates, Technical Support: BMTPC and Delhi State Industrial and Infrastructure Development Corporation (DSIIDC)

Source: *Delhi Development Authority, Master Plan for Delhi-2021*

Kathputli In-situ Slum Rehabilitation Project

The Kathputli Colony in the West Delhi is inhabited by the puppeteers, street artists, snake charmers and magicians. The area is located near Shadipur and had come up on public land in 1950, when the wandering artists settled at the vacant land near railway tracks, which was then on the western fringe of the city. The Kathputli Project covers 5.22 hactares and is planned to provide about 4,000 EWS (Economically Weaker Section) flats for squatter families. According to the plan the community of puppeteers and performers who stay in the colony will be temporarily shifted to transit camps till the private developer constructs multi-storey flats to accommodate the estimated 3292 families. Planned under the public-private partnership with Raheja Developers, the project was first announced in 2009 but was delayed due to many hurdles. Part of the land would be used by the private developer to build residential and commercial pockets for sale market rates. With an area of 36 square meters, the flats would be located in six 15 storey towers. Each household will be given a permanent unique number to ensure transparency.

Fig. 6.20. Model/View of Kathputli Slum Rehabilitation Covering 5.22 Ha, New Delhi

Fig. 6.21. Kathputli Transit Camp at Anand Parbat

Management and Maintenance

Effective management and maintenance of the slum redevelopment and social housing schemes can be brought by partnership among private sector, NGOs and community-based organisations and slum co-operative societies. The salient areas pertaining to improved management of slum rehabilitation and social housing development are the following:

(*a*) Innovative land management strategies with respect to land information, assembly, protection and tenure rights.

(*b*) Better financial management and exploring new areas of resource optimization, reducing administrative overheads, affordability as a major concern, promoting micro-financing.

(*c*) Flexibility in planning and management to facilitate design solutions for affordability and evolutionary upgradation of services/facilities.

(*d*) Better control over time, bridging gap between demand and supply, overcoming delays and cost over-runs.

(*e*) Decentralization, horizontalisation, constitution of project management groups and new ways of contracting, monitoring and maintenance.

(*f*) Technological interface and new procedures for contracting out with reference to specifications, physical/social infrastructure, construction and maintenance.

(*g*) Capacity building, competitiveness, training, motivation and participatory decision-making process.

(*h*) Transparency in process of planning, finance, construction, management and disposal.

(*i*) Legal reforms, including Acts, building bye-laws, regulations and procedures.

The management and maintenance of the services can be ensured through the involvement of the local communities as partners, contracting out the maintenance of certain components of infrastructure services and by a systematic maintenance cycle (daily, weekly, monthly, etc.) and its monitoring.

For a coordinated management, it is necessary to work out an accountable structure and take up regular monitoring of the physical and financial targets on short term, mid-term, and long term basis. Effective involvement of the community organisations at grass root level will help in the process of motivation and the beneficiaries to sustain and manage day-to-day issues such as drainage, solid waste management, water supply, electricity, public health, sanitation, education, skill development, etc. A continuous interaction with the service agencies should be maintained, so as to address the priorities and the needs of the community. Slum rehabilitation need to be linked with poverty reduction, livelihoods, physical and social infrastructure, which enables empowerment and transformation of the slum dwellers. This requires a comprehensive approach, of which some key action areas are the following:

- Building Database on Slums, Poverty and Livelihoods, GIS Mapping of Slums.
- Visioning Slum-Free Cities Integrating Slums with City-wide Infrastructure.
- Reforming Master Planning, Inclusive Zoning, Reservations for the Poor and Informal Sector.
- Involving the poor at all stages through participatory planning, peoples' estimates & social audit; addressing resettlement and rehabilitation issues.
- Incentive Zoning Using Land, Floor Space Index (FSI) and land use as the resources.
- Employment, Livelihood & Skill Development.
- Launching Skills Initiative, Linking Micro-finance to Livelihood and Shelter, Community Empowerment with women and child focus.
- Strengthening Institutional Capacity to address urban poverty and slums, building Resource Centres and Advocacy Forums.
- Convergence of health, education, social security, etc.
- Learning from best practices: some examples include Kudumbashree, Kerala, Gruhakalpa, Andhra Pradesh, Town Planning Model of Gujarat, Transfer of Development Rights and Accommodation Reservation Models of Maharashtra, Gujarat, Premium FSI/Incentive Zoning in Mumbai, Delhi and Andhra Pradesh Urban Poverty Alleviation Fund, Andhra Pradesh.

- Preference in transfer and allocation of Government/Municipal Lands for slum rehabilitation.
- Shelter Fund with dedicated revenues, earmarking of Municipal Funds for the poor (P-Budget).
- Security of tenure.

Tenure System

The challenge of land tenure and transfer of ownership of government land under slum clusters and illegal colonies is a major issue and a determinant of its planning and development. This needs to be reviewed with reformed law and procedures of ownership/tenure rights so that the poor become the legitimate owners. An overview of various tenure systems and their advantages and limitations is given in Table 6.3:

Table 6.3: Alternative Tenure Systems and their Characteristics

Tenure system	Characteristics	Advantage	Limitations
Freehold	Ownership perpetuity	High degree of security, freedom to dispose off use as collateral for loans.	Costs generally high, collateral value may not be relevant if incomes are low and financial institutions are weak. Property values go up and trap the unwary.
Delayed freehold	Conditional ownership. Title granted in completion of payment of development	High security, Freedom to dispose, or use as collateral for loans. Maximum commercial value.	Failure of payments may result in eviction. Collateral value may not be relevant if incomes are low. Expectation of increased value triggers marketing of assets.
Registered leasehold	Ownership of a specified period from a few months to 99 years	As secure as freehold but only for the period specified in the lease.	Requires legal framework. Costs generally high.
Public rental	Rental occupation of publicly owned land or house	Provides a high degree of security, provided terms and condition of occupation are met.	Limited supply may restrict access. Terms are often restrictive. Deterioration results if maintenance costs not met.
Private rental	Rental of privately owned land or property	Good security, if protected by legally enforceable contract. Provides flexibility.	Open to abuse by owners. Deterioration may result, if maintenance costs not met.
Shared equity	Combination of delayed freehold and rental in which residents purchase a stake in their property and pay rent on the remainder.	Combines security and potential increase in value of delayed freehold and flexibility of rental. Residents can increase their stake leading to full ownership.	Requires a legal framework and efficient management.

Cooperative tenure	Ownership is vested in the cooperative of which residents are co-owners.	Good security, maintains social cohesion.	Requires a legal framework. Restrictions may reduce incentives to invest. Requires registration of land and association.
Customary ownership	Ownership is vested in a particular community, land allocated by customary authorities.	Widely accepted, Simple to administer, social cohesion.	Vulnerable to abuse, poor customary leadership may weaken its legitimacy.
Non-formal tenure system	These include regularized and unregularised squatting, unauthorized sub-division, and unofficial rental arrangements, which may coexist on the same plot.	These mostly cover non-formal areas, such as squatting, which are not catered by public authorities.	These informal tenure categories have become commercialized, so that access by low income groups is restricted.

***Source:** UNCHS (2000)*

Annexure 6.1

Asian Development Bank (ADB), Extracts of Guidelines for Preparing Cities Without Slums Program (2004)

Introduction: These guidelines were prepared under an Asian Development Bank (ADB) Regional Technical Assistance (RETA) project to assist the participating cities in drawing up City Without Slums (CWS) Program. The CWS Program and a City Development Strategy (CDS) were the two main outputs of the RETA Project.

Need for Flexibility : These guidelines need to be used flexibly, in a manner consistent with such realities as (*i*) the dimensions of poverty and slum-related problems, (*ii*) the availability of resources, (*iii*) the availability and reliability of data, (*iv*) the relative status of CDS preparations, (*v*) the existence and impact of pro-poor initiatives, and (*vi*) the priority given to other, competing development initiatives.

Full account will also have to be taken of the validity of alternative approaches to slum eradication, which in some instances may not support conventional slum upgrading solutions based on land ownership.

Maintaining Momentum : CWS Program interventions must be implemented in tandem with other pro-poor initiatives, building on their experience and at the same time having an impact on them–an iterative process that maintains the momentum in this critical sector.

An important consideration in preparing these guidelines, was to keep them as simple and easily understood as possible. The intent as to ensure their practical use especially to stakeholders, many of whom lack experience and familiarity with the CWS approach. Comprehending guidelines prepared in a foreign language would moreover be a daunting prospect.

CWS Program–CDS Links : To succeed, the CWS slum upgrading program must be part of a comprehensive urban development strategy, addressing all aspects of development that affect poverty. In that sense, the CWS Program is a localized application of the CDS in poor urban communities those now living in slum and scutter settlements, and those who will form slum settlements in the future. For this reason close links need to be maintained between the CDS and the CWS Program. These guidelines should therefore be read in conjunction with those for CDS preparation. The CDS guidelines diagrammatically illustrate these links at various stages of preparation of the CDS and the CWS program.

In addition to physical and environmental improvement, the CWS Program will have to (*i*) stimulate regeneration in slum settlement to create employment and income; (*ii*) promote social development and improve governance and empowerment in poor urban communities; (*iii*) help create more skilled and productive communities through better pubic education, health, and welfare service; and (*iv*) support enterprise development and livelihood training.

The CWS Program must also create the policy framework and condition that will be conducive to greater private investment and stakeholder participation in the slum upgrading process to sustain the program over the longer term.

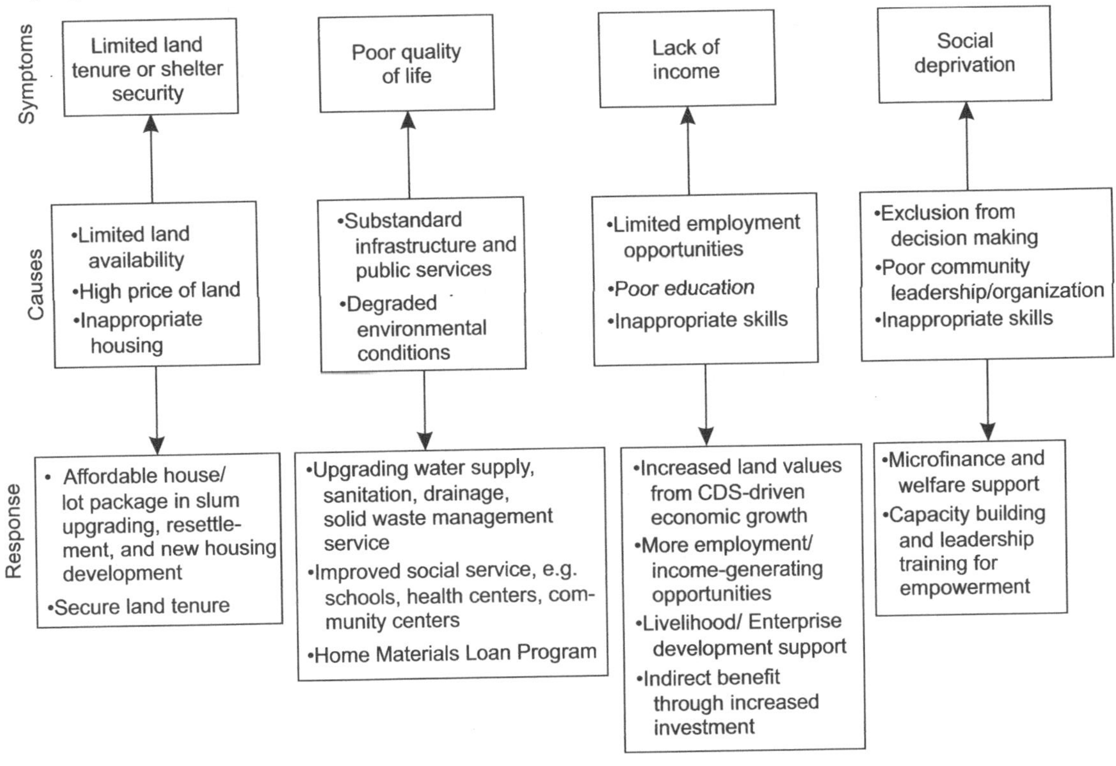

Fig.2.26: Symptoms and Causes of Poverty

Guidelines : There are six main stages in the CWS Program preparation process:

- Stage 1: Preparation
- Stage 2: Data Collection and Analysis
- Stage 3: Formulation of CWS Program Goals, Objectives, and Targets
- Stage 4: Preparation of CWS Strategic Framework
- Stage 5: Implementation of CWS Program and
- Stage 6: Program Monitoring and Evaluation.

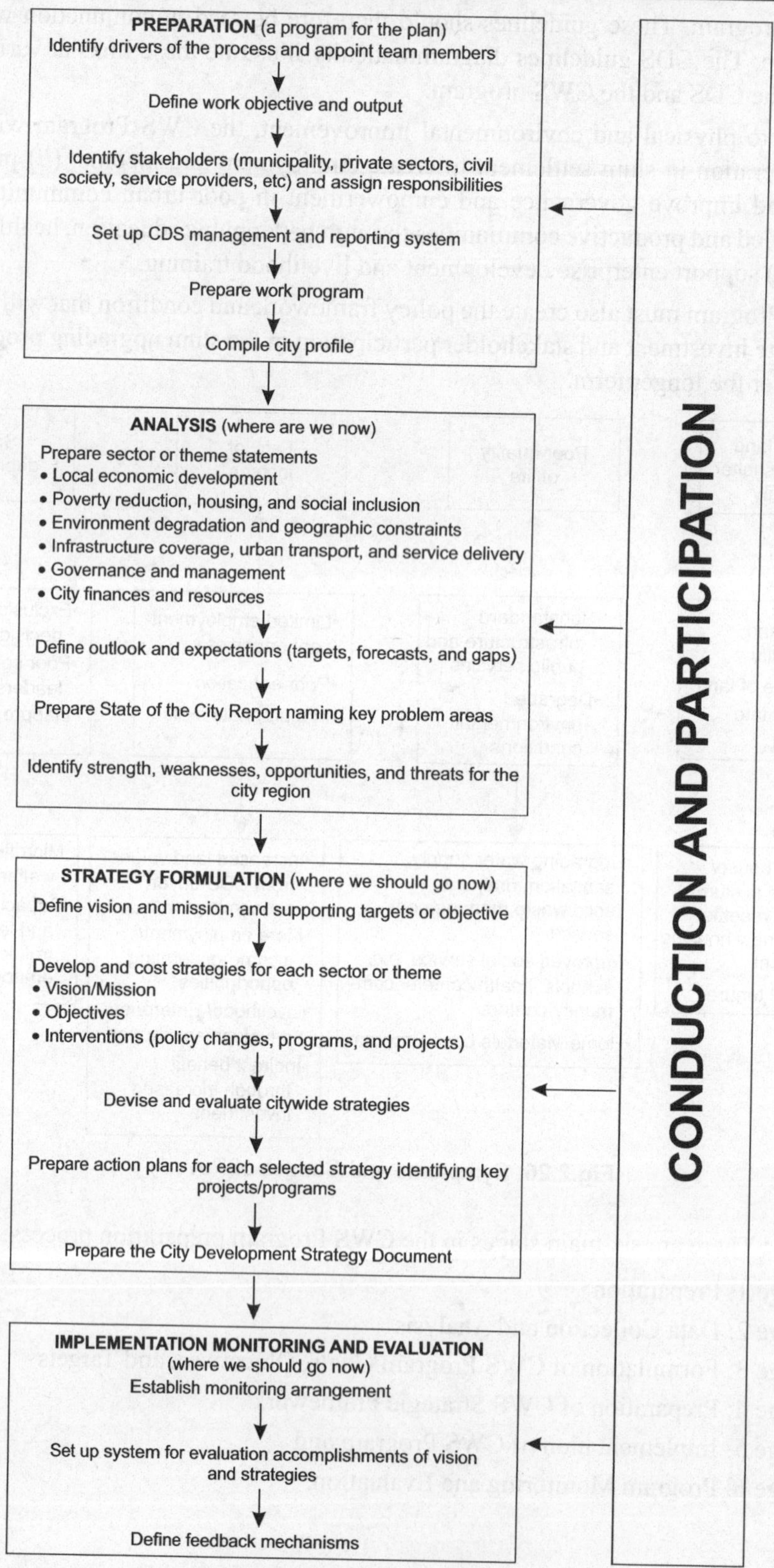

Fig. 6.23. The CDS Process

All these stages will involve a high degree of participation by consulation with stakeholders. A CWS Program Steering Committee or a similar group will endorse the program preparation of key points in the process.

Stage I : Preparation and Institutional Arrangement

The city, under the direction of the mayor, will lead the preparation of the CWS Program preparation will operate at three levels:

- **Technical Task Force:** to lead CWS Program preparation;
- **Housing Board (or equivalent body):** to provide support and overall guidance: and
- **Sub-project Stakeholder Group:** to make inputs into the preparation and implementation of specific site/community sub-projects.

Box 1: CWS Program: Potential Stakeholders at LGU Level

- Governement (national, provincial and local) departments involved in pro-poor shelter program and projects;
- People's organization (POs): broad LGU-level representation in CWS Program preparation, as well as participation of specific, as well as participation of specific POs in community subproject design and implementation;
- NGOs imvolved in the pro-poor shelter sector and related sectors;
- Private sector business interests, especially developers of socialized housing and others in the construction industry;
- Private or public infrastructure and service providers;
- Government and private landowners;
- Civil society;
- Academics;
- Media representatives; planning and implemetning public awareness initiatives; and
- Special interest groups.

Housing Board

If not already established, a Housing Board (HB) (or an equivalent body) will be formed by the LGUs to provide overall policy guidance and direction to CWS Program preparations. The mayor may chair the HB, which should also include senior representatives of key LGU departments and selected national housing agencies, as well as broad stakeholder representation extending to representatives of people's organization (POs) and non-governmental organizations (NGOs) involved in pro-poor shelter initiatives and the private business sector (usually developers of low-cost housing).

The TTF will act as the HB Technical Secretariat and will make the necessary technical presentations for review and endorsement, in the process drawing on relevant stakeholder intereset group.

The HB will approve and endorse CWS Program outputs at key junctures of the preparation process, including (*i*) the agreed work program and the monitoring and reporting system; (*ii*) the shelter needs and resource assessment; (*iii*) agreed objectives and targets (*iv*) policy and program initiatives forming part of the strategic framework (*v*) the implementation plan, including prioritized community and site subprojects; and (*vi*) applications for funding support including those submitted to the CA.

Box 2 : CWS Program: Required Outputs

- Analysis of city/municipal and informal settlements data (Stage 2)
- Urban poor shelter needs assessment and resource analysis (Stage 2)
- CWS Program goal, objectives, and targets (Stage 3)
- Strategic Framework, comprising policy and program initiatives to support the CWS Program (Stage 4)
- Long-Term and Phase I (CWS) Implementation Plan (Stage 5)
- CWS Program Action Plan and priority/Pilot subproject(s) (Stage 5)
- Application for CA funding (where applicable).

Box 3 : Validating the CWS Program Approach

The comparative analysis of survey data at the LGU and informal settlement levels can be used to validate the focus of the poverty reduction efforts of the CWS Program on informal settlements. This comparative analysis should be based on agreed poverty indicators, possibly determined nationally to allow broad mind nationally to allow broader nationwide or even across CA cities comparison of condition in urban areas, such as the percentage of household in informal settlements.

- Base line Information (*i*) income poverty threshold, (*ii*) unemployment or underemployment rates, (*iii*) access to safe drinking water and acceptable sanitation, (*iv*) primary/secondary school enrolment and adult literacy.
- Average (*i*) household size and occupancy, and (*ii*) infant mortality and malnutrition.

Stage 2: Data Collection and Analysis: Review of CDS City Profile

The city profile will cover the demographic, geographical, physical, social and economic characteristics of the city. It will document present conditions and chart future development trends. Because limited time is allowed for compiling the profile, available data will be used as much as possible.

Physical and Environmental Conditions

- Location and identity of all informal (slum and squatter) settlements;
- Location of all vacant and potentially developable lands;
- Current and proposed land use;
- Land ownership and value;
- Dangerous, hazardous, and otherwise undevelopable land (including flood prone areas and steep slopes);
- Existing and proposed infrastructure and services (especially the coverage and capacity of water supply, sanitation, drainage, roads, schools, health centers); and
- Ongoing and committed development proposals.

Demographic and Socioeconomic Conditions

- Existing and projected population and growth rates (for the defined CWS Program period);
- Average household size;
- Household income profile, including the LGU poverty threshold;
- Primary and secondary school enrolment and attendance;
- Adult literacy; and
- Infant mortality and malnutrition rates.

Other Data Requirements

Physical and socioeconomic data will be prepared for each identified informal settlement (and where appropriate, vacant developable land). The data will comprise the following:

- Physical condition: land area, ownership, and value; number, use, and condition of structure; existing and proposed infrastructure and service (especially water supply, drainage, sanitation, roads and footpaths, and garbage collection, as well as access to education and health facilities); main physical features, especially those that could inhibit site development, such as slopes, rivers, and drains.
- Population and household characteristics: present and projected population and growth rates (within the defined plan/program period); number and average size of households; household income profile (especially in relation to defined poverty threshold); employment/unemployment rates; educational attainment; economic activity and occupations.
- Social services: type and location of education, health, welfare, and recreational facilities serving the community; school enrollment and attendance level; typical reported health problems.
- Profile of urban poor communities: details of people's organization (POs) and membership; supporting NGOs; Private business interests; priority issues and concerns of each community.

Assessment of Shelter Needs of Urban Poor

The assessment will give an overall picture of present and future shelter needs of the urban poor against which local governments can measure their response. The assessment will be based on data collection and analyzed at the city level and in relation to existing informal settlements. More specifically, it will look into (*i*) the present shelter backlog, represented by the number of poor urban households living in slum and squatter settlements; and (*ii*) future shelter needs of population growth, new household formation, and immigration, could increase the size of the slum/squatter settlements or form new ones if these needs are not met. The assessment of shelter needs will include the need for (*i*) secure and affordable land and housing; (*ii*) appropriate standards of housing, considering such factors as size, occupancy, condition, and materials; (*iii*) minimum basic standards of municipal infrastructure and services, with emphasis on water supply, drainage, sanitation, and garbage collection; (*iv*) essential social services and facilities, including schools, health care, and welfare facilities; (*v*) improved employment and income-generating opportunities; and (*vi*) better governance and representation.

CWS Program will be based on a two-pronged shelter delivery approach comprising wherever possible, in-situ upgrading of existing informal settlement with minimum displacement; and development of affordable new serviced plots and housing units to accommodate households resettled from existing settlements and the new households as a result of population growth.

Present Shelter Needs of the Urban Poor

Present shelter needs in informal settlements will be further defined in terms of (*i*) upgrading will be further defined in terms of (*i*) upgradable or non-upgradable housing units; and (*ii*) retained or displaced households, as follows:

Type 1: Upgrading housing units/retained households

(*a*) Housing units on either government or private land that can be upgraded in-situ.

(*b*) Resident households that can remain because of acceptable occupancy ratios.

Type 2: Upgradable housing units/displaced households

(*a*) Housing units on either government or private land that can be upgraded in-situ.

(*b*) Resident households that will be displaced and resettled in new serviced site because of overcrowding (occupancy ratios above acceptable standards).

Type 3: Non-upgradable housing units/displaced households

(*a*) Housing units that cannot be retained because they are in (*i*) danger zones or otherwise hazardous areas such as rivers, waterways, flood-prone land, steep slopes, electricity transmission areas, and road reservations; (*ii*) lands officially reserved in approved national, provincial, or local development or local development or land use plans (or in committed development projects) as (*a*) public domain; (*b*) public infrastructure services, and facilities; or (*iii*) sites for uses other than social housing.

(*b*) Resident households that will be displaced and resettled in new serviced sites for the same reasons.

Type 4: Non-upgradable housing units/displaced households

(*a*) Housing units that cannot be retained because they will be displaced in the upgrading process, to (*i*) create road, footpath and infrastructure/services, right-of way; (*ii*) reduce residential densities to meet development controls and building regulations, especially in respect of minimum plot sizes, fire regulation, and environmental consideration; and environmental consideration; and (*iii*) replace dilapidated housing units.

(*b*) Resident households that will be displaced and resettled in new serviced sites for the same reasons.

Future housing need is calculated on the basis of the need to accommodate those households forming part of all future natural population growth and immigration, which if not otherwise intercepted and provided for, will expand existing slum and squatter settlements or form that part of the population that as potentially urban poor.

From the preceding assessment of urban poor shelter needs, it is clear there are two main streams of shelter provision for the urban poor, viz. upgrading of informal settlements.

New Serviced Sites and Affordable Housing

New serviced housing sites for the urban poor will be provided on vacant land to accommodate the entire/future population.

Resources Needed

Land, infrastructure, buildings materials, labour and finance will be needed to meet projects of poor shelter needs.

Land

Estimates of the additional land required to meet urban poor shelter needs over the plan period will be based on the need for new serviced sites and housing. Assumptions will have to be made as to the average plot size and the proportion of net gross residential area in new sites, taking into account land needed for roads, footpaths, open space, and community facilities, as well as potentially undevelopable areas, such as creeks and rivers.

Municipal Infrastructure and Services

Water supply, electricity, sanitation, and solid waste management systems must be provided. Calculations of the capacity of public utilities required to support this provision will be based on agreed standards, taking into account those households and housing units to be retained in existing sites, which are already provided with some level of infrastructure and services. For example,

- Water supply; Assume one metered connection per housing unit, an acceptable housing occupancy ratio, and an average water consumption per household per day.
- Electricity: Assume one metered connection per housing unit, an acceptable housing occupancy ratio, and an average electricity consumption per household.
- Sanitation: In most cases it will be safe to assume that a high proportion of domestic sanitation in low-cost housing areas will use septic tanks. Assume one standard domestic septic tank per housing unit, an acceptable housing occupancy ratio, an average household size, and then determine the requirements for desludging.
- Solid waste management: Estimate the garbage generated weekly by each household, and thus the requirement for a sanitary landfill/disposal/processing site.

Building Materials and Labour

The analysis of building material requirements will be limited to material required for (*i*) civil works contracts, such as for the construction of roads, footpaths, drainage, and water supply works; and (*ii*) basic house construction materials, such as cement, GI sheets, bricks, blocks, plumbing and electrical materials. Under the CWS Program only appropriate and affordable forms of housing (such as core housing units) will be built in new serviced sites. All other aspects of housing provision will be the responsibility of individual owners.

Finance

Only broad estimates of the financial implications of meeting shelter requirement over the defined CWS Program period are needed. Detailed cost estimates will not be needed at the initial preparation stage because (*i*) 15-year cost projection are inherently unreliable; (*ii*) the assessed needs themselves are based in part on untested assumptions; (*iii*) there is a lack of specific detail regarding individual site development requirement and beneficiary affordability; and (*iv*) details of cost recovery mechanisms and funding arrangements shall have to be determined.

In most developing countries, available resources will invariably fall well short of those required to meet projected shelter demands. In preparing the long-term program, therefore, there will be a need to take into account the time needed to bolster resources through various policy and program initiatives, other parallel urban poor initiatives or approved planning and development document such as the CDS.

Both government and non-government capacity and capability are dependent on a range of variable factors, such as (*i*) the evolving political environment in each LGU, (*ii*) the commitment of successive teams of senior executives and senior staff, (*iii*) the effectiveness of organisational arrangements designed to support the CDS and the CWS Program, (*iv*) the role of the private sector in CDS/CWS Program implementation, (*v*) the level of community response and self-help involvement, (*v*) competing development priorities, and (*vii*) the impact of training and capacity building programs. It is therefore difficult to assess institutional performance as a determining factor in CWS Program formulation.

The only rational approach seems to be based on the assumption that the level of CWS Program delivery represents a reasonable and incremental increase over current levels of accomplishment.

Stage 3: Formulation of CWS Program: Goals, Objectives, and Targets

The overall CWS Program goal will comprise a broad definition of accomplishment that will support the attainment of a longer term multi-sectoral development vision. It is this vision that forms the basis of the CDS. CWS Program objectives will directly support the attainment of the goal and thus in turn, the overall development vision stated in the CDS.

The main factors that affect the poor urban household and define their condition are the following: (*i*) lack of secure tenure; (*ii*) poor quality of life due to inadequate infrastructure and service provision and degraded environmental condition; (*iii*) high levels of unemployment or underemployment, and therefore limited household income; (*iv*) limited access to education, health, and welfare services; (*v*) limited access to credit and financial services; and (*vi*) exclusion from key decision-making processes.

CWS Program objectives support the eradication or reduction of poverty, and are linked to the following :

- Security of tenure;
- Minimum acceptable standards of municipal infrastructure and social services;
- Improved employment and income earning opportunities;
- Improved education, skill training, and health care;
- Better access to credit and other financial services for house-plot purchase, home improvement, enterprise development, and livelihood activities; and
- Improved levels of community organization, capacity, and empowerment.

Table 6.4: Scope and Coverage of City Without Slums Program

Sector/Theme	Objective of Analysis	Coverage
Local economic development	To assess a city's economic prospects linked to output, employment, and regional national development and determine how its economic base can be improved	City income and employment analysis: economic base and cluster analysis: change, output, and markets: job growth and decline; rate of startup, survival, and failure of small businesses, barriers that impede growth among local business; availability of land premises, barriers to the development of key sites Unemployment and skills: Local unemployment rates, concentration (social or spatial groupings); economic inactivity, barriers to employability in particular areas or among particular communities; skills and experience of local labour force.
Poverty, housing, and social inclusion	To assess the extent and causes of poverty and housing shortage, and determine the need for social services.	Demography: Population and natural increase and migration, socio-economic profile including household income distribution and change Poverty: Profile poverty and changes over time poverty maps. Housing demand and supply: new household, housing backlog, upgrading and resettlement, and implications Social services: Education, health, and social development needs and deficiencies
Environmental degradation and geographic construction	To assess the status of urban environment and its management	Environment: Water resources and pollution, air quality, environmental hazards, solid and hazardous wastes, noise pollution environmental barriers to development
Infrastructure coverage, urban transport, and service delivery	To determine infrastructure and service deficiencies and prospects	Infrastructure: Water supply, sewerage and sanitation, flood control and drainage, solid waste management, energy demand, and supply Communications: Road space demand, traffic management, public transport issues, air and sea-port Social infrastructure: Shortage of school buildings, health facilities, etc.
Governance and management	To determine issues related to city governance	Governance and management: Quality and standards of public services, including transparency and accountability of the city government and other public bodies Participation: Involvement of community/ stakeholders and extent of consultations undertaken by the city, key non-government, people's and other organizations linked to poverty reduction and other civic issues

City finances and resources	To assess the financial sustainability of the city, its ability to raise resources, and the magnitude of capital investments made in the city	City financial analysis: Sources of funds and local revenues and transfer; analysis of expenditures, including capital investments, recurrent expenditures, and debt service; trends and changing structures Investments in the city: General trends in public and private investment in infrastructure, services and business

Performance Targets

Performance targets are quantified program objective against which relative accomplishment can be measured. The accurate determination of shelter needs will make it possible to define specific objectives and thus, it turn, performance targets. These targets are important monitoring tools. To facilitate monitoring, evaluation and program review, targets can be established for each year, or at least for each phase of the program.

Stage 4: Preparation of CWS Strategic Framework

CWS Program initiatives derived from the needs assessment will be concerned mainly with the legal, physical, and environmental condition of the urban poor, that is, security of tenure and the provision of acceptable minimum standards of municipal infrastructure and services, all of which are important performance indicators for the CWS Program. However addition, it will be necessary to:

Box 4: Typical Policy and Program Initiatives Under the CWS Program

- Address all other aspects of poverty including the full range of socio-economic development.
- Preparation of comprehensive slum upgrading policy will involve a review and, where necessary, the updating of pro-poor and slum upgrading policies and programs.
- Expansion of ongoing poverty eradication program will involve determining the relevance and impact of existing government, NGO, and private sector pro-poor programs and project on the CWS Program, and integrating these into the CWS Program as far as possible.
- Organizational and capacity strengthening of key institutions involved in poverty reduction and related sectors, including (*i*) relevant department of national, state, and especially local government agencies, (*ii*) CDS/CWS Program steering groups and technical support committees, (*iii*) NGOs, (*iv*) people's organizations (POs), and (*v*) microfinance and local banking institutions. Project interventions will include more targeted capacity building initiatives related to specific site/community condition, especially among NGOs and POs.
- Improved education, health-care, and welfare service will involve relevant government and private agencies in the provision of facilities, human and financial resources, and development programs in support of the CWS Program, including, preschool institutions and primary schools, primary health-care facilities, recreational facilities, and rehabilitation centers. There will be a targeted application of these programs to the specific needs of identified communities.
- General public and community awareness campaigns will include those related to (*i*) fight against crime, alcohol, drug abuse, and HIV-related problems; (*ii*) support for better health and environmental management practices such as advice on food and nutrition, sanitation, waste disposal, and recycling; and (*iii*) wider appreciation of the objectives and scope of the CWS initiative.

- Information sharing and dissemination on various aspects of the CDS and CWS Program through the development of a stakeholders's community based information network and links to other cities and programs.
- Strategic planning and programming to provide an evolving context for long term CWS Program development. This will be undertaken through the maintenance of close links and integration with ongoing CDS activities, such as studies and master plan of local economic development, transportation, sewerage, drainage/flood control and other key sectors.
- Preparation of CWS Program Operations Manual will be a valuable tool in scaling up the Program within the city, and then to the regional and national levels.

Concerns such as the need for more jobs, better education and health-care, access to credit, and greater representation for the urban poor shall focus upon facilitate successful shelter delivery through policy and program initiatives in such critical areas as land acquisition, and improved institutional and organizational arrangements to encourage private sector support and community self-help involvement. Each component of the strategy should be described in full and should indicate the following:

- Objective and scope in terms of CWS Program preparation and implementation, to include desired impact/outcome;
- Agency responsibility, including the allocation of technical and financial resources;
- Business plan, including scheduled start date, immediate action (next step), and time allowed for completion;
- Link to other national, provincial, or local government development initiatives; and
- Additional resources requirement and likely sources.

Stage 5: Implementation of the CWS Program

The preparation of the CWS Program Implementation Plan will consider a number of factors derived from previous preparatory stage, as follows:

- Total urban poor shelter needs, as determined through the assessment and the comparative analysis of required and available resources (Stage 2):
- Overall CWS Program objectives and performance targets (Stage 3):
- Realistic assessment of the impact of strategic policy and program initiatives (Stage 4); and
- CDS, other valid planning and development documents, and development initiatives in the annual budgets.

It is assumed that the Long-Term Implementation Plan (LTIP) will be designed to meet all existing and projected urban poor shelter needs within the defined (CWS) Program period.

The LTIP will be defined by the rate at which upgrading or serviced plots (housing units) can be delivered and poor households can be accommodated. It will be expressed in three main forms of shelter delivery:

Box 5: Typical Sub-project Initiatives Under the CWS Program

- Improved security of land tenure and structure tenure: this will involve (*i*) land owner ship mapping valuation of land in identified slum/squatter settlements, and vacant, potentially developable land; (*ii*) preparation of topographical, physical, and cadastral surveys; (*iii*) exploration of alternative land acquisition approaches and tenure arrangements; (*iv*) acquisition of land in accordance with funding constraints and technical, economic, and social project evaluation; and (*v*) issuance of titles or secure leasehold agreements to eligible beneficiaries.
- Upgrading or provision of basic infrastructure and services in informal settlements and in resettlement and new low-cost housing sites: the infrastructure and services will include roads, footpaths, drainage and flood control structures, water and electricity supply network, sewerage and sanitation systems, solid waste management systems, street lighting, schools, health centres, community and rehabilitation centres, and public open space and recreation facilities.
- Provision of affordable housing units in resettlement and new low-cost housing sites.
- Maximized opportunities for self-help improvement in site development and housing through training programs, access to micro finance support, and links to other established government pro-poor programs.
- Financial and microfinance support for house/plot purchase, and growth-oriented enterprise and livelihood development.
- Community training and capacity building: including programs to (*i*) empower and promote greater self-reliance in poor urban communities; (*ii*) improve community organization and management and livelihood activities; and (*iii*) promote more effective participation in CWS Program preparation, implementation, monitoring, and evaluation.
- Institutional strengthening and capacity building of specific stakeholder groups including appropriate LGU departments, NGO, and microfinance institutions.
- Education and awareness-raising campaigns (*i*) within the private sector to encourage investment in the CWS Program; (*ii*) of specific communities in matters related to the prevention of HIV, crime, and drug abuse; and (*iii*) to encourage community saving and loan programs.

- **Upgrading:** In situ upgrading of plots (housing units) in existing informal settlements.
- **Resettlement:** the development of new serviced site and affordable housing units to accommodate households displaced (*i*) from informal settlement in danger areas and strategic government reservations; and (*ii*) from existing settlements as a result of upgrading or over crowding in excess of acceptable occupancy ratios.
- **New site development:** serviced plots and affordable housing units to accommodate that proportion of future population growth during the CWS Program period that could lead to the formation of new slums and squatter areas or the expansion of existing ones.

Box 6: Land Acquisition

A high proportion of shelter needs will be for new serviced plots and affordable housing to accommodate resettlement or to forestall future demand. The acquisition of suitable and affordable vacant land for development is therefore a high priority. The identification of potentially appropriate land should be followed immediately by negotiations with landowners, as the acquisition of land in the Philippines (even within and between government agencies) is generally a complex and protracted process, which needs to be anticipated in LGU programming and budgeting as early as possible. The need to ensure that new serviced shelter development is in accordance with proposed development trends and use patterns, and is supported by mains infrastructure and services provision of adequate capacity, further reinforces the importance of maintaining close links with the CDS in preparing implementing the CWS Program. In instances where there are high urban densities and limited land availability to meet demand within city boundaries, there may be a need to seek suitable sites in adjacent areas.

The CDS will give a broad indication of proposed development trends and land uses that may extend beyond city boundaries and give some indication of external land availability and use. If the need for land acquisition likely, there will be great advantage in seeking out the appropriate site and making the necessary moves toward collaboration with adjacent local governments, private land-owners and other parties concerned, at the earliest possible opportunity.

Box 7 : Short Term Implementation Program (STIP) Selection Criteria for the CWS Program

- Land acquisition and development cost : It will be important to ensure that all land in identified upgrading and new sites can be acquired and developed within the Phase I time frame, at a cost consistent with beneficiary affordability and PIP funding constraints.
- Adequate resettlement site capacity : The development of adequate resettlement site capacity should be included in Phase I to accommodate the anticipated level of displacement and resettlement. The Long Term Implementation Program (LTIP) and shelter needs assessment will give an indication of this.
- Adequate mains infrastructure availability and capacity : This should be sufficient to allow upgrading and/or development of all STIP subproject sites and communities to agreed standards within the specified Phase I time frame.
- Demonstrably high levels of need : This will be especially critical in respect of communities living in danger zones and households living below the poverty line.
- High levels of community support : This will especially be critical in subproject requiring some measure of dislocation and resettlement.
- High impact and visibility : This is important in ensuring positive demonstration for ongoing CWS Program initiatives and as a means of increasing private sector involvement and community participation and cooperation, as well as general public support.
- General consistency with the CDS : LTIP agreed CWS Program performance targets, and other valid planning documents, supporting PIP and annual budget allocations.
- Links to other government, NGO, and private sector pro-poor initiatives : This will help maximize the use of limited resources.

The preparation of the Short-Term Implementation Plan (STIP) will be based on the first phase of the LTIP. The STIP will be prepared in significantly more detailed than the LTIP. It will adopt the broad mix of shelter types included in the LTIP (upgrading, resettlement, and new sites), but will apply these directly to specific informal settlement and new sites identified in the mapping and survey data prepared in Stage 2. This will inevitably involve some adjustments to the LTIP phasing and estimates, which can be accommodated over time as part of regular monitoring and review process.

Requirement for the CWS Program

- *Land:* area, ownership, and value, to determine the options and likely cost of acquisition, including links to other government pro-poor housing programs.
- Existing and proposed land and structure use, including that in adjacent properties.
- Physical features: especially rivers, creeks, flood-prone areas, steep slopes, vegetation, and other feature that affect subproject design and layout, as well as the upgradability or nonupgradability of structures.
- *Structures*: number, use, condition, and materials, to determine overall residential density and identify upgradable and nonupgradable structures.
- Existing and proposed infrastructure and service: especially roads and footpaths. water supply, drainage, sanitation, electricity, and garbage collection, to determine the need for on-site and offsite upgrading or additional infrastructure and service provision.
- Ongoing and committed development proposals: to assess the compatibility of CWS Program upgrading and new site proposals.
- Population size and projected growth rates throughout the CWS Program period, to estimate household growth and the demand for new affordable housing units in existing informal settlements.
- Household characteristics, including household size and composition, to determine occupancy ratios and the need for possible housing units to accommodate households displaced as a result of overcrowding.
- Household income, saving, and expenditure, to determine the affordability levels of potential beneficiaries.
- Employment, occupation, and levels of skill, educational attainment and literacy to establish the need for supporting socioeconomic programs and facilities, and other pro-poor development initiatives to support job creation and income generation.
- *Governance*: details of PO organizations, activities, membership, and support from LGU and NGOs, to judge the need for community empowerment and capacity building program, and the likely role of the community in the design and implementation process.

Box 8 : Program Monitoring and Evaluation

CWS Program monitoring and evaluation, although linked to specific CWS performance targets, will be best undertaken as an integral part of the overall monitoring evaluation and reporting systems set out for the CDS.

Essential Considerations for Program Monitoring and Evaluation.

Land Acquisition : No major outstanding issues of land acquisition should in any way obstruct site access or delay scheduled subprojects design and implementation, and the resolutions of land tenure issues. Selected sites should be owned by the local government unit (LGU) or by the community, or already part of formal sales agreements involving the community or an existing joint-venture agreement with the landowners.

Resettlement : Upgrading or development should not involve the relocation of any housing units or the resettlement of households that cannot be accommodated on site or in pilot subproject is feasible option. At the same time, there should be no in-situ upgrading of any community or site located in a dangerous or hazardous area, in a strategic government reservation, or in land officially designated for development other than residential.

Infrastructure/services availability: Upgrading or development should not be dependent on any form of major offsite mains infrastructure provision that could potentially obstruct scheduled subproject completion. Thus, the selected site should (*i*) already have all-weather pedestrian and vehicular access; (*ii*) already have access to water supply mains and drainage of adequate capacity; and (*iii*) not be subject to serious flooding and inundation requiring drainage works, such as seawall construction, reclamation, or river bank protection.

Demonstrable need: Any community selected for upgrading or resettlement should have a dominant percentage of poor households living at or below the poverty threshold.

Community support: The selected pilot should have a strong and genuinely representative people's organization, which supports the upgrading and development approach and has an established working relationship with the LGU.

Source: *Asian Development Bank (2004) Guidelines for Preparing Cities Without Slums Programs ADB, Manila, Philippines.*

DEBRIEFING QUESTIONS

1. How a slum is defined? Explain the extent of the problem of slums in urban India.
2. What are the different types of slums and approaches for their rehabilitation?
3. What are the slum indicators?
4. Explain and compare provision based and supports based approaches for slum rehabilitation. Give examples.
5. Write notes on the following:
   (*a*) Dharavi, Mumbai
   (*b*) Slum Rehabilitation under Mumbai Urban Transport Project
   (*c*) Ahmedabad Slum Networking Project
   (*d*) Site and Services Scheme
   (*e*) In situ Slum Rehabilitation
6. What are the broad contours of guidelines for making cities slum-free?
7. What options can be adopted for self-financing of a slum rehabilitation project?

7

HOUSING RENEWAL AND REDEVELOPMENT

The Indian city invariably comprises the following three kind of areas:

(*a*) Traditional city and villages

(*b*) Planned areas and colonies

(*c*) Unplanned areas, including slums and jhuggi-jhompri clusters, unauthorized colonies, encroachments, etc.

Generally, about half of the Indian city is unplanned having about two-thirds of its population. These areas provide affordable shelter to poor and offer the scope of redevelopment, densification and upgradation. According to the government statistics, out of total housing shortage of 18.78 million, 14.99 million comprise dilapidated, congested and cramped houses. As such, about 80 per cent of the total housing shortage involves urban renewal, upgradation, regularization, redevelopment, rehabilitation in-situ extensions or retrofitting of existing housing.

Fig. 7.1. Shahjahanabad, Delhi has a closely packed, self-generated, high density housing and mixed land-use

Source: *Rory Fonesca, 1976, The Walled City of Delhi in Shelter and Society*

In the traditional segments of Indian cities, it is common to witness a compact maze of houses, narrow roads where the bulk of poor live. The proximity of structures and the pattern of meandering and narrow streets help in maintaining the privacy. An outside observer sees the streets as a pattern of dark voids between buildings and is apt to arrive at an erroneous conclusion. Behind the narrow dark lanes are sunny courtyards where most of the activities take place. The traditional spatial structure has a sieve like porous form. Closely knit fabric of structures helps to keep out the harsh sun and provides shaded courtyards and streets. During the night, the open courtyards radiate out the heat and creating a cooling effect and providing thermal comfort through passive means.

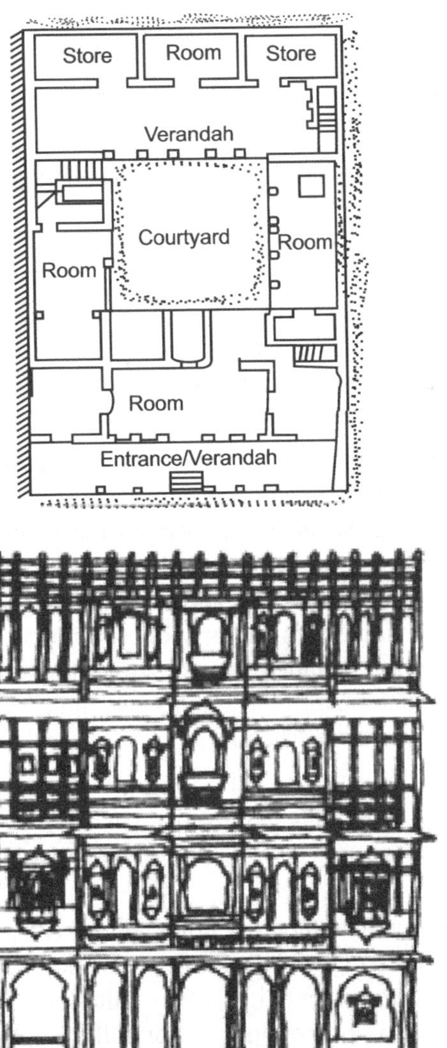

Fig. 7.2. Plan and elevation of Patwa Haveli, Jaisalmer

Source: *Shikha Jain, Haveli: A Living Tradition of Rajasthan*

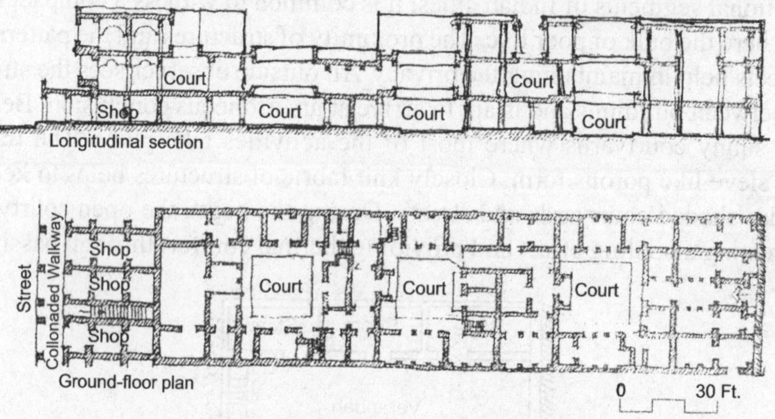

Fig. 7.3. A Large Haveli with multiple courtyards in Jaipur

Source: *Kulbhushan Jain*

The indigenous settlement is a working model of closely knit and self-contained community. Its spatial structure is a logical outgrowth of social and economic norms governing community and individual behaviour. Low-income groups and migrants, who constitute the bulk of urban population, find in the indigenous city an environment where opportunities exist for economic betterment and the life is often more compatible than the barren imagery of new areas.

The morphology of indigenous settlements demonstrates a variety of typologies and characteristics. Variations in physical, cultural and socio-economic conditions are discernible within every settlement. The marginal areas are distinguished by their poor inhabitants and migrants mostly working in the informal/service sectors. The dwellings are generally temporary in nature, having a low-rise, high density and compact pattern, yet reminiscent to rural form. The essential services like water supply individual taps and privies are generally non-available. The land tenure is usually disputed or it is under unauthorized possession of a non-resident landlord, who extracts rent from the residents. Low-income of the residents and status of tenure do not permit immediate improvement of the buildings or reconstruction.

The Census 2001 & 2011 indicate growth of population of peri-urban areas three times faster than the urban areas, which is mainly due to the emergence of unauthorised colonies on agriculture and semi-rural lands. The urban limits advance upon the fringe of the city, by which the villages are embraced or obliterated.

The peri-urban invasions or unauthorized colonies present a different typology. These have been comparatively of a recent origin. The form of development, which includes commercial and industrial activities, besides residential, is often imitation of modern planning patterns. The population in these settlements is predominantly formally employed migrants or having secure small business. Most of the structures/dwellings are owner occupied. The position of the services is comparatively better, as most of the structures have individual water supply, septic tanks and electricity. The development occurs through land grab or by purchase of erstwhile rural land which involves an organized, but informal market mechanism and a nexus of property agents, local politicians and officials.

Many a times the land is notified for acquisition by the Government under the Land Acquisition Act. However, the court cases, stay orders and pace of the acquisition induce the growth of unauthorised colonies, mainly by the land racketeers having a political clout around local power structure. The developers tend to sell off all the land with no parks, facilities and common areas, parking, etc. The buyers indulge in speculation, and illegally subdivide their plots, so that their investment is paid off by half of their land by its enhanced price after a couple of years.

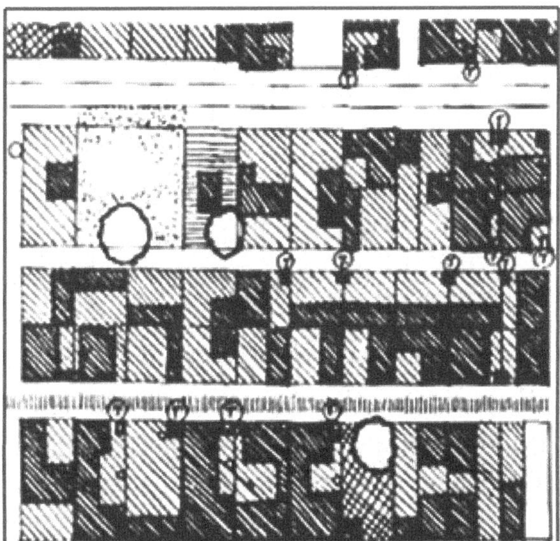

Fig. 7.4. East Angad Nagar indicating progressive sub-division of plots on narrow streets with no common space and having 90 to 95% area under plots

Fig. 7.5. Evolutionary growth of an unauthorised colony. The photograph indicates progressive construction and sub-division of plots as the land prices jump with political assurance of its regularization

Fig. 7.6. Layout Plan of Janakpuri Unauthorized Colony, Average Plot Size 100 to 200 sqm

The unplanned developments are broadly characterized by the following:

- Buildings are usually structurally unsafe and dilapidated, do not conform to the building byelaws and are deficient in basic services, facilities and open space.
- Encroachments and appropriation of public lands, roads, railways, and land earmarked for parks, public facilities and utilities.
- Illegal conversion of green areas and agricultural land in contravention of the Master Plan/Zonal Plan and DCR.
- Transactions of lands by Power of Attorney, non-legal tenure and non-payment of stamp duty.
- Violation of various laws, such as ULB/Development Authority Acts, Town Planning Act, Land Reforms Act, Stamp Duty Act, Property Registration Act, etc.

Fig. 7.7. Abul Fazal Enclave–an Illegal Colony in River Zone, which is a no construction zone. The Delhi Development Authority vide notification dated 28th September 2013 decided to exclude an area of 3109 Ha under 70 unauthorised colonies from 8070 Ha covered by the river (Zone 'O') by changing its boundary, which was nixed by the judiciary

Against the popular notion that it is the poor who squat on public lands, there is a growing trend of 'neo-colonisation' by the nexus of property dealers, officials, political leaders, middle income group and 'neo-rich.' In extreme cases, if the political pressure does not work, the people get stay orders from the courts for any punitive action and payment of development charges. This has made the process of unauthorised colonies unstoppable. The general impression is that punitive action and demolition are faced by the common-man, while the powerful manage to escape the law. This also raises a question on the relevance of the planning regulations and building bye-laws, while the large areas and colonies grow up without any planning compliances and building plan approval.

The unplanned areas have a huge population and illegalities are a major source of corruption and rent seeking. They are also vote banks and political patronage is always at hand. As such, in spite of court orders, the local bodies hardly take any punitive actions, to check the illegal buildings and spread of such colonies. On the contrary the regularisation of unauthorised colonies is announced from time to time and special laws are enacted to protect them. With time, these colonies are serviced by the public departments with roads, water supply, sewer lines and electric connections. Although sites for community facilities, such as schools, dispensaries, parks, etc. are shown in the regularisation plans, these are neither appropriated nor developed.

Fig. 7.8. Dwellings in unauthorized colony are non-engineered and without approval of building plan, having the risk of being unsafe

Irrespective of status of land and land use, the unauthorized colonies are regularized and constructions are exempted from safety requirements, many of which are dangerous. The local bodies under political pressures do not take any action for mandatory collection of development charges, penalties or land cost.

Fig. 7.9. An Unauthorized Colony in Delhi

Fig. 7.10. An unauthorized colony in East Delhi. Irrespective of land use, regularisation plan, building bye-laws and status of land, the individual structures keep growing

The process of regularization and redevelopment involves conducting physical surveys and socio-economic surveys, population, density, land use, ownership of land, etc. The preparation of development plan may require collection of development charges and acquisition of the pockets required for roads, community facilities and infrastructure services. The estimates of the development works are proposed for undertaking site development, levelling, dressing, construction of roads, laying of services, viz. water supply, sewer lines, drainage and electric lines, etc. However, in spite of an approved regularization plan, the buildings continue to be built without any approval and compliance to the plan. The area earmarked for parks, schools and other facilities got built up, no one surrendered any land for widening of roads, nor paid the development charges.

Khirki Extension

Khirki Extension came up during late 70s when builders constructed houses on agricultural land belonging to Khirki village without any approval from the civic bodies. During 80s and 90s, hundreds of illegal buildings were constructed and sold to homebuyers. Khirki village, which used to be within the limit to Khirki Fort, also expanded its boundaries by constructing houses on the agricultural lands. Today Khirki Extension has approximately 15,000 buildings having upto seven floors.

Spread over eight blocks, half of the population of Khirki Extension comprises people living in rented accommodations. People from Nigeria, Uganda and some other African countries started settling here five to six years ago, most of them living in J-3 and J-4 block. The biggest problem is lack of civic amenities, water, sanitation and roads. Groundwater has almost depleted and water connections have not been provided. RWAs allege that their repeated requests to various authorities against ongoing illegal construction went unheard.

Concept of Urban Renewal

In spite of various issues like dilapidation and congestion, the Indian cities have a huge stock of housing, large number of which are self built and serve the poor. Low income households are capable of improving their own housing conditions and to supply rooms or accommodation for their extended family. The people themselves, against the plans, have demonstrated a potential for investing and gradually developing housing, adequate to meet their needs. Their resources can be matched with public resources to increase the speed and efficiency of housing delivery process. This requires a radical change in the planning process that involves people in the delivery system and transforming unplanned housing development into planned development. Thus, transformation can be seen to be a means of renewing the housing stock and adding accommodation and services. This reminds us that planning and design is setting the context for a process rather than completing a product.

The concept of urban renewal had its bearings in Europe in 1940s after the cities were destroyed by bombardment during the Second World War. Large scale clearance of old, runaway part and destructed areas of a city was undertaken and new housing, commercial centers, roads and facilities were planned and built with the aim of economic and social revitalization. However, Jane Jacobs, the author of Death and Life of Great American Cities, in the fifties observed that *the city planners sought to modernize the civic landscape, bulldozing old building and erecting 'super block' filled with high rises and elevated highways, which caused large scale displacements and eviction of the poor.*

The concept of urban renewal as a process of re-development and upgradation of old city and unplanned areas gained currency in India in the 1960s in Delhi Master Plan. It aimed to regenerate the old city by redevelopment, rehabilitation and conservation, along with augmentation of infrastructure services, amenities and greens, while retaining the existing communities and their livelihoods.

Fig. 7.11. Master Plan for Delhi (1962) introduced the concept of urban renewal for old city of Shahjahanabad and adjacent areas

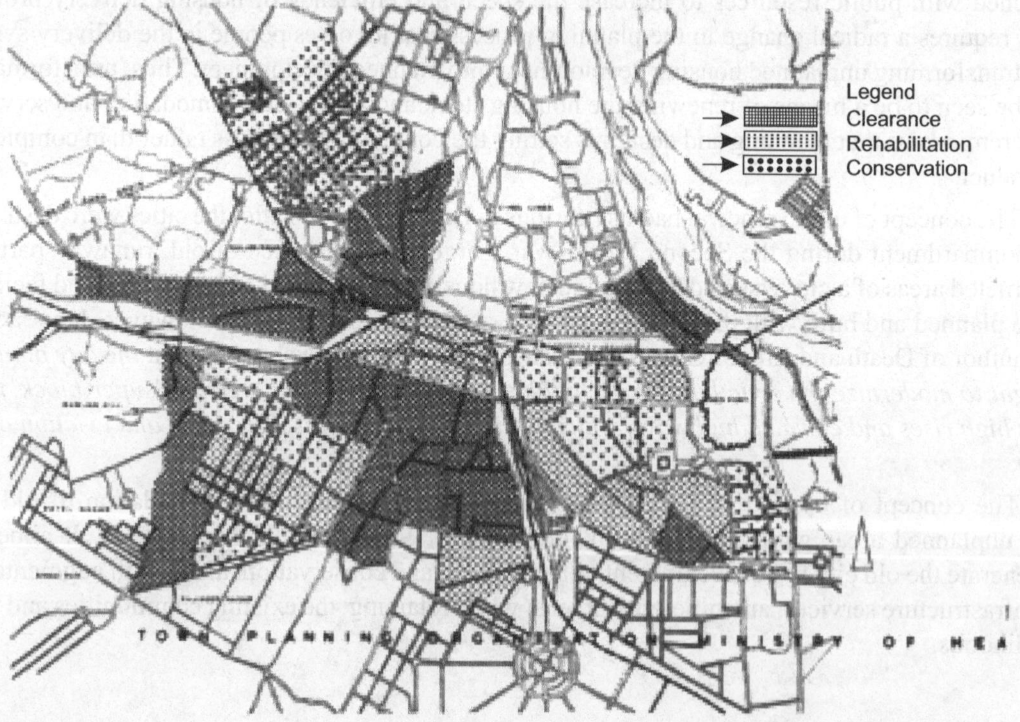

Fig. 7.12. Identification of clearance, rehabilitation and conservation areas in Old Delhi in Master Plan for Delhi (1962)

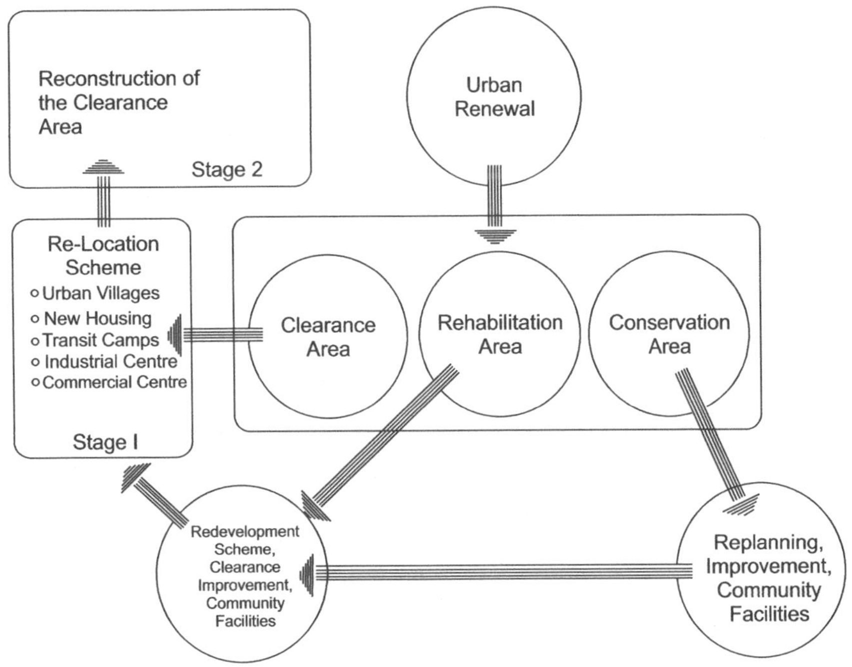

Fig. 7.13. Functional Affinity of Urban Renewal

Source: *Draft Master Plan for Delhi (1960), Work Studies*

Fig. 7.14. Chawri Bazaar in Shahjahanabad, Delhi

The urban areas were identified into Clearance, Rehabilitation and Conservation zones, based on an empirical analysis as given below:

Table 7.1: Multiple Index-Walled City Zone (Delhi)

Indicators	I		II		III		IV	
	%	Index	%	Index	%	Index	%	Index
% of households with income less than Rs 100	67	160	23	55	24	57	29	69
% of households living in temporary structures	82	820	24	240	14	140	8	80
% of household without water	64	152	33	79	8	19	5	12
% of household without latrine	79	304	12	46	4	15	8	31
% of household without electricity	88	154	44	77	23	40	8	14
% of household without kitchen	86	139	23	37	43	69	50	81
Average number of persons per living room	3.5	103	3.9	115	4.2	124	3.1	91
Multiple index		262		93		66		54
Rank		14		8		3		1

Evaluation Criteria: >125 Clearance Area

75 to 125 Rehabilitation

< 75 Conservation

Source: *Draft Master Plan for Delhi–Work Studies (1960)*

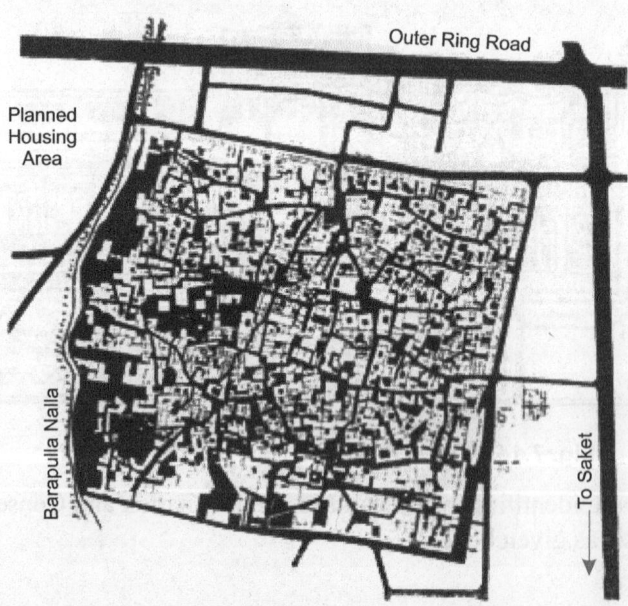

Fig. 7.15. Morphology of Village Chiragh, Delhi—low rise, high density with shops along main roads. A large number of squares (chowks), temples and mosques dot the streets. Closely knit fabric of structures keep out harsh sun and hot winds

However, the Master Plan proposals of urban renewal could not be implemented, except in some isolated projects, like Dujana House and Turkman Gate, mainly due to political and public resistance, financial and other problems.

The replacement of traditional, organic and indigenous urban form of the Old City by formal, modern apartment blocks has not been welcome by the people. It is a mute edifice which reminds that the concept of urban renewal, pigeonholed under the physical manifestations, like slums, overcrowding and blight have marginalized the core issues of housing for the poor. The priorities, such as decongestion, open space, land use zoning, building bye-laws and physical accessibility do not coincide with those of the local community. This is a clear expression of separation of planning program from the priorities of housing the poor and cultural and social values.

Jawaharlal Nehru National Urban Renewal Mission

The Government of India undertook a countrywide program of urban renewal under the Jawaharlal Nehru National Urban Renewal Mission (JNNURM), which comprised the following:

- Basic Services for Urban Poor, Slum Rehabilitation and Housing:
  - Water Supply
  - Sewerage
  - Road Network and Transportation System
    Storm Water Drainage
  - Solid Waste Management
  - Heritage and Conservation
  - City Environment
- Urban Infrastructure and Governance

The raison-d-etre' of urban renewal has been to conserve, rehabilitate, regenerate and revitalize the existing urban areas. However, under the urban renewal mission and its sub-mission, half of the total investments were made on urban transport and buses. Urban Housing and Slum Rehabilitation received only 18% and urban heritage and conservation meager 2% of JNNURM investments. Many cities could not avail financial assistance due to complex procedures.

Urban Renewal in China

During the Cultural Revolution in China, housing situation in the city of Beijing stagnated. It was of poor quality and unplanned with inadequate infrastructure. The number of rundown houses continued to increase and housing standards in new construction were reduced. In 1973, the Municipal Government was forced to deal with the housing crisis in the city and some development took place, including the notorious high rise blocks built in contravention to height limits, just a few hundred meters from the Tiananmen Square.

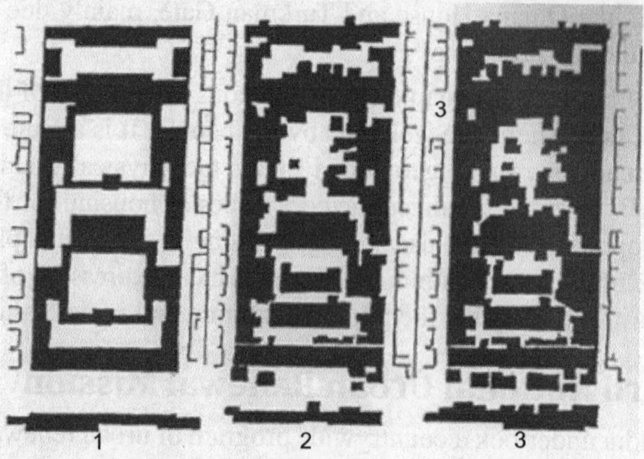

1. 1950s floor space 2440 sm, courtyard complex
2. Late 1970 floor space 3196 sm multi-household compound
3. 1987 floor space 3796 sm 155% of that in early 1950s, Courtyardless compound

Fig. 7.16. Infilling of Courtyards in traditional housing clusters in Beijing

Source: *BSHF (1995) Housing in Beijing, BSHF, London*

A survey of the run-down housing districts of Beijing was carried out in 1990 and showed the following:

- There were more than 20 million square meters of single storey houses in the city, which accounted for 44 per cent of the built up area.
- 10 million square meters of these single storey houses were in condition of grade III, IV or V (on a scale of five grades, number I being the best).
- There were 128 separate areas of run-down housing in the inner city, accounting for 60 per cent of the low grade housing.
- Two officially preserved areas of the city's old housing account for only 3 per cent of this 10 million square meters, the rest is virtually abandoned.
- General conditions of roads, infrastructure and services in and around these areas are poor and most houses have no sanitation, kitchen or other basic facilities.
- Very high densities lead to severe overcrowding with floor area per person of less than 2 square meters. This led to deterioration of dwellings, over-use of services and courtyards, public square-corridors, stairways, plumbing, etc. The balconies were converted into store-rooms or living space that created a dismal appearance.

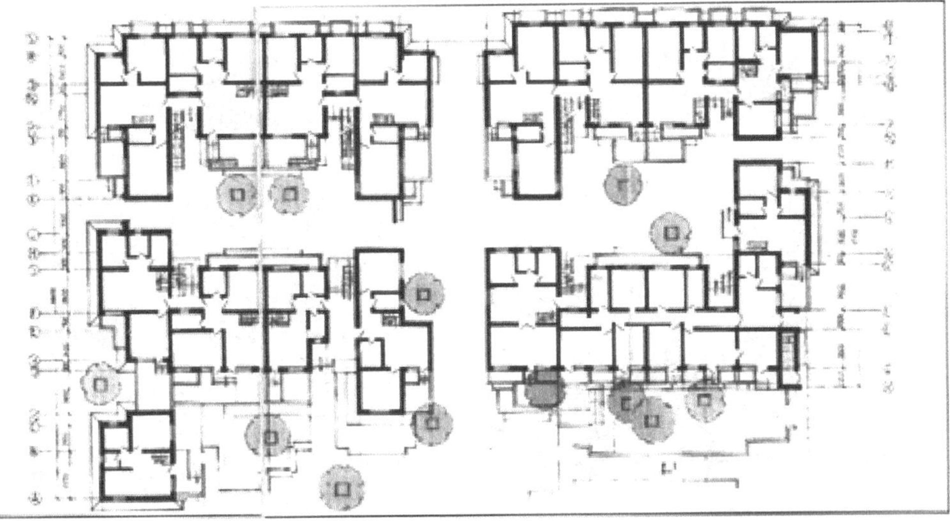

Fig. 7.17. Urban Renewal Plan of four storied courtyard housing for the inner city, Beijing

Source: *BSHF (1995) Housing in Beijing, BSHF, London*

In the year 2000, a comprehensive housing plan was developed for China, and the housing standards prescribed a minimum area of 7.5 square meters per person (8 square meter in Beijing). Gross density of population was increased to 600-800 persons per hectare (from an average of 300 persons per Ha). The industrialised building systems were encouraged for housing. It was mandated that an average apartment size shall have 56 sqm in low-rise and 62-64 sqm in high-rise blocks, with water and electricity, sewerage, gas supply, heating and ventilation system, wardrobe, kitchen range, basin, bath and WC.

Increased emphasis was placed on wide range of facilities—health, social, commercial, sports, recreation, parks and better environmental conditions in the residential districts. Redevelopment of run-down housing areas was given a high priority, which improved the living conditions of the poor.

Housing Renewal in Japan

Cities like Tokyo, Osaka and Kyoto in Japan during the 1960s-70s faced huge shortage of land and housing. On the other hand, its economy was developing rapidly. It faced a paradox of conservation of cultural heritage, while meeting the goal of modern, comfortable and spacious housing. To address these issues a strategy for housing transformation was developed based on minimum intervention in the areas of cultural significance while keeping in view the constraint of non-availability of lands. Based on demographic, economic, social and physical surveys, including housing and land records, a voluntary strategy was developed for self-starting housing renewal. The government agencies developed the local area plan indicating widening of the roads, common facilities, parks and the services—water, power, sanitation, drainage and solid waste management with minimum interventions, and appropriation of lands for these against incentive Floor Area Ratio. Such developments were guided by Special Regulations, and were exempted from general building bye-laws. The government agencies facilitated joint development and also provided financial help and subsidies. These resulted in optimum utilization of urban land and better and more spacious housing.

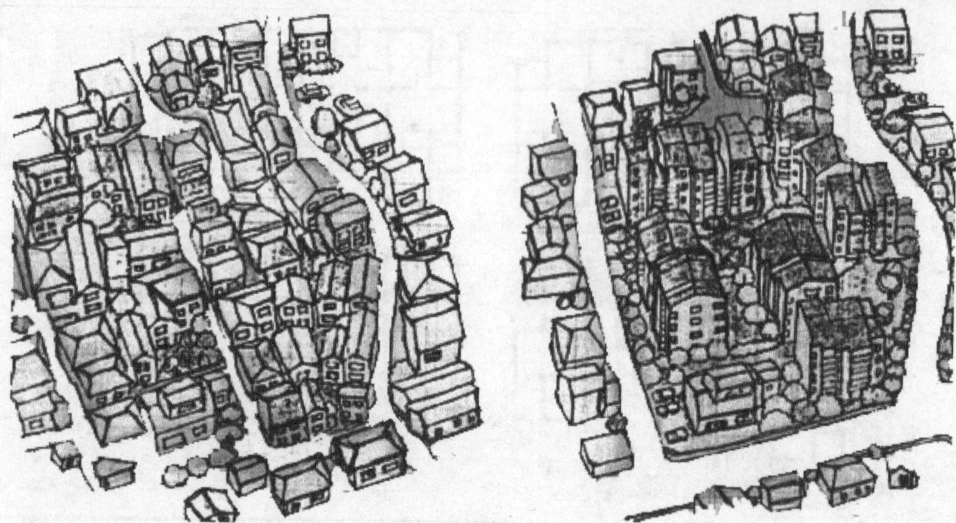

Fig. 7.18. Urban Renewal in Japan: Congested housing areas with single storied houses were replaced by multi-storied housing releasing ground for roads, parks and common facilities. Special regulations enabled combination of properties for joint development, with certain exemptions from general building bye-laws

An Agenda for Housing Transformation

The key point of success of housing transformation in China, Japan and elsewhere indicates that it is necessary for the government and planning authorities to set up a facilitating environment for the process, and not to be an actor by itself. This needs special regulations and certain exemptions from the conventional legal framework. The process has to be local, participatory, community led and voluntary. As such, the housing transformation is guided by the following principles:

1. **Community as an integral part of the shelter process and the city:** In the upgrading process communities should plan and implement their improvements as part of a comprehensive, collaborative process. This involves surveying the settlements and then preparing upgrading plans which attempt to resolve the tenure, housing and infrastructure problems. This is a way to link the housing problems of the city's poorer citizens with the larger town planning process. This is very different than the conventional project-by-project approach, in which a few scattered communities may be improved, but because they are neither linked with each other, nor linked to the other development processes in the city, they have no strength. In the alternative model, it is the communities who take decisions and do all the work, whereas the government takes the role of facilitator and supporter. In this way, the upgrading process can trigger transformations in the city's larger development process, in which communities are increasingly accepted as legitimate and valuable partners.
2. **Secure tenure:** An important aspect of the upgradation program is to secure land tenure, which is seen as the foundation of secure, sustainable communities. It should be up to the communities to negotiate their own tenure arrangements as a pre-condition to participate in the upgrading program, through such strategies as cooperative land purchase, long-term lease contracts, land-swapping or user rights. These negotiations can be made

individually by communities or collectively by larger networks, but the main emphasis is on obtaining collective, rather than individual land tenure.

3. **Communities and their networks as core actors:** Most conventional housing programs for the poor run into trouble because they depend upon the government agency, and not the people to do all the work. In most cases, that agency cannot keep up with the scale of need. The strategy of using the strength of the communities and city-based partnerships in which communities take the lead to solve the problem of housing, should be the starting point in the process of developing capacities to resolve local housing problems.
4. **"Demand-driven" approach rather than "supply driven":** The new approach should allow the communities that are ready to implement the improvement projects themselves and evolve a program that creates a "demand driven" approach to community upgrading. This is something different from the more conventional "supply-driven" approach, in which the State constructs housing units or infrastructural facilities according to the plans.
5. **Let people control the money:** A radical innovation of the program should be that the money is controlled by the communities, once they have developed their upgrading plans and negotiated their land tenure status. By placing the money directly into people's hands, the program would put communities in control of the upgrading process, instead of a government agency or an NGO. The people themselves would decide how to use the subsidies. A community may decide, for example, to set up a special fund to buy building materials cheaply in bulk. A flexible financial management process would allow communities to make these decisions themselves, and to manage their construction in ways that match the realities of their lives, while its multi-party participation provides transparency and self-assessment at every step of the process.
6. **Make efficient use of state resources:** In an upgrading model the communities are the implementors and control the finances. When communities plan and decide together how to use the budget, they get very thrifty and very creative, a thousand variations and innovations occur naturally, bringing out all the untapped resourcefulness. Besides improving their roads, drains and water supply systems, they could build a community centre, plant trees or anything the whole community identifies as priorities.
7. **Allow people to choose their own helpers:** An important aspect of the program should be that the communities and the local actors have the freedom to select NGOs, architects, institutions or builders they would like to assist them in the process of developing their community improvement plans. In this way, new partnerships between communities, local governments and other organisations can be established together with more flexibility in the program management.
8. **Promote a broader concept of upgrading:** In order to promote a much broader, holistic and more integrated process of community improvement. Beyond physical improvements and tenure security, it is necessary to integrate social, environmental and economic well-being of the local communities. Because physical change is something immediately tangible, it can be a potent means to bring about other deeper, but less tangible changes to social structures, managerial systems and confidence within the poor communities.
9. **Promote variations rather than standard solutions:** Existing upgradation and new relocation sites usually follow a rigid set of planning/design standards and engineering norms. As a result, all these layouts look the same, regardless of where they were or who

lived there. In fact, it is possible to upgrade old communities and design them in the spatial patterns which can often bring charm and delight to informal settlements, winding lanes, houses built in clusters around quiet cul-de-sacs, shady places to get together and sit, places for markets and temples, playgrounds, etc.

To improve the living conditions and tenure security of about one-third of urban population is a staggering task. The big challenge is how to ensure that the communities lead the process, with local cooperation between stakeholders for implementing the upgradation plans.

The Strategy

Care has to be taken in privatization of the housing market, which often leads to enhanced homelessness due to economic marginalization and vanishing affordable shelter. The ongoing economic restructuring and reforms may result in dismantling or reduction of the welfare services. The programmes to enhance efficiency and productivity in a competitive model via transfer of land, assets and services to the private sector may endanger the sustenance of the homeless and very poor. Indian cities are witnessing a new order of high wage occupations and emergence of affluent families which are claiming the urban territory and buying out the prime areas occupied by the poor. Low-cost housing areas are getting replaced by non-residential or expensive housing units.

To promote a comprehensive housing upgradation and development, which brings about improvements in all aspects of people's lives, it is necessary to take into consideration the comprehensive upgrading plans. Pilot upgrading projects should be organized in as many clusters as possible to demonstrate how community-driven upgrading can be done and provide a set of examples of how upgrading can provide opportunities for "learning by doing" through actual implementation.

Synchronize Shelter and Poverty Reduction: A major priority area of intervention in promoting a synchronised development of shelter and poverty reduction is to evolve a new policy and planning framework, and removing barriers in the development of low income housing linked with micro-enterprise. There is a need for the state/local bodies to formulate decentralized programmes, which allow various options for community based shelter, with the technical, administrative, legal and financial supports from the State.

In order to establish closer links between shelter and poverty reduction, it is necessary to revise the concepts of planning, land tenure and building regulations. It involves a transformation in the relationship among the people, government, urban planners/managers and the land/resources/ financial institutions.

Writing about home-based enterprises and hawkers in Delhi, Surbaya and Pretoria, Graham Tipple of the University of Newcastle upon Tyne, concludes that "*they should be accorded more attention by policy-makers – not to control them, but to find ways of cooperating with entrepreneurs to assist them to be effective and efficient. Other reason why cities need vendors on streets and not in designated food courts, is because hawkers are the eyes of the street and prevent violent crime. Our city roads are safer because of them.*"

These provide self-employment opportunities to a large number of the poor and the middle-income groups and also make the residential areas more secure and comfortable. On other hand environmental degradation, structural and fire risks, overstressed infrastructure services and parking are the downsides of Home Based Enterprises.

It is necessary to adopt a comprehensive approach towards housing transformations, keeping in view the tolerance levels from environmental, traffic/parking and availability of services. A fundamental premise could be to exempt small enterprises and housing extensions in low income settlements from the ambit of conversion/permission charges, licensing, commercial charges for electricity and revision of property tax. This will obviate the harassment to the poor and small entrepreneurs and strengthen the city economy.

Fire and structural safety for every building /house cannot be compromised. These can be delinked from building plan approval, land tenure/ ownership and layout plan approval. This would enable every building owner to procure a structural and fire safety certificate, which is segregated from the regularisation of construction and occupancy/completion certificate.

Optimum Utilisation of Urban Land

Most of the Indian cities witness gross under-utilization of urban land. In Delhi, for instance, residential developments by DDA have under-utilized land, both in its plotted and group housing schemes. On the other hand, public owned lands under encroachment and irregular/unauthorized colonies are written off by sweeping regularization. The regularization of unauthorized colonies in Delhi and such developments in the guise of cooperatives in Jaipur are illustrative examples.

Attempts at densification of under-utilized built-up lands in the cities have usually met with little success largely due to the absence of an adequate implementation framework. These are also hijacked for real estate development. For instance, the government policy of permitting release of land under-polluting, sick mills in Delhi, Mumbai and Kolkata was intended to increase the housing supply. However, in Delhi the prime areas under DCM land at Bara Hindu Rao and industrial areas on Najafgarh Road have been used for providing low density posh housing. Tatas have built 4-bedroom houses in the poshest location in Mumbai for the rich, and other prime lands are being used for spacious luxury residences. Thus a major opportunity for conserving scarce land and providing houses for the poor is lost.

It is common to witness multi-storied and expensive housing under the policies of redevelopment and Transit Oriented Development (TOD), where enhanced FAR is granted. The conversion of houses on plots to apartments and so called farm houses and low density residential policy for their conversion violate the principle of equity, restrictions imposed by development control norms and property transfer rules. These overlook the principle of mandatory reservation of land for social housing. The market pressure and process of redevelopment often result into infrastructural stress and inequities.

A Comprehensive Framework

There is a need to rethink and review the redevelopment, TOD and Infill Development norms, guidelines and principles, which are equitous, promote affordable housing (both rental and ownership), and discourage speculative 'property development.'

The increase in FAR and density should synchronize with enhanced green/open spaces, social/community facilities, infrastructure services, parking, etc. The concept of "accommodation reservation," *i.e.* allowing incentive FAR to land-owner against the provision of community facilities in private plots, can be invoked for built-up area and regularised unauthorised colonies. In this way the community facility would be made available free of cost and without putting burden on the urban local body. Land Pooling and Transfer of Development Rights can also help in making lands available for roads, parks, facilities and social housing. Such techniques are viable alternatives to compulsory land acquisition. Mixed use and commercial activity in part of the plot can be allowed against compensation for land appropriation.

The concept of housing transformation cannot take off, unless the municipal bye-laws for approval of building plans are reviewed. There is a great scope to upgrade and redevelop old, dilapidated housing areas, urbanized villages and irregular colonies, which should be taken up in a comprehensive planning framework and their integration into the wider urban system as "self-serviced" settlements. Such comprehensive framework should be differentiated according to the type of area. As an example, these norms may be on the following lines:

- Gradual and voluntary transformation of dilapidated, unplanned housing areas by collective and joint redevelopment.
- Facilitating the conversion of isolated plots into group housing with incentive FAR (say 50% over and above permissible) and additional FAR (15 to 20 per cent) for mandatory EWS/LIG housing.
- 10 per cent of land or FAR for commercial use, 10 per cent of land or FAR for social facilities and 15 to 20 per cent of land for greens.

Incentive FAR and the concept of Accommodation Reservation can be effective tools in provision of community facilities without land acquisition. Often in view of the disputed land ownership, non-approval of building plans of existing buildings and lack of an approved layout plan, the ULB does not find it possible to approve the redevelopment and building plans. There is a need to work out a more pragmatic procedure for the approval of redevelopment/regularization plans and building plans. This requires certain exemptions from the existing building bye-laws which should focus more at the cluster level, whereby the owners come together and reorganize their individual properties so as to provide minimum roads, common green, soft parking and common facilities. The amalgamation and reconstitution of the individual plots may be permitted and incentivized with an extra FAR and density. The standards of minimum width of roads and community facilities can be relaxed, wherever justified by planning considerations.

For augmenting the physical infrastructure, it is vital to work out a phased and evolutionary programs and plans of facilities and services, which allows improvement at a later date. The introduction of decentralised system of sewerage, water treatment, power generation, waste recycling and spatial characteristics of infrastructure, including the cost of installation, maintenance and distribution system should be the determinants in the mode of aggregation of the housing redevelopment. It is necessary to promote 'area-wise' decentralised services for water treatment, sewerage and solid waste management, for which technology is already available in the country. Such systems can be installed and managed by the residents themselves, without burdening the state exchequer and local bodies.

Capacity Development and Financial Resources

Housing transformation cannot be accomplished without raising the capacity, skills and financial resources of the ULB/housing agency. The ULB/municipal authorities are responsible for preparation of urban renewal, regularization plans and redevelopment schemes. However, they suffer from severe capacity constraints. The setting up a SPV and outsourcing on a continued basis may be considered, and responsibility for this purpose may be decentralized. Pilot redevelopment projects can be taken up by the government/ULB to demonstrate the principles and viability of such projects.

Mobilising private capital can be done through various instrumentalities, such as using land as a resource and by levy of development and betterment charges. A crucial aspect in this regard relates to the methodology of assessment and capture of the value of land in the process of redevelopment. It may be necessary to raise the resources from the market by issue of bonds and through various financial and asset management processes by enabling the ULB to get Credit Rated.

At present there is no system of a centralized and digital registry or record of rights in respect of urban properties, leading to disputes, under-taxation and various other problems. As observed by the Working Group on Financing of Urban Infrastructure, there should be a comprehensive registry of urban lands at all levels of government as a first step towards putting land based instruments to good use.

DEBRIEFING QUESTIONS

1. Explain the type of housing areas in a city.
2. What do you understand by the concept of Urban Renewal?
3. About 80 per cent of housing shortage in urban India is due to dilapidation, lack of space and services. How such areas can be transformed?
4. Write notes in the following:
   (*a*) Multiple Index System for urban renewal
   (*b*) JNNURM
   (*c*) AMRUT
5. Briefly explain the following:
   (*a*) Process of public participation in Housing and Urban Renewal
   (*c*) Demand driven approach
   (*d*) Decentralised services
   (*e*) Bankable approach to urban renewal.

8

SHELTER FOR ELDERLY, DISABLED, HOMELESS, MIGRANTS, WOMEN AND STUDENTS

A city caters to everyone both—young and old, poor and rich, and labourers and professionals. They all have right to city and shelter. Care of the elderly, handicapped, poor migrants, transit labour, women and students is a moral and ethical responsibility of the society for which housing has a major role. Accordingly, inclusive housing should provide the shelter to all.

Senior Citizens : The population of senior citizens as a percentage of total population, which stood at 7.5 per cent as per the census, is likely to increase to 12.4 per cent in 2026, as per the report *of the Technical Group* constituted by the National Commission on Population. According to UN projections, the overall population in India by the year 2050 will grow by 55 per cent, but that of 60 + people will increase by 326 per cent. Alarmingly, there would be a 700 per cent increase in the 80 + age group, making India an ultra-age society.

The Maintenance and Welfare of Parents and Senior Citizens Act, 2007 seeks to ensure that the elderly are not deprived of basic amenities like food, healthcare and housing. However, the parents, grandparents and senior citizens are sometimes dispossessed of their property and find themselves unable to maintain themselves.

Disabled : It is estimated that in India about 27 million, that is about 2% of the population, are disabled. A large section of these people are poor and lack appropriate housing. The Person with Disability (Equal Opportunities, Protection of Rights and Full Participation) Act, 1996 mandates non-discrimination, equal opportunities and protects the rights to full participation for persons with disabilities. This, therefore, requires that spaces be designed to suit the needs of all persons with disabilities. Also, Model Building Bye Laws, 2015 mandate that barrier free environments are maintained to ensure inclusive cities and universal design. Different types of disabilities as categorized below, need special types of housing and barrier free environment:

(*a*) **Non-ambulatory :** Impairments that, regardless of cause or manifestation, for all practical purposes, confine individual to wheel chair.

(*b*) **Semi-ambulatory :** Impairment that cause individual to walk with difficulty or insecurity. Individuals using braces or crutches, amputees, arthritis, spastics, and those with pulmonary and cardiac ills may be semi-ambulatory.

(*c*) **Sight :** Total blindness or impairments affecting sight to an extent that the individual functioning in public areas is insecure or exposed to danger.

(*d*) **Hearing:** Deafness or hearing handicaps that might make an individual insecure in public areas because he is unable to communicate or hear warning signals.

Migrants and Transit Households : As per census, 2011 there are 487 million workers in India of which around 30% are migrants. A large population of these are urban poor and destitute, who are either homeless or lives in shacks, slums or share accommodation with their relatives or friends. They not necessarily need a permanent home nor may afford it, but transit, rental accommodation would meet their immediate needs. Besides the migrants, the families affected by natural disasters also need transit, temporary or emergency shelter.

An Expert Group set up by the Ministry of Urban Affairs and Employment estimated that about 3.9 million houses are susceptible to earthquakes of very high intensity, about two crore houses are susceptible to damage due to winds and about 9.3 million houses are susceptible to damage due to floods. The kutcha houses built from clay–mud, unburnt bricks and blocks, random stone in mud, mortar and burnt brick built in mud mortar are liable to damage and destruction under sustained heavy rains. Some 49 per cent of the total housing stock is liable to very high damage from one or the other natural hazard; while about 1% of the total housing stock gets destroyed every year. In an earthquake, 80% of the deaths are due to collapsing buildings. Brick and stone buildings without proper reinforcement, tiled/wooden roofs, built without proper framework and bracing are liable to collapse. Non-engineered buildings continue to be built in the areas prone to natural disasters. Driven by unemployment and poverty, millions of people are occupying disaster-prone areas. As per estimates the number of people affected by disasters has been increasing by 6% every year since 1960.

The Homeless : The Census of India defines homeless people as those not living in "census houses," *i.e.* a structure without a roof. Planners charged with providing housing land to deserving cases classify a person as eligible for the housing and land allocation programmes if they do not have a roof or land. Thus, residents of 'Jhuggi and Jhompri' clusters (squatter areas) are entitled to a plot in a regularised area only if their housing is cleared. However, if a household has a plot in a regularised area but only a poor and insubstantial shack on it, he is not regarded as homeless because of the land holding.

Only those people having no form of roof and shelter are homeless. They include people living on the street, without cover. Homeless people have poor quality shelters made of plastic, fabric, cardboard, bamboo, discarded construction and demolition waste, etc. These are often without water supply and sanitation facilities and may have an illegal power connection. They often :

- Have little physical security,
- Do not have address or identity,
- Develop few social networks,
- Have little access to government assistance,
- Tend to gravitate to the centre of the cities to support opportunistic lifestyles.

The two fundamental causes of homelessness are :

- Poverty.
- The failure of the housing supply system.

In India rural poverty has driven large number of people to seek employment in cities. Most often a single man will move to the city to work and send money back to the family home. In this case they prefer to save money for their families rather than spending on accommodation. The homeless prefer to stay in a shack, with a relative. In some cases other family members follow them to the city and live on or near the place of work in rudimentary shelters.

Poverty and housing shortage alone do not necessarily lead to homelessness. A number of other issues make these things worse:

- Rural to urban migration
- Social causes
- Political unrest
- Evictions.

Homeless people are moved generally because :

- They are perceived as a nuisance
- They disturb the attractiveness of the city
- They offer a poor image of the city during important civic events.

In India, it is quite common for government to use their powers to evict people who have neither the money nor the power to defend themselves. People are evicted to:

- Clear land for more valuable development
- Improve the city's image for special civic events

Often such evictions:

- Are violent
- Disrupt newly formed social networks
- Cause trauma amongst the evicted
- Affect children
- Cause greater poverty amongst the evicted

The Mumbai, Prevention of Begging Act is used to clear the streets of homeless people when important events are to take place or for cosmetic clearing of the streets.

The importance of shelter was highlighted by the deaths of several hundred people in Delhi in January 2003, when the temperature dropped to minus 2 degree centigrade at night. The night shelters provide bedding, water and sanitation. As a temporary measure, schools and government buildings provide additional support services to the homeless people.

The shortage of housing is often the root cause of homelessness and the poorer households are hit hardest as they miss out in the market. As such, there is a need for housing that the poorest households can afford. It should be:

- Cheap and rental.
- Built with local, low cost technologies.
- Situated close to places of work.
- Serviced to a minimum level.

An innovative approach was adopted in Mumbai where the police trained street children in traffic control. They were given uniforms and put to work for the city. The scheme was so successful that it was extended after the first year. Many NGOs also provide support for street children and youth by the provision of food and healthcare. The street children project in Bangalore offers a combination of accommodation, education and employment training within a fairly rigid timetable. The project is always so much crowded that there is a suspicion that parents might abandon their children. Aashray Adhikar Abhiyan, Delhi is a shelter rights campaigning organisation, which works with homeless people. It provides legal advice as well as one-to-one support to access a range of services, such as doctors.

Another NGO, the Society for the Promotion of Area Resource Centre (SPARC), has an alliance with the National Slum Dwellers Federation and Mahila Milan. Together they support 60,000 low-income people to move voluntarily from their settlements besides the railway tracks of Mumbai to safer and legitimate areas. The people help to plan settlements without forced eviction and without further impoverishment.

Working Women and Widows: With rising education levels large number of women employed in urban areas face the chronic shortage of safe and affordable housing. Many of them are unmarried/ single, widowed. As per Census 2011, there are 56 million widows (4.6% of population) in India, many of whom face the problem of housing.

University Students: During last decades, India had a galloping enrollment in higher education, which is in order of 28.56 million. Many of them are migrants and are not provided with the hostel accommodation. As a result, they pay through their nose for paying guest accommodation or live in sub-let substandard rooms. They do not require the standard dwelling unit, but affordable, clean and quiet hostels with day-to-day services, such as food and laundry would suffice.

Young Professionals and Workers: It is estimated that one-third of the urban working population (33 to 40%) comprises single, young professionals and workers. Most of them seek shelter in sub-letting room, barrack or a garage. Well to do among them may find temporary rental accommodation in an expensive paying guest house, dormitory or a small hotel. They neither need nor can afford to buy a house in view of transit nature of the job.

Housing for Elderly

Meeting the housing needs of older people is a tremendous challenge for the governments and to civil society. In the built-environment, the needs of the older persons include the following pertinent areas of concern:

(*a*) Housing;

(*b*) Health and community facilities;

(*c*) Services and transport; and,

(*d*) Open space, recreation and outdoor environment.

Various schemes for construction of old age homes and multi-service centres for older persons have been worked out. It is proposed that housing schemes for urban and rural lower income segments should earmark 10 per cent of the houses/house sites for allotment to older persons, besides easy access to loans for purchase of housing and for major repairs. The layouts of housing clusters should ensure that there are no physical barriers to mobility and accessibility to shopping complexes, community centres, parks and other services, which should be safe and easy. A multi-purpose centre for older persons should be provided in housing clusters. Segregation of older persons in housing area has to be avoided as it prevents interaction with the rest of the community. Preference should be given to older persons in the allotment of flats on the ground floor.

In housing of older persons, common service facilities for meals, laundry, common room and rest rooms should be provided. They should have easy access to community services, medicare, parks, recreation and cultural centres. The design should be carefully considered the prevention of accidents and enhance safety, taking cognizance of reduced physical capacity and infirmities. Noise and other forms of pollution affect children, the sick and older persons more adversely, which should be controlled and enforced. Older persons should be given consideration in promptly dealing with matters relating to transfer of property, mutation, property tax and other matters.

The theme of "Adding Life to the Years" is replacing the conventional 'Adding Years to Life.' The aspect of health is becoming increasingly important for both older persons and society at large for the lifelong enjoyment of active and happy lives. This implies launching health promotion programmes dedicated to the older persons with the joint efforts of the NGOs/voluntary agencies, government, local bodies and the private sector in a bid to advance the health-promotion activities and the creation of an environment to support such activities. There is a need to identify the needs of the older people and work out norms for the development of such facilities. For spreading the awareness Citizens' Council on Health Promotion can be constituted to further health promotion activities on a local basis.

For dissemination of information, education and awareness of health promotion, health festivals and other relevant events can be very helpful. Model health promotion projects at the community level, including the conduct of health campaigns and the preparation of manuals for the health promotion movement can be regularly taken up by the voluntary groups and government/local bodies. Yoga, meditation centers, indigenous health systems and lifelong sports facilities should be promoted for healthy living of older people. A 'Life Plaza' can be established in each zone of the city to support health promotion, nutrition and to provide information with regard to indigenous health systems.

A comprehensive approach will be to design a system comprising norms and standards for health and community facilities. Construction of geriatric hospital facilities, including nursing homes for the elderly should relate to easy accessibility. Health facilities include nutrition, recreation and other supports for the elderly.

Besides health facilities, the development of special community facilities for serving the elderly is equally important. For an environment of convenience, a system of essential facilities and services should be evolved integrating the community, accessibility, transport and housing with the facilities. A system for supporting elderly people's life may comprise comprehensive social welfare centres, Silver Human Resource Centre/Training Institutions, institutions for protecting the rights of disabled and the elderly healthcare information centres, Rehabilitation and Medical Centers, Geriatric Hospitals, nursing homes, information counseling, household services, community welfare services, emergency communication, clubs, sports and swimming pools and, home-care service centres.

Older people can, and already do, make a significant contribution to society in a variety of ways. It is necessary to provide support and expand contribution in both scope and scale. This will help provide a sense of value and purpose, which is so essential for older population. A variety of organizations foster the use of their skills. The greater involvement of older people in society is one of the many ways in which they can remain busy, productive and active. They can be involved in teaching, in school management, either paid or as volunteers. This serves the purpose of increasing contact between the generations and pass on the skills and experience of the older people, as well as improving efficiency of the older people.

Other forms of destitute and transit accommodation prevalent in India have been ashram, dharmshala, orphanage, etc.

Ashram : Traditionally, the cities in India had ashrams which are philanthropic and are linked with the spiritual practices. These monasteries were locus of cultural activity such as yoga, music or religious meditation, etc. and were ideal places for retreats for the elderly to rest and relaxation.

As such, traditionaly ashram were located far from human habitation, in forests or mountainous regions, amidst natural surroundings conducive to spiritual instructions and meditation. Many ashrams also serve as gurukuls, residential schools for children under the guru-shishya tradition. These imbibe the values of simple living, service, devotion and discipline.

Temporary/Transit Shelter

There are four basic types of temporary transit settlements :

(*a*) **Reception or Transit Centre:** where displaced people or refugees stay for short periods. A reception and transit centres should be treated in the same way as a planned settlement, if it is large, having a population over 2,000, or is expected to last a long time. Environment resources will have to be carefully assessed to make sure that both displaced and local populations have enough water, fuel, and construction material and that the local economy and environment are not adversely affected.

(*b*) **Camps:** where people have settled spontaneously, yet require partial relocation, provide of infrastructure and sustainable environmental resources.

(*c*) **Temporary or Transit Barracks:** The barracks or tenements are constructed and serviced for a temporary period (say 2 years) before households are permanently resettled.

Military dormitory accommodation is generally in the form of barracks. It was for two persons per room, which has been phased out in favour of single occupancy. The toilet facilities were generally common, which is changing towards individual toilets. The 'mess' *i.e.* dining room is a prominent facility in a barrack. In hard areas open-bay barracks may house 10 to 12 persons per room. The model of barracks with variations has been extensively used in India for temporary rehabilitation of refugees, disaster victims and destitute. Private builders/ contractors also provide temporary barracks for their construction labour.

Night Shelter : Many migrants, labourers, workers, beggars in the city do not have shelter and live on pavements near their jobs. As a human right, they deserve to be accommodated in the night shelters, which should be located near the Railway Stations, Bus Terminals, major markets and work centers. Existing facility buildings can also be used for night shelter. Besides night shelter, there is a need to provide a network of old age homes, orphanage, women's hostel, anangwadi, transit-camps and dormitories.

Fig. 8.1. A modular prefabricated night shelter

General Guidelines for Transit/Temporary Shelter

The social structure and gender roles of the displaced population should be reflected in the planning of the settlement which should take into account needs for markets, meeting places, recreational areas and so on. These facilities are essential in supporting the re-establishment of the displaced communities. Existing forms of social representation should also be supported, given the importance of consultation with displaced people, particularly women, and their involvement in humanitarian interventions.

- The overall site should provide 20 to 40 sq.m. space for each person. This includes infrastructure (*e.g.* roads, sanitation, schools, offices, water systems, security fire-breaks, markets, storage facilities, shelter locations), but excludes land for agriculture.
- Clusters of modular units may be established.
- Land for possible further expansion may be identified.
- Ensure that is provision for social facilities such as markets, places of worship, cremation grounds, graveyards, health facilities, solid waste disposal, water, community nutrition centres, workshops and recreational areas.
- There may be provision for facilities required by humanitarian/local government and service agencies such as administrative offices, warehousing and staff accommodation.
- There should be adequate firebreaks of at least 2 metres between dwellings, 6 metres between clusters of dwellings, and 15 metres between blocks of cluster.
- Quarantine camps may be established, or sites be identified in isolation from general residential areas, in order to minimize the spread of an epidemic.
- Plastic sheeting: Plastic sheeting provided for shelter should meet specifications defined by UNHCR or BSI. Plastic sheeting for weather proofing damaged buildings should be followed BSI specifications/local building bye-laws.
- Damaged homes: Displaced people returning to homes damaged by war or natural disasters must be adequately supported. It is preferable to help people to make one room habitable, rather than providing collective accommodation. Victims of earthquakes should be discouraged from inhabiting damaged buildings.

Shelter Standards: Although shelter standard depends on the climate and the size of the household, on an average covered area of 3.5 to 4.5 sq. m. per person should be provided.

In warm, humid climates, shelter must be oriented and designed to maximize ventilation and prevent entry of direct sunlight, so the door and windows should preferably face north and south. The roof should have a good slope for rainwater drainage and have large overhangs. Appropriate orientation is important to maximize airflow; it should not be obstructed by neighbouring shelters. Shaded space outside the shelter is recommended for cooking. Ventilation and surface water drainage are extremely important.

In hot dry climates construction must ensure high thermal capacity, allowing with changes in night and day temperatures to cool and heat the interior alternately. Windows should be small. If only plastic sheeting or tents are available, a double skinned roof with ventilation between the layers to prevent radiant heat transfer should be considered. Alternatively, use of insulation materials should be supported. In a light structure, maximum ventilation is not an objective but should be easily controlled, *e.g.* by opening opposite doors to prevent heating by hot winds and radiation from the surrounding ground, and to prevent coming into the shelter. Shade can be gained from surrounding shelter or trees.

During site planning, trees and other vegetation are spared as far as possible. Road and drainage patterns are planned in such a way as to make use of natural contours in order to avoid erosion and flooding.

Measures may be required in shelters in both hot and cold climates to prevent infestation by vectors such as mosquitoes, rats and flies. The pattern of shelter for use by displaced people and material selection should form shelter programmes and subsequent control measures.

Guidelines for resettlement planning

- Total overall area of a camp 30 sq.m. per person (including area under roads, services, shelter, etc. depending on the layout and terrain).
- Minimum covered emergency shelter area : 3.5 sq.m./person.
- Area for support services : 7.5 sq.m. per person. This is for initial planning and will depend on the level of support providing administration, number of feeding centres, clinics, water storage and treatment areas, waste disposal, etc.
- Fire breaks : Minimum distance between buildings 2 × height of building (preferably greater, especially if the construction materials are highly combustible).
- Distance between blocks : 30 m minimum. Provide a fire break around the perimeter of the camp to protect against bush fires.
- Administration: 1 centre per camp
- Communal latrine usage: 15-25 users/cubicle
- Minimum distance to latrine from shelters: 30 m
- Desirable number of private latrines: 1 per family
- Minimum distance of latrine to a water source: 15 m
- Distance between water point and users: 150 m maximum
- Minimum number of water points: 1 tap/250 users
- Health post and feeding centre: 1 per 20,000 people
- Hospital: 1 per 2,00,000 people
- Solid waste container: 1 per 10 families
- Distance from users to food and fuel market: 150 m max.

Source: *Compiled from UNHCR, WHO and other sources.*

Dharamshala: A unique institution of residential accommodation in India had been dharamshala. These are usually built at religious pilgrimages for a specific community, caste, ethnic group, profession or persons from a specific region. The pilgrims and travelers are generally charged minimal or allowed free stay for a limited duration at a dharamshala. It also provides a hall for conference, ceremonies, marriage, discussions and preaching.

Pension: Pension is popular in providing affordable accommodation to the travelers in continental European countries. Now, they can also be found in North Africa, Middle East and in part of South America (such as Brazil and Paraguay), South Korea, Japan, and the Philippines. These may be located in historic buildings, can be family-run, and are generally cheaper than other lodgings, such as hotels.

Dormitory: A dormitory (dorm) or hall of residence is a building primarily providing sleeping and boarding quarters for large number of people and students. Many colleges and universities provide variety of dormitories for their students, such as hostels and single room with several beds. Usually dormitories have communal bathroom facilities. These generally have internet facilities, a central computer room, Wi-Fi, catering and kitchen facilities, laundry room, etc.

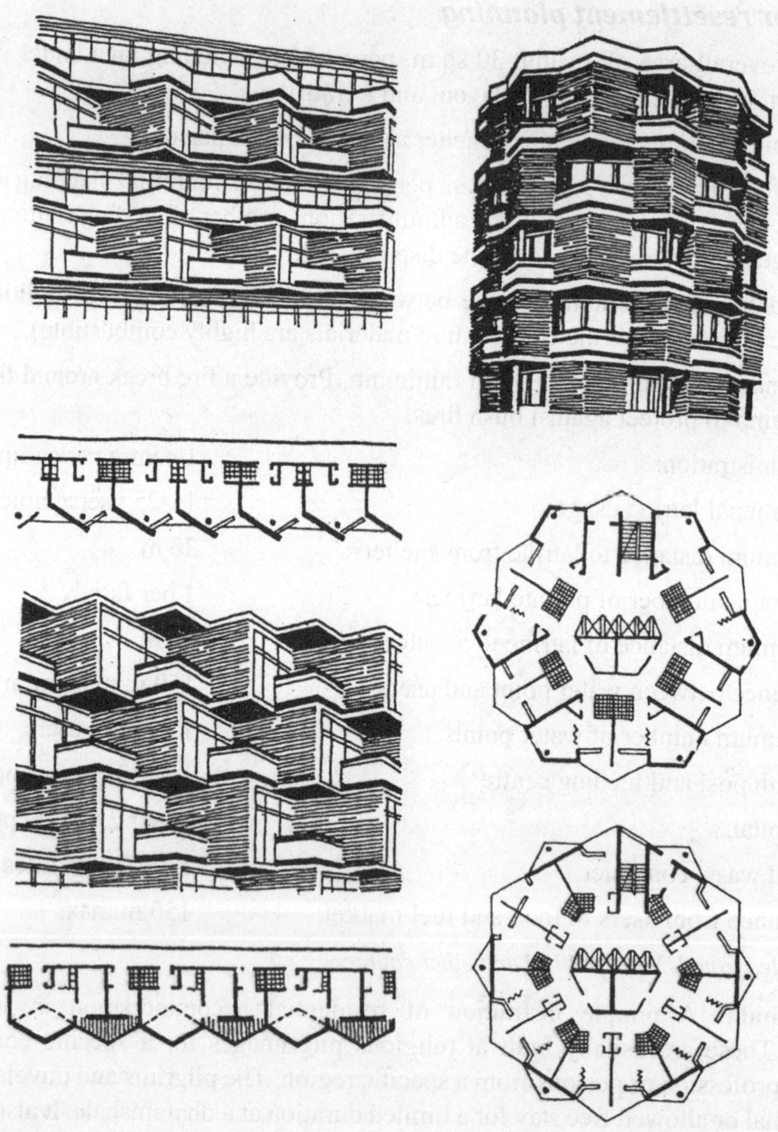

Fig. 8.2. Dormitories and hostels cater to the housing needs of the single professionals, working women, students, etc.

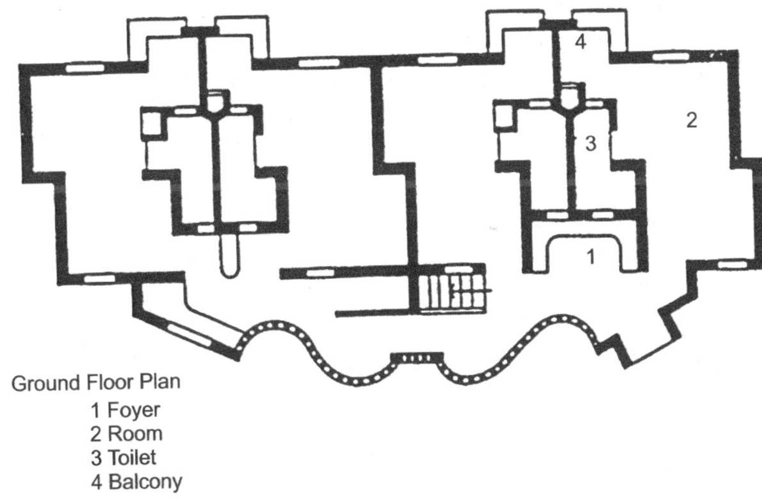

Fig. 8.3. Trivandrum, Women's Hostel, Laurie Baker, Architect

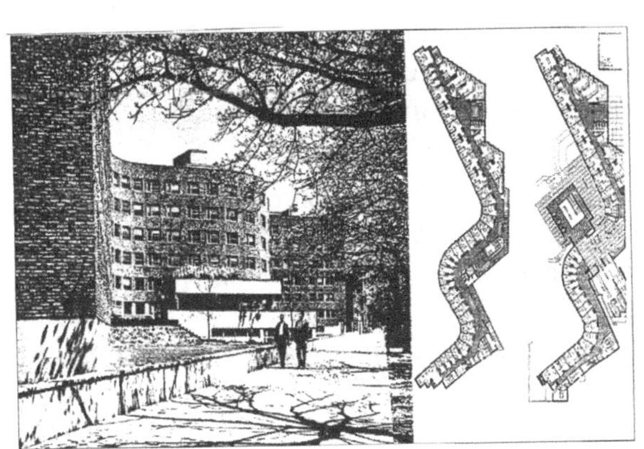

Fig. 8.4. MIT Dormitory, Alvar Aalto Architect

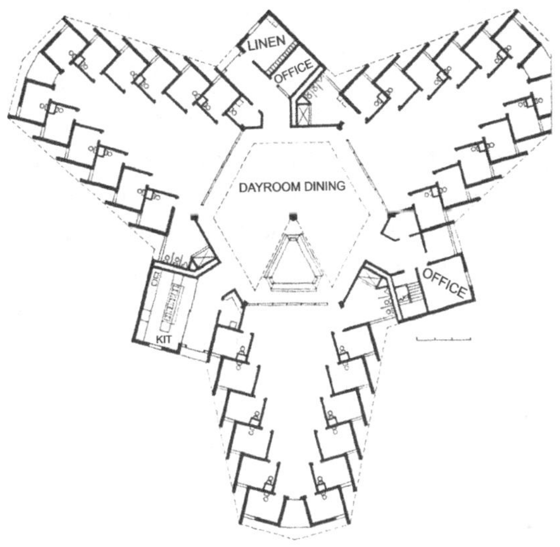

Fig. 8.5. Cheshire Community in Connecticut provides a large dining/dayroom space, and three clusters of twelve cells each. Each cluster has its own toilets and recreational space

Boarding and Lodging: Boarding schools generally provide dormitories, hostels and residents' halls to accommodate large number of children in minimum space. These may have bunk beds with common toilet facility. As per the norms, the minimum floor area of a dormitory per student varies from 2.3 sq. m to 4.2 m^2 plus 1.2 m^2. A minimum distance of 0.9 m should be maintained between any two beds in a dormitory. A bedroom for a single student should have a minimum floor area of 6.0 m^2. Such accommodation should be provided with the help of private sector for students coming to urban areas. It may also be upgraded to serve the young professionals and working women.

In coastal areas, the idea of floating dormitory can be explored. Dormitory ships and vessels can provide water-borne housing for temporary events, such as sports, fairs, training courses, conferences, etc. Notable among floating dormitories is SS Stevens, a 473-foot, 14,893 ton ship operated by Stevens Institute of Technology in Hoboken, New Jersey. From 1968 to 1975, Stevens served as the floating dormitory for as many as 150 students of the institute.

Hostels for students and tourists : These may have bunk bed, share a bathroom, lounge and sometimes a kitchen. Hostels are often cheaper for both the operator and occupants and provide a long-term shared accommodation to students, travelers and backpackers. Various NGOs, such as YMCA, YWCA, Youth Hostels of India and Hostelling International (UK) provide hostels.

Youth hostels were an exponent of the vision of the German Youth Movement to let poor city youngsters breathe fresh air outdoors. The youths were supposed to manage the hostel themselves as much as possible, doing chores to keep the costs down and build character, and be physically active outdoors. Because of this, many youth hostels closed during the middle part of the day. Very few hostels still have a "lockout" or require chores beyond washing up after self-catered meals.

Though very uncommon, a mobile hostel is a hostel with no fixed location. It can exist in the form of a camp site, a temporary building, bus, van, or a short term agreement in a permanent building. Mobile hostels have sprouted up at large festivals where there exists a shortage of budget accommodation. Mobile hostels generally provide dormitory accommodation for backpackers or travelers on a shoe string budget. An example of a mobile hostel is Hostival. These have sprouted up at Oktoberfest, Carnival, San Fermin, Las Fallas and the 2010 World Cup.

Guest House : Guest house is a kind of lodging which is similar to a hostel, bed and breakfast, or inn, which provide inexpensive lodging. It can be within private home which has been partly or fully converted for the guest accommodation. The owner usually lives within the property and may serve the guests with homemade food.

Bed and breakfast and guest houses are usually family owned live-on premises. The family members may work 10 to 12 hours and may employ part-time service staff. Hotels maintain a staff presence of 24 hours whereas a guest house has a limited staff. A guest-house may provide meals in room or in a restaurant attached. In recent years, especially in Delhi after the Commonwealth Games 2010, the perception changed and guest house accommodation has improved now they are offering 3 star equivalent facilities like fully furnished room, comfortable bed, food, air-conditioner, TV, wi-fi, hot and cold water supply and security.

A Bed and Breakfast is a small lodging establishment that offers accommodation and breakfast. Bed and breakfasts are often private family homes and typically have between four and eleven rooms. Some B&Bs operate in a niche market, such as boats with floating bed and breakfast. The CCGS Alexander Henry museum ship was one example. With enormous growth of cities like Delhi, Kolkata, Chennai, Hyderabad, Ahmedabad, Pune, Bangalore and Mumbai, facing acute housing shortage, Bed & Breakfast is becoming a favourite option among the young professionals and business persons.

A Serviced Apartment is a fully furnished apartment available for both short-term as well as long-term stays, providing the amenities, such as room service, a kitchenet, a fitness centre, a laundry room, dining room and recreation room. Serviced apartments are rented for short periods of time, usually by the month as opposed to annual rentals in the unfurnished apartment rental market. They are seen as an alternative to hotels. The apartment may vary from studio apartment to luxury apartment.

An Apartment Hotel is a serviced apartment complex that uses a hotel-style booking system. It is similar to renting a furnished apartment, but with LPG connection, kitchen equipment, air-conditioners, furniture, hot and cold water, internet/wi-fi, laundry machine, gym, indoor games, etc. allowing occupants to do everything they would do at home, such as cleaning, washing, and cooking. The kitchens may include utensils, crockery, pressure-cooker, a sink, a refrigerator, a microwave oven, a stovetop, dishwashers, etc. The concept of serviced apartment in India is still at a nascent stage, which has been introduced in Delhi, Bangalore, Mumbai, Chennai and few other cities. However, it offers a large scope in meeting the accommodation needs of executives, young professionals and others.

A holiday cottage, holiday home, or vacation property is a small home, a cottage that vacationers can rent. Renting a holiday cottage gives vacationers the freedom to eat in, eat out, stay in bed all day and generally come and go as they please. In contrast to this, accommodation in a bed and breakfast or hotel usually involves some sort of restriction on the time of day, guests need to vacate their rooms for cleaning and so on.

The rapid development of the internet and technologies such as telephony and personal digital assistants allow people to work from home. This has blurred the division between office and residence. Many business people, including the British entrepreneur Richard Branson, use their residence for both business and living purposes. This involves a change in planning regulations where mixed use is liberally permitted in residential use zone and service apartments are not categorized under commercial use. This relaxed property tax and other overheads on service apartments would trigger their development on a larger scale. This would also help in meeting the acute urban housing shortage.

Open Space, Recreation and Outdoor Environment

The importance of development of greenery and conservation of natural environment are very relevant for a healthy, clean and green ambience. Besides city level forest, river-front, greenery, district/regional parks, sports complexes, etc. about 10 per cent to 15 per cent of the neighbourhood area should be planned for parks and playgrounds within the residential areas. A system of landscaped linkages connecting various activities in a city or neighbourhood should be provided where people can go for long walks without interruption by vehicular traffic. The parks and open spaces should provide a sense of oasis and shelter from oppressive climate. Green belts also act as noise buffers and can be utilized as wind-breakers, and These also reduce the pollution, dust and high SPM levels in the urban atmosphere. By proper land use planning, such as location of public, semi-public and commercial activities along major transport arteries, a buffer can be created for residential zone. The green buffer with thin leave trees, land formations, mounds, embankments, noise screens, rubberized roads, etc. provide effective barriers to transmission of noise.

Urban transport usually contributes nearly two-thirds of the total air pollution in the form of suspended particulate matter. This is causing a serious threat to the environment and health of the people. The objective should be to provide access by green modes of urban transport, such as walking, bicycling, intermediate public transport modes, exclusive bus ways, dedicated mobile tracks, CNG powered vehicles, trains, etc. Important considerations of public transport should be easy access, last mile connectivity and mobility with comfortable boarding and embarking for the older people and handicapped. Bus stops, vehicle design and facilities like toilets, public telephones, etc. should be carefully and sensitively designed so as to meet the needs of elderly and disabled people.

Barrier-free Environment

A major consideration in the planning and design of outdoor and indoor environment should be that people with disabilities and older persons with arthritis, or on wheel chair could move around without much difficulty. This means that level differences shall be evened out to enable people in wheelchairs to move about without help from others. This also requires that:

- Paths and pavements shall be flat, uniform and slip-free;
- Orientation points and guide routes must be provided for usually disabled people;
- Paths and pavements shall be free from unnecessary obstacles;
- Information and warning signs must be understandable, clear and well lit.

Areas where passengers alight from vehicles should be close to building entrance, preferably within 10 m. The line of vision between alighting area and entrance shall be free so that people waiting can see each other. The network of pathways should be continuous and easy for older/disabled to follow and perceive. Paths shall be clearly distinguished from the roads for motor vehicles.

Large open areas should be provided with guide routes, guide surfaces and orientation aids. Guide route should be without obstacles or hazards, where a disabled person can walk. Guide rails are used by people who have difficulty in walking, to provide support and assistance and by visually disabled people as orientation aid. Guide rails should continue past resting sections and at least 300 mm past the beginning and end of the flight of steps or the ramp.

Fig. 8.6. Pedestrian Bridge and Ramp for Wheelchair Users

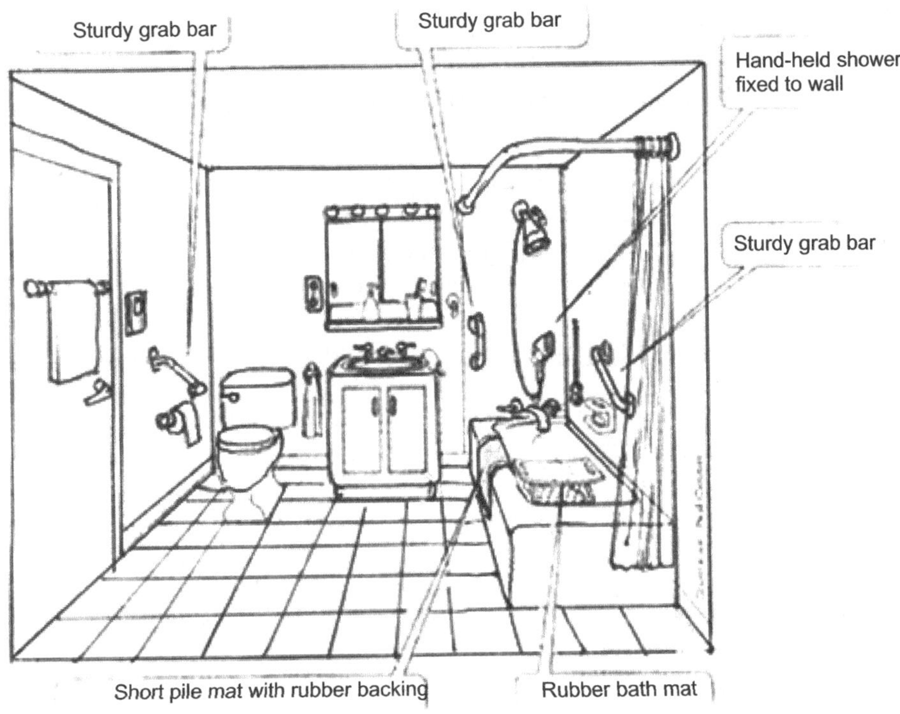

Fig. 8.7. A Toilet with Handles on Walls for Safety of Elderly, Disabled and Children

Source: *www.gvbtx.com (Grand New Builders, Texas, (USA)*

Ramped approach : Ramp shall be finished with nonslip material to enter the building. Minimum width of ramp shall be 1800 mm. with maximum gradient of 1:12, length of ramp shall not exceed 9.0 m having double handrail at a height of 800 and 900 mm on both sides extending 300 mm. beyond top and bottom of the ramp. Minimum gap from the adjacent wall to the hand rail shall be 50 mm.

Lavatories

Lavatories should be designed to allow access by wheel chairs and double buggies. Separate unisex facilities enable helpers to assist disabled people of the opposite sex. A unisex facility should not be entered from a single sex facility. In premises such as theatres or sports stadia where large numbers of people arrive and depart at the same time, it is desirable to have wheelchairs accessible units in the male and female lavatories in addition to a separate unisex unit. Lavatories providing facilities for people with disabilities should measure no less than 2000 mm × 1500 mm. The door to any compartment designed for disabled users must have a minimum clear opening width of 900 mm but 1000 mm is preferred. The floor surfaces of lavatories should be non-slip in both wet and dry conditions. An outward-opening, side-hung door is better than a sliding door. It should always be possible to open doors from the outside in an emergency.

A healthy environment plays a major role in the welfare of the people especially disabled, destitute and elderly. As per WHO, environmental sanitation is a health-related package, which includes the following:

- Safe disposal of wastes (human, solid, liquid and gaseous waste),

- Safe drinking water,
- Personal hygiene,
- Clean house and pollution free indoor and outdoor air, and
- Barrier free, safe movement for all.

It is essential to adopt the environmental and physical norms and standards for various services. The system should be based on participation by the residents. Stand-by arrangements and complaint redressal mechanism should be integral part of the services. At housing level, 24-hour service centres should be provided and managed by trained personnel.

DEBRIEFING QUESTIONS

1. What special considerations are required while planning, designing and developing housing for the following:
   (*a*) Elderly
   (*b*) Disabled
   (*c*) Homeless
   (*d*) Transit workers
   (*e*) Students
   (*f*) Working women
2. Explain how the following types of accommodation can help to meet the housing shortage in a city:
   (*a*) Dormitories
   (*b*) Guest houses/PGA
   (*c*) Hostel of Working Women
   (*d*) Night Shelter
   (*e*) Old Age Homes

9

HOUSING AMENITIES, FACILITIES AND SERVICES

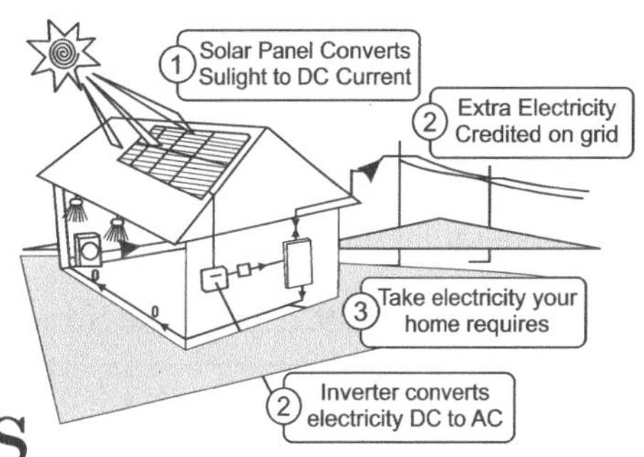

The quality of housing largely depends upon the standards of housing amenities, open space, physical and social infrastructure, including water, power, sewerage, drainage and solid waste management, health, recreation, education and community facilities.

Housing Standards aim to achieve sustainable and wholesome development by a process of organizing people and their activities over space and time. These envisage optimum use and efficiency of land and resources and setting of buildings, together with services and communication and transport routes so as to secure a sustainable environment, community welfare, economy, convenience and beauty. The planning is a dynamic, continuous and cyclic process. It encompasses implementation, monitoring and review. Planning can be seen as a matrix of its three levels–policy, strategic and action planning, and 5 spatial scales, viz. Regional/sub-regional, City, Zone/Sub-zone/ sector, Ward/local area, and Project Area Planning. The Community Plans or Wards Plans establish the specific area-wise requirement of the resources and detail out the exact manner in which a certain plan must be accomplished. Housing Area Plan combines goals, policies, procedures, norms and resources necessary to carry out given functions.

Hierarchy of Urban Development

A city should be planned so as to create a hierarchical structure for self-sufficiency. The smallest planning unit is conceived as Housing Area for 5000 population with a primary school, convenience shopping, open area, Anganwadi and milk booth as the minimum provisions. The higher level of facilities are to be provided at Neighbourhood, Community, District, Zonal, Sub-City and Regional levels. The hierarchy of development on the basis of population is given below:

Table 9.1: Hierarchy of Urban Development

Sr. No.	Planning Unit	Population
1.	Housing Cluster	5000
2.	Neighbourhood	5000-15,000
3.	Community	Up to 100,000
4.	District	5 Lakh
5.	Zone	10 Lakh
6.	Subcity	20–25 Lakh
7.	City	50 Lakh

Source: *UDPFI Guidelines, 1996; MPD 2021.*

The provision of amentities in the hierarchy of urban development can be planned according to the standards, requirements, and resources.

Land use Structure

The general land use structure for urban centres is as given below:

Table. 9.2. Land use Structure for Urban Development (Master Plan Level)

Balance	Land Use	Percentage of Development Area			
		Small	Medium	Large Cities	Metropolitan Cities & Megacities
1.	Residential	45 – 50	43 – 48	36 – 39	36 – 38
2.	Commercial	2 – 3	4 – 6	5 – 6	5 – 6
3.	Industrial	8 – 10	7 – 9	7 – 8	7 – 8
4.	Public & Semi-Public Facilities	6 – 8	6 – 8	10 – 12	10 – 12
5.	Recreational	12 – 14	12 – 14	14 – 16	14 – 16
6.	Transport & Communication	10 – 12	10 – 12	12 – 14	12 – 14
7.	Agriculture, Water bodies and Special Areas	Balance	Balance	Balance	Balance
8.	Total	100	100	100	100

Source: *URDPFI, 2016 Guidelines*

Community Planning

The concept of community planning attempts to create physical and social units of manageable modules of population. As a planning concept, the neighbourhood unit signifies the natural human tendency for relationships to have a territorial expression. The idea is to conceive a city composed of a number of sizeable units, each unit as a comprehensive entity by itself. This intends to allow the growth of a community spirit fostered by sustained social interaction and at the same time to function as a modular unit, which contains the basic utilities, services and community facilities. It provides shops for day-to-day needs, recreation, parks and open spaces, education, health and cultural sites and a circulation network for the movement of people and goods.

A modular pattern of spatial organization can help in organizing the community and design of housing cluster. The housing cluster may comprise about 750 to 1000 persons which is analogous to the traditional "mohalla." Three to four such units form a Primary Community Unit with a population of about 5000, which is planned around a Primary school, park and convenience shopping. At the next level, the residential planning area with a population of 15,000-20,000 population can be planned around a Senior Secondary School, neighbourhood park and playground, community facilities and a local shopping centre. A Sector comprising of three to four residential planning areas can be organized around a Community Centre, college, sports complex and a transit hub. A Planning District may comprise three to four sectors with a District Centre, District Park, University, Cultural Hub, Work Centres, etc.

The size of a residential sector is governed by (*a*) the area required for various land use components; (*b*) the population required to support the sector level services and facilities; (*c*) accessibility to such facilities; and (*d*) the existence of physical boundaries. The sector must be large enough to support the community facilities such as the primary school, senior secondary school, local shopping centre, health centre, park, etc. At the same time, it should not be so large as to loose the advantage of a compact and integrated community life.

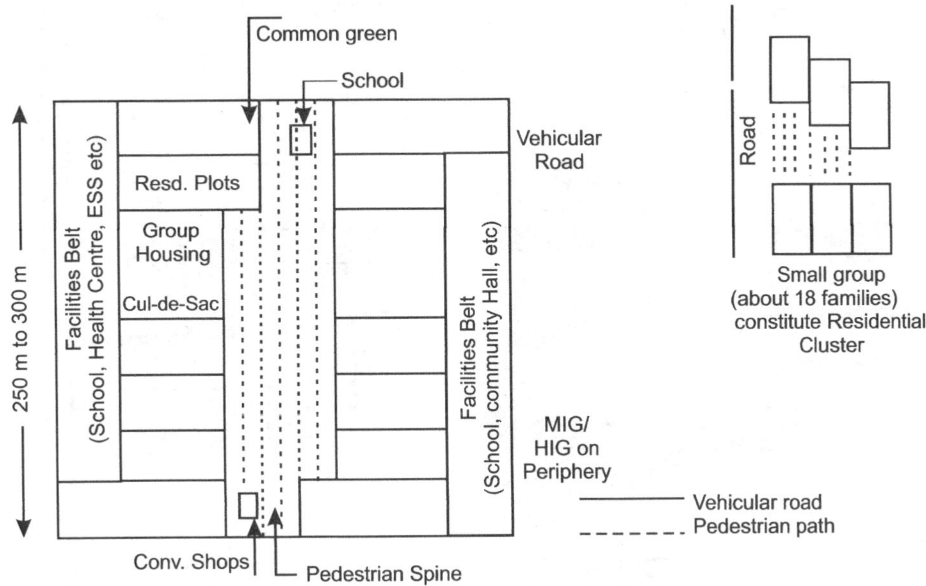

Fig. 9.1. Primary Housing Unit

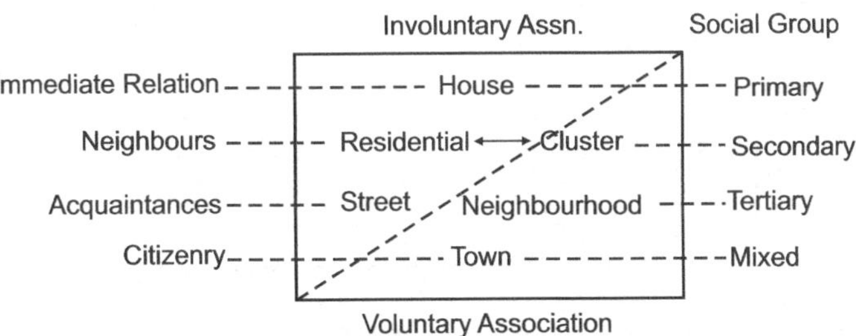

Fig. 9.2. Levels of Association

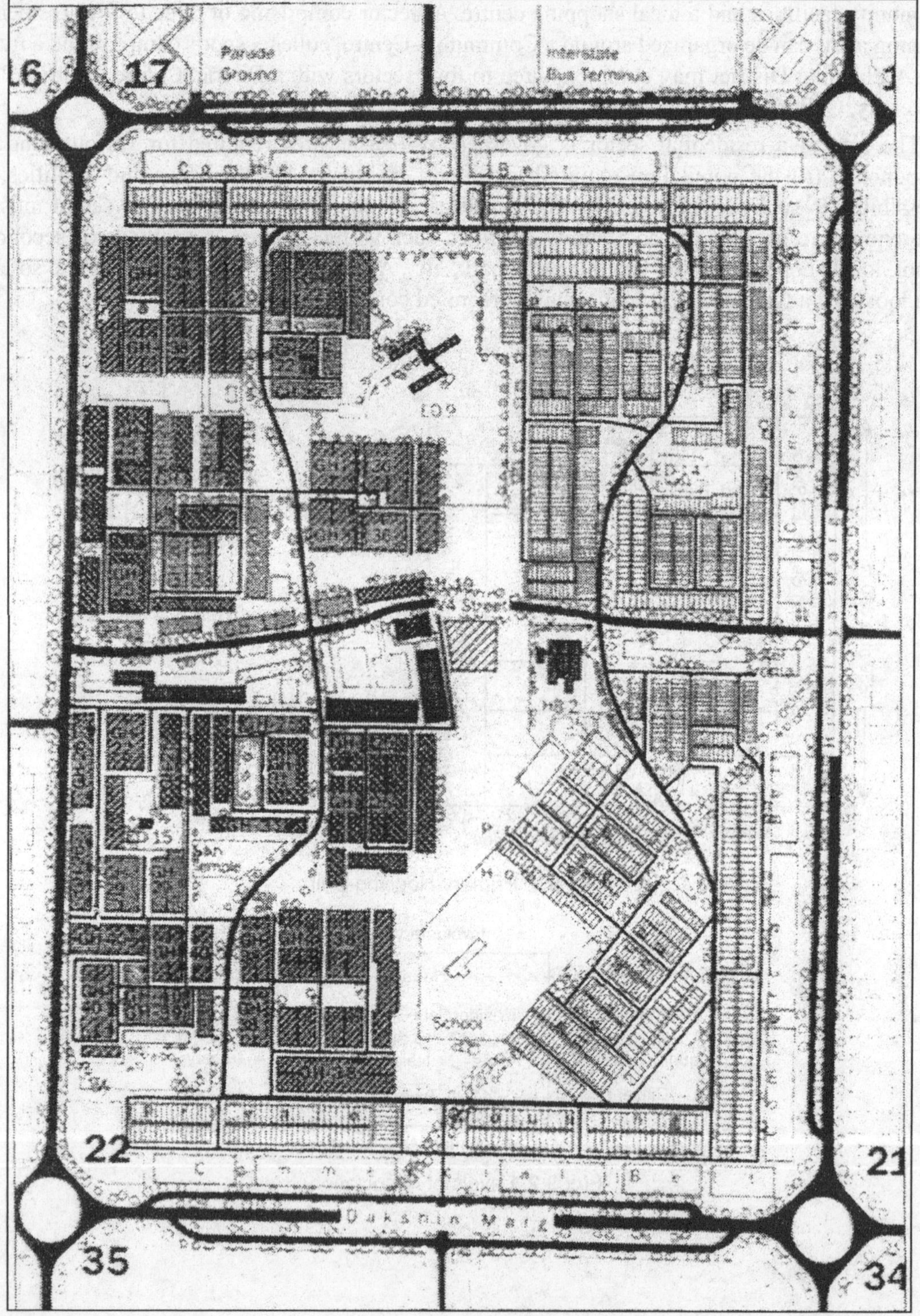

Fig. 9.3. Plan of Sector 22 (800 × 1200 m) Chandigarh. It has been planned with variety of housing and educational, recreational, health, cultural and commericial facilities for a population of 15,000 and three density groups of 25, 50 and 75 ppa

Fig. 9.4. A Walkable community provides access to the facilities and bus stop at a maximum 5 to 10 minutes walk (400 to 800 m). Pedestrians and wheelchair/pram users should be able to move safely without conflict with vehicular traffic

Certain facilities are provided for a group which establish an interrelationship among the various neighbourhoods and sectors. Some of the facilities may be located in the core area of the sector whereas facilities of smaller size and which cater to a smaller number of people, need to be well distributed within it.

The suggestive norms for various facilities are mentioned below:

Table 9.3. Norms for Community Facilities at Sector Level (About 30,000 population)

Social Infrastructure	Number of Unit	Area (Sqm)	Total (Sqm)
Primary School	6	2000	12000
Senior Secondary School	4	16000	64000
Dispensary	4	1000	4000
Nursing Home	1	1000	1000
Health Centre	1	2000	2000
Tot-lot	120	480	57600
Housing Area Park	6	5000	30000
Housing Area Playground	6	5000	3000
Neighbourhood Play area	2	15000	3000
Convenience Shopping Centre	6	1100	6600
Local Shopping Centre	2	3000	6000
Milk Booth	6	150	900
Community Hall & Library	2	2000	4000
Electric Substation 11 KV	4	120	480

***Source:** DDA, Delhi Master Plan, 2021 and other sources*

Chandigarh provides an excellent example of Sector Planning (800 m × 1200 m) with a system of community facilities for various groups (Fig. 9.3).

Circulation Network

The circulation pattern of a community must be designed so as to fit into the overall road pattern of the city. The sector level road system should be such that no road within the sector can be used as a shortcut for a thoroughfare. The circulation system should give safe and easy access to residences, shops, schools, public buildings and recreational facilities. The peace of the sector must be preserved by avoiding traffic hazards, noise, glare and automobile pollution. The mass-transit system of the city should be so planned so that the buses, metro monorail, suburban trains, etc. run on the major traffic arteries and feeder streets, but not on the residential streets of a sector. Special attention should be paid to silence and safety zoning. Cul-de-Sac, loop streets, bikeways and footpaths may be laid out to link residential areas with community facilities and to connect the sectors with one another so that pedestrians and cyclists may be free from the hazards of vehicular traffic.

Along the major transport corridors on the edge of a sector there is propensity of mixing of residential and commercial uses. In order to eliminate the possibility of the misuse of residential areas along the edge of a sector, such areas should be pre-planned for mixed use, institutional buildings, commercial centres, organised open spaces, etc.

The internal road network of the sector should discourage through traffic and vehicles which do not have their origin and destination within the sector to pass through it. The road network should have a clear hierarchy in terms of collector/distributor, access roads and pedestrian paths. The arterial and sub-arterial roads should form the boundaries of the sector and should not subdivide it. The width of a collector/distributor road can be 30 m and an access road can be 20 m or 12 m wide, depending upon the expected traffic load. As far as possible intersections should be avoided. The junctions of collector/distributor roads with arterial/sub-arterial roads bounding the sector should be in the form of T-junctions and staggered junction of arterial/ sub-arterial road, with the collector/ distributor to discourage flow of external through traffic. Separate cycle tracks should be provided without conflict with fast moving vehicles and obstacles. Corridor planning is a preferred way to relate transit with land use, greenery, development control and provision of parking. Geometric design of roads, cross-sections, junctions and intersections, grade separators, along with associated details such as spacing, camber, gradients, super-elevations, turning radius, sight distance, widening on curbs, shoulders, median strips, etc. should adhere to standards.

The width of the roads and streets and the number of traffic lanes depend upon the anticipated volume of traffic during the peak hours projected for next 2 decades, and also composition of traffic. The following table shows the recommended road standards:

Table 9.4. Road and Street Standards

Type of Road	Right of Way	Number of Lanes
Major road	24 m to 30 m	Two lanes to start with and four lanes ultimately
Neighbourhood road	14 m to 18 m	Two lanes
Residential street	9 m to 14 m	Two lanes
Cul-de-Sac (not to exceed 180 m length)	8 m to 9 m	Two lanes

Loops	3 m to 5 m	As may be necessary
Service lane (in case of row housing)	5 m to 6 m	As may be necessary
Cycle track	2 m to 3 m	As may be necessary
Footpath	1.5 to 3 m	

Source: *IRC*

Footpaths of adequate width should be provided on the arterial roads, major roads and some of the sector roads. Cycle tracks may be provided along major roads. Recommendations for minimum and maximum distances for access to schools, recreational areas, parks, shops and various public buildings in a residential sector made by the COPP (Committee on Plan Projects) are given below:

Table 9.5. Access Standards for Community Facilities

Community Facilities	Suggested Distance
Nursery School	0.40 km
Primary School	0.40 to 0.60 km
Secondary School	Up to 1.60 km
Tot-lot	0.20 km
Children Park	0.40 to 0.50 km
Playground	0.80 to 1.60 km
Neighbourhood Park	0.80 to 1.60 km
Local Shopping	0.40 to 0.80 km
Health Centre	0.80 to 1.60 km

Source: *Committee on Plan Projects, Govt. of India*

Street Lighting

There are many factors which influence the planning of street lighting. Generally, a good installation is the result of achieving the best visibility consistent with a relatively low cost unit of light and power consumption. In designing street lighting the governing factors are layout, type of road surface and junctions. Street lighting should be designed in such a way that motorists can drive at the desired speed without the use of headlights. The motorist should be able to see an object on the road within safe stopping distance. In places where the speed limit varies from 40 to 50 km per hour, the safe stopping distance is about 40 m.

Single row lighting for sector roads up to 24 m Right of Way and double row lighting for main roads may be provided. The lighting poles should be spaced at 30 to 35m intervals. LED, halogen, mercury, sodium vapor and solar lamps could be used with advantage over incandescent lamps and fluorescent tubes.

Landscaping

The best way to organize a city is through the design of its landscape rather than the buildings. The cities need to be designed in sync with the landscape which should generate its urban form. As a thumb rule, a city should have about one fifth of the land under organized greens. At sector level the green areas should be at least 10 per cent, and preferably 15 per cent of total area. The landscape plan should be based on site analysis and climate, soil, and land use zoning for identifying recreational open spaces with the following considerations:

- Pattern and use of open space, water availability, drainage pattern, topography, air pollution and noise control.
- Species of vegetation and trees and their location/planting.
- Footpaths and roadside planting, connectivity and access for all.
- Paved and unpaved spaces, landscape furniture and facilities.
- Passive and active recreational areas.
- Treatment of transmission lines, conservation of water bodies and other natural landscape areas.
- Details of landscape space, their maintenance, security, lighting, etc.

Fig. 9.5. A network of parks and playgrounds is the focus of housing development

Fig. 9.6. A playground can be developed as a mini stadium-cum-amphitheatre

Norms for Informal Sector and Street Vendors

Large sections of unemployed and under-employed population depend upon jobs and livelihood in the informal sector. They bring forth multitude of small enterprises, petty trading and casual labour. This vernacular and disorganized sector with highly reduced needs of space, services and investments is a major source of employment in the economic fabric of a city. Realising the fact, that they have right to the city the following planning provisions are necessary to cater to this sector:

- Earmarking of 'Hawking' and 'No Hawking' zones, Spaces for stationary and mobile street vendors. Reservation of 10 per cent of space for street vendors, hawkers, etc. in every shopping centre.
- The weekly markets to be identified and improved with proper services and facilities.
- New areas for Janta markets, repair shops and workshops be developed with basic amenities.
- Provision of common basic services, like solid waste disposal, urinals/toilets, water point and lighting.
- Innovative design of stalls, push-carts and mobile vans of various sizes and with cleaning facilities.
- Adopting mandatory norms of space for hawkers/vendors, and their legal protection.

Table 9.6. Norms for the provision of informal sector of trade

Area	No. of Units
• Planned Commercial Centers	3-4 units per 10 formal shops
• Govt. and Commercial Offices	5-6 units per 100 employees
• Wholesale Trade & Freight Complex	3-4 units per 10 formal shops
• Hospitals	3-4 units per 100 beds
• Bus Terminal	1 unit per 2 bus-bays
• Primary School	3-4 units
• Sr. Secondary School	5-6 units
• Regional/District Parks	8-10 units at each major entry
• Neighbourhood Park	2-3 units
• Residential Area	1 unit/1000 population
• Industrial Area	5-6 units per 1000 employees

Source: *DDA, Delhi Master Plan-2021, New Delhi.*

Repair Shops/ Workshops

The proliferation of unplanned automobile repair shops has been causing traffic and environmental problems. Mandatory norms are necessary for provision of automobile workshops, and also reservation of at least 10% of industrial and commercial areas for service and repair shops. The average area of repair shop may be 15 to 30 sqm with common repair open space/courtyard @7.5 to 15 sqm /shop. Informal repair shop area may be average 2.16 sqm (1.8 × 1.2 m) with provision for disposal of solid waste, metallic oil, paints, and liquid wastes, lighting, signage and noise control.

Waste/Water Recycling and Watershed Management

The urban areas in India are suffering from shortage of potable water. There is a need to improve the potable water supply, exploit new opportunities and promote community driven water conservation measures. These include the following:

(*a*) **Recycling of treated wastewater** with separate lines for potable water and recycled water by dual pipe supply system may be introduced.

(*b*) **Ground water recharging** may be ensured through rain water harvesting, conserving water bodies and controlling groundwater extraction. Groundwater extraction is to be controlled through registering boreholes and recharging according to test yields.

(*c*) **Rain water harvesting schemes** should be mandatory in all development, parking, roads and building projects.

(*d*) **Dovetail watershed management, arrest the run-off** ensure the conservation of natural valleys, water bodies and aquifers. The concept of 'zero run-off drainage' with retention ponds, sediments traps and balancing lakes should be adopted, with a segregated wastewater disposal system. A green network overlapping the blue network would protect the ecology of aquifers, and also provide a pleasant environment. Simple methods of site planning, which incorporate porous/semi-permeable paving, drop inlet/down-pipe, sediment trap, retention ponds, etc. contribute in maintaining ground water table.

(*e*) **Pollution control** of rivers, major drains and canals which have become polluted due to indiscriminate dumping of wastes. These need strict pollution control measures and eco-sensitive land use controls. Water flow needs to be controlled and stabilized and marked at each kilometer station. The valleys should be zoned as water portals, so that these are flanked with greenery, farmlands and forests, where the hazard of pollution exists, the charges for operating permits should cover the expenses of policing and mandatory performance and liability insurance.

(*f*) **To improve the quality of river-water** secure its continuous flow and encourage the return of aquatic life. This needs improvement of drainage, waste water treatment and pollution abatement by sewerage improvement. The surplus water during the monsoons should be retained in balancing ponds along the riverbed rather than allowing it to the downstream areas.

(*g*) **Landscaping of the drains and waterfront** may be taken up in the form of interconnected parkways with simple and natural landscaping. Such trails could be one of the cheapest forms of drainage and recreation. The drainage basins can be made self-sustainable by integrating water-sewerage-drainage systems.

1. Secondary treatment of rainwater
2. W.C.
3. Washing machine.
4. Garden water outlet/tap
5. Rainwater channel at roof
6. Rainwater storage after primary treatment
7. Municipal water inlet
8. Rainwater tank
9. Bathtub inlet
10. Kitchen sink

Fig. 9.7. Rainwater Harvesting and Recycling

(*h*) **Water supply in new housing** should incorporate separate lines –one for washing, WC flushing, water coolers and garden taps, the second for supplying potable water. All residential complexes having a discharge of over 10,000 liters per day should incorporate wastewater recycling.

(*i*) **Efficient methods of water conservation, use and recycling** may be adopted by using water saving appliances and waterless flushing system.

(*j*) **Controlling leakages and UFW:** All measures should be taken to reduce unaccounted flow of water (UFW) and production losses. About half of the water that is treated and distributed at public expense is non-revenue, due to unrecorded usage or illegal taps and water connections. To ensure a minimum amount of potable water to the poor, by an equitable distribution system is necessary. Leak detection and rectification works should be assisted by the utilities. Meters should be installed for consumers of municipal water and ground water and also for waste water discharge.

(*k*) **Microdrip irrigation and xeriscaping** can be adopted to save water for irrigation and gardening. To discourage mosquito breeding in stagnant water, small fountains and cascades can be provided.

Energy Efficiency and Net Zero Energy

To meet growing power requirement, it is necessary to enhance renewable energy and reduce its demand by energy efficiency. Net zero energy and energy chains, passive micro-climatic design, intelligent energy controls, heat recovery, etc. can result in energy saving. In domestic sector energy saving can be about 20% by adopting measures such as replacement of low efficiency incandescent lamp with high efficiency fluorescent tubes (CFLs), LED and solar lamps. Light-emitting microchips work longer, use less power and allow the use of light in new ways. These consume 80 per cent less electricity than the incandescent bulbs and have longer life.

The following are some critical Low Energy Building Design principles:

- Compliance of building with Energy Conservation Building Code
- Integration of energy concept from project outset, demand management, compact shape to minimize power requirement
- Daylight design
- Using energy labelled equipment, efficient lighting, ventilation and space conditioning
- Shading, green roof, building envelope
- Fenestration, window/openings and glazing design
- Efficient use of passive solar energy, renewable energy
- Energy-efficient, easy-to-use technical systems
- Low-energy electrical appliances
- Use of low embodied energy, recyclable construction materials
- Increased insulation, elimination of thermal bridges, wherever possible
- Safety against fire and other hazards.

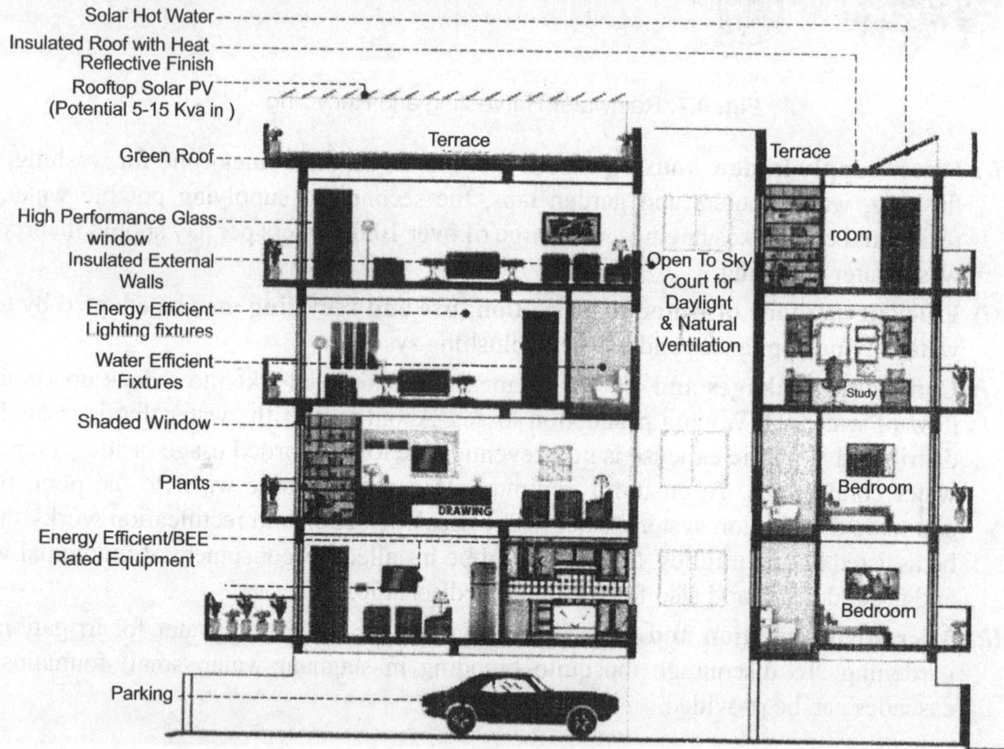

Fig. 9.8. Typical section of a Residential Building in Compliance with Energy Conservation Building Code

Source: *DUAC/Amit Ghosal (2015) Punjabi Bagh, DUAC, New Delhi.*

Alternative cooling and air-conditioning systems, such as passive evaporative cooling micronisers (PECM), passive downdraft evaporative cooling (PDEC), earth air tunnel shafts and courtyards are adopted for natural cooling and ventilation. Average earth temperature at 4 m depth below earth is around 25 to 27°C. This can condition the space by passing air through buried pipes or earth tunnels.

India is endowed with abundance of sun. The roof area of 100 sq. meters receives about 500 KW per day from eight hours of sunshine. Photovoltaic systems can be integrated into the building through the mechanical integration (multi-functionality of a PV element), and electrical integration (grid connection and/or direct use of the power, and system control). Solar roof can produce electricity in buildings for their own use. Solar electricity can be collected through a decentralized smart grid for integrated and uninterrupted power.

Drainage and Storm Water Management

Drainage in ecological context goes beyond construction of conventional drains and the control of flood flows. Lining of drainage channels with hard materials also increases discharge rates and increases the risk of erosion, risk of damage to drainage banks, structures and foundations. On the other hand vegetation of catchments reduces soil erosion and increase run-off times, water retention and infiltration, as well as making a general improvement to the environment. The use of paving materials such as bricks or concrete block in place of asphalt and other smooth materials can have similar effects, although to a lesser degree.

As a principle, planning of drainage should follow the line of natural drainage. Drains should be in straight lines, or in easy curves. Laterals should be laid in the line of greatest slope. Intercepting drains are an exception generally being placed across the slope. Three principal types of lateral sub-drainage systems are common—the herring bone, grid iron and parallel systems. The parallel system is most economical because it involves the least duplication of drainage by laterals and mains. The preferable arrangement is short mains and low laterals rather than the reverse. A minimum slope of 1 per cent (1 ft in 100 ft) is recommended. Steeper slopes are better. The quantity and flow of run-off also depends upon land use and type of surface.

Check dams and retention lakes may be designed for increasing ground water table and as storm water holding points, wherever needed. Drainage should be linked with the ecology and green networks, by adopting the concept of "bio-drainage."

The following measures are essential for proper drainage planning:

(*i*) Drainage to be integral part of layout plan, housing scheme, redevelopment plan and Road Development Plan. One of the fundamental issues often neglected is the integrated design of roads, drains, sewers and other utility networks, like water supply, electric and communication cables, etc. Bad surface of the roads lead to accumulation of rain water, waste water and debris. Suitable ducts/pipes should be provided by the side of carriageway for cables, pipes, etc. so that the road is not dug up time and again.

(*ii*) A proper database, GIS based drainage mapping and planning should be promoted.

(*iii*) Sub-wells may be developed under flyovers for trapping rainwater.

(*iv*) Pump houses in low-lying areas should be provided with back-up power.

(*v*) Remodeling of some drains may be required considering the upstream flow in the region.

A well planned system of retention lakes, balancing ponds and porous paving can lead to avoidance of the construction of huge storm water drains. Its advantages include the availability of greenery, recreational and water reserves for recreation, and the enrichment of the underground aquifer by continual replenishment.

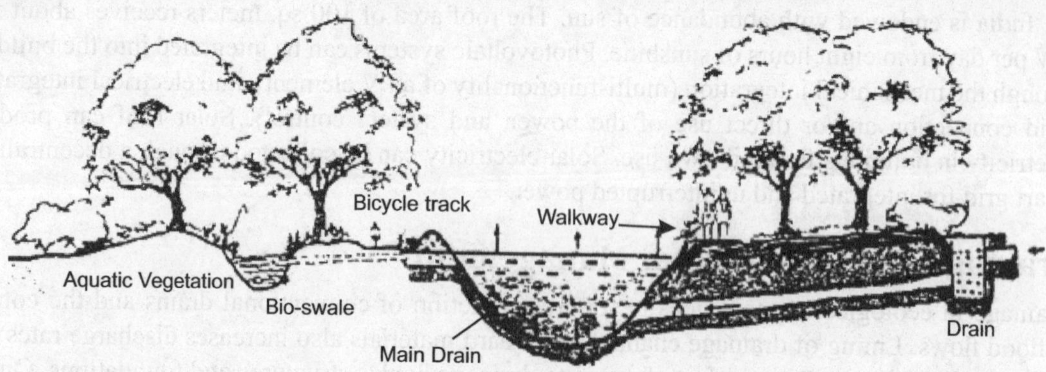

Fig. 9.9. Najafgarh drain in Dwarka sub-city, New Delhi was originally Hindon River, which is now badly polluted. It is proposed to be recovered by pollution control, boating facilities, walk-ways, jogging and bicycle tracks, vegetation and adoption of the concept of bio-swale and balancing reservoirs to harvest the storm water

Fig. 9.10. On-channel treatment of polluted water flow in Palam Drain, Dwarka, New Delhi, by bacterial biom mediation, Daphnia treatment and Floating Wetlands reduced pollution levels and foul odour

Source: *INTACH*

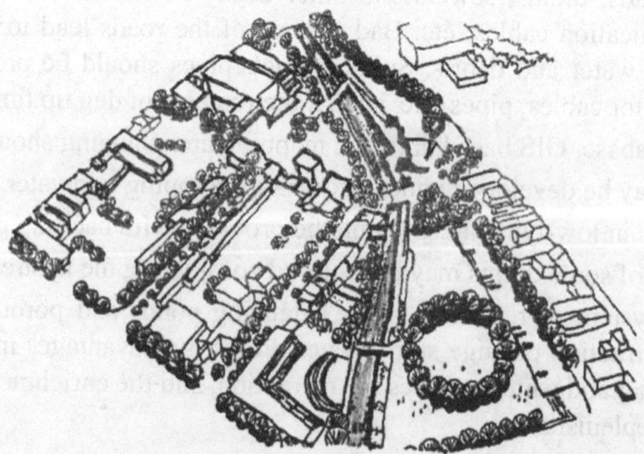

Fig. 9.11. Bio-Remediation and landscaping of Palam drain provided an attractive jogging track and freedom from foul odour, mosquitoes, etc.

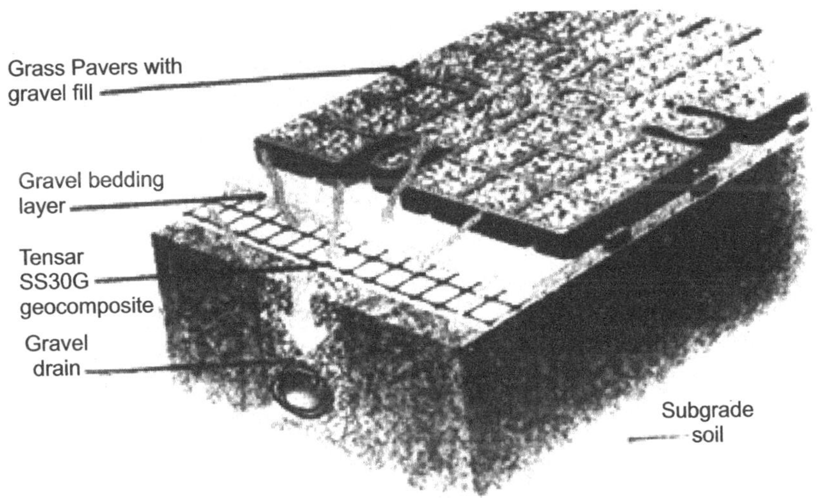

Fig. 9.12. Drainage of Parking Area/Footpath Combined with Rainwater Harvesting

The various options of retention systems are given below:

Low area drain (soakway): Water collects at the lowest part of the site. It is generally designed as an extension of the lawn where the soil can become highly saturated during rain. Visually the area under drain functions like a lawn and can be used a green trail.

Ditches and swales: These can also be grassed, planted with water-loving plants and to provide a habitat for animals. Ditches will form temporary water features after rainfall. They take up less space than a low area drain. They are permanent features and cannot easily perform a different function when dry. Swales should be vegetated for optimizing infiltration into the ground which should be part of a surface water collection network.

Permanent retention ponds: These are permanent water features that have a higher amenity values. Ponds require more space than ditches as water levels need to fluctuate and more water is permanently retained on site. Retention ponds can be well supplemented with reed-bed filtration system prior to discharge into a local drain or river. They score slightly higher than ditches and swales in environment terms as they combine aesthetic values with filtration.

Underground collection cistern: This is an expensive option with the lowest environment rating and also limited capacity. Its strongest point is the minimal space required. Water is collected and slowly discharged into the groundwater through a sand and gravel pit by filtration.

Improving the quality of water: Storm water and waste water should be segregated, so that storm water can be stored and used for horticulture and irrigation, whereas waste water can be recycled after primary and secondary treatment. To improve the quality of drainage water falling in to water bodies/river, effluent treatment plants should be provided at outfall of drains and aeration units at interceptions with advanced techniques for maintenance of drains.

Waste water recycling: By using root-zone beds, bio-remediation, oxidation ponds, aeration, etc. treated waste water can be used for non-potable purposes, thereby reducing demand of fresh water. For treatment of pesticide traces, the sand filter with bituminous charcoal or coconut shells can be an economical method. However, the best way to get rid of the pesticides (non-point) and industrial toxins is through source protection at the catchment itself through methods such as organic or biological farming, etc.

Strict enforcement of Water Pollution Act and enforcing the installation of treatment facilities by polluting units/ industry, and ensuring efficient functioning of the STPs and the ETPs are essential. In the absence of proper waste disposal system and controls, many drains are choked with solid waste. As such, improved solid waste management is essential for efficient drainage. Regular desilting of drains and control of dumping of solid waste/ malba into the drains should be taken up. Public awareness program need to be taken up in association with NGOs and RWAs to make the people aware about the consequences of dumping the solid waste in the drains.

Sanitation

In India, a large number of families in the slums, resettlement colonies and villages do not have access to toilets. According to Urban Sanitation Policy and Vision (2015) of the Union Ministry of Housing and Urban Affairs, one out of six urban Indians is compelled to defecate in the open every day; 26 to 50 per cent urban households suffer inadequate access to sanitation facilities; and only 30 per cent of urban households have access to sewerage systems. The sewage generated in slums remains unconnected to city system and the service agencies or the municipalities refuse to handle it. Some of the sewage plants do not function or have become derelict.

The Centre for Civil Society in its survey (2008) revealed that Delhi had only 132 public toilets for women, many of them barely functioning, compared with 1,534 for men. This severely limited the mobility of women and their right. The issue of toilets affects most the poor women who live in slum areas and girls who drop out of school due to lack of toilets. Community toilets often suffer from lack of cleanliness, water supply and may be without a door, forcing people to use walls, open space and drains for toilet. Toilets are essential not simply as a convenience for the students, workers, travellers and shoppers, but also in crowded slums that are characterised by lack of toilets.

The public toilets need to be well maintained, regularly cleaned and sanitized with proper and regular water supply, electricity and sewage disposal. In Delhi most of the high profile public toilets built during Commonwealth Games 2010 are lying locked, due to management deficit and lack of proper maintenance agreement with the concerned agency.

Ecological Sanitation: Sanitation is a major ecological issue which is intimately linked to soil and sub-soil water contamination, pollution of surface water and extensive use of water in disposal of excreta. The Centre for Science and Environment (CSE) in its landmark study of the 71 cities 'Excreta Matters' (2012) found that while 23 per cent people live in slums, the waste discharge from slums is only five per cent of the total sewage. The slum areas by and large remain un-served by sewage networks and wastes are conveyed through open drains. These are the human settlements without kidneys.

The present scenario of sanitation is characterized by:

- The use of biocide hygiene inputs which are a burden on the environment;
- Wastage of water;
- Energy-intensive and expensive waste water treatment;
- Waste of plant nutrients and organic matter;
- Capacity constraints of the operators and frequent breakdown of systems resulting in transfer of pollution instead of elimination; and
- Discharge of sewage into rivers and water bodies causes their pollution.

In conventional water-borne disposal of human wastes, large amounts of clean water are used to flush and transport human waste to distant sites for treatment. The disadvantages of centralized large sewage treatment plants and extensive sewerage include high capital costs, high energy requirements, contamination of groundwater or piped drinking water, and use of large volumes of water.

This calls for revisiting the sanitation technology, planning and design standards and evolve eco-san practices for sanitation. Composting toilets can operate if fed with urine and faeces (and small amounts of wash water), or they receive faeces only and composting becomes a simple operation manageable by the user. Fully composted human faeces can be handled like any other compost. Composting toilets make ecological and economical sense. In Auroville and some other cities in India there are examples of composting toilets at the level of households, as well as public facilities.

Waterless Urinals

Waterless urinals can save 1000 liters of water per day (per 100 users). The new generation urinals does not need oil sealed cartridge. The surface of urinal is glazed using a special nano-technology based chemical which makes it highly hydrophobic, *i.e.* it repels urine and does not let dust or other impurities stick, making it stain free. The ammonia in urine is responsible for foul smell due to breakup of urea bacteria by water. In waterless urinal, urine is flushed down the drain through a non-returning valve which does not allow the vapours to come back. Due to anti-bacterial coating, pathogens cannot survive in the urinal. The oxidizing effect and lack of water kill the bacteria in the urine. This also reduces the volume of sewerage and thus the capacity requirement of the STP. The maintenance cost of cartridge free Kupple waterless urinal is very low as compared to conventional urinals.

Sewerage

High density of septic tanks in a habitat make aquifers susceptible to infiltration. Without proper sanitation and sewerage treatment, extreme pressures are exerted on natural resources and safe water supply. In the settlements of the poor without municipal sewerage, it is necessary to work out alternative options without depending upon the municipal system.

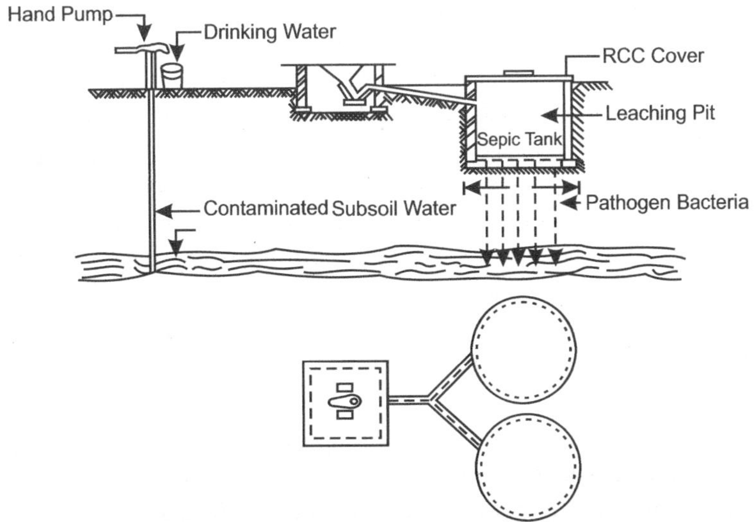

Fig. 9.13. A Conventional Septic Tank and Latrine Contaminating Sub-Soil Water

Decentralized STPs with smaller capacities can be provided at the community level, besides the possibility of recovering energy/ gas as fuel from sewage can be explored. The sewerage has to be designed to handle sewerage @ 80 % of the water supply. The waste water and sewerage capacity is linked with provision of recycling infrastructure. Mini Decentralized Treatment Plants, apart from reducing the sewerage load, can yield recycled water, which can be used for gardening, washing, cooling towers, etc. and also gas for generating power.

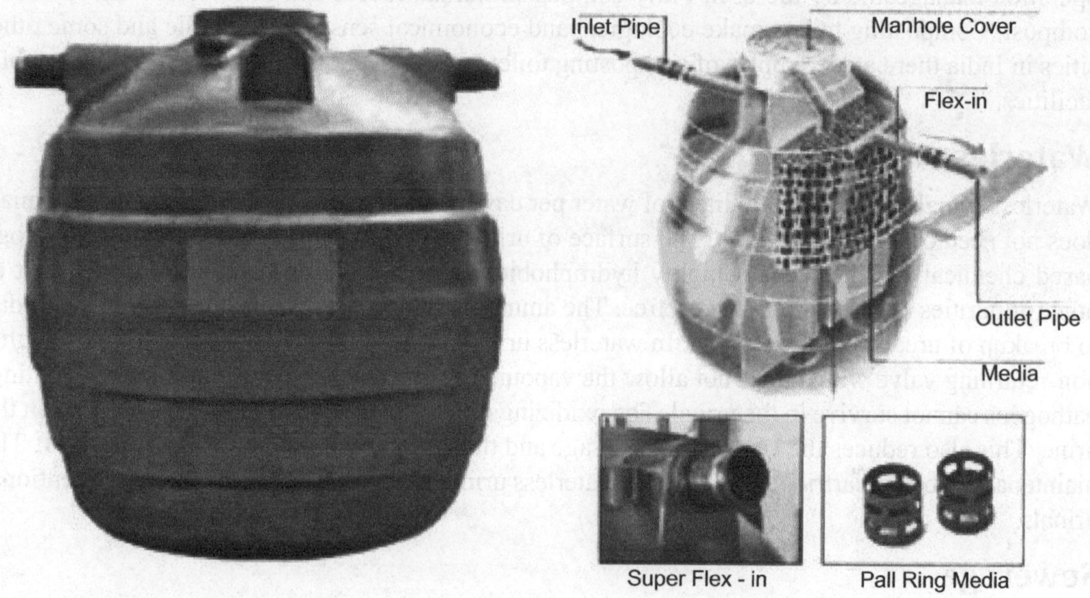

Fig. 9.14. Septic tank for first level treatment of black water from households
Source: *DUAC/M.N. Ashish Ganju, 2014, Ayanagar Urban Development*

Root Zone System : The Root Zone Process is emerging as an economical and efficient method to treat industrial and domestic effluents. More than 2000 types of bacteria and tens of thousands of fungi exist in the reed bed. These microbial organisms oxidise impurities in the waste water. In this process, aerobic and anaerobic zones exist side by side, inducing different types of chemical reactions and balancing bacterial growth, thus decomposing the contaminants to their basic form.

Three integrated components are essential to the system—the reeds, the reed bed and microbial organisms. The system involves running contaminated water through the root zones of especially designed reed beds. The reeds and the reed bed together provide efficient effluent treatment, and the released water is environmentally acceptable. Phosphates, sulphur compounds, nitrogenous materials reduce to their elemental forms, while BOD and COD are drastically brought down. Heavy metals precipitate from solution and are bound into the soil matrix. What comes out of this constructed marsh is treated waste water which is much cleaner than possible with any other technique.

The capital cost of the Root Zone System is roughly half of the conventional systems while operation and maintenance costs are around one fifth. The technology has the potential to reduce treatment costs considerably and therefore may gain wide application.

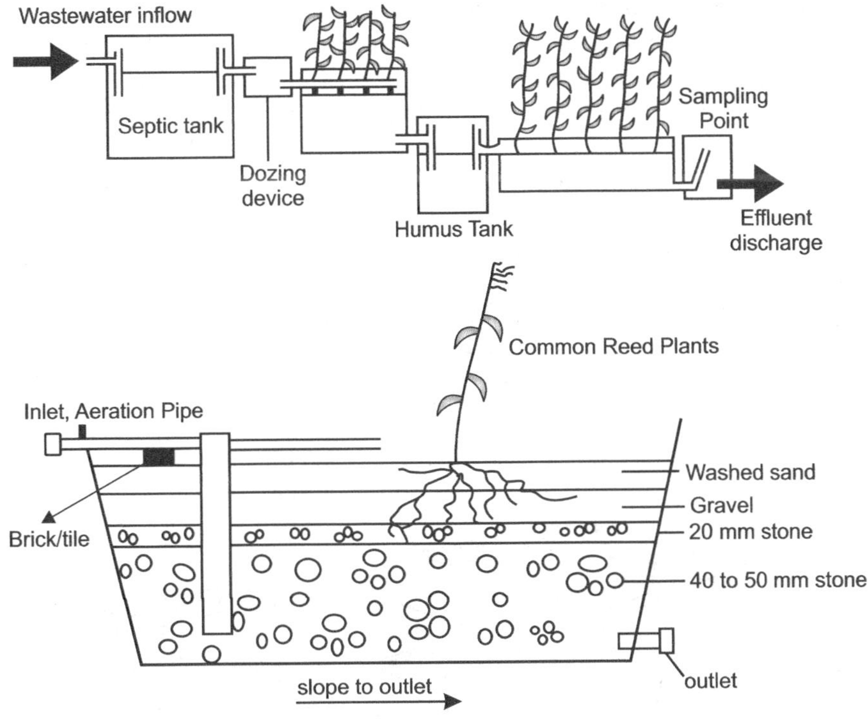

Fig. 9.15. Root Zone System Using Reed Beds as Constructed Wetland

Source: *Centre for Alternative Technology Publications, www.cat.org.uk*

Biological Composting System : For isolated areas, where municipal sewerage is not available, Biological Composting System provides a viable solution. The process uses oxygen in the air which converts sludge and organic wastes into carbon-dioxide, water and energy. The energy thus produced enables the microbial cells to divide, to move and utilize yet more sludge and waste. This is a natural process by which fallen leaves get converted into humus and revitalize the nutrition of the soil. Based on this principle, continuous bio-reactor composting system is a new generation technology for treatment of the sludge and organic wastes. The aerobic bacteria are faster, thus the process is more efficient and also the capital cost is reduced. The heat is generated in a vessel or a tunnel by bacterial action, raising the temperature to 70° C, which kills all the pathogens. Thus, the bio-reactors convert the sludge into pollution and germs free material, which is not possible in the digestion process.

The reaction chamber, which can be constructed in masonry and concrete, is comprised of two main components. The first is the compaction chamber with delivery hopper to feed the material, a pusher plate pushes the water/sludge into the compression chamber. The reactor is closed on all the sides having smooth surface on the inner walls. Ventilation ducts or channels in the floor supply air to dry the sludge. The compressed material is then delivered to the maturation chamber, where micro-organisms process the sludge. Heat produced by composting process, or if necessary, by artificial heating to 60° to 70° C ensures a pathogen free end-product. The final product can be used for local parks, agriculture or for treatment of wastelands. The reactors can be designed and installed in standard modules or batteries. This system eliminates pathogen contained leachate. As such, there is no danger to pollution and contamination of sub-soil water.

Extended Aeration Technique: An innovative system of sewage treatment is extended aeration technique. The processing unit can be designed in the form of a compact, modular and a self-contained system. It can be installed independent of the overall city system and is suitable for sewerage needs of scattered unauthorized colonies, villages and other areas. The process is based upon the phenomenon of self-oxidation by the bacteria. When the bacterial cells reach their ageing stage, the consumption of organic matter is maximised. The bacterial cells draw their own oxygen for additional energy which they require. The process of self-oxidation leads to stabilization of sludge and purification of the effluents. A sequence of the treatment process viz. screening, aeration, settling and thickening take place within the package unit. Thus, open land can be saved from spillover of sullage and waste. The unit can be installed underground and the site can be landscaped from above. It is protected against electrical currents and corrosion. The unit can also be constructed in the masonry/ concrete over the ground.

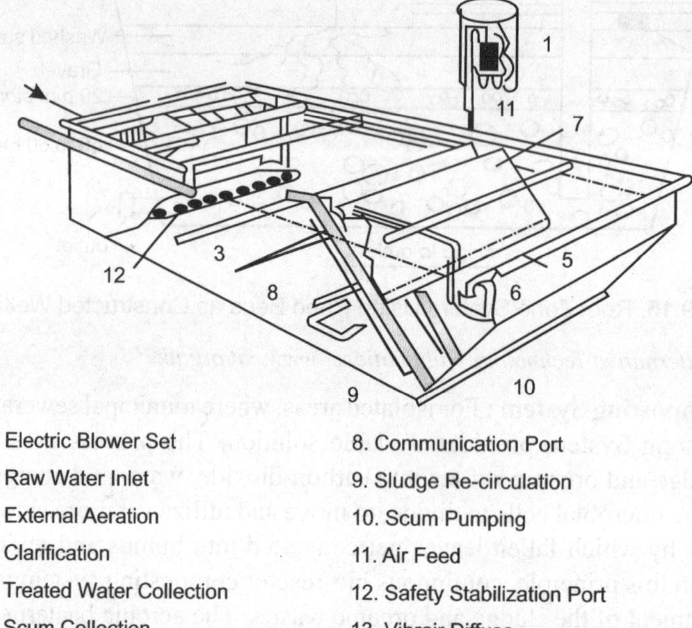

1. Electric Blower Set
2. Raw Water Inlet
3. External Aeration
4. Clarification
5. Treated Water Collection
6. Scum Collection
7. Baffle
8. Communication Port
9. Sludge Re-circulation
10. Scum Pumping
11. Air Feed
12. Safety Stabilization Port
13. Vibrair Diffuse

Fig. 9.16. Extended Aeration Technique

Solar Aquatic Septage Treatment System : In a typical septic treatment plant, effluent is discharged into a head works consisting of a receiving station and digester. From there it flows by gravity into in-ground tanks where the effluent is blended to compensate for variations in loads and is preconditioned. Following equalization and preconditioning, effluent is pumped to a clarifier. From here sludge is pumped to the sludge stabilization tank where it is aerobically stabilized. It then flows to the reed bed for passive composting. Underflow from the reed bed is recycled by pumping it back into the equalization tank for further treatment.

Liquid from the clarifier enters a series of solar silos that contain the plants and worms involved in the clean-up operation. After moving through the silos by gravity flow, the liquid enters a second clarifier. Solids from this clarifier are recycled back to the equalization tank, where they re-enter the system, reseeding microbes as they travel.

Next, the liquid moves through a gravel filled de-nitrifying marsh planted with grasses and is then sterilized with ultraviolet light before being discharged. Depending on total suspended solid limits, a sand filter may be required for final polishing before purified water is discharged.

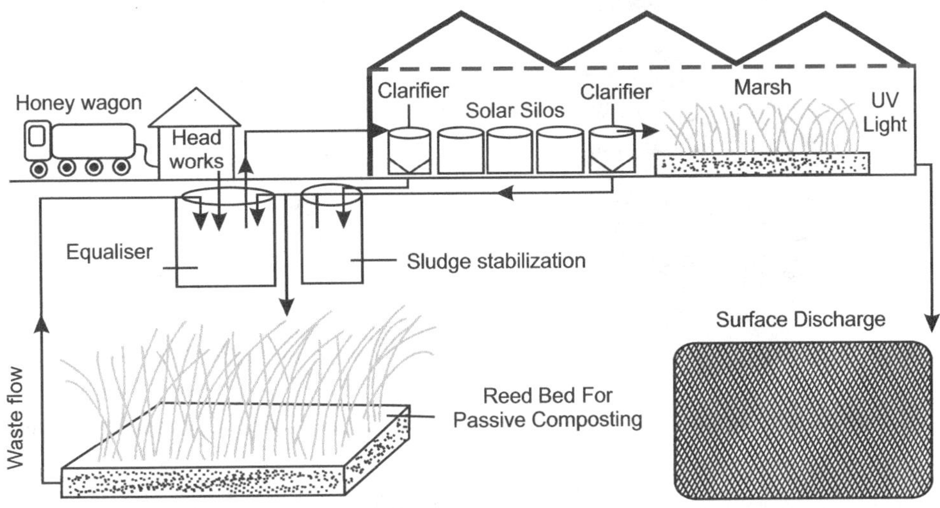

Fig. 9.17. Solar Aquatic Septage Treatment System

Source: *Ecological Engineering Associates & William E.Soper, Surface Application of Sewerage Effluent and Sludge, Madison, Wisconsin, 1979*

Biopaq-UASB Technology : The heart of the Biopaq system is the anaerobic reactor based on Paques Up flow Anaerobic Sludge Blanket (PAQ-UASB) process. The reactor consists of a large corrosion resistant tank which incorporates a unique 3-phase settler to separate the sludge, biogas and effluent. The settler is located at the top of the reactor and is designed for specific COD reactor loadings and hydraulic throughout. A flow distribution network is located at the base of the reactor. This network is designed to distribute the flow evenly throughout the bottom of the reactor. This eliminates short-circuiting and promotes the proper formation of the granular sludge which is a critical factor in reactor operation. The distribution network is designed to facilitate easy cleaning, thereby eliminating potential plugging problems.

The anaerobic process comprises a UASB reactor called Biopaq. The raw effluent is first taken to the buffer tank. The capacity of the buffer tank is calculated such that acid genesis phase is triggered immediately. The effluent is then pumped to Biopaq reactor through a series of distribution pipes. The multiple distributions ensure a uniform flow of liquid throughout the sludge blanket making maximum use of available high bacterial population. The liquid rises to the top of Biopaq reactor along with biogas generation and also some sludge particles.

Solid Waste Management

The problem of solid waste management is becoming acute due to increasing population, urbanisation, changing lifestyles and consumption patterns. The garbage from unauthorised developments, slums, Jhuggi-Jhompri (JJ) settlements, etc. is hardly collected which further adds to the environmental degradation. According to Aseem Burman Committee (1998), the informal waste pickers are the backbone of waste management. They not only help in cleaning the neighbourhood, but also reuse, recover, recycle and remanufacture an estimate about one-third of garbage.

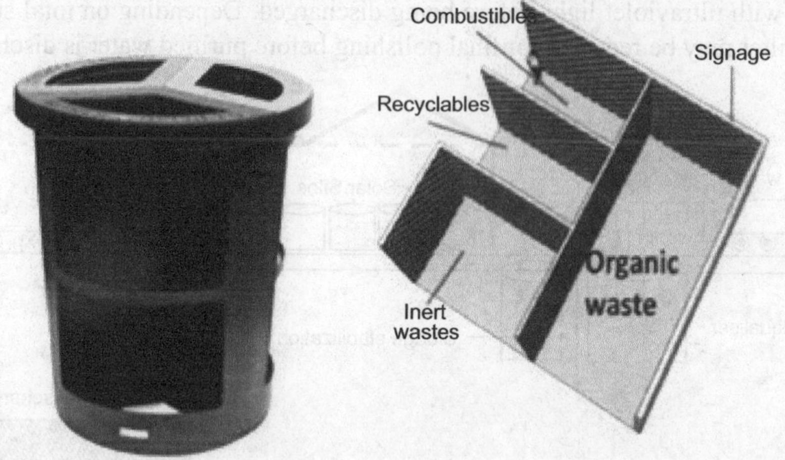

Fig. 9.18. Dustbins with Separate Chambers for Organic, Combustible, Recyclables and Inert Waste

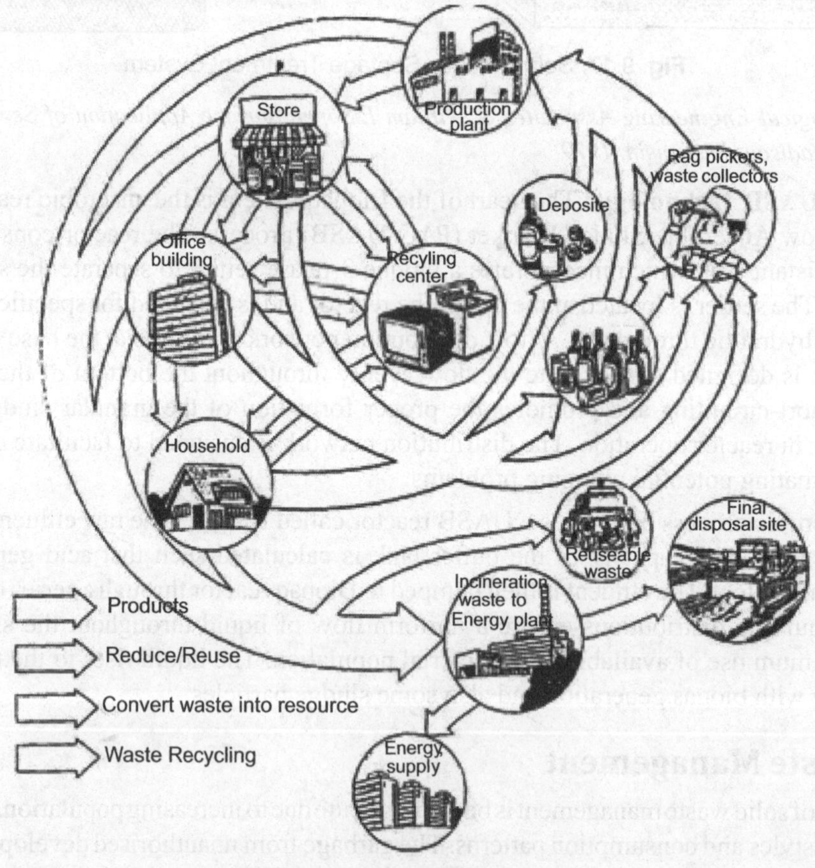

Fig. 9.19. Sustainable Waste Recycling

Other than domestic and office garbage, the waste includes bio-medical waste; electronics waste plastics, hazardous waste from abattoirs, markets and industries; construction debris and fly ash, etc., which requires specialized handling, disposal, recycling and reuse. Major part of solid waste is disposed of in sanitary landfills, which are often saturated and finding new sanitary landfill sites has become extremely difficult. There is no option but to resort to alternative, decentralized methods of waste treatment, reduction, recycle and use, which include solid waste energy and recycling facility (SWERF), vermiculture, fossilization and composting.

Various studies conclude that recycling waste is by far the cheapest alternative to landfills, and plants that convert garbage into other products are cheaper than those that burn garbage. As such, it may be more practical to build several small, decentralised waste facilities rather than a large one.

Energy Recovery from Waste: By adopting scientific methods energy can be recovered from waste. As the organic matter decays it produces biogas, known as landfill gas (LFG). Landfills have to be managed so that the LFG does not pose a threat to the surroundings. Rather than discharging it to the atmosphere, LFG can be recovered as useful energy. Indian municipal waste has a potential to generate 150-250 cu.mt. of biogas/LFG per ton depending upon the quality of wastes. By employing a set of generator and transformer, bio-gas can be converted in electrical energy.

Bio-methanation Technology: In this process organic matter of solid waste is segregated and thereafter it is fed directly into a bio-reactor, where in presence of methanagenic bacteria, and under an aerobic condition, the fermentation takes place and bio-gas is produced. In addition high quality organic manure is also produced. Energy can be recovered by digesting certain organic wastes and recovering the methane rich bio-gas which provides heat and electricity.

Fuel-Pellets: Municipal Solid Waste (MSW) comprises various materials such as paper, plastics, glass, metals, food and vegetable matter, rags, rubber, etc. By segregation of the organic materials from MSW, it can be dried, ground and pelletized. This can be added by biomass to enrich calorific value of fuel pellets.

A pilot project of the Department of Science and Technology has been set up at Mumbai for producing about 80 tons per day of refuse derived fuel pellets as a coal substitute. In Gujarat, Vadodara Municipal Corporation has taken up the production of petro-coal pellets from combustible garbage, plastic, dry leaves, discarded clothes and vegetable waste supplemented by oil or petro-waste available from oil refineries. After dehydrating and pulverizing the garbage, it is mixed with petro-waste and converted into the Pellet, which is about half the price of coal and emits lower levels of sulphur dioxide and carbon monoxide.

Incineration Technology: Incineration is a process of controlled combustion of solid wastes and residue. During combustion moisture is vaporized whereas the combustible portion produces heat, whereas carbon dioxide, water vapour, ash and non-combustibles, are the end products. The heat generated during incineration is recovered and utilised for the production of steam, heating water, and generating electricity. Incineration technology is economical for the treatment of large quantities of solid wastes by thermal process.

Pyrolysis/Gasification Technology: In this process segregated combustible matter is allowed for drying and thereafter it is shredded in a hammer mill. The combustion/pyrolysis of shredded matter takes place in a fluidized bed reactor without any fuel support. The end product includes combustible "producer" gas, which can be utilised for production of power. The heat produced in the process can also be employed for production of steam and ultimately generating power. Although not fully competitive with conventional electricity at today's prices, extracting energy from wastes offers environmental benefits, help to reduce fossil fuel consumption and, amongst other things, mitigate the problem of methane emissions from landfill sites.

Composting: Incineration is an effective solution, but it is expensive for wastes having a high proportion of vegetable and putrescible matter. Economic constraints favour composting, as the city wastes contain a significant amount of nitrogen, phosphate and potash, as well as organic soil supplements. For bio-degradable matter composting is one of the most popular systems of garbage disposal. Apart from saving land, valuable products like compost, biogas, heat, electrical power, recycled paper, plastics, glass, metal, etc. are obtained. Composting can be done in different ways, such as Aerobic window composting, Anaerobic trench composting and Vermi-composting.

Vermi-Composting: Composting of bio-degradable waste by earthworms is gaining popularity. Organic waste is allowed to be decomposed by micro-organisms already present in the waste. Earthworms degrade the organic waste by both physical and chemical breakdown in their gut. The gut of an earthworm acts as a bio-reactor providing ideal conditions for temperature. pH and oxygen concentration help in speedy growth of aerobic bacteria. These micro-organisms produce useful compounds like antibiotics, vitamins and plant growth hormones. Worms use about 5 to 10 per cent of the organic material for their growth and excrete the rest in the form of granular cast which is known as vermin-compost. The granular loose vermicast provides oxygen rich, nutrient rich media for aerobic microbes which further promote decomposition process. About 2,000 worms are required for a waste volume of 1 × 1 × 0.5 m. On an average 5 kg of waste is partially digested by 1,000 worms in a day.

Solid Waste Energy and Recycling Facility (SWERF): A sustainable solution for the management of municipal solid waste is by setting up a Solid Waste Energy and Recycling Facility (SWERF). SWERF reduces the need for land for landfills by 90 per cent odours and health risks are reduced as the SWERF process is totally enclosed. There is sterilized handling of recyclables and rejects as the municipal solid waste is first processed in an autoclave. Greenhouse gases are reduced to the maximum by efficient conversion technology.

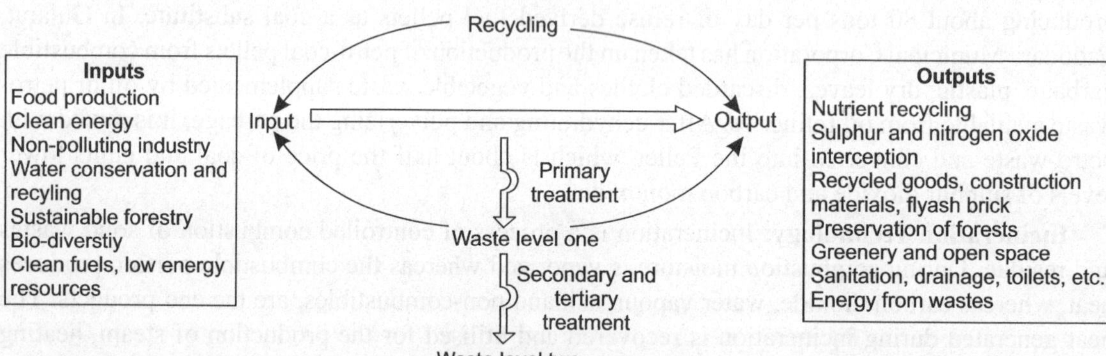

Fig. 9.20. Circular Metabolism

The SWERF system has the following features:

- Waste Reception
- Autoclaving of waste
- Mechanical separation of recyclables
- Organic pulp,washing,drying and storage
- Gasification of organic pulp to create syngas
- Electricity generation from syngas

About 30 to 35% of solid waste in urban areas comprises construction and demolition waste. The SWERF provides its segregation from other wastes and encourages its recycling, which can be used for land filling, road soling, pavement base material, production of pre-cast tiles, blocks and recycled concrete aggregate.

Pneumatic Solid Waste Management : Garbage transportation is one of largest overheads of the local bodies and overloads the roads. Pneumatic waste collection can mitigate these problems. It consists of an integrated collection station, piping system and discharge valves that are situated below vertical chutes. Waste of one type is collected into the garbage chute, where it is stored above a garbage valve between the emptying cycles. There is a main pipe network under the valve that connects all valves and transports the waste to the collection station. These systems work best in a radius of about a kilometer. Pneumatic waste collection offers a cleaner solution that can alleviate traffic congestion and encourage recycling. It also would improve the overall city hygiene, aesthetic, and fewer garbage trucks lead to a reduction in CO_2 emission, traffic noise, pollution and reduced haulage costs. This system has been adopted in Mecca Grand Mosque. Completed in 2013, Mari-Matic's Metro Taifun System is one of the largest automatic solid waste collection system in the World. The system conveys 900 tons of solid waste per day during peak seasons. Waste bags are fed into gravity chute intakes linked to a network of 30 km of pipelines running beneath the grand mosque complex. Transporting waste through airtight pipelines instead of using trucks minimizes problems of noise, smell and dust and uses much less energy.

Safety from Disasters and Emergencies

Natural disasters, such as earthquake, hurricane, floods and landslides cannot be prevented. However, by prudent planning and preparedness and relief measures, it is possible to minimize the loss of property and human lives to a great extent. It is essential to establish support systems to deal with major disasters, including the organization and dissemination of information, assistance and training. Fire, traffic accidents, outbreak of infectious diseases, collapse of structures, stampede, etc. are some of the man-made disasters, which can be avoided by proper planning and preventive measures. The areas of vulnerability need to be identified for proper planning and effective enforcement, including the following strategies:

(*a*) Micro-zonation surveys should be referred for land use planning, layout plans and building design.

(*b*) Building bye-laws should incorporate the aspects of multi-hazard safety and retrofitting. Priority should be given to public buildings such as hospitals, educational, institutional, power stations, infrastructure, heritage monuments, lifeline structures, and those which are likely to attract large congregation.

(*c*) Disaster Management Centers with a common platform for various safety and security services (*e.g.* police, disaster, structural, health, fire services, etc.) should be established. Media campaigns, educational and publicity about disasters and emergency should be taken up to promote safety culture and behavior.

(*d*) The key communication centers should be protected from natural disasters, *i.e.* flood, fire and earthquake, etc. and services restoration should be taken up on top priority.

There is a need to focus on strategic issues of how to prevent accidents and measures to be taken. It is necessary to investigate the cause of the accident and why it happened. Adequate steps should be taken to prevent accidents, mishaps or failures and to contain its aggravation in the city at construction site, power project, roads, rails, buildings, mines, embankments which may be due to geological failures, landslide, embankment failure, flooding, earthquake or other natural disasters, human and machine failures, and lack of adoption of environment, health and safety norms and protocols. The countries which have been successful in reducing the dangers tackled it through structured programs as part of their national missions with sustained implementation at local level.

The cities frequently witness building collapses. Most of the buildings in the unplanned areas, slums, the old city and unauthorized colonies are non-engineered, sub-standard, old and dilapidated and face the risks of structural safety. There is a need to check and retrofitting all such non-engineered buildings. The local bodies along with structural engineers and fire safety organizations can help the occupants in this task. It is also necessary to review, simplify and enforce the building codes. Fire can be prevented by building use and design, specifications, construction materials, process control, maintenance and better engineering practices.

DEBRIEFING QUESTIONS

1. What is the meaning of (*a*) Physical Infrastructure, (*b*) Social Infrastructure?
2. What are the main considerations in provision of schools, dispensaries and parks in a neighbourhood?
3. How the shortage of water supply can be overcome in housing areas?
4. Explain the following:
   (*a*) Renewable Energy
   (*b*) Energy Efficiency
   (*c*) Net Zero Energy
   (*d*) Biological Composting System
   (*e*) Waste Recycling
   (*f*) Circular Metabolism
5. What do you understand by community planning? Explain briefly.
6. What is understood by disaster resilient planning?
7. Write short notes on the following :
   (*a*) Standards of community facilities
   (*b*) Building Standards of Low Income Housing
   (*c*) Drainage and storm water management
   (*d*) Public Toilets

10

BUILDING RESOURCES AND TECHNOLOGY

India is bestowed with rich traditional building crafts and has abundant natural building materials. However, with the industrialisation of building construction, this wealth is depleting and building crafts are becoming obsolete. There is a tremendous potential to rediscover and revive the conventional materials, methods and diverse crafts of construction for low cost housing. The popular methods and local materials together with modern technology are the cornerstones of low cost housing. Recently, based on traditional materials and techniques, quite a few systems for roofing, walls and floor have emerged.

The use of local materials is generally more appropriate to the climate and costs. Brick, tile, lime, surkhi, plam thatch, stones and country timber can replace cement, steel and glass. Generally these are more suited to the hot humid climate. They do not make the local masons and craftsmen redundant, are generally less expensive and also minimises the use of the country's scarce and non-renewable resources.

Mud Housing

For conservation of building cost and energy, there has been considerable interest in mud housing during recent years. However, its acceptability depends on changing the image associated with the huts and rural houses. If you build low cost houses only for the poor, people think that it is good or just temporary. To conserve energy we have to stop cutting down trees, and conserve heat and oil needed for making modern construction materials. Compressed mud is a suitable material for walls. An essential requirement is to impart training to build regular mud bricks. One can teach how to make adobe bricks more regular by adding a stabilizer like lime. A machine can help to compress it to produce regular sized mud bricks. The problem of mud walls is their protection from rain, dampness and climate. The way to protect a mud house is to build an extended roof. The mud walls can be half the cost of the regular walls and one-twelfth the cost of doors and windows.

The pioneer architect Laurie Baker advocates use of mud, stabilized earth and adobe bricks for low cost house construction. However, he feels that the government should take the lead by changing the codes, standards specification, working methods and techniques.

The late Hasan Fathy, Egyptian Architect, had been another phenomenon in low cost housing. While the architects and building industry were busy in finding new techniques, materials and industrialised system for low cost housing, he was looking back at the traditional methods, crafts and materials. Some called him the "Messiah of the shelterless", while the people impressed by his beautiful forms called him the "Picasso of the earth." Fathy found the solution to acute housing problem in mud brick structures. Not just by talking, but by his designs he demonstrated and convinced many that mud is as glamorous as concrete. He had deep respect for the tradition and appreciation for ancient Egyptian housing, where in his words, "the tradition and appreciation for ancient Egyptian housing were yet to clash with modern technology." He continues....

> *"Every house is a wonder, every house different. A whole village of specious, lovely, clean and harmonious house, each more beautiful than the last. How can people so poor that they cannot even afford to buy bread even dream of a factory made house. It is pity that the government authorities think of people as millions to be shoveled into various boxes, loads of gravel."*

During the 1940s the Egyptian government invited Fathy to rehabilitate 6000 inhabitants of Al-Qarna, a village on the west of the Nile, opposite the tourist resort of Luxor. Fathy wanted each house to be different to suit the individual family. He had a difficult time to change the conventional approach of evolving standard designs and bureaucratic notion that the poor were too ignorant to decide the individual requirement for themselves. Fathy, however, prevailed and new village grew on the sands of A1-Qarna. Built by local artisans with local and cheap materials, mud-bricks, sand and pebbles, it is a pilgrim centre for the new breed architects. It is a beautiful composition of arches, domes, pastel colour walls - all set in a human scale. *"People say to use mud bricks for housing is to take a step backwards but in reality it is step forward,"* he recalled in an interview. *"Concrete blocks bear no human reference. The answer is underfoot,"* Fathy said.

Fig. 10.1. Queen Hatshepsut Making Mud Brick.

Fig. 10.2. Adobe Construction from Egyptian hylograph.

The calculations of firewood consumption show that each brick consumes about 0.32 kg of wood. This means that the construction of a small 50 sq mt house will need about 5 tonnes of firewood. The use of bricks, thus, involves continuous depletion of forests and fuel. By using mud, lime, sun-burnt bricks, bamboo roof and other materials like polythene sheets, etc. the energy consumption of a house would come down to about 0.3 tonnes of firewood. At the same time the cost may reduce by about 30%. Sun burnt brick or adobe has a high resistance to erosion and given additional inputs to prevent moisture absorption, this will go a long way in providing an energy efficient and a cheaper house. Lime rendering provides an enormous improvement in the performance of the walls, as calcium carbonate is known to be a very good waterproofing agent. If a layer of calcium hydroxide is provided on wall, it acts as a very good impervious layer. Such cheaper measures can substantially contribute to conserve the existing housing stock. It is not enough to build new housing; there are so many old buildings whose life needs to be extended.

By adopting several simple techniques, the quality and durability of mud brick structures can be substantially enhanced to conserve the existing housing stock.

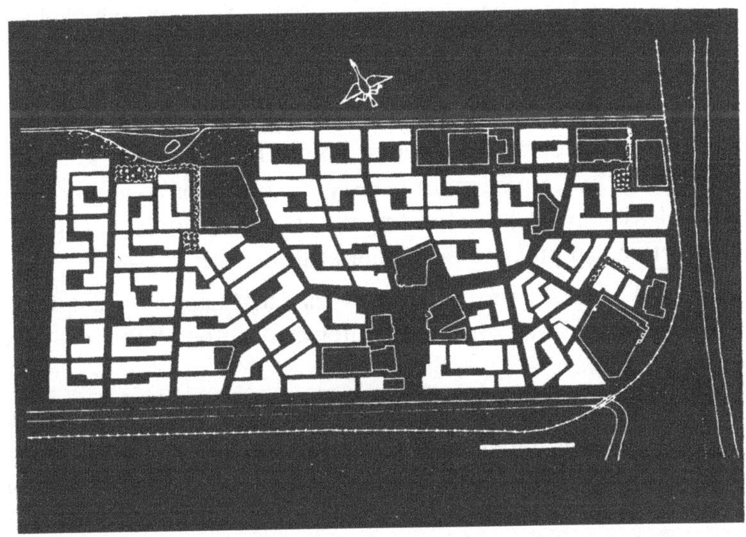

Fig. 10.3. Hassan Fathy Plan of Al-Qarna recreated traditional mud brick village architecture. He was able to produce a vocabulary, which became a living experiment in rural housing

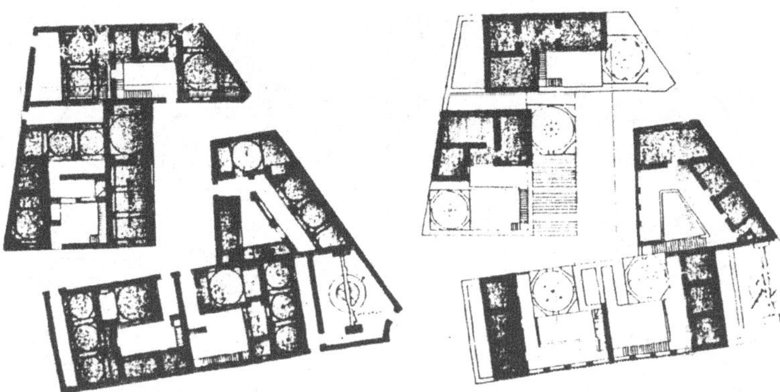

Fig. 10.4. Al-Qarna, Egypt, Hasan Fathy, architect. The houses respond to desert climate and living pattern of peasantry communities

By using binding and stabilizing agent like lime, cement, gum, cow-dung, rice husk, resin, organic fibre, etc. the adobe construction can be substantially improved. To densify the soil ramming or compaction are the common methods. Not only the soil being used for making bricks or walls should be compacted but also the earth below the foundation should be well rammed before erecting the foundations and walls. This helps in strengthening of the structure and avoids pores and cavities, which are dangerous for dampness and seepage. Insertion layers of brick tiles in the walls protect them from rain and dampness. They also provide extra strength to bear the impact of load and earthquake.

Projecting the roof with overhang helps protect the walls against rain. In case of areas with high dampness, it is necessary to build the sub-structure and foundation with fired brick, stone, or stabilised earth and provide a higher level of plinth. By plastering the walls mud stabilized with cow-dung or white lime composite, or painting makes them more durable and smooth in finish. In extreme soil and weather conditions, only stabilised mud bricks should be used. Compacted soil blocks have greater compressive strength as compared to country bricks and are often cheaper. Earth bricks and blocks are very poor in tensile strength. As such, while designing structures, the effort should be to minimise eccentricities and to make best use of compressive property by adoption of arches, vaults and domes for spanning. In case walls are subjected to tensile loads, these should be reinforced with steel bars, bamboo or other appropriate material. By proper detailing and rendering, walls can be protected from water. This is important as the saturated wet strength of earth structure can be less by 25 percent of the dry strength. For economy it is suggested to use short spans of roof (say less than 4 m). By limiting the area of opening (say upto 15 percent of wall area) the adobe construction can prove to be economical.

The use of plain mud blocks with no additives is satisfactory for single-storeyed building. Waterproof coatings based on animal glue and whitewash can be effectively used to protect mud block walls against rain erosion.

Soil cement blocks can be load bearing and made water-proof. Un-plastered external soil-cement block surface can perform satisfactorily when the annual rainfall is in the range of 900 to 1,000 mm. Use of lime or cement and lime combination is also quite feasible for manufacture of the blocks.

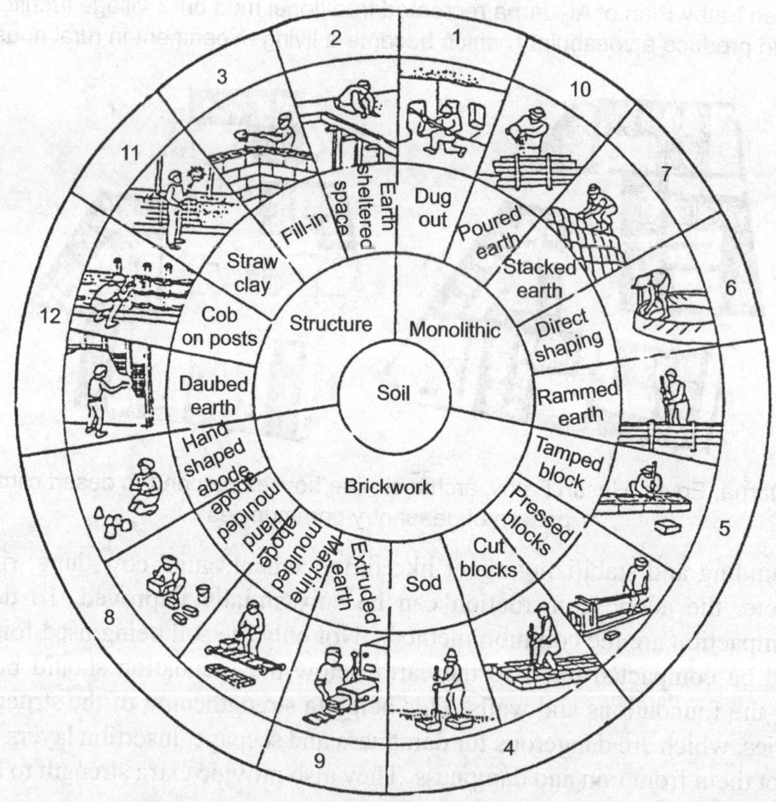

Fig. 10.5. Use of earth as a building material

Well made soil cement blocks do not need plastering in most cases. The front portion of mud blocks can be stabilised by the addition of lime surkhi. This gives a built-in plaster for the mud blocks which withstand the heavy rains.

Mud blocks may not be successful if there is too much sand in the soil which is prone to erosion. Otherwise, they should be protected with a coating of tar and a wash of lime and surkhi on top. Simple lime soil plaster, using lime, red soil and sand makes them resistant to rains. Such plaster is cheapar and sticks to the wall better than cement plaster.

Mud bricks are made from unusable clay or pond clay which shrinks and cracks on drying. They are made stable by adding 2.5% of cement. The conventional mud brick making machine has been modified to create holes in the bricks which ensure a greater compaction and when baked, dry more uniformly throughout. As such, they require lesser time and fuel than conventional bricks.

Other Local/Low cost Building System and Components.

The other systems and components developed include bricks and tiles, hollow concrete blocks, precast Tee-block, precast funicular shells, cast-in-situ funicular shells, thermocole core RCC panels, paper honeycomb core door/cladding panels, eggcrate core door/cladding panels, fibre concrete, etc.

Bricks & Tiles

Brick is the most sought-after building material, and is widely manufactured and used locally. The clay available in river basins, water tanks and coastal areas are plastic in nature. For proper moulding, drying and burning of bricks and tiles. The clay requires addition of some non-plastic material like sand, stone dust or flyash. Clay–fly ash bricks have the advantages of saving clay and fuel.

The future trends in brick making go in three directions : (*a*) to reduce the weight by making perforated or hollow bricks and consequently reduce the consumption of clay and fuel, (*b*) to improve thermal efficiency of brick kilns, and (*c*) to produce bricks made of sand and lime or fly ash sand-lime or stabilised soil bricks by pressing and/or steam curing, requiring much less energy than in burnt-clay bricks. Perforated bricks show as good compressive strength as solid bricks, and are used for load bearing structures. Hollow bricks with over 30% hollow space, are mainly used for non-load bearing walls and partitions. Burnt clay flooring, terracing tiles, glazed/non-glazed ceramic tiles are produced extensively in different shapes, sizes and designs.

Burnt-clay bricks: Colour: generally blood-red or brown. Shape: should be regular with sharp edges which is better achieved in machine-made bricks.

Dimensions (as per IS specification): Modular: length 190 mm, width 90 mm, height 90 or 40 mm, Standard Dimensions: length 210 mm, width 110 mm, height 70 mm. Locally manufactured bricks may have different dimensions.

Dimensional tolerance: On testing a lot of 20 bricks the length, width and height should not vary more than 2% on average, and not more than 2 mm on individual brick in length, width and height.

Efflorescence: On immersion of a brick in water drying a white scum or salt gets deposited on the brick surface known as efflorescence. It indicates the low quality of brick.

Lime bursting: Burnt-clay bricks contain unburnt limestone (kankar) particles which cause expansion in volume, bursting and cracking in bricks.

Other bricks: They are (*i*) Sand-lime bricks, (*ii*) Flyash sand-lime bricks, and (*iii*) Stabilised-soil bricks. Sand-lime bricks are available in compressive strength of 75-250 kg/cm^2 and water absorption of 10-15%. These bricks are produced by high-pressure forming steam curing. In fly ash sand-lime bricks, fly ash is substituted for sand, the process of manufacturing being the same as for sand-lime bricks. Stabilised-soil bricks, produced by using about 5% cement as stabiliser, give compressive strength, of 35-40 kg/cm^2 depending upon the forming pressure applied during production. The above three types of bricks are generally free from the defects of efflorescence and lime-bursting of burnt-clay bricks.

Table 10.1: Classification of Burnt-Clay Bricks

Brick Class (IS)	Average compressive strength kg/cm^2	Water absorption after 24 hr immersion%	Uses
350 300 250 200 175 150	350-400 300-350 250-300 200-250 175-200 150-175	15 (for all classes)	Structural brick-work, reinforced brick masonry in multi-storey construction, heavy duty flooring, class above 300 for heavy engineering foundations
125 100 75	125-150 100-125 75-100	20 (for all classes)	For load bearing brick walls, 3-4 storey building, flooring, foot paths, etc.
50 35	50-75 35-50	20 (for both classes)	For general 1-2 storey residential building, boundary walls, etc.

Source: BMTPC (1997)

Table 10.2: Classification of Flooring, Walling & Terracing Tiles

Type of Tiles	Breaking load kg	Water absorption after 24 hr water immersion %	Uses
• Clay roofing tile – Mangalore pattern AA Class A Class – Allahabad pattern – Country	 90-100 90-100 100-85 60-85	 12-14 14-16 12-15 13-18	Roofing of residential and other buildings. All types are generally locally produced and used.
• Clay flooring tile	110-120	12-15	Residential/commerical building floors
• Acid resistant clay/ floor tiles	200-350	5-7	Industrial building with floors exposed to acid spillage
• Ceramic tiles – Wall (glazed) – Floor Tiles (glazed) (unglazed)	 100-150 300-350 300-350	 0-0.5 0-0.5 3-5	Decorative and common tiles for bath rooms & walls. Decorative and common unglazed vitreous tiles for floors

Source: BMTPC (1997)

The quality of construction depends on the quality of bricks. The deteriorating quality of bricks witnessed during the past few decades has been a serious setback to the building industry. There are various reasons for this. One reason is that the construction activity and consequently the requirement of bricks has been increasing at a very construction activity and consequently the requirement of bricks has been increasing at a very fast pace resulting in expansion in brick manufacture without adequate attention to quality. Insufficient attention of earth quality and blending. Inadequacy of trained operators and lack of care and attention in the manufacture are factors responsible for the deterioration.

The changes in the dimension of bricks witnessed during the last hundred years have also been responsible for the deterioration. It is common knowledge that thin bricks bake better and as such it is easier to manufacture quality bricks if they are thin. Since ancient times till the Mughal period bricks were no thicker than two inches. The excavations from Harappa and the monuments of the Mughals testify this. The British were responsible for introducing the three inch brick and along with it the bond known as the English bond and the Flemish bond. The reason is not known but it would appear that it was intended to reduce the courses and speed up construction. The three inch thickness allows reasonable baking. Almost the entire production is now in 9" × $4\frac{1}{2}$" × 3" size which has come to be accepted as the standard construction dimension.

The Central Building Research Institute has been promoting the modular brick measuring 8"×4"×4" (20×10×10 cm). The brick manufacturers refused to accept this. They argued that a four inch brick would never bake well. The requirement of coal would be also increased, if energy required increase in proportion with the thickness. Further, the masons found it difficult to hold it in one hand. The modular brick never could take off.

Table 10.3: Comparison of Different Bricks and Bonds

Wall 100 sq.ft	**British Brick 9" × 4" × 3"**	**Modular Brick 8" × 4" × 4"**	**Cladding Brick 9" × 4" × 2"**	**Classical Brick 12" × 4" × 2"**
Bond	English	English	Hudco	Hudco
Wall Thickness	9"	8"	6"	6"
Bricks	1200	900	1200	900
Mortar (sqf)	525	500	416	400

Source: *Sharma, SK, Efficient Brick Size and Bond, Hudco, New Delhi*

According to the HUDCO, the manufacture of bricks in the country should revert back to the classical brick which after allowing for mortar joint should be 29 × 11 × 5 cms. Reckoning one centimeter mortar, the finished dimension would be 30 × 12 × 6 cms giving a grid of six centimetres mortar to work on. The thickness of the basic wall in Hudco Bond would be 17 cms or 6.7".

The bricks, low cost, locally available, recyclable and user friendly. They are climatically more comfortable as compared to concrete, steel, stones, etc. and offer unlimited variety of design, uses and alternatives.

Due to the uneven hand-made bricks and the presence of underfired bricks which disintegrate during the monsoon, cement plastering is commonly adopted. Baker developed strong walls and attractive brickwork by introducing new bonding technique which can accommodate dimensional variations. Underfired bricks can be eliminated by thoroughly soaking them before use. Interesting texture and patterns can be created by skillful use of ordinary bricks which do not need any plastering.

Flyash Bricks

Flyash, sand, and lime small quantity of chemical accelerator are mixed in a suitable proportion. A homogenised mix of raw materials is prepared by adding water. The mix is subject to a pressure of approximately 250 kg/cm^2 in hydraulic or manual press. The compressed bricks are then exposed to natural drying for 48 to 72 hours. Semi-dried bricks are then cured under saturated or atmospheric pressure of steam (also known as auto-claving or hydrothermal treatment). Steam cured bricks are then stacked in the open, during which they gain further strength. Flyash bricks of various types can be manufactured by this process. These can also be manufactured on a small scale by manual presses. The manufacturing process involves the following stages:

(*i*) Procuring raw material, viz. flyash from thermal power stations, sand and lime.
(*ii*) Mixing lime, flyash and accelerator with clean water in a prescribed proportion.
(*iii*) Forming green bricks by block presses.
(*iv*) Drying the bricks.
(*v*) Fixing the bricks or steam curing.
(*vi*) Stacking.

The process of making flyash-sand-lime bricks is quite simple. The plant and machinery are easily available all over the country. For steam curing water and power are required. Diesel can also be used for steam generation.

Flyash bricks are of light gray colour, uniform in shape and size, having strength and absorb less water. The bricks have low coefficient of variation, enabling the design of brickwork with a low factor of safety. Since the bricks have uniform and smooth surface, a saving in the mortar and plastering can be expected. The bricks can be used within 24 hours of their manufacture. They are free from efflorescence and stains. The cold crushing strength of flyash bricks is 150 kg/cm^2 as compared to 75 kg/cm^2 for class-1 bricks. Their water absorption is 13 to 15% as compared to 20% for conventional bricks.

Lime pulveriser, electrical hoists, storage bunker, vibrators, screw feeders, belt conveyors, mixer, hydraulic press, transfer buckets, trolley, curing chambers and boilers are the main items of equipment and machinery required for a plant of flyash bricks.

Besides large mechanised plants, hand operated, small scale presses for production of flyash bricks at local levels are also available. The Building Centre, Society for Technology and Action for Rural Advancement and various other organisations provide technical help and equipments for manufacture of flyash bricks at the local level.

Following types of flyash brick can be manufactured:

(*i*) **High Strength Brick:** Such bricks have three times higher crushing strength, low water absorption and are accurate in dimensions, with better surface finish.

(*ii*) **Perforated Bricks:** Perforations in the bricks ensure a better compaction and a more uniform baking and drying. Such bricks require lesser time and coal/fuel than the conventional solid bricks. They are lighter and allow better bonding and handling. In the advanced countries 70% of the bricks produced are perforated bricks. These bricks allow a saving in raw material and fuel/energy consumption. These are 30% lighter and as such result in economy in construction, reduction in the deadweight and transportation costs.

(*iii*) **Hollow Clay Bricks:** These are used as filler block in the floor and roofing slabs with a considerable saving in cement and steel. These also have insulating properties.

(*iv*) **Heavy Duty Bricks and Paving Bricks:** These are used in heavy engineering works such as piers, bridge works and abutments of retaining walls. These have a high strength of more than 600 psi and low porosity, which is below 5%.

(*v*) **Sewer Bricks:** These are used for lining of sewers and drains for disposal of sewerage, industrial wastes and storm water.

Stones

A variety of stones quarried, cut and dressed, either polished or rough textured, are used in foundations, masonry, flooring, roofing, as well decorative facing panels/ veneers. Stones as coarse and fine aggregates are required for concrete and concrete products. Stones are still extensively used in various parts of the country as they are locally available with proven durability. There is a good export market for polished marble, granite are slate stones. Serpentine and soap stones have no specific classification. The stones are classified as given under:

Table 10.4: Classification of Stones

Rock Type	Stone
Igneous Sedimentary Metamorphic Natural stones are identified by : (*a*) compactness, (*b*) size, shape and strength (*c*) colour & aesthetic appeal.	Granite, basalt Limestone, marble, Sandstone, laterite Slate

Table 10.5: Stone Types, Properties and Uses

Properties						
Stone	**Density kg/m^3 (min)**	**Water absorp-tion % max.**	**Compressive strength range kg/cm^2**	**Resistance to abra-sion**	**Re-sist-ance to Acid**	**General use**
Granite & basalt	2500	0.04	1400 - 2400	VG	G	Decorative facing, flooring; walls, foundation; concrete slabs & tiles
Limestone a. Low density b. High density	1700 2400	7.5 3.0	200-500 500-1500	G	P	Aggregates for concrete & tiles, walls, special types for flooring

Marble a. Compact & white b. With flaws & colour	 2500 2200	0.75	500 - 1800	G	P	Flooring, decorative facing; slabs & tiles; aggregates for concrete tiles.
Sandstone a. Standard b. Quartzite c. Bluestone	 2200 2400 25500	 5.0 3.0 1.0	250-1500	G	VG	Aggregates; decorative facing; slabs & tiles; walls
Slate	2400	0.5	700-1000	G	G	Roofing; fine aggregates; decorative facing
Laterite	1700	20.0	500-800	P	F	Walling blocks
Serpentine & Soapstone	1500	1.5	800-1000	F	F	Decorative facing hearths & metals, fillers & ceramics

Key: VG : Very Good, G : Good, P : Poor, F : Very Poor
Source: *BMPTC (1997)*

Binding Materials

A house has thousands of joints, maximum being in the masonry work. From simple soil and lime mortar, cement has become the most common material of joining blocks, bricks and plastering. Very often low income families cannot afford Portland cement, which is becoming out of their reach. It is necessary to promote the development of the alternatives and less costly binding agents. Albeit somewhat less efficient, these alternative may also reduce energy consumption and the level of technical complexity.

Lime

Lime has multiple uses, *e.g.* in agriculture for the enrichment of soils, for stabilisation of roads, for sugar refining, etc. In the field of construction, lime provides coarse plaster for masonry and in the preparation of soft surface coating. The production of siliceous limestone bricks using lime as a binder can be competitive, compared with the production of clay bricks. Lime is easy to produce, even on a small scale. Except under certain situations, it is generally available at a lower price than cement. However, with the advent of portland cement, use of lime has been more or less relegated to rural areas of the country.

Lime is used in conjunction with other materials, like sand, pozzolana (surkhi), gypsum, etc. for making mortar or plaster. Several varieties of lime, like quicklime, hydraulic lime, fat lime, magnesium lime and kankar lime can be used according to availability and purpose.

Basically, all limestones contain calcium carbonate together with some other ingredients and impurities. Quicklime is manufactured from limestone, which is mixed with coal (6:1 ratio) and is fired in a vertical shaft kiln. Limestone is calcined at about 1000-1100° centigrade. Quicklime is slaked with proportion of water to form hydrated lime. Aluminous hydraulic limestone contains a high proportion of aluminium silicate. It has hydraulic property, by which it hardens by itself in dampness and humidity. It is quite strong and can be used in masonry and mortar with pozzolana, gypsum etc. Semi-hydraulic limestone is not as pure as eminently hydraulic lime. It is suitable for simple structures.

Fat lime has high calcium contents and less impurities. It can be readily slaked and bears good strength. Although, it takes a long time to set, it facilitates easy working. It can be used with pozzolana, gypsum, etc. for mortaring and plastering.

Magnesium lime is obtained from limestone containing magnesium carbonate. It slakes with difficulty and needs much attention in working.

Kankar lime is prepared from round pebbles and stones commonly available in the riverbeds. Besides lime, this limestone has several other chemicals and impurities. This is cheaply available and is commonly used in rural areas.

For slaking of lime generally the following methods adopted:

(*a*) Tank slaking,

(*b*) Platform slaking, and

(*c*) Mechanical slaking.

Slaking process involves cleaning of limestone, hydration, grinding, dehydration and drying, sieving and then finally packing/storage and use.

Traditional production of lime involves wastage of energy and fuel. Uncertainty and unreliability of its quality often lead to a lack of confidence on the part of users. Providing quality marking, standardisation and technical assistance in modernisation of lime industry can help to revive its popularity.

Details of different types of limes, their application and recommended lime-gypsum mixture for internal plastering are provided in Tables 10.6 and 10.7:

Table 10.6: Building Lime: Classification and Application

Lime class (BIS)	Type of lime	Application	Compressive str. of mortar kg/cm^2
A	Eminently hydraulic lime CaO min 70%	• Structural purpose • Mortar with sand alone, usually 1:3, by volume. • Sets fast when mixed with water but slower than cement.	22.5
B	Semi-hydrualic lime CaO, min 60%	• Masonry mortars with sand along • Usually 1:3 by volume • Sets moderately fast	17.5
C	Fat lime (High calcium lime) CaO min. 85%	• Finishing coat in plastering • White washing • Cement or pozzolana (surkhi, cinder, fly ash) as mortar 1:1:6	30-55

D	Magnesium limes (*a*) Dolomitic MgO min. 15% max. 40% (*b*) High magnesium MgO min. 5% MgO max. 15%	• Finishing coat in plastering • White washing mortar 1:1:6 or 1:2:9 • Finishing coat in plastering • White washing with cement as mortar, 1:1:6	30-40
E	Kankar lime (*a*) Medium CaO, 40% (*b*) Low CaO, 30%	• Self-setting with water for hydraulic structures; 1:3 mortar • Actual performance depends on the type of clay materials in kankar.	20-25

Source: *NBO*

Table 10.7: Recommended Lime-Gypsum Mixes for Internal Plastering

Background	Undercoat (by vol.)				Finishing coat (by vol.)			
	GP	**PC**	**L**	**S**	**GP**	**PC**	**L**	**S**
Brick work	1/2	1/4	1	2-4	1/2	-	1	1/2
Precast concrete	2	1/4	1	5	1/2	1/4	1	-
Fibre board	1		1/4	1	1/2	-	1	1

GP = Gypsum Plaster, PC = Portland Cement, L = Lime, S = Sand.

Source: *BMPTC, 1997*

There are several types of Portland Cement, varying in mineralogical composition, fineness, rate of hardening strength development and amount of heat generated during setting and hardening. These variables, depending on specific construction, need to be taken into account during the manufacturing process. Blended cement contains Portland cement and admixture, such as flyash calcined clay, pozzolana, granulated blast furnace slag to improve impermeability or corrosion resistance of concrete against sea and sulphate water. Cement is supplied in bags and also in steel drums for bulk uses. Cement gets easily deteriorared quality on long storage. Particularly in damp conditions or when exposed to air. Major types of cement and their application, their physical and chemical requirements and functions and uses of admixtures are given in following tables:

Table 10.8. Classification of Cements and Applications

Major types of cement	Application
Ordinary Portland (33 grade)	General purpose, concrete plaster in construction work
Ordinary Portland (43 grade)	Special grade high strength for structural concrete
Ordinary Portland (63 grade)	Special grade high strength for structural concrete
Low heat Portland	Initial setting time is longer; used for mass concrete
Rapid Hardening Portland	Strength gain is fast; used for precast concrete

Hydrophobic Portland cement	Resistance to moisture on storage; used for general purpose
White Portland cement	Flooring and precast terrazzo tiles
Slag cement	Provides mild sulphate resistance in concrete work
Super sulphate cement	Provides high sulphate resistance in marine construction
High alumina cement	Provides high sulphate resistance in marine construction
High alumina cement	Provides mild chemical resistance for furnaces and chemical storage areas
Sulphate resistance cement	Special types used in sulphate water foundation and structures
Pozzolana cement	Mild chemical resistance; used in mass concrete; provides better impermeability
Masonry cement	Used for masonry only

Source: *BMTPC, 1997*

Table 10.9: Physical & Chemical Requirements of Cement

Properties	**Ordinary Portland cement**	**Low heat Portland cement**	**Rapid hardening Portland cement**	**High strength ordinary Portland cement**	**Hydrophobic Portland cement**	**White Portland cement**
Specific surface cm^2/gm	2250	3200	3250	3500	3500	2250
Setting time minutes (Vicat) initial (minimum) Final (max)	30 600	60 600	30 600	30 600	30 600	30 600
Soundness Lechatelier (max.) mm.	10	10	10	10	10	10
Fleet of hydration 7 days (maximum) 8 days (maximum)	—	65 cal/g 75 cal/g	—	—	—	—
Compressive str. kg/cm^2 min. at 7 days 28 days	220	160 350	—	330 430	220 310	Not less than 90% of specification
MgO (%)(max.)	6.0	6.0	6.0	6.0	6.0	6.0
SO_3 (%) (max.)	3.0	2.75	2.75	3.0	2.75	2.75
Insoluble residue (%) (max.)	4.0	2.0	2.0	2.0	2.0	2.0

Loss on ignition (%). (max)	5.0	4.0	4.0	4.0	4.0	5.0
Specific surface cm^2/g (min)	2250	3000	—	4000	2250	3000
Setting time minutes Initial (minimum) Final(maximum)	 30 600	 30 600	 90 1440	 20 600	 30 600	 30 600
Compressive str. (kg/cm^2 (min) 7 days 28 days	 220 —	220 310	 50 —	220 300	— —	220
Soundness Lechatelier mm (max.)	10	10	10	5 (Cold)	5	10
Expansion soundness autoclave (max) %	0.8	0.8	1	-	-	0.8
Slag content %	25-65	-	-	Min 70	-	-
Pozzolana content %	-	10-25	-	4.0	-	-
Insoluble residue (max.) %	4.0	Related to Pozzolana content	-	4.0	-	4.0
MgO (max.)%	8.0	6.0	-	10	-	6.0
SO_3 (max.)%	3.0	3.0	-	6	-	3.0
Loss on ignition %	4.0	5.0	-	-	-	4.0

***Source:** BMPTC, 1997*

Table 10.10: Functions, Ingredients and use of Admixtures in Cement Concrete

Functions	**Main ingredients**	**Dosage % by wt. of cement**	**Use**
Workability aid Air entraining Set retarder Water reducer Plasticizer	Wood resins, detergents, sugar carboxylic acid; silicone sulphonated hydrocarbon, polymers, etc.	0.5 1.0 1.0 0.5	To reduce water/cement ratio in concrete but improve workability and slump properties
Accelerator	Calcium chloride Trichloroethanal amine	1-2 0.5-1.0	Improving corrosion resistance of steel reinforcement

Corrosion inhibitors	Sodium benzoate, stannous chloride, Sodium nitrite	1-2.0	Improving corrosion resistance of steel reinforcement
Pozzolana	Fly ash, calcined clay, Surkhi, volcanic ash	1.5 to 2.0	To produce Portland - Pozzolana cement or in-situ admixture effect low heat of hydration, improve impermeability and sulphate resistance
Curing compound	Vegetable or mineral oil emulsion	1 to 1.5	Sprayed on set concrete to protect loss of water

Source: *BMPTC; 1997*

Pozzolana and other binders

There are various siliceous aluminous materials, like flyash, clay, surkhi, reactive surkhi, fine silica and gypsum. When combined with lime they develop cementing properties. Depending on the material, this property can be exploited by certain methods like autoclaving, calcining and hydraulic reaction. The pozzolana raw material can be calcinated by various methods. Different kinds of kilns, like downdraught rotary kiln and fluidised bed calciners are employed in the manufacture of pozzolana.

An admixture of lime or cement is usually used with pozzolana for preparation of mortar. The strength and quality of mortar depends on the admixtures, method of mixing and proportion of various ingredients, viz. sand, surkhi, water, lime, pozzolana, cement, etc. Sea shells, reefs, and industrial or agricultural wastes also have pozzolana properties, which include fired tiles, rice husk, ashes, flyash, etc. With the addition of these ingredients, lime pozzolana blocks can be produced at a much less cost than cement blocks.

The mortar should be used as early as possible after mixing. In any case, the mortar should be used the same day. Eminently hydraulic lime or mortars mixed with cement should be used within four hours of preparation.

The Bureau of Indian Standards have recommended the specifications and proportions for various binding materials and mortars. Generally cement, lime and sand ratio should be 1:1:6 or 1:2:8 for general mortars.

In spite of the possibility of replacing cement by other binders, the price of binders continues to be substantial. Cement is becoming out of the reach of the poor. Cement and other binding materials should therefore be used to their maximum potential. This calls for adoption of well worked out standards, proper detailing and design, proper supervision and workmanship for reducing the quantity of binding materials. Self-aligning, interlocking blocks, made of concrete, flyash or pozzolana, can be used in place of conventional bricks. These blocks do not require any mortar joints. Educational Design Inc. (EDI) have developed thermo-mud blocks which are self supporting upto a height of three storeys. Corners, vertical joints and edges can be bonded either by poured concrete with reinforcement, or by sulphur fibre. The size of the blocks or bricks also affects the quantity of bonding material. Larger the block, lesser would be the joints and quantity of binding material.

Cement and other binders are the keystones of building industry. Concerted action should be taken for increasing their production, improving the quality and their optimum use without any wastage.

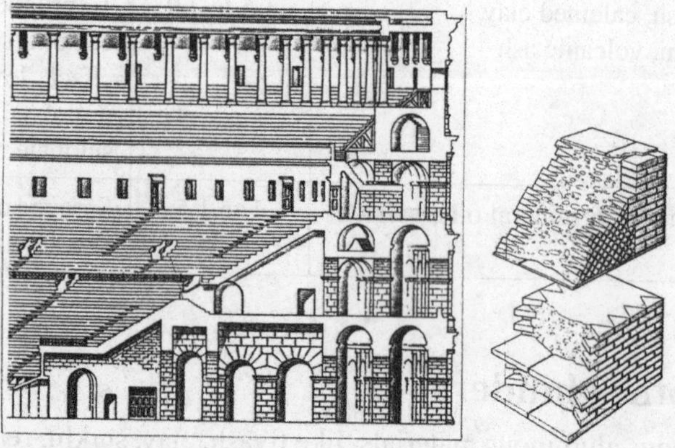

Fig. 10.6. During the first century, the Romans established bricklaying wherever they found plentiful supplies of clay. Their bricks look more like large tiles rarely more that 4 cm thick, 18 × 9 inches (46 × 23 cm). They were well-burnt and durable. They also developed concrete pozzolana which was used extensively in the structural core of buildings. Brick, stone and marble were used as facing materials to provide permanent shuttering to concrete pozzolana

Limestone Calcined Clay Cement

The Development Alternatives (Tara) have developed Limestone Calcined Clay Cement as an alternative binding materials. Calcined clay reacts with hydration product of clinker and limestone reacts with calcined clay, that make the microstructure denser. Calcined clay pozzolanic material and limestone as a semi-reactive filler create a synergy with the reaction of calcined clay and limestone producing carbo-aluminate that improves the strength and durability of the cement.

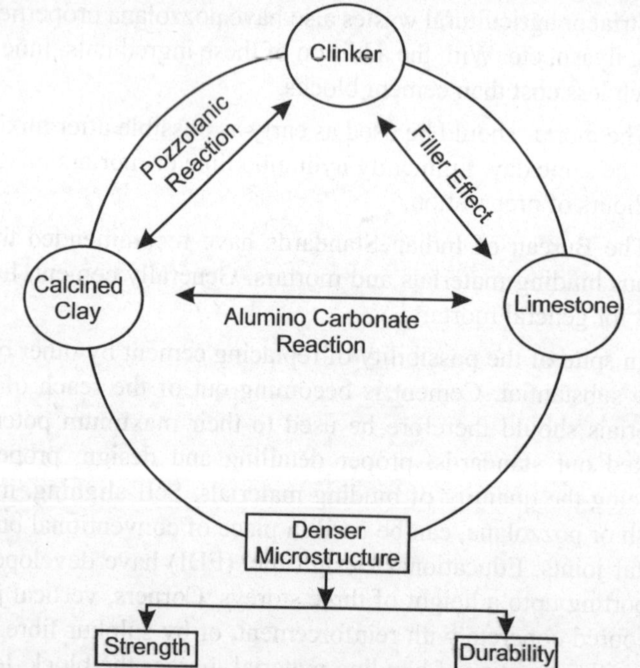

Fig. 10.7. Limestone Calcined Clay Cement (LC^3) Process

Source: *Tara/Development Alternatives*

Normal portland clinker is used in the production of LC^3. Clays containing 40% to 70% kaolinite are ideal for the production of LC^3 which are abundantly available as waste in mines. The clays are calcined at 750°C to 850°C to make them reactive. Calcination requires less than half the energy required for clinker production. Limestones with as little as 65% carbonate content and even with impurities such as quartz and dolomite can be consumed in LC^3. No calcination of the limestone is required. Waste material from marble and kota stone production can be used in place of limestone.

LC^3 contains 40% to 65% clinker by weight of 30% to 38% calcined clay, 15% to 20% of crushed limestone and 3% to 7% of gypsum. The calcination of clays can be carried out using rotary kilns. Due to lower temperatures and lower energy, the capital investment required for these rotary kilns is less than that of cement kilns of the same capacity. Flash calcination and fluidised bed reactor technologies can also be used for the calcination of clays. Flash calciners are similar to preheaters commonly used in cement plants.

LC^3 develops ultimate strength similar to that of Ordinary Portland Cement (OPC). Strength development in LC^3 has generally been observed to be faster than OPC and PPC. LC^3 cement satisfy all the requirements of physical characteristics laid down in the Indian Standards.

LC^3 has a high chloride penetration resistance and produces a dense microstructure with high resistivity making it ideal for harsh conditions like in marine environment.

The production of LC^3 emits as much as 30% less CO_2 than OPC and 11% less CO_2 than PPC. The energy consumed in producing LC^3 is also significantly lower than OPC and even lower than PPC in many scenarios. LC^3 also offers solution for the utilisation of low grade mine reject and other waste materials. Due to the lower calcination requirement, LC^3 is more economical to produce than OPC for similar performance, especially at locations with shortage of high quality fly ash.

Sulphur

Some other binders are organic binders, synthetics, magnesia-based binders and sulphur. Sulphur can be a viable bonding agent and a reinforcing material. It can be used with chopped fibres, wherever tensile strength is required. It can be applied hot or as a sulphur-sand grout. Tests show that sulphur bonding works as well as the standard cement mortar in low rise construction. It is a very good water proofing agent in wet areas and hence suitable for humid regions. Sulphur adds colour and texture to surface and can be tinted in various colours, other than its own yellow colour.

Sulphur Concrete

Sulphur can be an economical substitute for portland cement. It is available in many parts of the world and it is associated with volcanic rocks. There are many minerals containing sulphur in a combined state: Phyrite, Calena, and Gypsum are some of these Sulphur can also be recovered from natural gas and fuels. Sulphur used in construction does not need to be of high purity.

The properties of sulphur:

- It adheres strongly to a wide range of materials.
- It is a fast-setting and a high-strength cement.
- Good water impermeability and unsoluble in water.
- Poor conductor of heat and electricity.
- It is remeltable and reusable without changing its chemical properties.
- Techniques for melting and casting are inexpensive and simple. (Sulphur melts at 120° centigrade.)

- It helps in improving other building materials by impregnation (wood, concrete).
- Sulphur is an excellent waterproofing material and when mixed with plastics it becomes a flexible coating, useful for keeping humidity out.

The basic equipment required for producing sulphur concrete has multiple functions:

- To melt sulphur (120°-140° centigrade), electricity, gas or wood can be used.
- To mix molten sulphur with aggregates, a regular concrete mixture is adequate.
- Moulds for casting molten sulphur-concrete can be made from metal, wood or plastic.
- Small tools, rubber hammer, spatula, shovel, bucket, ladle, plastic beaker can be used.

Constructing with sulphur concrete involves precautions similar to those encountered in operations with hot-mixed asphalt. Normal precautions for handling hot fluid materials must be observed, such as wearing proper protective clothing, safety glasses, goggles or face shields.

Roof and the Floor

Perhaps the most costly item in a house is the roof, accounting for about one-fourth of the total cost. Mindless application of modern technology and indiscriminate standardisation of public works have replaced the vernacular and low cost roofing methods and materials. Pitched roofs made of Mangalore tiles and country tiles are being ousted by the RCC slab. Tile roofing is considered old fashioned in an apparent desire to imitate the West. However, it is not always possible to afford the tradition. With the rising cost of timber and due to the vertical expansion of housing in the cities, new materials and techniques have to be adopted. Recent research has made the asbestos out of question because of health hazards. Galvanised tin sheets conduct heat too rapidly and are unsuitable for our hot climate. That leaves only reinforced concrete for roofing. There are ways of using reinforced concrete and minimising costs. Baker uses reinforced cement filler slab with light-weight materials in the concrete to reduce costs and heat.

Fig. 10.8. Waffle/filler slab for roofing

Fig. 10.9. Parabolic corrugations in the vault roof by Laurie Baker

Concrete absorbs heat and emits it in the night—half of it downwards into the house and half of it upwards. Most of the concrete has to be filled and shuttered. By replacing the non-structural concrete by waste or cheaper materials like, coir, waste wood, thermocole and tiles as fillers, it is possible to save on cement and provide insulation. For flooring, red chips, surkhi, brick bats, broken glazed tiles and other waste materials can be used, which are much cheaper than cement and mosaic. These surfaces give an unusual look and make the interiors lively.

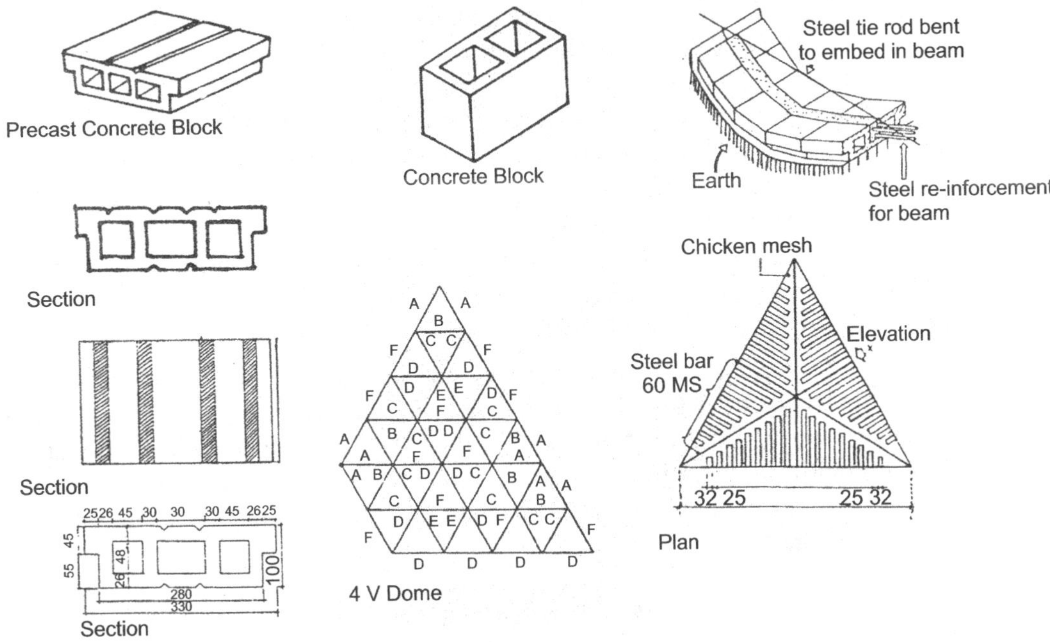

Fig. 10.10. The geometry of geodesic dome, Bhartiyam Gram, New Delhi, Anil Laul, Architect

Jack Arch Roofing

Jack arch roofing is a traditional technique. It can be adapted by using hollow clay tile panel for the floor. Old brickbats can be shaped and used to make an arch, with the help of wooden moulds. This can be assembled on the ground by laying the tiles into a curved shape, with two rods in the centre and mortaring the joints. The arch can be lifted next day. The corners of the walls of soil-cement tend to chip off and get damaged. Rounded corners can avoid this problem.

A preset arch panel built with hollow burnt clay tiles can be used as a roofing element. A variety of spans can be covered with different types of roofing systems, *e.g.* precast RC beams for a shorter span of 3 m, cast in situ RC for a wider span of 5 m and jack arch for the corridor. A barrel vault can be adopted for shorter spans like the toilets and garage.

Tarfelt-cum-thatch Roof

Tarfelt is a fairly cheap material. It comes in rolls and is easy to transport. With a few layers of tarfelt supported by closely spaced thin wooden members we can make a light roof. The layer of thatch can be very thin because the tarfelt layer provides the waterproofing. The thatch on the top can also be treated to further extend its life. Thin plastic membranes and polythene, which are made locally, can also provide waterproofing.

Bamboo Roof/Floor

Unsplit bamboos of requisite length are placed close to each other and tied together with a metal wire. Bamboo ties are also placed at the supports to strengthen the structure. This work can be done on the ground itself. It is not necessary to select bamboos of equal diameter, as a slight variation in thickness is tolerable. Straight lengths of bamboo are essential for raft-like construction. Once the bamboo raft is assembled, it is lifted and positioned on the supporting brick structure and anchored firmly to the brickwork. A muddy mixture of local earth and water is prepared at this stage. A 5 cm thick layer of mud mortar is laid evenly on the raft, rammed gently and allowed to dry. To render the construction waterproof, bitumen and kerosene are mixed with mud. If the bamboos are of unequal thickness, a hessian cloth must be spread over the entire raft prior to laying the wet mud so that it does not leak through the gaps. The joints are filled with locally available binding materials like mud and lime or cement. The choice of binding materials will depend upon the degree of the structure's exposure to rain and other climatic conditions. A gradient is provided in the surface for rainwater to run off. Brick joints can be sealed with IPS (Indian Patent Stone), and internal floor can be finished with mud, cow dung or cement plaster.

The bamboo roof has several advantages like being cheap, quick and durable. However, the main limitation of the technique is that the usable length of bamboo restricts the span. With the time the bamboo may warp which can create cracks in the flooring and opening up of the joints. In some cases, the deterioration of the bamboo by insects and fungi may cause structural weakness. To avoid sagging, it is advisable to divide the total span with intermediate supports, battens or rafters. To provide resistance against warping, the bamboos should be tied very close together with a good number of nodes. To protect the bamboo structure against insects, rot, fungi and fire, the bamboo should be given a fire retardant treatment and treated by a preservative.

Bamboo roof needs careful treatment to prevent leaking. A layer of polythene sheet with stabilized soil covering or lime surkhi concrete with a layer of tarfelt should be provided to make it leakproof.

Bamboo Boards

Bamboo boards are available in standard sizes and thickness, like hardboards and particle boards. They are very strong and have the beauty of bamboo. They are manufactured from bamboo, which are abundantly available in the country. They are chemically treated and machine processed and bonded into a board. They can be used for various purposes like false ceiling, furniture, facade, doors, windows, partitions, panelling etc. They are waterproof and fungi resistant, and are quite cheap as compared to timber and even conventional hardboards.

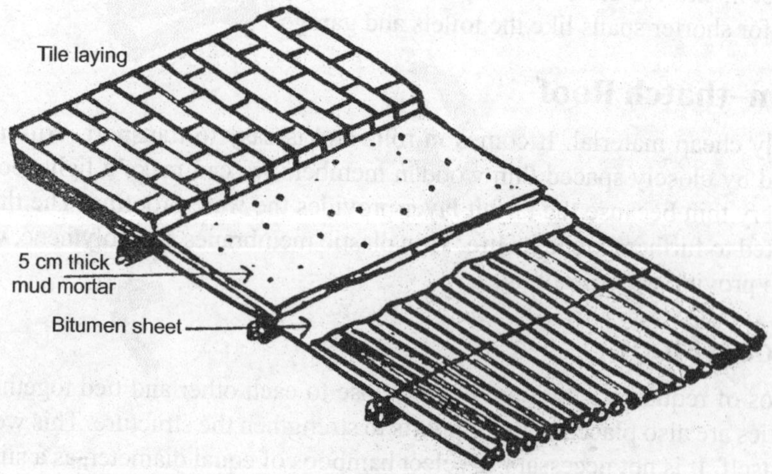

Fig. 10.11. Bamboo Raft Floor/Roof

Fig. 10.12. Arched Lintol

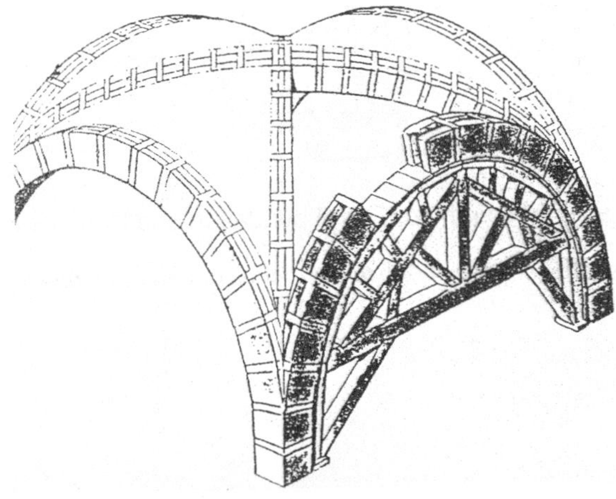

Fig. 10.13. Dome for Roofing

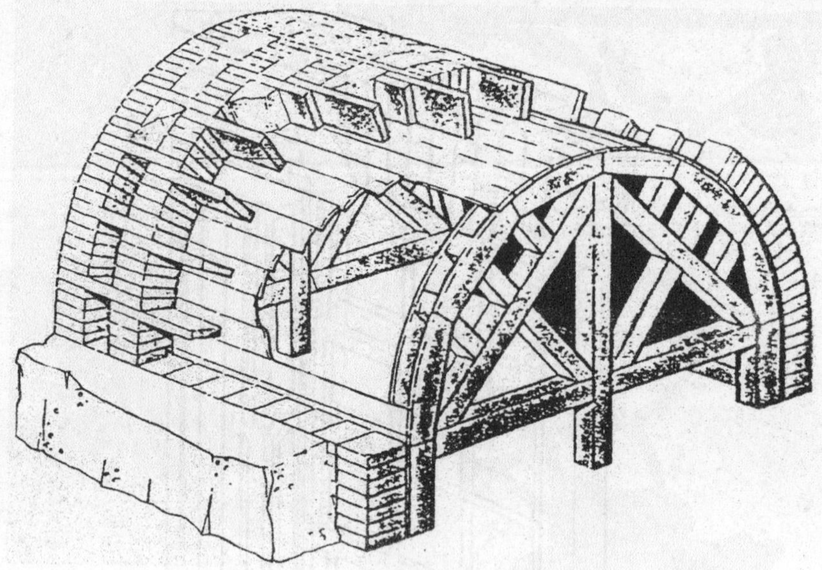

Fig. 10.14. Vault Roofing

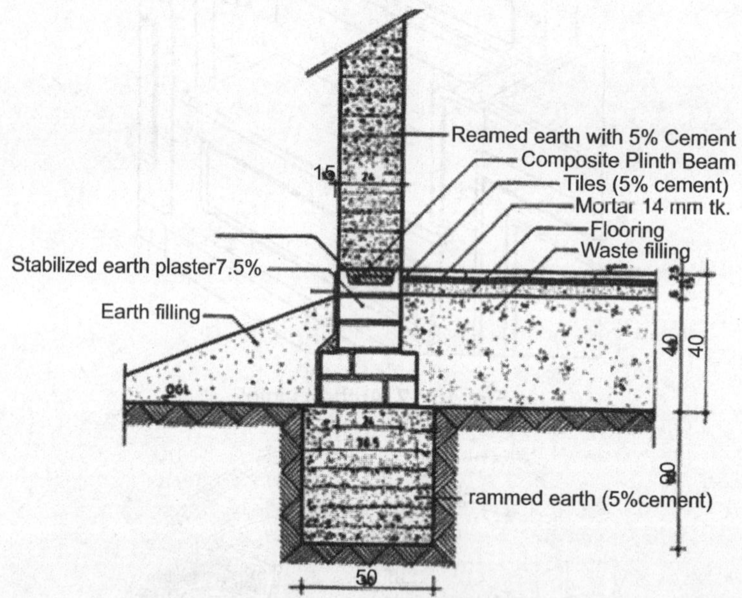

Fig. 10.15. Stabilized Rammed Earth Foundation and Composite Plinth Beam

Source: *Auroville Earth Institute, http:/www.earth-auroville.com maintenance/uploaded pics/37 serf/jpg*

Fig. 10.16. Inverted Arch Foundation

Source: *http:/www.stonepoplar heightsfarm.org/Foothing img011/jqp*

Funicular Shells

Funicular shells are doubly curved thin membranes which use very little materials, yet are strong. This structural property is used in optimising material usage and getting the maximum strength. This helps in increasing efficiency and consequently reduces the expenditure.

Jute fabric stretched on a square wooden frame takes its natural sag. This sag provides a strong shell like geometry. Once concreted and upturned, this curvilinear shell becomes a stable load-bearing structure. In this manner, rectangular and triangular shells can be cast. Larger shells can be cast in situ, but need mechanical hoisting, as they are much too heavy to lift manually. The negative shells can be cast in plain cement mixed with red oxide, chips, broken clayware etc. As flooring, they are economical, time saving and durable. These can also be used for foundations of walls and columns saving time and cost.

Funicular shells with sides over 2 m should normally be cast in-situ. Beams are arranged in a criss-cross pattern, leaving square voids into which a fibreglass mould is fitted from below. The shell is then cast over, with bricks, blocks, waste materials, broken materials, stones and other substances: often laid with mortar joints. Once the shell sets, its base is separated from the overlaying shell with the turnbuckles. The standard framework may be used for about 1,000 applications. Precast concrete funicular shell units can also be used for passing of rods. These are turned on hard ground and flash slurry is poured through a small hole in the shells and tamped down. The water eventually dries off, leaving behind a compacted mass that resists shifting of the shell units and supports the concave hollow of the shell. To avoid erosion due to onslaught of rain, it is necessary that proper drainage and berms are provided.

Thrift beam has a hollow core which is filled with a light weight, insulating material. Thermocole, which can be obtained as waste packing material, is quite suitable as a filler. Welded wire mesh all around is used for reinforcement. The square beam, rotated by 45 degrees allows individual or sub-beams to rest on longer sides with a bird's mouth joint. The funicular concrete or brick panels can be placed in position once the frame of beams is erected.

This concept permits adoption of modular units of small geodesic or shell panels, which can be manually handled. Their slight curvature allows use of roof as a flat surface. Roof panels, clustered together are quick in erection, strong and allow flexibility of space planning.

Cast in situ funicular shells mini-geodesic dome or slab can be manufactured in a fibreglass mould, which is fitted in between a grid of beams. Bricks, waste material, stones etc., are laid on the fibre-glass mould with mortar joints. Turnbuckles at the bottom of the mould release it from the cast shell once it has set. These moulds can be used for thousands of applications.

Thermocole Core RCC Panels

In RCC a large amount of material is superfluous, which does not contribute to its structural strength. In construction, we cannot afford wastage of cement, steel and other costly materials. Hollow panels are designed on this concept by removing material from the core, while providing reinforcement in the areas under tension and on the surfaces. The hollow core can be filled up with thermally insulating thermocole.

Thermocole is covered by steel mesh on both sides, with steel wires spot welded at intervals for connection between the surfaces. Continuity bars join all the panels in a single panel of significant strength. It is lightweight and can be placed in position easily. Thermocole core RCC panel system facilitates saving of time as all prefabrication work can be completed off site, before or parallel to on-site construction. The wall and roof panels are joined together by placing in position continuity, bars, binding steel and with their concreting. This needs to be done with care to avoid any leakage from the joints. Reinforced hollow concrete or flat brick panels can also be used for staircase treads. A plastic mixture of lime-soil-cement-sand provides a sound mortar for plastering. Red mud can be used as a pigment in flooring, which is extremely low cost and is available locally.

Prefabricated reinforced roofing panels made with hollow tiles can be fabricated on the ground and assembled over the beams/trusses. Such roofing eliminates framework completely and is much lighter than the reinforced concrete roof (75 kg per sq. mt). The same concept can be developed and extended for an improved jack arch roofing.

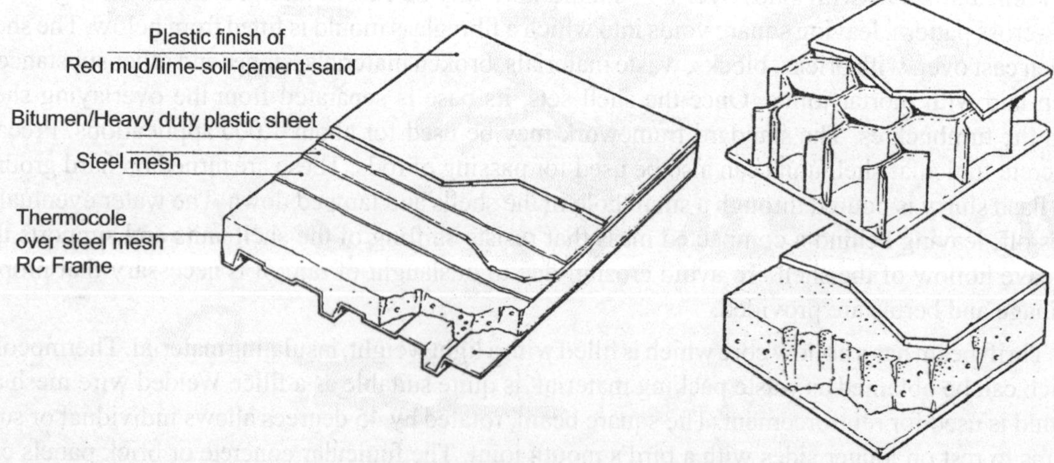

Fig. 10.17. Honeycomb sandwich and thermocole core panels

Geodesic Dome

Geodesic dome allows quick and cheap enclosure of space and construction of shelter. In Delhi it has been tried at few places. As a standard unit, it is a square (26 ft/8.4 m each side) with 30 × 30 cm (12" × 12") RCC posts at the four corners supporting a skeletal and segmental geodesic dome frame. The triangular infill units are 12 mm medium density fibre board with good insulation value, which can be cut rapidly and screwed into place.

At the apex is a pyramidal ventilator. The roof can be finished with flat, cross-lapped, red mud or plastic shingles. The walls are interesting combination of brick and hollow rice husk concrete blocks which are independent of the columns and ceiling. Being non-load bearing, these may not need any excavated foundations.

Fig. 10.18. Geodesic dome, Bhartiyam Gram, New Delhi (Anil Laul)

Lintels and Arches

By reverting back to corbelling and arches, the expenditure on lintels, steel, cement and framework can be avoided in house construction. Baker uses corbelled arch or simple stepped brickwork wherever small openings are needed. Reinforced brickwork or flat arch can be adopted to allow a plain soffit in a rectangular opening.

Usually the openings in a house are excessive to the needs of living and for climatic comfort. In many cases it is found that doors and windows are kept permanently closed or paper is pasted over the glazing. As such, in order to save cost it is necessary to rationalise the size and number of openings.

Fig. 10.19. Flat arch for door/window opening (Laurie Baker)

Doors and Windows

Doors and windows are among the costliest items in the construction of building. This is because expensive materials and a lot of skilled labour are involved in their manufacture besides additional expenditure on items such as hinges, locks, bolts, sills, lintels, etc.

According to Laurie Baker, "Many doors need not be there at all. Often an opening in the wall is all that function and usage requires. Typical examples are the link between sitting and dining areas or between children's and parent's bedrooms. If a door is not necessary, do not put. Considerable and immediate cost reduction is achieved."

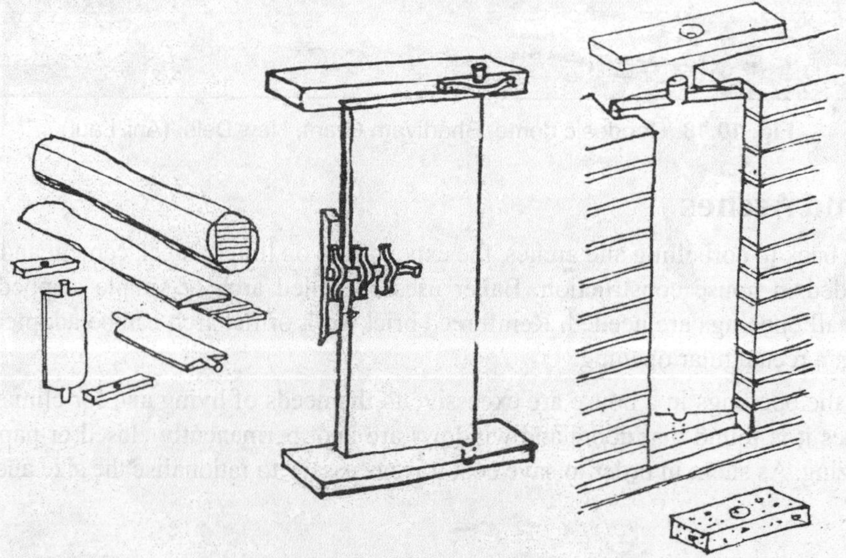

Fig. 10.20. Inexpensive door and dowelled windows made from waste wood (Laurie Baker)

Laurie Barker adds further: "We can seriously consider whether any part of the normal door unit is necessary. In many parts of houses we do not require a tight fitting door, and a simplified or contemporary version of the old traditional door can be used effectively with some cost reduction." "If the window is only shut for security reasons "why introduce glass into the shutter when it could be a simple pivoted leaf of planks and battens?"

Steel Doors, Windows and Railings

The alternatives to wood are steel doors, windows and railings, which are extensively used in buildings. It is not the ordinary steel but is generally galvanised, phosphated and pre-painted. Special steel requires no maintenance. The manufacturing process is hi-tech which makes the doors and windows rustproof and maintenance free. They are available in bright colours, such as red, blue, beige, white and brown. The windows are available mainly in three varieties. The first variety is a complete set with glass panes. It has a hollow section of tubular frame with shutters, openable or fixed, complete with regulation wings and brackets for attachment. Another variety has an extra attachment and that is mosquito net. The third variety is the ornamental window. These are decorative windows suitable for private buildings and for special architectural effects. They have a rolling shutter box, which can be made in wood, plastic, or metal. These do not need curtains or pelmets.

Prepainted and prefinished railings are also available with a modular kit, which facilitates on-site installation. These can be fabricated in various metals like aluminium, copper and brass, besides steel alloy. Recent developments in technology have made it possible to have non-rusting, corrosion free, permanent finish/painted railings, suitable for both interior and exterior.

Phenotherm Insulated Panels

These are fire resistant and are suitable for false ceiling, under-deck installation, air-conditioning ducts, partitioning and panelling. In case of continuous fire, it turns brown but retains its shape. It is an excellent fire resistant material and prevents spread of fire.

Rubberwood

Among the secondary timbers, the rubberwood is fast emerging as a substitute for the expensive teak, sagwan and kail-wood. It is cheap, durable and easily available. It can be used for high quality furniture, doors and windows. Rubberwood is treated with chemical impregnation and irradiation, which make it immune to fungi attack. Untreated rubberwood is prone to fungal infection and rots quickly. It is subjected to kiln drying, a process by which wood is seasoned under controlled temperature, humidity and air flow. Seasoned wood maintains its form and dimensional stability. Machining and moulding give it a smooth finish and proper adhesion. Once the rubberwood is seasoned, it is chemically treated for fungus and infections. Thus it acquires a long lasting life.

Rubberwood can be used as a substitute of timber in many applications like doors, windows, shutters, frames, furniture, cabinet, partition walls and rafters. Fire resistance of wood is improved by using treatment with sulphates, chlorides and nitrates of ammonia.

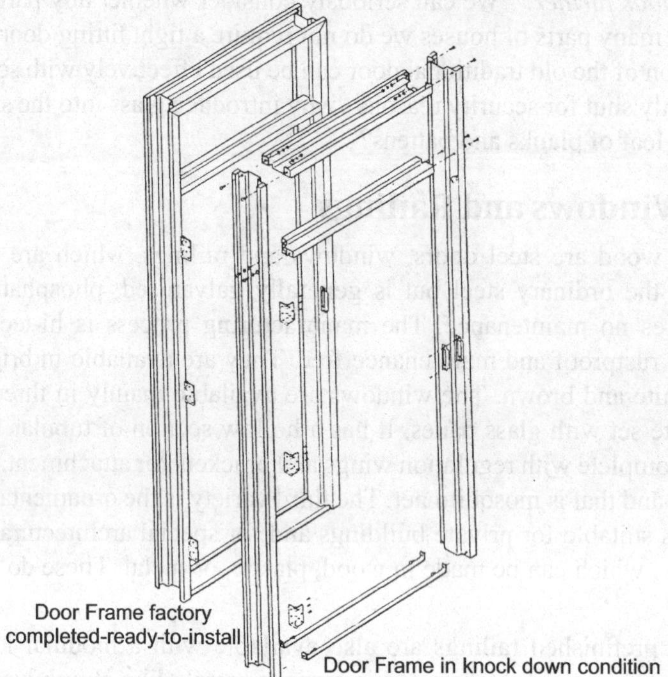

Fig. 10.21. Pressed Steel Frame Door

Wood and Reconstituted Wood

Imperative to reduce the consumption of timber in building involves the identification, development and promotion of alternative materials which can be substitutes for wood. A wide range of economical and versatile wood substitutes like ferrocement, plastics and metal based products and techniques of construction are available. Wood lumbers, sawn wood sections, plywood, particle boards, fibre board, blockboard and wood-wool boards made from wood chips and fibres are the main products. These are used for structural elements, roofing, ceiling, partitions, panelling, doors windows, ventilator frames and shutters. Wood and sawn wood / timber are generally seasoned by air, solar heat, steam or electricity to remove moisture and make the sections dimensionally stable, free from cracks and bending etc. Many types of wood, particularly secondary species and soft wood, are chemically treated for preservation against decay caused by moisture, fungi, insects and termites.

Particle board

The development of the particle boards traces back to the Second World War. It is reconstituted wooden panel and an excellent substitute for natural wood. Being prefabricated, it saves lot of time in woodwork. It is used extensively for partitions, cabinets, shelves, ceiling, doors, sideboards etc. It is made from low grade waste-wood or agricultural ligneous waste. Waste wood and synthetic resins are the two basic raw materials of the particle board. It is much cheaper than timber, yet it gives the effect of wood. It is universally available in various sizes and thickness. The carpenters all over are familiar with its use, as it is user friendly and facilitates easy and quick workmanship.

Fibre board

Like particle board, fibre board is also based on the recycling of waste materials. Fibre board is manufactured from separate fibres or bundles of waste wood, glued by synthetic resins. It utilises the woods of inferior quality, residuals, waste wood from saw mills and plywood plants and agricultural wastes like bagasse, rice husk, cotton stalk and jute stalk. There are various qualities of hardboard and insulation fibre board. Available in various sizes, these are extensively used for furniture, partitions, shelves, cabinets, ceiling, doors, etc.

The standard hardboard is a homogeneous fibre building board whose surface texture is usually smooth on one side and with a fine mesh pattern on the reverse. It is used for ceiling lining, panelling, kitchen units, furniture, etc. Tempered hardboards are those which are subjected to oil tempering. This improves its strength and weathering properties. It is water resistant and abrasion resistant. Tempered boards are used where strength and higher resistant to abrasion and moisture are required. The insulation boards are light coloured files or sheets manufactured from bagasse or wood-waste. They are used where good thermal insulation is necessary such as walls, ceiling, roof lining and for permanent shuttering for concrete.

Medium density fibre boards have been recently developed. The process involves several stages, viz. defibration, refining, drying of the fibre, blending with resin, board forming and dressing. These can be made in any thickness and are good for furniture and household construction.

Due to the facility of easy working, universal availability and quick output, fibre board is a favourite material of architects, designers and carpenters. Apart from interiors and furniture, it is a popular material for putting up temporary structures and exhibition stalls.

Plywood

Plywood utilises the secondary species of timber. Shelvings of secondary timbers and synthetic resin are the two basic raw materials. It is used for furniture making, wall panelling, door panels, shelves, cupboards and other household items. It had been developed in Europe during the First World War, when there was a dire need of economy in construction, materials and time. It is universally available in various qualities, sizes and thickness. Plywood allows easy and quick working as compared to timber.

Rice Husk Boards

Rice husk boards are superior in quality and cheaper than the wood based particle boards. These are suitable for tropical and hot climate. These can be used for panelling, doors, furniture, cabinets, table tops, partitions, false ceiling and flooring. Rice husk boards utilise rice husk which is a waste material and have sound insulating quality. This makes them suitable for record room, auditoria, cinema halls etc. They are termite proof and fire resistant.

Chemical treatment of wood: The main chemicals used for treatment of wood are creosote, creosote-coal tar, penta-chlorophenol, zinc chloride, boric acid and copper sulphate-potassium dichromate - arsenic pentoxide. While using chemical preservative treatments, precautions like use of hand gloves and face masks have to be taken as these chemicals are highly toxic and poisonous.

Table 10.11. Classification of Wood and Reconstituted Wood

Type	Properties				Uses
	Shrinkage resistance	Bending strength	Resistance to decay	Resistance to weathering	
Natural Wood					
Hard wood	P	F	F	F	Strip flooring, stair treads, panels and frames, structural members, piles
Birch yellow	G	F	G	F	
Deodar	P	VG	VG	F	
Rose	F	G	G	G	
Teak	F	G	G	G	
Soft wood					
Fir	VG	VG	G	F	Chips for laminated wood, flooring, roofing shingles
Pine	F	P	F	F	
Red	P	F	VG	G	
Spruce	F	P	F	F	
Secondary Species					
Mango	P	F	P	P	For most of the application as above after proper seasoning and chemical treatment
Neem	F	F	G	F	
Jamun	F	P	P	F	
Jack	F	F	P	P	
Reconstituted Wood					
Laminated wood					
Plywood	F	F to G	G	F	Panels, shutters, shuttering, partition, ceiling, etc.
Laminated lumber	G	VG	G	F	
Sandwich panel	G	G	G	F	
Particle boards					
Fibre board	VG	G	G	F	Panels, shutter, shutters, partition, ceiling, interior panelling, etc.
Insulation board	VG	F	G	F	
Hardboard	G	VG	G	F	
Wood wool board					
Cement bonded	G	G	F	G	Partitions, panelling core, shutters, ceiling, etc.
Oxychloride bonded	G	G	F	P	

P = Poor, F = Fair, G = Good, VG = Very good

Source: *BMPTC, 1997*

Fibre reinforced concrete (FRC) roofing sheets are of the following types : (*i*) Asbestos cement, (*ii*) Wood wool/coil/fibre cement, (*iii*) Ferrocement, (*iv*) Steel fibre small pieces (0.5 to 2.5 cm long) and cement concrete, and (*v*) Glass fibre cement. They are flat or corrugated. In the selection of FRC bonded roofing sheets, the service life (durability) aspect must be ensured. All organic (vegetable) fibres in cement concrete matrix as well as glass fibre deteriorate in alkaline media. The fibres lose their tensile strength and become brittle. Hence, care is taken in treating the organic fibres with a coating or by boiling in water to remove the harmful contents (lignin, etc.) which adversely affect the strength of cement concrete. In glass fibre cement concrete, it must be ensured that only alkali resistance 'E' type fibre is used. In steel fibre reinforced concrete roofing sheets such as ferrocement or steel (small size) reinforced types, there is always a fast rate of corrosion of the reinforcement. Hence most of the above types, except AC sheets, are suitable for short span and semi-permanent shelters/sheds or houses.

Glass Fibre Reinforced Plastic Products (GFRP): are available as roofing sheets, tiles, prefabricated shelters, cabins, almirahs, door and window shutters, glazing, etc. There is a variety of glass fibre products along with many emerging plastic composites.

Although synthetic fibres in plastic matrix are more compatible, natural fibres like wood, sisal, coir, jute, cotton-lintel, mesta, etc. are also used in a variety of fibre reinforced composite products. Among the fillers in these products exfoliated perlite, exfoliated vermiculite, asbestos, rockwool, etc. are quite common. Among the plastic matrix besides epoxy and polyester other plastic being used are polypropylene, polystyrene, acrylic and polycarbonates.

Fibre reinforced and other plastics are used in panels, glazing and door shutters. They are of three types: (*a*) Acrylics base using Poly Methyl Methacrylat (PMMA), (*b*) Poly Carbonate (PC) and (*c*) Fibre Reinforced Polyester (FRP). Several other plastic glazing materials with or without fibres such as cellulose acetate, fluorinated ethylene-propylene, polyvinyl fluoride and polyvinyl chloride are also used.

Acrylics, although easily scratched, have a good resistance to weathering, salt spray and corrosive atmosphere. Poly-carbonate glazing has high impact resistance and provide a light transmission of 82 to 90%.

Fibre-glass reinforced polyester has light transmission up to 85% and has a good impact resistance. Plastics generally need an anti-oxidant ingredient to avoid yellowing and cracking of FRP on prolonged exposure.

Fibreglass Reinforced Plastics

Recently there had been extensive production and use of fibreglass and plastics for buildings and interiors. Fiberglass reinforced plastic integrates the good qualities of the two materials. This is available in sheets, panels and in moulded form. It is waterproof, insect proof and free from any chemical reactions, corrosion, rusting, etc. It has good insulating properties. It can be cut by ordinary tools and facilitates easy and fast working. Fibreglass enforced plastics are available in various shades and finishings. These do not need any surface painting and are lightweight. These can be used for roofing, partitions, panelling, handrails, storage bins, cabinets, door shutters, etc.

PVC Door and Window

PVC doors and windows are lightweight, impact resistant, self-extinguishing and high technology product. This hardware is designed for functional needs and for security. Double locking systems are available to provide maximum security. An adjustable friction stay enables the window to remain open to any desired extent. It can be fitted directly on the masonry without a timber frame. This product does not have the problems of rotting, rusting, peeling, warping, swelling or painting. For specific and special buildings, certain accessories like sealed cavity, rubber gasket, double glazing, shutters for control of heat, dust and noise are available. They can be used in any climate and are designed to withstand wind loads, and can bear temperatures from –10° C to + 50° C.

Construction and Demolition Waste

Discarded paper, boards/cartons, plastics agro-wastes, wood and construction and demolition wastes can be recycled into furniture, fibre pipes, electrical and drainage systems, asphaltic corrugated roofing sheets, soling material for roads, pavements and foundations, etc. The building industry can gainfully utilise wastes for a variety of application, and in many cases, substitute of the use of timber through products made from agro-waste processed along with suitable binders under pressure. These can be used for making several kinds of insulation boards and roofing sheets.

Table 10.12. Energy Saving in Recycled Building Materials

S.No.	Process	Use of Industrial & other wastes	Approximate (%) saving in energy
1.	Portland-Pozzolona & portland	Flyash, mining wastes, blast furnace slag	15-20
2.	Lime-Pozzolana Mixtures	Lime Kiln Rejects, Industrial Ashes	30-40
3.	Lime Rice-Husk Pozzolana	Rice Husk Ash or Rice Husk	30-40
4.	Lime-sludge, Rice Husk Pozzolona	Rice Husk Ash or Rice Husk	40-50
5.	Sand Flyash Bricks	Flyash/Mining Waste	30-50
6.	Masonry Cement Wastes	Lime Sludge & Mining Mineral	10-20
7.	Cement Concrete Tiles	Mixing and Mineral Waste	10-15

Source: *BMTPC 1997*

Table 10.13. Energy Saving in the Manufacture of Building Materials Using Industrial Waste

Building Material	Composition	Energy(kJ/kg)	% Saving
Portland Pozzolana Cement	75% portland cement 25% Burnt clay pozzlana	6945 6280	+20
Portland flyash pozzolana cement	75% portland cement 25% flyash	5945 5945	(+) 25
Portland Blast furnace slag cement	60% portland cement 40% BFS	4473 4773	(+) 40
Waste lime sludge & rice husk ash cement	70% waste lime sludge 15% rice husk ash	9839 9839	(+) 25
Masonry Cement	50% portland cement 50% Mineral Tailing	3977 nil 3977	(+) 20

Note: (+) Donotes saving.

Source: *BMPTC, 1997*

Low Embodied Energy and Low Cost Building

In a typical house in India, it has been observed that about 30% of construction cost accounts for brickwork, 20% for roofing and 15% for doors/windows. Labour consumes 27% of total construction cost.

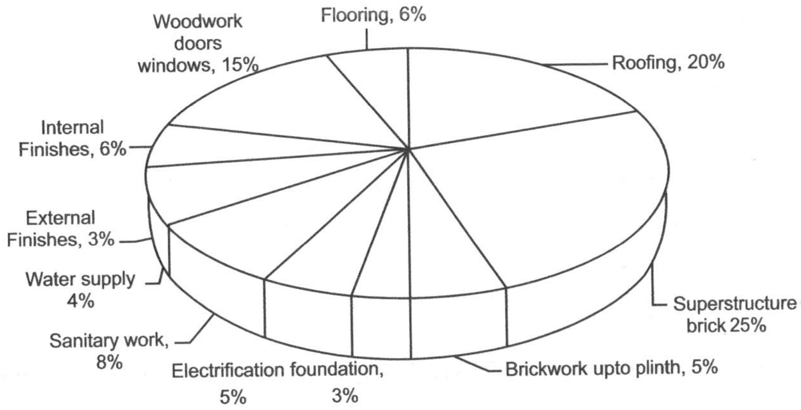

Fig. 10.22. Approximate Break-up of total Construction Cost for different elements of building

Source: BMTPC, 2010.

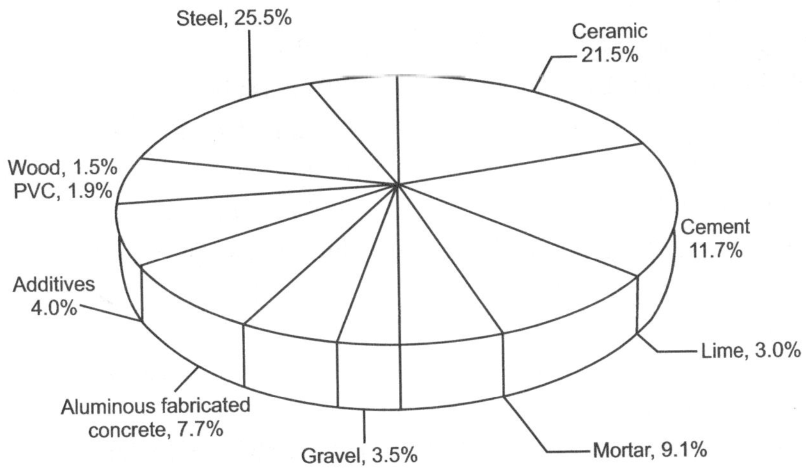

Fig. 10.23. Building Materials–Embodied Energy

Source: *Report of Centre of Research for Energy and Consumption Report (2010) Down to Earth (Jan 16–31).*

Nowadays, plethora of alternative building materials with low energy contents, such as blended cement, bricks from different waste materials, steel from recycled steel, replacement of partial sand component are produced in India. Hand molded bricks per 1000 nos. consume about 880 × 10 kcal/kg in fully mechanised plant, assuming the average calorific value of bituminous coal used as 5500 kcal/kg.

Similarly, conversion of wet process in cement manufacturing results in 37 to 40 per cent reduction in fuel consumption. Wet process in cement manufacturing to dry process results in 37 to 40 per cent reduction in fuel consumption. Considering reduced energy consumption a number of cement manufacturers in India have converted their wet process plants to the dry process. The basic approaches towards reducing embodied energy and resource depletion include the following:

- Use locally sourced materials, those found on site or vicinity and minimise use of imported materials
- Keep use of materials from non-renewable sources to minimum
- Use low energy materials, keeping high embodied energy materials to a minimum
- Use second hand/recycled materials
- Re-use existing building and structures instead of virgin new building materials.
- Use non-toxic and low emission materials
- Avoid fibers from insulation material getting into the atmoshphere
- Avoid materials which produce damaging chemicals/toxins
- Do not dump waste materials off site but re-use on site

DEBRIEFING QUESTIONS

1. What do you understand by Building Resources?
2. Explain how local materials, conventional construction techniques infused with modern technology and systems.
3. Write short notes on :
   (*a*) Mud-brick housing (*b*) Bricks
   (*c*) Soil-cement blocks (*d*) Flyash bricks
   (*e*) Stones (*f*) Lime mortar
   (*g*) Pozzolana (*h*) Limestone Calcinated Clay Cement
   (*i*) Gypsum (*j*) Embodied Energy
4. Describe the approaches of the following architects towards low cost housing :
   (*a*) Laurie Baker (*b*) Hasan Fathy
   (*c*) Anil Laul
5. What kinds of roofing can be built without use of cement and concrete?
6. Explain the following :
   (*a*) Arch Foundation (*b*) Bamboo roof/floor
   (*c*) Hollow Concrete Block (*d*) Funicular Shell
   (*e*) Geodesic Dome (*f*) Wood Substitutes
   (*g*) Recycling construction waste and Agro-waste
7. What cost effective and alternative technologies can be adopted for low-cost housing?

11

BUILDING AND HOUSING SYSTEMS

Low productivity, high costs, long building cycles, high energy contents, non-standardization and poor quality are the main challenges of building and housing. At present a large proportion of building activity in the country is carried out by the individuals in a sporadic, semi-industrial manner, outside the monetary sector, employing mostly the local resources. It is necessary to change these traditional methods by innovative technologies. Building and supporting economic activities represent about 10% of the gross national product, which deserve integrated systems approach.

The importance of construction is both direct and tangible. It plays multiple roles in national growth and development :

- Construction's contribution to gross domestic product;
- Its linkage to other industrial sectors;
- Its direct demand for labour:
- Its contribution to national capital formation;
- Its importance in socio-economic transformation;
- Leveraging the economy, amenities and transport.

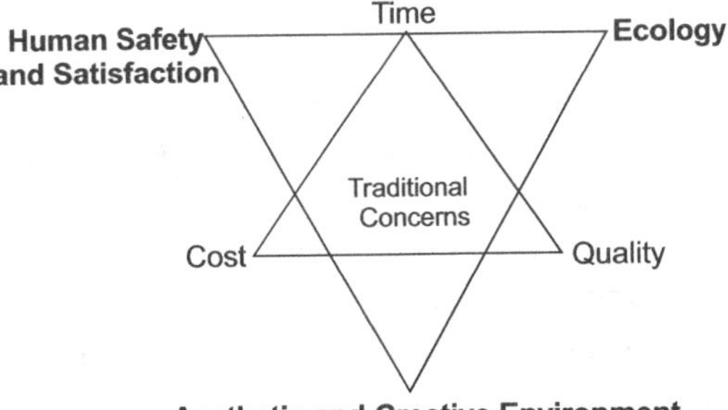

Fig. 11.1. New Paradigm

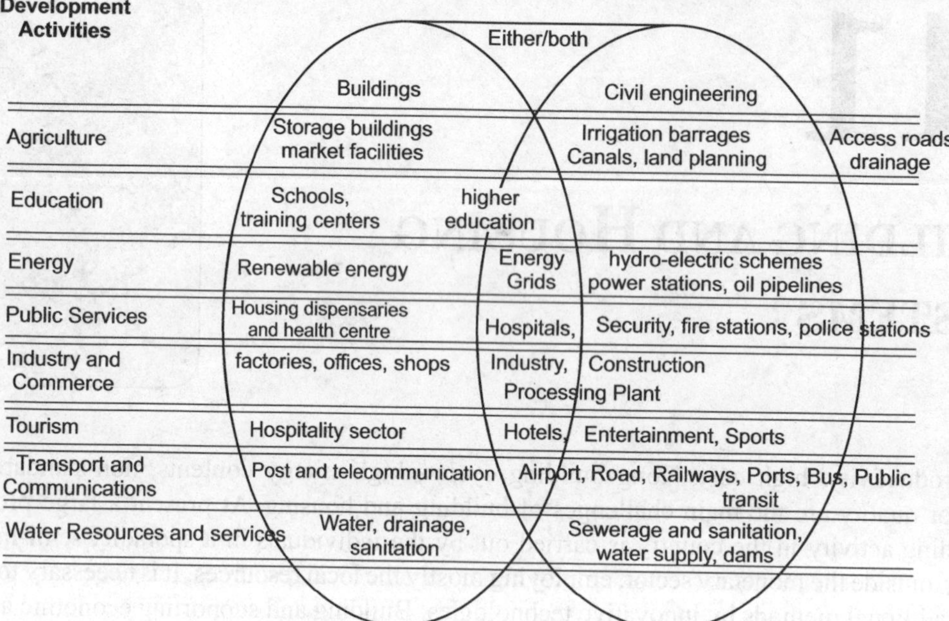

Fig. 11.2. Construction Output Required by Major Economic Sectors

Source: *A.D. Austen and R.H. Neale (eds), (1984) Managing Construction (Geneva, ILO)*

Time, quality and cost have always been the traditional factors in materials and construction. Today a new value system is emerging which is enveloping these concerns. These are human safety and satisfaction, ecological sustainability and aesthetics.

A major concern of housing in India is optimization of the use of land and building resources. While dealing with the reduction of the cost of housing the plinth area of dwelling is reduced and specifications are lowered. In spite of subsidies, such housing continues to be beyond the reach of the target population. While saving the cost of construction, attention needs to be given on the cost of land development and services. The cost of land and its development form a sizeable component of dwelling cost. This is increasing mainly due to the following factors :

- Increasing cost of land and services, viz. water supply, sanitation, sewerage, drainage, power, solid waste disposal, roads and parks, etc.
- Increasing overheads, departmental charges, interest and delays.
- Inefficient layout and design.
- Indiscriminate privatization and commercialization of services, without an effective, regulatory mechanism and controls.

The housing development, construction and materials should aim to achieve the following :

- Reduction in cost of construction
- Reduction in labour utilized
- Reduction in time
- Reduction in transportation cost by reduction in weight of materials and shorter distances.
- Lower rates of pollution, dust, noise, accidents, GHG emissions, etc.
- Higher standards of performance, quality and durability

Based on local conditions and regional variations, a package of systems and technologies can be evolved :

- Small scale prefabrication based on local labour, materials and machinery
- Partial prefabrication, combining standardized and optimized precast components
- Full-fledged/complete prefabrication which involves large panel construction and industrialized components.

Modular Coordination and Systems Approach

Systems approach represents a technological leap from conventional to industrialized building methods. Modular coordination and standardisation should be simultaneously adopted. The idea of 'systems building' must facilitate the pooling of mutual cooperation. As a solution to overcome the problem of coordination, the integration of design, production and assembly operations is necessary for good results, both in the centrally-planned and market economies, particularly in the case of a closed system.

Close coordination and consistency between planning, design, production and management of buildings are indispensable pre-requisites of systems approach. This is difficult to obtain since quite often the objectives and interests of architect, builders, investors and users are not identical. To overcome this problem, an interdisciplinary approach together with modular coordination and standardization is necessary. Systems building aims to meet the functional, structural and design requirements in an efficient, quick and economical way. Art, science and technology in their inter-relation are the basis of architecture. This implies that a system building need not be a dull, box like structure, but can be designed beautifully. The basic principles of "less is more", efficiency and economy are the pillars of "systems building."

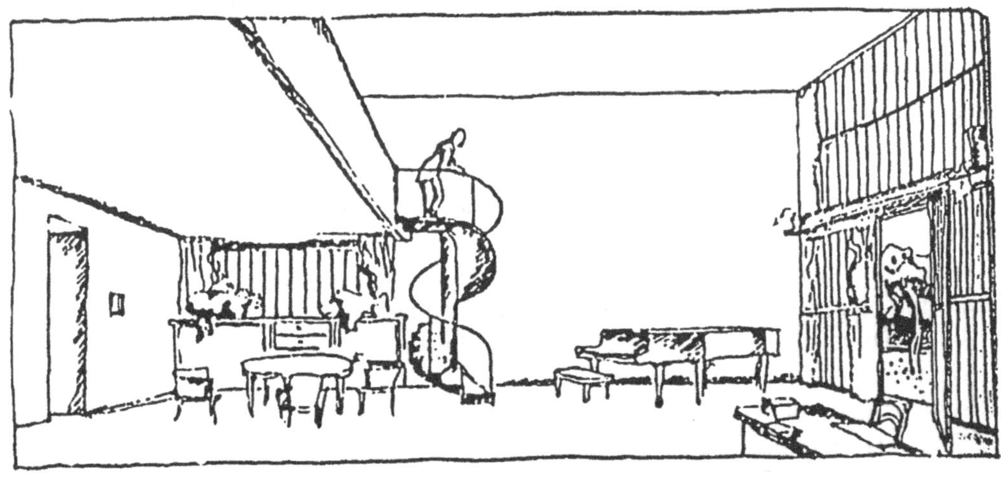

Fig. 11.3. Le Corbusier (1921) Mass Production House

According to Le Corbusier *"Citrohan, is to say a house like a motor-car, conceived and carried out like a ships's cabin. The actual needs of the dwelling can be formulated and demand their solution. We must fight against the old-world house, which made a bad use of space. We must look upon the house as a machine for living in or a tool. When a man starts any particular industry, he buys the necessary equipment and tools; when he sets up a house, the fact is a ridiculous dwelling, an incoherent grouping of a number of rooms."*

Fig. 11.4. Le Corbusier, 1922 Mass Production Villa-framework of concrete a large living-room 30 feet × 16 feet, kitchen, maid's room, bathroom, two bedrooms and a "solarium"

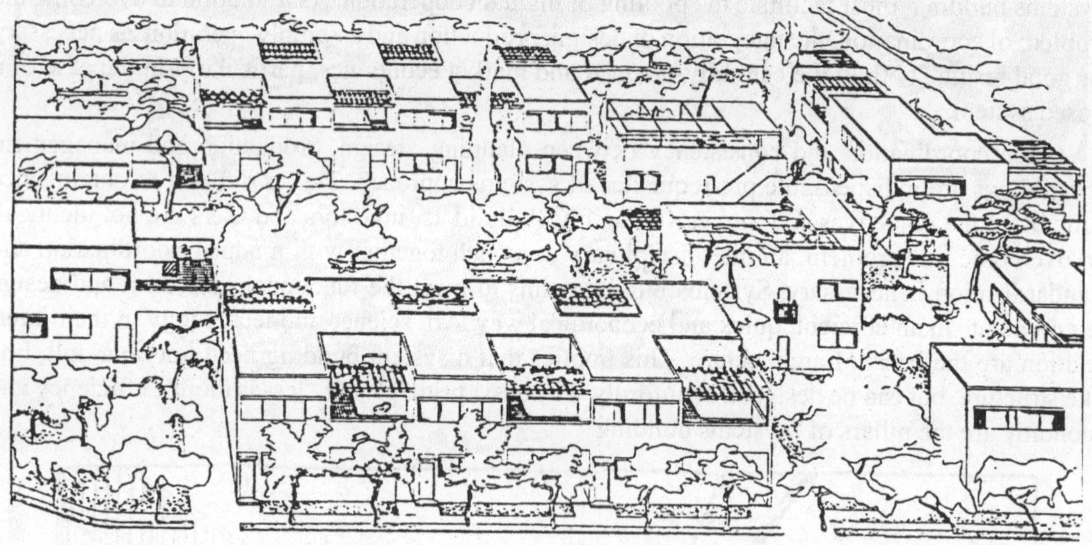

Fig. 11.5. Le Corbusier, Bordeaux-Pessac, 1924 Modern Dwellings. The primary elements have been minutely fixed and are multiplied with endless variations

In spite of the fact that India is the third largest bank of technological skills in the world and has achieved a high level of industrial development, in building construction the innovations are limited and sporadic. Although there are efforts to industrialise the building process largely emerging from individual entrepreneurship, these have not proved adequate. There is a general lack of confidence among the professionals, industry and state establishment in terms of their relevance, utility and production. In the absence of general acceptability, they are subject to many limitations. The main reason is status quo attitude and assessing the innovative building systems by the yardstick of century old PWD codes, manuals and specifications.

The National Committee on Science and Technology (NCST) panel on 'Prefabrication including industrialised system of buildings', spelt out a strategy for introducing industrialised building in our country. In its report, it states:

"There is a scope for introducing full-fledged prefabrication (either on-site or off-site) for mass housing, industrial and institutional buildings in metropolitan cities with a population of a million and more. In urban areas with a population of less than one million and in rural areas there may not be continuing demand for residential and institutional buildings to justify setting up of capital intensive factories. Partial prefabrication combining standardised and optimised precast components such as solid or hollow concrete blocks, light-weight concrete blocks, columns, beams, lintels, doors and windows, parline roofing units, sanitary core units etc., produced on-site or off-site, combined with in situ walls may be the solution. This makes standardisation and modular coordination inevitable and a preliminary step for the industrialisation of building activity. Modular coordination properly applied to various components that enter into the construction of housing and building would reduce the cost through greater efficiency in the use of labour and less wastage of construction materials. As the smaller number of standard types that would result from the use of modular materials would create a bigger market for each of them, this would make large scale production possible. This too would bring down prices."

Coordination and Continuity

Close coordination and consistency between design, production and assembly of buildings is an indispensable condition for the success of systems building. This is difficult to obtain since quite often the objectives and interests of the architects, builders, investors and users are not identical. To overcome this problem, a possibility is to establish an interdisciplinary team of all those directly involved, in order to develop a 'common language.' The idea of systems building may facilitate pooling of mutual cooperation. It is a promising outlook which may bring building industry closer to the pattern of other advanced industrial branches. The systems building, as a solution to overcome the problem of coordination, involves the integration of design, production and assembly operations. Such a 'package deal' is used with good results, both in the centrally planned and market economies, particularly in the case of a specific closed system.

Standardisation and Modular Coordination

Standardisation and modular coordination are the basic tools and language of systems building, which lead to prefabrication. The application of modular coordination may eliminate or reduce many processes like shaping, forming, scaffolding and mixing of materials at the site. The increase in productivity is the most obvious and spectacular effect of prefabrication. It can be affected by finishing operations and by proper organisation, planning and management.

Finishing works such as plumbing, electrification, wiring, tiling, plastering, painting, flooring, decorating, etc. represent about one-third of the total cost of an average residential building. Most of these operations are labour intensive. Generally, the development of finishing works is not balanced with the industrialised operations, including many systems of complete prefabrication. Although many on-site finishing works cannot be avoided, some of them can be carried out industrially. Apart from wall and partition panels which can be finished in the plants, other items such as fittings, furniture, doors, windows, etc. can be prefabricated.

In Europe, as compared to traditional building systems, complete prefabrication of large projects has yielded about 30% reduction in the labour component, while the productivity of on-site operations almost doubled. This resulted into higher speed of construction, reduction of manpower problems, and expansion of building capacity. A dwelling of 100 sq m built by traditional methods in Europe requires about 1800 manhours while by modern methods it needs only 800 manhours. In some developing regions, the same area requires between 4700 to 12600 manhours. Thus, the advanced systems of prefabrication can substantially reduce the building cycle.

Long back, in 1967 the Economic Commission for Europe's Second Seminar on Building Industry at Paris, it was pointed out:

> "A considerable part of the benefits associated with a breakthrough of industrial development in the component sector may not bring a direct return to the investors who initiated this development but will accrue partly to those factors of production who are engaged in management and operations on site, partly to clients and to users of building and partly to society in general as an increment to the gross national product."

These benefits or 'external economies' do not enter into the profit calculations which are the basis for the decisions made by manufacturers of components on the scale and technology in which they will invest. For this reason it may well happen that investments which are optimal for society as a whole may not appear as profitable to the independent decision maker in the market. Thus the price system which is conventionally supposed to work out an optimal and harmonious solution to decentralised decision making may be a poor solution instead.

The social and market conditions of the country require that the approach towards industrialisation of building should not be aped by the Western model of 'organised centralisation', but on the concept of 'decentralisation'. India, with its diversity of living patterns, skills and decentralised production and market system, needs to adopt the 'prefabrication by the masses' rather than 'massive prefabrication'. This had been discernible in the crafts and production of standardised building components in the traditional markets like carved stone pillars, balustrades, stone slabs for roofing, doors, windows, shutters, wooden and concrete grills, battens and many other items. What is needed is a suitable system and technology for prefabrication which is gradual, local and appropriate for the society, and its popular crafts and skills. It should not make redundant all those who are already engaged in marketing, production, assembly and building construction.

A basic prerequisite for developing building systems involves extensive rationalisation, development and expansion of building materials production and progressive industrialisation. The initial phase of industrialisation of building had been defined by the Committee on Housing, Building and Planning as follows:

> "The Committee considered that among the measures which might be quoted as an example of first steps in the industrialisation of building were the establishment of small and medium scale mechanised plants for the production of small and medium-standard elements suitable for handling by small cranes (panels, door and window units, roofing units) and for use in houses with walls made of traditional materials such as, bricks, stones blocks, etc. The organisation of centralised facilities for the production of cement and mortar should be encouraged so as to achieve economy in materials, time and cost. The modernisation of existing plants and the establishment of new ones in large towns for the production of standard building units by industrialised means also be promoted."

Rationalisation does not impose restrictions on variety of building components, nor it means superimposition of standards. The aim is to evolve a common language and parameters for diverse building components and methods. As such, rationalisation and partial prefabrication can be successfully managed with traditional methods and materials. This can result in improved ways of conventional building methods and systematisation of the building industry. This can also help in small-scale industrial production of standardised doors and windows, precast concrete components, such as blocks, lintels, trusses, beams, columns, slabs, etc. At the same time, the production of new materials like lightweight concrete, hollow tiles, etc. can be encouraged. The production of fibreboards, paints, glues and preservatives for finishing operations can also be established.

Simple fittings, hardware and hand tools would provide another possibility. In the course of further development, a variety of new and improved materials and prefabricated components can be gradually introduced. It is generally believed that building costs can be minimised by concentrating on the mass production of building components and materials.

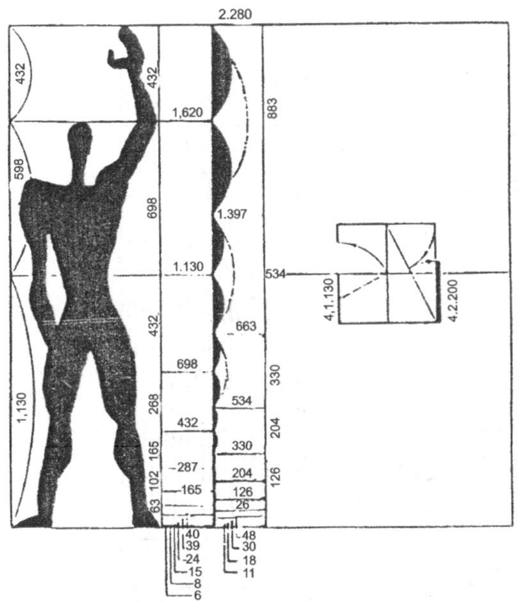

Fig. 11.6. Modular figure by Le Corbusier is the basis of standardisation of building components

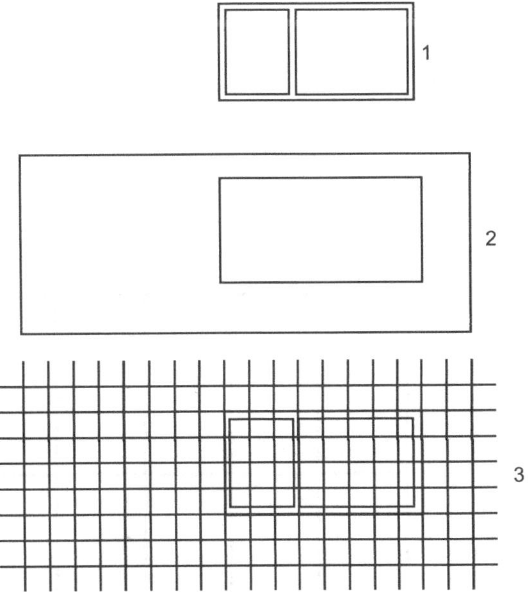

Fig. 11.7. Modular systems in building design:
1. The component
2. Location of components in the Building
3. Modular coordination

Fig. 11.8. Division structure of the Janko Swiss Building Block System based upon the Golden Section

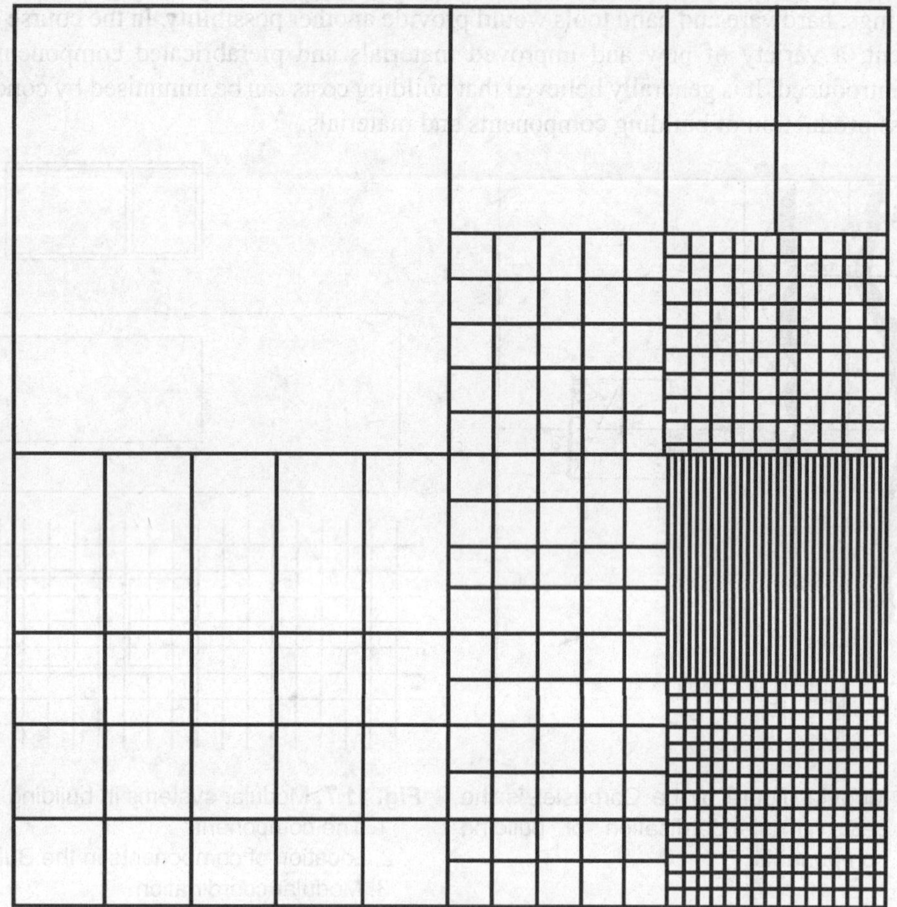

Fig. 11.9. The Modular System of Soviet Union–Basic module 0.10 m/0.30 m, Planning module: 3.00 or 6.00 or 9.00 m

It is necessary that a design approach is evolved for the industrialisation of building construction. Building systems should be based upon well conceived designs which allow various permutations and combinations. Modular coordination and rationalisation thus become the prerequisites in evolving the building materials and component industry into an integrated process.

Standardisation of structural elements would permit the adoption of mass production industry for construction and consequent reduction in the cost of production. Standardisation is closely linked with the introduction of a unified modular system, coordinating sizes of structural components, tolerances and basic parameters of various purpose buildings. Another advantage of standardisation and modular coordination is simplification of design process. The production of prefabricated elements and operations on the construction site become more simple, systematic and organised.

Standardisation is a complex process of formulating and applying rules for an orderly approach to a specific activity with cooperation of all concerned, taking due account of functional conditions and safety requirements. A standard is the result of a detailed planning and engineering efforts. In addition to the dimensions and tolerances, the standards of building materials and elements also establish the performance criteria with respect to acoustics, water tightness, fire resistance and other provisions, including testing methods.

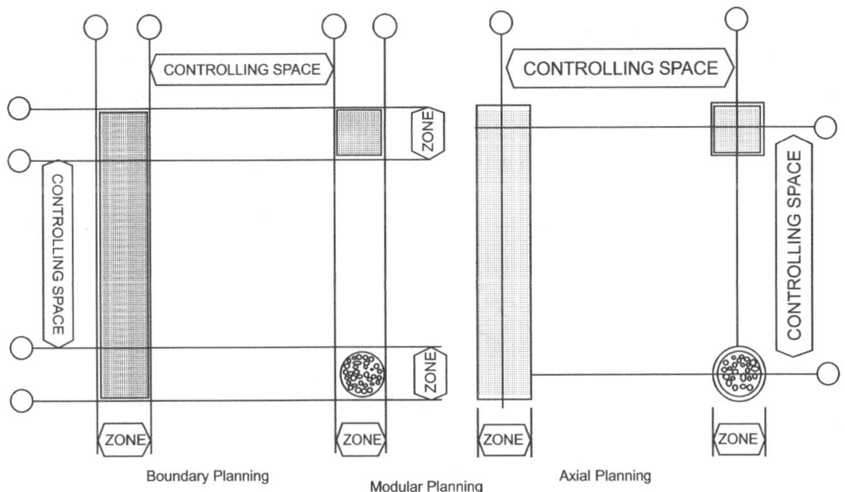

Fig. 11.10. Modular Planning

Source: *National Buildings Organization*

The performance of building can be standardised in accordance to the building regulations within parameters such as permissible loads, natural lighting, ventilation, thermal and acoustic conditions, minimum dimensions of rooms and parts of buildings, distances between buildings etc. In all cases the dimensions should be coordinated on a modular basis.

Dimensional coordination means the establishment of a range of related dimensions for common use in sizing building and components which make up these buildings. Modular coordination is a method of sizing the dimensions of building components and of building on a basic module, *e.g.* 10 cm (four inches).

Modular coordination offers several advantages. It simplifies and unifies the process of standardisation, bringing into building operations a kind of discipline which is typical for advanced industrial technologies. Consequently, it creates conditions for mass production, production of the number of similar sections, units and prefabricated components, inter-changeability of the products, material economy, simplification and rationalisation of operations and increased productivity. Ultimately, better economy in the whole building process is achieved.

Modular coordination, no doubt, reduces to some extent the freedom of design, if one considers individual tastes and creativity. However, 'creative discipline' does not mean uniformity or monotony. There is always a broad range for the achievement of innovative results, in terms of the functional aesthetic parameters of buildings even by standardisation and modular coordination. Modular coordination also offers opportunities for technological development and overcomes the impediments in remodelling the existing system.

Standardisation and modular coordination result into simplification of the operations including design and execution, reduction of material and labour consumption and better performance of buildings. The initial phase of standardisation and modular coordination may be developed bin uilding elements, which are produced in series and have an important impact on building economy, such as bricks, tiles, concrete blocks, doors, windows, roofing materials, fittings and other prefabricated components.

Lack of uniformity in standardisation and modular coordination inhibits development of the building industry and reduces its productivity. The existence of multiple systems of measurement present difficulties. For this reason, it is essential to encourage standardisation of the dimensions and quality of commonly used products at the national level. It is also desirable at the international and regional levels to establish a common link in building materials and components, equipments, tools, machines and plants. Subsequently, standardisation and modular process should become a continuous process leading eventually to a full national or regional system of building standards.

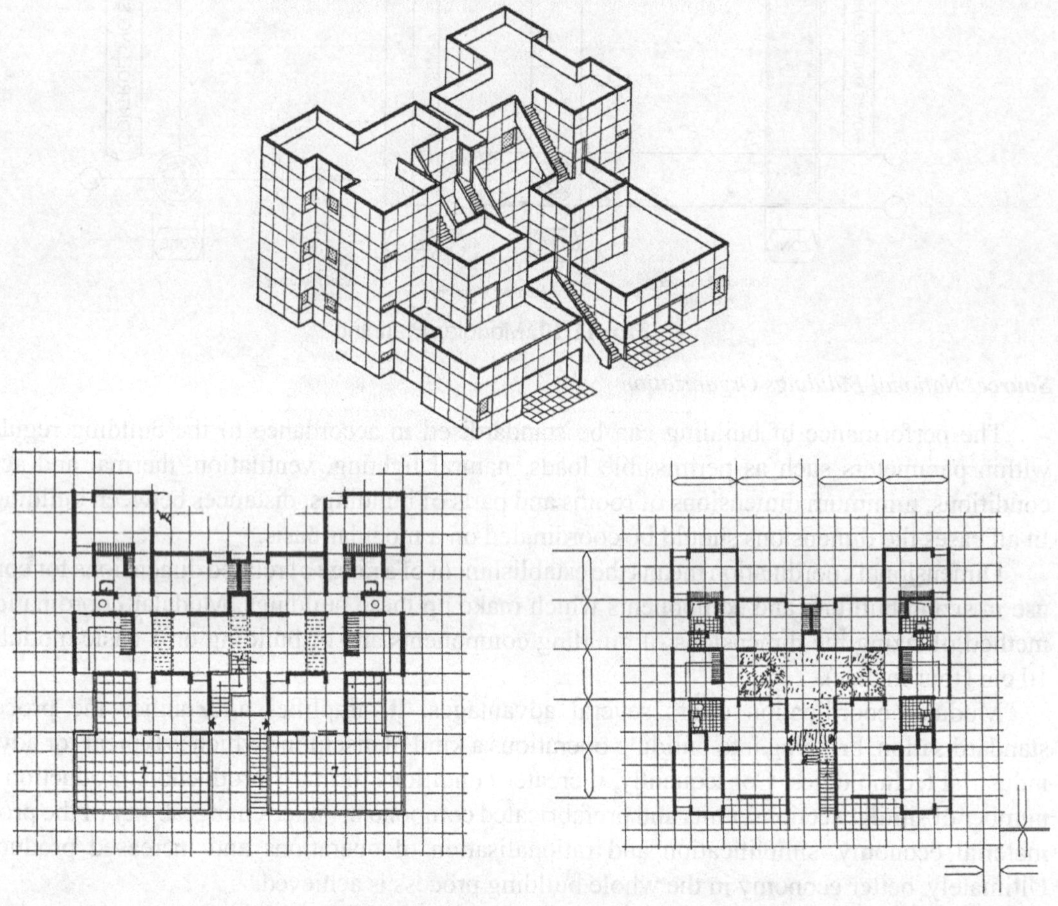

Fig. 11.11. Modular Housing

Source: *Ministry of Works and Housing, 1998, Group on Prefabrication and Modular Co-ordination.*

A highly effective means of rationalising the industry is through the architectural design. In a note to the Committee on Housing, Building and Planning at its second session, the Secretary General commented as follows:

> *"Based on the norms and standards prescribed by the central authority, standard type design may be worked out by teams of experienced designers, taking into consideration, among other things, climatic and geological conditions, local living habits, economical specification and improved design and construction techniques. The floor spans may be standardised and the design for houses of different sizes and structures interrelated by identical architecture and technical planning. Maximum cost per unit area may also be laid down for construction in different localities on the basis of the standard design."*

Even in the first stage of industrialisation a close collaboration between designers, suppliers, producers and users should be maintained. For sophisticated industrialised techniques, a professional reorientation of engineers and the designers is inevitable.

A well conceived layout plan and design of materials management circulation, storage facilities, workshops, location of machines and equipment, etc. should be prepared before any site operations are started. It must be based on the technologies which will be used in construction.

Site-work schedules, coordinating in time and space and related operations, like delivery of materials, labour engagement, use of machines and participation of sub-contractors, need pre-planning for a systematic building project. The work programme must assess the needs and functions of the team of workers for specific and repetitive operations, such as, brick laying, plastering, carpentry, insulation, works etc. Specialised building gangs, which are typical for the so called 'flowline' building method, can be engaged for large projects.

Better utilisation of local materials should be preferred to imported or expensive ones, provided the requirements on the performance are fully satisfied.

Progressive Transformation

Improvement of currently used hand tools, machines and other equipment and the introduction of new and more effective ones represent an important part of rationalisation measures. Containers for transportation and handling of bricks and tiles, standard reusable shuttering and scaffolding, jacks, mobile cranes, concrete and mortar mixers, compressors, vibrators, steel bending and welding equipment, etc. would greatly increase the productivity and improve the quality and economy of building. Easy availability and expanded use of tools such as saws, braces, screw and nail drivers, pipe wrenches and others for carpentry, masonry, plumbing, plastering and painting, are equally important for the productivity and quality of work.

Establishment of temporary plants and workshops for the production of building components, such as carpentry and joinery, mortar and concrete mixing, steel bending shops, precasting of concrete blocks, etc. can be organised on larger building sites.

By means of the design, it is possible to create favourable prerequisites for rationalisation. Based on the contemporary state of the skills, material and technical possibilities, the appropriate design influences the standard of organisation, the productivity of labour and the cost of construction. The designs based on modular coordination make it possible to apply more easily new materials and products, assembly of components and mechanisation. The flowline method of construction and repetitive processes bring about economy in building. These measures mainly involve design, technical and organisational adjustments to utilise more efficiently the available resources, without much additional investment.

Rationalisation measures can be gradually amplified by the expanded use of prefabricated components such as beams, lintels, trusses, wall blocks, slabs, stairs, doors, windows, roofing and flooring units, partition and sanitary panels, etc. Initially, when the market is small, these components can be conveniently produced on the building site or in small scale industries.

Prefabrication, during this phase, may account for 20 to 30% of the total construction value of the buildings. Prefabrication, combined with rationalised measures, can help in the reduction of building costs and time. Partial prefabrication can gradually become more advanced, transforming itself into full scale industrialisation. Simple components can be complemented by more elaborate load bearing and non load bearing panels for walls, partitions, roofing and ceiling and sanitary installations.

A widespread misconception is that industrialised systems make the traditional systems and technologies obsolete or redundant. A prefabricated building system may coexist and even collaborate with the traditional one. In fact, if properly adopted, the two systems can be complementary. This, however, imposes rather strict requirements on the design and standardisation so that the industrialised systems become open to architectural and structural variations.

Appropriate technology is an important factor for the success of industrialisation. In spite of high technological inputs, the record of success of industrialisation in the country has been dismal. The reason might be that the industrialisation of building process is complex and requires integration of economic, cultural, administrative and managerial actions. A well conceived organisation, marketing strategy and efficient management cannot be a sideline in this pursuit.

Operations research, application of network diagram, mathematical models and computer techniques are becoming important in the preparation, programming and control of the building process. With their use, it is possible to introduce progressive forms of organisation and management as they allow a rapid analysis of complex situations, comparison of various methods of production, variations of design and selection of alternatives.

Various Stages of Planning

Any scheme for building construction has to pass through several stages which are predominantly following:

(*a*) Programming, surveying and finalising the requirements for design and planning
(*b*) Planning and design
(*c*) Structural design, specifications, services, quantity and material management
(*d*) Execution, including project management.

Each stage has potential for cost reduction. Considerable economy can be achieved at the following stages:

(*i*) Planning, detailing and rationalisation for the requirement at pre-design stage
(*ii*) Reducing ancillary areas and optimisation of functional areas
(*iii*) Providing multiple use of the facilities
(*iv*) Standardisation of repetitive items
(*v*) Managerial optimisation of resources, time and materials.

At the stage of structural design and specifications, adoption of functional design and economical use of local materials can result in cost reduction. At the stage of execution, economy can be affected by proper programming and efficient review so that the men, materials and machinery are fully utilised and time and cost overruns are minimum.

The design stage is most crucial for achieving efficiency and cost optimisation, which involves the following:

(*i*) Optimisation of land use, Floor Area Ratio and Density
(*ii*) Design of building evolved on the basis of conceptualisation of an economical structure
(*iii*) Standardisation of dimensions, components and openings
(*iv*) Optimal use of building materials and their augmentation

(*v*) Rationalisation of specifications and use of new techniques of construction

(*vi*) Improved management of projects, including computer aided design of space, structure and programming.

Industrialisation of Building Process

The key concept involved in the industrialisation of building begins with the standardisation, rationalisation, production of new and improved building materials and components and the introduction of effective tools, machines and site equipment. A variety of prefabricated components can be evolved according to local needs, materials and skills. Partial prefabrication in this development stage should represent a significant technological breakthrough from conventional to industrialised building methods.

The foundations, walls, doors and windows and roof are the most important components of a structure. These components can be designed and oriented to the needs of general coordination of the dimensions improving thereby the speed of construction and reducing the construction cost. The various types of foundations normally adopted are:

(*a*) Spread foundations

(*b*) Pile foundations

(*c*) Columns and footings

(*d*) RCC raft foundations

Because of the varying soil conditions prevailing in different parts of the country, it is generally more practicable to make foundations by conventional methods, using in-situ techniques rather than adopting prefabrication. In-situ foundations have been found economical in most cases. In seismic regions, special attention needs to be paid in designing the foundations. Prefabrication for foundation is rare and adopted only in special cases.

Walls

Stabilised soil, bamboo and wooden panels, rammed earth, bricks, soil cement blocks, light weight concrete blocks, panels, etc. are used in the construction of walls. However, bricks continue to be the backbone of the building industry. At present, bricks are produced in different shapes and sizes. Most of the bricks produced are non-modular, having conventional size of 23 cm × 11.5 cm × 7.5 cm (9″ × $4\frac{1"}{2}$ × 3″). During the construction the number of bricks broken into different sizes to fit into position is very large. As a result of this, in addition to wastage of materials and labour, quality of construction also suffers. Efforts should be made to standardise the dimensions of bricks, their production and use. The present brick size is based upon British practice. It would be pertinent to study if we could revert back to traditional brick size (12″× 2″ × 4″) which would facilitate construction of hollow walls, variety in bonding, saving of dead weight and space of the walls and lesser breakage.

Fig. 11.12. Geodesic dome by standard components is based on the principle of enclosing maximum space with minimum surface area and materials. It is formed by small, manually handable components which assemble to give a 3-D structural framework. Buckminster Fuller is credited to have invented the geodesic dome for buildings

Adoption of large size blocks would improve the speed of construction and reduce mortar consumption, as compared to walls with standard bricks. The low density of concrete, light weight concrete, permits use of bigger size wall blocks. For manufacturing medium size and large blocks, use of agriculture and industrial wastes like rice husk, blast furnace slag, flyash and thermocole, can economise costs and give better insulation to the walls.

Though in India, several prefabrication techniques have been developed for walling, such as, small, medium and large panels, yet these have not proved economical for low income housing as compared to traditional bricks. Large panel construction and similar prefabrication techniques could be appropriate at a later stage. At present, partial prefabrication appears to be a significant area in the transition of conventional construction to industrialised systems.

Floors and Roof

Structural floors/roofs account for substantial cost of a building. Any saving achieved in floor/roof reduces considerably the cost of buildings. Traditional cast in-situ concrete roof cost involves the use of temporary shuttering which adds to the cost of construction and time. Use of standardised roofing components where shuttering is avoided prove to be economical, fast and better in quality. Prefabrication of such components (on-site or off-site) can be introduced to achieve quality, speed and economy.

The common prefabricated roofing/flooring components are:

(*i*) Precast concrete battens and hollow clay or concrete blocks (*ii*) Precast elements such as channel units, hollow cored units cellular units, funicular shells, thrift beams, sandwich panels, etc.

(*iii*) Precast concrete solid slabs

(*iv*) Light weight concrete slabs

(*v*) Reinforced brick panels

(*vi*) Reinforced concrete T-units

(*vii*) Roofing tiles

(*viii*) Precast reinforced and prestressed hyperboloid shells

(*ix*) Geodesic domes, segmental skeletal shells, etc.

At present, most of the factories are producing their products in different dimensions, which lack flexibility and inter-changeability. With the adoption of modular coordination and standard sizes, these components would give greater flexibility with lesser number of components.

Doors and Windows

Innumerable types and sizes of doors and windows are being used in buildings. This involves wastage of labour and materials. To minimise these wastages, it is essential to standardise and optimise dimensions of doors and windows. This will enable economical manufacture of limited types of doors and windows. It will also reduce the dependence upon skilled labour at site and minimise the wastage of materials. Precast reinforced concrete and steel door and window frame also economise the cost. Synthetics, PVC, fibreglass and non-ferrous metals like aluminium are now being used for manufacture of doors and window frames. However, their use is limited for low cost housing. The efficiency of space can be achieved by a systems/modular apparels.

Modularisation

Successful modularisation must be based on detailed knowledge of the underlying parameters of the structure, standard sizes of building components, coordination, etc.

As the properties of the system and the modules become better understood, the design rules will tend to become more clear. The innate interdependencies can be addressed by the design rules, integration and coordination of the systems. Eventually, the process may become standardized and simple. The design rules address the following:

- architecture defining various systems.
- interfaces, that is, how different modules and elements will interact, including how they fit together, connect, communicate, and integrate.
- integration procedures that allow the system to work.

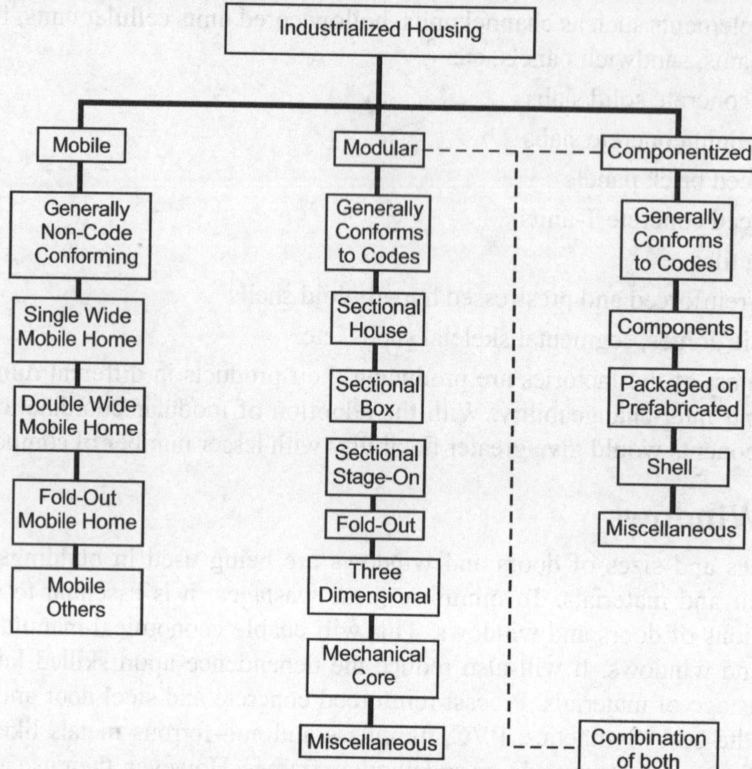

Fig. 11.13. The industrialized housing industry covers three major segments—mobile building, modular design and components

Source: *Reidelback, John A. Jr. (1971) Modular Housing, Massachusetts*

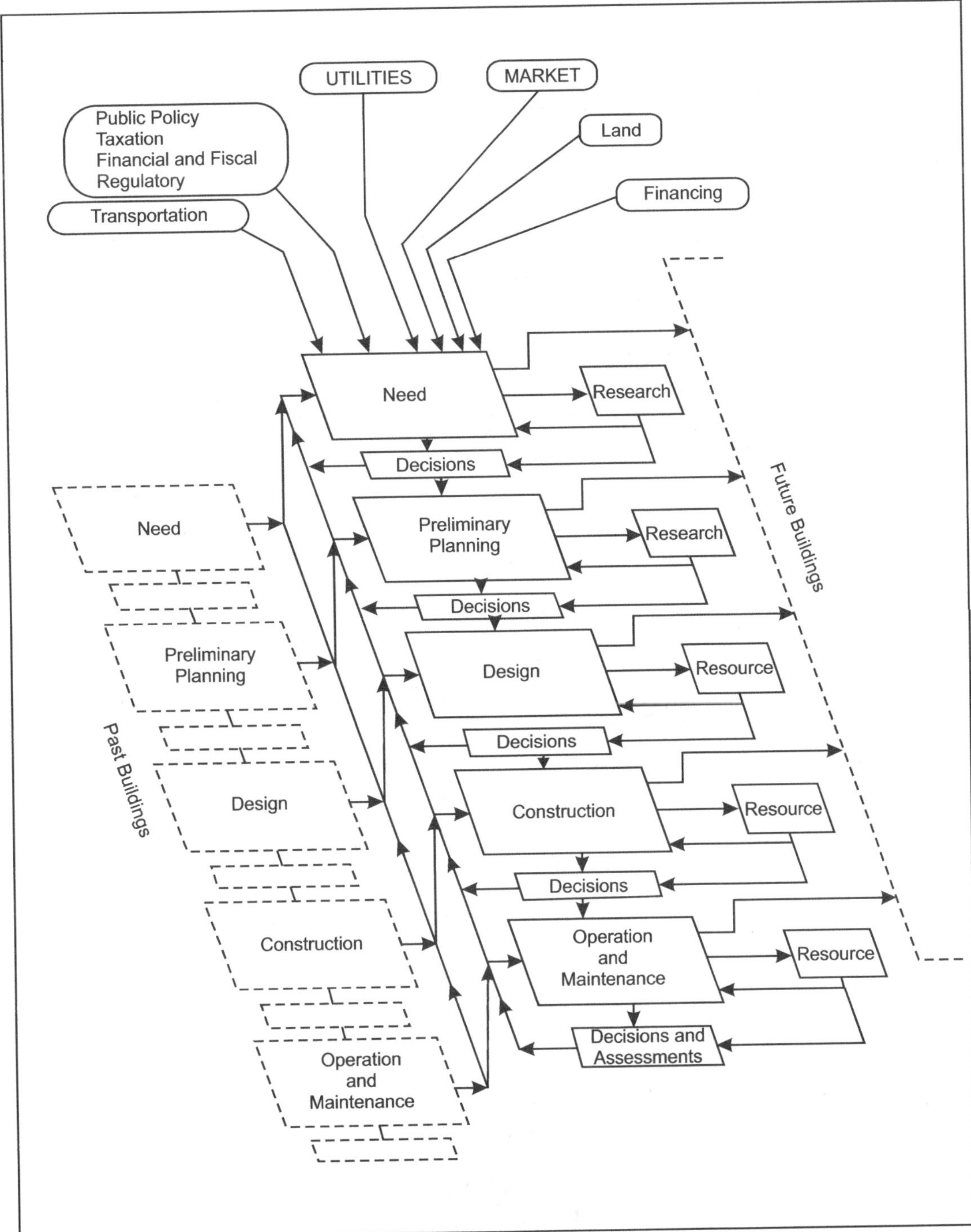

Fig. 11.14. The Building Process as an integrated system of building operations

Source: *Albert GH Dietz (ed) (1961) Components in House Building (NAHB Components Study), MIT, Massachusetts*

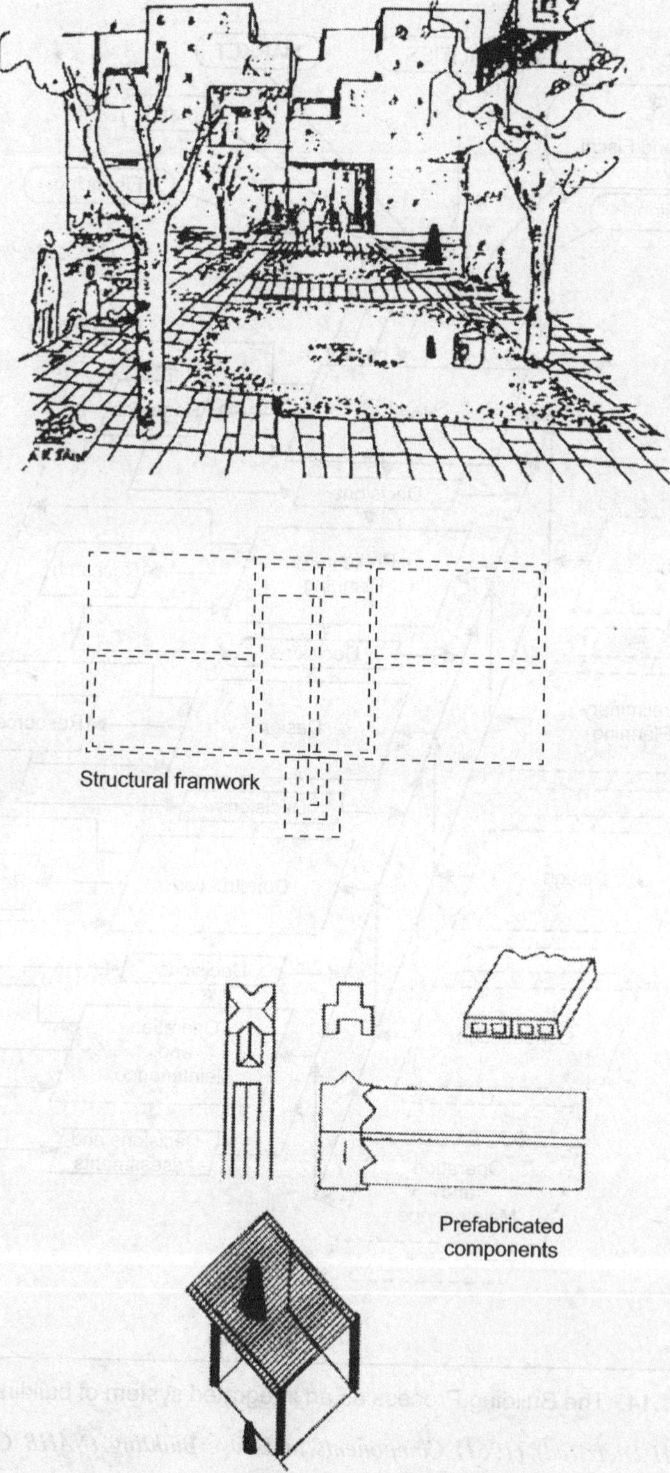

Fig. 11.15. Skeleton Prefab Social Housing, Architect, A.K. Jain

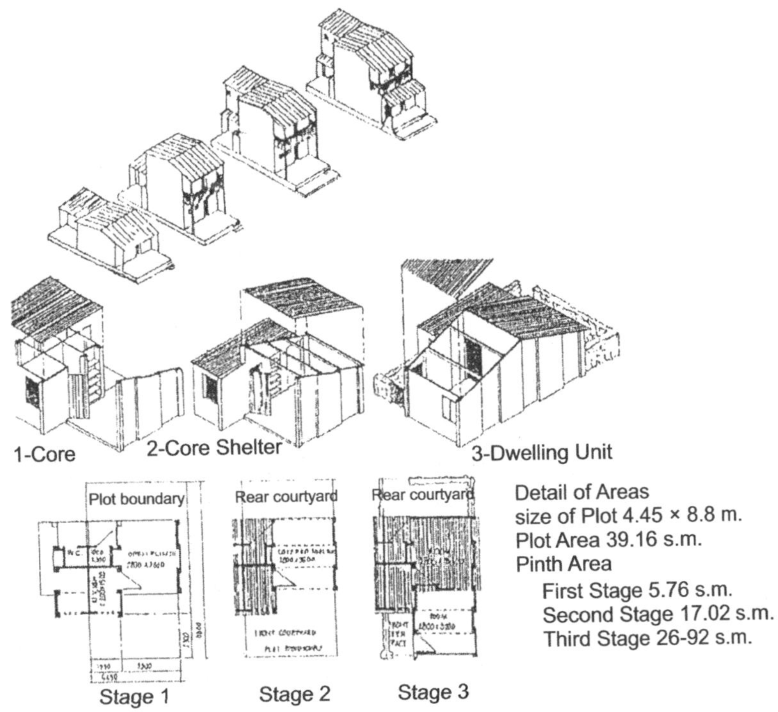

Fig. 11.16. Core Housing which grows from 5.76 sm to 92 sm dwelling unit is based on standardised and evolutionary components

Source: *Florian Steinberg, Concept Evolutionary Housing Design for India, HUDCO, New Delhi*

Systems Approach

Fig. 11.17. Slum Dwellers Housing Scheme, La Puntilla at San Juan Puerto Rico, Puerto Rico Urban Renewal and Housing Administration. The skeleton is built by the Housing Administration, whereas the households finish and furnish their own dwelling units in accordance with their resources, taste and needs

The plans and designs manifest a synthesis of the complex factors, programme of requirements and various stages of construction. Uniform standards that are set too high can price poor households out of formal housing. It may be better to provide basic, safe shelter in appropriate locations, even with limited space. Existing housing, even in poor condition, can be upgraded and retrofitted which may serve residents better, where they have social connections and access to employment. Housing design should enable systems approach in its production and upgradation.

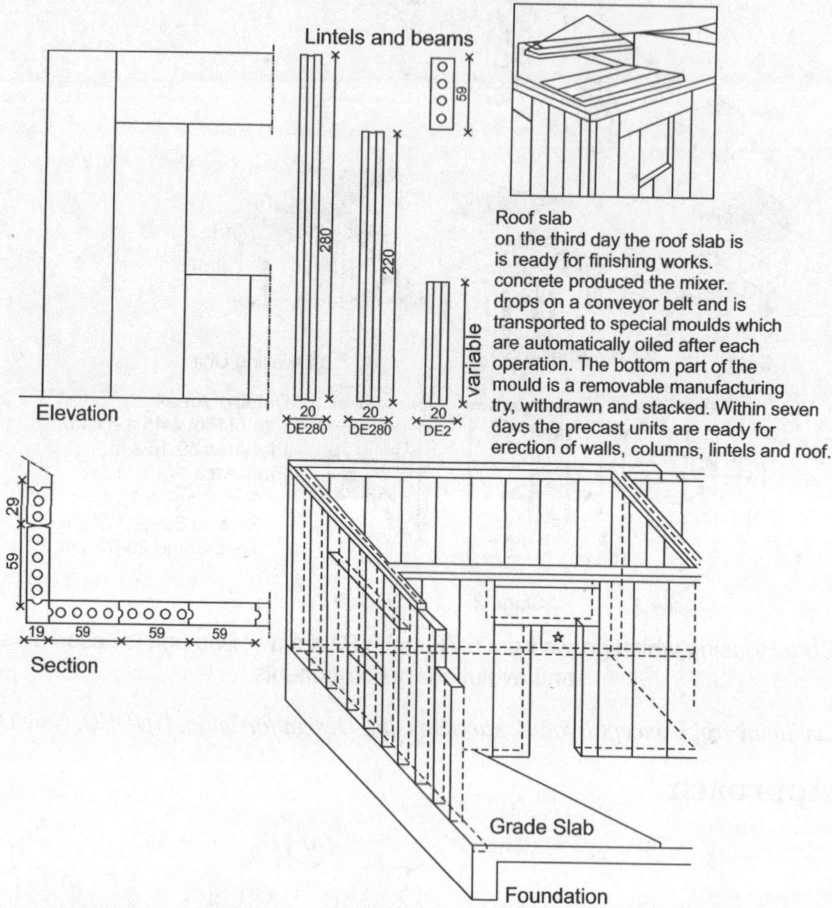

Fig. 11.18. Readymade Housing for Disaster Prone Settlements

Source: *Jaggi, I R, Readymade Housing, Indian Architect and Builder, October 1991*

Affordable housing need not be a replica of standardised units, but should incorporate flexibility of space by creating living platforms with roof or skeleton, where the dwellers can furnish and finish their dwellings according to their taste, needs and resources. Ground floor can be kept for parking, shops, community space and common facilities.

The concept of evolutionary housing is based on two major criteria: the right of each family to develop its own dwelling according to its own priorities, needs, and resources and introducing time into the process of design for gradual development and changes. Evolutionary design defines the plot-core relationship, *i.e.* the design of a built core, its location on the plot and the development alternatives for various stages of growth, both horizontal and vertical. The core is the cell through which the dwelling unit is generated. The 'composite development' constitutes the combination of the plot and the core, *i.e.* the placing of a particular core in a particular position within a particular plot. Growth options indicate the direction as well as the feasible transformation offered by a given initial core.

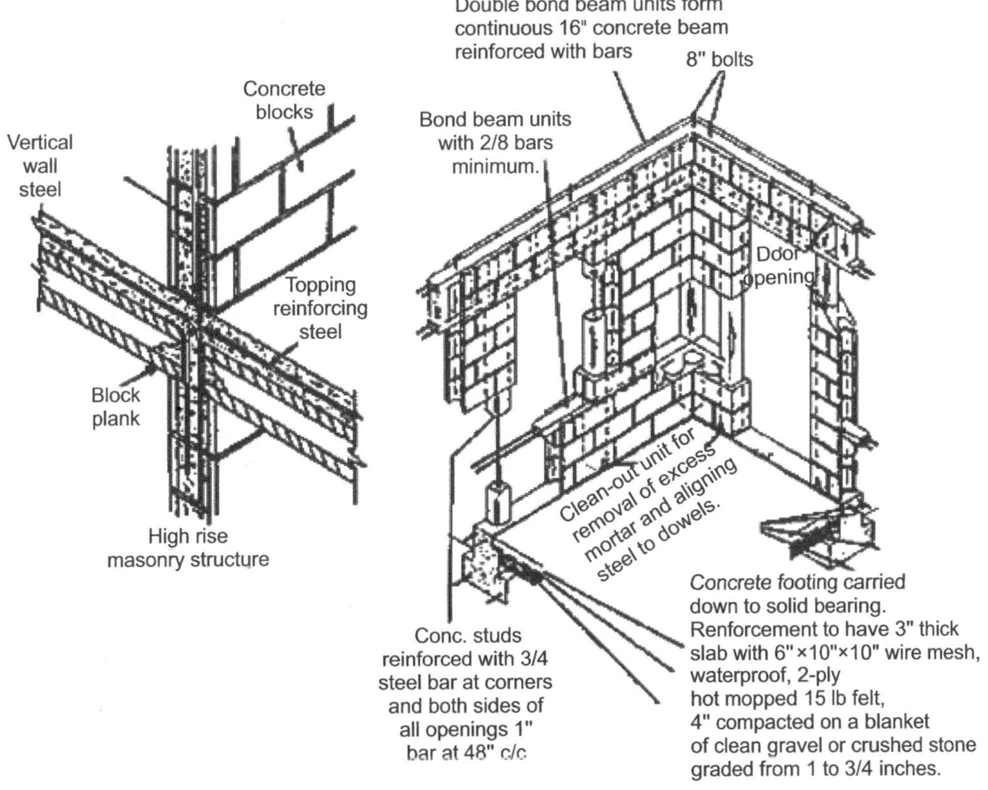

Fig. 11.19. Multi-storied Masonry Structure for Housing

Source: *Dr. P. K. Rao, Safeguards for Sound Concrete, Indian Architect and Builder, October 1991*

Systems Based Technologies

Proven technologies and regulatory supports can enable large-scale, low-cost housing production. Industrial approaches (using components manufactured off-site), standardization, and improved purchasing and other processes can reduce cost by 30 per cent. Uniform building codes can spread these practices and government and developers can scale up the industrial production.

Pre-cast and prefabricated systems include steel and concrete frames, pre-cast panels, and structurally insulated panels. Tunnel form and light weight metal form works enable the casting of horizontal and vertical elements simultaneously so that walls and slabs can be cast in one operation in a daily cycle. This approach combines the speed, quality, and accuracy of off-site production with the flexibility of on-site construction.

Table 11.1: Systems Housing Options

Approach	Type	Description
Precast systems and Framework	Light gauge steel frame Pre-cast concrete frame Pre-cast concrete panels Structurally insulated panels	Galvanized steel sheets, roll formed into profiles used for framing Reinforced concrete framing elements, including columns and beams pre-cast in factory (not commonly used in housing).
Prefabrication Panels/ Components	Glass fiber-reinforced panels Volumetric Pre-cast Modular Homes	Large concrete walls and slab panels prefabricated in factory. Insulating foam core sandwiched between two structural facings, typically metal sheet or cement.
Superstructure	Complete factory-built homes. Lightweight/ foam concrete block, Tunnel framework (In-situ), Lightweight/reusable framework (In-situ), Insulated concrete forms.	Concrete masonry units laid dry and subsequently grouted, partially grouted, or surface bonded. Lightweight reusable panel forms made from aluminium or plastic polystyene foam or beads, used as stay-in-place forms, dry stacked and filled with concrete.

Walling Components

Bricks are often moulded in clay and fire. Their compression strength ranges from 20 to 60 kg/cm^2. Hollow blocks bricks can be produced by stretcher-levellers and extruders.

For solid stone blocks, moulding corresponds with the cutting process which is done after extraction with cutting machines or block sawing. As a bye-product of cutting stones, a large quantity of aggregate stone dust and mortar are obtained. These can be recycled for manufacturing concrete blocks.

For bricks, concrete and cast gypsum blocks, drying is an important phase of the production process. Artificial drying consumes a large quantity of energy. Sun is an ideal source of heat for drying. Depending upon the climatic conditions, it may be possible to combine the use of solar energy and heat recovered from the kilns.

Precast concrete blocks

Essential ingredients of concrete blocks are the aggregates, binders and water. The aggregates include various materials, such as natural gravels, crushed stone, sintered/pulverised fuel ash, pumice, clinker, foamed or air-cooled slag, expanded clay, shale, clay and wood sawdust. Usual binding material is ordinary or rapid hardening portland cement. Lightweight concrete blocks can be either load bearing, or self supporting which are used for the partitions. For external and load bearing walls dense blocks are more suitable.

Concrete blocks can be solid, hollow or cellular. Solid blocks are essentially without voids, but can have small cavities, grooves or finger holes for ease of handling and laying. In hollow blocks cavities are through and through, while in cellular blocks the cavities are closed at one end.

Several variations are possible within the above categories of blocks. Interlocking blocks are most innovative, as they provide a stronger bond, use less mortar and offer interesting patterns on the facade. 'T', 'L', 'Z' shaped lightweight concrete blocks can be manufactured in various profiles. They offer interlocking joints, interrupting horizontals or verticals to form a self-locking pattern. Insulating materials like thermocole and fibreglass can be sandwiched within the cavity for better insulation during the construction of wall by concrete block. Perforated block are also becoming popular, as these are suitable for tropical climate. These diffuse sunlight but permit air flow.

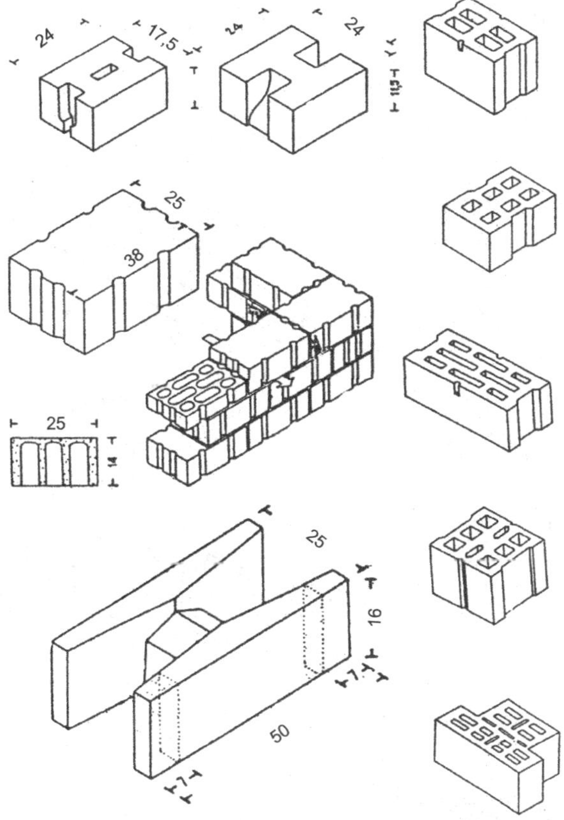

Fig. 11.20. Concrete Blocks

Source: *United Nations, 1972*

Joints

Thin, uniform and fine joints give better strength to a wall. Joints should be resistant to moisture penetration. The strength of the joints depends upon the area of bedding. The greater the area of bedding, the higher would be the strength of the wall. Though joints are not critical features of block work, they can provide a neat and beautiful appearance. Untidy and careless joints make the facade of the wall ugly.

With wetting and drying all masonry materials undergo dimensional changes. Although these changes are minor, they can cause cracking or damage the structure unless precautions are taken. To allow dimensional changes due to shrinkage, wetting, expansion, moisture movement and changes in temperature, joints and binding mortar should allow certain flexibility.

The other causes of cracking are often an uneven settlement of foundation, deflection, impact and thermal movement. Cracking and damaging can be minimised by adequate curing of blocks, joint control, reinforcement and by proper detailing and design.

Surface Texture

Mass produced, machine made concrete blocks offer an interesting and a wide range of patterns, finishes, relief, colours and texture. Alternatively, if they are to be painted, care should be taken that their texture and bonding pattern are not obliterated.

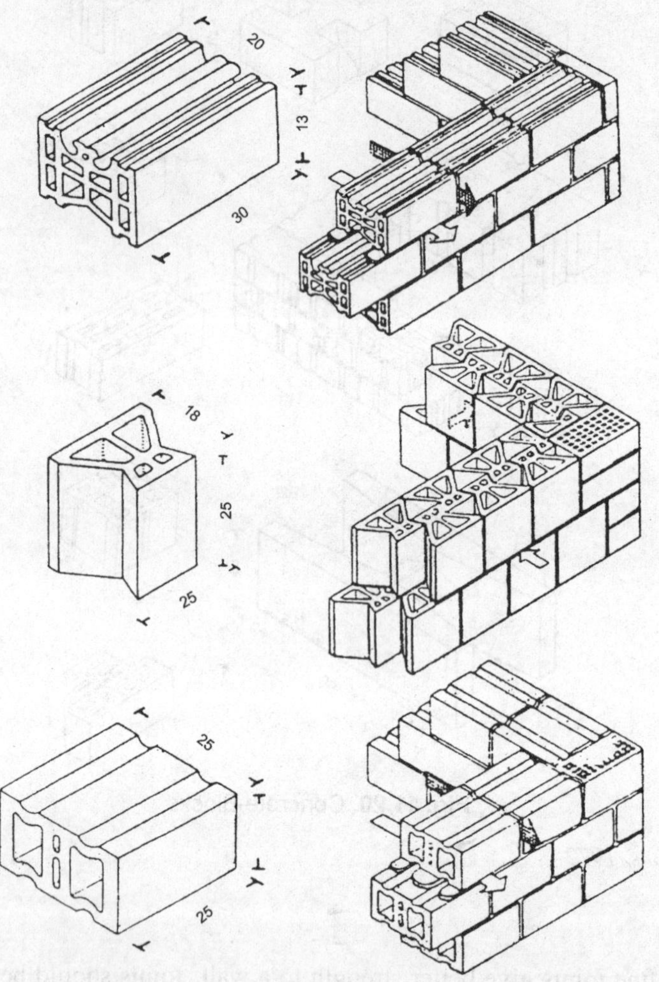

Fig. 11.21. Bonding of lightweight concrete blocks

Source: *United Nations, 1972*

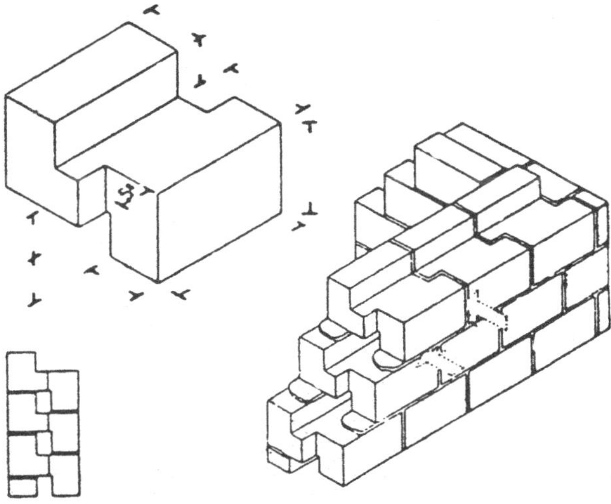

Fig. 11.22. Z-shaped lightweight concrete units interrupting vertical and horizontal joints

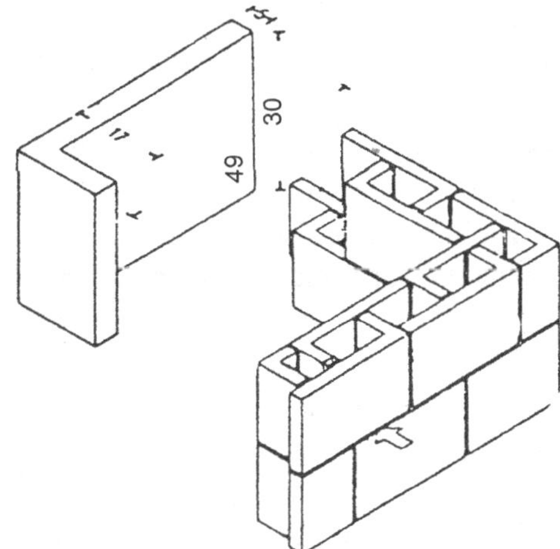

Fig. 11.23. L-shaped lightweight concrete unit filled with heat insulating material

Source: *United Nations, 1972*

The choice of the type of finishing of blocks depends on various factors like durability, rain penetration and weathering conditions. Different treatments are available to minimise rain penetration and to protect the wall from atmospheric and chemical reactions. A bold profile and rough texture are suitable for external walls. The walls under shade require a more pronounced texture than the walls exposed to bright sunlight. Various kinds of built-in surface textures, commonly adopted for concrete blocks are given below:

Plain Concrete Blocks - which may be dense, lightweight or aerated can have uniformity of simple texture and sharp edges.

Split Block - high density concrete unit is split in smaller blocks, exposing and splitting the aggregates in the process. The colour and texture of the surface depends on the intensity of split and the aggregates used. They are both coarse and fine texture and can be adopted for facing work, as per design requirements.

Sawn Blocks - lightweight blocks are sawn after manufacturing, which gives them a woodlike texture.

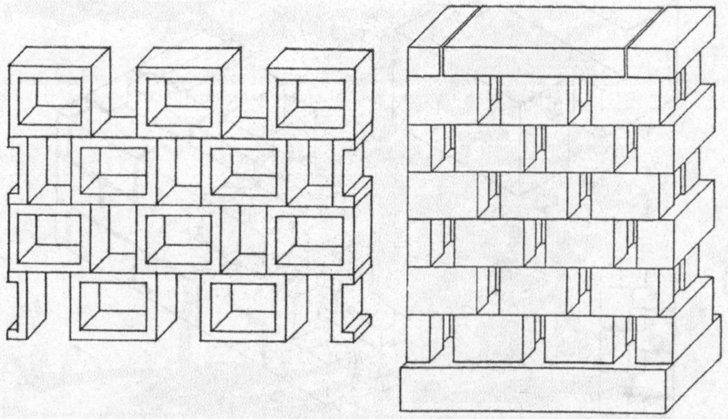

Fig. 11.24. Concrete blocks perforated wall

Profiled blocks - are moulded by casting against a profiled face. Geometrical patterns and rock-faced profiles are popular, though custom designed relief, composition and artistic profiles can also be casted.

Exposed aggregate blocks - are manufactured by deliberately exposing the pattern or lining of wooden framework as done in precast concrete. Alternatively sand bed and blast techniques can also be adopted. Block recessed joints emphasise the form of separate blocks while flush joints make the whole wall to appear as a unit. An attractive pattern can be obtained by exposed aggregate and mortar joints.

Glazed blocks - have a smooth and reflective finish, which is obtained by curing and glazing of the block by resin. Such blocks have a very low co-efficient of absorption and condensation. However, to avoid the concentration of water joints, which may risk moisture penetration, joints should be well finished. These are easier to clean and more hygienic, resistant to acids, stains, spots, alkalis, oxidizing agents, petroleum and solvents. These qualities make them suitable for service stations, breweries, buildings in high traffic zones and for external walls.

Pierced concrete blocks - have good insulating qualities as these blocks diffuse sunlight, filter dust and noise and permit free flow of air. A wide range of attractive patterns, colours and finishings can be provided in such blocks.

Sprayed blocks - a special finish can be applied by spray to blocks, after they have been moulded and are still green. The surface can then be coated with a clear lacquer. This makes the finishing smooth and long lasting.

Slump blocks - are produced by releasing the unit slump from the mould in such a manner as to obtain an irregular face. An interesting facade can be obtained by proper design and by the play of light and shade on the surface.

Finishing

Building of walls with blocks involves binding and surface finishing. Mortars are used by mixing binders, *i.e.* lime, cement and sand. The function of bonding mortar is to convey and distribute loads. Their thermal and physical characteristics must therefore correspond with those of the masonry. Non-traditional, ready to use mortars for concrete blocks can be laid dry. The blocks should be moistened beforehand for adequate bonding. Saving of mortar, to a large extent, depends on the form of block, its size, precision of joints and workmanship.

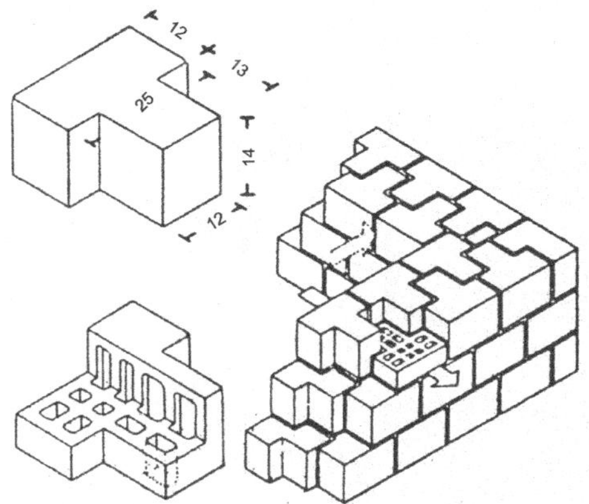

Fig. 11.25. T-shaped lightweight blocks with closed cavities

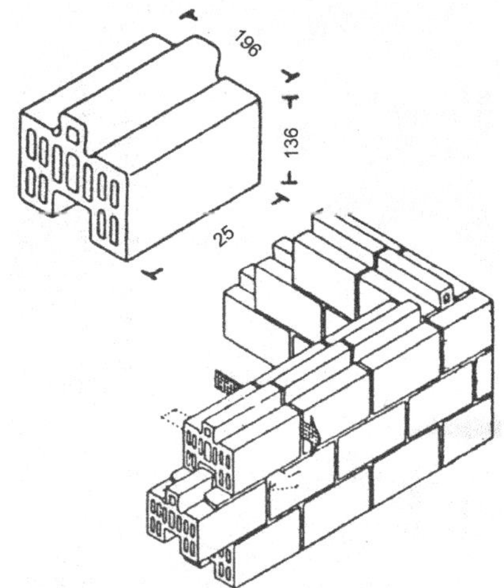

Fig. 11.26. Wall block interrupting horizontal joints

Source: *Deptt of Economic and Social Affairs (1972). Use of Precast components in masonry building construction, United Nations*

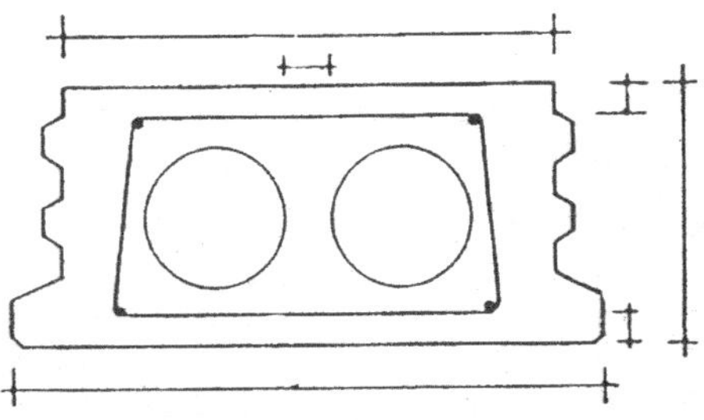

Fig. 11.27. Precast R.C. core unit

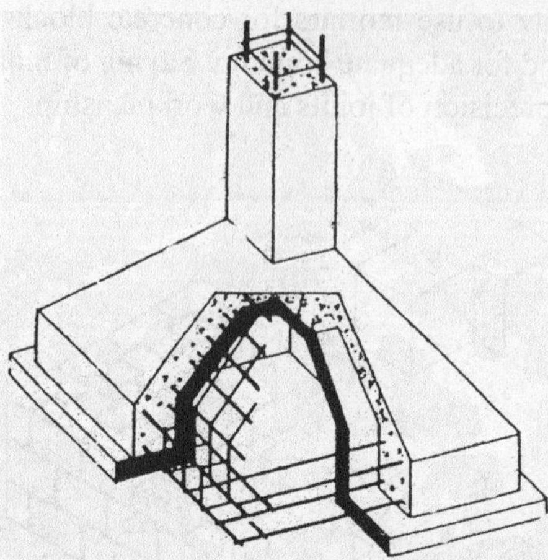

Fig. 11.28. Hyperbolic Paraboloid footing

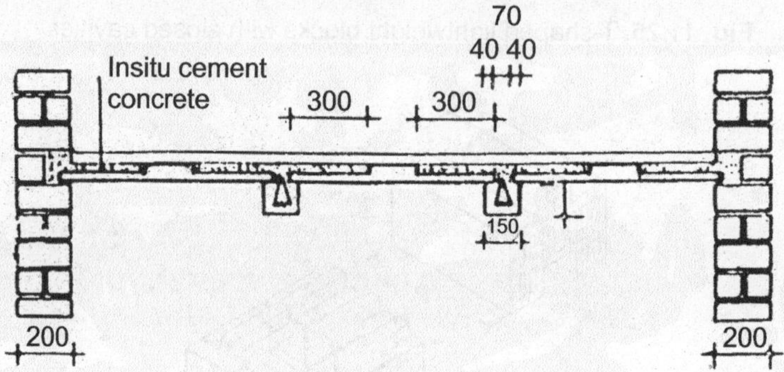

Fig. 11.29. Precast R.C. Plank

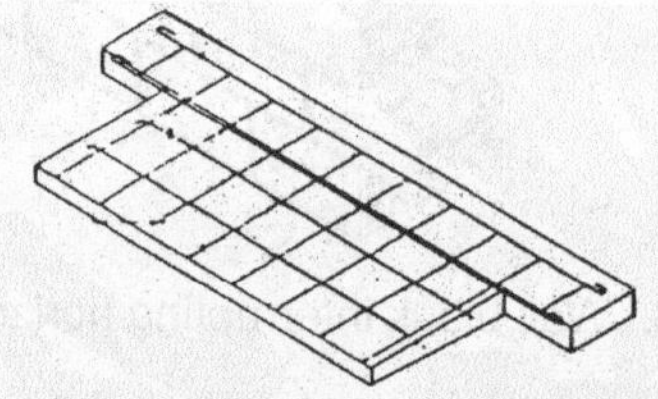

Fig. 11.30. Thin precast R.C.C. lintel

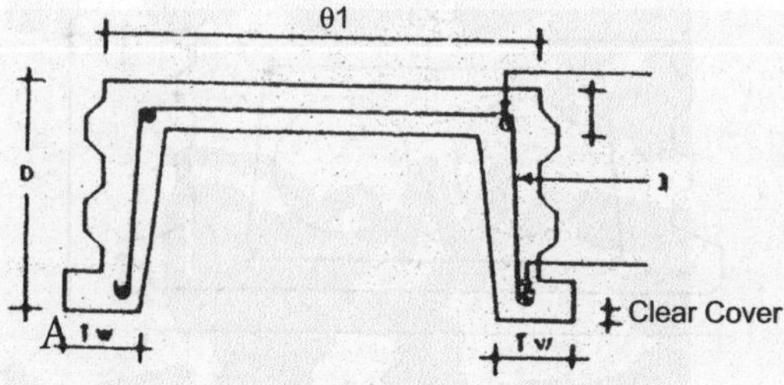

Fig. 11.31. Section of a channel unit

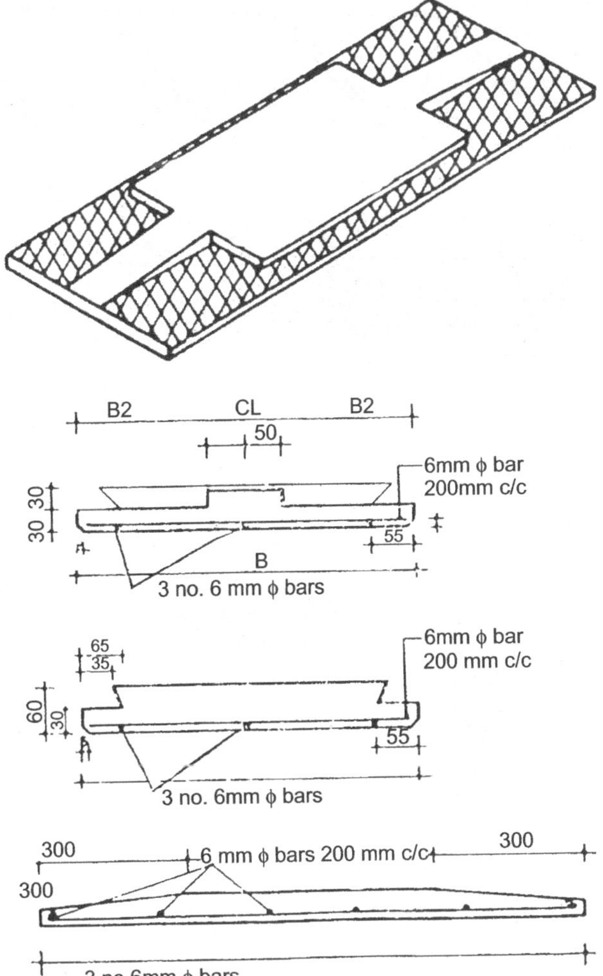

Fig. 11.32. Precast R.C. plank and joist system

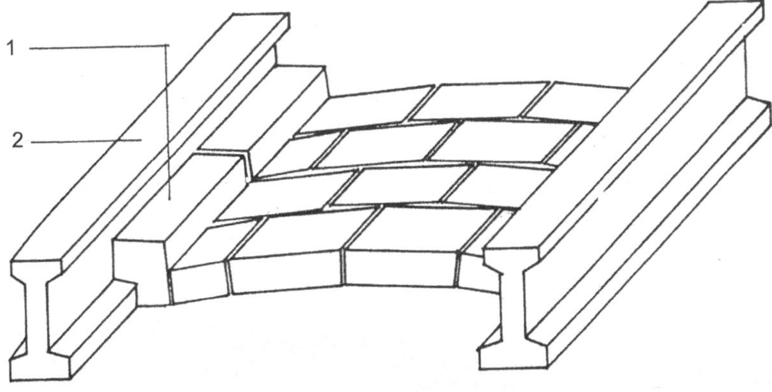

Fig. 11.33. Floor block vault constructed between beam (2) with masonry units and joined by bricks of special shape (1)

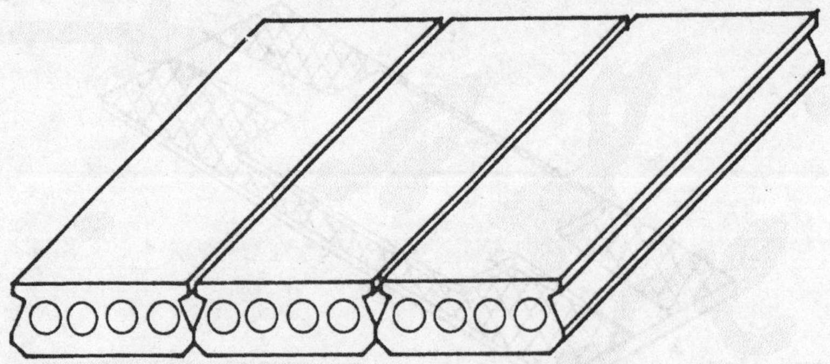

Fig. 11.34. Precast concrete slab with circular holes

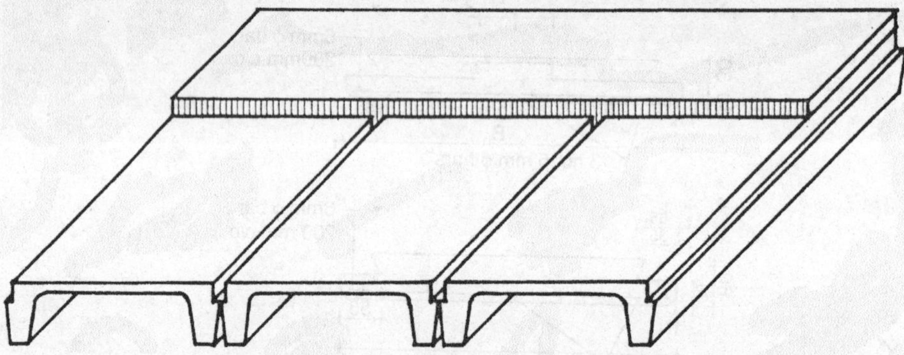

Fig. 11.35. Ribbed regular concrete slab

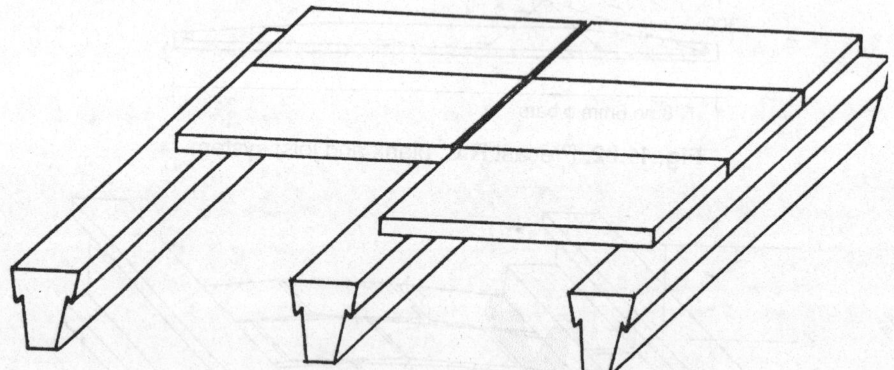

Fig. 11.36. Floor block on the top of the beams

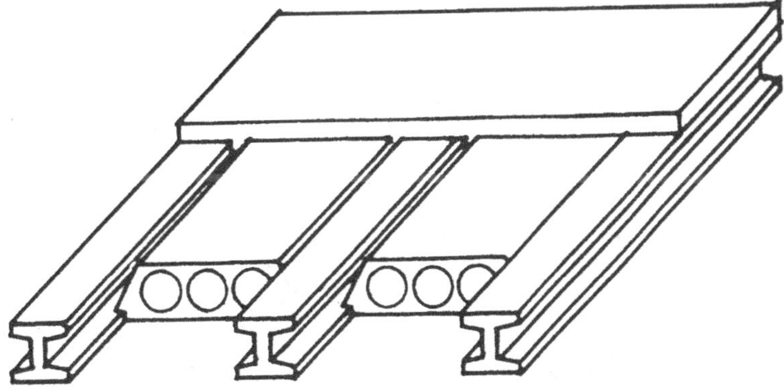

Fig. 11.37. Floor block on the bottom flanges of the beam

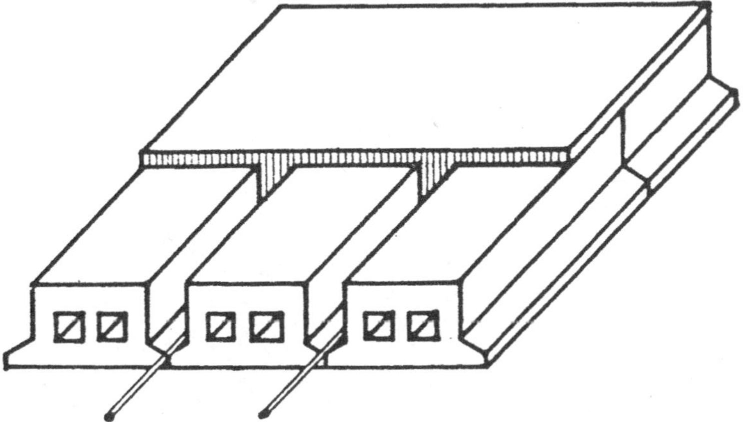

Fig. 11.38. Beam cast in situ between the floor block

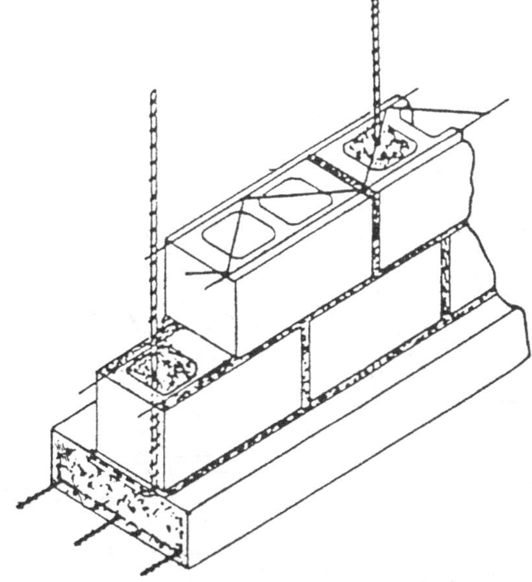

Fig. 11.39. Typical concrete block wall and footing detail

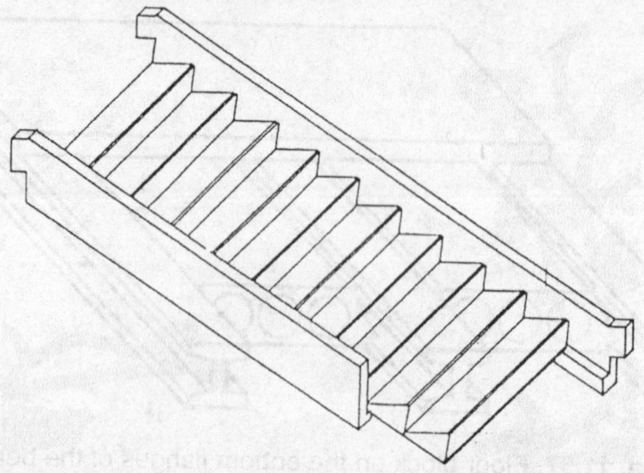

Fig. 11.40. Prefabricated stair composed of supporting beam

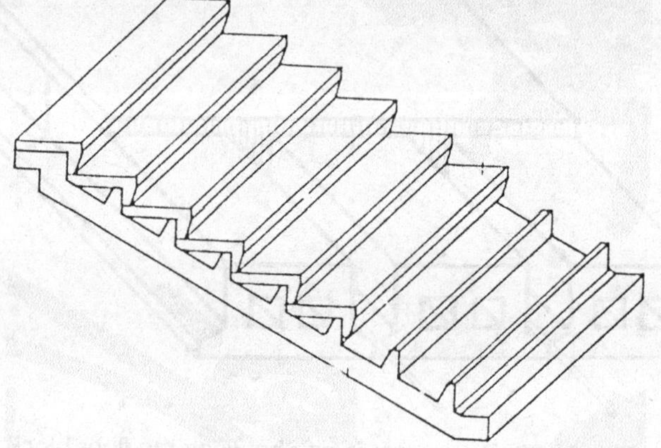

Fig. 11.41. Prefabricated stair composed of structural slab

Fig. 11.42. Stair–Prefabricated flight and landing unit

Zero Energy Housing

Electricity consumption in India is increasing rapidly and the buildings account for one-fourth of total energy consumption. This has serious implications on the ecology and climate, besides a financial burden on households. Zero energy housing aims to significantly lower energy consumption. It aims to produce as much renewable energy as consumed from the grid. System automation is the brain and heart of a zero-energy house. Modular in-situ construction, such as prefab components, concrete blocks, precast roofing planks and joints and Steel Core Panels are opening up new possibilities in building projects. Such construction produces less than half the carbon emission of the industry average and does not require heavy machinery, cranes and lifts. Completely recyclable, the light-weight building components allow energy efficient, rapid construction.

Methodology
- Pre-assembled panels (3.9 by15.6 meters), including flooring, ceiling,and embedded shafts, water, electricity, lighting, ventilation, and drainage

Keyfacts
- 93% of construction completed off-site
- 1% construction waste

Fig. 11.43. Assembling a high-rise in 15 days (from prefabricated components that took six months to manufacture)

Source: *McKinsey Global Institute (2014), "A Blueprint for addressing the global affordable housing challenge"*

Computerization and Automation

A new surge has led to Computer Aided Manufacturing (CAM) and Computer Integrated Manufacturing (CIM) prefabricated components, ceilings, walls, roofs, etc. Construction robots range from simple tools to fully automated robot. In Japan and other countries single task and automated construction systems are becoming common. To address the shortage of skilled labor and workforce in construction sector, single task robots are developed to supplement skilled labour and to achieve construction speed, precision and quality. Various single task robots are used for jobs like concrete and steel structural erection, external and internal finish work, maintenance and demolition work, etc.

Construction automation has 4 fundamental components:

- An on-site, all weather enclosed factory

- Automated jacking system
- Automated material conveying system
- Centralized information system.

These systems use JIT principle for delivery of materials and bar coding for tacking and materials management at site. The simulation of construction process by automation gives information about time, expenditure and the number of various workmen, skilled tradesmen and other staff needed. This way the time of on-site construction could be reduced at least by half to one-third in comparison to the conventional construction. However, it demands increasing efforts in project planning, process planning and logistics. Accordingly the on-site staffs have to be more specialized as most of the non-ergonomic work on site is reduced.

Precast Building Systems

Depending on the structure, precast systems are divided into the following categories:

- Large-panel systems
- Slab-column systems with walls
- Frame systems
- Mixed systems

Large-Panel System: "Large-panel system" refers to multistory structures composed of large wall and floor concrete panels connected in the vertical and horizontal directions so that the wall panels enclose appropriate spaces for the rooms within a building. These panels form a box-like structure. Both vertical and horizontal panels resist gravity load. Wall panels are usually one story high. Horizontal floor and roof panels span either as one-way or two-way slabs. When properly joined together, these horizontal elements act as diaphragms that transfer the lateral loads to the walls.

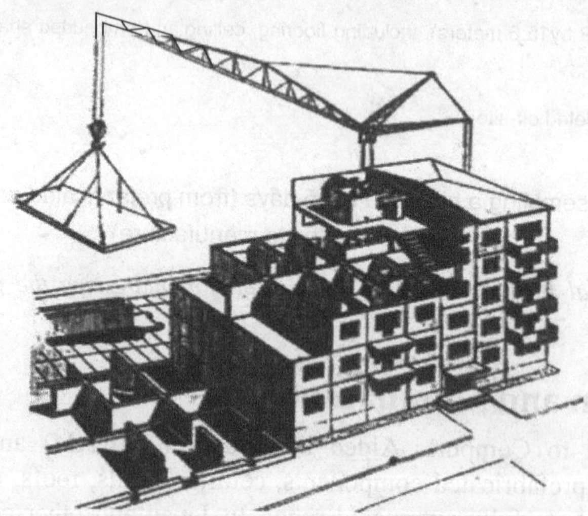

Fig. 11.44. A Large-Panel Concrete Building under Construction

Depending on the wall layout, there are three basic configurations of large-panel buildings:

- Cross-wall system. The main walls that resist gravity and lateral loads are placed in the short direction of the building.
- Longitudinal-wall system. The walls resisting gravity and lateral loads are placed in the longitudinal direction; usually, there is only one longitudinal wall.

- Two-way system. The walls are placed in both directions.

Thickness of wall panel ranges from 120 mm for interior walls to 300 mm for exterior walls. Floor panel thickness varies from 60 mm to 150 mm. Wall panel length is equal to the room length, typically on the order of 2.7 m to 3.6 m. In some cases, there are no exterior wall panels and the facade walls are made of lightweight concrete.

Panel connection represents a key structural component in these systems. Based on their location within a building, these connections can be classified into vertical and horizontal joints. Vertical joints connect the vertical faces of adjoining wall panels and primarily resist vertical seismic shear forces. Horizontal joints connect the horizontal faces of the adjoining wall and floor panels and resist both gravity and seismic loads.

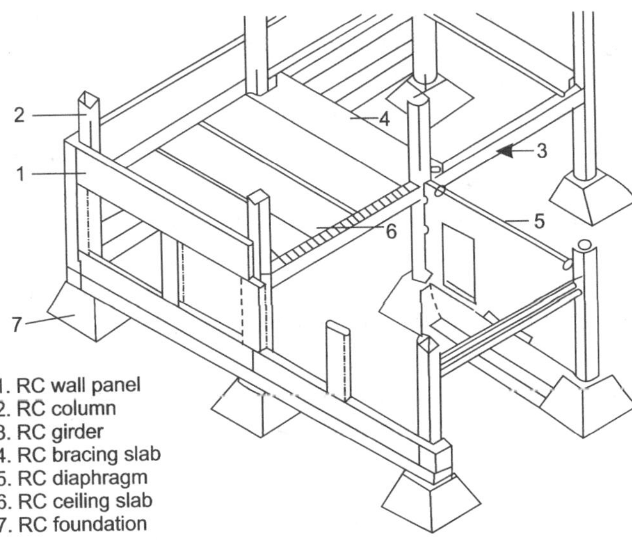

Fig. 11.45. Components of a precast reinforced concrete frame system

Joints: Depending on the construction method, the joints can be classified as wet and dry. Wet joints are constructed with cast-in-place concrete poured between the precast panels. To ensure structural continuity, protruding reinforcing bars from the panels (dowels) are welded, looped, or otherwise connected in the joint region before the concrete is placed. Dry joints are constructed by bolting or welding together steel plates or other steel inserts cast into the ends of the precast panels for this purpose. Wet joints more closely approximate cast-in-place construction, whereas the force transfer in structures with dry joints is accomplished at discrete points.

Frame System: Precast frames can be constructed using either linear elements or spatial beam-column sub-assemblages. Precast beam-column sub-assemblages have the advantage that the connecting faces between the sub-assemblages can be placed away from the critical frame regions; however, linear elements are generally preferred because of the difficulties associated with forming, handling, and erecting spatial elements. The use of linear elements generally means placing the connecting faces at the beam-column junctions. The beams can be seated on corbels at the columns for ease of construction and to aid the shear transfer from the beam to the column. The beam-column joints accomplished in this way are hinged. However, rigid beam-column connections are used in some cases, when the continuity of longitudinal reinforcement through the beam-column joint needs to be ensured.

Slab-Column System with Shear Walls: These systems rely on shear walls to sustain lateral load effects, whereas the slab-column structure resists mainly gravity loads. There are two main systems in this category:

- Lift-slab system with walls
- Pre-stressed slab-column system

In the connections, the steel bars (dowels) that project from the edges of the slabs are welded to the dowels of the adjacent components and transverse reinforcement bars are installed in place. The connections are then filled with concrete that is poured at the site. Most buildings of this type have some kind of lateral load-resisting elements, mainly consisting of cast-in-place or precast shear walls, etc. In case lateral load-resisting elements (shear walls, etc.) are not present, the lateral load path depends on the ability of the slab-column connections to transfer bending moments. When the connections have been poorly constructed, this is not possible, and the lateral load path may be incomplete. Properly constructed slab-column joints are essential for transferring moments, as shown by several full-scale vibration tests.

Another type of precast system is slab-column system that uses horizontal pre-stressing in two orthogonal directions to achieve continuity. The precast concrete column elements are 1 to 3 storeys high. The reinforced concrete floor slabs fit the clear span between columns. After erecting the slabs and columns of a storey, the columns and floor slabs are pre-stressed by means of pre-stressing tendons that pass through ducts in the columns at the floor level and along the gaps left between adjacent slabs. After pre-stressing, the gaps between the slabs are filled with in-situ concrete and the tendons then become bonded with the spans. Seismic loads are resisted mainly by the shear walls (precast or cast-in-place) positioned between the columns at appropriate locations.

In any structure equilibrium, resistance and stability are the basic pre-requisites. In the past the gravity was added to defeat gravity, resulting in massive masonry, compression structures, such as the pyramids. The new materials like steel and carbon fiber have brought higher values of tension capability of structure, reducing the consumption and weight of building materials. Pre-engineered building is based on the dictum of 'less is more' that is enclosing the given space with more flexibility and stability by using lesser materials. This implies the adoption of Newton's law in design of a structure, that is, counteract the pull and push forces by ranging them off against each other, a game of action and reaction.

Emerging Technologies and Resources

With ever increasing need to build efficient, more sustainable and economic housing and buildings, various technologies are emerging, such as:

- Welded wire fabric rapid wall panel systems
- Glass panel reinforced gypsum panel
- EPS and wire reinforced panel
- Light gauge steel framed structure with concrete panels
- Precast large panel system
- Modular tunnel framework
- Prefabricated building modular system
- Steel frame modular building system
- Total open prefab system

- Large elements/small elements systems
- Gypsum unit housing systems
- Fiber cement board with expanded polystyrene (EPS) blocks and concrete
- Fiber cement board with expanded polystyrene (EPS) blocks, light gauge steel studs and concrete
- Light-weight interlocking sandwich panels
- Reinforced cement boards, aerated cement core, with silaceous and micaceous material aggregate.
- 3-S Prefab system with hollow structural components

Fig. 11.46. QuikBuild Panel System of Beardsell Ltd. consists of a welded wire space frame integrated with expanded polystyrene insulation core

Welded Wire Fabric Rapid Wall Panel System: The wall panel is placed in position and a wythe of concrete of required thickness is applied to both sides. The wall panel receives its strength and rigidity from the diagonal cross wires welded to the fabric on each side. The shell of the structure is built manually by erecting the panels directly onto the slab with protruding reinforcement rods and then finished by plastering using the traditional method or by shotcreting to create a monolithic structure.

Glass Fibre Reinforced Gypsum (GFRG) Panel System is an integrated composite building system using factory made prefab load bearing cage panel and monolithic cast in-situ RC infilled for walling and floor/roof slabs, suitable for single storey to ten storey building. It is made of calcined gypsum plaster, reinforced with glass fibres and panels manufactured to a thickness of 124 mm under carefully controlled conditions to a length 12 m and height of 3 m, with cavities.

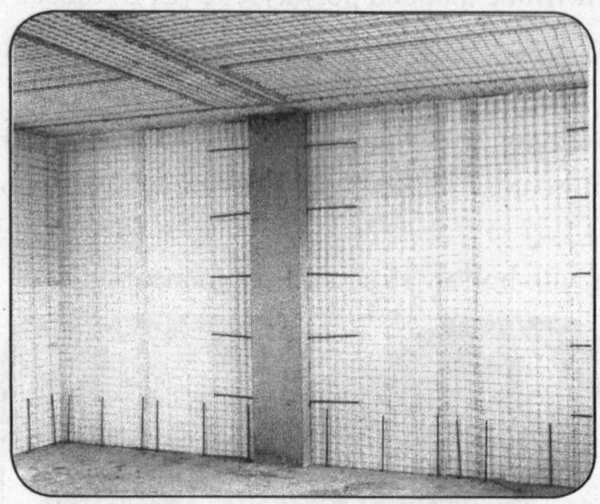

Fig. 11.47. Reinforced Expanded Polystyrene Core Panel System

Reinforced Expanded Polystyrene Core Panel System is a factory produced sandwich panel system for the construction of low rise buildings up to G+3 and as filler walls in high rise RCC and steel frame buildings. These panels are being produced by Jindal Steel & Power Ltd. A core of undulated polystyrene is covered with interconnected zinc coated welded mesh on both sided reinforcement and shotcrete. The panels are finished on site by pouring concrete (double panel, flooring and stairs) and spraying concrete to realise the different structural elements *i.e.* Vertical Structural Walls, Horizontal Structural elements (slabs/floors) and non-structural cladding elements.

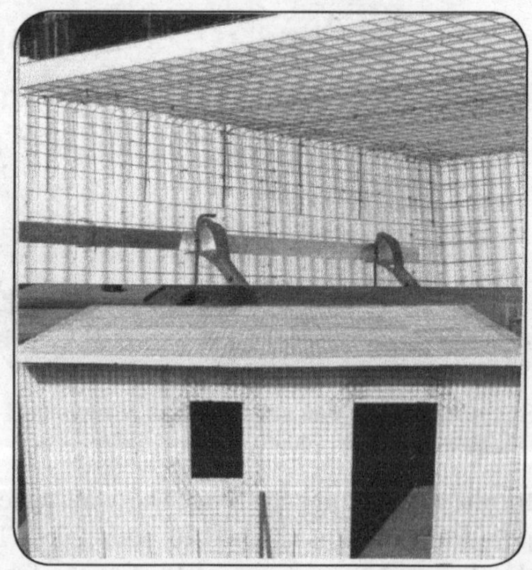

Fig. 11.48. Rapid Panel by Worldhaus Construction Pvt. Ltd., patented EPS Core Panel System

Rapid EPS Panel System is a prefabricated assembly of high-strength steel wire forming a panel with core of expanded polystyrene (EPS). The basic unit of the Rapid Panel is the zig-zag truss. Steel wire is bent into a zigzag shape to form a continuous chain of web members. This bent wire is then welded to continuous chord wires at every node to form the truss. During construction,

Rapid Panels are installed as walls and/or slabs. Specified mixtures of the panels complete the structure.

Fig. 11.49. The Concrete wall is a patented system of Schnell Wire System

Concretewall comprises panels of expanded polystyrene (EPS) insulation and steel reinforcement which are site applied with concrete. A layer of welded wire mesh on either side of EPS core is welded together by steel orthogonal trusses which penetrates through EPS core. The panels are joined together in a desired configuration on site and sprayed on both sides with shotcrete to form a sandwich type construction. The exterior of the panels may be finished with weather proof coating such as plaster while interior surface (walls) and ceilings can either be plastered or lined with conventional lining material.

Fig. 11.50. EMMEDUE Advance Building System

EMMEDUE System is based on factory made panels consisting of self extinguishing expanded polystyrene core (generally corrugated) sandwiched between two welded wire fabric mesh made of high strength galvanized wire. A galvanized steel truss wire is pierced completely through the core at an offset angle for superior strength and welded to each of outer layer welded wire fabric mesh. The panels are finished at site using shotcrete mix of cement and coarse aggregate of required thickness on both sides. The panels are used for load bearing walls and floors and are suitable for 3 to 4 storey buildings.

Fig. 11.51. Light Gauge Steel Frame Structure with Infill Concrete Panels (LGSFS-ICP)

Factory made Light Gauge Steel Framed Structure (LGSFS) comprises precast panels filled with light weight concrete at site. The LGS frame is a "C" cross-section with built in notch, dimpling, slots service holes, etc. Produced by computerized roll forming machine. The frames are assembled using metal screw at site to form wall on pre-built concrete floor. The door cut outs as required are incorporated in the frame. The roof structure is conventional RCC slab.

Source: *BMTPC*

Fig. 11.52. Light Gauge Steel is cold form steel which has an advantage over hot rolled steel as it is lighter in weight and thin sections of any form can be manufactured normally

LGSFS is factory made galvanized light gauge steel structure assembled as panels at site and are suitable for 3 to 4 storey structures. The infill walls can be of any material ranging from precast boards, EPS panels or an external layer of insulation material and outer leaf of CP Board or dry mix shotcrete. The floor/roof can be RCC/steel truss/steel deck on joints as per the requirement.

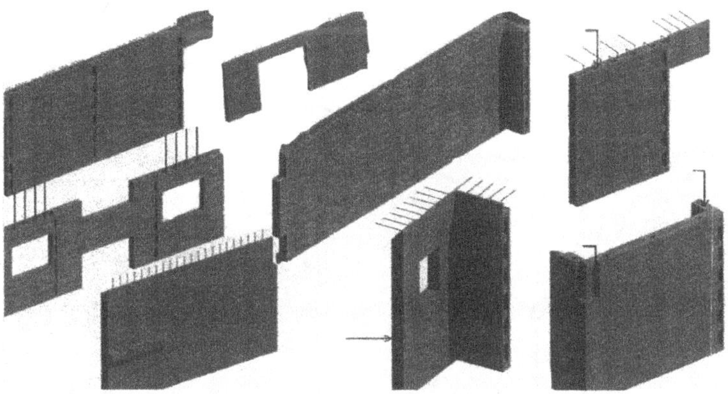

Fig. 11.53. Light Gauge Reinforced Panels

Precast Large Construction Panel (PLCP) system is a structural system comprising various precast elements such as walls, beam, slabs, columns, staircase, landing and other customized elements There are two types of precast concrete elements, namely precast reinforced concrete elements and precast pre-stressed concrete elements, prefabricated in a precast yard or site. The precast elements are installed on site and supported by temporary jacks. Shims are used to carefully align the elements which are grouted after the final adjustment. A typical construction involves design, strategic yard planning, lifting, handling, transportation and assembly of precast elements.

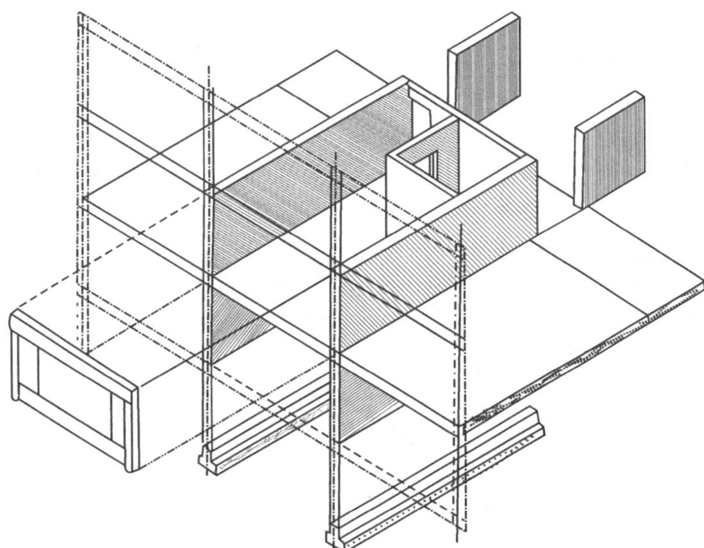

Fig. 11.54. Total System–Panelized units are large enough to constitute entire walls, partitions and floors

Source: *Engineering News-Record*

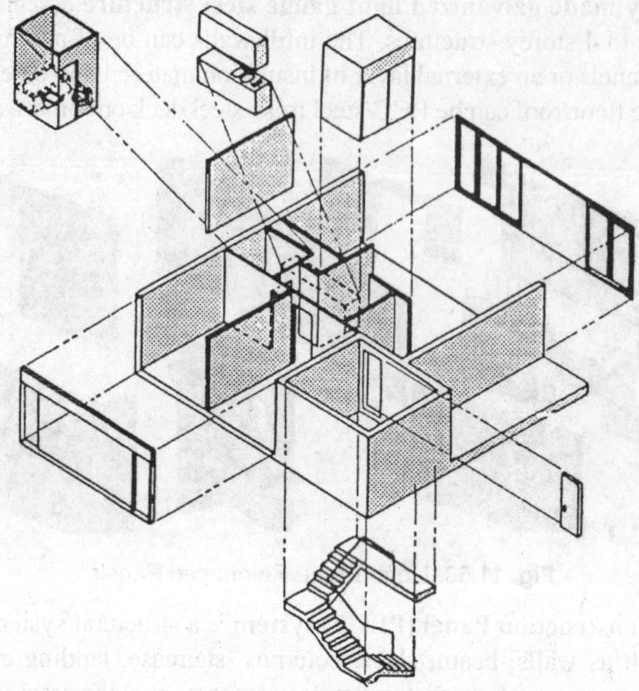

Fig. 11.55. The rationalization and application of modular coordination and assembly line techniques are the pre-requisites of prefabricated construction

Source: *Engineering News Record*

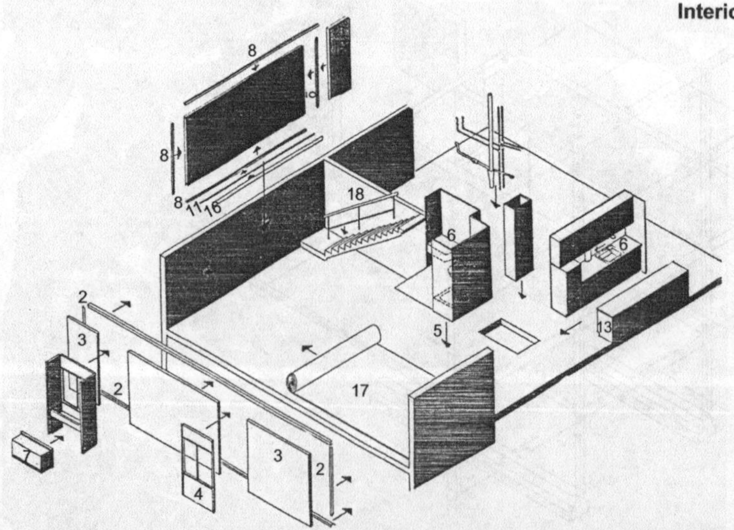

Interior Erection Sequence:

1. plumbing vent, duct, mech. services
2. frame for curtain wall
3. curtain wall panels
4. window panels
5. bath unit: walls and lavatory
6. tub, toilet, and kitchen sink
7. heating/air-conditioning unit
8. runners for interior partitions
9. interior partitions, panels
10. door post
11. electric services, cables, fittings
12. door panel
13. kitchen cabinets
14. painting
15. vinyl wall covering
16. vinyl base
17. finish flooring
18. stair-rail

Fig. 11.56. Carl Koch Concrete Assembly System. Modular Components are so designed that enable several permutations and combinations of space design

By proper sequencing, it has been possible to erect and complete the interior of a nine-storey units in 32 weeks. What makes this possible was due to the design of the structural system, which not only enabled laborers to work virtually indoors, but also of few components, combined in numerous ways to form different types of buildings.

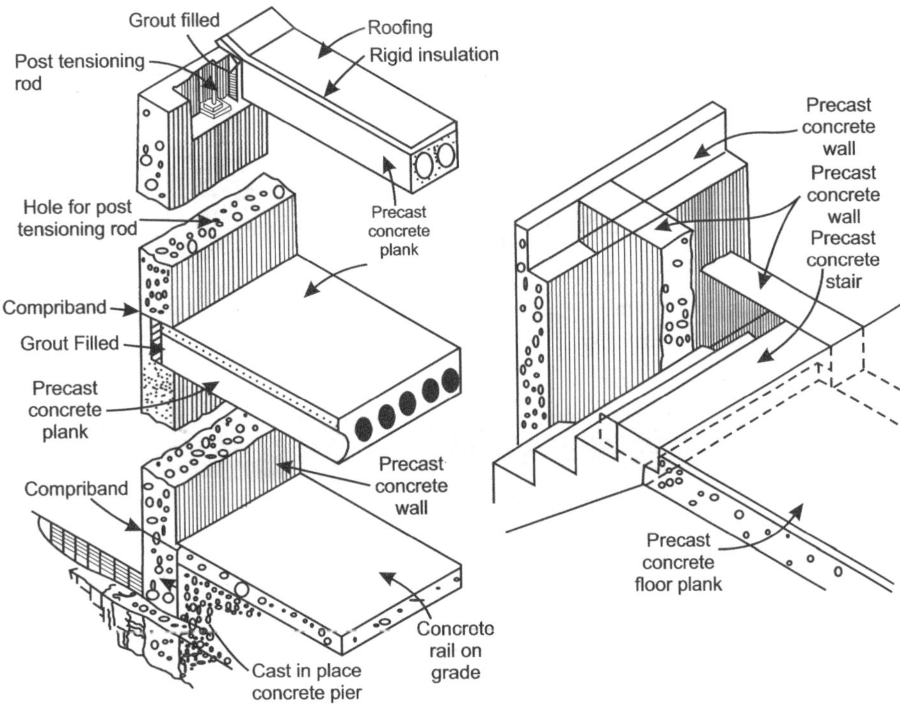

Fig. 11.57. Structural System (Carl Koch System)

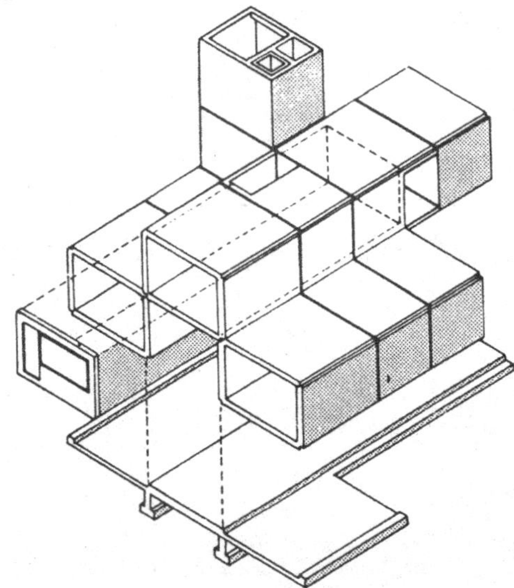

Fig. 11.58. Monolithic Units (Boxes). Factory-produced units are preassembled with volumetric elements provided with a high level of finish, that reduces the on site finishing time to a minimum

Source: *Engineering News Record.*

Fig. 11.59. Moshe Safdie's Habitat 67, Montreal, Canada comprising prefab box units stacked vertically and projecting out, creating an interesting high density, compact pattern

Fig. 11.60. Modular Tunnel formwork is a mechanized system for cellular structures. It is based on two half shells which are placed together to form a room or cell. Several cells make an apartment. With tunnel form-work, walls and slab can be cast in a single day.

Source: *BMPTC*

Fig. 11.61. The Moducast@ System combines a series of modules to create the overall building, which provides complete flexibility in the layout. The structure is designed in splitable transportable modules. These panels are assembled on specially designed steel beds and floor concrete is done linking the panels to the floor reinforcement forming a monolithic structure. This module is moved to various stages to complete the secondary operations and finishing works. Finished module is then transported to site and erected to form the final structure. It is suited for low to medium rise housing projects

Source: *Moducast Pvt. Ltd.*

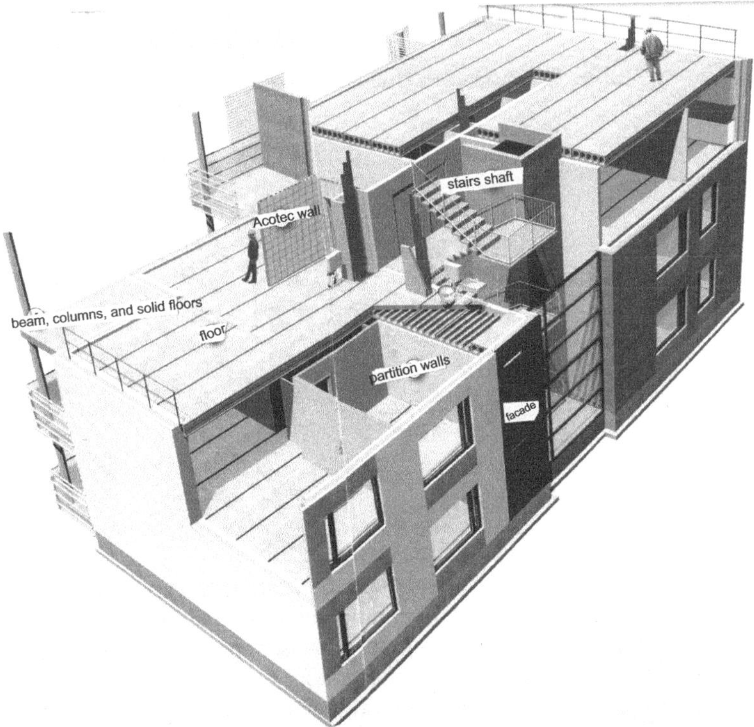

Fig. 11.62. Prefabricated Building Modular System

Source: *Moducast Private Ltd.*

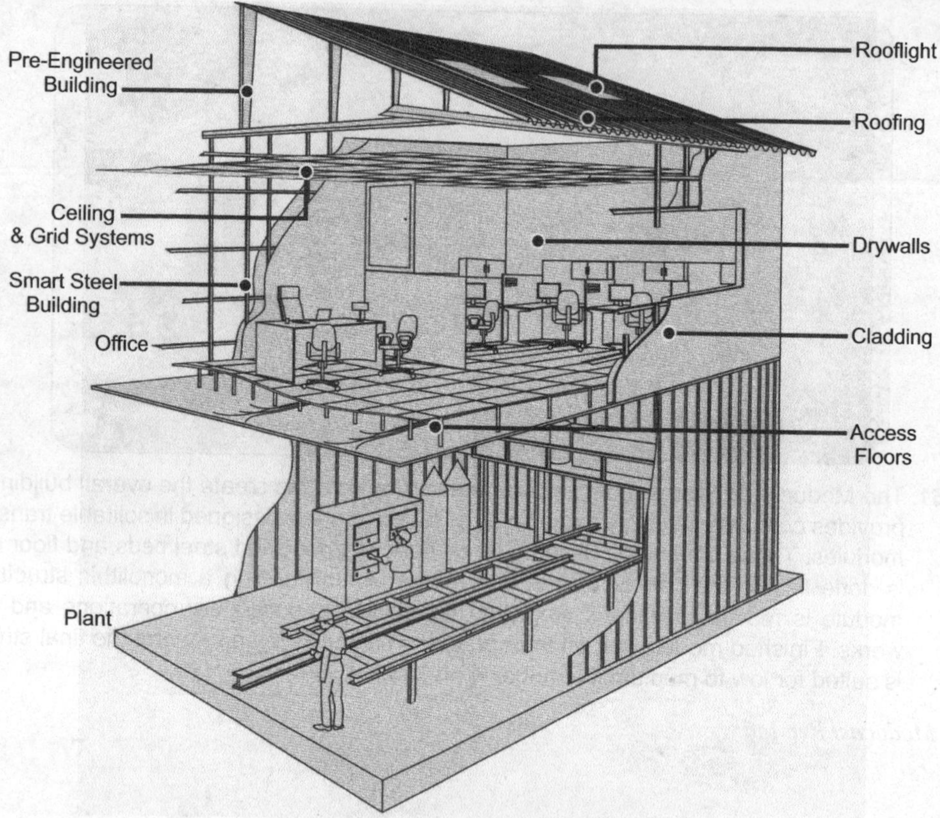

Fig. 11.63. Prefab Building Modular System

Source: *Moducast Pvt. Ltd.*

Fig. 11.64. Fast Track Modular Building Construction System is a hot rolled steel frame structure with different walling components, manufactured and fabricated in a controlled factory environment. The steel-modules pre-fitted with flooring, ceiling tiles, electrical and plumbing fittings are transported to the site for installation. Once all the components are assembled and erected at site, shortcreting is done on factory made 3-D Expanded Polystyrene (EPS) panel walls making it a monolithic structure.

Source: *BMTPC*

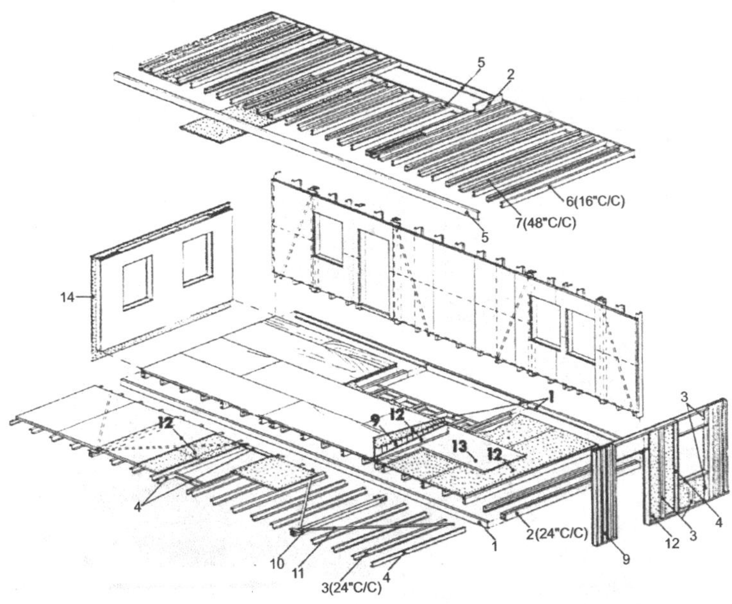

Fig. 11.65. Exploded view and component parts of 36 foot-long first-storey module for a prototype house. Components: 1. edge beam; 2 floor joist; 3 wall study; 4 multi-use channel; 5. ceiling edge beam; 6. ceiling joists; 7. ceiling angles; 8. wall angles; 9. corrugated steel decking; 10. structural steel tube; 11. steel straps; 12. gypsum wallboard 13. shiplap plywood; 14. woodrock siding.

Source: *United States Steel Corporation.*

Fig. 11.66. The industrialized open prefab construction technology is based on factory manufactured structural components

Industrialised Open Prefab System

In this system, precast dense concrete hollow columns of appropriate size are used in combination with precast dense concrete rectangular T shape/L shape beams and lightweight reinforced autoclaved cellular concrete slabs for floors and roofs. The hollow columns are grouted with appropriate grade of in-situ concrete. All the connections and jointing of various structures are accomplished through in situ concreting along with secured embedded reinforcement of appropriate size, length and configuration to ensure monolithic continuous resilient ductile behaviour.

Fig. 11.67. The Speedfloor System is a suspended concrete flooring system using hot rolled steel joints as an integral part of the final concrete and steel composite floor

Source: *BMTPC*

Speed Floor System

It is a hydrid concrete/steel tee-beam in one direction and an integrated continuous one-way slab in other direction. The joist of different depths are manufactured from pre-galvanized high tensile steel. These joists are roll formed, punched, pressed and slotted in a fully computerized machine.

The joint's depth and the concrete thickness are varied depending on the span, imposed loads and other functional considerations and are custom manufactured.

Low Cost Housing Systems

Primarily housing prefab systems are of two kinds—Large Elements and Small Elements. Large elements are generally recommended in the areas where machinery is available and labour costs are high. These are also speedier as compared to small elements system. However, small elements systems are cheaper and facilitate community self help and small contractors to participate in housing construction.

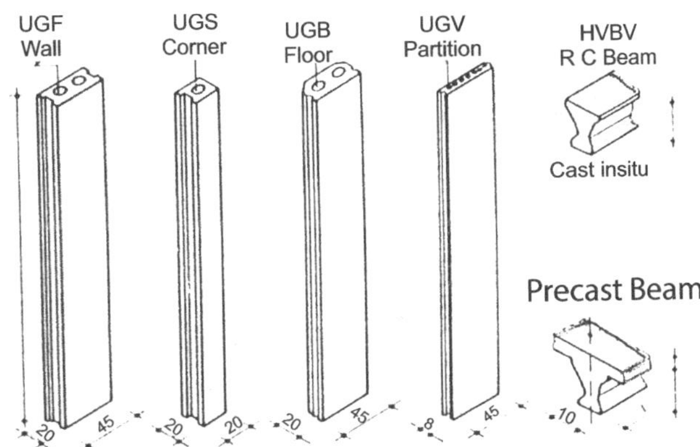

Fig. 11.68. Basic Elements for Construction with Large Elements

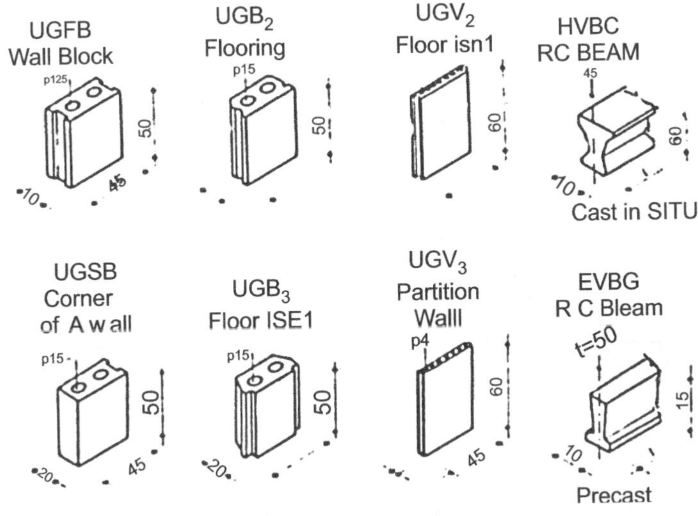

Fig. 11.69. Basic Elements for Construction with Small Elements

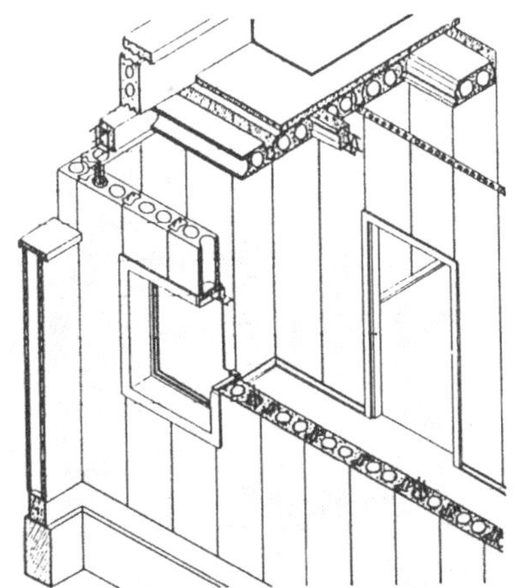

1. Concrete Foundation
2. UGF
3. R.C. Column
4. Window
5. Door
6. Lintel
7. UGV_1
8. Suspension Stirrup
9. UGS
10. R.C. HVBG
11. Tie Beam
12. Concrete Topping
13. Insulation
14. Coping
15. UGB_1

Fig. 11.70. Large Element System

1. Concrete Foundation
2. UGFB
3. UGSB Corner Elements
4. Door
5. Window
6. Lintel
7. UGV_2
8. Suspension Stirrup
9. R.C. Tie Beam
10. EVBG
11. UGB_3
12. Concrete Topping
13. Insulation
14. Coping

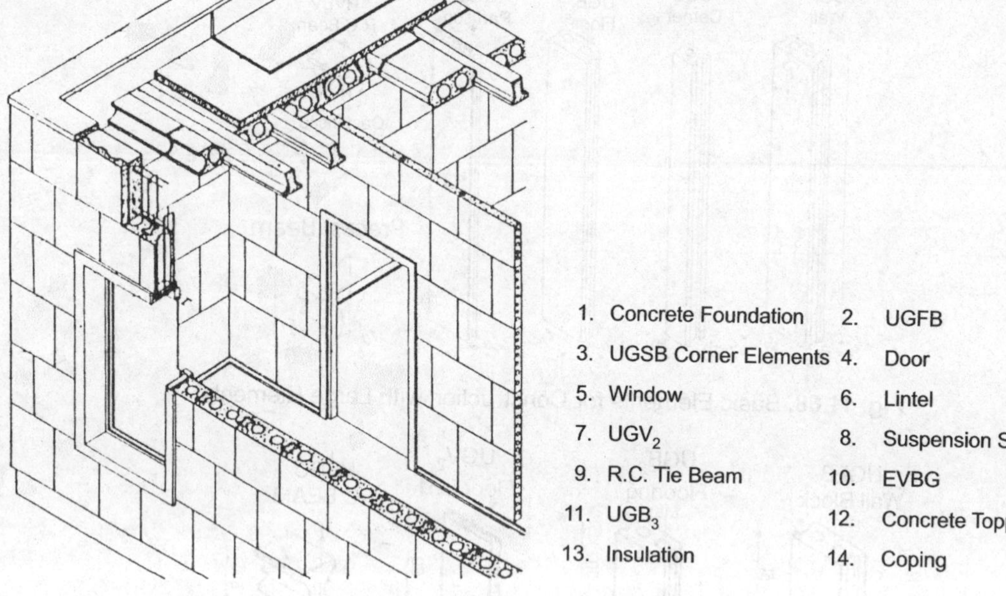

Fig. 11.71. Small Element System

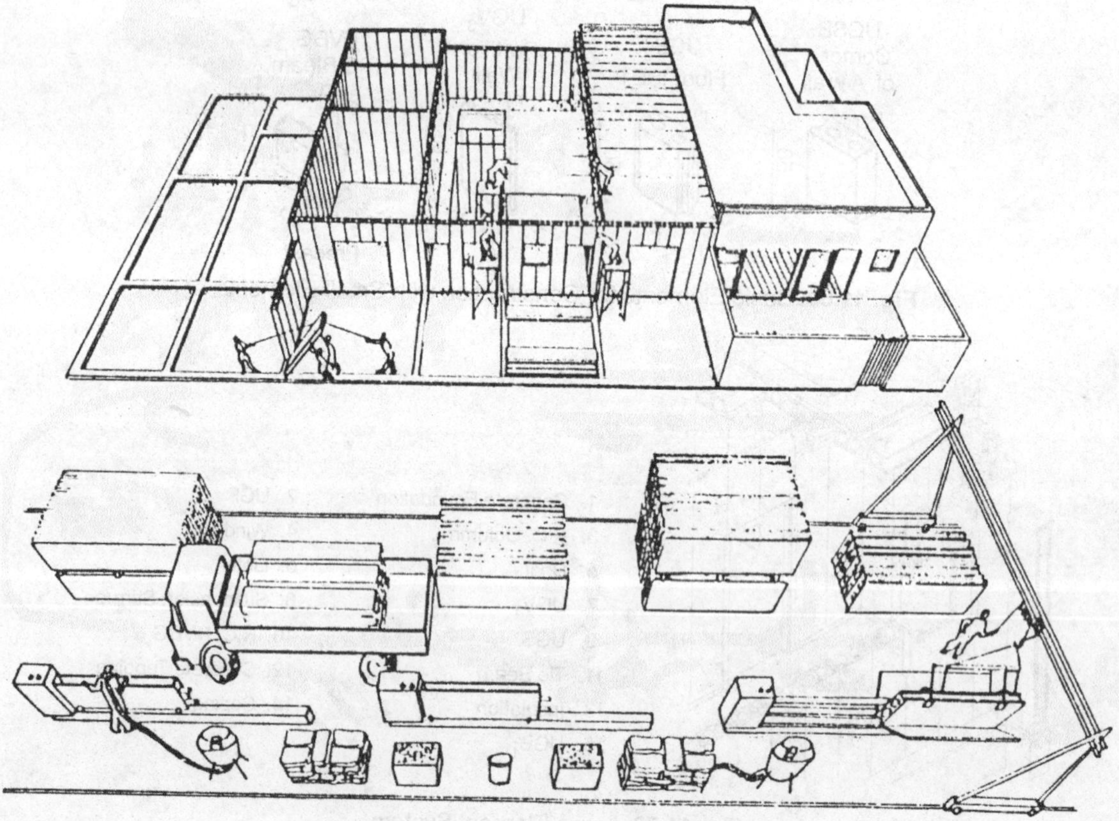

Fig. 11.72. Large Element System

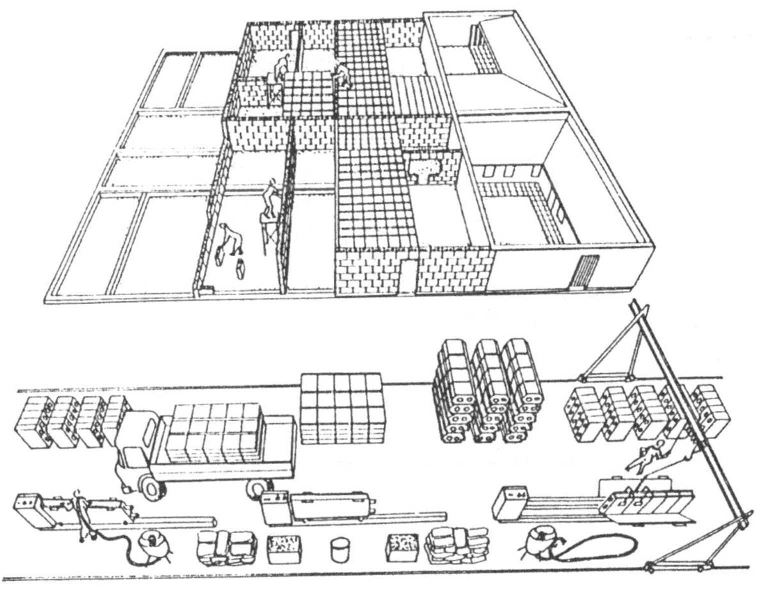

Fig. 11.73. Small Element System

Execution of the building is simple and quickly carried out, so it does not require and special skill even in as the large element system. During the execution very limited amount of materials are needed, such as gypsum concrete, and reinforcing bars. The assembly of a house of 80 square metres without foundation, but including the positioning of the gypsum walls, floor and partition elements placing of doors and windows takes only 140-160 hours.

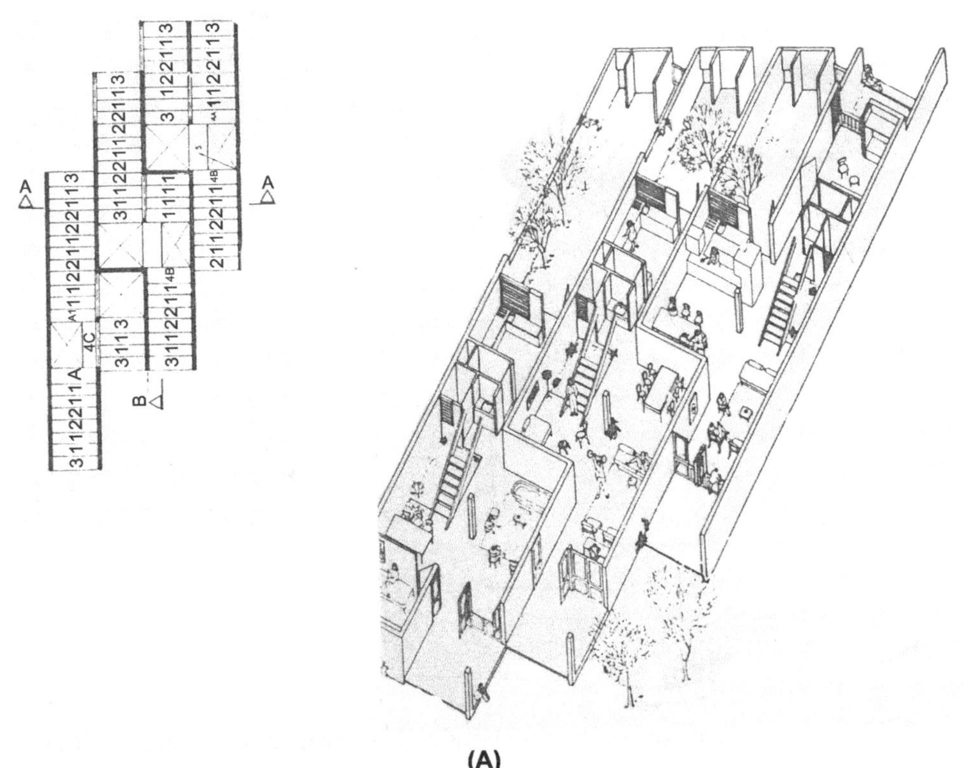

(A)

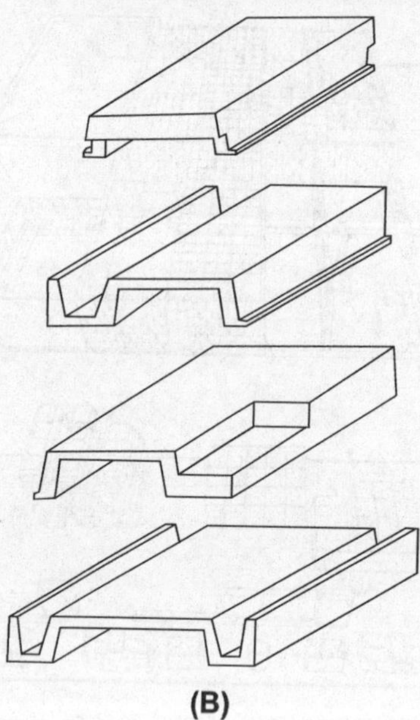

(B)

Figs. 11.74 (A and B). Charles Correa, Entry for low income housing international competition for UN Centre for Human Settlements (1976)

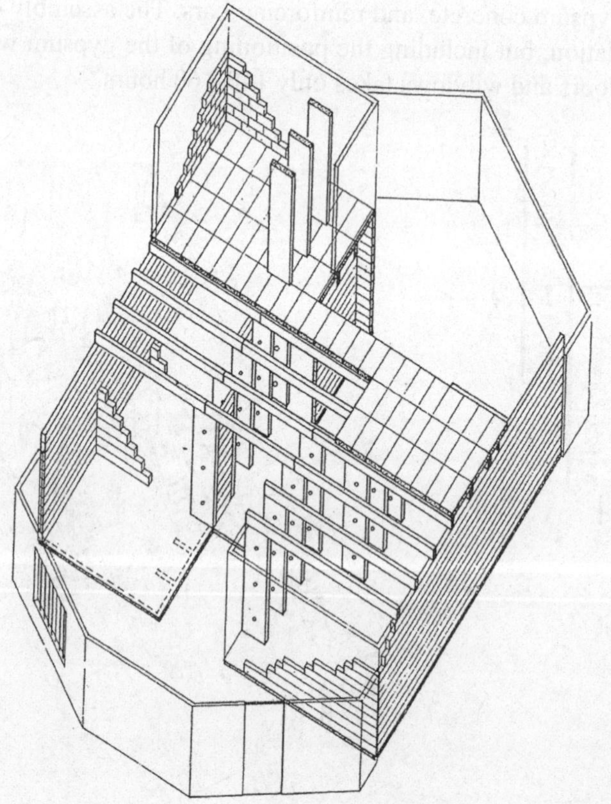

Fig. 11.75. E Van Eyck, Entry for Low Income Housing International Competition, UNCHS, 1976

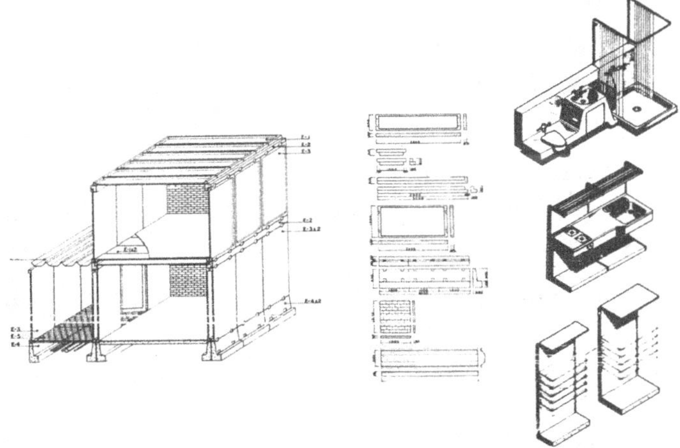

Fig. 11.76. Maki and Kikutake, Entry for Low Income Housing International Design Competition, UNCHS, 1976

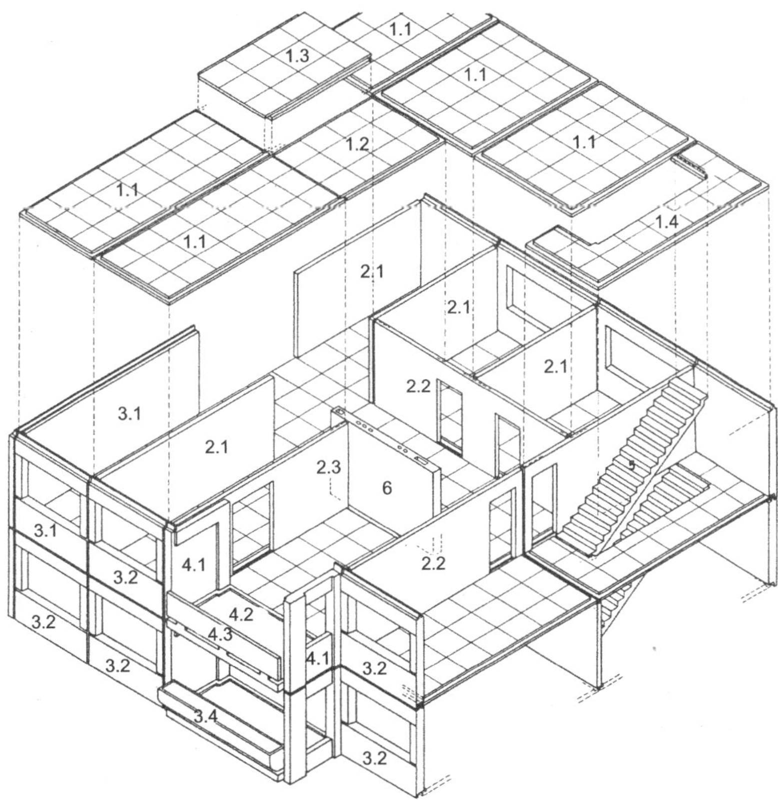

1.1 Normal Floor
1.2 Suspended one side
1.3 Suspended two sides
1.4 Stairway opening
2.1 Wall Units
2.2 Door Opening
2.3 Passage
3.1 Facade/Parapet/Fenestration
3.2 Load-Bearing Wall
3.3 Facade
3.4 Flower Box
4 Internal Partitions
5 Stairs
6 Internal Walls

Fig. 11.77. Carcass System

***Source:** EIC, SA, Zurich*

The Carcass System comprises:

- Load-bearing and stiffening wall elements
- Load-bearing facade elements
- Lift, stairway and special elements
- Room-sized floor elements
- Window + balcony elements

The vertical loads between the load-bearing wall elements are transmitted by elastic support strips. The horizontal loads in the floor elements are transmitted to the wall-elements by steel dowels. The floor elements are welded together after placing and aligning and from a stiff, horizontal slab.

The technical installations comprise the sub-system for electrical installations, ventilation, plumbing and heating.

Gypsum Housing

The hydrophobisation of gypsum has enabled its use for building construction, which is low cost, simple and widely available. The 45 cm modular grid of the elements facilitates a simple, flexible design of houses and public buildings for various functional and technical demands. The building system can satisfy the architectural requirements and the surfaces of the elements need no plastering. The outside surfaces can be provided with interesting finishing. The gypsum elements can be easily transported and cut on the site.

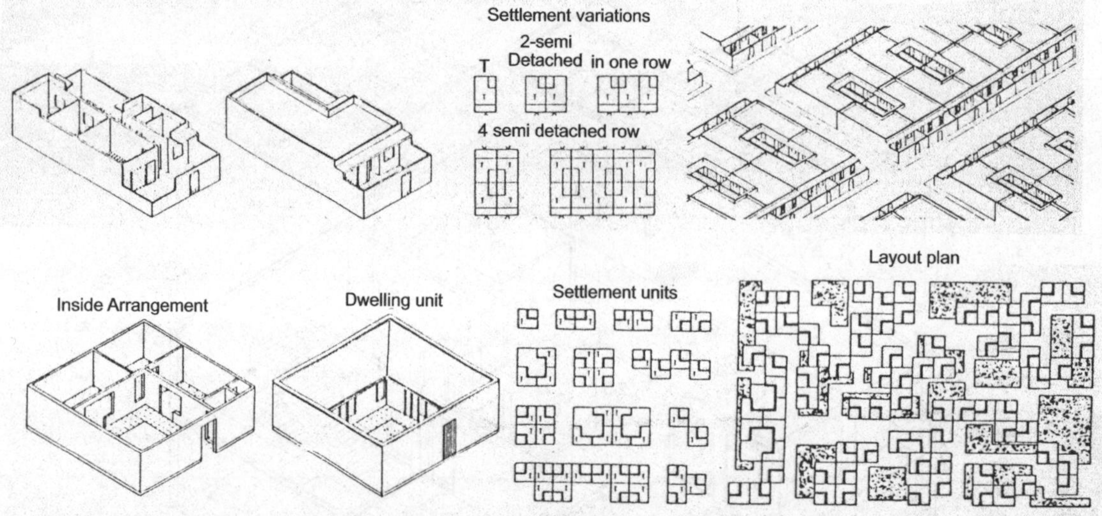

Fig. 11.78. Gypsum Housing: Large Element System

Source: *Shelter for the Homeless: Hungary Report by Creative Innovations Association and Heavy Industrial Trading Co., Hungary.*

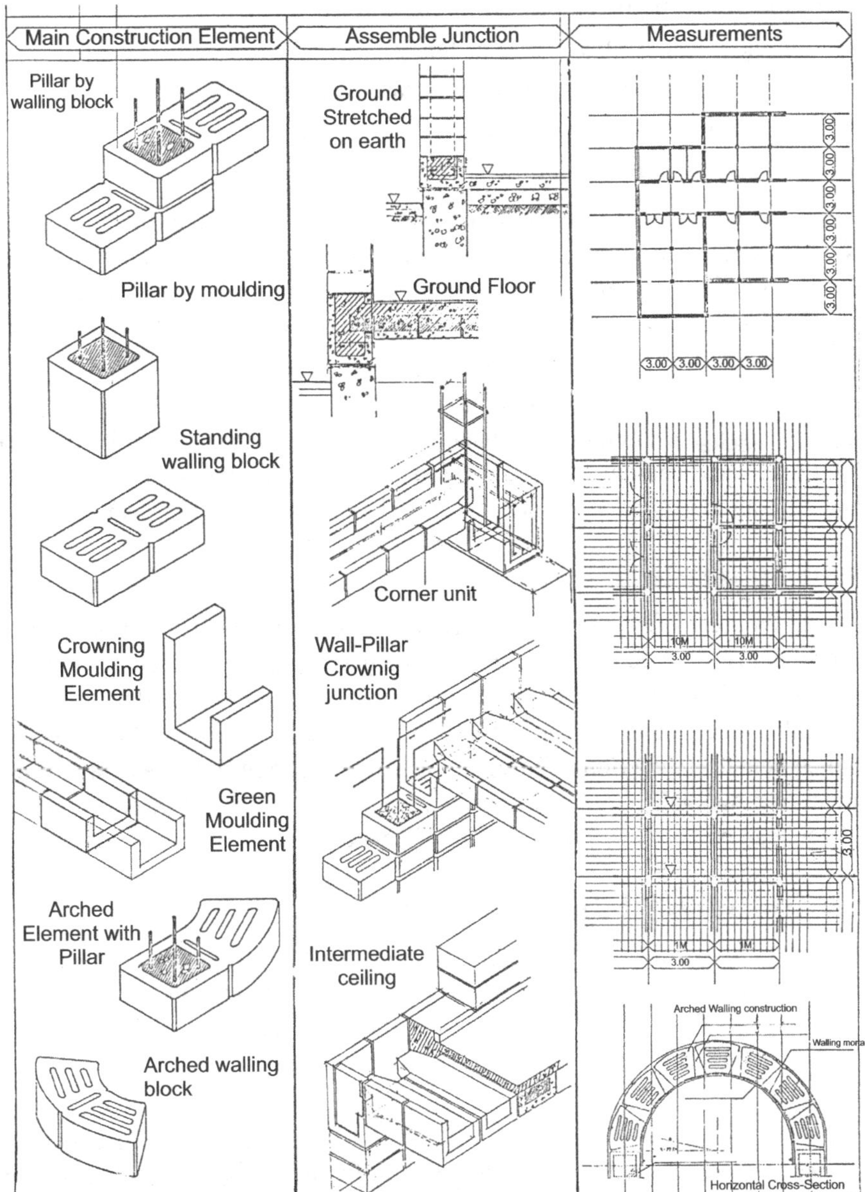

Fig. 11.79. Construction and Assembly of Gypsum Building Components

Source: *"Shelter for the Homeless", Hungary Report Creative Innovations Assn, and Heavy Industrial Trading Company, Peoples Republic of Hungary*

Production of Concrete Panels and Components

Precasting of concrete elements for systems building is basically a repetitive process of moulding fresh concrete, which involves the following operations:

- supply and storage of raw materials
- mixing of fresh concrete

- preparation of the mould and insertion of reinforcement and necessary fittings
- casting of elements, followed by finishings
- hardening, followed by the grinding process
- removal of elements from the mould
- Storage, handling and transportation of elements.

All these need to be done in an economical way, as the cost of the finished product depends upon the cost of raw materials, the cost of the plant and installations and the labour cost. The system builder has to strike a balance between labour costs, the cost of investment and the cost of maintenance and running of the machinery. Without adversely affecting the quality, the improved techniques should lead to improved economics.

A modern concrete mixing plant should have the facilities for the supply and storage of basic raw materials, viz. aggregates, cement and water. It should facilitate weight batching and volume batching of aggregates and cement for their mixing. The facilities may include forced flow mixing of concrete and central control of machinery or partial automation of the plant.

Hand Mixed Concrete

When the materials required for the manufacture of precast concrete are available on the building site or in its close vicinity, the quarrying, crushing and grading of the aggregates can be done at the plant. In case only small quantities of concrete are required, the mixing is done with a drum mixer or a forced-flow plan mixer having a capacity of 150-250 litres. It is advisable to weight-batch the aggregates and cement and the volume batching of water. The aggregate is charged into the mixer by a hand shovel or a manually operated dragline. Cement is fed to the mixer from a cement silo. The fresh concrete can be conveyed with the help of hand-barrows or wheel-barrows.

Portable & Stationary Concrete Plants

A portable plant is useful in manufacturing precast concrete units at the building site, from where it can be shifted after the work is over. The production system and the plant equipment are designed to facilitate the transfer of the whole equipment to a new building site quickly and economically. The capacity of such a plant is generally 20 to 60 cubic meters of fresh concrete per hour.

Plants of this order are mostly arranged horizontally. Aggregates are stocked on the ground which depending on the number of grades may be subdivided into several compartments. The aggregates are charged to the batch-weigher by means of a manually operated or fully mechanised dragline scrapper, and conveyed by a feed-chute to the batch-weighing hopper. The continuity of feed and the weighing accuracy may be improved by a vibratory feed-chute or a belt feeder. Weighing is cumulative, that means different grades are weighed at the same place.

From the weighing hopper, the aggregate is transferred to the mixer either directly through a chute or a skipbucket. The mixer is fed by a conveyor or a charging carriage.

Cement is stored in pneumatically filled cylindrical silos. From the silos it is transferred to batch-weighing by a worm feeder, an aeration duct or a rotary feeder and then by gravity directly into the mixer or into the skip-bucket of the mixer. Cement should be batched on a separate scale as the accuracy of the aggregate batcher is insufficient for this job. Water is fed into the mixer of which quantity control is usually volumetric. Fresh concrete is discharged by gravity.

In larger precasting factories, the concrete plant is a separate production unit. Its technological system and mechanical equipment have the character of a stationary plant. In order to utilise the equipment fully and to achieve efficient operation, these plants often fully and to achieve efficient operation, these plants often act as suppliers of ready-mixed concrete in the region. The output generally varies from 60 to 500 cubic meters of fresh concrete per hour.

Larger plants should have the facility of moisture control of the mix and correction by appropriate batching of water. The plant may have instruments for recording the composition and quality of concrete mix, which makes quality control possible. Such plants are generally fully automatic. Such type of plants are arranged vertically in the form of a tower. The aggregates and cement are lifted in one operation to the top level of the plant, from where they are transferred by gravity through several stages of processing. The power used in lifting the materials is considerable and expensive. However, an advantage of this system is that it requires only one lifting mechanism.

The mixing tower has four or five levels, fresh concrete is discharged at the lowest level. The mixers occupy the second level, on the third are the scales, the batchers and the controls of the plant. The hoppers for cement and the aggregates are on the fourth level. The incoming aggregates are received and distributed at the fifth level.

Aggregates are lifted to the top of the tower by a conveyor, a bucket elevator or a skip. Different grades of aggregates are charged into separate compartments through a multi-branch chute provided with baffle plates or through a revolving chute. The cement compartment is fed by a pneumatic system. Separate weighing facilities may be provided for each grade of aggregate. The weighed aggregates are charged through a chute into one of the mixers. A separate scale is required for cement and additives. The moisture contents of the aggregate should be taken into account when establishing the water/cement ratio.

The mixing cycle of forced-flow mixers is approximately 50 to 70 seconds, which as compared to the relatively small capacity of the mixing plant, yields a high output of fresh concrete.

Conveying Concrete

Trucks are swift and easy to manoeuvre and well adapted, so they are the most appropriate means of conveying concrete. Tanker type small dumpers and fork-lift trucks are also available for the purpose. A sophisticated, efficient and built in transportation method within the plant is the provision of belt conveyors. With belt conveyors, concrete can be discharged at the points of moulding or throw off carts. Greater distances can be spanned by an arrangement of several belt conveyors with a revolving chute system to discharge concrete. The operation of belt conveyors is usually by electricity. The breakdown of power or a fault in one conveyor may stop the whole production cycle. Trolleys and cableways may be suitable where considerable slack is involved or on a hilly site. For smaller plants, trolleys may not be suitable for conveying concrete.

Electrically driven trolleys running on a tract carry containers which are emptied by tipping or by a bottom discharge system. Trolleys on overhead rails provide a flexible arrangement and the containers can be discharged at any point on the tract. The floor of the workshop remains free which can be effectively used for production. The trolleys may be controlled by remote or automatic switches.

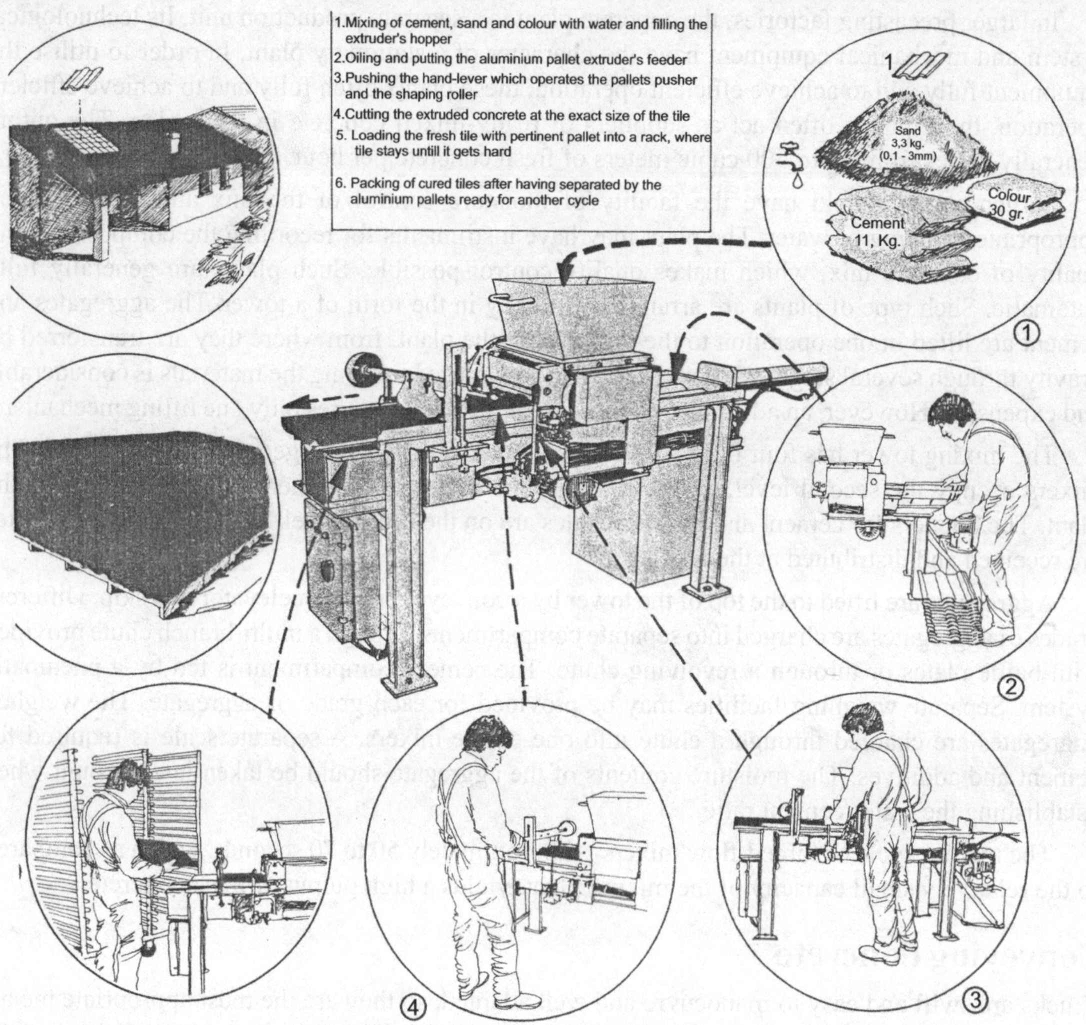

Fig. 11.80. System Unit for Manufacturing Concrete Roof Tiles

The compacting effect of the vibration is proportionate to the frequency used. Immersion vibrators/platform vibrators or vibrating table can be used for this process, depending upon the needs. After the period of curing, the forms are disassembled and the precast units are transferred to the storage area. There are various methods for removing the castings from the forms. Slip off system, stripping system, rolling method, etc. can be adopted as per the production capacity, requirements and level of mechanisation.

For the production of precast solid or hollow wall blocks, floor blocks, ducts, etc. automatic or semi-automatic presses and moulds are used. The press-box, which opens at the top and the bottom, moves upwards and downwards along guiding rails. Generally a mobile press, the so-called egg-laying machine, is used in which the press boxes move forward, while concrete products are left behind. After the concrete has set, the units are conveyed to the storage yard. Another kind of press used for manufacturing precast blocks is the stationary press. The finished products roll out from the underplates and transferred for curing. This technique is used where large series of precast units are manufactured.

For a serial production of wall blocks, floor beams, floor panels, slabs, girders, lintels and other long precast units, stripping system is widely used in stationary or on-site plants. Artificial curing is built in the system, which helps in increasing the production capacity. A variation of the stripping system, known as the rolling method, is widely used in the production of coffered floors and beams. In this method the compaction and forming of the concrete are carried out in one operation. This is done with the aid of moulding cylinders, which are shaped according to the required profile of the precast unit.

In a slipping form, either the form is stationary and the fresh concrete moves, or the form moves and the precast unit remains stationary. This technique is useful for manufacturing large and huge size concrete components, which are cast on the site workshop, With this method, girders, pillars, homogeneous floor panels, prestressed beams etc. are manufactured.

The precast units produced by mobile slip-forming machine are cut to size by disc wheel cutter after the concrete has set. These cutters can be rolled across the surface of the precast units on pneumatic type wheels, and the cutting disc can be lifted mechanically or hydraulically.

The slip-form system requires utmost consistency in the concrete mix, otherwise the thickness of the units may not be uniform in size and strength. The concrete mix must be designed to develop an early strength and thus prevent deformation of the precast units due to shifting of the form. However, acceleration of hardening of concrete is an expensive process and uses much electricity/ fuel.

Handling, Assembly and Transportation

A major consideration, which is often a constraint for adopting large panel system, is the necessity for mechanised loading, transporting, handling and installing equipment. The manufacture of large precast units involves handling and loading at the plant. After this, transportation to the building site or stores has to be organised. Again, at the building site handling and installation of the precast units is required to be done. Generally the precast units are transported by motor vehicles *i.e.* truck, tractor and trailer, lorry and semi-trailer tractor. For large plant, railways are more economical for which the plant should be located along the railway siding. Large size precast units can also be transported by waterways, if the plant is located close to such a facility.

Loading and unloading can be done either manually or with the help of mechanised equipment. Precast units can be handled within the working radius of the lifting equipment/cranes. Forklift trucks and lorry-mounted cranes can also be helpful in this task. Mobile platform cranes may run along the fixed tracks so as to serve a larger area. Most platform cranes are equipped with a separate flexible pipe which leads to the far end of the jib and serves to operate grasping attachments.

Small precast units can be conveniently handled with wheel-barrow, handcarts, self-propelled trucks or small dumpers. For large precast units, it is preferable to use mobile cranes or forklift trucks. For small installations and lifting jobs, manually operated lifting devices can be manufactured locally. The standing derrick can be such a facility. Weights upto 250 kg may be lifted with a hemp rope using block and tackles. The top and the foot of the standing derrick may be equipped with rope pulleys and manually operated winches. The lifting capacity of such winches can be upto 5,000 kg.

Hoists can be another simple method to supplement the workers. The lifting capacity of a hoist may range upto 1,000 kg. Hoist can be easily assembled at the site or a self-erecting hoist with a steel frame, can be used. Mobile hoists can be moved on pneumatic wheels to another location in a short time. The platform of the hoist can be rotated which makes it easier to handle the materials. A crane jib can be fitted at the top of the hoist. It can be used to hoist the material to a height of 7 to 10 metres. Crane is the most popular and versatile equipment for handling of large precast units. Various kinds of cranes can be used for the purpose:

(*a*) Mobile or trailer mounted crane

(*b*) Rail mounted tower crane

(*c*) Gantry crane

(*d*) Small building cranes

The cranes are usually self-erecting, with telescopic tower sections. Modern cranes are often lorry mounted and mobile. The jib of such cranes can be lengthened by puhsing forward telescopically arranged tower by a mechanical or hydraulical operation. Gantry crane can be used for construction of two to three storey building. A gantry crane moves on tracks laid alongside the building. The load is lifted and positioned by a trolley. The trolley may be suspended on girder or run along the tracks from the top.

To allow safe and easy lifting, all the large precast components, like floor beams, panels, lintels and roofing units, should be provided with cast-in hoisting loops. They can be suspended from the loops or lifting beams having hooks or cables. Cast-in-loop is an important feature of panel structure and should be strong enough to take the load and lifting jerks.

DEBRIEFING QUESTIONS

1. Explain the concept of 'Systems Building'.
2. What is the role of housing in economic development?
3. Explain the salient features of housing construction systems by the following architects:
   (*a*) Le Corbusier
   (*b*) Charles Correa
   (*c*) Laurie Baker
4. Explain the concept of Modular Coordination and Standardization of dimensions/sizes of components in housing.
5. What are the pre-fabricated components which can be easily and economically adopted for housing?
6. Write notes on the following:
   (*a*) Industrialized housing process
   (*b*) Evolutionary/Skeleton housing
7. Explain the options for superstructure technologies (walls, roof, openings, lintels, chajja, staircase, etc.).
8. What is the role of computerization and automation in housing production?

9. Explain the following:
   (*a*) Large Panel System
   (*b*) Frame System
   (*c*) Slab Column System
   (*d*) Mixed System
   (*e*) Modular Tunnel Framework
   (*f*) Steel Frame Modular System
   (*g*) Glass-fiber Reinforced Gypsum Panel
   (*h*) EPS and Wire Reinforced Panel
   (*i*) Fiber Cement Board with Expanded Polystyrene Blocks
   (*j*) Light-weight Interlocking Sandwich Panels
   (*k*) 3-S Prefab System with Hollow Structural Components.

12

RENTAL HOUSING

A significant percentage of the weaker section and lower income groups can't afford housing on ownership basis, even when such housing is subsidized. Rental housing has been an important instrument for provision of housing at affordable price to general public, working women, low wage casual labour and employees, migrants, students and others, such as short term/contract professionals.

As per Census 2011, over 27% of urban residents of the country are living on rent and most of them are informal in nature. The NSSO 65th round report has highlighted that 25% of the hired dwelling units have informal and only 5% have legal agreement. All the States in India are governed by their respective Rent Control Acts (RCA), which are skewed towards tenant protection. A fixed rent with limited options to increase rentals has made the rental housing economically unattractive.

Though there is no precise definition of rental housing, it could be taken as residential property wholly or partly available to individuals or families for living, on payment of mutually agreed amounts and on terms and conditions of tenure agreed on between the owner of property and tenants, legally or otherwise. The residential rental properties include flats, part of the house, barsati, hostel, independent houses, bungalows, paying guest accommodation, apartments, rooms within the house and time share property. Housing tenure can be defined as arrangement under which someone has the right to live in a house.

According to Model Tenancy Act, 2019 'a tenant means a person by whom or by whose account or behalf the rent of any premises, or, would be payable for any premises as a sub-tenant and also any person continuing in possession after the termination of his tenancy whether before or after the commencement of this Act, but shall not include any person against whom any order or decree for eviction has been made.'

Tenant may not receive utilities, maintenance and other services as a part of package. In order to meet the unfulfilled need of affordable housing for low income groups, the augmentation of rental housing supply has been emphasized from time to time. The National Urban Housing and Habitat Policy, 2007 emphasizes on encouraging supply of houses on both ownership and rental basis. Draft National Urban Rental Policy, 2015 aims to promote rental housing market by providing incentives to housing finance institutions (HFIs) by revamping the rental legislation by Model Tenancy Act,

2019. The National Shelter Fund under the control of National Housing Bank also provides subsidy for the housing for the underprivileged sections and gives a thrust to rental housing.

Despite government efforts to promote rental housing, it remains the speculative outcome of the market. While the government lacks the fiscal resources to directly subsidize all rental households, there exist a distinct prospect of improving the investment climate, regulate the housing market and revamping the rental laws. However, other challenges which need to be addressed include the availability of housing stock on rent for diverse income groups, transparency in transaction and information sharing on rental practices, rental accommodation for special groups, such as unorganized workers, women, students, etc., financial incentives, property tax and income tax rebates, defining the responsibilities of tenants and owners, and security issues related to rental properties.

Other factors such as unrealistically low rental, poor maintenance, and low quantity of housing constructed for rental purposes; holding back unoccupied houses for fear of loosing control, etc. are resulting in substantial reduction in residential construction for rent. Significant number of renter's live in physically deteriorated, dangerous or hazardous structures. Many low income renters are concentrated in distressed areas of high poverty, with no or poor water supply, electricity, parks, sanitation and cleanliness. Sometimes these may exist on encroached or disputed lands which are patronized by slum-lords.

Renting of homes is treated as a "commercial" activity which increases property tax, electricity charges and service taxes. Housing loan payments can be deducted from Income Tax, but not rent paid specially by the poor and informal renters, who do not get the receipt against the payment. Accelerated deterioration of physical condition of the rental housing results as the landlords are not able to maintain rented properties out of their meager rent. A conservative estimate puts the number of landlord-tenant litigations half of the total litigations in the country.

International Experiences in Rental Housing

Significant proportion of residents in developed and developing countries are tenants. Housing tenure in Germany, for example, is 57 per cent rental and 43 per cent of houses are owner occupied, while Berlin has 89 per cent of houses occupied on rental basis. The housing tenure in different countries and major cities of the world are shown in the following table:

Table 12.1: Percentage of Rental Housing in Developed Countries

	Percentage of total housing stock*		**Percentage of social housing stock by****	
Country	**Social rental**	**Private rental**	**Public sector**	**Housing assoc. (profit/non-profit)**
UK	20	10	54	46
Ireland	7	11	90	10
USA	3	29	31	69^
Australia	5	22	85	8

Canada	6	28	34	66
Austria	23	17	43	53
France	16	24	Some^	90^
The Netherlands	35	12	1	99
Denmark	19	18	-	100
Germany	6	51	18	Some^
Switzerland	6	9	Some^	Some^
Singapore	10^	-	100	-
Republic of Korea	9	35	Some	-
Hong Kong	31	-	100	-

Note: Housing associations are the organisations that build and/or manage rental, low-cost or 'social' housing

*Remainder of total housing stock is predominantly ownership

**The social housing stock includes both social rental and ownership units

^Includes not for profit associations, co-operatives, modern rent agencies and regulated private landlords. Some associations have tenant shareholders.

***Source:** International experience in providing affordable housing, IDFC 2011*

A number of countries have employed tax provisions to enhance after tax yields as a way to increase private investments in the rental housing. Direct subsidy expenditures are also used in some countries, *e.g.* the Netherlands employs small capital grants, while Japan and Sweden sustain pre-existing interest rate subsidies (a mechanism used in the 1960s and 1970s in both Canada and United States). Australia and New Zealand have implemented and maintained healthy investment environments without direct subsidy. Notably, neither country has onerous rent control, both permit depreciation and deductability of rental losses against other income.

The US government has tried to empower tenants with rent vouchers allowing them to seek their own housing from private landlords, rather than confining low income tenants to public housing ghettos. Housing vouchers or rent vouchers are administered locally by public housing agencies (PHAs) who receive federal funds from the US Department of Housing and Urban Development (HUD) to administer the voucher program. Under the program, a housing subsidy is paid to the landlord directly by PHA on behalf of the participating family. The family then pays the difference between the actual rent charged by the landlord and the amount subsidized by the program. In addition, the Low Income Housing Tax Credit (LIHTC) of US is the nation's largest and successful affordable rental housing production program. LIHTC program is an indirect Federal subsidy used to finance the development of affordable rental housing for low-income households.

In United Kingdom, Housing Associations have promoted 'rent to buy' scheme, whereby an aspiring buyer can let/rent an affordable home for up to five years, while arranging to secure a loan to buy the same. These government-backed schemes offer discounted rent of not more than 80 per cent of what tenants would pay on the open market often less, and some tenants even return some of the rent for use as part of the deposit when they graduate to ownership.

In Australia, the Government has launched the National Rental Affordability Scheme (NRAS) to help increase the supply of affordable rental dwellings. Rent for these properties is charged at 20 per cent below the market rate for eligible tenant. Under this scheme the Australian Government provides funding to increase the supply of affordable rental dwellings, reduce rental costs for low to moderate income households and encourage large scale investment in affordable housing.

Canada has pursued a systematic long term devolution of social housing and rental allowances to the provinces and some local governments accompanied by funding transfers. Ireland has introduced a shared ownership scheme which enables the purchase of new or second hand homes in the open market with the local authority or the not-for profit housing agency initially taking at least 40 per cent stake, which they rent to the beneficiaries. The individuals fund their equity stake through the local authority loan and committed to take out all the equity in the property over 25 years. They make a payment on a mortgage for the part they own and pay rent to the local authority for the other part. Social security recipients may be entitled to receive a 'rent supplement' to cover the substantial part of the average market rent in the local area. Another scheme called 'Rental Accommodation Scheme' was introduced in 2004 under which the local authority will progressively takes over responsibility for procuring new rental accommodation on a long term basis. A key procurement mechanism for securing additional accommodation is through long term partnerships with the private sector to acquire, own and operate dwellings for the recipients using funding transferred from the rent supplement program.

In France, investors in private rental housing may gain access to subsidized loans. They can claim capital depreciation and may obtain a tax credit equal to 10 per cent of the interest paid on mortgage for two years.

In the Netherlands, the rent for the cheaper rental homes is kept low through governmental oversight and regulation. In practice this is accomplished by non-profit private housing foundations or associations.

In China, the government provides old flats which are rented at a very low price, called 'Lian Zu Fang' (literally 'low rent house' or 'low rent housing'). China has another popular scheme called the 'Public Rental Housing' (PRH) scheme, first attempt to use which is non-ownership housing to solve the housing problem of the people, mainly focusing on relieving the accommodation stress of local young staff and migrant workers who have relatively low income. China has introduced a series of tax exemptions for companies responsible for building and managing public rental housing projects, in the latest sign of the country's increasing reliance on state subsidized housing to cool its overheated property market.

Need for Rental Housing

Renting offers many benefits such as:

- Moving to and from rental housing involves much lower transaction costs than home ownership both for tenants as well as landlords.

- Renting transfers primary responsibility for upkeep and maintenance of the house to the landlord
- Renting does not tie up funds in the form of a down payment, nor does it expose households to the risk of loss of that investment
- The rental market allows labour force mobility and geographic shifts in the search for the job
- In a position of acute shortage, rental housing provides a staging post to the tenant, to the owner, it enables a steady source of income that converts urban land into an investment
- Another financial benefit to renting over buying a house is having access to amenities, such as pool, fitness centre, tot-lots, tennis court, etc. that would otherwise be a huge expense
- An obvious benefit that renters have over homeowners is that they do not have to pay property and other municipal taxes which can be a significant financial burden
- The renters have not to pay huge down payment for the property
- By renting, citizens avoid owing a mortgage that is more than the house's worth
- The fluctuation in property values, affect home owners, but it does not affect renters
- By renting, citizens have the option to choose a more affordable living space as per their budget and income. They can also choose their neighbours to some extent.

Reforms in Rental Housing Legislation

Rental housing is particularly essential for migrant labour, industrial workers, working single women, widows, working men, students and other groups. This needs several measures, such as to repeal/amend Rent Control Acts and to adopt the Draft Model Tenancy Act, 2019, which facilitates income tax concessions for institutional owners that create mass rental housing, providing subsidies for low income tenants. There is need to develop economically viable rental housing models, such as Rent-to Own Scheme, Shared Ownership Scheme, PPP Model, Rental Voucher Scheme, Rental Allowance Scheme etc. An online portal of database on rental housing stock, vacant houses/ properties can streamline the optimum utilization of such housing.

The Model Tenancy Act, 2019 drafted by Union Ministry of Housing and Urban Affairs Alleviation suggests:

- Entering into contractual agreements balancing the rights and responsibilities of both the owners and tenants.
- Introducing smooth online registration process and grievance redressal mechanism to enable growth of rental housing.
- Provide for fast adjudication process for resolution of disputes through rent tribunals.
- Repossession of the premises by the owner through rent courts.
- Adopt/amend/formulate appropriate legislations/rules for creation of institutions to operate, maintain and management of rental housing stock, both social and market based.
- Prepare customised strategy/action plan to address the issues of vacant/locked houses through a time bound action plan.
- To promote Residential Rental Management Companies (RRMC) to bring efficiency, especially in operation, maintenance and management of large scale rental housing projects/schemes.

- To encourage formation of cooperative societies, municipal housing companies, neighbourhood associations, not for profit entities or other entities that would create, operate, maintain and manage rental housing stock.
- To take initiative towards a gradual shift from existing rental market to formal vibrant rental housing market by promoting voluntary registration drives through appropriate fiscal and non-fiscal incentives at local level.
- To encourage employers to offer Rental Housing/ Rent-to-Own facilities to their employees (*i.e.* specific grants/ financial assistance, loans at lower interest rates, etc.).
- To encourage corporate houses, charity organisations, RWAs, NGOs to initiate rental housing projects targeting the urban poor.
- Initiate programmes to create/support system that accelerate rental housing projects speciality social/need based rental housing category.
- Build capacity of various stakeholders in planning and implementation of housing projects/schemes with special focus on Rental Housing.
- Promote use of local technology/design based on the local knowhow and needs for housing in general and rental housing in particular.

Promoting Rental Housing

The Central and State Governments and all the stakeholders have to follow a coordinated approach towards removing the impediments and introducing following financial and taxation changes to enable the provision of social rental housing:

(*a*) Rental housing should be mandatory in the urban housing agenda and in all government housing programs

(*b*) Rent Control Act may be abolished

(*c*) Subsidy for low income tenants may be provided, along with finances for private landlords providing low-income rental housing may be provided

(*d*) Property tax may not increase due to its renting

(*e*) Security of tenure may be promoted without discouraging rental supply

(*f*) Innovative Rental Housing Schemes may be devised

(*g*) Tax incentives may be provided to rent paid and also for private investment in rental housing

(*h*) Formation of high speed Special Courts and Rent Tribunals for rental litigation.

Rental Housing Projects can be facilitated by creating Special Purpose Vehicles (SPVs) offering loans on lower interest rates allocate certain percentage of fund especially for Social Rental Housing / offer opportunity to buy back from private sector affordable housing builders and to make it available on rent, rent to own.

Banks and Housing Finance Institutions (HFIs) can promote innovative financial instruments and co-operative Housing Sector and Non-Government Organizations' (NGO) can play a role in promoting rental housing and provide information to tenants and encourage development of tenant associations.

The promotion of rental housing needs working out a comprehensive strategy and coordinated actions, as demonstrated by the MMRDA's affordable rental housing scheme. In 2008, MMRDA launched an affordable rental housing scheme to build 5 lakh 160 square foot (sq.ft.) homes in 5 years. The scheme is based on relaxing Floor Space Index (FSI) in order to cross-subsidize the construction of low income rental units, and also the option of Transferable Development Rights (TDR). Under the scheme, developers receive an FSI of 4, with 15 per cent as commercial space, if they use 1 FSI to build rental homes on one-fourth of their plot. These rental flats are handed over for free to MMRDA to allocate. MMRDA rents out units at a rent between Rs. 800-1,500 per month. Eligible applicant households must have monthly income over Rs. 5,000, have lived in Maharashtra for 15 years and not own a home in the MMR. The project received a good response initially with 215 applications to build over 9 lakh rental units. Of these, 50 applications were approved for 2.6 lakh units, of which few developer's applications were withdrawn, some due to delays in getting government clearances. MMRDA is considering outsourcing maintenance and management of the properties to third party, rental management associations (RMAs),who would be paying a fee to MMRDA for the right.

Key Action Points

The following can be the key triggers for rental housing:

- Rental Housing Policy needs to be more closely integrated with the housing programmes like the Pradhan Mantri Awas Yojana. This also involves amendments in the Rent Control Acts.
- For a city-wide spread of housing, provisions of one-third of total housing units have to be rental in all housing schemes. The developer shall hand over such housing units to the government against reimbursement of cost of construction.
- Bonus FSI, as done by MMRDA, can incentivize the development of rental housing
- Schemes such as Rental Housing vouchers and similar to Low Income Housing Tax Credit (LIHTC) of the US, which give rebate in income tax against investment in low income rental housing, can have a multiplier effect in the creation of rental housing.
- Non profit associations may own and manage such properties.

The Draft NURHP, 2019 is a stepping stone towards creating a vibrant and inclusive rental housing market in India. Government of India along with State Governments may develop various models of rental housing and earmark budget to mainstream rental housing. The States/UTs will have to frame their own rental housing policy along with different models of rental housing (*i.e.* rent to own, shared ownership, model on management of rental properties with private partners in raising necessary funds, resources, etc. This also requires developing the criteria of identification of target tenants for whom it would like to provide rental housing.

Debriefing Questions

1. What is the importance of rental housing in the access of housing?
2. Explain the salient features of Model Tenancy Act, 2019.
3. What policy, financial and legal reforms are necessary to promote rental housing?
4. Explain the Draft National Urban Rental Housing Policy of the Ministry of Housing and Urban Affairs.
5. What lessons can be learnt from international experiences to boost rental housing market in India?

13

LAND FOR HOUSING

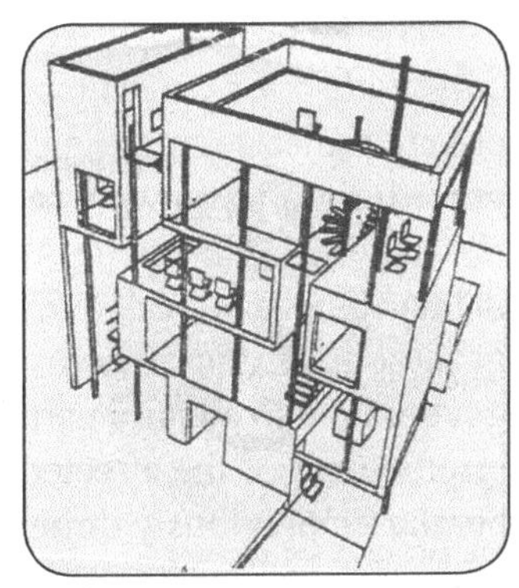

Urban land is the most expensive and critical component of housing. In large cities, if land cost is excluded, social housing would become affordable and viable. This implies mandatory reservation of land for affordable housing (EWS/LIG) in all housing projects/layouts, the cost of which is excluded from the cost of the house that could be as much as 60 to 90% of total house cost. Nevertheless, the acquisition of land under the Right to Fair Compensation and Transparency in Land Acquisition, Rehabilitation and Resettlement Act, 2013 has become too difficult and too costly.

In view of the various issues in Land Acquisition Act, 1894 and also due to changing political situation, the Parliament in 2013 replaced the Land Acquisition Act, 1894 by a new Act. In its preamble, the spirit of the Right to Fair Compensation and Transparency in Land Acquisition, Rehabilitation and Resettlement Act, 2013 (RTFCTLARR Act, 2013) has been articulated:

> *"...An Act to ensure, in consultation with institutions of local self-government and Gram Sabha's established under the Constitution, a humane, participative, informed consultative and transparent process for land acquisition for industrialisation, development of essential infrastructural facilities and urbanisation with the least disturbance to the owners of the land and other affected families and provide just and fair compensation to the affected families whose land has been acquired or proposed to be acquired or are affected by such acquisition and make adequate provisions for such affected persons for their rehabilitation and resettlement thereof, and for ensuring that the cumulative outcome of compulsory acquisition should be that affected persons become partners in development leading to an improvement in their post-acquisition social and economic status..."*

The RTFCTLARR Act, 2013 defines "public purpose" which includes acquisition by appropriate government (state or central) for (*a*) own use, hold and control (including public sector undertakings); (*b*) for PPPs where land continues to vest with the government; and for private companies for public purpose (excluding private hospitals, educational institutions and hotels). Public purpose projects include acquisition for strategic defence purposes; infrastructure projects as notified by the GOI; agriculture related projects; industrial corridors, mining and the national investment and manufacturing zones (NMIZs); water and sanitation, educational, sports, healthcare, tourism, transportation and space programme related projects; and housing development plans of various categories. The Act allows acquisition of multi-crop irrigated land, which shall not be more than 5% of the state's total cultivable area. The RTFCTLARR Act states that such land shall be acquired only under "exceptional circumstances" as a "last resort".

The RTFCTLARR Act, 2013, allows for the acquisition of the scheduled areas and tribal land, only with prior consent of Gram Sabhas or councils. In all other areas consent is required for private projects requiring 80% consent and PPPs requiring 70% consent. However, there is no clear procedure as to how consent may be ascertained and Gram Sabhas and urban local bodies are to be consulted. Under the Act, private companies shall provide for rehabilitation and resettlement if they purchase or acquire land, through private negotiations, equal to or more than 100 acres in rural areas and 50 acres in urban areas. In addition, if such companies request the appropriate government to acquire part of an area for public purpose, they shall be liable for rehabilitation and resettlement of the affected persons, for the area acquired by the government, as well as the land purchased previously through private negotiations. Further, a maximum of five per cent of irrigated multi-cropped land may be acquired in a district, with certain conditions; and every acquisition requires a Social Impact Assessment (SIA) by an independent body.

Under the Act, the minimum compensation shall be 2 times the market price of land in urban areas and 4 times the market price of land in rural areas, besides mandatory rehabilitation and resettlement of those whose land is acquired. The provisions of this Act do not apply to 16 existing legislations that provide for land acquisition, which include: the Atomic Energy Act. 1962, the National Highways Act, 1956, SEZ Act, 2005, Land Acquisition (Mines) Act, 1885, the Railways Act, 1989, etc.

Alternatives To Compulsory Land Acquisition

With the difficult and expensive acquisition of land under the 2013 Act, together with ever- increasing shortage of urban land, it is necessary to evolve the alternative approaches to land acquisition/ assembly, and urban planning. From the experience of several cities in India, one notices several alternative strategies towards urban land, as given below:

(*a*) Guided land development for townships, industrial areas and special economic times (such as urbanisable blocks, National Manufacturing Hubs, SEZs, satellite townships, etc.);

(*b*) Land pooling with compulsory reservation of land for social housing, public facilities and amenities (Town Planning Schemes in Gujarat and other States);

(*c*) Land reconstitution/redevelopment (for in-situ upgrading in small parcels in core areas);

(*d*) Joint sector and partnership models of land assembly and development (Greater Noida, New Mumbai, etc.).

(*e*) Transferable Development Rights (mainly for built-up areas).

(*f*) The concept of 'Excess Condemnation' can be used for major roads/transport, facility corridors and metro terminals and cross subsidisation of non-remunerative projects like social housing, slum rehabilitation, development of infrastructure services, parks, public facilities and transport hubs.

(*g*) Redevelopment and redensification of existing urban areas.

Land being a state subject, various options of land banking/ assembly, development and disposal operate in India. Most of the States have adopted the policy of public-private partnership and licensing the developer for housing/township development. For example, in Haryana, the Haryana Urban Development Authority (HUDA) issues licenses for the acquisition and development of land by the private developers who purchase it directly at market prices. The private developer/colonizer takes up the development and gets the land use converted by paying certain charges.

The cities should explore the options of redevelopment and recycling existing urban areas, including slum and squatter settlements and encroached lands. This involves a more participatory and sharing the benefits of development with the farmers and land owners. The developer may work out an arrangement or a Memorandum of Understanding (MOU) with the land owners. The MoU or agreements spell out the commitments and time-frame for development, redevelopment, housing and ancillary facilities, services, etc. The cost of the development of land, water supply, sewers, storm drainage, roads and amenities like parks, schools and hospitals could be met through free sale of 10-15 per cent out of the housing units and part commercial development of the land. In built-up/redevelopment areas where land is required for road widening, services or community facilities, the tools of Transferable Development Rights (TDR) and Accommodation Reservation (AR) can be used. Rather than adopting a single model, it is suggested to work out a hybrid model of land assembly and development keeping in view the needs and priorities of development.

Table 13.1: Alternative Land Assembly and Procurement Strategies

Predominant Considerations	Land Policy Option
Regularisation of existing development on private lands	Town Planning Scheme/Land Pooling and Land Sharing, land owner as partner
Obtaining land for public facilities in developed areas	Transfer of development right and accommodation reservation
Mobilising financial resource for social housing and slum rehabilitation	Development of part of land for market sale, optimum FAR/Development Controls, use of air right, Incentives based slum redevelopment, co-operatisation, market sale component and bonus FSI/FAR

Town Planning Schemes in Gujarat and Maharashtra

Land Pooling, Town Planning or land readjustment approach enables the developer or public authority to assemble land parcels, to prepare a plan and develop roads and other infrastructure, common services and amenities. These approaches have been used in some States in India. The origins of this approach data back to early 20th century, taking its roots from the "Lex Adickes" in Germany. During the development, a project organization, either public or private, readjusts lots based on a publicly approved plan and develops infrastructure such as roads, parks, and water systems. The plan requires approval by a specified share of the development. The owners benefit from land-value increases after development. Japan applied land readjustment extensively after the Kanto earthquake in 1923 and after World War II, helping close postwar housing shortage of more than two million units by 1964. By 2000, around 30 per cent of total urban area in Japan had been developed through this method. India has also implemented the land pooling policy in several States, such as Maharashtra, Gujarat, Tamil Nadu, Punjab, Andhra Pradesh (especially for Amravathi, the new capital) and Kerala. This policy is expected to result in availability of lant for development of residential, commercial, public and semi-public segments through private sector participation.

The States of Gujarat and Maharashtra have adopted a two-stage Town Planning Scheme to develop lands in the urban peripheries or to redevelop unplanned settlements. In the first stage, an overall development plan is created for the city by identifying areas of urban growth and primary infrastructure expansion. In the second stage, detailed micro-plans and a sequence for development are created for a number of smaller areas, usually between 100 to 200 ha. Then the government or local authority builds roads, public amenities, utilities, and social spaces within the area and may reserve some land for sale to recover its infrastructure costs. Some land is set aside for development of affordable housing. The land required for all these elements is then proportionally deducted from the land area of each land owner.

With the new infrastructure, the land value of the entire area increases significantly. The government raises additional funds to pay for infrastructure costs by charging landowners a betterment levy based on a per cent age of the increase in land value. Once the process is completed, the landowner is free to develop, retain, or sell the land.

The process creates incentives for land owners to pool their parcels by letting them participate in land-value gains, which shortens implementation time. Care is to be taken that the development of infrastructure services proceeds in tandem with housing construction. With inclusionary zoning in readjustment projects, land can be unlocked for affordable housing development and can open up housing stock within the city for lower-income segments.

From 1999 to 2009, the Ahmedabad Urban Development Authority managed to develop about 700 hectares a year using the Town Planning Scheme, equivalent to about 3.2 per cent of the built-up area of Ahmedabad. The readjustment program has also been effective in developing infrastructure projects such as the Ahmedabad Ring Road. However, in spite of various successes, it cannot be applied all over. Some of the issues inherent in the policy and legislation need to be addressed.

Table 13.2: Major Issues in Compulsory Land Acquisition and Town Planning Scheme

Compulsory Land Acquisition	Town Planning Scheme
• Resistance from farmers for acquisition inadequate compensation, litigations/court cases • Encroachment on govt. land/road • Piecemeal development due to withholding of land by the owners/farmers/speculators • Disputed land ownership • Speculative holding of land/projects • Delay in obtaining approvals • Huge profits by developers despite ceiling • Scattered location of projects/urban sprawl • Redevelopment of existing urban areas not covered by external services • Lack of inter-departmental coordination • Speculative projects in remote locations • EDC/cost recovery not related to development of services	• Compromise with planned development • Long time in finalization and approval of TP Scheme • Poor land bank of government/ULB • Perceived bias in favour of land owners • ULB subsidizing TPS development by 50 to 80% • Slow land supply against fast urban growth • Access to land for social infrastructure/utilities difficult and inadequate • Time consuming planning and regulatory controls • Inefficient resources use, poor cost recovery • Poor infrastructure standards, environmental quality, Administrative/political interference • Illegal subdivision of land • Poor recovery of betterment charges • Poor maintenance of the project • Lack of external & internal development

Land Pooling in Vijayawada, Jakkampudi for Social Housing

Jakkampudi village is situated at the foothills, at a distance of about one km from Veeranjaneya Swamy Temple on Vijayawada-Kotturu, Tadepalli road. The population of this village is about 1000. The main occupation of the people in this village is agriculture. Its proximity to Vijayawada city has made the village a potential site of development. Under the Basic Services for Urban Poor Scheme (BSUP), the Vijayawada Municipal Corporation (VMC) in collaboration with the district administration took up a land pooling scheme in partnership with land owners. Under this partnership, land has been shared between farmers and VMC in the ratio of 60:40, without cash compensation to the farmers.

Kerala's Plot Reconstitution Scheme

Plot Reconstitution (PR) is a land development technique which has been adopted in Kerala. Trichur Urban Development Authority (TUDA) carried out a PR technique in Kannankulangara area during 1982-86 covering an area of 7.5 ha and incorporating proposals for development of a central municipal bus stand, market complex, shopping centre, hotel complex and other uses. Initially the planning authority had moved with proposal to acquire land through Kerala Land Acquisition Act, 1961. Strong objections were raised against the land acquisition by nine land owners of land and obtained a stay order against acquisition. The TUDA, instead of going for litigation, decided to resort to the technique of land reconstitution inviting the land owners for negotiation.

Re-allotment of plots was made to individual owners as per plan, considering the extent of their original land, location and land value. Also commercial land use benefit was given to land owners. The average land value enhanced to average 7.7 times after plan finalisation and reallotment. Formulation and implementation of this scheme took 6 years. TUDA received more than two ha land free of cost and without lengthy legal procedure.

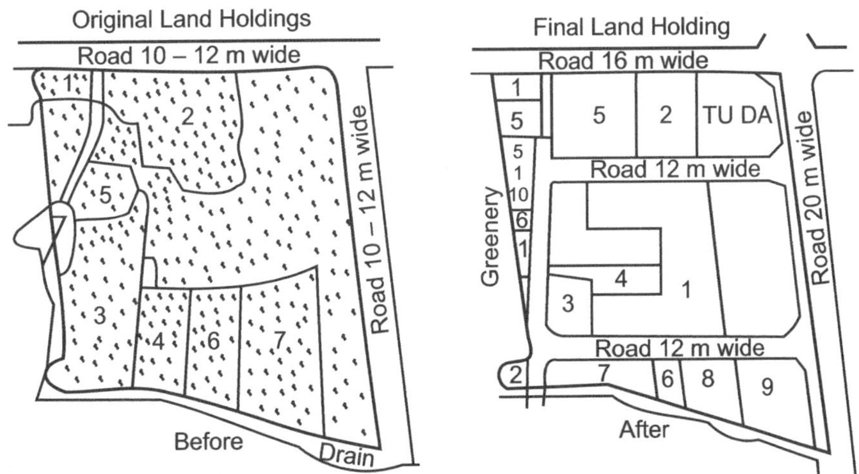

Fig. 13.1. Plot Reconstitution Scheme at Kannankulangara Trichur, Kerala

Source: *Mitra, Banashree (1984) Urban Land Development Strategies and Analysis, Urban and Rural Planning Thought (SPA), New Delhi*

The Concept of Excess Condemnation is another method which can be employed to serve the twin objectives of providing a public road, highway or such facility and generate revenue by the acquisition of additional lands which are directly affected by such provision. The adjacent area is developed by the local body, the land value of which increases as a result of facility/ road, and accrues to the local body.

The Concept of White Zoning: As adopted in Singapore, white zoning allows flexibility in land use. Depending upon the feasibility of land use and floor area permissibility, the developer pays the land use and FAR charges. This concept can be adopted to strengthen the financial base for infrastructure development and urban local body, as well as to provide innovative services/ facilities. The facility corridor and Influence Zone along metro corridor can be the starting point for white zoning.

The Concept of Transferable Development Right (TDR): This is being adopted in various cities in India, such as Bangalore, Chennai, Hyderabad, Mumbai, Nagpur, Pune and Pimpri Chindwada for appropriation of land without compulsory acquisition under the Land Acquisition Act, but against the grant of Development Right.

In Nagpur, a model has been evolved wherein vacant government or private lands have been used for construction of affordable housing. In some areas private lands have been used for affordable housing by acquisition by the Municipal Corporation in lieu of TDR. Construction is generally carried out by private operators, which is partly funded by Government of India through BSUP and partly by the municipal corporation. This model is a good example of providing social housing in the cities/areas wherein government lands are not available in enough quantity and in right locations.

Regulations have been framed for TDR for roads, slum rehabilitation, heritage, amenities and reservations, such as parks. The following Table provides a comparative status of TDR for various uses in various cities.

Table 13.3. Transferable Development Right (TDR) in various Indian Cities

City	Bangalore	Chennai	Hyderabad	Mumbai	Pune	Pimpri-Chinchwad
Implementing agency	Bruhut Bangalore Mahanagar Palika	Chennai Metropolitan Development Authority	Municipal Corporation of Hyderabad	Municipal Corporation of Greater Mumbai	Pune Municipal Corporation	Pimpri-Chainchwad Municipal Corporation
TDR (Genert)	Development Right Certificate (DRC) shall be used in the same zone or in the less intensified; one but not vice versa. TDR shall not be considered in receiving plots abutting less than 12m width Additional floor area in the receiving plot shall not exceed 0.6 times the existing FAR	The FSI in the form of DRC shall be equal to the surrendered land area multiplied by an FSI of 15, further by a factor arrived by dividing the guideline valve of the land at which development regulations transferred is proposed to be received/utilised Wherever land surrendered qualify for FSI of 2.00 or more the extent of additional FSI allowed in TDR shall he 0.25	The TDR is arrived at on the basis of relative land valve and equivalent amount in both export and import areas. The TDR shall not be allowed in unauthorised building/structures constructions. TDR is only applicable to high rise building above 15m. The max. FSI/built up area not exceed 1/3rd of the permissible FSI.	Resultant FSI on utilising plot not to exceed 0.4 times of originally permitted on the plot Any TDR receiving plot shall not be eligible for more than 100% additional FSI in whichever combination TDRs are received provided at least 20 per cent of the FSI shall be reserved for slum rehabilitation.	DRCs shall not be used in zone 'A' and congested area In other sectors of the city. DRCs shall not be used on plot for housing schemes of slum dwellers for which additional FSI is permissible and the area where the permissible FSI is less than 1.0. be used on receiving plots to exceed more than 0.4.	The receiving plot shall be allowed maximum of 2.00 FSI. If the proposed plot is affected by DP road or road widening. The receiving plot-in the BRT corridor shall be allowed such additional FSI (0.4) along with TDR so that the permissible FSI shall not exceed 2.00.

Road TDR	If any plot is acquired for road widening than 50% relaxation in setback and coverage is permissible either in same plot or receiving plot	As above	Land required for master plan roads equivalent to 100% of built are a of such and surrendered.	TDR for road reservation, FSI can be exceeded by another 0.8 times the original FSI. 40% of FSI can be utilized on a in-situ. The remaining 60% elsewhere in the form of TDR.	The FSI on receiving plot shall be allowed to exceed equivalent to land surrendered or road widening.	
Slum TDR	—	—		The maximum FSI is 2.5, includes 1.5 FSI for social housing and rest for free sale.		
Heritage TDR	—	—	For heritage buildings and heritage precincts equivalent to 50% of built up area of such site area.	The FSI of a receiving plot is allowed to exceed by not more 0.4 in respect of heritage building and up to a further 0.4 in respect of land surrendered for road widening.		
Amenity TDR	—	—		Within the FSI of 0.4, the land owner can construct designated amenity on 40% of land, and hand it over to the concerned department free of cost. Remaining 60% of land is allowed full permissible FSI.		
Greens Reservation	—	—	For reservation of area under lakes/ water bodies/ nalas, or recreational buffer greenery, equivalent to 50% of recreational area allowed for building.			

Source: Mahendra B., Veena N. and Harikrishnan K., BMRDA, Department of Town Planning, Government of Karnataka, Bangalore

Land Management Tasks and Techniques

Land management is critical for housing development, redensification, slum rehabilitation, regularisation and infill development. This involves coordinated development of service networks (water supply, sewerage, drainage and power), common facilities, parks and utilities, planning of lands, reservation of lands for social housing, and its development. These require strategic interventions, such as given below:

- Preparation of plans of redevelopment, slum rehabilitation, social housing, land pooling and development, services plans, mobility plans and projects, based on digitized land records and GIS, adoption of waste water recycling and renewable energy, water conservation and energy efficiency.
- Preparation of financial and organisational plans, programmes and Detailed Project Reports (DPRs)
- Enhancing organisational efficiency, legal back-up and procedural reforms.
- Time-lines and action programmes

Table 13.4: Land Management Tasks and Techniques

Tasks	Techniques and Measures
Increased and coordinated construction of the networks, main roads, and utilities	• Funding raised from the related increase in urban land values. • Flexible land use planning and work programming for road and utilities • Preparation of a housing land supply programme • Financial planning of services, development and upgradation.
Availability of land for public, social and government uses	Payment of fair compensation (market value or reinstatement value) • Increased funding, raised from anticipated increase in land values. • Development of streets, facilities, services and public open spaces. • Land pooling/readjustment projects.
Timely Planning of land and publication of the plan and programme	Publication of draft plans and programmes : • Promotion, persuasion and information sharing • Land banking • Finalization of Land Poolings Sharing Plans.
Timely subdivision of land into streets, open spaces and building plots for planned development.	Planning of housing projects : • Subdivision regulations and land use zoning. • Efficient administration of subdivision regulation. land banking, and sale of land with planning and development controls. • Land pooling/readjustment/sharing projects. • Planning of land for infrastructure, amenities, public roads.
Supply of land for affordable/social housing.	• Review of subdivision regulations to allow compact and dense development • Allocating land from land banking project and from land pooling/ readjustment project for low-income housing. • Upgrading squatter and slum settlements.

Time bound development approvals and use of land and financing	• Time lines and action programmes. • Simplifying and on-line approval procedures. • Financing plan. • Building materials, specifications and codes. • Service charges and property tax on all building plots. • To improve self-help housing, regularization of illegal settlements, conferring property titles, recovery of development and conversion charges

Land and Housing Tenure

'Tenure' is a pre-requisite to empower the poor in transforming their lives and climbing up in the socio-economic ladder. Without a legal right, poor cannot use their property as collateral and do not get a loan. As such, granting ownership rights is essential in all slum resettlement and low income housing schemes. A common fear is that the formal housing of the poor changes hands and is bought over and the poor remain homeless. To overcome this problem, it may be suggested that such housing may be leased out to the cooperatives or in the name of joint family members at nominal rents, instead of sale. This also needs redefining the concept of shelter which should include transit accommodation, dormitory, hostel, paying guest, etc. The industry, educational, offices and other establishments may be encouraged to provide residential accommodation to the workers.

The challenge of land tenure and transfer of ownership of government land under slum clusters and illegal colonies is a major issue and a determinant of its planning and development. This needs to be reviewed with reformed law and procedures of ownership/tenure rights so that the poor become the legitimate owners. This will encourage seeking the approval of the layout plans and building plans, facilitating a gradual conversion of informal/illegal settlements into planned areas. In slum areas rental tenancy can be given for an initial period which can be subsequently converted into ownership rights. For the promotion of collective community development, land can be jointly owned by all the residents.

Land registry systems verify the validity of existing deeds, confirm its valid ownership, land use, location and extent of property area, described in title documents and deeds. The land-registration authorities require a purchaser to execute a title search (which may also be guaranteed by title insurance) to prove that the title is clear of liens, mortgages, and other encumbrances.

Effective land registration system is also related with the planning controls, land use and building rules regarding height, density, sub-division/amalgamations of plots and so on. Land use agencies require the owners to obtain the approval of their construction, and pay the requisite charges. Land-use agencies are responsible for granting variances and may negotiate with owners and developers to provide public improvements in return for permission to build non-conforming projects.

To meet the specific and pressing needs of assembling land for affordable housing land-registration system should have strong mechanism for registering unregistered land. One approach is to publish a notice of the proposed deed tor previously unregistered land and, if no one comes forward with a prior claim, the deed is deemed irreversible subject to whatever compensation the government and private-sector developers are required to pay to avoid delays from challenges to titles.

Adoption of digitized, on-time, comprehensive, and reliable property registry can have immediate beneficial effects. In Dubai, for example, the volume of land sales jumped by more than 80 per cent, from an average of 180 properties per month to 330 per month, after reforms to the land-titling system were adopted. The government digitized records, required brokers to register, and simplified land registration processes. It also created a secure database to ensure the reliability of records and created a public authority to oversee the real estate industry. This also helped in locating many parcels of under-utilized or idle land, including government owned land, that could support affordable housing development. Land can be freed for development trough idle-land regulations, land readjustment and pooling and transit-oriented development. Simultaneously, it is essential to reserve at least 15% of residential FAR/FSI or 35% of dwelling units for EWS/LIG categories, with a system of cross-subsidisation in all future housing projects and Land Pooling projects. It necessitates the simplification of legal and procedural framework for conversion of agricultural land for non-agricultural purposes.

Tenure Rights

Tenure models broadly fall under three categories, namely, Property Rights, Use Rights and Community Ownership, as discussed hereunder, along with their salient features, advantages and disadvantages. Land tenure regularization schemes are carried out as a part of urban renewal, redevelopment and upgrading projects to provide security of tenure.

Table 13.5: Types of Tenure

Type of tenure	**(*a*) property ownership rights**	**(*b*) use rights**	**(*c*) community ownership**
Approach	Direct titling of plots/other Arrangments including joint holding/land sharing/ long term leasing	Only right to use the land-no ownership	Land belongs to community-just like a cooperative. Members have undivided interest, cost of land not included in sale price
Objectives/ perceptions	• Best perceived form of security • Beneficiary is encouraged to invest through self/ community • Product is a marketable/ transferable entity	Prevents eviction, beneficiary is encouraged to invest through self/community.	• Self/community investments on short term • Communities have long term control over use of land
Targeted beneficiaries	Residents of particular notified slums for upgrading those occupying pubic land		
Financing and transfer modalities	• Direct sale with service charges	User charges can be used in case of use right being upgraded to full ownership.	• Community land trust adopts lease fees for its members • Loans are provided to members/lease holders for home improvements, lessee can use their subleases for loans to improve their units

			• Members pay for land surveys to register bona fide structure owners
Role of NGOs/ CBOs	NGOs may organize communities and help CBOs in accessing tenure rights		
Advantages	• Encourages investment in housing • Construction and improvements-Improves access to formal channels of credit • Widens property tax revenue base of local authorities • Encourages efficiency of land and housing markets and allows transaction of property • Can address sectoral policy and institutional issues	• Makes it easier for the poor to geplots • Decreases likehood of land price increase and consequent forced moves of tenants • Easy to apply since it does not create political and social conflicts	• Makes it easier for the poor to afford • Likehood of land price increase and consequent forced move of tenants • Control of speculation in land transactions • Participation and • empowerment of the community
Disadvantages	• Government may be reluctant to provide tenure for squatters as this is seen to be protecting property rights of people who break the law. Issuance of land documents can create considerable conflict, especially in places where squatters have paid, and when more than one owner exists for the same land. • Property rights can push up land and housing values and may force tenants to move out. Administratively complex and time consuming.	• Does not provide the user with access to formal credits • Does not contribute to increased revenue base of local authorities • Conflicting results regarding house improvements • Cannot be sold, bought, and bequeathed officially; property (housing or a part of the land) cannot be transferred into case easily • Perceived as 'less safe" and 'less free'.	• A new modality, not much experience • Perceived 'less safe' and less free • Can be complex to administer, the land trust should get registered and get a trust deed, several committees need to be established to coordinate the ownership of plots, loans, etc.

Source: *Urban Poverty (October, 2006) National Resource Centre on Urban Poverty, Mumbai*

To curb the resale of social housing and its speculation, it is necessary to review the tenure options of the dwelling clusters with a view to:

- Reduce the cost and enhance afford ability;
- Provide common spaces, in a manner, which would dissuade the beneficiaries to go for quick sale of independent units;
- License shelter units initially on rental basis, convertible into tenure after 10 years, or so. Alternatively, the land tenure can be given jointly to husband and wife/parents, or to the co-operatives/resident associations;
- An evolutionary pattern of dwelling which can be expanded with the need and resources.

Tenure of slums and Jhuggi Jhompri cluster is an important issue. Various options are available which can be adopted with a view to shift from non-formal/illegal tenure to a freehold/shared tenure:

- Free-hold
- Delayed freehold
- Leasehold
- Public Rental
- Private Rental
- Shared Equity
- Cooperative Tenure
- Customary Ownership
- Non-formal tenure

Depending upon the situation, the form of tenure can be worked out. However, it should empower the women (joint tenure) and promote cooperative/shared tenure, so that the sale and transfer of property becomes difficult, hence the housing of poor does not become a commodity.

DEBRIEFING QUESTIONS

1. Explain the salient provisions of Right to Fair Compensation and Transparency in Land Acquisition, Rehabilitation and Resettlement Act, 2013 and its impact on housing production.
2. What are the alternatives to compulsory land acquisition?
3. Explain the concepts of:
   (*a*) Land Pooling and Land Sharing
   (*b*) Compulsory reservation of land for social housing
   (*c*) Transferable Development Right
4. Explain the different forms and issues of land and housing tenure in India and how these can be streamlined?
5. What measures can be adopted to prevent resale of subsidized housing?

14

HOUSING FINANCE

Housing and economy are inextricably linked. This is more true in respect of the poor who can be more productive by having a house. With this aim the Pradhan Mantri Awas Yojana seeks to build 10 million houses for urban poor. The program envisages an expenditure by the exchequer to the tune of Rs 3 lakh crore and 4 times of this amount by the construction industry/ private sector and individuals. The mission provides an interest subvention of 6.50 per cent on housing loans to beneficiaries belonging to economically weaker section (EWS), including slum dwellers and low income group (LIG). It will benefit urban poor by an amount of Rs 2.30 lakh each with reduced EMI, estimated at Rs 4050 pm as compared to Rs. 6,632 per month for a loan of Rs 6 lakh over 15 years at 10.50 per cent interest rate. The central assistance works out in the range of Rs one lakh to Rs 2.30 lakh per beneficiary. Under the redevelopment plan of slums, a central grant of Rs 1 lakh on an average per beneficiary is being provided to the States/Union Territories. Under affordable housing in partnership with public and private sectors or by the individual, central assistance of Rs 1.50 lakh to each beneficiary is provided.

Financing of social housing is a critical issue. The real beneficiaries do not have funds nor the credit worthiness to access bank loans. The private sector, by and large, does not find the social housing sector profitable. The government housing agencies also face financial crunch, besides other problems such as procurement of land, regulatory issues and capacity building. The increasing cost of urban land has become a major barrier. Time taken in approval of project and other delays further add to housing cost.

Issues of Housing Finance

The issues of housing finance can be seen from the following stand points:

- General public/consumers
- Developers and Housing Agencies
- Housing Finance Agencies

According to the surveys and interviews some of the findings and issues in affordable housing are the following:

- The housing is a human right, provision of which should be facilitated by the government.
- Prices of social housing should be controlled and made tax free.
- The government should encourage improvement and additional space in existing old houses, for which subsidy and loans should be available.

- Local small cooperative societies should be encouraged for affordable housing.
- The dream of the housing for all may get abrogated by adoption of business oriented, bureaucratic approach in its implementation.
- Government land and subsidies should be available upfront for affordable housing projects. The government land for housing can be retrieved from idle SEZs, industrial estates, etc.
- The administrative work in accessing finance, and land for affordable housing needs to be streamlined.
- The regulation of affordable housing projects should be delegated to an empowered committee comprising the ULB, Developers, Service Agencies, and Associations of Housing Buyers.
- One window approval of building plans is necessary.
- The land use controls should be liberalized and made flexible for affordable housing.
- FAR/FSI and density for affordable housing should be enhanced to incentivises the Private sector.
- In the affordable housing and slum rehabilitation schemes, exemptions be given from GST, stamp duty, VAT and other taxes.
- Easy housing loans at low interest rate and tax concessions can boost the affordable housing sector.
- Legal tenure is a pre-requisite, without which the poor cannot use their property as collateral and do not get a loan.
- Legal and procedural reforms are necessary to boost housing dcvclopmcnt.
- Risks of Housing Finance Companies (HFCs) in giving loans to the poor, especially non-salaried class should be covered by insurance.
- The concept of Reverse Mortgage can be adopted more widely.
- Frequent hikes in interest rates make the loans costlier for the home loan borrowers. This dampens the demand for housing and also leads to creation of delinquencies.
- Slowdown of industrial growth, business and trade, and the IT industry are impacting the housing market which needs urgent intervention of the government.

There is a need for a fast approval mechanism, reduction in bureaucratic interventions and proper dissemination of information.

As regards financing for housing, the following are the critical issues:

- Availability of affordable urban land
- An effective and efficient regulatory mechanism
- Access to housing finance, especially for the EWS/LIG categories
- A coordinated approach to housing

Land Issues

Availability and accessibility of land and explicit titles are the principal issues. It is connected housing finance. Greater part of the urban poor are engaged in informal sectors whose income alongside with creditworthiness is not straightforwardly confirmable.

A number of unauthorized colonies and illegal clusters have mushroomed in and around various metropolitan centers in haphazard and unplanned manner, which are without services and other essential facilities. The land parcels belonging to the government bodies, public-private institutions or areas meant to be green belts, are usually encroached upon. The upgradation of overcrowded, unplanned and un-hygienic housing areas and bringing them within the legal planning framework and their upgradation are the serious challenges.

To build 12 million EWS and LIG houses, about 30,000 hectare of net residential land is required at a density of 400DU/ha. Another 30,000 hectare of land is required for MIG and HIG dwelling units at average densities of 300 dwelling units per hectare and 150 dwelling units per hectare respectively. At 300 Floor Area Ratio (FAR) the average dwelling unit size of 50 sqm, 100 sqm and 200 sqm would be available for three income categories. Assuming 50 per cent of city area is required for social infrastructure, transport, utilities, parks, playgrounds and work centers, there is a need to assemble, plan and develop about 1.2 lakh ha or 1200 sq. km of area. Looking at the exorbitant price of the serviced urban land, it may not be possible to acquire the required land for housing. Affordable housing is not possible without affordable land. On an average there had been 10 times increase in land cost in Delhi during last 10 years. The Government notified land rates given in the following table indicates an unviable ratio of land and construction cost which varies from 11:1 to 35:1.

Table 14.1: Notified Minimum Circle Rates for Residential Land and Construction, Delhi

Category	Minimum Land/Circle Rate per sqm	Minimum Construction Rate per sqm	Ratio of land: construction rate
A	7,74,000	21,900	35:1
B	2,45,520	17,400	14:1
C	1,59,840	13,920	11:1
D	1,27,680	11,160	11:1

***Source:** GNCTD Gazette Notification dated 4.12.2014*

The land prices being 11 to 35 times the construction cost, point out towards the need to make optimum use of the land, achieving the stipulated Floor Area Ratio (FAR) and density. It is also necessary to consider compulsory recovery of 15 per cent of land, (with a choice to pay equivalent money) as per the circle rates, by the users of land for low density villa, farm houses, or vacant urban land kept for speculation.

For social housing (EWS/LIG) land cost should be exempted from dwelling unit cost, MIG dwelling units to include the actual price of land, and HIG (dwelling size above 120 sq. m.) pay 15 percent over and above market price of land, that would cross-subsidise the social housing land component.

According to National Urban Housing and Habitat Policy (2007) in every housing scheme at least 15 per cent of the saleable net residential land and FAR should be reserved for social housing and pooled on a zonal basis to have an even spread in different parts of the city and not concentrate at one place. Accordingly, in all residential areas and townships sufficient land should be reserved for housing of low income and weaker sections.

To recycle existing urban areas by redevelopment, infill development, densification, and renewal, it is necessary that slum rehabilitation and affordable housing projects may be deemed as a 'public purpose' for acquisition of land.

The social housing projects should be based on using land as a resource, whereby market sale component of housing can subsidise social housing. Part commercial use, optimum FAR and density pattern can also subsidize and reduce the cost of housing. The concept of land pooling/ adjustment can overcome the problem of land acquisition.

Incentive FSI/FAR, ground coverage and density norms are necessary to create more housing stock, while reducing the cost of land per housing unit. Transferable Development Rights (TDRs) is another tool to obtain land for public activities/facilities free of cost.

The city should provide a network of rental housing, dormitories, hostels and night shelters for the migrants, young, singles, retired and homeless population, especially the poor. It is imperative to evolve a new rental social housing policy with well defined roles of government in building rental housing stock.

Planning and Regulatory Issues

There are several regulatory issues which range from lengthy approval processes and delays, eventually escalating housing costs. To accelerate the delivery of affordable housing the following reforms are necessary:

- Reforms in the planning legislation, regulatory and fiscal frameworks;
- Planning and development controls for efficient use of land,
- Upgradation of infrastructure services in existing slums, old housing areas;
- Mandatory enhancement of the availability of the rental housing;
- Addressing the special housing needs of elderly, disabled and homeless persons;
- Support system for provision of services and their maintenance;
- Use of best available construction technologies and adaptability to changing needs;
- Promoting improvement of the public and private housing stock, rehabilitation/ resettlement schemes for rundown housing areas.
- Revisiting, Stamp Duty Act, Rent Control Act, Property Registration System, Building Bye-laws, etc.

With a tendency towards market led housing, the housing output of the government sector has been diminishing progressively. This is resulting in non-affordable and profit-oriented housing market. It is therefore necessary that as a rule in any government facilitated housing scheme, at least one-fourth of housing is built/developed by individuals/plot owners, one-fourth by cooperatives/ community groups, one-fourth by government/PSU/local body and one-fourth by the private sector/ PPP.

The Approach

Despite having an extensive network of financial institutions, banks and apex housing cooperative societies, low-income groups lack access to home finance. According to the India Exclusion Report (2013-14) prepared by the Action Enterprise, Bangalore 95 per cent of financing in housing sector flowed to middle and high income group housing from public sector banks and housing finance companies, where the shortage is mere 4 per cent. Compared to this, only 5 per cent of the financing flowed to weaker sections and low income group housing from these sources, where the unmet need is of the order of 96 per cent. This demands a paradigm shift whereby the public sector banks and housing finance companies have to reverse their policy of housing finance. It should be mandatory to give 75 per cent of total budget of the banks and government bodies under loans for social housing.

Besides the contribution of the Central government, the State governments and financial institutions have to be mobilised to finance social housing. Under the Home Owners' Mortgage Equity Subvention Scheme (HOMES) loan limit has been raised from Rs 5 lakh to Rs 10 lakh for EWS and Rs 8 lakh to Rs 15 lakh for LIG categories, along with 5.5 per cent interest subsidy on these loans. To make loans available to the poor a Rs. 1000 crore Credit Risk Guarantee Fund (CRGF) has been established. Under CRGF money will be given as collateral security to those who seek loans from the banks for EWS or LIG houses. It is estimated that with this fund around 1.2 million affordable housing units will be financed.

The funding pattern of social housing projects can be four layered, Government of India, State Government, Municipal Corporation/Housing Agency and the beneficiary. Transfer of Development Rights (TDR), Floor Space Index (FSI) and part Commercial use can help in bridging the viability gap funding.

Land is the most expensive component of cost of housing, which needs to be excluded from social housing cost to make it affordable. This has been demonstrated by Greater Vishakhapatnam Municipal Corporation (GVMC). The rehabilitation of Vishakhapatnam slum population (6.48 lakh) is the responsibility of the GVMC and Andhra Pradesh State Housing Corporation. The GVMC has been able to build about 15,320 EWS/LIG houses on the 10 per cent lands obtained from private residential layouts free of cost.

The financing of the social housing can be further supplemented by mortgage guarantee fund, social housing fund, micro-financing, land-housing-infrastructure bundling, Mutual Fund, Provident, Insurance and Pension Funds, and General Obligation Bonds.

Rationalization of Stamp Duty, both in terms of uniformity and reduction to a reasonable level of maximum 5 per cent, as stated in National Urban Housing and Habitat Policy, and exemption of EWS/LIG dwelling units from Stamp Duty (as already done by the Government of Rajasthan) are necessary for reducing the cost of EWS/LIG housing. Value Added Tax (VAT) for Stamp Duty would avoid repeated taxation. It is also necessary to review the definition and cost ceilings of low income and slum resettlement, taking into account the realistic costs. According to McKinsey Global Institute, the following three main factors can help in making the investment in affordable housing financially viable:

(*i*) Reduce loan origination costs:
- Improve assessment methods to quality borrowers
- Introduced standardized property valuation methods
- Initiate mortgage–guarantee schemes

(*ii*) Reduce cost of funding mortgages:
- Establish liquidity facilities
- Expand capital market funding (with covered mortgage bonds or mortgage–backed securities)
- Increase use of micro deposits

(*iii*) Leverage collective savings to reduce rates:
- Launch housing provident fund
- Offer contractual savings schemes

Since the government has budgetary limitations and resource constraints there is an increasing tendency to go for partnership and private sector development. As an alternative, the efficiency of government and private housing agencies needs to be enhanced. This can be done by saving the time and resources, especially by using industrial approach and computerized operations. Deployment of an industrial approach demands certain magnitude to achieve scale efficiency. Simultaneously it is also essential to optimise land use, density and floor area ratio and using innovative tools for housing finance, such as REITs.

To tackle the huge problem of investments, it is suggested to adopt a collective community approach in financing and loan repayment. A small group of families come together and form a joint housing group for sanction of loans, acting as a social collateral. They built together and pay together. This would reduce the hassles in loan procurement, paperwork and dealing with land, construction, suppliers and contractors. The credit -cum-subsidy model together with eco-housing approach will reduce the government burden, ensure community participation and promote housing delivery.

Whilst price of residential projects are largely guided by land costs, construction costs have a significant share in the price of affordable housing. During the past decade, construction costs have increased by nearly 80-100% due to the appreciation in prices of construction materials and skilled labour.

For an efficient and effective delivery of affordable housing project, the selection of technology, developers, contracting procedures and operational model are critical. These are essential not only for economy, speed and quality of construction, but also for ecological sustainability and inclusive growth.

This is a unique opportunity to introduce state of art processes, such as digital planning, spatial data infrastructure for land management and land pooling, benchmarking, infill development, Building Information Modeling, single window plan approvals, intelligent and smart services, especially sanitation, water and energy, and recycling of solid and liquid wastes. It is also essential to introduce new management tools, such as smart cards for property transactions, together with e-governance and capacity building of housing boards, and companies, housing finance organizations and banks, labour, legal and procedural reforms, especially those dealing with land acquisition, stamp duty, property registration, rent control, VAT and building bye-laws.

Land and housing are mainly the State subjects and the State governments have to initiate the reforms and develop the housing strategies, secure lands and prepare housing schemes, which can be provided with the Central government assistance. The housing projects should be meticulously planned, programmed and regularly monitored in real time by computerised project management software. Appropriate, efficient and speedier systems and building technologies could be invoked for high quality and green housing development.

In view of need to upgrade about 15 million dwelling units in congested, unserviced, dilapidated areas and difficulty in acquiring new lands, the focus for next decade should be on the brown-field development and housing renewal. It is essential to explore the options of infill development, redevelopment and redensification, enhancing the Floor Area Ratio and residential density, so as to optimise the land potential. The tools of Land Pooling and Transferable Development Right (TDR) can be the alternatives to acquisition of land under the Land Acquisition, Rehabilitation and Resettlement Act, 2013. This would enable the availability of land without monetary compensation, for roads public facilities, parks, playgrounds, civic amenities, etc. Such schemes have been implemented in Ahmedabad, Mumbai, Hyderabad and Bangalore.

Urban housing and subsidized slum redevelopment can be financed through award of part of project land for market sale, and by enhanced FAR and density along with adequate infrastructure and public transportation facilities. Gains in property values can be recouped for social housing and infrastructure development.

To overcome the delays and cost overruns action planning and effective monitoring are necessary. Technological, energy and environment concerns should interface with the standards and specifications, infrastructure services, construction and maintenance. There is a need to adopt new contracting procedures for efficiency, quality of service and sustained maintenance. To meet the huge urban housing targets there is no option, but to optimize and synergize the resources of both public and private sectors. A gradual transition by a hybrid approach can integrate best of the two worlds.

As a broad principle, the financing of social housing, slum rehab and redevelopment may be structured as a joint responsibility among the Central Government, State Government and project agency /ULB, each contributing one-third of the costs, besides part of the cost of construction to be borne by the beneficiary.

The concept of bundling of land-infrastructure-housing can subsidise slum rehabilitation and social housing. In every housing project 35% of dwelling units are mandatory for social housing units below 40 sqm, against additional FAR.

The JNNURM-BUSP project in Thane is a typical example, where only 10 to 16 per cent of the house cost is borne by the allottees. The funding pattern of the project is four layered-Government of India contributed 50 per cent, Government of Maharashtra 25 per cent, Thane Municipal Corporation (TMC) 9 per cent and remaining 16 per cent by the slum families. TMC has also used Transfer of Development Rights (TDR) and Floor Space Index (FSI) for funding the viability gap. Smart cards were issued to slum families so that benefits reach to the genuine people.

Part of financing of affordable housing or slum redevelopment can be met by the incentives like additional FAR, development rights, commercial components, etc. To make social housing schemes bankable, it is necessary to take advantage of mandatory reservations, optimize utilization of land by higher density and FAR, besides reducing the cost and time in land development, construction and infrastructure provision. The mixed land use/part commercial or market sale development can also help in financing affordable housing projects. Home Owner's Mortgage Equity Subvention Scheme (HOMES) can provide easier housing loan and interest subsidy.

Alternative Sources of Housing Finance

Housing finance is a long-term investment and asset liability mismatch is a major problem for housing finance companies. Access to long-term funds from schemes such as Real Estate Mutual Fund (REMF) would boost supply of funds to housing sector. National Housing Bank can raise funds through capital gain bonds. The banking industry and the HFCs can address the needs of poor sections by subsidizing interest rates, pooling funds and relaxing mortgage requirements, as also through instruments such as micro-financing, community pool funding, land mortgaging, and annual installments for loan repayments.

Besides presently available avenues of access to housing finance, several options can be explored for raising resources. Some of these are given below:

(*i*) Provident/Insurance Funds: Access to these funds can be made available to social housing sector through financial institutions or other approved intermediaries which can ensure the safety of these funds. It can also be used for subscription to mortgage backed securities provided they are declared "approved securities" by the government.

(*ii*) Real Estate/Property Mutual Funds: Such funds can be launched to channelise investments for social housing. The funds will have to function as per the regulations of SEBI.

(*iii*) Property Linked Indexed Bonds: These may be structured as an instrument of secured debt of a specific duration. These can be refunded on maturity linked to the appreciation of a proportion of certain properties under development based on an index which may be formulated by an independent valuer.

(*iv*) Foreign Direct Investment (FDI): Foreign investors mainly look for safety and liquidity of a reasonable return on their investment. There have been suggestions that FDI should be permitted for the housing sector subject to a minimum lock in period of three years.

(*v*) Securitization of Loans: In case where assets (properties) acquired with loan funds are held by builders over a long term period, these loans could be passed on to a Special Purpose Vehicle (SPV) for sale at the market. However, for the securitization to take place, it is necessary to have legal reform and make the transfer of rights less costly and less time consuming.

(*vi*) Debt Equity Ratio: Presently loans from FIs are considered on the traditional concept of debt equity ratio. However, in many cases land is developed jointly under development rights granted by the owners. The land is, therefore, not on the balance sheet of the developer. In such cases, the debt equity ratio needs to be adjusted appropriately to increase the availability of funds to the developer.

(*vii*) Specialized Institutions: The question of setting up specialized institutions to cater to the financial needs of the social housing sector needs to be looked into. This is crucial, as bulks of the loans at present are in favour of MIG, HIG and luxury housing.

(*viii*) REITs and InvITs can be the alternative avenues of funding and sourcing institutional capital. Real Estate Investment Trusts (REITs) and Infrastructure Investment Trusts (InvITs) can act as a key enabler for capital markets in real estate sector while providing investors with exit options. Both REITs and InvITs have the potential to bring it nearly Rs. 3000 billion over the next few years.

(*ix*) Life insurance companies are typically both owners of real estate for their own account and permanent mortgage lenders. They may be joint-venture financial partners with developers.

(*x*) Tax-exempt bonds can be used for special economic zones industrial projects and low-income housing projects. From a real estate finance perspective, they serve as lower interest lending sources for both construction and permanent financing because the interest on the bonds is exempted from income tax. Their use is quite complex and subject to numerous rules and in periods of low interest, the benefits are more limited than in periods of high interest rates.

Table 14.2: Real Estate Investment Trusts (REIT)

Legal form (minimum capital requirement)	Trust (Rs. 2500 crore)
Restriction on Investors	Minimum of 3 sponsors, each holding at least 5% of the units. Together, the sponsors should hold on less than 25% of units for a period of no less than 3 years from date of listing. Minimum 200 unit holders from public.
Restriction of Assets	At least 80% must be invested in completed and avenue generating properties. Property development and investment in under construction property should not exceed 10% of the fund value.
Distribution Requirement	At least 90% of the net distribution cash flow, at least once every six month.

A key feature that makes the REIT structure attractive is that it provides an avenue for individuals to foray into the real estate market with minimal investment commitment. Due diligence is conducted by REIT managers prior to an investment, saving individual investors the hassles of carrying out background checks of property builders and developers. As units of the REIT are listed investment in the trust also provides liquidity to an individual investor. Investors get an opportunity to invest in a diversified portfolio in the reality sector. The Union Budget (2016-17) has exempted Dividend Distribution Tax (DDT) for SPV of REITS. This would make the REITS feasible and profitable to the investors.

(*xi*) Micro-Finance: Housing microfinance delivers housing finance to low-income people for the delivery of micro-enterprises and housing.

- Its size varies, but generally 2–4 times larger than average working capital loans (income generation loans tend to be Rs. 3000-10000).
- Term usually is 2–24 months for home improvements, and 2–5 years for land purchase or construction.
- Collateral is mostly unsecured; co-signers often used; real guarantees may be used; formal ownership of dwelling or land may be required; savings sometimes used as a guarantee (may be compulsory).
- Targeted clientele are low-income salaried workers, micro-entrepreneurs, and poor people. This is sometimes accompanied by land acquisition, land registration and construction.

SEWA Bank's Housing Microfinance (HMF) Programme

SEWA Bank is an excellent example of an NGO to facilitate microfinance in a formal manner. SEWA Bank is a registered bank permitted to make loans, accept deposits, and perform all normal banking services. SEWA bank was established in 1974 at the initiative of 4000 SEWA members who each contributed Rs. 10.0 as share capital which has grown astronomically. SEWA Bank provides secured and unsecured loans to women for housing, home repair, micro enterprise, education and health.

National Housing Bank

In India the housing finance companies are growing steadily. The reasons for this include better access to products with varying features such as offer of different interest rate on loans, decreasing equal monthly installments (EMI's) suiting the needs of individuals. Some of the banks and HFC's have come up with such innovative products known as home equity loans. These loans are offered against the mortgage of the existing property. The mortgage loan portfolio of 20 HFCs has crossed over Rs. 1 trillion.

However, it is necessary to address some of the issues that include transparency and full dissemination of information to customers. Many financiers have been lobbying for developers to move towards a mandatory rating of builders and development projects. Such a move would have a two-fold effect. First, it would make it easier for a consumer to know which builder is credible and would help the financier to ensure that the borrowers project will not get stuck in needless litigation or land acquisition issues. This would enable financiers to identify riskier propositions early on and pre-empt a possible default. Secondly, it would force builders to be much more forthcoming about their projects and financials, thus allowing only viable projects to attract investment.

Mortgage Insurance, mandatory in some countries if the loan to value ratio is high, is almost missing in India. Mortgage insurance would enable the customer to get funds on easier terms, without putting high down payments on the mortgage. In India, there are no regulatory restrictions on loan to value ratios. When done with ratios as high as 90-95 per cent, lending poses a major risk to financiers if the borrower defaults. Further, most mortgages in the Indian market are given primarily to salaried individuals. Mortgage insurance could enable financiers to tap into other categories like low-income groups or self-employed individuals. Secondly, in some countries where mortgage insurance is available, those mortgages generally attract a lower risk weight. Lower risk weights would help financiers have more resources to lend out. The National Housing Bank has initiated the process of setting up a Mortgage Credit Guarantee Company which is being examined by the Reserve Bank of India is examining the regulatory framework and risk norms.

Financing Options for Affordable Housing

1. **Indian Mortgage Guarantee Company (IMGC):** IMGC is India's first mortgage guarantee company set up by NHB (38% stake) in collaboration with Genworth (36%), IFC and ADB (13% each). A mortgage guarantee, also known as mortgage insurance, is primarily designed to offer credit protection to lenders. Lenders can seek a guarantee cover, either partial or full, on its mortgage portfolio against payment of a fixed premium, determined at the time of taking the cover. The guarantee can be invoked on the underlying loans turning NPA. The risk transfer to IMGC (or other mortgage guarantee companies) releases lenders' capital and enables higher leverage.

   India Mortgage Guarantee Company (IMGC) concluded its first mortgage guarantee transaction for a Rs. 378 million pool of priority sector housing loans originated by Dewan Housing Finance Company Ltd (DHFL). As per the transaction, IMGC has offered a first loss guarantee of 10% for the pool which, along with 7.5% credit collateral, has earned an 'AAA' rating for the pool. The cash flow and first loss support provided by IMGC to the pool of housing loans has reduced the level of credit enhancement requirement which would result in release of Tier I capital for the originator.

2. **Establishment of CERSAI:** The Government of India in 2011 set up the Central Registry of Securitisation Asset Reconstruction and Security Interest of India (CERSAI) under the SARFAESI Act, 2002 to have a central database of all mortgages created by lending institutions. The objective of this registry was to compile and maintain data relating to all transaction secured by mortgages. All banks and HFCs which fall under the purview of SARFAESI Act were advised to register with CERSAI and the data in respect of all properties mortgaged in its favour. The lending institutions were also required to pay fees for uploading of the data.

   There have been challenges in terms of all the participating members not being able to load the complete data into the central registry as the conversion of historical data into specific formats is time consuming and requires upgradation of the existing system. Thus, the system has not been utilised its potential so far.

3. **Credit Risk Guarantee Fund for Low Income Housing:** The Credit Risk Guarantee Fund Trust for Low Income Housing (CRGFTLIH) was setup in May 2012 by the Government of India to address the housing needs of the LIG/EWS segment of the urban population. While mortgage guarantee companies address the general default guarantee requirements of housing finance institutions, the CRGFTLIH specifically addresses the urban LIG and EWS population. The Fund provides credit default guarantees up to 90% of the loan outstanding for loans upto Rs. 0.2 million and 85% for loans between Rs. 0.2-0.5 million for an upfront guarantee fee of 1% of loan amount. This would absorb a significant share of the credit losses faced by lenders.

4. **Issuance of long term bonds:** The RBI has allowed the banks to issue unsecured, long tenure bonds with a minimum maturity of 7 years, for financing infrastructure and affordable housing. There is no restriction on the amount that can be raised by banks under this programme. Several regulatory incentives have been provided to banks for issuance of such bonds, which include:
   - To keep effective cost of such bonds low, such bonds have been exempted from CRR/SLR requirements to remove any negative carry for the issuing bank.
   - Relaxation from priority sector lending requirements through reduction of outstanding bonds from Adjusted Net Bank Credit.

   More importantly, for the first time affordable housing has been given uniform importance as the infrastructure sector and the term has also been formally defined for the first time by a financial sector regulator. According to RBI, lending to affordable housing is defined as housing loans eligible under priority sector lending by the RBI, and also housing loans to individuals up to Rs. 5 million for houses of values up to Rs. 6.5 million located in the six metropolitan centers viz. Mumbai, New Delhi, Chennai, Kolkata, Bengaluru and Hyderabad and Rs. 4 million for houses of value up to Rs. 5 million in other cities for purchase/construction of one dwelling unit per family.

Fiscal Incentives

Government of India has extended a range of fiscal incentives for investment in affordable housing. Toward this, some of the key initiatives include Interest Subsidy for Housing Urban Poor (ISHUP) where 5% Interest Subsidy is given for loans up to Rs. 1 lakh and the NPV of the subsidy amount is given to the lending Bank upfront; operationalisation of Credit Risk Guarantee Fund Scheme

(CRGFS) which will act as a risk-mitigation for lending to the urban poor for housing whereby the lending institution can get a guarantee cover of 90% for a loan of up to Rs. 2 lakh and 85% for a loan of between Rs. 2 lakh-Rs. 5 lakh; allowing issuing of Tax-free Bonds for low cost housing and core infrastructure projects to HUDCO and other Financial Institutions and permitting Banks and Financial Institutions to raise resources through External Commercial Borrowing (ECB) route for Affordable Housing and Slum Rehabilitation.

Direct Tax Rebates for Affordable Housing Projects

The Central Board of Direct Taxes (CBDT) has amended Income Tax Rules under Section 35 AD to include Affordable Housing projects w.e.f. 1st April, 2011. This allows for investment linked deductions to businesses, which develop Affordable Housing under a notified scheme. The section 35 AD (5) (ac) of the Income Tax Act, provides that where the specified business is in the nature of developing and building or housing project under a scheme for slum redevelopment or rehabilitation framed by the central government or a state government, and which is notified by the Board (CBDT) in accordance with guidelines which state that the project shall have prior sanction of the competent authority empowered under the Scheme of Affordable Housing in Partnership framed by the Ministry of Housing and Urban Affairs, Government of India are entitled to receive a 100% tax deduction on capital expenditures.

In housing projects, whether slum redevelopment or affordable housing schemes, the expenses specifically related to the projects, whether revenue or capital, are debited to the concerned projects and are deductible from profits of such projects. However, this concession is targeted at equipment used for construction of the project. The examples of equipment and other capital expenditure for which benefit of 35AD could be availed by the developers are shuttering material, concrete mixtures/ batching plant, bar binding/ welding machines, transit vehicles, pumps and motors, tower cranes etc. This concession would have a greater significance in projects that use mass construction technologies, such as industrialised construction methods, which have high initial investment on equipment.

Rental Housing

As many poor families cannot avail loan nor can pay down payments, it is essential to make available a large proportion of affordable housing on rental basis. This essentially involves a different financial structuring with the following features:

(*a*) Rental subsidies: Provide subsidy which covers a portion of monthly rent.

(*b*) Renter protection measures: Institute measures which provide additional protection for renters against eviction, rent hikes, and negligent landlords.

(*c*) Rent to own initiatives: Allow tenants to build equity without having to qualify for mortgage or make initial down payment.

(*d*) Energy and water efficiency measures.

(*e*) Consortiums for maintenance and services.

(*f*) Homeownership associations/ rental management companies charges for rent collection.

Financing the Private Sector Projects

In India, the usual practice of developers is to collect the cost of the building in installments from the buyers, so that the builder finances the cost of the project. Individual buyers can approach either their employer or a financial institution for a loan against mortgage which usually ranges from 75% to 85% of the property. The builder often enters into an arrangement with financial institutions and helps the buyers to get loans.

The Reserve Bank of India (RBI) has also issued guidelines to the scheduled banks regarding lending to building industry and also public housing agencies, Housing Boards, Local Bodies, Individuals, Cooperative Societies, Employers etc. These loans are linked to specific projects for a stipulated period (generally 18 months). The banks have to ensure that no part of such funds is used for any speculation in land and the prices are based only on the documented price of land, actual cost of construction and a reasonable profit margin.

Developers tend to launch affordable housing projects in multiple phases, where developers realize returns due to the appreciation in prices over a project lifecycle. A working capital model is usually followed, wherein cash inflows from sale receipts fund the construction of the project. The developer needs to de-risk himself from costs of land acquisition.

For an investor land cost is the single biggest factor in affordable housing development. Land cost may exceed 50 per cent of total property prices, and in some large cities like Delhi and Mumbai as much as 90 per cent of property cost. This requires alternative approaches, such as underwriting, partnership and profit sharing with the land owners. Higher rate of returns and shorter breakeven period can be achieved in an affordable housing project by adopting the following measures:

- Entering into a Joint Development Agreement (JDA), Joint Venture (JV) with landlord or Public Private Partnership (PPP) with government authorities for land where approvals are in place.
- Shortening the period of construction (within 12 months for a particular phase).
- Lowering the cost of construction (below Rs. 1,000 per sq. ft.).
- Low ticket size to ensure 100% sales within a short time period (below Rs.10 Lakh per EWS/LIG unit and Rs. 30 lakh per MIG unit) or as may be defined by Affordable Housing Policy of the State so as to obtain state incentives.

The most effective way to reduce origination cost is to reduce the risk of lending to lower-income buyers. Risks can be better assessed by establishing credit bureaus and certified property appraisal schemes. Mortgage Guarantee programs can reduce the risk to lenders (and allow them to lend at lower rates) by protecting them in case of default.

One way to reduce the costs is to make best use of the land. Many cities in India have introduced the concept of Transit Oriented Development (TOD), with enhanced Floor Area Ratio ranging from 200 to 400 along with high densities. Higher FAR and densification have direct implications on urban housing supply and its prices.

Housing Potential in Metro Cities

According to the Census 2011, there are 53 metro cities which are having a population more than a million each. Their incomes and housing demand are commensurate with the population and growth rate. Hence these cities provide viable markets for affordable housing. Per capita income can be another index for the selection of the cities. However, it should be seen in conjunction with the housing demand, which may be higher in the cities with medium or even lower income.

Given that micro-mortgages are in great demand, collateralized, affordable and commercially sustainable, it is believed that the market has extremely high potential. The impact on low-income households could be even greater than that of microcredit, possibly with an even faster track to scale. Still there are many challenges that need to be addressed, specifically around credit assessment, transaction costs and access to long-term debt. In the long run, HFCs that develop the most cost effective, robust and scalable models will become the leaders in this large and fast growing market.

A proportionately high number of slum households, generally reflects affordable housing shortage. Another relevant aspect for consideration is the Basic Infrastructure Index. It also shows a relationship with slum population – higher slum population being inversely proportionate to low infrastructure index. Asset Holding Index also shows a close similarity with the Basic Infrastructure Housing Quality Indicators. Amongst the mega cities, Greater Mumbai has an acute housing problem and lack of space, with 7.7 per cent (the highest in India) having no exclusive room and 57.3 per cent living in just one room. The situation of adequate housing is also critical in Kolkata and Chennai. Amongst the megacities, the situation in terms of adequate housing is best in Delhi and Hyderabad. Greater Mumbai has the largest percentage of one-room houses (57.3 per cent) and Kannur the lowest (3.5 per cent) among the metropolitan cities. Srinagar has the largest percentage of houses with six rooms or more (22.6 per cent); and Greater Mumbai and Greater Vishakhapatnam the least (0.7 per cent). On an average, 63.2 per cent of houses in metropolitan India have two or more rooms.

Amongst the 53 metropolitan cities, Bangalore and Madurai have the least percentage of owned houses as a percentage of the total number of houses (37.0 per cent each); while the highest percentage of owned houses as a percentage of the total number of houses in Srinagar (96.2 per cent). More than 50 per cent of the households live in rented accommodation in eight metros (out of the total 53): Madurai, Bangalore, Vijayawada, Coimbatore, Tiruchirappalli, Chennai, Hyderabad and Chandigarh. On an average 68.9 per cent live in owned houses, while the rest 31.1 per cent live in rented accommodations. The prevalence of rented accommodation is much higher in the Class IA or mega cities with only 59.4 per cent of them living in owned houses, while the rest 40.6 per cent live in rented houses. The prevalence of rented accommodation is much lower in the cities of Class IB, with only 29.4 per cent living in rented accommodation, while the rest 70.6 per cent live in their own houses. Amongst the Class IA mega cities of India, the highest prevalence of rented accommodation is found in Bangalore (63.0 per cent), and is lowest in Ahmedabad (22.6 per cent).

Aggregate housing quality index value is highest for Surat, while Dhanbad is the worst. On an average, 9.7 per cent of the census houses in metropolitan India were vacant in 2011, while the rest 90.3 per cent were occupied. As per Census 2011, the total number of census houses in urban India is 110.14 million, out of which 11.09 million are vacant and another 0.73 million are occupied but kept as locked. A total of 19.84 million are used as shop/office; school/college; hotels/guest houses; hospital/dispensary; factory/workshops; places of worship; and other non-residential uses. There are 76.13 million houses used for residential purposes and 2.35 million houses used as residence-cum-other use; the two together giving the housing stock of 78.48 million.

Housing Market and Financial Capacity

According to NIUA & HUDCO report (2013) the 16 metros namely Amritsar, Bhopal, Coimbatore, Dhanbad, Durg-Bhilai Nagar, Faridabad, Gwalior, Jamshedpur, Kannur, Kollam, Kota, Kozhikode,

Madurai, Nagpur, Thiruvananthapuram and Thrissur are in a housing crisis, but are "good" in terms of their economic performance. According to the report, 11 metros namely Allahabad, Asansol, Jabalpur, Kanpur, Lucknow, Meerut, Patna, Raipur, Ranchi, Srinagar and Varanasi are found in a housing crisis but also have shown a very "bad" economic performance. 11 metros namely Ahmedabad, Aurangabad, Chandigarh, Delhi, Greater Visakhapatnam, Indore, Kochi, Ludhiana, Rajkot, Tiruchirappalli and Vadodara are "good" both in terms of their economic performance, as well as their housing quality. Further, another 15 metros namely Agra, Bangalore, Chennai, Ghaziabad, Greater Mumbai, Hyderabad, Jaipur, Jodhpur, Kolkata, Malappuram, Nashik, Pune, Surat, Vasai Virar City and Vijayawada are "good" in terms of housing but "bad" in terms of their economic performance.

Table 14.3. Matrix of probability of paying back the housing loans across the 53 metros

	Metros in housing crisis	Metros not in housing crisis
Metros with good economic performance	Amritsar, Bhopal, Coimbatore, Dhanbad, Durg-Bhilai Nagar, Gwalior, Faridabad, Jamshedpur, Kannur, Kota, Kollam, Kozhikode, Madurai, Nagpur, Thiruvanthapurm, Thrissur	Ahmedabad, Aurangabad, Chandigarh, Delhi Greater Visakhapatnam, Indore, Kochi, Ludhiana, Rajkot, Tiruchirappali, Vadodara
Metros with bad economic performance	Allahabad, Asansol, Jabalpur, Kanpur, Lucknow, Meerut, Patna, Raipur, Ranchi, Srinagar, Varanasi	Agra, Bangalore, Chennai, Ghaziyabad, Greater Mumbai, Hydrabad, Jaipur, Jodhpur, Kolkata, Malappuram, Nashik, Pune, Surat, Vasai Virar City, Vijayawada

Source: *NIUA & HUDCO, 2013, Metropolitan Cities in India, Phase I Report, 2013, New Delhi*

Basic Infrastructure Matrix

Table 14.4. Matrix of Basic Infrastructure Index and Economic Performance

	Metros in basic infrastructure crisis	Metros not in basic infrastructure crisis
Metros with good economic performance	Bhopal, Coimbatore, Dhanbad, Durg-Bhailainagar, Faridabad, Greater Visakhapatnam, Jamshedpur, Kannur, Kochi, Kollam, Kota Kozhikode, Thiruvananthapuram, Thrissur, Tiruchirappalli	Ahmedabad, Amritsar, Aurangabad, Chandigarh, Delhi, Gwalior, Indore, Ludhiana, Madurai, Nagpur, Rajkot, Vadodara
Metros with bad economic performance	Agra, Asansol, Jabalpur, Kanpur, Lucknow, Malappuram, Meerut, Patna, Raipur, Ranchi Srinagar, Vasai Virar City	Allahabad, Bangalore, Chennai, Ghaziabad, Greater Mumbai, Hyderabad, Jaipur, Jodhpur, Kolkata, Nashik, Pune, Surat, Varanasi, Vijayawada

Source: *NIUA and HUDCO (HSMI), 2013, Metropolitan Cities in India, Phase-I Report, New Delhi*

The NIUA/HUDCO study (2013) "Metropolitan Cities in India" concludes:

(*a*) There are 8 metros which are "good" in terms of economic performance and status of housing and infrastructure: Ahmedabad, Aurangabad, Chandigarh, Delhi, Indore, Ludhiana, Rajkot and Vadodara.

(*b*) 9 metros (Asansol, Jabalpur, Kanpur, Lucknow, Meerut, Patna, Raipur, Ranchi and Srinagar) are found to be "bad" both in housing as well as infrastructure and economic performance.

(*c*) 19 metros are "good" in terms of economic performance; but not necessarily in housing or infrastructure. These are: Amritsar, Bangalore, Chennai, Ghaziabad, Greater Mumbai, Greater Visakhapatnam, Gwalior, Hyderabad, Jaipur, Jodhpur, Kochi, Kolkata, Madurai, Nagpur, Nashik, Pune, Surat, Tiruchirappalli and Vijayawada.

(*d*) 12 metros namely Bhopal, Coimbatore, Dhanbad, Durg-Bhilainagar, Faridabad, Jamshedpur, Kannur, Kollam, Kota, Kozhikode, Thiruvananthapuram and Thrissur have poor basic infrastructure and housing, but due to their economic performance the potential to emerge.

(*e*) The 5 metros are economically under-performing, and have either housing or infrastructure problem. These are: Agra, Allahabad, Malappuram, Varanasi and Vasai Virar City.

Table 14.5. Categorization of metropolitan cities based on economic performance and status of basic infrastructure and housing

Achievers (8) in Economy & Infrastructure Development	Ahmedabad, Aurangabad, Chandigarh, Delhi, Indore, Ludhiana, Rajkot and Vadodara
Achievers (19) Economy–God Housing & Infrastructure – OK	Amritsar, Bangalore, Chennai, Ghaziabad, Greater Mumbai, Greater Visakhapatnam, Tiruchirappalli and Vijayawada
Achievers (12) Economy – God Housing & Infrastructure-Poor	Bhopal, Coimbatore, Dhanabad, Durg, Bhilainagar, Jamshedpur, Kannur, Kollam, Kota, Kozhikode, Thiruvananthapuram and Thrissur
Achievers (5)	Agra, Allahabad, Malappuram, Varanasi and Virar City.
Non-achievers (9)	Asansol, Jabalpur, Kanpur, Lucknow, Meerut, Patna, Raipur, Ranchi and Srinager

Source: *NIUA and HUDCO (HSMI), 2013, Metropolitan Cities in India, Phase-I Report, New Delhi*

According to Jones Lang LaSalle report absorption was skewed towards projects in the Rs. 4,000 per sq ft band across all the seven metros in India, which comprised affordable and mid-segment. Absorption in projects with units priced below Rs. 4,000 per sq ft increased from 78.0% in the 1st quarter 2009 to 86.0% in 3rd quarter 2010. This was because buyers were capitalising on the bottomed-out prices of projects after the economic recession, with the fall in prices being sharper in projects in fringe areas of select cities. Oversupply and poor buying sentiment during the recession increased the stock of residential units and this kept residential prices under pressure across most cities in India. However, when interest rates were increased by the RBI at end-2010 it affected home buyers' ability to purchase, and this resulted in a slowdown in sales across price segments.

The absorption share in projects priced above Rs. 4,000/sq ft improved from 3Q10 onwards going from a mere 15.0% in 3Q10 to about 36% by 1Q12.

Since buyers of projects in the price band of Rs. 3,000 per sq ft or below are price sensitive 'Need Based Buyers'.Their ability to afford houses diminished during the times of hardening interest rates. Similarly, the segments of buyers in the price band of Rs. 7,500 per sq ft or more were predominantly 'Aspirational Buyers' or second home buyers who could choose to postpone their buying decision. Hence projects in the price band of Rs. 3,000-7,500 per sq ft have a relatively lower percentage of unsold stock as compared to the other two categories.

Expected Returns and Selection of Cities

Typical pre-tax IRRs achievable in an affordable housing project, where a developer has himself purchased land, can range from 40-45%. The breakeven period for a hypothetical project studied below is nearly 24 months, which is due to land acquisition costs borne by the developer. Developer could enter into a Joint Development Agreement or Joint Venture with the landlord to reduce upfront land-acquisition costs and improve breakeven period.

The Government of India has launched the 100 Smart Cities, 500 Cities under Atal mission for Rejuvenation ban Transformation and 12 cities covered by the Heritage Redevelopment for Integrated Development and Augmentation Yojana (HRIDAY). These are likely to emerge as the hubs of urban development, and offer ample opportunities to build Affordable Housing, PG Accommodation, Service and Studio Apartments, etc.

The selection of cities for affordable housing projects can be done by a multiple index system based on the following critical parameters:

1. Economic - per capita income, economic infrastructure index, etc.
2. Development potential, identification of city ranking parameters
3. Policy support and regulatory environment
4. Housing Demand, slum population, housing quality index
5. Land – cost, title, transactional transparency
6. Housing finance access and safety

The ranking of the cities can be done on the basis of weighted index. It is important that the index is based on the correct data and perceptions, and not on the impressions. It is necessary to explore the potentials for affordable housing projects dedicated to slum dwellers, industrial workers, informal sector, etc. This needs creating new business models and redefining the role of the developer as a catalyst and facilitator. There is a tremendous scope for such initiatives as most of the present business models focus only on the formal, organized sector where profitability is the central theme.

Multiple Index System to Evaluate a Housing Project

A multiple index system can help in comparative selection of a real estate project. This implies that values (from 1 to 10) are assigned for critical factors, such as:

• Profitability	1-2	High Risk/loss making
• Location and land	3-4	Break even, low priority
• Ease of approvals	5-6	Moderate

• Law and order threats	7-8	Good
	9-10	Very Good

If the value of even one component is below 20, the proposal falls in rejection zone and may not be pursued. The total of critical components (maximum 40) can be assessed as under:

Below 20	–	Not viable
20-25	–	Not very attractive
26-30	–	Can be considered, needs some compromises
31-35	–	Recommended
36-40	–	To be grabbed

This only demonstrates a general approach and critical factors would vary from place to place, from project to project. After a project is shortlisted after due diligence, the next phase is working out a programme for planning and design by selecting the land and project management experts, surveyors and an architect/planner.

Marketing Strategy

When defining the target market, it is important to engage with the present demand and a futuristic vision. This should be based on the following information and analysis:

- Distinguishing characteristics of the major/primary market, information about the critical needs of potential customers, the degree to which these needs being met, the demographics, geographic location, the identification of the major decision-makers, and any seasonal or cyclical trends which may impact the business.
- Size of the market, including the customers in the primary market, their purchasing capacity, the geographic area they reside in, and the forecasted market growth. The extent to which the market share can be gained and the reasons why, number of customers expected, and competitors profile.

Market studies include following:

- Competitive supply profile, including occupancy, rent, selling price, absorption pace, unit sizes, amenities and features.
- Growth trends in the market, including population, households, income, age, education, jobs, and other characteristics, population trends, household formation, and age characteristics with associated lifestyle choices.
- Capture the potential, competitive penetration analysis for housing projects. Many different techniques are used depending on the product type or land use under study and the kinds of data that are available.
- Development program, product and absorption potential, defining the types of spaces or housing products, including sizes, character, style, estimated absorption, and pricing.

An overall marketing strategy should include the following four sub-strategies:

- A market penetration strategy.
- A growth strategy might include an internal strategy such as how to increase human resource and acquisition strategy, a franchise strategy for branching out, a horizontal strategy to provide the same type of products to different users, or a vertical strategy where the same products is offered at different levels of the distribution chain.

- Channels of distribution strategy, choices for distribution channels, existing agencies, internal sales, distributors, or retailers.
- Communication strategy, promotion, advertising, public relations, personal selling, and printed materials such as brochures, catalogs, flyers, etc.

Business Models: A major advantage of taking up affordable housing is its huge demand and potential market, almost all over the country. However, due diligence is necessary while adopting a business model. The critical considerations of such a business model include the following:

(*i*) Location and land

(*ii*) Ease of approvals

(*iii*) Investment vis-à-vis profitability

(*iv*) Housing market potential demand and supply situation

(*v*) Policy support

(*vi*) External Infrastructure Services

Broadly, the following models can be considered for affordable housing:

- PPP/Jt. Development Model
- A public sector housing development agency would be interested in partnership if it finds it advantageous to mobilize investments, speedy delivery and efficient development, and also if it provides PMC support to cover the risks.
- Collaboration with the private developers /land owners
- Self-development where the company takes up the project itself and manages the land, finances and all other activities on its own.
- Hybrid Model which combines the government housing agency, international agency, private sector and / or a cooperative society.

In a crowded housing market, it is important to stand out by offering USP (unique selling proposition), specialized goods and services that are attractive to buyers. Systematic understanding of the sequence of housing project is essential for a viable business model.

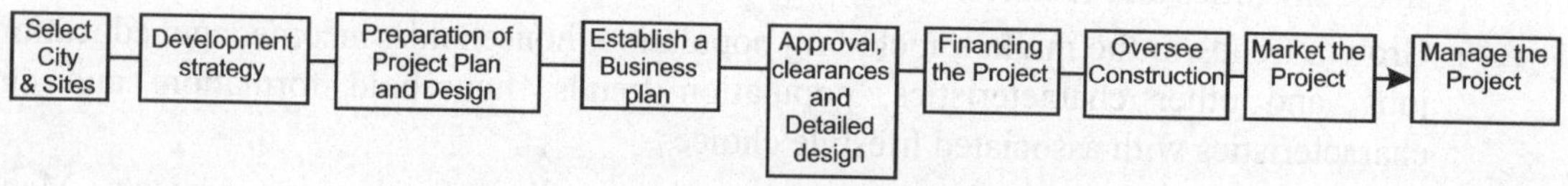

Fig. 14.1. Housing Development Process

Professional advice is necessary from the experts to ascertain various issues involved in a project, such as:

- Land use, floor area ratio, zoning regulations, water and power, planning permission, approval of building plans, etc.
- Financial cost, benefit assessment, sources, risks, returns, etc.
- Possible threats, such as heritage zone, airport zone, CRZ regulations, environmental clearance, political risks, and extortion risk, delays, etc.
- Land tenure issues, rehabilitation, court cases, legal and constraints.
- Market demand and potential.

It is always handy to prepare a checklist and a comparative matrix charts for the preliminary assessment of various options, such as housing, villas, plotted development, redevelopment and other choices. These help in giving a clear idea of various factors which are critical for a real estate project.

Planning and Project Design

Site Location Details: Land, area, site dimensions, physical surveys, maps, digitized information concerning the site and its surroundings, infrastructure services, traffic and transport, local climate environmental information, heritage zone, existing trees, reserved forest (if any), eco-sensitive areas around the site, geological/hydrological data, soil, ground water, airport/air-funnels, noise levels, etc.

Development Controls: Planning authority/municipal regulations for land use, floor area ratio, maximum height, ground coverage, road widths within and outside the site, setbacks, parking availability and requirement, planning and zoning controls, bye laws with respects to fire safety, structural and earthquake safety, rainwater harvesting, services, basements, projections, ventilation, stipulations concerning trees/ reserve forest, infrastructure services, heritage zone, air funnel, etc. A city development plan or Master plan includes the development controls, such as land use zoning, land sub-division and building controls. Land use zoning broadly specifies the configurations of different types of land uses. Sub-division and building controls are used to regulate development in order to secure acceptable spatial standards.

Property constraints, such as topography, floodplain, wetland, environmental issues; site views and proximity to other land uses should be considered. Net buildable area depends upon specific land use of site, Floor Area Ratio and development obligations, such as parking requirements and services.

A detailed project plan addresses the following issues:

- Land, planning issues and physical infrastructure.
- Resources (financial, human, system, land, management, etc.)
- Organisational and Regulatory system
- Project implementation, delivery, financing and marketing.

Force-field analysis and SWOT analysis are helpful in ascertaining project specific strategies, issues, risks, constraints and opportunities. The resources and the potential investments, their sources should be worked out. Evaluate various options vis-à-vis resources and cost benefit analysis including risks. This leads to an action plan comprising strategies, key result area and action points in a time frame. It addresses all the critical issues pertaining to land, planning and physical infrastructure, organizational, regulatory process, project implementation, delivery and marketing.

Project Financing and Economic Viability

Based on the detailed design and plans, the economic feasibility can be worked out. This process is typically iterative with modification to the program based on economic results. Key elements of the economic feasibility include the following:

- Development Costs
- Land
- Site improvements

- Utilities
- Off-site requirements
- Hard construction costs
- Soft costs
- Development revenues
- Sales proceeds or rental income
- Investment/profitability assessment
- Rates of return on investment property
- Margin on sales
- Potential sources of Investments

This would lead to financial structuring of the project. Many developers now-a-days do not hold the property, but the partner with land owners. They often sell to an investor-owner at a favorable price because the risk is lower, with a typical target profit level of 20 per cent.

Financial Plan for Affordable Housing

The following critical issues may be considered by a developer:

(*a*) Value for Money/Consumer Focus

- Adopt the principle of transparency in business, no ambiguity in floor area, plinth area, super area, etc.
- Guarantee no increase in announced dwelling price, do not cross the committed time lines of construction and delivery.

(*b*) Explore New Financing Tools

- REITs can be adopted for funding social housing
- Optimise cost of land, development and construction.

(*c*) Planning and Design

- A composite view of social, cultural, economic, environmental and technology aspects, synthesised by planning and design
- Affordable housing projects should be inclusive, integrated and inter-connected

(*d*) Technology and Innovation

- Rapid Assembly Line industrialized construction whereby 10 to 15 storey buildings can be put up within few months
- Quality and Safety Assurance and Audit
- Intelligent services, e-management
- Solar energy smart grid, waste water recycling, pneumatic solid waste management, etc.

(*e*) Social Dimension

- Provisions for unorganized sector, street vendors, helpers, etc.
- Spaces for livelihood and common facilities, especially for women and children, socio-cultural facilities, laundry, convenience store, dispensaries/health centers, gym, play area, roof garden, etc.
- In-situ slum rehabilitation and infill housing projects

(*f*) Actioning

Start shortlisting the cities for affordable housing and slum rehabilitation along with due diligence of the following factors:

- Availability of land, either upfront or in partnership with the land owners.
- Affordable Housing Policy of the State government which offers incentives such as stamp duty exemption, relaxed land use conversion and development charges, easy loan, etc.
- Prepare a financial structure and plan.
- Prepare a Project Management Plan, timelines/spreadsheet.

It is necessary to network with housing agencies, private developers and financing agencies for mutual accumulation of capacities in the housing sector.

DEBRIEFING QUESTIONS

1. What are the current major sources of finances for social housing?
2. What subsidies are provided under PMAY?
3. What are the major issues of financing the social housing?
4. What are the major roles of housing finance agencies.
5. What are the ways to leverage micro-savings for low-cost housing?
6. What are the alternative sources of housing finance?
7. What fiscal incentives are available and can be proposed to promote social housing in India?
8. Write short notes on:
   (*a*) Housing Market
   (*b*) Financial capacity
   (*c*) Finances for slum rehabilitation
   (*d*) Housing micro-finance
9. What are the business model options for affordable housing?

15

Housing Management Strategies

Several countries have formulated affordable housing policies and strategies such as given below:

- Countries like Singapore, the Netherlands, Sweden and Denmark are followers of universal approach where the whole population is provided with decent and affordable housing.
- Canada, Malaysia, United States and most of the European Union have a more common approach wherein housing is provided to the weaker sections of the society, which otherwise are excluded from the housing market distribution system.

In spite of contrasting approaches and policies, these countries have been able to meet their housing needs.

Enabling Levers For Housing

The RICS in its study "Making Affordable Housing Work in India" (2010) has shown the results of the data collected about the six enabling levers used to improve housing conditions in the eight cities, rating each "high", "medium", or "low" when compared with the other cities. These levers are (*a*) degree of capacity, (*b*) land title security, (*c*) housing finance system, (*d*) growth rate accommodation, (*e*) transactional transparency, and (*f*) supply responsiveness.

The first column shows the degree to which the affordable housing program is centralized. Hong Kong, London and Singapore are identified as having highly centralized affordable housing programs, with governments almost completely driving the affordable housing programs in these cities. Government is less involved in the medium rated city of Johannesburg, with market forces playing a much larger role in Amsterdam, Adelaide and Vancouver's affordable housing programs. The next six columns show data for six enabling conditions. For example, the degree to which land titles are secured in each city. Land titled security is rated as "high" in Amsterdam, Adelaide, San Francisco and Vancouver and "medium" in Hong Kong, Singapore and Johannesburg. These ratings mean those cities rated as "high" have the higher degree of land title security than those rated as medium (or low). The appropriate degree of centralized government control can be assessed by considering the level of these six enabling conditions.

Thus, a city with high land title security, a sophisticated housing finance system, very good transactional transparency, adequate industry capacity, adequate planning controls and land availability, needs very little government control. Instead the market provides sufficient housing stock at an acceptable affordability rate. Conversely, if the six enabling factors are not adequately provided for, then increasing government control is required to maintain a sufficient and balanced housing supply. The international review identified that none of the cities selected could entirely rely on market control.

	Hong Kong	London	Singapore	Johannesburg	Amsterdam	Adelaide	San Francisco	Vancouver
Degree of Centrality	High	High	High	Medium	Low	Low	Medium	Low
Land Title Security	High	High	Medium	Medium	High	High	High	High
Housing Finance System Sophistication	High	High	High	High	High	High	High	High
Growth Rate Accommodation	High	High	High	High	High	Low	Low	Low
Transactional Tranaparency	High	High	High	Medium	High	High	High	High
Supply Responsiveness	High	High	High	Medium	High	High	Medium	High
Other Interventions	High	High	High	Medium	Medium	Medium	Medium	Low

High Medium Low

Fig. 15.1. Enabling Levers that make Affordable Housing Work in Eight Global Cities

Fig. 15.2. Degree of Government Involvement

Source: *RICS (2010) Making affordable housing work in India.*

The Netherlands has one of the most regulated housing markets in Europe. It has a large social rental sector, and gives rent allowance for low-income dwellers and tax benefits for owner-occupiers. It has the largest share of social housing within European Union and social housing accounts for about 31% of the total housing stock as well as around 75% of the rental stock. The social rental sector in fact accounts for about 35% of all dwellings, larger than any other country of Western Europe. Though not specifically defined, the social housing sector caters to the needs of low income households, both on rent and ownership basis.

Whereas low rentals support the lower income groups to continue renting, the tax benefits allow higher income group to mortgage and buy. Home owners can fully deduct interest payments on their mortgage loan from their taxable income, though it is not a common practice in most European countries. In the Netherlands, the responsibility for adequate housing has been decentralized from the central government to the local authorities (mainly municipalities) and housing associations. This was done because the ULBs have a better idea of the needs of local housing market and hence greater efficiency in targeting the local needs. In contrast, in India housing market is largely unregulated, public housing agencies lack capacity, resources and coherence between Centre and State policies.

Affordable Housing in Brazil (Minha Casa, Minha Vida): Brazil is one of the emerging economies globally. Like many other countries, Brazil is also facing housing problems, especially for the population at bottom of pyramid. Official estimates suggest housing deficit varying from 5.4 to 6.3 million households. The Brazilian Government has taken several measures to tackle the housing problem.

Traditionally, the Brazilian Housing Finance System relied on two basic funding sources: saving deposits held by the public with financial institutions authorized by the Central Bank of Brazil; and mandatory deposits made by employers in accounts held in the names of their employees in the Fundo de Garantia do Tempo de Servico or FGTS. However, many potential borrowers were deemed ineligible to receive loans from these sources of financing due to concerns over the difficulty and expense involved in foreclosing on property. This ineligibility led to the creation of a new source of funding. Law 9514 of 1997 changed the face of the Brazilian mortgage industry, principally through the introduction of a new securitization vehicle (CIBRASEC-Companhia Brasileira Securitização or the Securitization Company) that improved liquidity in the mortgage marketing and a new type of real estate investment instrument-the CRI (Certificado de Recebiveis Imobiliarios or Certificate of Real Estate Receivables), which is a note issued by securitization companies.

In April 2009, the Brazilian Government launched National Housing Plan named Minha Casa, Minha Vida scheme ('My House, My Life') to build one million houses in Brazil for those earning low wages. More than 400,000 units were built for families each with a monthly income of less than GBP 416 on payment of 10 to 20 per cent of their monthly income. Families with a monthly income between GBP 416 and GBP 1388 are eligible to receive subsidies from the Government and pay 20 per cent of their monthly income for the access to the new homes. The program has also devised a back-up plan for families, who lose their jobs on allocation of homes, with a special fund of GBP 294 million for covering their defaults.

Malaysia: In Malaysia, need for low cost housing is deeply felt in Kuala Lumpur, capital of Malaysia. Kuala Lumpur occupies 0.07% land of the country's total area and accommodates about 10% of Malaysian population. Considering high population density, housing is costly in relation to incomes. As a result, about 12% of people are living in squatter settlements.

Under 5 yearly Government plan for low cost housing, families whose household income does not exceed RM 750 per month are provided units at a cost RM 25000 or less. The type and size depends on whether it is a walk up flat or high rise flat. Built up area is between 45-56 sqm having at least 2 bedrooms, a hall, a kitchen and a bathroom/toilet.

Until 4th Malaysia Plan, provision for low cost housing was the sole responsibility of public sector. But as public sector failed to achieve the targeted supply, private sector was called upon to play an important role in 4th, 5th and 6th Malaysia Plans. In the Fifth Malaysian Plan period, to increase the supply of low cost houses, the Government launched Special Low Cost Housing Programme (SLCHP) in 1986 with target of 0.24 million units and by the year 1989. Special privileges accorded under the scheme were:

- Establishment of one stop approval agency
- Flexibility in rules, regulations and standards
- Greater accessibility to financial facilities from commercial banks.

The private developers undertake such housing projects and at least 25% of the project is devoted to low cost units. The scheme received good response from private sector but was average in terms of target achievement.

China: Being a socialist economy, China has followed 'low income and low rent' policy. Urban housing is mainly provided by work unit so that low wages are compensated by cheap rental housing and rationed commodities. There was not much choice for the urban workforce other than to concentrate on industrial production and live and work unit housing provided by the state enterprises. Low rentals often resulted into the minimal maintenance and substandard buildings. Political leadership in China then realised the need to raise rentals to market levels and consequent raise in wages.

The Housing Reform Plan (1988) recognized that housing could bring economic and social benefits. The housing marketisation became the government policy, which sought to continue raising rents to competitive level and began the sale of public sector housing.

In tandem with the 8th Five Year Plan (1991-1995), the State Department endorsed the Shanghai Housing Reform Plan in May 1991. Based on the subsidy model, it was characterized by innovative devices such as the Housing Provident Fund, rent subsidy, and housing bonds. Thus, there was a shift of housing finance burden from central government and work units to individuals and the market.

In 1994, the State Department issued a policy, called 'State Department's Decision on the Deepening of City and Township Housing Reform,' in a bid to push ahead the housing reform process towards the market. Five policy measures were proclaimed:

(*i*) Co-ownership of Housing Responsibility: which would be shared by the State, work unit and the individual.

(*ii*) Housing Provident Fund: The state made use of the Housing Provident Fund to assist home finance. Both the work unit and the individuals would contribute to a common account. Designated banks supplement the fund with individual loans through a mortgage system.

(*iii*) Socialization and Professionalization of Housing Management – diminishing role of the State and work unit in housing production and allocation. The housing stock is managed by professional bodies.

(*iv*) Selling of Former Public Rental Housing to Sitting Tenants: The State progressively sells all existing public housing stock to sitting tenants at a discount rate of 50% and down payment not less than 30% of the purchase price.

(*v*) Housing for Middle and Low Income Groups: The State would continue to produce economic comfort housing for those groups who could not afford to buy.

The 1994 policy provided a framework for monetization of housing subsidies in 1998. It involved termination of welfare housing allocation, which would be replaced by direct housing subsidies in cash. The government paid the workers money to allow them to buy or rent from the market.

Singapore: Over the half-century since gaining self-governance, Singapore's comprehensive approach to developing housing has produced more than one million homes, housing more than 80 per cent of the population. When Singapore's Housing and Development Board (HDB) was created in 1960, less than 9 per cent of Singaporeans lived in government housing, and the previous housing agency completed construction at the meagre rate of one unit per 150 families each year. More than half a million people, nearly half the population, lived in dilapidated housing or squatter communities. Singapore's Housing and Development Board (HDB) has succeeded in providing housing at affordable rates for a booming population. Singapore housing is dominated by the public sector, with more than 80 per cent of the population housed in Housing and Development Board Units. However, despite HDB's success in providing affordable housing on a large scale, it has been criticized for expropriation of land, limited choices for residents, and low yields for savers in the HDB central provident fund.

Table 15.1. Singapore Housing Development Approach

Technological innovation	Improved procurement	Labour management	Process efficiency	Quality control
• 70 per cent prefabricated parts, allowing for quick assembly and production at scale • Metal framework for efficient shaping of concrete • Standardization across building types	• Managing supply chains handling most crucial resources • Negotiate contracts and specifications with suppliers	• Heavily managed licensing and registration process • Training of workers	• Audits and new production methods for efficiency • Streamlining permit process to avoid delays	• Assess construction against CONQUAS system • Review sample set of units for initial rating and then adjust final payment.

Note: Construction Quality Assessment System (CONQUAS) is a construction quality rating system developed by Singapore.

Source: *"Provision of public housing in Singapore," in Good Practices and Innovative Experiences in the South, Vol. 2: Social Policies, indigenous knowledge and appropriate technology, Martin Khor and Lim Li Lin, eds., 2001; McKinsey Global Institute (2014).*

Hong Kong: HDB offers mortgage loans to eligible buyers, which are funded by government and offered at the Central Provident Fund saving rate plus one percentage point. By making loans directly from guaranteed funds, the government is able to lower origination costs and the risk premium on housing loans. Buyers are expected to use all available funds (excluding those protected for retirement) for a down payment on a home, further reducing the mortgage risk by lowering the loan-to-value ratio. Typical loans are for 80 per cent of the home value with 25 year term. Monthly loan payments can be covered out of a Central Provident Fund account for up to a 120 per cent valuation limit, or the purchase price of the flat. This cap forces some buyers to seek additional financing. Additional subsidies are available to qualified low and middle-income buyers in the form of HDB housing grants.

Baan Mankong Programme in Thailand: Thailand had almost 2 million slum dwellers in 1990; by 2005 this figure had slashed to just 119,900. This dramatic decrease in slums is attributed largely to the government's long-standing commitment to slum upgrading, accompanied by strong strategic development planning and monitoring. But it was largely the activities of CBOs that led the government to establish a nationwide slum upgrading programme. Thai urban community organizations had organized sound savings and credit, but also through their networking approach, linking different communities with each other in order to strengthen their development capacity and learning. The government supported the mobilisation of slum communities, initially through savings and credit and subsequently through a broad variety of development activities. This created a sound basis for scaling up to a national community upgrading programme, called Baan Mekong, and launched in 2003 that set out to achieve 200 cities without slums within five years. It operates through the Community Organizations Development Institute (CODI), a nationwide public organization that provides loans to organized communities for land acquisition, housing construction, neighbourhood improvement, and income generation. In the meantime, slum upgrading has become a part of the national development agenda.

Affordable Housing in Sri Lanka: With an annual decline of 3.7 per cent, the total number of slum dwellers in Sri Lanka in 2005 stood at half a million, down from nearly 900,000 in 1990. The provision of housing has been considered a major priority by successive governments since independence in 1948. In 1977, the government ventured into significant and ambitious attempts to increase the housing stock in the country and increase home ownership. A distinct and separate organization, the National Housing Development Authority, was established to implement and promote mass housing programmes such as the One Hundred Thousand Housing Programme and the One Million Housing Programme, and provide long-term subsidized loans for new developments and upgrading activities. In 1994, it focused its attention on high density housing in urban areas in view of the increasing land scarcity, the government decided to stop slum upgrading and initiate a programme to relocate slum and shanty dwellers in apartments built by the government.

Housing and Slum Upgrading in Vietnam: Vietnam has developed five-year housing and investment plans with financing proposals. The central government plans to work with donors to address the financing gap. The government has taken up a number of pilot projects, local community-financed 'alley upgrading' schemes, and the Vietnam Urban Upgrading Project. A key element of these projects is the preparatory process of citywide, inclusive workshops to discuss the merits of in-situ upgrading and the challenges it offers in urban development for the country as a whole. The Vietnam Urban Upgrading Project includes the four cities of Can Tho, Haiphong, Nam Dinh, and Ho Chi Minh City. The initiative deals with in-situ urban upgrading, the provision of loans for housing improvements, and the provision of tenure security through the issuance of land-use certificates to slum dwellers. It attempts to prevent the creation of new slums, and active public participation through the People's Committee in each city. The local women's unions and local banks for housing and micro-finance are the active partners.

Community Development and Poverty Alleviation in Bhutan: This project focused on the Olep ethnic group who lived on the western fringes of an important national park in the west central part of Bhutan. Originally a nomadic hunter, gatherer community, the Olep were encouraged by the government to settle in Rukha in the early 1970s, so that they could benefit from the development initiatives that were taking place in the country. With no experience of settled living and their earlier means of living off the forest no longer available, the community fell into extreme poverty. This project, run by the Tarayana Foundation, has developed skills and encouraged a self-help ethos that has successfully helped the community to recover and prosper.

Originally focusing on the village of Rukha, the project has spread to 150 other villages across Bhutan.

Fig. 15.3. Community, Self Help House in Bhutan

Source: *www.worldhabitatawards.org*

Fig. 15.4. Housing built by TECHO-Habitat in Chile

Source: *www.worldhabitatawards.org*

Techo-Development of Habitat, Chile: Techo is an NGO working with residents and young volunteers to overcome the poverty covered which thousands of people live in informal settlements across Latin America and the Caribbean. TECHO's 'Development of Habitat' projects aim to implement permanent solutions in the settlements in the different countries in which it operates. 'Development of Habitat' projects are currently in place in Chile, Argentina, Uruguay and Colombia.

The projects have had a direct impact on the lives of the participating families. Besides improved living conditions, people are also trained in management which allows them to lead their own projects and deal with issues.

Slum Dwellers Housing in San Juan: Puerto Rico Project demonstrated that slum housing need not be a replica of standardized units, but should incorporate flexibility of space by creating living platforms and roof, where slum dwellers can furnish and finish their dwellings according to their own needs and resources. A simple prefab system provides economical and fast development. Ground floor is kept for parking, shops, community space and common facilities. Each family can complete and furnish the dwelling unit according to their own needs and resources. To accommodate all the slum dwellers, the project was developed on a high density, compact and low rise patterns.

Cano Martin Pena Community Land Trust, San Juan: The Martín Pena Channel was once a waterway that ran through the middle of the Puerto Rican capital San Juan. Impoverished squatters settled on the mangrove swamps along its banks, building more than 5,000 informal homes. The swamp was filled with debris and silt, and with no sewer system became highly polluted. It provides a new model for improving informal settlements without them becoming unaffordable for the original residents. Around 1,500 families were made eligible for the right to occupy land in the District.

Fig. 15.5. Flooded swamps in San Juan, Puerto Rico

Fig. 15.6. New houses built by rehabilitated squatters in San Juan

Source: *www.worldhabitatawards.org*

Zero Energy Housing for European Union: Electricity consumption in India is increasing rapidly and building accounts for one-fourth of total energy consumption. This has serious implications on the ecology and climate, besides a financial burden on households. Zero energy housing aims to significantly lower energy consumption.

Fig. 15.7. Zero Energy Housing

It aims to produce as much renewable energy as consumed from the grid. System automation is the brain and heart of a zero energy house. Modular construction, such as prefab components and Steel Core Panels are opening up new possibilities in building projects. Panel construction produces less than half the carbon emission of the industry average. Completely recyclable, the light weight and durable panels allow energy efficient, rapid construction.

Rent to Buy Scheme, United Kingdom: The Highlands Small Communities Housing Trust (HSCHT) 'Rent to Buy Scheme' helps people on low income living in the remote highlands of Scotland to find an affordable home. At the heart of the scheme is a financial mechanism which enables low income families to save up to buy a home whilst they are renting it.

Part of the rent is retained by the HSCHT and is available as a lump sum that is used as a deposit to buy the house. The affordability of the housing has been protected by the Rural Housing Board, ensuring that the new properties remain available to local people and are not sold in the open market.

Grameen Bank Housing Programme, Bangladesh: Bangladesh is one of the world's poorest, most densely populated and least developed nation. With a population in excess of 125 million, it is the eighth most populous country in the world. Situated in low-lying delta where four major river systems come together, the country also suffers from regular and severe problems of flooding.

Grameen Bank grew out of an action research project initiated by Professor Muhammed Yunus in 1976, who recognized that it is the poor people's lack of access to capital rather than their capacity of repay that perpetuates their poverty. The action research project started in Chittagong University provided credit facilities for a small number of poor families and enabled them to set up small income-generating businesses. These tiny loans of a few dollars, issued without formal collateral, enabled the poorest of the poor to get out of their downward spiral of poverty and exploitation by money-lenders. Building on the success of this and subsequent projects, the Grameen Bank was formally incorporated in 1983 and is today the largest rural credit institution in Bangladesh with 240000 borrowers, 95 per cent of whom are women. It provides services in 38659 villages (more than half of all villages in Bangladesh).

In 1984 the Bank started to lend money for housing loans and to date 450,000 houses have been built using these loans. An average of 7,000-8,000 new loans are made every month. The housing loans are available only to existing Grameen Bank borrowers who have a 100 per cent repayment record and have completely repaid their first two income generation activities, but after a natural disaster the Grameen Bank evolved a special housing programme in which the above criteria were relaxed. The housing loans are usually repaid over a 10 year period with a simple interest rate of eight per cent.

Micro-Banking Programme in Indonesia: The Unit Desa Programme of the Bank Rakyat Indonesia consists of about 3,600 disbursement centres for micro-credit. It is a combination of following models:

- Self-Help Group Model: Members of the SHG save and pool their deposits and lend to the members from the deposits and collect interest thereon.
- Individual Banking Programme (IBP) Model: In this model, an individual is directly assisted by a co-operative bank.
- Community Banking Model: In this model, the NGOs-MFIs facilitate the local community to pool their savings and provide loans to its member from its kitty.
- SHG-MFI-Bank Model: In this model, Self-Help Group (SHG) gets linked with a MFI which in turn is linked with a bank. The MFI borrows funds from banks and lends to the SHGs.

Mexico: In Mexico, a legislation known as the Special Statute for the promotion of the micro-enterprise was passed in 1988. Economist Hernando de Soto spearheaded the movement to offer government guaranteed title over the property. The think-tank he founded, the Institute of Liberty and Democracy, prevailed in one of the most radical make-overs of a society that brought an informal economy and thereby bulk of the populace within the regulatory fold through the effort of providing land titles. Ever since, Hernando de Soto had been consulted by several governments world over to spread this philosophy and ensure that the growth process becomes more inclusive.

An Overview of various international experiences: The following table provides a snapshot of some lessons from best practices to help and service the slums and informal settlements in various countries.

Table 15.2. Slums and Informal Settlements–Some Best Practices

Country	Pilot project	Legal status	Main drivers		Process	Best practice/lessons learned
			Utility	Other		
Venezuela	"Barrio Election project" (electricity only)	Land ownership and amendments to laws and regulations	Created a 'payments culture' Turned informal users into customers	Improved quality of life Created Inclusion into society improved safety conditions	Identified and established relationship with target communities. Installed prepaid meters in a low-cost grid	Carefully plan a pilot Assured data use engineering with sociology on scalability
South Africa	PN Energy Service (Pty) Ltd. Electricity only	All citizens earning less than the national minimum wage are eligible for up to 50 kwh of power supply free of cost	National energy planning objective and targets ESKOM push to install safe and legal connection	Specific target to Increase township programming. Pre-payment meters proved a success	Sealing meters to prevent tampering. Conduct sweeps and audits in the area to identify illegal connections	Prepaid meters are preferred by low-income customers. Sweep teams are in the area identify illegal connections
Brazil	LIGHT: Programme for Normalization of Informal Area (PRONAI)	LIGHT provided, documentation of proof of residence for favela (slum) residents. Granted amnesty from prior electricity debts and fines for theft.	Programme was self-financing	Improved quality of service Reduced safety hazards	Made grid connections and legal purchase of electricity affordable through subsidies. Distributed free efficient light bulbs.	Strengthened buy-in by using community-based agents to create a payment culture.
Morocco	LYDEC-electricity, water and sanitation connection	Under the Cities without Slums programme-30% of informal settlements improved in-situ. Remaining residents of slums shifted into legal landholdings.	Break-even investment 96% collection rate in temporarily electrified slums, losses reduction and improved service.	Office National de l' Electricite aimed at full national connectivity, Slum restructuring policy.	Most slum/informal settlement residents moved to mixed-income housing developments. Some smaller urban slums upgraded in-situ	Provided bundled services. Only 3 of 14 Discoms were privatized. Developed a partnership with the housing department and local authorities

Colombia		Established a "pila publica"- a communal connection point. If area is not habitable, the inhabitants are relocated to secure areas.	Once regularised, collect service charges similar to rest of population. Positive cost/ benefit for EPM and consumers	Area based integrated planning and execution, lowered total costs by 15-25%	Conducted census of houses. Each house given a fixed subsidy, regularise the area and install individual meters.	Electricity is supplied to everybody. Individual metering is essential.

Source: *Jain AK (2009) Urban Housing and Slums, Readworthy Publishers.*

Partnerships in Affordable Housing

The following abstracts taken from Hala S. Mekawy's paper "Effectual Role of Local Level Partnership Schemes in Affordable Housing Delivery", outlines the experiences of some countries in development of partnership in affordable housing delivery.

In developing countries, partnerships are still emerging. The partnerships accomplished remarkable success in housing low-income people in countries like India, Turkey, Kenya, Zimbabwe, Malawi, Nigeria, Malaysia and the Philippines. However, the partnership model failed in some other countries like Pakistan and had modest achievement in South Africa and Nigeria.

The Philippines' experience represents a model program that can be adopted in Egypt. It is a demonstration of government play's a key role in providing land, and curtailing government non-necessarily high housing standards, while private-sector partners handle land development, construction of housing units, and provisions of infrastructure services.

Another significant experience is that of India, where there is a wide-spread co-operative housing movement. Partnerships between the government and civil society organizations have recorded remarkable success at varying levels in different states; they worked more effectively where the focus was on drawing in private investment rather than contracting out various responsibilities to the private developer. This was also demonstrated in the experiences of Kenya, Zimbabwe and Malawi, where land is inaccessible due to being of high value and government-owned. The Indian experience also shows that in order to facilitate greater private and co-operative sector participation, there is a need to undertake legal/regulatory, institutional, and land policy reforms, provide suitable financial measures and incentives to encourage investment in housing (for both households and the corporate sector), and widen existing housing related databases. Also, banks and housing finance institutions extend/intensify their coverage in low income neighbourhoods, devise innovative flexible housing finance schemes for targeting low-income groups with suitable subsidy support from the central and local governments, and encourage potential beneficiaries to form cooperative housing societies. The Indian experience revealed that NGOs are key actors; they empower communities, assist in the formation of community organizations, and sometimes even develop. It was found that partnership schemes between state agencies and private partners bring together the efficiency in production and technical and marketing expertise of the private sector with the accountability of the public sector. The experience shows that the government must pave the way for a constructive expansion of partnership by assuming the role of facilitator, implementation agency and 'moderator', balancing market incentives with community interests. Also setting affordable housing policies, ensuring the primacy of state regulation, effecting capacity building to increase awareness, and minimizing risks are the major challenge for the private sector partners.

A replicable model is that of Turkey, where the government employed a special public private partnership approach to deliver mass housing projects through a special approach housing development administration (TOKI). This housing is on government owned land where private developers provide a proportion of developed units back to TOKI for the government to rent or sell to those in need of public housing. This approach avoids the problems of land speculation and the constraint that high land values have imposed in delivering affordable public housing. Its long-term arrangements (sometimes up to 30 years) also transfer risk to the private sector. It also helps to minimize local/central government costs on social rental housing and increased rental housing supply. The model proved to be successful in delivering mass market housing, and could be applied in other markets where the government has control of large areas of land, as in the case of Egypt. Another model of public-private partnership schemes, successfully applied in Turkey, is joint venture land banking. This scheme expropriates or purchases land, then releases it at affordable prices for low income groups.

In Morocco, public private partnership arrangements between the government and private developers, have worked well, especially when they applied inclusionary zoning. Factors of success included the ability of the government to offer subsidized land and tax breaks to make affordable housing projects more attractive to private developer.

The experience of Mexico, where a new generation of partnership "Hybrid Value Chain" collaboration are commercial in nature, shows that although business-social collaborations may not always be the most cost-effective approach, they are superior solutions provided certain conditions apply, namely identifying the right partners and visionary leaders, involvement of low-income communities through empowerment/mobilization, and availability of necessary resources.

The Iranian experience also illustrates the increased capacity for public-private partnership schemes in housing provision for lower-income groups; that they are more effective than leaving the entire process to the market. Moreover, it demonstrates that government could bring about construction of new low-income housing by delivering land to co-operatives and private-sector firms, and working directly with them. The main attributes enhancing the outcomes of partnership schemes in affordable housing delivery are: first, key partners; second, attributes related to the national context; third, attributes related to the local context (local authority-local community - NGOs - housing organization); fourth, formulation steps, basic arrangements, principles and features of the scheme.

Various international development organizations such as the World Bank, International Finance Corporation and Asian Development Bank, international non-governmental organizations such as Michael and Susan Dell Foundation and some private equity players have also funded low-income housing, for example, Carlyle invested USD 26 million in Value Budget and Housing Corporation (VBHC) in 2011.

The partnerships that build upon capabilities of all partners with an understanding of local market capacities, and the ability to organize the local community/citizen groups, proved to have the potential to generate a "win-win" for affordable housing delivery.

Source: *Hala S. Mekawy, Ettative Role of Local Level Partnership Scheme in Affordable Housing Delivery.*

Strategic Management

The origins of strategic management can be traced back to the period when international donor organizations begun to consider the financing of the urban sector, either as a series of large scale projects or as "sector loans" that aimed to establish national level financial intermediaries to provide an assured flow of capital. The urban investments were scrutinised for how their equity and efficiency of urban growth as well as for its replicability in the future. The"banker's" approach of stimulating a sustained capacity of urban growth management differed sharply from the prevailing practice. The effective utilization of the capital injected in the urban system requires the following preconditions:

- rapid assessment of prevailing problems and priorities, leading to project identification
- strengthening or creation of institutional structures which could oversee the detailed planning and implementation of a set of major projects which often incorporated technical, financial and management innovations;
- resource mobilization which ensured that the benefits created by the project will be translated to finance streams that directly or indirectly will cover the cost of investment leading to sustained repairability.

Action Planning

The generic features of action planning and management appear in a 1988 monograph of the World Bank:

"The Action Planning approach supplements conventional development planning and implementation techniques in improving institutional capacities for effectively plan and manage the implementation of their development programmes. It is a powerful means for achieving seven fundamental objectives:

(*a*) Identifying local perceptions of problems and constraints to be addressed by development programs/projects;

(*b*) Revealing values and attitudes to which the program/project approach must be adopted;

(*c*) Arriving at a procedural, analytical and operational framework that meets the development goals of the country;

(*d*) Mobilizing a critical mass of local supporters and implementers for the development strategy as a whole or particular program/project elements of the strategy;

(*e*) Generating sufficient commitment and ownership by appropriate supports;

(*f*) Starting a process for team functioning to be used throughout planning,implementation and evaluation; and

(*g*) Improving the capacity of project or program management teams to plan and manage on an ongoing basis during implementation."

Action planning aims to address the problems which are self-evident, persistent and where sufficient social commitment exist for their solution. The legitimacy of action planning is derived from the generally shared assessment that solutions must be found rather than just the problem identification. Action planning searches for an active network of actors whose goal orientation coincides. While institution moulding and influencing goal adjustment may be a legitimate long term aspiration, it is the initial cohesion of constituency that provides the impetus for successful action. It operates within a clearly defined (spatial and administrative) territory, where the power to act is not substantially challenged by other actors. Action planning reinforces the freedom of exercising choices,which is not eroded by interference.

Action planning is investment induced. It starts with a plan which lends credibility to the development of a resource base. It seeks to break new grounds in technical, managerial and financial areas where conventions in the past prevented solution generation. It avoids institutionalising techno-bureaucratic routines, but looks at each situation as new. In action planning explicit attention is paid to the financial implication of macro developmental projects, their contribution to sustainable expansion of programmes on the basis of their resource mobilizing impact. In fact, demonstrated 'affordability' at the user, institution or broader governmental level is the elementary justification for investment commitments which allows linkage between planning and implementation. It aims to introduce the element of 'changing course', both in terms of existing practices and opening new opportunities. The feasible vision of alternative futures (urban growth, technological and administrative innovations) will require the adjustment and change management of existing practices.

Action planning recognizes the essential ingredient of political support, and builds upon the participatory process of its own planning subjects. The political support may be obtained through the visibility of party politics or through the mobilisation of powerful institutions,individuals or media. The macro scale orientation of action planning derives its rational from the synergic outcome of coordinated and integrated projects, the evident added benefits accruing to the participant agencies in the achievement of their objectives. This integration in macro spatial planning becomes a motivating force, reinforcing the commitment by a number of institutions to contribute to the implementation of the micro-projects.

Project Management

Housing development process is a complex and creative activity. However, for the sake of simplicity the key steps involved are explained below:

Obtain a Site: The developer must obtain a site through purchase, lease, contract agreement, or venture agreement with the owner. This is the first step in the development process. One should undertake the time and expense of planning a site only if reasonably certain that the site can be developed. Approaches to obtain site include acquisition, partnership with the owner or outright punches.

The developer takes the risk of obtaining entitlements or other approvals. Prior to acquisition, there would typically be a due-diligence period during which investigations can be made into environment, soils, floodplain, wetlands, legal status, encumbrances, and other factors that have a basic impact on the development potential of a site.

Sometimes, particularly when there are uncertainties, a developer signs a contract with the owner to obtain site control for the period necessary to determine whether he can proceed with the desired development. In a contract to purchase, there is typically an initial period of due diligence and planning. Depending on the terms of the contract, earnest money provided is refundable with in a given period.

Development and Planning Team: This step may include engaging the architects, engineers, planners, financial consultants, and other professionals with skills and expertise, including construction and marketing in addition to general development expertise. They undertake the preparation of development plan according to mandatory controls, developers brief and market demand. This undergoes, the process of government/local body approvals.

Business Potential Study: The developers test market potential by both formal and informal studies. Market studies include several key elements:

- Competitors profile, market demand, rent, selling price, absorption pace, size, amenities, and features.
- Growth trends in the area, including population, households, income, age, education, jobs, and other characteristics, such as changing age characteristics and lifestyle choices.
- Capture site potential and requirement; including cost-benefit and penetration analysis for projects, product types or land user.
- Development program/product and absorption potential, defining the types of spaces or housing products to be provided, including size, character, style, estimated absorption, and pricing.

An overall marketing strategy should include the following:

- A market penetration strategy.
- A growth strategy which may include an internal strategy such as growth of jobs, land acquisition strategy, buying another business, a franchise strategy for branching out a horizontal strategy, or a vertical strategy whereby providing the products with a different distribution chain.
- Channels of distribution, internal sales force, distributors or retailers.
- Communication strategy.

Project Selection Process: There is a wide range of choices and housing opportunities in urban India. For a developer the most important considerations are profitability, land availability at right location, government/local body approvals and convenience in construction, development, obtaining infrastructure services and marketing. A developer has to be a visionary. He should be able to see the future. This requires a keen eye for the market, and a logical, rational approach while taking a decision. Decisions based on vague assumptions, astrological advice, intuition, etc. may be fatal and pose unforeseen risks and losses. Professional advice may be necessary from the experts to ascertain various issues involved in a project, such as:

- Land use, floor area ratio, zoning regulations, water and power, planning permission, approval of building plans, etc.
- Financial cost, benefit analysis, sources, risks, returns, etc.
- Possible threats, such as heritage zone, airport zone, CRZ Regulations, environmental clearances, political risks, extortion risks, delays, etc.
- Land tenure issues, court cases, legal constraints.
- Marketing demand and potential.

It is always handy to prepare a checklist and comparative matrix charts for a preliminary assessment of various options, such as group housing, plotted development, hotel, shopping mall, and other choices. These help in giving a clear idea of various factors which are critical for a project.

Design Brief

A housing project needs to have a consistent and harmonious design theme, urban form and structure, interiors, etc. Accordingly, a design brief is evolved keeping in view of the following:

Breakup of various functional areas, inter-relationship of different areas (*e.g.*, shops, theatre, restaurants, recreation, common facilities, rest rooms, administration, security, canteen, workshop, parking, circulation corridors, lifts, escalators, and staircases, fire security, transformer/generator, water supply, electricity, generators, renewable energy, maintenance staff room, etc.).

The planning and design brief should be as comprehensive as possible. This makes the consultants focused and helps them to faithfully translate the developer's requirements in the design. It may be remembered that to make a project stand out, always go for the best architect. She or he may be bit expensive, but would give value for money. Always insist for a time frame from the consultants and monthly reports on MS project that would help in timely progress, approvals, preparation of bill of quantities, tender documents, estimates, and appointment of the contractors.

Site Potential and Detailed Design: Site studies determine what and how much legally can actually be built on the land involved. These studies must consider, among other things:

- Master Plan/Zonal Plan, land use, FAR/FSI density and other controls and regulations.
- Opportunities and constraints, including location, area potential, zoning, transportation, access and capacity, availability of utilities, site constraints, such as topography, floodplains, wetlands and other environmental issues, soil problems, particularly for redevelopment sites), and site opportunities, such as views, proximity to other land uses, and attractive features.
- Streets, open space, and public facilities, and other standards to be considered for the specific site.
- Net buildable areas, considering the opportunities and constraints of the site.
- Buildable parcels/lots to achieve housing development that is appropriate.
- Development quantities, including parking, street requirements, and other physical features.

At this stage a detailed programme is developed for planning and design and for seeking the approvals of the government/local body.

Improved Performance, Accountability and Capacity Building

To improve the 'management accountability' in respect of delivery of social housing by Government Housing Agencies (GHAs), there is a need of adopt an accounting and budgetary system. Both, the private and public sectors will have to adopt established and accepted accounting practices uniformly in order to ensure transparency. The industry will have to incorporate strict financial discipline in its routine functioning so that the resources generated for specific projects, whether by way of investors' fund, loans from financial institutions or any other borrowing, are deployed for the project and not diverted for other uses. The practice of ESCROW account can be adopted, wherein funds are placed in banks in specific project accounts and are released only for use in the project. Adoption of such practices will considerably inspire confidence for the builders amongst investors and financial institutions.

The annual budget of Government Housing Agency (GHA) or an urban local body (ULB) should be built up using 'building block' approach by cost centers.The identification of the cost centers has two main purposes:

(*a*) To facilitate the measurement of the efficiency with which resources are expanded by identifying costs and output data to specific and recognizable centers.

(*b*) To provide a sound basis for fixing charges through the allocation of costs of cost centers to various services. In this way, the total cost of providing each housing unit or service can be established.

In accordance with the principle of management accountability, expenses should be identified, the costs should be apportioned in accordance with the volume of services provided, like planning, design and development services, maintenance, transport, workshop, mechanical and electrical services, etc.

The concept is that the cost center allows for direct control of activity costs via the budget system. In this way, principle of management accountability may be extended to support activities as well. The cost center principle can be applied to control both capital and revenue expenditure. It must be emphasized that the overriding concern should be the efficiency in the use of total resources.

To define and assess performance, it may be necessary developing appropriate output measures. The monitoring of the operating efficiency can be done in the following ways:

(*a*) By providing the means of comparing the performance over a period of time;

(*b*) By providing the means of tracing the performance on a real time basis;

(*c*) By allowing the actual performance to be measured against a standard or target which has been as an integral part of the budgetary control process.

Although unit cost provides an important source of output measures, non-financial measures should not be neglected. The accountability of management for achieving 'value for money' can be secured by the careful development of output measures within a framework of management accounting. The budgetary control reports produced by such a system will be more informative and conducive to the taking of corrective action in problem areas, so that the financial performance of the GHA/ULB and a real estate sector as a whole can be improved.

This also needs a matrix of the relevant skills, encompassing knowledge, reflection, conceptualizing and action. A balance needs to be maintained between the idealism and academic skills and the actual delivery on the ground.

DEBRIEFING QUESTIONS

1. What are major challenges of housing management in the context of affordable housing?
2. What critical lessons can be learnt from Singapore, Netherlands, Brazil, Mexico, Thailand, Sri Lanka, Vietnam, Malaysia, Bhutan, Chile, San Juan, Bangkok, Indonesia, Venezuela and Colombia in providing access to affordable housing?
3. Write short notes on the following:
   (*a*) Land Management for housing
   (*b*) Financial Management for housing
   (*c*) Legal Reforms for housing
   (*d*) Management of Slum Rehabilitation
   (*e*) Land Information System and GIS
   (*f*) Housing/Property Transaction Reforms
   (*g*) Housing Maintenance
4. What are the six levers for housing development and delivery?

5. Write short notes on:
   (*a*) Action Planning
   (*b*) Strategic Management
   (*c*) Capacity Building of a Housing Organisation
   (*d*) Housing Project Management
   (*e*) Housing Marketing
   (*f*) Sources of Housing Finance

16

Regulatory Reforms for Housing

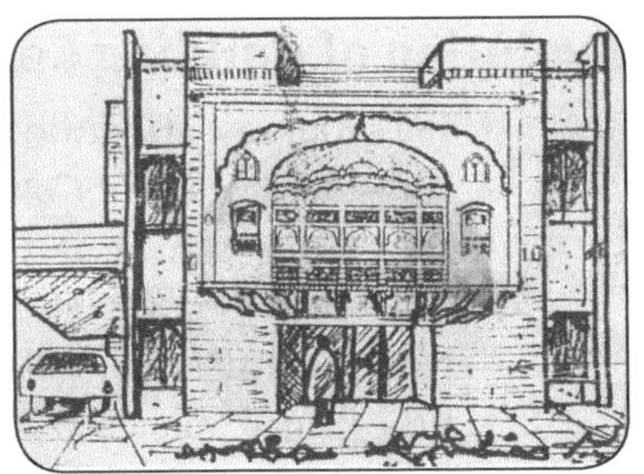

A major issue in housing development is the regulatory regime and the building bye-laws. Even if all the resources—land, finances, technology, building materials, manpower and machinery are available, the delivery of houses can be delayed, unless the development control regulations and building regulations are reformed.

McKinsey Report (2001) states that *'land approval related hurdles are costing 40 per cent higher to home cost. By removing these hurdles GDP growth can be added by 1.5 per cent.'* According to a report by World Bank, if the building approval procedures are too complicated, the builders tend to proceed without permit. By some estimates 60 to 80 per cent of buildings in developing economies are undertaken without the proper permits and approval'. India, in spite of recent elevation, still ranks very low in ease of getting building and construction permits.

The Tenth Five Year Plan had alluded to such a system by stating that *'another serious malaise affecting investment in real estate sector and housing development is the tardy process of planning approvals. A system of deemed approvals for all planning permissions by registered architects operating on the basis of self-regulation much like chartered accountants do, would enormously speed up the entire plan approval process. This will ensure that far larger quantum of housing stock is supplied every year at more reasonable prices.'*

The regulation of building activity started in India during 1880s. The industrial revolution in big cities like Bombay (Mumbai), Calcutta (Kolkata), Madras (Chennai) and Delhi, triggered large scale building activity, as a result of which there was a need to ensure safety, health and convenience of the residents. As such the original purpose of building bye-laws was to ensure structural safety, public health and convenience by way of regulations pertaining to:

- Light and ventilation, size of rooms, openings, etc.
- Public Health, plumbing, sanitation and water supply standards.
- Building use and occupancy, construction materials, structure, passages, lifts, staircase, etc.
- Conveniences, toilets, etc.
- Use controls

With the passage of time, the building bye-laws have expanded to cover town planning, slum rehabilitation, pollution control, conservation of heritage, urban design, structural safety, disaster management, environment impact assessment and energy efficiency.

Evolution of Building Controls and Regulations

- 1864-Railways, Highways, Sanitary, Commissions in Madras, Calcutta and Bombay
- 1870-Industries Start Coming up
- 1887-Delhi Municipal Committee framed Building Bye-laws, piped water supply, electricity, sewerage introduced
- 1888-Bombay Municipal Corporation Act
- 1914-Punjab Municipal Act
- 1913-Patrick Geddes in India, Conservative Surgery, Survey and Urban Improvement
- 1919-UP Improvement Trust Act, improvement trusts formed in various cities
- 1948-Master Plan for Greater Bombay
- 1950-Refugee Rehabilitation
- 1950s-Low cost housing, sanitation, Slum Areas Act
- 1954-Bombay Town Planning Act
- 1957-1960s-Creation of Delhi Development Authoritiy, Municipal Corporations, Building Bye-laws
- 1973-Delhi Urban Art Commission Act passed by the Parliament
- 1980s-Environment Acts & Environment Impact Assessment, Revised Building Bye-laws
- 1990s-Rainwater Harvesting, heritage conservation, disaster management, Barrier-free built environment
- 2000s-Green Buildings, energy efficiency, smart cities, urban governance

The Building Regulations now encompass a complex range of controls, such as given below:

Planning Controls/DCR

- Development Controls
- Land use zoning
- Sub-division Regulations, infrastructure services, traffic/mobility and parking plan, landscape plan, etc.

Building Controls

- Height
- Ground coverage
- Setbacks
- Floor Area Ratio
- Density
- Parking/road in front

Architectural Controls

Hoardings

Fire safety, earthquake and structural safety

Airport Regulations

Environment Regulations

Urban Design Regulations

Heritage Regulations and Archaeological Stipulations

Currently a builder requires as many as 34 kind of permits before starting construction which takes anywhere between six months to three years. The developer has to run to over two dozen Central Government ministries and agencies, including Environment and Forests, Archaeological Survey of India, National Highways Authority, fire department, electricity department, Airport Authority of India, Ministry of Labour, Ministry of Mines, Central Ground Water Board, etc. to get no objection certificates.

Table 16.1. Number of Approvals Required and Time Taken

Country	No. of Approvals Required	Time Taken
India	34	6 month to 3 years
Hong Kong	6	Over two months
Singapore	11	26 days

The development control regulations and building bye-laws are made primarily for green-field development and not for redevelopment which is a major thrust of Housing for All, AMRUT and other programmes of urban development. Regulations have to respond to the need of redevelopment and provide a facilitating framework. The constraints of redevelopment are the requisition of proof of land ownership, mechanism for approval of plans, joint ownership and development of small plots being amalgamated together. The regulations do not provide any system of assembly of small plots, so that the old dilapidated areas can be developed with proper layouts, adequate roads, services, amenities, parking and open spaces.

The building regulations are almost exclusionary with no concept for the slums, hutments, poor households, small vendors and manufacturers. These often ignore the vital aspect of public importance, like public toilets, dustbins, drinking fountains, footpath design, street furniture, locating street vendors, utility booths, signage, public spaces, conservation of cultural heritage, etc.

Building bye-laws are based upon an absolute normative set of regulations, and do not permit location specific variations and flexibility. This is due to general apprehension that discretion leads to rent seeking behavior. On the contrary, rigid regulations impel developers to bypass the regulations by rent paying.

Real Estate (Regulation and Development) Act, 2016

The Real Estate (Regulation and Development) Act aims to create a Real Estate Regulatory Authority (RERA) and an Appellate Tribunal that will act as the watchdog for the housing and real estate sector. This would protect the consumer's interests, while creating an alternative redressal mechanism for any disputes that may arise. The Act demands greater disclosure from the developer community and a higher level of project accountability to remove the information asymmetries in the housing market. The Act mandates the compulsory registration of real estate agents, and prevents money laundering by the non-organised brokers. A major provision of the Act is the standardization of area measurement, with carpet area to be the measure. Developers would need to provide the status of all approvals as well as sanctioned plans, to buyers and will not be able to sell their project without obtaining the required approval. The Act also seeks to ensure that the buyer's payment is utilized for the development of the particular project by necessitating the creation of an escrow account, where 70% of the customer advance will be used only for that project. The Act makes the developer responsible for adhering to the timelines and conditions committed for the project. The Real Estate Regulatory Authority (RERA) acts as the central agency to coordinate the development of the sector, as well as to promote transparency, efficiency and competitiveness.

The bottlenecks and overlapping regulatory jurisdictions can be reduced by a careful mapping of the regulatory jurisdictions, regulatory authority and regulatory laws. The Real Estate (Regulation and Development) Act, 2016 seeks to provide a uniform regulatory environment, creation of Real Estate Regulatory Authority and a unified regulatory framework to fast track and re-engineer the process.

The Act aims to reduce frauds and delays, and enhance the efficiency, professionalism and standardization. The Act covers both residential and commercial real estate and envisages:

- Establishment of Real Estate Regulatory Authority
- Registration of Real Estate Projects and Registration of Real Estate Agents
- Mandatory Public Disclosure of all project details
- Adherence to declared plans
- Fast Track Dispute Settlement Mechanism
- Establishment of Central Advisory Council
- Establishment of Real Estate Appellate Tribunal
- Bar of Jurisdiction in Courts, and,
- Power to make Rules and Regulations.

Reforms in Building Regulations

The Government of India has initiated certain reforms to fast track clearances for construction which include the following:

- The Union Ministry of Environment, Forests and Climate Change has come out with revised and simplified environmental laws. These have been notified vide Gazette of India dated 9th December 2016.
- The notification brings building projects of the size of less than 20,000 sqm within the ambit of fulfilling "environmental condition" through self-declaration and certification procedure. Local authorities will have the power to take a final call on compliance of green norms. The local authority may issue the building permission incorporating environmental norms and allow the project based on self-declaration. Project of the size above 20,000 sqm and less than 1,50,000 sqm will be exempt from the existing procedure of prior environmental clearance from the State-level Environment Impact Assessment Authority. This category of residential buildings will not require State Level Environmental Assessment Authority.

  However, commercial projects will have to take SPCB consent, and prior clearance from the Central Environment Impact Assessment Authority. Specified empanelled environment auditors will assess and certify the projects. There are also provisions of penalty on the owner and blacklisting of the auditors in case of false declaration or certification.
- The Ministry of Civil Aviation has asked the Airport Authority of India to standardize the norms for building heights around airports. The authority has issued Color-Coded Zonal Maps (CCZMs) for 12 airports which account for 58 per cent of such applications and

make them available to the respective urban bodies. The Ministry has also commissioned an improved version of online NOCAS (No Objection Certificate Application System), eliminating human interface and expediting issue of NOC through automatic calculation of permissible height in airport zone, and also enabling the applicants to track the status of their applications.

- Online filing and NOC for buildings falling outside restricted areas of national monuments can be obtained using 'app' developed by ISRO. Heritage bye-laws of 281 major monuments have been fast tracked by the Ministry of Culture.
- Local military authorities and units have been directed to provide details and maps of restricted and unrestricted areas.
- Formulation of Model Building Bye-laws by the Ministry of Urban Development, 2016 with on-line approval on single window.

The Expert Committee appointed by Government of India for Streamlining Approval Procedure for Real Estate Projects (SAPREP) came up with six areas of reforms:

- Bring transparency, predictability and accountability to protect consumer interest
- Review existing systems and procedures by removing duplicity and conflict between regulations, bringing in automation process and delegation of approvals
- Single window or 'one-stop shop', enabled by IT
- Reforms to promote affordable, green housing
- Sharing of best practices, and incentivizing States and cities
- Creating capacities in public (ULB's and UDAs and TP Departments), private sector and professionals (architects, engineers, urban planners, structural and other specialists) to carry out development responsibility.

In view of the complexity of getting building permit, loss of time and corruption involved, there is a need to consider on-line processing, simplification and deregulation of planning and building controls.

A graded and differential approach may be a possibility, comprising the following stages:

- No sanction/waiver
- Instant Prototype Sanction (on-line)
- Sanction of architectural plan and structural design by Registered Architects and Structural Engineers under intimation to the ULB, and within BBL, NBC and DCR of Master Plan
- Planning and development permissions by the ULB

This involves the devolution of powers and responsibility to registered Architects/ Engineers and deletion of micro-details from the Building Regulations, which can be attended and certified by the architects and engineers.

The Urban Local Body (ULB) should primarily deal with Planning and Development Permission, which are concerned only with the external and broad aspects of buildings. The Planning and Development Permission Regulations may comprise three sections: (*i*) Planning and Development Control Regulations, (*ii*) Building Design, and (*iii*) Building Safety and Structural Design. For (*ii*) & (*iii*) the registered panels and agencies of architects and engineers can be delegated the powers of deemed sanctions. The development controls should cover the following aspects:

- Land use zoning, layout plan, redevelopment plan, housing cluster plan, Sub-division Regulations, Mixed use, mandatory provision of social housing, social and physical infrastructure, urban design and heritage control, etc.

- Floor Area Ratio, density, parking and road in front, height, urban form
- Ground coverage, setbacks and mandatory green/open space be regulated as per the area specific character of the area on the basis of the local development plan and area specific urban design guidelines. All these plans and details should be available on the web site.

Larger plots (say 4 Ha and above) may involve the approval of Services Plans, Transport and Parking Plans, urban design, heritage, environmental and other clearances. The Planning & Development Regulations should also cover the approval of land pooling schemes, sub-division plans and building proposals.

For Planning and Development Permission, an inter-disciplinary on-line platform representing Architects, Planners, Engineers, Service Agencies, representatives of Fire Department, Civil Aviation, NMA/ASI, Pollution Control Committee and other concerned authorities can be created, the delegation of powers for approval and clearance under various acts.

For the unplanned areas (unauthorized colonies, urban villages, etc.) Planning and Development Permission should aim to bring them within the fold of planned development. This will need evolving comprehensive guidelines for amalgamation of plots, infill development, and conversion of isolated plots into development of group housing, with proper facilities, parks and parking.

The local authorities should ensure that on-street parking, congestion and traffic bottlenecks are avoided and provision of greens mixed land use, utilities and amenities are adequately provided in all built up areas.

A major emphasis of the Housing for All is on brown-field, densification and redevelopment with additional/ incentive FAR. This needs the preparation and approval of redevelopment scheme, taking into consideration the surrounding area, mobility, parking, greenery and services. To ensure availability of common areas, the tools of Transferable Development Rights and Accommodation Reservation are essential. Also, it should be ensured that through the redevelopment schemes and Transit Oriented Development, the poor are not priced out and at least one-third of the dwelling units are provided to EWS/LIG categories, against grant of incentive FAR.

The architectural design of the building up to 8 storied (height 26 m) and up to 1000 sqm plot in a planned colony may be approved by the registered architect under intimation to ULB. The Structural Design, Civil and Services Plan may be approved by a registered engineering, professional agency under the delegated powers. The reforms in Building Regulation should make it redundant for an inspector to enter a private building, and the regulations concerning the internal features, like room size, ceiling height, ventilation; sanitary fittings, etc. may be the mandatory responsibility of the Architect.

However, in the unplanned areas, unauthorised /regularised colonies, village abadi, etc. the Completion Plan / Occupancy Certificate may be issued only by the concerned local body. The devolution of powers to registered panel/agencies of architects and engineers would not work unless they are made responsible and accountable to the local body, who delegate them with such powers.

The city should not have any unsafe building irrespective of status of a colony, land ownership or land use. As such, it is necessary to delink building safety from the process of the planning and development permission or approval of building plan. Every building should have a Structural Safety Certificate which need not be linked with land use, approved layout and ownership. As mandated in the Master Plan for Delhi-2021 (MPD 2021), a structural safety certificate be submitted for all buildings in the built-up areas, including the unauthorized colonies, villages and Special Area. The

Local Bodies can proactively help the building owners in making available the services of a panel of structural engineers/ institutions for guiding the owners to ensure the structural safety of non-engineered buildings. A simplified Structural and Fire Safety Code for existing non-engineered buildings can be introduced along with other regulations, such as setbacks and minimum road width.

Online Building Plan Scrutiny System

The computerised scrutiny system named "AutoDCR" is being brought in use by various municipal corporations in India. The system has been adopted by Pune Municipal Corporation, Thane Municipal Corporation, Meera Bhayandar Municipal Corporation, Kolhapur Municipal Corporation in Maharashtra. The SUDA, AUDA and Hubli Dharwad Municipal Corporations are also implementing the system. Products are designed to get faster and accurate approval of building proposals. It brings uniformity and standardization of drawings and process to eliminate lengthy manual process and human errors. It reduces the time and effort of the architect and the authority.

Building Information Modelling, (BIM) can bring various departments on a common platform for approval/scrutiny of Building Plans. The BIM reads data from CAD drawing, establishes relationship between various entities, imposes specific proposal conditions, geometrically maps each and every entity by corresponding with complex and interlinked rules. Tables and reports are saved with the drawing.

The BIM generates various scrutiny reports dynamically based on the DC rules in a user friendly, viewable/printable format. As a result, time required for sanction of building proposal can be reduced to a maximum of 7 days.

It is also important that administrative procedures are simplified and streamlined. For this, it is imperative to rely on modern management practices and best technological tools, such as digitized drawings and photographs of construction are introduced via Building Information Modelling system.

Debriefing Questions

1. Explain the regulatory systems for buildings plan approval in India, highlighting the barriers.
2. Write short notes on:
   (*a*) Planning and Development Control Regulations
   (*b*) Building Bye-laws
   (*c*) Real Estate (Regulation and Development) Act, 2016
   (*d*) Environmental Regulations
3. Explain the concept of one-window, on-line approval of building plans.
4. Explain the following:
   (*a*) Civil Aviation Clearance for Construction Projects
   (*b*) National Monuments Authority, ASI/Heritage Conservation Committee
   (*c*) Fire Safety Regulations
   (*d*) Model Building Bye-laws (2016)
   (*e*) National Building Code of BIS (2016)

BIBLIOGRAPHY

Acioly, Claudio & Forbes Davidson (1996) Density in Urban Development, Building Issues, Vol. 8, Lund Centre for Habitat Studies, Sweden

Action Enterprise (2013-14) "India Exclusion Report", BFC, Bangalore

Adrian and Gordon Gill (2011) Towards Zero Carbon, Image Publications, Australia

Archer, R.W. (1988) An outline urban land policy for the developing countries in Asia. Bangkok: Asian Institute of Technology.

Arimah, B.C. (1992) Hedonic Prices and the Demand for Housing Attributes in a Third World City: The Case of Ibadan, Nigeria. Urban Studies, Vol. 29, no. 5, 639-651.

Bala, R. (1986) Trends of Urbanization in India: 1901-1981. Jaipur: Rawat Publication.

Bank, W. (1972) Urbanization; sector working paper. Washington, D.C.: World Bank.

Baross, P., & Linden, J. J. (1990) The Transformation of land supply systems in Third World Cities, Avebury, Hampshire: Ashgate Publishing Group.

Bartholomew, H. (1955) Land uses in American cities. Cambridge: Harvard University Press.

Barton, H., Davis, G. and Guise, R. (1995) Sustainable Settlements: A Guide for Planners, Designers and Developers, the Local Government Management Board, London.

Barton, H. et al (2003) Shaping Neighbourhoods, Spon Press, London.

Benninger, Christopher (2011) Letter to a Young Architect, CCBA Pvt. Ltd., Pune.

Benninger, Christopher (2016) Architecture for Modern India, CCBA Pune and Skira, Milan.

Bertaud, Alain (2014) "Converting land into affordable housing floor space," Policy Research Working Paper Series 6870, The World Bank, Washington.

Bhatia, Gautam, (2014) For the New Prime Minister, Times of India, 25th May 2014, New Delhi.

Bhatia, Gautam, (1991) Laurie Baker-Life, Works and Writings, Viking, HUDCO, New Delhi.

BIS, (2016) National Building Code of India SP:7, Bureau of Indian Standards, New Delhi.

BMTPC (2018) Compendium of Prospective Emerging Technologies for Mass Housing, BMTPC, Ministry of Housing and Urban Affairs, New Delhi.

Boelhouwer, PJ & Hoekstra, JSCM (2009). Towards a Better Balance in the Dutch Housing Market-Analysis and Policy Propositions. European Journal of Housing Policy, 9(4), 457-475.

Bose, A. (1967) Delhi's Urban Sprawl. Land Development and Land Price. 1947-67 (Mimeo). New Delhi: Institute of Economic Growth.

BSHF (1995) Housing in Beijing, BSHF, London.

Census of India (2011) House Listing and Housing Census., Government of India, New Delhi.

Census of India (2012) H-Series Tables on Census Houses, Household Amenities and Assets, 2011, Registrar General and Census Commissioner, India, Ministry of Home Affairs, New Delhi.

Charles, B. J. (1993) Private Sector Participation in Land Development Guidelines for Increasing Cooperation Between Local Government and Private Developers. Habitat , Vol. 17, pp. 53-62.

Clonts, H. J. (1970) Influence of Urbanization on Land Values at the Urban Periphery. Land Economics, Vol. 46 (Issue: 4).

Cody, E. (June 1996) Poverty and Environment—A Problem or a Solution? In Habitat Debate (Vol. 2, p. no.2). Nairobi: UNCHS.

Darin-Drabkin, H. (1977) Land policy and urban growth. Oxford ; New York: Pergamon Press.

Dave, Bharti (2018) Mapping the Quality of Living Spaces in India, Indian Research Academy, New Delhi.

DDA, (2007) Master Plan for Delhi – 2021, Ministry of Urban Development, New Delhi.

Davey, K. J. (1988) Municipal development funds and intermediaries. Washington, D.C.: Working Paper No. 32, World Bank.

Delhi Development Authority (2004) Delhi without Slums - An Action Plan, draft report of Madhukar Gupta Committee constituted by the Ministry of Urban Development, Government of India,unpublished, New Delhi.

De Soto, H. (2000) The Mystery of Capital: Why Capitalism Triumphs in the West and Fails Everywhere Else, Basic Books, New York.

Dillinger, W. R. (1995) Better urban services : finding the right incentives. Washington, D.C., World Bank.

Doebele, W. A. (1994) Urban Land and Macro Economic Development Moving from Access for the Poor. In G. J. (eds), Methodology for Land and Housing Market Analysis. UCL Press.

Dougles, S. A. (1993) Land and Stock Prices in Japan. Journal of Economic Perspectives, Vol.7, pp.149-160.

Dowall, D. E. (1995) The land market assessment : a new tool for urban management. Washington, DC: The World Bank.

Dreze, Jean, and Amartya Sen (1996) India, Economic Development and Social Opportunity, New Delhi: Oxford University Press.

Dupont V. (1997) Residential and Economic Practices of Pavement Dwellers in Old Delhi. Working Paper Series, No E/186/97. Delhi: Institute of Economic Growth.

Dupont, V., & Mitra, A. (1995, January-June). Population Distribution. Growth and Socio-Economic Spatial Patterns in Delhi: Findings from the 1991 Census Data. Demography India, 24, no. 1 & 2.

Durand-Lasserve, A. (1987) Land and Housing in Third World Cities: Are Public and Private Strategies Contradictory, No.4, pp.325-339.

Falvo, Rosa Mario & Ramprasad Akkisetti (ed.) (2016) Christopher Benninger, Architecture for Modern India, Rizzoli, New York.

Fanning, D. (1989) This Land is My Land or is it, Forbes Vol. 43, Issue: 2 January 23. Vol. I, No. 7.

Florian Steinberg, Concept of evolutionary housing design for India, HUDCO, New Delhi.

Fonesca, Rory, (1976) The Walled City of Old Delhi in Shelter and Society.

Gareth, J. (1992) The Impact of Government Intervention Upon Land Prices in Latin American Cities: The Case of Puebla, Mexico, University of Cambridge.

George, P. E. (1974) The Influence of Zoning Regulation on Land and Housing Prices. Washington. D.C. Urban Institute.

Gleson, M.E. (1979) Effects of an Urban Growth Management System on Land Values. Land Economics, Vol. 55 (Issue: 3).

Government of India (2007) National Urban Housing and Habitat Policy, Ministry of Housing and Urban Poverty Alleviation, New Delhi.

Government of India (2009) Tendulkar Committee Report, Planning Commission, Government of India, New Delhi.

Government of India (2008) PM's council on climate change, National Action Plan for climate Change, New Delhi.

Government of India (2009) National Mission on Sustainable Habitat, MOUD, New Delhi.

Government of India (1956) Slum Areas (Improvement and Clearance) Act, Government of India, New Delhi.

Government of India (1988) Report of National Commission on Urbanisation, New Delhi.

Government of India (1965) Report of the Committee on Urban Land Policy, Ministry of Health, New Delhi.

Government of India (1983) Task Forces on Housing and Urban Development: Shelter for the Urban Poor and Slum Improvement, Planning Commission, New Delhi.

Government of India (2012) Task force on promoting affordable housing, Ministry of Housing and Urban Poverty Alleviation.

Government of India (2013) Twelfth Five Year Plan, Planning Commission, New Delhi.

Government of NCT Delhi (2013), Delhi Human Development Report, Oxford, New Delhi.

Government of Rajasthan (2009) Affordable housing policy 2009, Department of Urban Development, Housing and Local Self Government, Jaipur.

Gupta, D. B. (1993) Housing and India's Urban Poor, Har-Anand Publication, New Delhi.

Hanes, J. H. (1991) Price Profiles for Land in Danish Urban Areas. Urban Studies, Vol. 28, No. 2, pp.277-287.

Hebraken, R. J., & Linden, J. J. (1992) Land delivery for low income groups in Third World Cities, Avebury, Hampshire: Ashgate Publishing Group.

Help Age (2000) Older People in Disasters and Humanitarian Crises: Guidelines for Best Practices, Helpage, New Delhi.

Hommes, R. (1995) Conflicts and Dilemmas of Decentralisation. Washington, DC: The World Bank.

HUDCO (2001) The State of the Indian Cities, Housing and Urban Development Corporation, New Delhi

Human Settlement Management Institute (HSMI)/Institute for Housing and Urban Development Studies (IHS) (1996) Profile of NGOs in Urban India-Institutional, Legal, Financial Framework and Related Issues. Capacity Building for the Urban Environment, New Delhi.

IDFC (2011) International Experience in Providing Affordable Housing, New Delhi.

IHS (1997) Capacity Building for Better Cities After Habitat II. Rotterdam.

IPCC (2007) Climate Change, Impacts, Adaptation and Vulnerability, IPCC, Cambridge and New York.

IYSH (1987) International Symposium on Housing Yokohama Japan, Japan: U.N. Publications.

Jack, H. (1987) Urban Land Economics—The Economics of Real Properties. London: McMillan Educational Ltd.

Jaggi, I.R. (1991) Readymade Housing, Indian Architect and Builder, October 1991.

Jain, A.K. (2009) Urban Housing and Slums, Readworthy Publications, New Delhi.

Jain, A.K. (2011) Making Infrastructure Work, Discovery Publishers, New Delhi.

Jain, A.K. (2014) Revisiting Land Acquisition and Urban Process, Readworthy Publications, New Delhi.

Jain, A.K. & Bansal Anil (1999) The Role of Private Sector in Urban Development: Case Study of Gurgaon. ITPI Journal.

Jain, A.K. (2001) Ecology and natural resource management for sustainable development. Dehradun: Management Publishing Company.

Jain, A.K. (2008) A Practical Guide to Disaster Management. New Delhi: Pragun.

Jain, A.K. (2008) Low Carbon City—Policies, Planning and Practice. Delhi: Discovery Publishers.

Jain, A.K. (2007) School Buildings—Planning, Design & Management. New Delhi: JBA Publishers.

Jain, A.K. (1996) The Indian megacity and economic reforms. New Delhi: Management Pub. Co.

Jain, A.K. (2018) Urban Transformation, Discovery Publishing House, New Delhi.

Jain, A.K. (2018) City Planning for a Changing India, Synergy Books, New Delhi.

Jain, A.K. (2016) Building Twenty Million Homes, Discovery Publishing House, New Delhi.

Jain, A.K. (2017) Landscape Architecture–Planning Engineering and Horticulture, Discovery Publishing House, New Delhi.

Jain, A.K. (1990) The making of a metropolis: planning and growth of Delhi. New Delhi: National Books Organisation.

Jain, A.K. (2008) Urban Transport Planning & Management. New Delhi: APH Publishing.

Jain, A.K. (2007) Water—A Manual for Engineers, Architects, Planners and Managers. Delhi: Daya Publications.

Jain A. K. (2009) Urban Land Policy and Public Private Partnership for Real Estate and Infrastructure Projects, Readworthy Publications, New Delhi.

Jain, A.K. (2011) the Informal City, Readworthy Publishers, New Delhi.

Jain, A.K. (2012) Dillinama, Synergy books New Delhi.

Jain, A.K. (2013) Sustainable Urban Transport and Systems, Khanna Publishers, New Delhi.

Jain, A.K. (2014) Right to Toilet, Readworthy Publication, New Delhi.

Jain A.K. (2003) Making Planning Responsive to and Compatible with Reforms, Cities Journal (UK) Vol. 20, No.2,

Jain, A.K. (2015) The Idea of Green Building, Khanna Publishers, New Delhi.

Jain, A.K. (2015) Smart Cities: Vision and Action, Discovery Publishers, New Delhi.

Jain, A.K. (2010) Urban Planning and Governance, Bookwell Publishers, New Delhi.

Jain, A.K. (2015) Conservation of Cultural Heritage, Discovery Publishers, New Delhi.

Jain, A.K. (2016) River Regeneration and Water Resources, Discovery Publishers, New Delhi.

Jain, A.K. (2015) Towards Cleaner and Hygienic Cities and Villages, Discovery Publishers, New Delhi.

Jain, A.K. (2015) Transforming Delhi, Bookwell, New Delhi.

Jain, Kulbhushan and Meenakshi Jain (2000) Architecture of the Indian Desert, AADI Centre, the University of Virginia, US.

Jain, Shikha (2004) Havelis: A Living Tradition of Rajasthan, Shubi Publishers, Gurgaon.

Jain, Shikha, Presentation on Heritage Legislation in India, an overview, IHCN, second biennial conference, Hyderabad, AP, 18-20 Dec. 2008.

Jane Jacobs, (1961) The Death and Life of Great American Cities, Random House, New York.

Jones Lang LaSalle (2014), India's Stock of Commercial Real Estate, On Point Research Report, Jones Lang LaSalle, Real Estate Intelligence Services.

Kabre, C. (2010) A new thermal performance index for dwelling roofs in the warm humid tropics, Building and Environment, 45: 727-738.

Klaus, Daniel (1994) Technology of Ecological Buildings, Birkhauser, Verlag, Basel.

Koenigsberger, Ingersoll, Mayhew, Szokilay (1985) Manual of Tropical Housing and Building; Orient Longman.

KPMG (2012) Affordable Housing – A key growth driver in the real estate sector, Mumbai.

Kumar, Arjun (2013) Access to Basic Amenities in Urban India Status of Levels Across Castes, Ethnicity, Religion, Livelihood Categories and Poverty in Various Class Sizes of Towns and Cities, Urban India, July-December 2013, National Institute of Urban Affairs, New Delhi.

Kundu, A (1993) In the Name of the Urban Poor. Access to Basic Amenities. New Delhi: Sage Publications.

Kundu, A. (1994) Urban Land-Price Research and the Utility of Land Registration Data Kurokawa, N. (1990, October) Getting Serious About Land Prices. Japan Quarterly, Vol. 37 (Issue: 4).

Mahendra B., Veena N. and Harikrishnan K. (2013) Transferable Development Rights in Indian Cities, BMRDA, Department of Town Planning, Government of Karnataka, Bangalore.

Malpezzi, S. (1990) Rental Housing in Developing Countries, Issues and Constraints, Expert Group Meeting to Review Rental System and Rental Stability, United Nations.

Martin Khor and Lim Li Lin, (eds). (2001) "Provision of public housing in Singapore," in Good practices and innovative experiences in the South, Vol. 2: Social policies, indigenous knowledge and appropriate technology.

McHarg, Ian, (1969) Design with Nature, New York, Natural History Press.

McKinsey Global Institute (2010) India's Urban Awakening: Building Inclusive Cities, Sustaining Economic Growth, Mumbai.

McKinsey Global Institute (2014) A Blueprint for addressing the global affordable housing challenge, New York.

McKinsey Global Institute Report—Bird of Gold, New York.

McMillan, D. P. (1989, May) An Empirical Model of Urban Fringe Land Use. Land Economics , Vol. 65 (Issue: 2).

Mehta, M. (1988) Urban Housing Policies: An Appraisal in N. J. (eds.), Housing in India. Delhi: B.R. Publishing Corporation.

Mills, E. S. (1979) Urbanization and Urban Problems: The Republic of Korea 1945-75. Cambridge: Harvard University Press.

Ministry of Urban Development Government of India, New Delhi (2001) the Constitutional (Seventy-Fourth) Amendment Act, 1992, Power to the People: The Nagarpalika Act.

Ministry of Urban Development (2014): Swachh Bharat (Clean India) Campaign, Government of India, New Delhi.

Ministry of Urban Development (2015) HRIDAY (Heritage and Redevelopment for Integrated Development), Government of India, New Delhi.

Ministry of Urban Development (2015) Smart City Mission Guidelines, Government of India, New Delhi.

Ministry of Urban Development (2015) AMRUT: Atal Mission for Rejuvenation and Urban Transformation, Government of India, New Delhi.

Ministry of Housing and Urban Poverty Alleviation (2015): Pradhan Mantri Awas Yojana–Mission on Housing for All, Mission Guidelines, Government of India, New Delhi.

MOHUPA (NBO) (2012), Urban Housing Shortage, 2012-17, New Delhi.

MOHUPA (NBO) (2013), State of Housing in India: A Statistical Compendium, New Delhi.

MOHUPA (2016) Ministry of Law, Real Estate Regulation and Development Act, New Delhi.

Mitra, A. (1990, December 15). Land Price in Indian Cities— Dimensions and Determinants of Change, Economic and Political Weekly.

Mitra, Banashree (1984) Urban Land Development Strategies and Analysis, Urban and Rural Planning thought (SPA), New Delhi.

MMRDA (1996) Mumbai Regional Plan Document MMRDA, Mumbai. MoEF (2006). Environmental Clearances, Ministry of Environment and Forest, Government of India, New Delhi, http://moef.nic.in/modules/project-clearances/ehvironment-clearances.

Modi, Narendra (2011) Convenient Action, Macmillan Publishers, New Delhi.

MoEF (2006) Environmental Clearances, Ministry of Environment, Forests and Climate Change, Government of India, New Delhi, http://moef.nic.in/modules/project-clearances/ehvironment-clearances.

MOUD/ Wilbur Smith Associates (2008) Traffic and Transport Policies and Strategies in Urban Areas in India, Ministry of Urban Development, New Delhi.

Mohan, R. & A.R.V. (1982) The evolution of land values in the context of rapid urban growth : a case study of Bogota and Cali, Colombia. Washington, D.C. World Bank.

MOHUPA (NBO) (2010) Report of Committee on Slum Statistics, New Delhi.

MOHUPA (NBO) (2012) Urban Housing Shortage, 2012-17, New Delhi.

MOHUPA (NBO) (2013) State of Housing in India: A Statistical Compendium, New Delhi.

MOHUPA (2013) Report of Task Force on Housing Shortage in India, New Delhi.

Munjee, N. (1992) Financing Shelter: New Experiments in Formal and Informal Institutional Links in Shelter. A paper presented at the 13th International Earoph Congress, 14-18 September, Kuala Lampur.

Murphy, R. E. (2007) The central business district: a study in urban geography. New Brunswick, N.J. Aldine Transaction.

National Sample Survey Organisation (2010) Housing Condition and Amenities in India: 2008-09, Report No. 535, Ministry of Statistics and Programme Implementation, Government of India, New Delhi.

NCAER (2013) Evaluation and Review of Land Pooling and Development Models for Delhi, unpublished, New Delhi.

NIUA & HUDCO/HSMI (2013) Metropolitan Cities in India, Phase I Report, New Delhi.

NIUA (1989) Profile of the Urban Poor: An Investigation into the Demographic, Economic and Shelter Characteristics. In Research Study Series No. 40. New Delhi: National Institute of Urban Affairs.

Pandya, Y. (2007) Towards symbiosis of nature and architecture, Architecture + Design 24(10).

Patel, Shirish B. (2016) Housing for All by 2022-Assignment Delivered, Accountability Nil, Economic and Political Weekly March 5.

Patwari, S., Bo Tang and Maurice Mitchell (eds.) (2010) Learning from Delhi, Dispersed Initiatives in Urban Landscape, Ashgate, Surrey.

Planning Commission (2011) "Faster, Sustainable and More Inclusive Growth: An Approach to 12th Five Year Plan", Planning Commission, Government of India, New Delhi.

Priemus, H. and Gruis, V. (2011). Social housing and illegal state aid: The agreement between European Commission and Dutch Government, International Journal of Housing Policy 11(1).

Rajat Gupta, Sanjay Seth, Zeenat Niazi, Jesus S Villanueva, Sanjoli Tuteja, Megha Behal, Pratibha Caleb and Ayushman Banerjee (2018). Mainstreaming Sustainable Social Housing in India: Findings and insights from the Mas-SHIP Project, Oxford Brookes University, TERI, Development Alternatives and UN-Habitat, New Delhi.

Rao, P. K. (1991) Safeguard for Sound Concrete, Indian Architect and Builder, October.

Ratcliff, R. U. (1949) Urban Land Economics. New York: McGraw-Hill Book Co.

Ravindra, A. (1996) Urban Land Policy: A metropolitan perspective. New Delhi: Concept Pub. Co.

Report of Centre of Research for Energy Resources and Consumption Report, (2010) Down to Earth, Jan. 16-31, New Delhi.

RICS (2010) "Making Affordable Housing Work in India", RICS, CBRE and LEVVEL, London/ New Delhi.

Richmond, K. (June 1996) Education, Poverty and Equity in Habitat Debate (Vol. 2, P. 2). Nairobi: UNCHS.

Rogerio Almeida (2001) House for Rs one Lakh, Span, Jan-Feb.

Saly, A.W. (2001) Corporate Entrepreneurship; Antecedents and Consequences of Entrepreneurship in large firms Amsterdam.

Sanjay, P. (1992) Energy Conscious Architecture: An endless quest. Architecture + Design 9(3) 14-16.

Satterthwaite, D. (2007) The Transition to a Predominantly Urban World and its Underpinnings, Human Settlements Discussion Paper, IIED, London.

Siembieda, W. J. (1994) Measuring the Price and Supply of Urban Land Market: Insights On Sources. In G. J. (eds) Methodology for Land and Housing Market Analysis. England: UCL Press.

SPARC (1985) We the invisible, Report on Pavement Dwellers in Mumbai.

Suresh, V. (1997) India-Status on the Built Habitat, International Conference on Habitat. New Delhi.

Suri, Promila (1994) Urban Poor—Their Housing Needs and Government Response, Delhi, Haranand Publication.

Tipple, A.G. and Susan Speak (2003) Homeless in Developing Countries, DFID. London.

T.C.P.O (1981) Report on Informal Sector in a Metropolis. Delhi: Case Study, New Delhi: unpublished.

UNESCO (2010) Historic Districts for All, New Delhi, UNESCO.

UN-Habitat (2010) The State of the World's Cities: Bridging the Urban Divide, London, Washington D.C., Earthscan.

UN-Habitat (2011) Cities and Climate Change, Global Report on Human Settlements, Earthscan, UK/USA/Nairobi.

UN-Habitat (2013) Planning and Design for Sustainable Urban Mobility, Global Report on Human Settlements, Earthscan, UK/USA/Nairobi.

UN Habitat (2003) The Challenge of Slums - Global Report on Human Settlements, Earthscan, London.

UNHCR (2017) Age, Gender and Diversity, Report, UNHCR, New York.

United Nations (1977) Land for Human Settlements. United Nations: New York.

UN-Habitat (June 1996) Problems of the Urban Poor in Human Settlements, In Habitat Debate (Vol. 2, P. 2). Nairobi: UNCHS.

UN Habitat (2003) Rental Housing, An essential option for the urban poor in developing countries, Nairobi.

UN Habitat (2007) State of World's Cities 2006/07.

Urban Poverty (October, 2006) National Resource Centre on Urban Poverty, Mumbai.

Wadhava, K. (1983, April. 2) Land Use Pattern in Urban Fringe Areas: A Case Study of Ahmedabad. Economics and Political Weekly.

Wegelin, E. (1996) Options for Municipal Interventions in Urban Poverty Reduction, Habitat Debate (Vol. 2, P. 2). Nairobi: UN-Habitat.

Wilson, Richard, L. (1960, February). Land Values in the United States. Urban Land , Vol. 2.

World Bank (2012) India Urbanisation Review: Urbanisation beyond Municipalities, Washington.

World Bank (1986) India-Urban Land Management Study (1986) Washington.

World Bank (2007) Report on Low-income Housing in Latin America and the Caribbean, Washington.

World Bank (1978) Urban Land Policy Issues and Opportunities, Vol. 1 & 2, Washington, DC: World Bank.

www.greenspec.com

www.nubricks.com, Brazil Government Launches "My House-My Life", Housing Plan.

http://www.niua.org

http://www.ficcirealestatesummit.com

http://www.censusindia.gov.in

http://www.delhigov.nic.in

http://www.unhabitat.org/housing

www/gvbtx.com

HOUSING FOR ALL: DESIGN, CONSTRUCTION AND MANAGEMENT

A.K. JAIN

FEEDBACK FORM

1. Which topics from your examination point of view are inadequately or not covered in this book?

____

____

2. Is there any misprints/ mistakes/ factual inaccuracy in this book? If so, please specify.

____

____

3. What is your assessment of this book as regards the presentation of the subject-matter, expression, precision and price in relation to the other recommended books available on this subject?

____

____

4. Which competing books you regard as better than this? Please mention their author and publishers.

____

____

5. Any further suggestions/comments you would like to make for the improvement of the book?

____

____

PS: If needed, please attach a separate sheet.

Name : ______________________

College : ______________________

Address : ______________________

Email : ______________________

Mobile : ______________________

Please mail the feedback form at:

KHANNA BOOK PUBLISHING CO. (P) LTD.

4C/4344, Ansari Road, Daryaganj, New Delhi-110002

You can also email this feedback form at contact@khannabooks.com or Whatsapp at +91 – 99109 09320

BEST FEEDBACK WILL BE REWARDED SUITABLY